COLLINS
MINI
ATLAS
OF THE WORLD

This edition produced for WH Smith in 2002

Collins Mini Atlas of the World

Collins
An Imprint of HarperCollins*Publishers*
77-85 Fulham Palace Road
London W6 8JB

First published 1999
Reprinted 1999, 2000
Reprinted with changes 2001, 2002
Copyright © HarperCollins*Publishers* Ltd 2002
Maps © Bartholomew Ltd 2002

Collins® is a registered trademark of HarperCollins*Publishers* Ltd

The contents of this edition of the Collins Mini Atlas of the World
are believed correct at the time of printing. Nevertheless, the publisher
can accept no responsibility for errors or omissions, changes in the
detail given or for any expense or loss thereby caused.

Printed and bound in Germany
by GGP Media GmbH

ISBN 0 00 766518 0 (WH Smith)
0 00 448893 8 (hardback)
0 00 448909 8 (paperback)
PH11270 (hardback)
OH11092 (paperback)

www.**fire**and**water**.com
visit the book lover's website

COLLINS
MINI
ATLAS
OF THE WORLD

HarperCollins*Publishers*

COLLINS
MINI
ATLAS
OF THE WORLD

CONTENTS

HOW TO USE THE ATLAS 6-7

THE WORLD

PHYSICAL FEATURES 8-9
CLIMATE 10-11
COUNTRIES AND TIME ZONES 12-13
POPULATION AND CITIES 14-15

OCEANIA

OCEANIA Countries 1:70M 16-17
AUSTRALIA 1:25M 18-19
Southeastern AUSTRALIA 1:10M 20-21
NEW ZEALAND 1:10M 22

ANTARCTICA 1:60M 23

ASIA

ASIA Countries 1:70M 24-25
SOUTHEAST ASIA 1:30M 26-27
MALAYSIA and Western INDONESIA
1:15M 28-29
CONTINENTAL SOUTHEAST ASIA
1:15M 30-31
PHILIPPINES 1:15M 32
NORTH KOREA and SOUTH KOREA
1:9M 33
JAPAN 1:10M 34-35
CHINA and MONGOLIA 1:30M 36-37
Central CHINA 1:15M 38-39
SOUTHERN ASIA 1:20M 40-41
PAKISTAN, INDIA and BANGLADESH
1:15M 42-43
Central ASIA 1:20M 44-45
ARABIAN PENINSULA 1:15M 46-47
Eastern MEDITERRANEAN 1:15M 48-49
RUSSIAN FEDERATION 1:42M 50-51

EUROPE

EUROPE Countries 1:40M *52-53*
EUROPEAN RUSSIAN FEDERATION
1:20M *54-55*
Northeastern EUROPE 1:8M *56-57*
UKRAINE and MOLDOVA 1:8M *58-59*
SCANDINAVIA and ICELAND 1:10M *60-61*
BRITISH ISLES 1:8M *62-63*
SCOTLAND 1:4M *64*
IRELAND 1:4M *65*
ENGLAND and WALES 1:4M *66-67*
Northwestern EUROPE 1:4M *68-69*
Central EUROPE 1:8M *70-71*
FRANCE and SWITZERLAND 1:8M *72-73*
SPAIN and PORTUGAL 1:8M *74-75*
ITALY and the BALKANS 1:8M *76-77*
GREECE, ROMANIA and BULGARIA
1:8M *78-79*

AFRICA

AFRICA Countries 1:60M *80-81*
Northwestern AFRICA 1:26M *82-83*
Northeastern AFRICA 1:26M *84-85*
Central AFRICA 1:20M *86-87*
Southern AFRICA 1:20M *88-89*
REPUBLIC OF SOUTH AFRICA 1:10M *90-91*

NORTH AMERICA

NORTH AMERICA Countries 1:70M *92-93*
CANADA 1:30M *94-95*
Western CANADA 1:15M *96-97*
Eastern CANADA 1:15M *98-99*
UNITED STATES OF AMERICA 1:25M *100-101*
Western U.S.A. 1:11M *102-103*
North Central U.S.A. 1:11M *104-105*
South Central U.S.A. 1:11M *106-107*
Northeastern U.S.A. 1:11M *108-109*
Southeastern U.S.A. 1:11M *110-111*
MEXICO 1:13M *112-113*
CARIBBEAN 1:20M *114-115*

SOUTH AMERICA

SOUTH AMERICA Countries 1:70M *116-117*
Northern SOUTH AMERICA 1:25M *118-119*
Southern SOUTH AMERICA 1:25M *120-121*
Southeastern BRAZIL 1:10M *122-123*

PACIFIC OCEAN 1:120M *124-125*
ATLANTIC OCEAN 1:120M *126*
INDIAN OCEAN 1:120M *127*
ARCTIC OCEAN 1:60M *128*

WORLD DATA *129-160*
INDEX *161-253*

These pages help the reader to interpret the reference maps in the atlas. They explain the main features shown on the mapping and the policies adopted in deciding what to show and how to show it.

The databases used to create the maps provide the freedom to select the best map coverage for each part of the world. Maps are arranged on a continental basis, with each continent being introduced by a map of the continent. Maps of Antarctica and the world's oceans complete the worldwide coverage.

SYMBOLS and GENERALIZATION

Maps show information by using signs, or symbols, which are designed to reflect the features on the earth that they represent. Symbols can be in the form of points - such as those used to show towns and airports; lines - used to represent roads and rivers; or areas - such as lakes. Variation in size, shape and colour of these types of symbol allow a great range of information to be shown. The symbols used in this atlas are explained here. Not all information can be shown, and much has to be generalized to be clearly shown on the maps. This generalization takes the form of selection - the inclusion of some features and the omission of others of less importance; and simplification - where lines are smoothed, areas combined, or symbols displaced slightly to add clarity. This is done in such a way that the overall character of the area mapped is retained. The degree of generalization varies, and is determined largely by the scale at which the map is drawn.

SCALE

Scale is the relationship between the size of an area shown on the map and the actual size of the area on the ground. It determines the amount of detail shown on a map - larger scales show more,

smaller scales show less - and can be used to measure the distance between two points, though the projection of the map must also be taken into account when measuring distances.

GEOGRAPHICAL NAMES

The spelling of place names on maps is a complex problem for the cartographer. There is no single standard way of converting them from one alphabet, or symbol set, to another. Changes in official languages also have to be taken into account when creating maps and policies need to be established for the spelling of names on individual atlases and maps. Such policies must take account of the local official position, international conventions or traditions, and the purpose of the atlas or map. The policy in this atlas is to use local name forms which are officially recognized by the governments of the countries concerned. However, English conventional name forms are used for the most well-known places. In these cases, the local form is often included in brackets on the map and also appears as a cross-reference in the index. All country names and those for international features appear in their English forms.

BOUNDARIES

The status of nations and their boundaries are shown in this atlas as they are in reality at the time of going to press, as far as can be ascertained. Where international boundaries are the subject of disputes the aim is to take a strictly neutral viewpoint, based on advice from expert consultants.

Boundaries

▬▬▬▬	International
·▬➤▬➤	International disputed
▭▭▭▭	Administrative (selected countries only)
●●●●●●●	Ceasefire line

Settlements

POPULATION	NATIONAL CAPITAL	ADMINISTRATIVE CAPITAL	CITY or TOWN
over 1 million	□ **BEIJING**	o **Tianjin**	o **New York**
500 000 - 1 million	□ **BANGUI**	o **Douala**	o **Barranquilla**
100 000 - 500 000	□ WELLINGTON	o Mansa	o Mara
50 000 - 100 000	□ PORT OF SPAIN	o Lubango	o Arecibo
under 50 000	□ MALABO	o Chinhoyi	o El Tigre

Communications

═══════	Motorway
───────	Main road
- - - - -	Track
─┼─┼─┼─	Railway
✈	Main Airport
┴┴┴┴┴┴	Canal

Other features

∴	Site of special interest
∿∿∿	Wall

Physical features

	Freshwater lake
	Seasonal freshwater lake
	Salt lake
	Seasonal salt lake
	Dry salt lake
	Glacier / Ice cap
───────	River
- - - - -	Seasonal river
⤒120	Mountain pass
1234 △	Summit

Styles of lettering

Country name	**FRANCE**	Island	*Gran Canaria*
Overseas Territory / Dependency	**Guadeloupe**	Lake	*Lake Erie*
Administrative name	**SCOTLAND**	Mountain	*Mt Blanc*
Area name	PATAGONIA	River	*Thames*

8

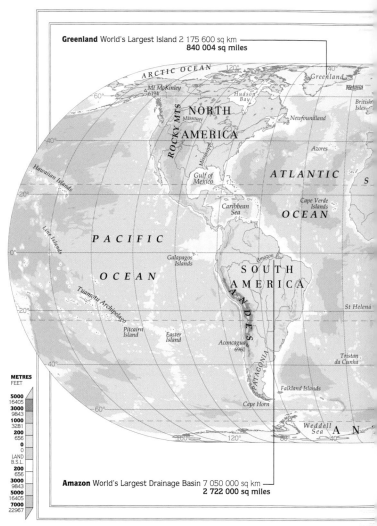

Greenland World's Largest Island 2 175 600 sq km
840 004 sq miles

ARCTIC OCEAN

Greenland

Iceland

Mt McKinley
6194

Hudson
Bay

NORTH

British
Isles

Missouri

AMERICA

Newfoundland

Azores

Hawaiian Islands

Gulf of
Mexico

ATLANTIC

S

Cape Verde
Islands

Caribbean
Sea

OCEAN

PACIFIC

Line Islands

Galapagos
Islands

Amazon

SOUTH

OCEAN

AMERICA

Tuamotu Archipelago

A N D E S

St Helena

Pitcairn
Island

Easter
Island

Aconcagua
6960

PATAGONIA

Tristan
da Cunha

Falkland Islands

Cape Horn

Weddell
Sea

A N

METRES
FEET

5000
16405
3000
9843
1000
3281
200
656
0
0
LAND
B.S.L.
200
656
3000
9843
5000
16405
7000
22967

Amazon World's Largest Drainage Basin 7 050 000 sq km
2 722 000 sq miles

Eckert IV Projection

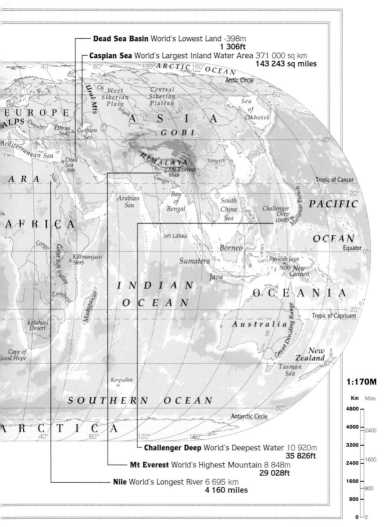

Dead Sea Basin World's Lowest Land -398m
1 306ft

Caspian Sea World's Largest Inland Water Area 371 000 sq km
143 243 sq miles

ARCTIC OCEAN

Arctic Circle

EUROPE

ALPS

Danube

Elbrus
5642

Caspian
Sea

Ob

West
Siberian
Plain

Irtysh

Central
Siberian
Plateau

Sea
of
Okhotsk

A S I A

GOBI

Ural Mts

Mediterranean Sea

Dead
Sea
-398

Nile

HIMALAYA

Mt Everest
8848

Ganges

Yangtze

Tropic of Cancer

ARA

Arabian
Sea

Bay
of
Bengal

South
China
Sea

Challenger
Deep
10920

Marianas Trench

PACIFIC

AFRICA

Congo

Kilimanjaro
5895

Great Rift Valley

Zambezi

Madagascar

Sri Lanka

Borneo

Sumatera

Java

Puncak Jaya
5030 New
Guinea

OCEAN

Equator

OCEANIA

INDIAN
OCEAN

Kalahari
Desert

Australia

Great Dividing Range

Tropic of Capricorn

Cape of
Good Hope

New
Zealand

Tasman
Sea

Kerguélen
Is

SOUTHERN OCEAN

Antarctic Circle

ARCTICA

Challenger Deep World's Deepest Water 10 920m
35 826ft

Mt Everest World's Highest Mountain 8 848m
29 028ft

Nile World's Longest River 6 695 km
4 160 miles

1:170M

Km	Miles
4800	
4000	2400
3200	1600
2400	
1600	800
800	
0	0

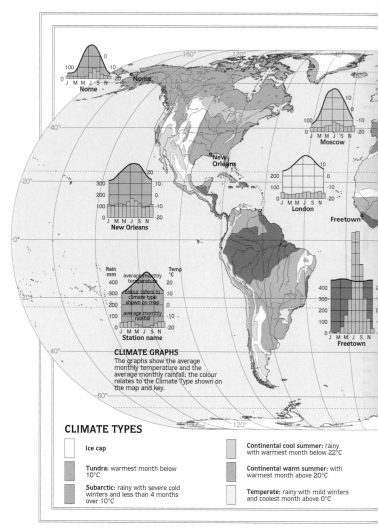

CLIMATE GRAPHS
The graphs show the average monthly temperature and the average monthly rainfall; the colour relates to the Climate Type shown on the map and key.

CLIMATE TYPES

Ice cap

Tundra: warmest month below 10°C

Subarctic: rainy with severe cold winters and less than 4 months over 10°C

Continental cool summer: rainy with warmest month below 22°C

Continental warm summer: with warmest month above 20°C

Temperate: rainy with mild winters and coolest month above 0°C

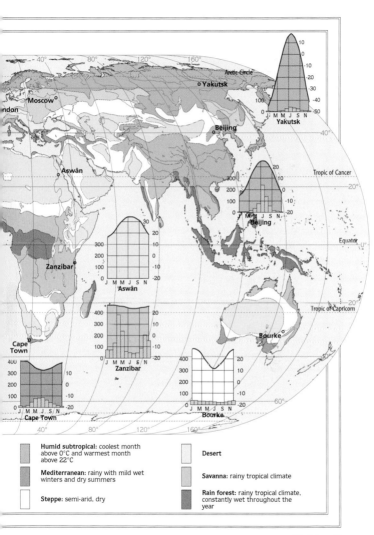

Humid subtropical: coolest month above 0°C and warmest month above 22°C

Mediterranean: rainy with mild wet winters and dry summers

Steppe: semi-arid, dry

Desert

Savanna: rainy tropical climate

Rain forest: rainy tropical climate, constantly wet throughout the year

© Bartholomew Ltd

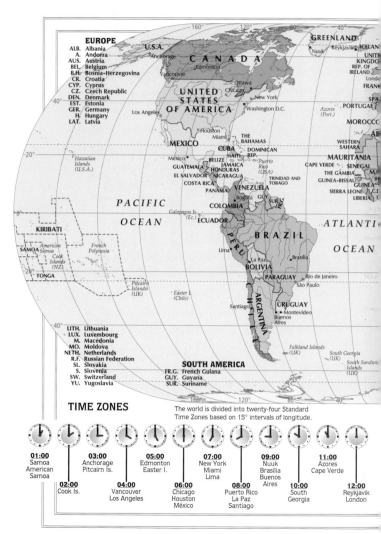

EUROPE

ALB. Albania
A. Andorra
AUS. Austria
BEL. Belgium
B.H. Bosnia-Herzegovina
CR. Croatia
CYP. Cyprus
CZ. Czech Republic
DEN. Denmark
EST. Estonia
GER. Germany
H. Hungary
LAT. Latvia

LITH. Lithuania
LUX. Luxembourg
M. Macedonia
MO. Moldova
NETH. Netherlands
R.F. Russian Federation
SL. Slovakia
S. Slovenia
SW. Switzerland
YU. Yugoslavia

SOUTH AMERICA

FR.G. French Guiana
GUY. Guyana
SUR. Suriname

TIME ZONES

The world is divided into twenty-four Standard Time Zones based on 15° intervals of longitude.

01:00 Samoa American Samoa	03:00 Anchorage Pitcairn Is.	05:00 Edmonton Easter I.	07:00 New York Miami Lima	09:00 Nuuk Brasilia Buenos Aires	11:00 Azores Cape Verde
02:00 Cook Is.	04:00 Vancouver Los Angeles	06:00 Chicago Houston México	08:00 Puerto Rico La Paz Santiago	10:00 South Georgia	12:00 Reykjavik London

Eckert IV Projection

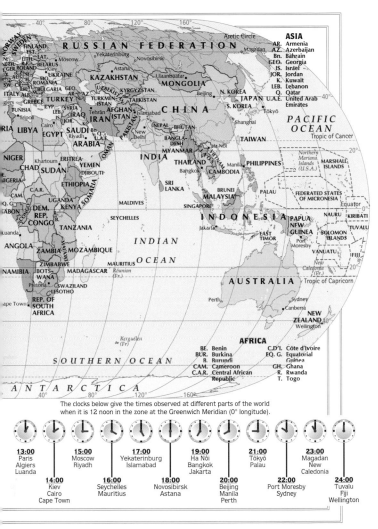

ASIA

AR.	Armenia
AZ.	Azerbaijan
Bn.	Bahrain
GEO.	Georgia
IS.	Israel
JOR.	Jordan
K.	Kuwait
LEB.	Lebanon
Q.	Qatar
U.A.E.	United Arab Emirates

AFRICA

BE.	Benin	C.D'I.	Côte d'Ivoire
BUR.	Burkina	EQ. G.	Equatorial Guinea
B.	Burundi	GH.	Ghana
CAM.	Cameroon	R.	Rwanda
C.A.R.	Central African Republic	T.	Togo

The clocks below give the times observed at different parts of the world when it is 12 noon in the zone at the Greenwich Meridian (0° longitude).

13:00	**15:00**	**17:00**	**19:00**	**21:00**	**23:00**
Paris	Moscow	Yekaterinburg	Ha Nôi	Tôkyô	Magadan
Algiers	Riyadh	Islamabad	Bangkok	Palau	New Caledonia
Luanda			Jakarta		

14:00	**16:00**	**18:00**	**20:00**	**22:00**	**24:00**
Kiev	Seychelles	Novosibirsk	Beijing	Port Moresby	Tuvalu
Cairo	Mauritius	Astana	Manila	Sydney	Fiji
Cape Town			Perth		Wellington

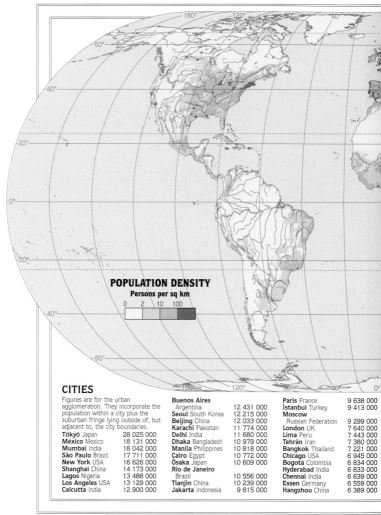

POPULATION DENSITY

Persons per sq km

0   2   10   100

CITIES

Figures are for the urban agglomeration. They incorporate the population within a city plus the suburban fringe lying outside of, but adjacent to, the city boundaries.

Tōkyō Japan		28 025 000
México Mexico		18 131 000
Mumbai India		18 042 000
São Paulo Brazil		17 711 000
New York USA		16 626 000
Shanghai China		14 173 000
Lagos Nigeria		13 488 000
Los Angeles USA		13 129 000
Calcutta India		12 900 000

Buenos Aires Argentina		12 431 000
Seoul South Korea		12 215 000
Beijing China		12 033 000
Karachi Pakistan		11 774 000
Delhi India		11 680 000
Dhaka Bangladesh		10 979 000
Manila Philippines		10 818 000
Cairo Egypt		10 772 000
Ōsaka Japan		10 609 000
Rio de Janeiro Brazil		10 556 000
Tianjin China		10 239 000
Jakarta Indonesia		9 815 000

Paris France		9 638 000
İstanbul Turkey		9 413 000
Moscow Russian Federation		9 299 000
London UK		7 640 000
Lima Peru		7 443 000
Tehrān Iran		7 380 000
Bangkok Thailand		7 221 000
Chicago USA		6 945 000
Bogotá Colombia		6 834 000
Hyderabad India		6 833 000
Chennai India		6 639 000
Essen Germany		6 559 000
Hangzhou China		6 389 000

Hong Kong China	6 097 000	Jinan China	4 789 000	Alexandria Egypt	3 995 000
Lahore Pakistan	6 030 000	Wuhan China	4 750 000	Washington USA	3 927 000
Shenyang China	5 681 000	Toronto Canada	4 657 000	Dallas USA	3 912 000
Changchun China	5 566 000	Yangôn Myanmar	4 458 000	Guadalajara Mexico	3 908 000
Bangalore India	5 544 000	Algiers Algeria	4 447 000	Chongqing China	3 896 000
Harbin China	5 475 000	Philadelphia USA	4 398 000	Medellin Colombia	3 831 000
Chengdu China	5 293 000	Qingdao China	4 376 000	Detroit USA	3 785 000
Santiago Chile	5 261 000	Milan Italy	4 251 000	Handan China	3 763 000
Guangzhou China	5 162 000	Pusan South Korea	4 239 000	Frankfurt Germany	3 700 000
St Petersburg		Belo Horizonte		Porto Alegre Brazil	3 699 000
Russian Federation	5 132 000	Brazil	4 160 000	Ha Nôi Vietnam	3 678 000
Kinshasa		Ahmadabad India	4 154 000	Sydney Australia	3 665 000
Dem. Rep. Congo	5 068 000	Madrid Spain	4 072 000	Santo Domingo	
Baghdâd Iraq	4 796 000	San Francisco USA	4 051 000	Dominican Republic	3 601 000

A B C D

1

East China Sea

A S I A

Northern Mariana Islands
Saipan (U.S.A.)
Guam (U.S.A.) □ Agana

2

Tropic of Cancer
Luzon
Caroline Islands
FEDERATED ST

Mindanao
Palau Islands
Halmahera

South China Sea
Bismarck Sea Rabaul
New Britain
New Ireland
Solo

Borneo
Sulawesi
Banda Sea
PAPUA NEW GUINEA
Port Moresby

3

Sumatera
Igva Sea.
Flores Sea
Timor
Arafura Sea
Coral S Island
Great Barrier Reef
Territo (Austr.)

Java (Jawa)
Bali
Timor Sea
Darwin
Gulf of Carpentaria
Cor Se

Christmas Island (Austr.)

Equator

0°

Broome
NORTHERN TERRITORY
Alice Springs
QUEENSLAND
Townsville

4

Cocos Islands (Aust.)

A U S T R A L I A

Brisbane
Gold Coast

I N D I A N O C E A N

WESTERN AUSTRALIA
SOUTH AUSTRALIA
Port Pirie
NEW SOUTH WALES
Newca

Geraldton
Great Australian Bight
Adelaide
Sydney

5

15°

Perth
VICTORIA
Canbe

Albany
Geelong ○ **Melbourne**
Bass Strait

SOUTHERN OCEAN

TASMANIA
Hobart

6

Tropic of Capricorn

30° 75° 90° 45° 105° 120° 135° 150°

A B C D

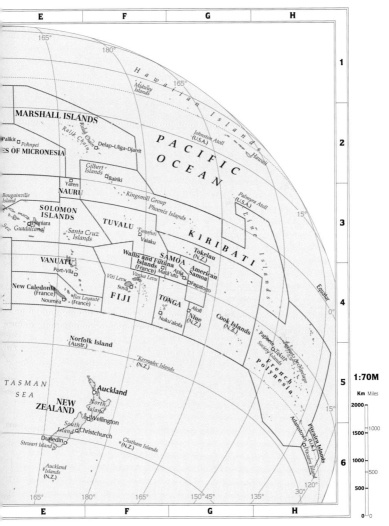

1:70M

Km Miles

2000

1500 — 1000

1000

500 — 500

0 — 0

© Bartholomew Ltd

18

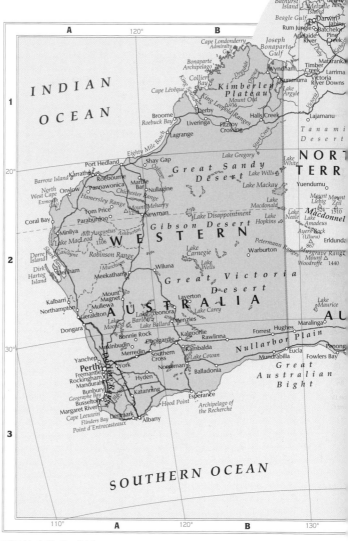

Lambert Azimuthal Equal Area Projection

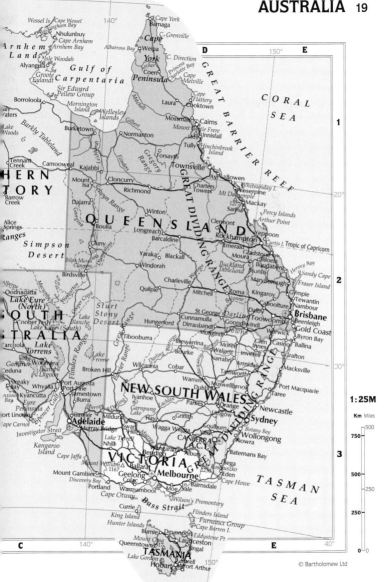

© Bartholomew Ltd

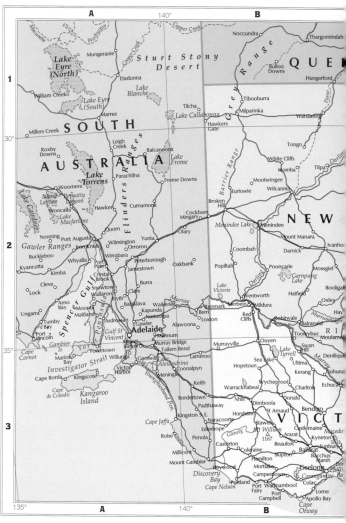

Conic Equidistant Projection

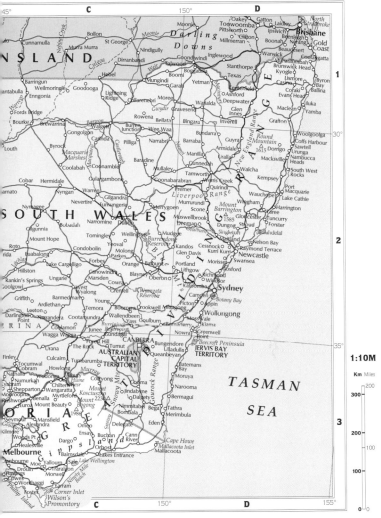

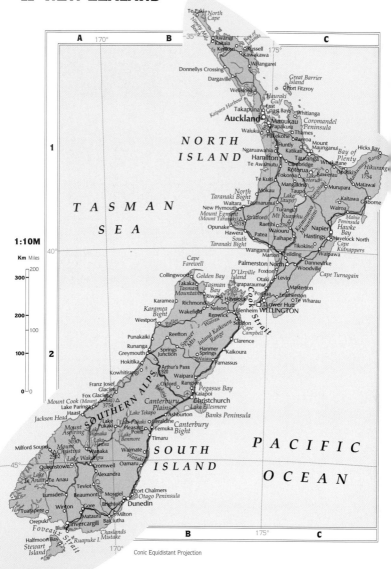

1:10M

Km	Miles
	200
300	
	100
200	
100	
0	0

Conic Equidistant Projection

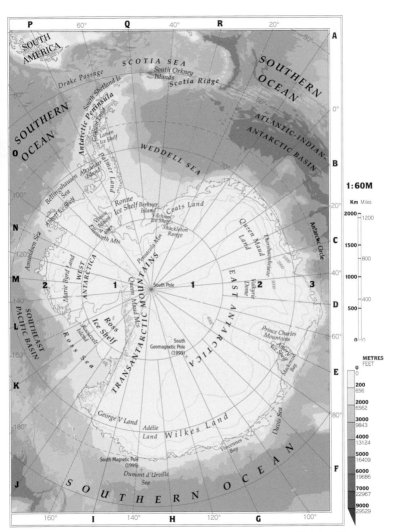

P 60° **Q** 40° **R** 20°

A

SOUTH AMERICA

SCOTIA SEA
South Orkney Islands
Drake Passage
Scotia Ridge

SOUTHERN OCEAN

SOUTHERN OCEAN

80°

0°

Antarctic Peninsula
Graham Land
Larsen Ice Shelf

ATLANTIC-INDIAN-
ANTARCTIC BASIN

WEDDELL SEA

70°

O

B

Bellingshausen Sea
Alexander Island
Palmer Land

100°

1 : 60M

Abbot Ice Shelf

Ronne Ice Shelf
Berkner Island
Filchner Ice Shelf
Coats Land

Shackleton Range

Queen Maud Land

Thorshavnheiane

Antarctic Circle

Km Miles

2000 — 1200

Amundsen Sea

Wilkins Ice Shelf
Ellsworth Mts
Pensacola Mts

20°

N

C

1500 — 800

120°

Marie Byrd Land
WEST ANTARCTICA

2 Queen Maud Mts **1**

South Pole

1 EAST

2 **3**

Valkyrie Dome

40°

M

D

1000 — 400

140°

SOUTHEAST PACIFIC BASIN

Roosevelt Island
Ross Ice Shelf

TRANSANTARCTIC MOUNTAINS

ANTARCTICA

400°

500

Prince Charles Mountains

150°

Ross Sea

South Geomagnetic Pole (1995)

60°

0 — 0

L

E

METRES
FEET

George V Land

Adélie Land

Wilkes Land

80°

Davis Sea

0 0

200 656

K

180°

Vincennes Bay

South Magnetic Pole (1995)
Dumont d'Urville Sea

2000 6562

3000 9843

F

160°

I 140° **H** 120° **G** 100°

SOUTHERN OCEAN

J

4000 13124

5000 16409

6000 19686

7000 22967

9000 29529

Orthographic Projection

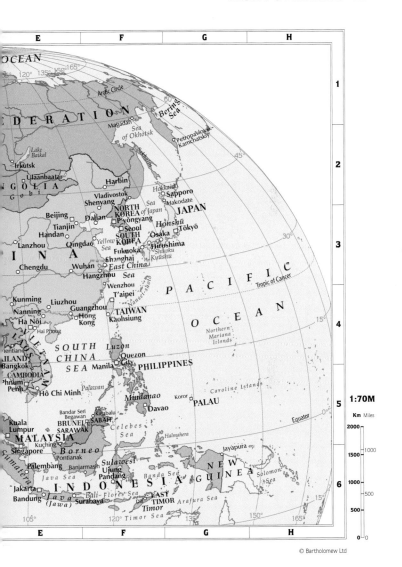

OCEAN

120° 135° 150° 165°

Arctic Circle

DERATION

Bering Sea

Magadan

Sea of Okhotsk

Petropavlovsk-Kamchatskiy

45°

Lake Baikal

Irkutsk

Sakhalin

Ulaanbaatar

Harbin

Hokkaido

NGOLIA

Gobi

Vladivostok

Sapporo

Shenyang

Sea of Japan

Hakodate

Beijing

NORTH KOREA

P'yŏngyang

JAPAN

Tianjin

Dalian

Seoul

Honshū

Tōkyō

Handan

SOUTH KOREA

Ōsaka

Lanzhou

Qingdao

Yellow Sea

Fukuoka

Hiroshima

30°

I N A

Shanghai

Shikoku

Kyūshū

Chengdu

Wuhan

East China

Hangzhou

Sea

Wenzhou

Tropic of Cancer

P A C I F I C

Kunming

Liuzhou

T'aipei

Nanning

Guangzhou

TAIWAN

O C E A N

Ha Nôi

Hong Kong

Kaohsiung

15°

Hai Phong

Northern Mariana Islands

ientiane

S O U T H

Luzon

ILAND

C H I N A

Quezon

Bangkok

S E A

Manila

City

PHILIPPINES

CAMBODIA

hnum Penh

Palawan

Hô Chi Minh

Mindanao

Koror

Caroline Islands

0°

1:70M

Davao

PALAU

Km Miles

Bandar Seri Begawan

Kota Kinabalu

Kuala Lumpur

BRUNEI

SABAH

Celebes

Equator

2000

SARAWAK

Sea

Halmahera

Singapore

Borneo

Kuching

Pontianak

Jayapura

1500

1000

Palembang

Banjarmasin

Sulawesi

NEW

Sumatra

Ujung

Banda Sea

Java Sea

Pandang

GUINEA

Solomon

1000

Jakarta

I N D O N E S I A

Sea

500

Bandung

Java

Bali

Flores Sea

15°

(Jawa)

Surabaya

Dili

EAST

500

TIMOR

Arafura Sea

Timor

105°

120°

Timor Sea

135°

150°

165°

0

E   F   G   H

© Bartholomew Ltd

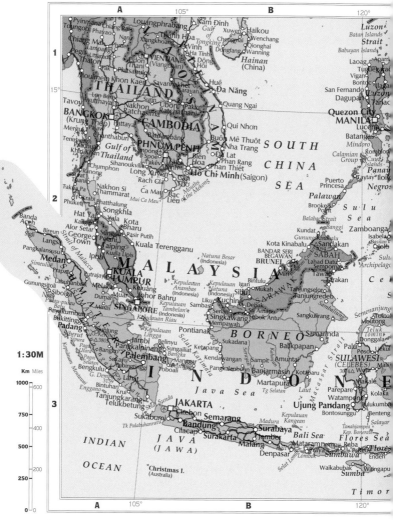

1:30M

Km Miles

1000 — 600

750 — 400

500 — 200

250 —

0 — 0

Albers Equal Area Conic Projection

C 135° D

PHILIPPINE
SEA

PACIFIC

OCEAN

Northern
Mariana
Islands
(U.S.A.)

Pagan

Saipan
Tinian 15°

Rota

Guam
(U.S.A.)

Dlillo
lands

PHILIPPINES

Catanduanes

Sorsogon
Catarman
Samar
Catbalogan
Tacloban

Bacolod
Cebu

Surigao
Butuan
Cagayan de Oro
Mindanao
Davao
Mati
General Santos

Ulithi
Fais

Yap
FEDERATED STATES
OF MICRONESIA

Ngulu
Sorol

Eauripik

Caroline
Islands

PALAU
KOROR

Kepulauan
Talaud

Morotai

Equator 0°

bes
Kepulauan
a
Sangir

Pellolohu Is

Hermit Is

Manado
Tondano
Gorontalo
Ternate
Halmahera

Sao-Siu
Tobelo

Waigeo
Pellelu

Jayapura
Vanimo

Aitape

Schouten Islands

Manam
Long
Island

Wewak

Dampir Kwoka
Sorong Doberai
Ransiki
Yapen

Jaziran
Numfoor
Manokwari Biak

Selat Yapen Tg d'Urville

Sarmi

PAPUA

Madang

Central

4000 4509

Umboi

Bacan
Obi
Misool
Salawati
Mafanlap
Inanwatan

Teluk Berau

Babo
Fakfak

Seram

Faulau

Nabire

Tg Vals

Van Rees

Pegunungan Tantau

Taritatu

Sepik

Mendi
Mount
Hagen
Kikori

Goroka

Pk Jaya
5030

Pk
Trikora
4730

Mandala
4700

Kison

Lae
Wau
Morobe

S

A

Kendari
Wowoni

Buton

Banda Sea

Ambon
Saparua
Banda

Kepulauan Kai

Sula

Kepulauan
Watubela

Amamapare

Kepulauan

Kai Kecil
Tual

Kai

Dobo

Wokam

NEW
GUINEA

Kerema

Kiköri

Bereina

Mt
Victoria
4073

Aru
Kobroör

PORT
MORESBY

Kepulauan
Alor

Kalabahi
Atauro

Kepulauan Barat Daya

Wetar
Damar
Roma

Huaki Kaiwatu

Wuliaru
Babar
Leti
Saumlakki

Kepulauan Tanimbar

Larat
Trangan

Sia

Benjina

Besar

Tg Deyong
Digul

Merauke
Morehead

P. Dolak

Balimo
Daru

Gulf
Papua

Dili
EAST
TIMOR

Selaru

Manatuto
Kefamenanu
Timor

Keci

Tg Vals

Arafura Sea

Kupang
Rote

AUSTRALIA

Melville
Island

Croker I.

Bathurst Island
Beagle Gulf

Van Diemen
Gulf

Darwin

Jabiru

C. Wessel

Wessel Is

Nhulunbuy
C. Arnhem

Gulf
of
Carpentaria

C. York

Bamaga

Weipa

Coen

C 135° D

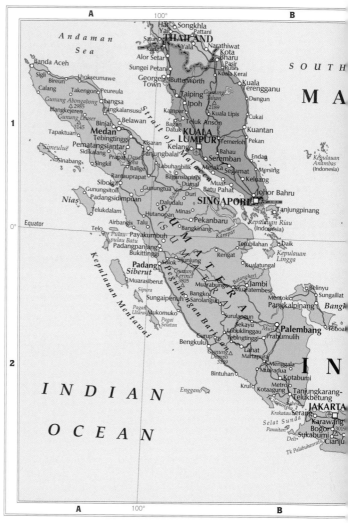

Albens Equal Area Conic Projection

30

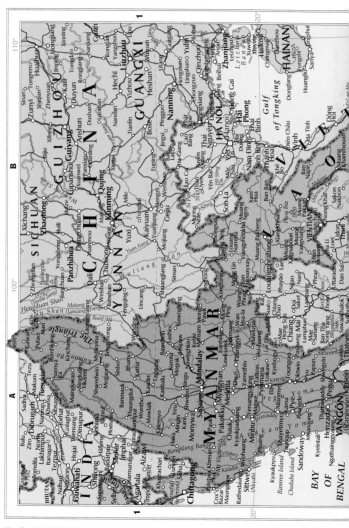

Albers Equal Area Conic Projection

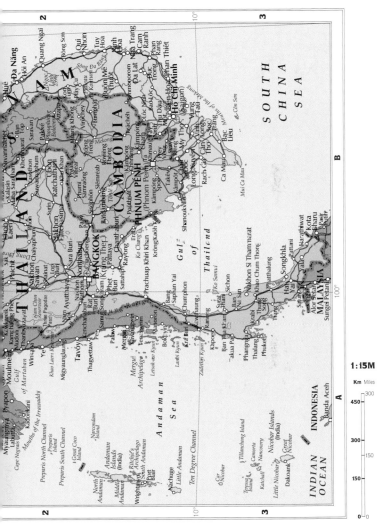

1:15M

PHILIPPINE SEA

PHILIPPINES

SOUTH CHINA SEA

CELEBES SEA

SULU SEA

Albers Equal Area Conic Projection

34

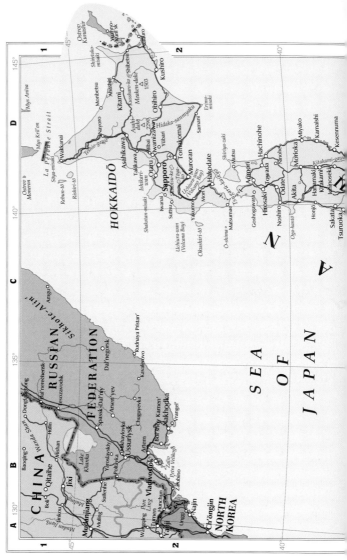

RUSSIAN FEDERATION

Sikhote-Alin'

Anyuy

Ol'ga

P'yatrechenskiy

Terechechenskiy

Geozavodsk

Dal'negorsk

Rudnaya Pristan'

Kavalerovo

Spassk-Dal'niy

Yaroslavskiy

Chuguyevka

Pokhaylovka

Arsen'yev

Ussuriysk

Bol'shoy Kamen'

Nakhodka

Vrangel'

Lake
Khanka

Partizansk

Vladivostok

Zaliv
Petra Velikogo

Zarubino

Ussro

CHINA

Baoqing

Qitaihe

Boli

Linkou

Jixi

Mishan

Suifenhe

Muling

Mudanjiang

Wanda Shan

Dongning

Hulin

Hunchun

Tumen

Tumen'

Hun

Mudan Jiang

Zaifu

Ling

Najin

Ch'ŏngjin

**NORTH
KOREA**

La Pérouse Strait

Mys Aniva

Mys Kril'on

Ostrov b
Moneron

*Ostrog
Kunashir*

Shiretoko-
misaki

Wakkanai

Rebun-tō

Rishiri-tō

Soya-misaki

Nayoro

Monbetsu

Kitami

Abashiri

HOKKAIDŌ

Asahikawa

Takikawa

Iwanai

Otaru

Ishikari-
wan

Sapporo

Shakotan-misaki

Suttsu

Yakumo

Uchiura-wan
(Volcano Bay)

Okushiri-tō

Matsumae

Wakkanai

Teshio-zaki

Kussharo-ko
Abashiri

Meakan-dake
1503

Asahi-
dake
(2290)

Yubari

Iwamizawa

Tomakomai

Muroran

Mori

Hakodate

Tsugaru
Strait

Obihiro

Hidaka-sammyaku

Samani

Erimo-
misaki

Kushiro

Tokachi

O-shima

Oma-zaki

Shiriya-zaki

Mutsu

Aomori

Towada

Ōdate

Noshiro

Akita

Goshogawara

Hirosaki

Honjō

Oga-hantō

Hachinohe

Noheji

Towada

Miyako

Morioka

Hanamaki

Kitakami

Kamaishi

Kesennuma

Kitakami-gawa

Ichinoseki

Sakata

Tsuruoka

K

N A

S E A

O F

J A P A N

Albers Equal Area Conic Projection

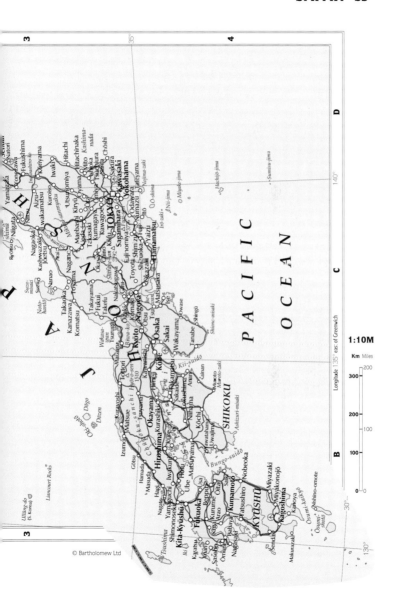

3

D

4

35°

140°

Sendai
Natori
Yamagata
Yonezawa
Shinjō
Niigata
Nagaoka
Joetsu
Kashiwazaki
Sanao
Suzu-misaki
Noto-hantō
Takaoka
Kanazawa
Komatsu
Takayama
Fukui
Tsuruga
Wakasa-wan
Kyōto
Ōtsu
Shirakawa
Fukushima
Kōriyama
Iwaki
Aizu-wakamatsu
Kuroso
Utsunomiya
Maebashi
Kiryū
Takasaki
Nagano
Matsumoto
Ōmiya
Nakatsugawa
Toyota
Gifu
Ōgaki
Nagoya
Komaki
Ichinomiya
Tsu
Matsusaka
Ōwase
Hitachinaka
Mito
Kashima-nada
Chōshi
Tsuchiura
Kawagoe
Kawasaki
TŌKYŌ
Yokohama
Fujisawa
Sagamihara
Odawara
Numazu
Fuji
Shimizu
Shizuoka
Yaizu
Hamamatsu
Okazaki
Kodwara
Itō
Ōshima
Nojima-zaki
Nii-jima
Miyake-jima
Mikura-jima
Iro-zaki
Omae-zaki
Hachijō-jima
Sumisu-jima

Kuwana
Kameyama
Kasai
Himeji
Akashi
Kōbe
Ōsaka
Sakai
Wakayama
Arai
Tanabe
Shingū
Shimo-misaki
Muroto-misaki

Tottori
Matsue
Izumo
Kurayoshi
Chūgoku-sanchi
Ō-san
1510

Hagi
Hamada
Masuda
Iwakuni
Gotō
Kurashiki
Kure
Okayama
Hiroshima
Fukuyama
Onomichi
Takamatsu
Sakaide
Marugame
Niihama
Kōchi
Iyo-nada
Matsuyama
Uwajima
Ōzu
Iwatehana
Iwanmi
SHIKOKU

Ashizuri-misaki

Kii-suidō

Bungo-suidō

Nagato
Yamaguchi
Shimonoseki
Ube
Kita-Kyūshū
Fukuoka
Nōgata
Iizuka
Beppu
Kurume
Ōita
Saiki
Saga
Nobeoka
Karatsu
Tsushima
Iki
Nagasaki
Sasebo
Ōmuta
Isahaya
Unzen
Kumamoto
Yatsushiro
Hitoyoshi
Miyazaki
Miyakonojō
Kagoshima
Sendai
Kanoya
Makurazaki
Ōsumi-shotō
Nishino-omote
KYŪSHŪ
Ariake-kai

Ullŭng-do
(S. Korea)

Liancourt Rocks

Oki-shotō
Dōgo
Dōzen

PACIFIC

OCEAN

130°

30°

Longitude 135° east of Greenwich

1:10M

Km Miles
300 — 200
200 —
100 — 100
0 — 0

© Bartholomew Ltd

Albers Equal Area Conic Projection

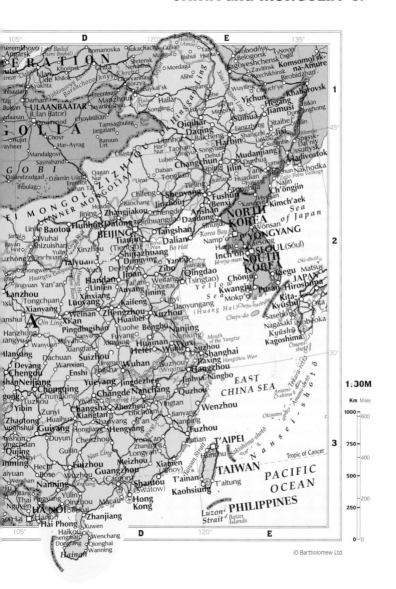

© Bartholomew Ltd

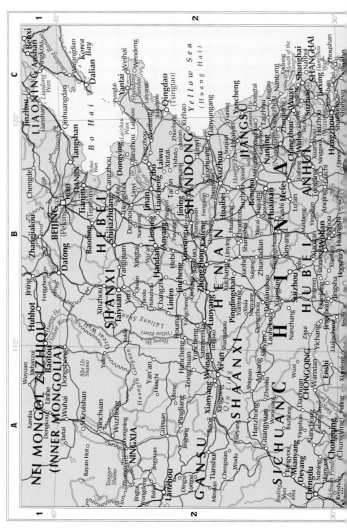

Albers Equal Area Conic Projection

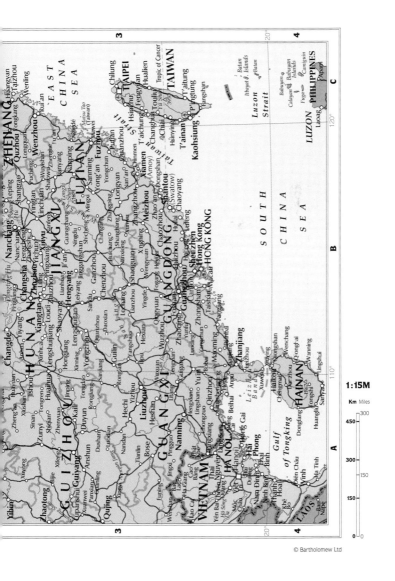

1:15M

Km Miles

450 — 300

300 — 150

150

0 — 0

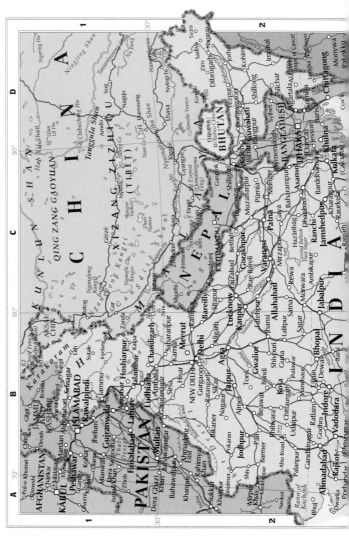

Albers Equal Area Conic Projection

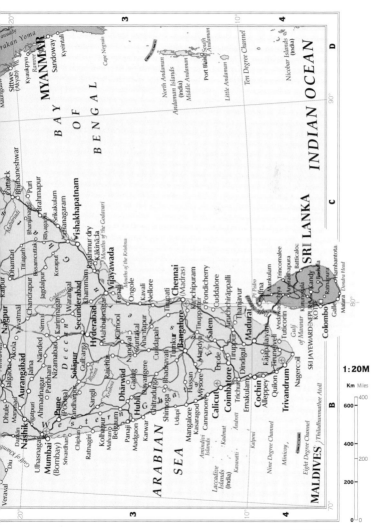

SOUTHERN ASIA

MYANMAR
Maungdaw · Sittwe (Akyab) · Kyaukpyu · Ramree · Sandoway · Kyeintali · *Cape Negrais* · *Arakan Yoma* · *Irawaddy*

BAY OF BENGAL

North Andaman
Andaman Islands (India)
Middle Andaman
Port Blair · South Andaman
Little Andaman

Ten Degree Channel

Nicobar Islands (India)

INDIAN OCEAN

Cuttack · Bhubaneshwar · Puri · Brahmapur · Titlagarh · Bissamcuttak · Jagdalpur · Koraput · *Mahanadi* · Dhamtari · Chandrapur · Raipur · Nagpur · Yavatmal · Akola

Srikakulam · Vizianagaram · **Vishakhapatnam** · Rajahmundry · Kakinada · *Mouths of the Godavari* · *Godavari*

Eluru · **Vijayawada** · Khammam · Warangal · Karimnagar · Nirmal · Nizamabad · Nanded · Parbhani · Jalna

Mouths of the Krishna · **Secunderabad** · **Hyderabad** · Kurnool · Mahbubnagar · Gulbarga · Raichur · Bidar · Solapur · **Aurangabad** · Ahmadnagar · Patpuri

Machilipatnam · Ongole · Nellore · Kavali · Nandyal · Anantapur · Gooty · Cuddapah · Bellary · Gadag · Navalgund · Bhadravati · Chitradurga · Davangere · **Hubli** · **Dharwad** · Belgaum · Panaji · Karwar

Chennai (Madras) · Tirupati · Kanchipuram · Pondicherry · Cuddalore · Tiruchchirappalli · Vellore · Salem · Mandya · Erode · Tiruppur · Karur · **Bangalore** · **Mysore** · Hassan · Kasaragod · Cannanore · **Calicut** · Trichur · Ernakulam · **Cochin** · Alleppey · Quilon · **Trivandrum** · Nagercoil

Madanapalle · Tirupattur · Dindigul · **Madurai** · Kalapalayam · Thanjavur · Nagapattinam · Tuticorin · *Gulf of Mannar*

SRI JAYEWARDENEPURA KOTTE · Puttalam · Kurunegala · Kandy · Anuradhapura · Trincomalee · Batticaloa · Medawachchiya · Negombo · **Colombo** · Ratnapura · Hambantota · Galle · Matara · *Dondra Head* · *Pt Pedro* · *Jaffna*

ARABIAN SEA · Mumbai (Bombay) · Ulhasnagar · **Pune** (POONA) · Kolhapur · Sangli · Ratnagiri · Chiplun · Mahad · Srivardhan · Nashik · Dhule · Malegaon · Jalgaon · *Western Ghats* · *Kaveri* · *Krishna* · *Bhima*

Daman · Damão · Veraval · *Gulf of Khambhat*

Laccadive Islands (India) · Aminidivi Islands · Kadmat · Amindivi · Kavaratti · Androt · Kalpeni · Minicoy

Nine Degree Channel · Eight Degree Channel

MALDIVES · Thiladhummathee Atoll

1 : 20M

Km | Miles
— 400
600 —
— 200
400 —
200 —
0 — 0

Albers Equal Area Conic Projection

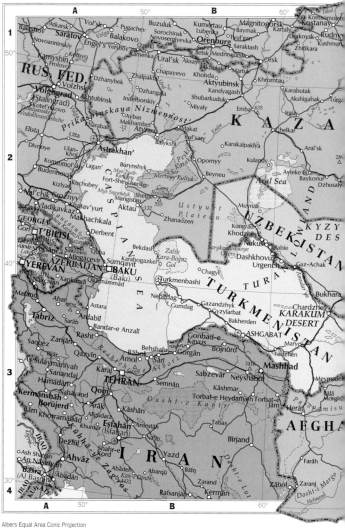

A 50° **B** 60°

1

50°

Atkarsk Vol'sk Pugachev Buzuluk Kumertau Magnitogorsk Komsomol's Kostanay
Balashov Saratov Volga Balakovo Sorochinsk Lubenka Baymak Kartaly Rudny
Novoannninskiy Engel's Yershov Oziniki Novosergiyevka Sol Orenburg Lisakovsk Zhitikara Kushmur
Kamyshin Kotovo Kamenka Ural'sk Aksay Akbulak Mednogorsk Orsk Saraktash Tobol Kushmur
Frolovo Chapayevo Khobda Martuk Khromtau
RUS. FED. Dzhanybek Zhalpaktal Aktyubinsk Kandyagash Emba 635 Karabutak
Volzhskiy Volgograd Akhtubinsk Inderborskiy Shubarkuduk Akshiganak Turga
(Stalingrad) Dzhangala Miyaly Irgiz Shelkar
Kotel'nikovo Tsimlyanskoye Vodokhranilishche Kharabali Aybas Makhambet -12 Atyrau Makat Karakalpakiya Aral'sk 285
Elista Utta Balykshi Oporniy Kulandy Ayteke Bi
Divnoye Ulan- Astrakhan' Burynshyk Sor Beyneu Baykonur Dzhusaly

2

40°

Khol Lagan' Mys Tyub- Pesk Merteyy Kultuk Mangistau Aral Sea
Komsomol'skiy Karagan Fort-Shevchenko Gora Besshoka Kulandy KYZY DES
Budennovsk Kizlyar Mys Sagyndyk Mangistau Shetpe Muynak UZBEKISTAN
Nal'chik Groznyy Kochubey Aktau -132 555 Ustyurt Khodzheyli Nukus Turan KAZA
Vladikavkaz Khasav'yurt Makhachkala Plateau Kungrad Dashkhovuz
GEORGIA Gori Derbent Kumugrad Urgench Gaz-Achak
T'BILISI Bekdash Zaliv Kara-Bogaz Gol Ozero Dashkhovuz Bukhara
ARMENIA Ganca Säki Karabogazkel Chagyl Chardzhev
YEREVAN Qusar Mingäcevir Sumqayit Turkmenbashi TURA Chardzhou KARAKUM
AZERBAIJAN BAKU (Baku) Qazimämmäd Nebitdag TURKMENISTAN DESERT
Naxçivan Länkäran Astara Gazandzhyk Gyzylarbat Bakherden ASHGABAT Maryp Teжен
Maraga Ahar Ardabil Bandar-e Anzali Gumdag Gazandzhyk Tedzhen Meymanel

3

30°

Tabriz Saräb Rasht Gonbad-e Bojnurd 341 Mashhad Para
Saqqez Zanjan Qazvin Behshahr Kavus Neyshabur Hala Morgha Herat
Äs Sulaymaniyah Bijar Karaj Amol Babol Sari Gorgan Sabzevar Torbat-e Heydariyeh Torbat-e Jam misu
Sanandaj Hamadan TEHRAN Semnan Kashmar Jam AFGHA
Kermanshah Nahavand Qom Dasht-e Kavir Tabas
Borujerd Aligudarz Arak Kashan Ardestan Birjand
Khorramabad Khunsar Esfahan (Isfahan) Na'in Yazd Dasht-e Lut
Dezful Shahr-e Kord Abarqu Farah
Ash Shatrah IRAQ Ahvaz IRAN Kuh-e Dinar 4432 Bafq Zarand Zabol Zaranj
An Nasiriyah Abadeh Rafsanjan Kerman Dasht-i Margo
Basra (Al Basrah) Abadan Helmand

4

A 50° **B** 60°

Albers Equal Area Conic Projection

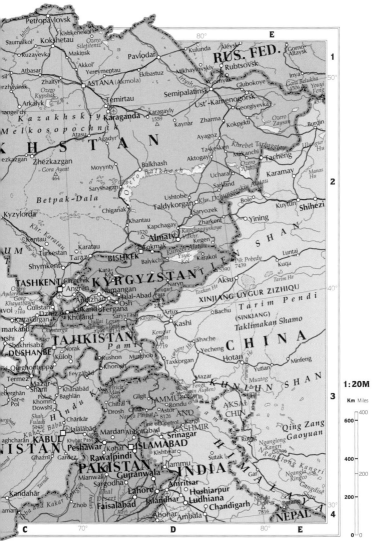

Petropavlovsk
kishkeneköl
Saumalköl Kokshetau Ozero
Siletiteñz
Ruzayevka Makinsk Pavlodar Kulunda Aléysk Gorno-
Atkol' Yereymentau Ekibastuz Mikhaylovskiy Rubtsovsk Altaysk
Atbasar Zhaltyr ASTANA (Akmola) Ust'-Kamenogorsk Inya Gora Belukha
Kypshak Temirtau Semipalatinsk Georgiyevka Youyi Feng

RUS. FED.

Arkalyk Karaganda Karagayly Kaynar Zharma Kokpekti Ozero Burqin
Zhezkazgan Gora Ayeat Moyynty Balkhash Aktogay Zaysan
Gora Ayeat Saryshagan Ushtobe Karamay Manas
Betpak-Dala Chigañak Taldykorgan Saryozek Bole Kuytun Shihezi

Kyzylorda Khantau Kapchagay Zharkent Yining
Kentau Turkestan Karatau Almaty Tokmak Kegen
Shymkent Taraz BISHKEK Balykchy Ysyk-Köl Karakol Luntai

TASHKENT chirchik KYRGYZSTAN Naryn Aksu Tarim He Kuqa
Angren Namangan Jalal-Abad Torugart Pass XINJIANG UYGUR ZIZHIQU
Gulistan Andizhan Osh Artux Tarim Pendi
Khŭjand Kokand Fergana Kashi (SINKIANG) Taklimakan Shamo
Kattakorgan Dzhizak Shache
markand TAJIKISTAN Pamir Yecheng CHINA
DUSHANBE Norak Kŭlob Rushon Murghob Taxkorgan Hotan Minfeng
Termez Feyzabad Mazar Yutian
Mazar-e Sharif Khanabad KUN LUN SHAN
Pol-e Baghlan Gilgit AKSAI
Dowshi Chitral Astor CHIN Qing Zang
Charikar Drosh Nanga Parbat Gaoyuan
KABUL Jalalabad Mardan Abbottabad Srinagar HIMALAYA
ISTAN Peshawar Kohat ISLAMABAD KASHMIR
Ghazni Gardez Rawalpindi Jammu
PAKISTAN INDIA
Mianwali Gujranwala Hoshiarpur
Kandahar Sargodha Lahore Amritsar Ludhiana Chandigarh
Zhob Faisalabad Jalandhar NEPAL
Abohar Ambala

1:20M

Km Miles
400
600
400 200
200
0 0

© Bartholomew Ltd

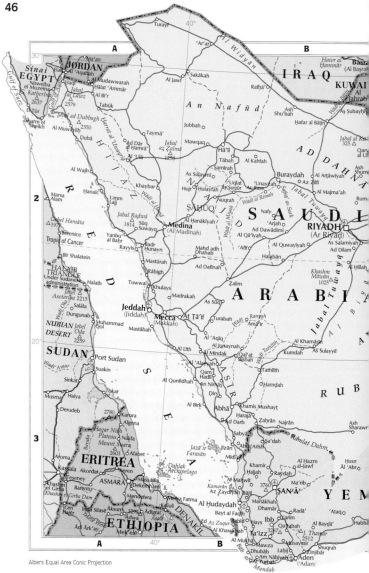

Albers Equal Area Conic Projection

1:15M

Km Miles

© Bartholomew Ltd

This map image contains the following labels:

A   30°   **B**

Sibiu, Sfântu Gheorghe, Artsyz, Odesa, UKRAINE, Armyans'k, Gulf of Taganrog, Râmnicu Vâlcea, Focşani, Brasov, Bilhorod-Dnistrovs'kyy, Skadovs'k, Novooleksiyivka, Staromynskaya, Yeysk, Pitesti, Ploieşti, Brăila, Bolhrad, Izmayil, Karkinits'ka Zatoka, Krasnoperekops'k, Komorom-Komarske-Pavlovskaya, Tihmashevsk

ROMANIA, BUCHAREST (Bucureşti), Slatina, Roşiori de Vede, Caracal, Dâmbovița, (Dunăre), Giurgiu, Silistra, Călăraşi, Constanța, Chornomors'ke, Crimea, Yevpatoriya, Dzhankoy, Simferopol', Feodosiya, Kerch, Temryuk, Slavyansk-na-Kubani, Krasnodar, Maykop, Khadyzhensk

Arabia, Craiova, Ruse, Razgrad, Dobrich, Mangalia, Sevastopol', Roman-Kosh 1545, Sudak, Novorossiysk, Tuapse

Pleven, Shumen, Lovech, Varna, Kavarna, BLACK SEA, Sochi

BULGARIA, Kazanlŭk, Stara Zagora, Sliven, Burgas, Ineboli, Ince Burun, Sinop, Samsun, Ordu, Giresun, Trabzon

Plovdiv, Dimitrovgrad, Khaskovo, Bolu, Zonguldak, Bartın, Boyabat, Bafra, Vezirköprü, Terme, Sebinkarahisar, Anadolu Dağları, Kelkit Dağı, Bayburt, Erzincan

Smolyan, Kürdzhali, Edirne, Kırklareli, Saray, Karabük, Ereğli, Kastamonu, Tosya, Amasya, Niksar, Tokat, Reşadiye, Üskdar, Erzurum

Thasos, Gökçeada (Imroz), Keşan, Şarköy, Tekirdağ, Çorlu, Silivri, Istanbul, Kadıköy, Sakarya, Geyve, Düzce, Gerede, Çankırı, Çorum, Sungurlu, Yıldızeli, Sivas, Zara, Divriği

Limnos, Çanakkale, Can, Bandırma, Bursa, Bilecik, Muduma, Beypazarı, Kalecik, ANKARA, Kırıkkale, Yozgat, Akdağmadeni, Kangal, Elbistan, Malatya, Hazar, Engeni

Lesbos, Edremit, Balıkesir, Susurluk, İnegöl, Eskişehir, Sivrihisar, Kaman, Yerköy, Sürücü, Tunc

Mytilene, Ayvalık, Soma, Simav, Tavşanlı, Kütahya, Emirdağ, Cihanbeyli, Kayseri, 3916, Pınarbaşı, Diyarbakır, Sivere, Şanlıurfa

Chios, İzmir, Manisa, Uşak, Afyon, Sandıklı, Akşehir, Tuz Gölü, Aksaray, Niğde, Yahyalı, Kahramanmaraş, Mils, Çakale

Íkaria, Kuşadası, Aydın, Nazilli, Denizli, Çivril, Burdur, 2799, Beyşehir Gölü, Beyşehir, Karapınar, Bor, Dağları, TURKEY, T, GREECE

Dodecanese (Dodekánisa), Milas, Yatağan, Muğla, Kızılören, Eğirdir Gölü, Eğirdir, Bucak, Konya, Ereğli, Tarsus, Adana, Gaziantep, İskenderun (Alexandretta)

Marmaris, Dalaman, Elmalı, Serik, Karaman, Osmaniye, Aleppo, Halab (Al Ḥalab)

Fethiye, 3073, Kaş, Antalya, Manavgat, Alanya, Silifke, İçel, Antakya (Antioch) (Hatay), Ar Raqqah (Al Raqqa)

Rhodes (Rodos), Meğisti, Antalya Körfezi, Erdemli, Aegean Sea, Agios Nikólaos, Karpathos (Scarpanto), CRETE (KRITI), Cape Apostolos Andreas, Hilib, SYRIA, Euphrates

Lindos, NICOSIA (Lefkosía), Keryneia, Aglalousa, Al Lādhiqīyah, Hamāh, Dayr az Zawr, Cape Arnaoutis, Evrychou, Larnaca, Bāniyās, Tartūs, Pafos, Lemesos, Tráblous (Tripoli), Ḥimş, Tadmur

CYPRUS, MEDITERRANEAN SEA, BEIRUT (Beyrouth), Sidon, Zahlé, Sab' Ābār, Ar Ruţbah, Syrian Desert, Badiyat ash Shām

LEBANON, Soûr, DAMASCUS (Dimashq), Ar Zarqā, Ḥefa, Nazareth, Sea of Galilee (L. Tiberias), As Suwaydā', Ţurayf

Marsa Matrûh, Alexandria (El Iskandariya), El 'Amiriya, Baltim, ISRAEL, Tel Aviv-Yafo, Irbid, JORDAN, Sakākah, Tawīl

El Hammam, Damanhûr, El Mansûra, Dumyât, Port Said (Būr Sa'īd), El 'Arish, JERUSALEM, WEST BANK, AMMAN, Petra, Ma'an, SAUDI

Qattâra Depression, Shubrâ el Kheima, Ţanţa, Zagazig, Ismâ'iliya, Suez Canal, GAZA, Beʼer Sheva, Dead Sea, Al Karak

El Giza (El Gîza), Giza Pyramids, CAIRO (El Qâhira), Suez (El Suweis), Sinai, EGYPT, Memphis, Al 'Aqabah, Al Mudawwarah

1:15M

Km Miles

© Bartholomew Ltd

Conic Equidistant Projection

1:42M

Km Miles
1200 —
— 600
900 —
— 300
600 —
300 —
0 — 0

© Bartholomew Ltd

Orthographic Projection

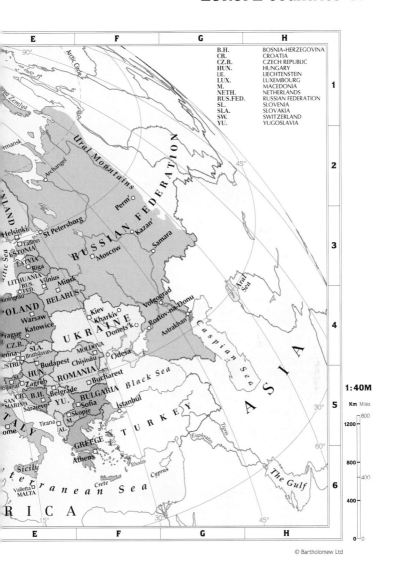

B.H.	BOSNIA-HERZEGOVINA
CR.	CROATIA
CZ.R.	CZECH REPUBLIC
HUN.	HUNGARY
LIE.	LIECHTENSTEIN
LUX.	LUXEMBOURG
M.	MACEDONIA
NETH.	NETHERLANDS
RUS.FED.	RUSSIAN FEDERATION
SL.	SLOVENIA
SLA.	SLOVAKIA
SW.	SWITZERLAND
YU.	YUGOSLAVIA

1:40M

Km Miles

© Bartholomew Ltd

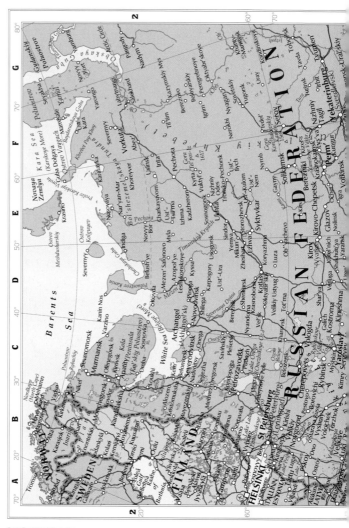

Conic Equidistant Projection

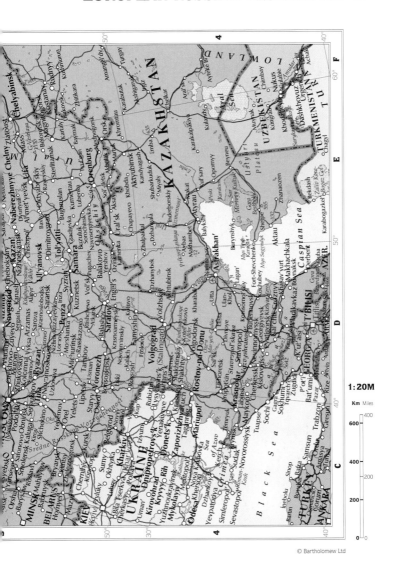

1:20M

Km Miles
┌ 400
600 ┤
     ┤ 200
400 ┤
     ┤
200 ┤
     ┤
0 ┴ 0

© Bartholomew Ltd

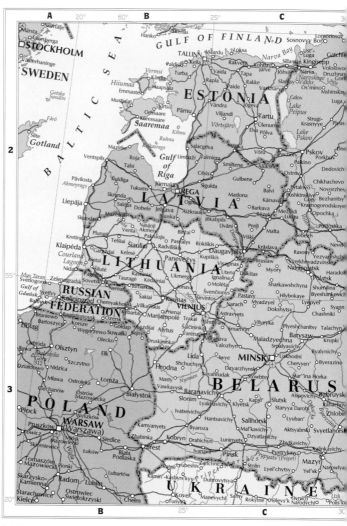

Conic Equidistant Projection

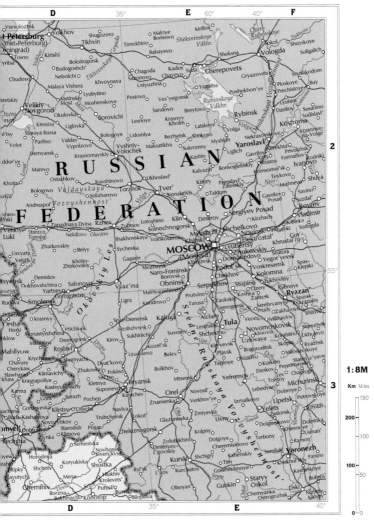

1:8M

Km Miles

150

200

100

100

50

0 0

Conic Equidistant Projection

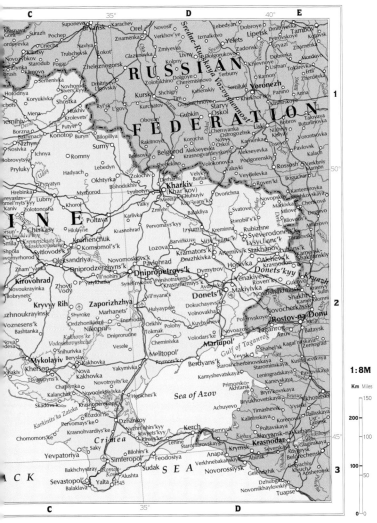

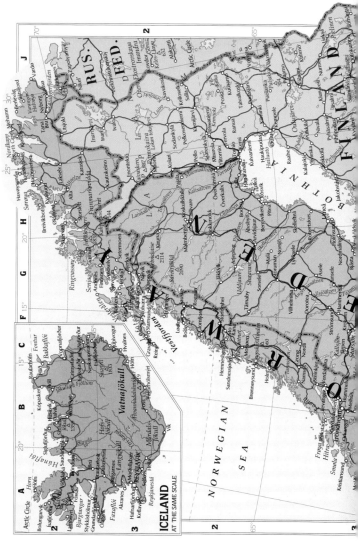

ICELAND
AT THE SAME SCALE

Conic Equidistant Projection

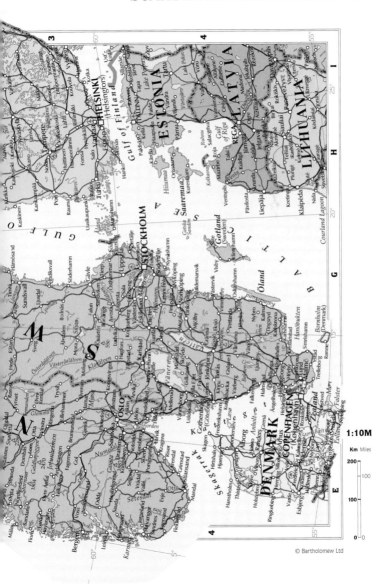

1:10M

Km Miles
200 —
— 100
100 —
0 — 0

© Bartholomew Ltd

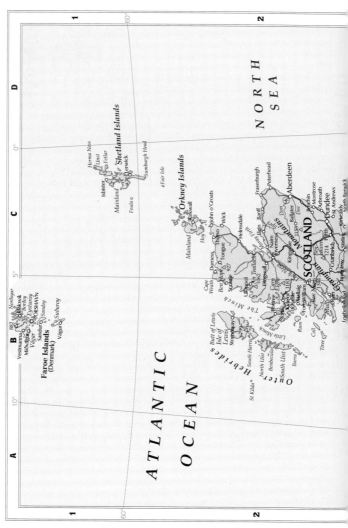

Conic Equidistant Projection

1:8M

Km Miles
- 150
200 -
- 100
100 -
- 50
0 - 0

A 6° B 4°

Orkney Islands
North Ronaldsay
Westray Sanday
Rousay Loth
Stronsay
Birsay Mainland Kirkwall
Stromness
Ward Hill Gritley
179 Hoy Stapla
South Ronaldsay John o' Groats
Pentland Firth
Dunnet Head Duncansby Head

Herma Ness
Unst
Yell
Isbister Uesta Fetlar
Ronas Hill Voe
450 Mainland
Walls Whalsay
Foula Lerwick
Bressay
Sumburgh **Shetland Islands**
Sumburgh Head
60°
2° Fair Isle

Cape Wrath
Durness
Ben Hope Tongue
927 Thurso Wick
Ben More Assynt Loch Shin
Scourie
Point of Stoer 998 Lairg Helmsdale
Lochinver Loch Broom
Ullapool Dornoch
An Teallach Golspie
1062 Ben Wyvis Dornoch Firth
Gairloch Loch Maree 046 Invergordon
Achnasheen Alness
Torridon Dingwall Black Isle Moray Firth
Carn Eighe Beauly Inverness Elgin Lossiemouth
1183 Loch Ness Findhorn Forres Buckie Banff Fraserburgh
Kyle of Lochalsh Aberchirder
Fort Augustus Monadhliath Mountains Grantown-on-Spey Dufftown Huntly Ellon Peterhead
Garry Spey Cairngorm Inverurie
Kingussie Macduff Dyce
Aviemore Cairngorm Mountains Don Aberdeen
Loch Lochy Ballater
1344 Fort William Braemar Lochnagar Stonehaven
Ben Nevis Blair Atholl 1155 Dee
Glen Shiel **GRAMPIAN MOUNTAINS**
Point of Ardnamurchan Salen Glen Coe Pitlochry North Esk Brechin
Morvern **S C O T L A N D** Kirriemuir Forfar Montrose
Tobermory Ben Lawers Tay Blairgowrie Sidlaw Hills Arbroath
Coll Arinagour Mull Rannoch Moor 214 Loch Tay Dundee
Ben More Killin Perth Firth of Tay
Tiree Scarinish 966 Crianlarich Crieff St Andrews **NORTH**
Iona Oban Callander Glenrothes Fife Ness **SEA**
Fionnphort Inveraray Ben Lomond Cupar
974 Loch Stirling Buckhaven
Colonsay Loch Awe Tarbet Lomond Alloa Kirkcaldy North Berwick
Helensburgh Dunfermline Dunbar
56° Beinn an Oir Greenock Dumbarton Falkirk **Edinburgh** St Abb's Head
Port 785 Clydebank Glasgow Cumbernauld Musselburgh
Askaig Paisley Coatbridge Dalkeith Berwick-upon-Tweed
1:4M Jura Gigha Rothesay Largs Motherwell Penicuik Duns Holy Island (Lindisfarne)
Islay East Kilbride Hamilton Peebles Galashiels Kelso
Km Miles Goat Fell Ardrossan Lanark Biggar Selkirk Newtown Coldstream
75 874 Irvine St Boswells Tweed
Mull of Oa Port Ellen Brodick Kilmarnock **SOUTHERN UPLANDS** Broad Hawick The Cheviot
Arran Prestwick 840 Law Jedburgh 815
Ayr Cumnock Moffat **Cheviot Hills**
100 Campbeltown Maybole Alnwick
50 **North Channel** Thornhill Kielder Rothbury
Giant's Merrick Water North Tyne
Causeway Portrush Ballycastle Mull 843 Castle Ashington
25 Portstewart of Kintyre Girvan Newton Douglas Lockerbie Longtown Morpeth
Coleraine Stewart Dumfries Newcastle upon Tyne
50 Ballymoney Stranraer Dalbeattie Annan Hexham Blaydon
Cullybackey Ballymena Wigtown Kirkcudbright Solway Firth Carlisle Gateshead Consett Durham
NORTHERN Larne Whitehead Luce Whithorn Cockermouth Penrith Spennymoor Wear
IRELAND Antrim Ballyclare Bay Workington **ENGLAND** 931 Cross Fell 893
0 Newtownabbey Bangor Donaghadee Mull of Galloway
A 6° B 4° C 2° D

Conic Equidistant Projection

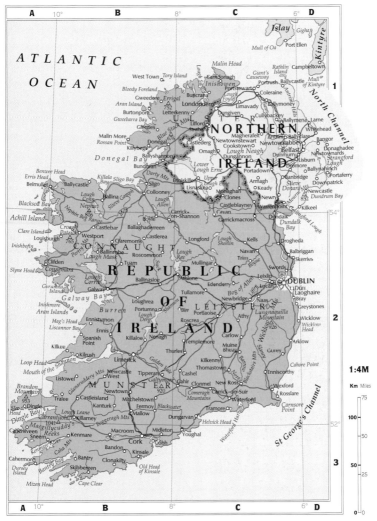

ATLANTIC OCEAN

NORTHERN IRELAND

REPUBLIC OF IRELAND

CONNAUGHT

LEINSTER

MUNSTER

Islay
Gigha
Mull of Oa
Port Ellen
Campbeltown
Rathlin Island
Giant's Causeway
Mull of Kintyre
North Channel

West Town
Tory Island
Malin Head
Carndonagh
Inishowen
Bloody Foreland
Gweedore
Errigal
752
Buncrana
Portrush
Portstewart
Coleraine
Ballycastle
Aran Island
Burtonport
Letterkenny
Londonderry
Limavady
Ballymoney
Gweebarra Bay
Lifford
Dungiven
Cullybackey
Glenties
Blue Stack Mts
676
Strabane
Magherafelt
Antrim
Ballyclare
Larne
Ballymena

Malin More
Rossan Point
Killybegs
Donegal
Castlederg
Newtownstewart
Cookstown
Newtownabbey
Bangor
Belfast
Donaghadee
Omagh
Lough Neagh
Dungannon
Lisburn
Newtownards
Strangford Lough
Ballynahinch

Donegal Bay
Ballyshannon
Bundoran
Lower Lough Erne
Portadown
Banbridge
Slieve Donard 852
Downpatrick
Newcastle
Dundrum Bay

Benwee Head
Erris Head
Belmullet
Ballycastle
Killala
Killala Bay
Sligo
Sligo Bay
Darty Mts
Enniskillen
Upper Lough Erne
Lisnaskea
Monaghan
Armagh
Keady
Newry
Warrenpoint
Kilkeel
Carlingford Lough

Blacksod Bay
Achill Island
Clare Island
Louisburgh
Croagh Patrick 765
Nephin Beg Range
Nephin
Lough Conn
Ballina
Ox Mts
Colooney
Lough Allen
Carrick-on-Shannon
Cavan
Castleblayney
Carrickmacross
Dundalk
Dundalk Bay

Westport
Castlebar
Boyle
Ballaghaderreen
Castlerea
Longford
Lough Sheelin
Kells
Drogheda
Balbriggan
Skerries

Inishbofin
Slyne Head
Connemara
Clifden
Partry Mts
Ballinrobe
Lough Mask
Claremorris
Roscommon
Lough Ree
Mullingar
Navan
Trim
Boyne
Swords

Gurumna Island
Galway Bay
Galway
Tuam
Ballinasloe
Athlone
Edenderry
Bog of Allen
Leixlip
Lucan
DUBLIN
Dun Laoghaire

Inishmore
Aran Islands
Oranmore
Loughrea
OFFALY
Tullamore
Naas
Bray
Greystones

Hag's Head
Liscannor Bay
Burren
Ennistymon
Portumna
Lough Derg
Birr
Portlaoise
Athy
Lugnaquilla Mountain 926
Wicklow
Wicklow Head

Spanish Point
Ennis
Killaloe
Nenagh
Roscrea
Carlow
Arklow

Kilkee
Kilrush
Limerick
Thurles
Templemore
Muine Bheag
Gorey

Loop Head
Mouth of the Shannon
Listowel
Newcastle West
Tipperary
Golden Vale
Cashel
Kilkenny
Thomastown
Clonmel
New Ross
Cahore Point

Brandon Mountain 953
Tralee
Galtymore Mts
Galtymore 920
Cahir
Comeragh Mountains
Carrick-on-Suir
Waterford
Enniscorthy
Wexford
Rosslare

Dingle
Dingle Bay
Castleisland
Mitchelstown
Fermoy
Blackwater
Tramore
Carnsore Point

Carrauntoohil 1041
Killarney
Macgillycuddy's Reeks
Lough Leane
Boggeragh Mts
Mallow
Dungarvan
Helvick Head

Cahersiveen
Sneem
Kenmare
Macroom
Midleton
Youghal

Caha Mts
Cahermore
Dursey Island
Bantry
Bantry Bay
Clonakilty
Bandon
Cork
Cobh
Kinsale
Old Head of Kinsale

Skibbereen
Mizen Head
Cape Clear

St George's Channel
Waterford Harbour

1:4M

Km   Miles

© Bartholomew Ltd

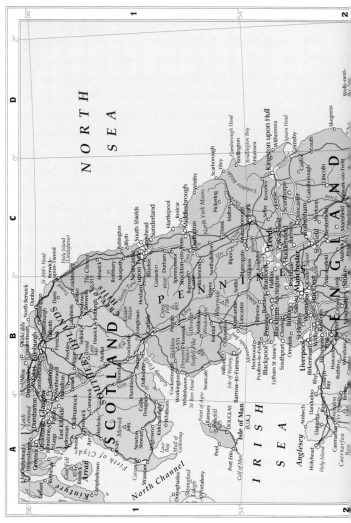

Conic Equidistant Projection

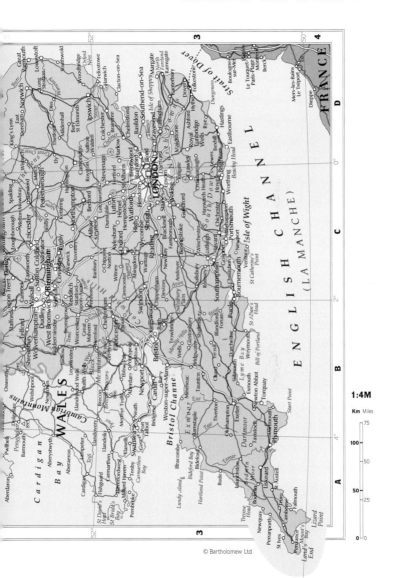

1:4M

Km Miles

Conic Equidistant Projection

Conic Equidistant Projection

1 : 8M

Km   Miles

A · 5° · B · 0° · C

1

50°

2

45°

3

A · 5° · B · 0° · C

Conic Equidistant Projection

Bude · Exmoor · Taunton · Salisbury · Winchester
Tiverton · Yeovil · UNITED KINGDOM · Crawley Folkestone · Dover · Dunkirk (Dunkerque)
Newquay · Exeter · Dorchester · Southampton · Worthing · Brighton · Ashford
St Ives · Truro · Bodmin · Dartmoor · Exmouth · Poole · Bournemouth · Portsmouth · Hastings · Calais
Penzance · Plymouth · Torquay · Lyme · Bay · Isle · Le Touquet-Paris-Plage · Étaples · Bruay-la-Bussière
Land's End · Falmouth · Start Point · of Wight · Berck · Doullens · Arras
Isles · Lizard · English Channel · Dieppe · Abbeville · Péronne
of Scilly · Point · (La Manche) · Neufchâtel- · Amiens
· Cap de la · Fécamp · en-Bray · Montdidier
· Hague · Cherbourg · Le Havre · Bolbec · Rouen · Beauvais
· Alderney · Baie de Seine · Compiègne
Guernsey · ST PETER PORT · Arcenes · Deauville · Honfleur · Évreux · Senlis · Chantilly
(U.K.) · Le Havre · Lisieux · Marne-la-
Channel Islands · Jersey · St-Lô · Caen · Vallée · PARIS
(Îles Normandes) · ST HELIER · (U.K.) · Coutances · Versailles
Roscoff · Golfe de · Granville · Flers · Séés · L'Aigle · Dreux · Chartres · Mennecy
Lesneven · Lannion · St-Malo · Avranches · Nogent- · Étampes
Île d'Ouessant · Guipavas · Morlaix · Cap · Dol-de-Bretagne · Alençon · le-Rotrou · Artenay · Nemours
Plouzané · Guingamp · Fréhel · Mayenne · Châteaudun · Orléans · Montargis
Brest · St-Brieuc · Dinan · Fougères · Vitré · La Flèche · Vendôme · Châteauneuf-sur-Loire
Châteaulin · Pontivy · Loudéac · Rennes · Laval · Le Mans · Château- · Gien
Douarnenez · Quimperlé · Vitré · du-Loir · Salbris
Pte du Raz · Quimper · Lorient · Baugé · Vierzon · Bourges
Ploemeur · Vannes · Châteaubriant · Ancenis · Angers · Tours · Avrillé · Romorantin- · Vatan · Sancoins
Île de Groix · Carnac · La Baule-Escoublac · Nantes · Vertou · Cholet · Saumur · Chinon · Lanthenay
Belle-Île · Quiberon · St-Nazaire · Loire · Loches · Indre
La Baule-Escoublac · Pornic · Bressuire · Thouars · Châtellerault · FRA
Noirmoutier-en-l'Île · Challans · La-Roche- · Parthenay · Poitiers · Le Blanc · Montluçon
Île de Noirmoutier · sur-Yon · Montmorillon · sur-Creuse
St-Jean-de-Monts · Île d'Yeu · Fontenay- · Niort · Civray · Bellac · Le Dorat · Guéret
Les Sables-d'Olonne · Talmont- · le-Comte · La Rochelle · Confolens · St-Junien · Ahun
St-Hilaire · Île de Ré · Charente · St-Jean-d'Angély · Limoges · Aubusson
BAY · Pte de Chassiron · Rochefort · St-Yrieix- · Uzerche
St-Pierre-d'Oléron · Saintes · Cognac · Angoulême · la-Perche · Ussel
OF · Pte de la Coubre · Royan · Montendre · Périgueux · Brive-la- · Tulle · Égletons
Pte de Grave · Soulac-sur-Mer · Ribérac · Montignac · Gaillarde · Aurillac · C
BISCAY · Pauillac · Coutras · Le Bugue · Souillac · Pleaux · E
· Libourne · Bergerac · Gourdon · Figeac · Espalion
· Mérignac · Bordeaux · Sarlat · Rodez
· Arcachon · Pessac · Marmande · Lot · Cahors · Camaux
· La Teste · Langon · Castelnau · Villeneuve-sur-Lot · Rodez
Gulf · Bazas · Agen · Moissac · Albi
of · Mimizan · Casteljaloux · Nérac · Lectoure · Montauban · Gaillac
Gascony · Mont-de-Marsan · Labouheyre · Roquefort · Condom · Colomiers · Grenade · Castres
· Soustons · Tartas · Aire-sur- · Auch · Toulouse · Puylaurens
Cantabrian Sea · Gijón · Santander · l'Adour · Muret · Carcassonne · Mazamet
Cabo de Peñas · Ribadesella · Torrelavega · Laredo · Donostia-San · Dax · Bayonne · Maubourguet · St-Gaudens · Pamiers · Limoux
Oviedo · Peña · Sebastián · Biarritz · Tarbes · Lourdes · Bagnères- · Foix · Durban-Corbières
Mieres · Cerredo · Gexto · Bilbao · Irún · Oloron- · Pau · de-Luchon · Quillan · Rivesalte
Pola · 2648 · Llodio · Tolosa · Ste-Marie · Echam · PYRÉNÉES · ANDORRA
de Lena · CORDILLERA CANTÁBRICA · Durango · Arañaz · 3404 · LA VELLA
Guardo · Vitoria-Gasteiz · Miranda de Ebro · Jaca · ANDORRA · Céret
León · Aguilar · Estella · Pamplona · Aragón
Saldaña · de Campóo · Briviesca · Logroño · Najera · Ejea de los · Arguis · Graus
Osorno · Burgos · SPAIN · Tafalla · Caballeros
Benavente · Sahagún · Duero · Sierra de la Demanda · Calahorra · Alfaro
Palencia · Carrión · Alfaro · Graus

1 : 8M

Km Miles

© Bartholomew Ltd

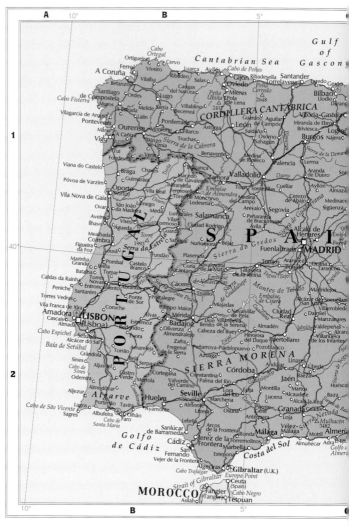

A   10°   B   5°

Gulf
of
Gascony

Cabo
Ortegal

Cantabrian Sea

Ortigueira
Ferrol
Cervo
Cabo de Peñas
A Coruña
Viveiro
Luarca
Avilés
Gijón
Ribadesella
Santander
Vilalba
Ribadeo
Oviedo
Torrelavega
Laredo
Gexto
Betanzos
Salas
Pola
Mieres
de Lena
Peña
Bilbao
Cangas
del Narcea
Ubiña
Llodio
Durango
Santiago
Ordes
Lugo
2411
CORDILLERA CANTÁBRICA
Vitoria-Gasteiz
de Compostela
Melide
Sarria
Becerreá
Guardo
Miranda de Ebro
Cabo Fisterra
A Estrada
Lalin
Ponferrada
Astorga
León
de Campóo
Aguilar
Brivlesca
Logroño
Vilagarcía de Arousa
Monforte
O Barco
Saldaña
Nájera
Pontevedra
Ourense
Osorno
Burgos
Marín
A Cañiza
Sahagún
Vigo
Winzo
Truchas
Benavente
Palencia
Lerma
Aranda
Tui
Verín
Sierra de la Cabrera
Medina
de Rioseco
de Duero
Sor
Fondevila
Braga
Chaves
Bragança
Zamora
Valladolid
Cuéllar
Almaza
Viana do Castelo
Guimarães
Macedo
Tordesillas
Cerezo
Ayllón
de Cavaleiros
Toro
de Abajo
Póvoa de Varzim
Mirandela
Medinace
Oporto
Vila Real
Embalse
Medina
Sigüenza
Sierra de Guadarrama
(Porto)
de Almendra
del Campo
Arévalo
Fermoselle
Segovia
Vila Nova de Gaia
São João
Lamego
Torre de Moncorvo
Ledesma
Ovar
da Madeira
Meda
Lumbrales
SPAIN
Peñaranda
Alcalá de
40°
Aveiro
Viseu
Vilar
Salamanca
de Bracamonte
Henares
Ílhavo
Formoso
Ávila
MADRID
Mealhada
Sabugal
Ciudad Rodrigo
Sierra de Gredos
Embalse
Coimbra
Guarda
Béjar
Fuenlabrada
Figueira
1993
Nuñomoral
da Foz
Lousã
Sierra de la Estrela
Fundão
Plasencia
Talavera
Torrijos
Aranjuez
Ocaña
Marinha
Pombal
Sierra de Gredos
de la Reina
Toledo
Tarancón
Grande
Oleiro
Castelo
Coria
Navalmoral
Batalha
Tomar
Branco
de la Mata
Tajo (Tejo)
Madridejos
Caldas da Rainha
Entroncamento
Alcántara
Montes de Toledo
Peniche
Torres
Abrantes
Cáceres
Embalse
Novas
de Valdecañas
Alcázar de
Socuéllamos
Torres Vedras
Santarém
Ponte
Trujillo
San Juan
Villarrobledo
Vila Franca de Xira
Coruche
de Sor
Portalegre
Miajadas
Ciudad
Daimiel
Amadora
LISBON
Crato Maior
Navalvillar
Real
Manzanares
Cascais
(Lisboa)
Elvas
Mérida
de Pela
Almadén
Valdepeñas
Alcaraz
Almada
Estremoz
Badajoz
Don
Villanueva
Hinojosa
Pozoblanco
Villanueva
Alcácer do Sal
Redondo
Olivenza
Benito
de la Serena
del Duque
Puertollano
de los Infantes
Cabo Espichel
Évora
Almendralejo
Cabeza del Buey
Baía de Setúbal
Setúbal
Zafra
SIERRA MORENA
Grândola
Torrão
Amareleja
Fregenal
Peñarroya-Pueblonuevo
Linares
Sines
Beja
de la Sierra
Azuaga
Cabo de
Aljustrel
Serpa
Córdoba
Andújar
Úbeda
Sines
Castro
Cortegana
Constantina
Jaén
Baeza
Odemira
Verde
Valverde
Palma del Río
Martos
Huéscar
Mértola
del Camino
Lora
Montilla
Alcaudete
Baza
Aljezur
Algarve
Huelva
del Río
Marchena
Lucena
Alcalá la Real
Albufeira
Portimão
Ayamonte
Almonte
Osuna
Puente
Granada
Guadix
Cabo de São Vicente
Lagos
Tavira
Seville
Genil
Antequera
Toja
Sierra Nevada
Sagres
Olhão
(Sevilla)
Mulhacén
Almería
Santa Maria
Cabo de
Lebrija
Arcos
Vélez-
3478
Faro
Sanlúcar
de la Frontera
Ronda
Málaga
Málaga
Motril
de Barrameda
Jerez de la
Torremolinos
Adra
Golfo
Cádiz
Frontera
Marbella
Costa del Sol
Almuñécar
de Cádiz
San
Estepona
Fernando
Vejer de la Frontera
Algeciras
Gibraltar (U.K.)
Cabo Trafalgar
Europa Point
Strait of Gibraltar
Ceuta
(Spain)
MOROCCO
Tangier
Cabo Negro
Asilah
(Tanger)
Tetouan

10°   B   5°

Conic Equidistant Projection

Conic Equidistant Projection

1:8M

Km   Miles
150

200
100

100
50

0 0

© Bartholomew Ltd

78

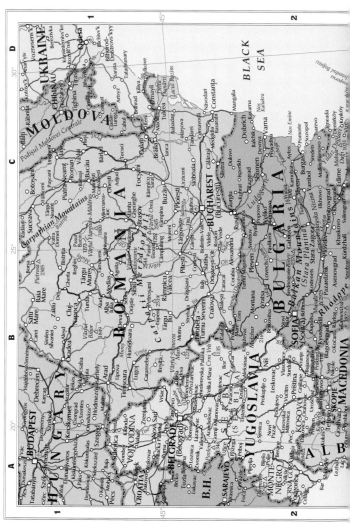

Conic Equidistant Projection

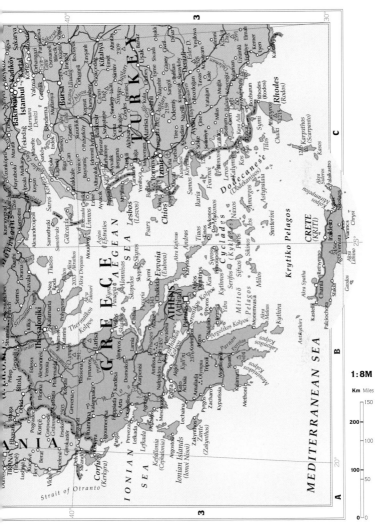

1:8M

Km Miles

150

200

100

100

50

0 0

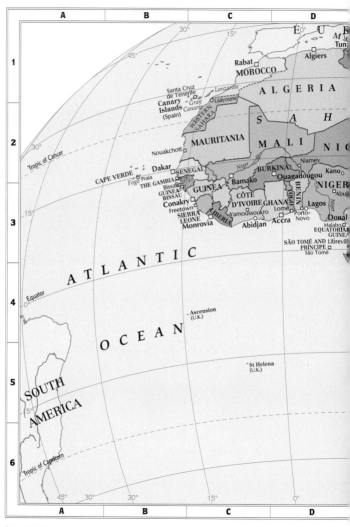

	A	B	C	D

Rabat □
MOROCCO

Algiers □

É° U
M
Tun

30°
15°
45°

Santa Cruz
de Tenerife
Canary Lanzarote
Islands Gran
(Spain) Canaria Laâyoune

A L G E R I A

WESTERN
SAHARA

S   *A*   *H*

MAURITANIA   **M A L I**   N I

Tropic of Cancer
30°

Nouakchott □

Niamey □

CAPE VERDE • •   **Dakar** □
Fogo □ Praia   □**SENEGAL**
THE GAMBIA □ Banjul
Bissau □
GUINEA- **GUINEA**   **Bamako**
BISSAU

Niger

BURKINA □
Ouagadougou

Kano ○

15°

Conakry □
Freetown □
SIERRA
LEONE
Monrovia

CÔTE
D'IVOIRE **GHANA**
Yamoussoukro   Lomé □
LIBERIA   **Abidjan** **Accra**

Porto-
Novo

Abuja

NIGER

Lagos □

Doual

Malabo □
EQUATORIA
GUINE

SÃO TOMÉ AND Libreville
PRÍNCIPE □
São Tomé

A T L A N T I C

Equator
0°

• Ascension
(U.K.)

O C E A N

• St Helena
(U.K.)

SOUTH
5°

AMERICA

Tropic of Capricorn

45°   30°   30°   15°   0°

	A	B	C	D

Orthographic Projection

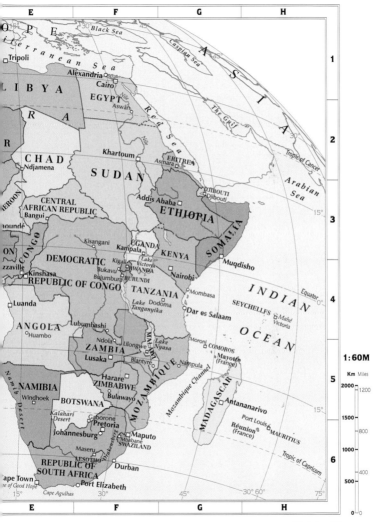

82

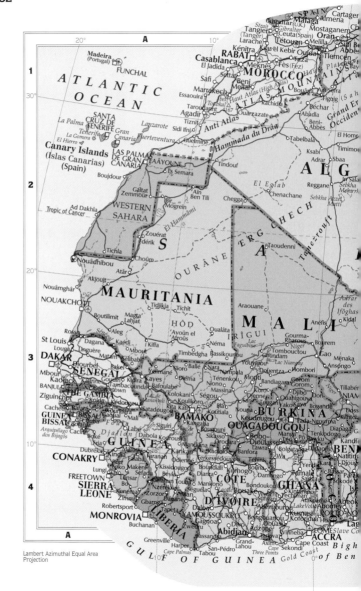

20°   A   10°

1

ATLANTIC
OCEAN

30°

Madeira
(Portugal)
FUNCHAL

La Palma
SANTA
CRUZ DE
TENERIFE   Gran
La Gomera   Canaria
El Hierro
Tenerife
Canary Islands
(Islas Canarias)
(Spain)

Lanzarote
Fuerteventura

LAS PALMAS
DE GRAN
CANARIA

Boujdour

RABAT
Casablanca
El Jadida
Safi
Essaouira
Marrakech

Kénitra
Meknès
Settat
Beni
Mellal

Tangier
(Tanger)
Larache

Strait of Gibraltar
Gibraltar (U.K.)
Ceuta (Spain)
Tetouan

SPAIN   Cartage
Málaga   Almeria
Mostagane
Oran   Sidi E
Tlemcen

MOROCCO
Fès (Fez)
Ksar el Kebir Ouida

Melilla

Plateau
(Saïd)

Béchar

Taroudannt   Ouarzazate
Agadir
Tiznit
Guelmim
Anti Atlas
Sidi Ifni

Haut Atlas (High Atlas)
Ifni   4167
Rachidia

Haut Atlas
Figuig   (Sah

Abâdla
Beni-
Abbès   Grand E
Occiden

2

Tropic of Cancer
Ad Dakhla

WESTERN
SAHARA

Aïn
Ben Tili

Gâltat
Zemmour
Bir
Mogrein

El Hammami

Es Semara

Tindouf

Hammada du Drâa
Tabelbala
Ksabi

Adrar
Sbaa
Chegga

El Eglab

Chenachane   Reggane

Timimo

El Homr

ALG

Sebkha
Mekerrh

Taoudenni

S

Tichla
Zouérat
Fdérik

Choûm

ERG CHECH

A

20°

Nouâdhibou
Atâr

Akjoujt

Nouâmghâr

NOUAKCHOTT

MAURITANIA

Tidjikja
Tîchît

Araouane

MALI

OURÂNE

Araouane

Anéfis

Adrar
des
Ifoghas
Kidal

Boutilimit
Magta
Lahjar

Aleg

HÔD

Ayoûn el
Atroûs

Tombouctou
(Timbuktu)

Gourma-
Rharous

Goundam

Gao
Ménaka

St Louis
Rosso
Dagana

Lougâ
Dinguère   Matam

DAKAR

Mbour
Diourbel

Kaolack   Kaffrine
Kidira

Kaédi

Mbout

Sélibaby
Kayes
Diéma

Néma

I Kiffa
Timbédgha

Nioro

Yélimané
Nara

Nampala

Ténenkou
Niono
Massina
Monti

Tourfa

Lac Niangay   Hombori

Ansongo

Tillabér

Djibo

NIAM

Mopti
Djenné   Bandiagara   Koro

SENEGAL

BANJUL

Ziguinchor

THE GAMBIA

BISSAU

GUINEA
BISSAU

Bignona
Cacheu   Bafatá
Kolda   Vélingara
Gabú

Arquipélago
dos Bijagós

Cacine
Boké

Kédougou
Kita Kati

Satadougou

Nioro
Kolokani

BAMAKO

Kangaba
Koutiala
Ségou

Koulikoro

Ouahigouya

Gorom-
Gorom

Dori

Bogandé

Kaya

Kantchari

Diapaga

Tenkodogo   Pô

Manga

BURKINA

Fada-Ngourma

OUAGADOUGOU

Sikasso

Bobo-
Dioulasso

Banfora

Bougouni

Bolgatanga

Gaoua

Lawra

Wa

Navrongo
Natitingou

BEN

Djoug

Tangoro

Boké   Kindia   Siguiri
Faranan   Kankan
Dabola

Mamou

GUINEA

Gaoual

Koundara
Labé
Djallon
Fouta
Dinguiraye

Kissidougou

Beyla
Odienné

Kadiolo

Kadiana
Tengréla
Terkessédougou

Boundiali
Korhogo

Katiola

Bondoukou

Tehini   Yendi

Yapei

Tamale

Basar

Parak

Sokode

Bimbila

CONAKRY

Dubréka
Kindia
Port
Loko

Benty
Forécariah   Kambia

Telimélé

Kamakwie

Kalabo
Faranah

Dabakala

Mankono

Séguéla

GHANA

Kpandu

Kintampo

Kumasi

Abomey

Kotoridua

PORTO-

Nkawkaw

Lag

4

FREETOWN

SIERRA
LEONE

Lungi

Makeni
Sefadu
Kenema

Koidu

Konema

Zimmi

Zorzor
Toulépleu

Touba

Man

Daloa

Nzérékoré
Danané

Duékoué

Bouaké

Gagnoa

Yamoussoukro

Bouaflé

CÔTE
D'IVOIRE

Sinfra

Divo

Bongouanou

Aboisso

Agboville

Abengourou

Cape
Coast

Winneba

Axim

LOMÉ
ACCRA

Slave Coast

Bigh
of Ben

Robertsport

MONROVIA

Buchanan

Greenville

Gbarnga
Zwedru
Tapeta

Harper
Cape Palmas

Grand-
Bassam

Grand-
Lahou

Sassandra

San-Pédro
Tabou

Three Points

Sekondi

Cape
Coast

Gold Coast

GULF OF GUINEA

0°

of Ben

LIBERIA

A

Lambert Azimuthal Equal Area
Projection

3

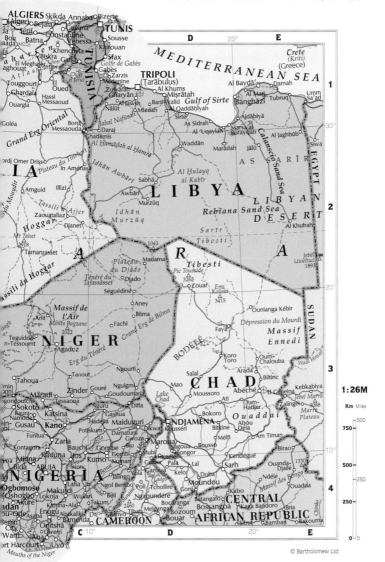

Northwestern AFRICA

ALGIERS (Alger) · Skikda · Annaba · Bizerte · Cap Bon
Bejaïa · Guelma · **TUNIS**
Bou · Sétif · Constantine · Tébessa · Sousse
aada · Batna · Khenchela · Kairouan
fa · El Meghaïer · Biskra · Gafsa · Sfax
aghouat · Tozeur · Chott · Golfe de Gabès
· Atlas · el Jerid · Gabès
Touggourt · El · Médenine · Zarzis
Ghardaïa · Oued · Zuwārah · **TRIPOLI**
Ouargla · Hassi · Gharyān · (Ṭarābulus) · Al Khums
Messaoud · Nālūt · Al Mawsh · Banī Walīd · Miṣrātah
Goléa · Bordj · Jabal Nafūsah · Mizdah · Al Qaddāḥīyah
Messaouda · Ghadāmis · Sirte · As Sidrah
ordj Omer Driss · Al Ḥamādah al Ḥamra · Al 'Uqaylah
· Plateau du Tinhert · In Aménas · Idhān Awbārī · Waddān · Marādah

Grand Erg Oriental

MEDITERRANEAN SEA
Crete (Kríti) (Greece)
Al Bayḍā · Darnah
Banghāzī · Al Marj · Tubruq · Umm Sa'ad
Gulf of Sirte
Ajdābiyā
Marsá al Burayqah · Al Jaghbūb · Sīwa

EGYPT

AS SARĪR

L I B Y A
Al Ḥulayq al Kabīr
LIBYAN DESERT
Rebiana Sand Sea
Calanscio Sand Sea
Al Khufrah

· Amguid · Illizi · Awbārī · Murzūq · Idhān Murzūq
· Sarīr Tibesti · Rebiana Sand Sea

A · Mt Tahat 2918 · Tamanrasset
Tassili du Hoggar
· Zaouatallaz · Djanet · Hoggar

Plateau du Djado · Madama · 1043 · Pic Toussidé 3265 · Tibesti · Emi Koussi 3415 · Jebel Uweinat 1893

· Ténéré du Tafassasset · Djado · Zouar
· Séguédine · Aney

SUDAN

Ounianga Kébir
Dépression du Mourdi
Massif Ennedi

· Massif de l'Air · Monts Bagzane 2022 · Bilma · Fachi
· Arlit · *Grand Erg de Bilma*
· Teguidda- · n-Tessoumt · Agadez · Erg du Ténéré
· Faya
· Koro Toro
· Oum-Chalouba

N I G E R
BODÉLÉ
Salal · Arada · Biltine · Kebkabiya
· Tahoua · Tanout · Ngourti · Mao · Moussoro · Ati · Abéché · El Geneina · Jebel Marra 3088 · Marra Plateau · Zalingeï
· Maradi · Zinder · Gouré · Nguigmi · Lake Chad · Oum-Hadjer · Abou · Zalingeï
gondoutchi · Tessaoua · Goudoumaria · Diffa
· Sokoto · Katsina · Nguru · Gashua
· Kaura · Namoda · Hadejia · Maiduguri
bi · Gusau · **Kano** · Potiskum · Damaturu · Dikwa · Kousséri · Bokoro · Déla

CHAD
Ouaddaï
· Am Timan
· Bitkine
· Melfi
· Bousso · Kendégué · Birao
· Ndélé · Ouanda-Djalié · Ouadda · 1330

NDJAMÉNA
· Gwoza · Maroua · Agoua · Am Timan

· Funtua · Zaria · Bauchi · Gombe · Biu · Mubi · Kaélé · Pala · Laï · Sarh
· Kontagora · Kaduna · Jos · Kumo · Numan · Guider · Kélo · Doba
Minna · **ABUJA** · Bida · Lafia · Ibi · Ngol Bembo · Poli · Tcholliré · Goré · Moundou
· Ogbomoso · Makurdi · Wukari · Takum · Yola · Garoua · Ngaoundéré · Bocaranga · Batangafo · Bossangoa · Kaga Bandoro · Bria

N I G E R I A
· Oshogbo · Lokoja · Katsina-Ala · Bamenda · Meiganga · Bozoum · Bouar
· Akure · Enugu · Abakaliki · Banyo · Tibati
adan · Onitsha · Obala · Bamban
u-Ode · Asaba · Iwerri · **CAMEROON** · Bakouma
City · Warri · Aba · Uyo

CENTRAL AFRICAN REPUBLIC
· Ndélé · Sibut · Bambari

rt Harcourt
Mouths of the Niger

1 : 26M

Km | Miles
750 — 500
500 — 250
250
0 — 0

© Bartholomew Ltd

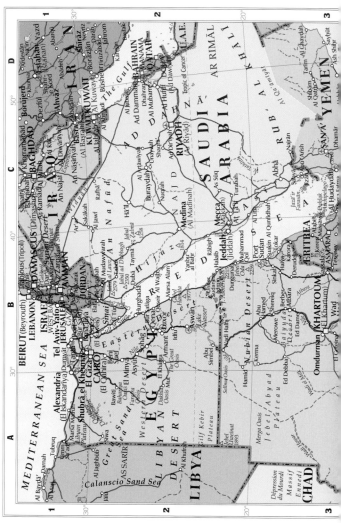

Lambert Azimuthal Equal Area Projection

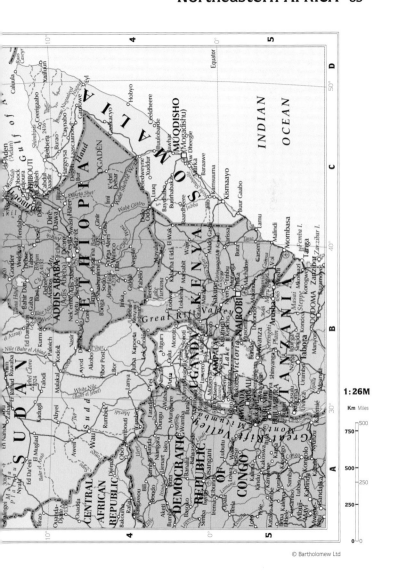

1:26M

Km Miles

500

750 — 500

250

500 — 250

250

0 — 0

© Bartholomew Ltd

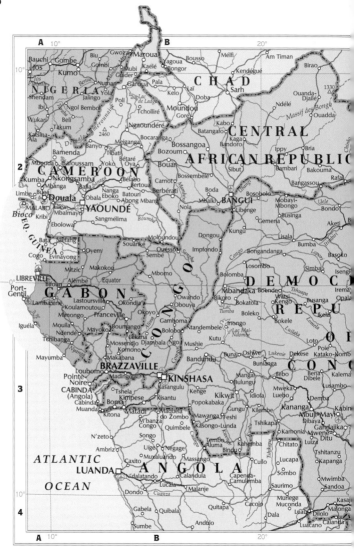

A 10°   B   20°

10°

Bauchi Gombe Biu Gwoza Maroua Bousso Mélfi Am Timan
Jos Gombi Mubi Kaélé Bongor Kendégué Birao
Kumo Güider Yagoua 1330
NIGERIA Numan Garoua Pala Lai CHAD Ouanda-Djallé
Benue Yola Kelo Doba Sarh Ndélé Massif des Bongo
Shendam Jalingo Poli Tchollíré Moundou Gore Ouadda
Ibi Ngol Bembol Lac Kabo Batangafo Kaga Ippy Bria
Wukari Beli de Ladeo Ngaoundéré Bossangoa Bandoro CENTRAL
Takum 2460 Meiganga Bocaranga Bozoum AFRICAN REPUBLIC Bambari Bakouma Rafa
Katsina- Mbere Banyo Tibati Bétaré Bouar Sibut Bangassou
Ala Bamenda Yoko Oya Belabo Bossembélé Boda Berbérati Carnot Bosobolo Mobayi- Bondo Uele Aketi
Mbouda Bafoussam Nkongsamba Nanga Eboko Abong Mbang Mbaiki BANGUI Mbongo Businga Bumba
Kumba Mbanga Bafia Batouri Nola Libenge Gemena Lisala Simba Isengi
Buea Douala Obala Bongandanga Basoko
MALABO Edea YAOUNDÉ Kungu Losombo DEMOC
Limbe Mbalmayo Dongou Bolomba Boende Watsi Opala Irema
BIOCO Kribi Ebolowa Sangmelima Bouma Impfondo Mbandaka Bikoro Tshuapa Busanga Ikela
EQ. GUINEA Bata Niefang Molondou Congo Bokatola REPU
Cogo Evinayong Oyem Souanke Ouesso Sembé Lomela OI
Mitzic Makokou Mbomo Boleko Lac Bokele
LIBREVILLE Alembe Equator Owando Ntandembele Tumba Loto CON
Port- Lastoursville Okondja Obouya Gamboma Imongo Mushie Poie Bena Kalema
Gentil GABON Mimongo Franceville Okoyo Lac Mai- Dibele Lusambo
Lambaréné Koulamoutou Boumango Ndombe Mweka Luebo Demba
Iguéla Mouila Bolobo Kutu Buna Oshwe Lukenie Dekese Kataka-Nomb Kananga
Ndende Mayoko Lékana Mossendjo Djambala Ngo Bandundu Bunianga Kamonia Mbuji-Mayi Kabin
Tchibanga Makabana Komono CONGO Mangai Bulungu Illebo Mwene- Gandajika
Mayumba Touboura BRAZZAVILLE Kasangulu Dibaya Ditu Tshitanzu
Pointe- Madingou KINSHASA Kenge Kikwit Idiofa Tembo Kahemba Chitato Luiza Kapanga
Noire CABINDA Tshela Kisantu Popokabaka Gungu Kilembe Aluma Bindu Lucapa
(Angola) Kimpese Maquela Mawanga Kasongo-Lunda Tshikapa Cullo Sombo Mwimba
Cabinda Boma do Zombo Feshi Kamonia Saurimo Sandoa
Muanda Matadi M'banza Quimbele Massango Capenda- Muriege Kasaji
Kitona Congo Songo Uige Negage Calandula Camulemba Muconda Dilolo Malonga
N'zeto Ambriz Muxaluando Bindu Cacolo Dala Luau Luacano Calantia
ATLANTIC Caxito ANGOLA Ndalatando Lucala Malanje Quitapa Andulo
LUANDA Dondo Cuanza Gabela Quibala Sumbe

OCEAN

A 10°   B   20°

Lambert Azimuthal Equal Area Projection

1 : 20M

Km | Miles
600 — | — 400
400 — | — 200
200 — | — 100
0 — | — 0

© Bartholomew Ltd

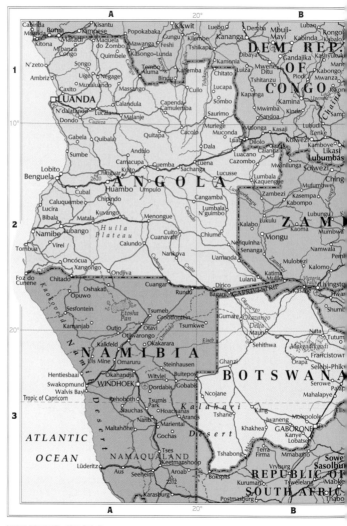

A   20°   B

Cabinda
Boma
Muanda
Kitona
Matadi
M'banza
Congo
N'zeto
Ambriz
Caxito
LUANDA
N'dalatando
Dondo
Gabela
Quibala
Sumbe
Lobito
Benguela
Lucira
Namibe
Tombua
Virei

Xisantu
Nimpese
Maquela
do Zombo
Quimbele
Songo
Uige
Negage
Muxaluando
Massango
Calandula
Lucala
Malanje
Cuanza
Andulo
Camacupa
Chinguar
Huambo
2620
Cubal
Chipindo
Caluquembe
Matala
Bibala
Lubango
Kuvango
Huila
Plateau

Popokabaka
Kikwit
Luebo
Demba
Mbuji-
Mayi
Lubao
Kongolo
Gungu
Kilembe
Kananga
Kabinda
Kabalo
Kashyukulu
Feshi
Mawanga
Tshikapa
DEM. REP.
Kasongo-Lunda
Dibaya
Gandajika
Kamonia
Luiza
Mwene-
Ditu
OF
Kabongo
Kikondja
Tembo
Aluma
Kahemba
Chitato
Piodi
Mwanza
Bindu
Cuilo
Lucapa
Tshitanzu
CONGO
Kamina
Capenda-
Camulemba
Sombo
Saurimo
Mwimba
Kinda
Muriege
Malonga
Kasaji
Lubudi
Quitapa
Cacolo
Muconda
Luau
Dilolo
Kolwezi
Tenke
Dala
Cuemba
Luacano
Cazombo
Caianta
Kambove
Likasi
Tuena
Sachanga
Lucusse
Mwinilunga
Solwezi
Lubumbas
Ching
Lumbala
Kaquengue
Mufumbwe
Cangamba
Zambezi
Kasempa
Kabompo
Menongue
Lumbala
N'guimbo
Kalabo
Kaoma
ZAM
Lubungu
Cuito
Cuanavale
Chiume
Mongu
Mumbwa
Caiundo
Nankova
Neriquinha
Senanga
Mulobezi
Namwala
Uamanda
Katima
Mulilo
Kalomo
Pemba

Foz do
Cunene
Chitado
Opuwo
Sesfontein
Kamanjab
Oshakati
Oncócua
Xangongo
Ondjiva
Cuangar
Rundu
Dirico
Bagani
CAPRIVI STRIP
Luiana
Livingstone
Victoria
Falls
Kasane
Hwar
Shumb

Etosha
Pan
Tsumeb
Grootfontein
Tsumkwe
iGumare
Okavango
Delta
Maun
Nata
Shumb

Outjo
Otavi
Otjiwarongo
Okakarara
Sehithwa
Makgadikgadi
Tutum
Francistowr

NAMIBIA
Uis Mine
Omaruru
Steinhausen
Ghanzi
Orapa
Selebi-Phik
BOTSWANA
Okahandja
Witvlei
Buitepos
Serowe
Palap
Hentiesbaai
Swakopmund
WINDHOEK
Dordabis
Gobabis
Ncojane
Mahalapye
Walvis Bay
Tropic of Capricorn
Rehoboth
Tsumis
Park
Kalahari
Kang
Molepolole
Ellis
Nauchas
Hoachanas
Aranos
Tshane
Jwaneng
GABORONE
Narib
Mariental
Desert
Khakhea
Kanye
Lobatse
Maltahöhe
Gochas
Tses
Keetmanshoop
Tshabong
Terra
Firma
Mmabatho
Sowe
Sasolbu
Lüderitz
Aus
Seeheim
Araob
2202
Bokspits
Vryburg
Tswelelang
Maoke
NAMAQUALAND
Karasburg
Kuruman
REPUBLIC OF
SOUTH AFRIC
Postmasburg
Thabo

ANGOLA

ATLANTIC
OCEAN

Kaokoveld

Namib Desert

A   20°   B

1

10°

2

20°

3

Lambert Azimuthal Equal Area Projection

© Bartholomew Ltd

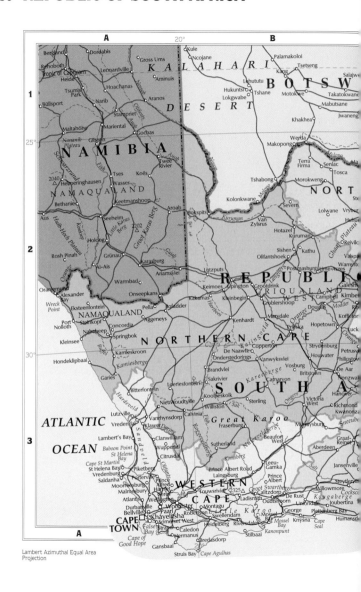

Lambert Azimuthal Equal Area
Projection

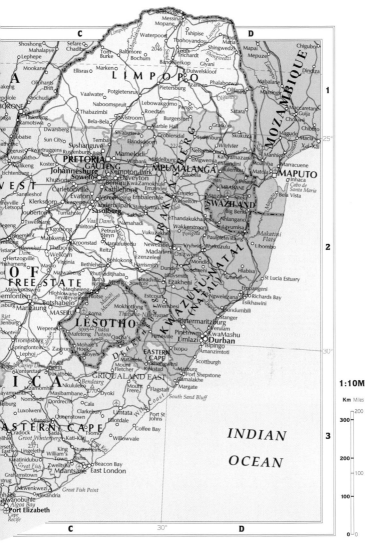

C · D

Beitbridge
Messina
Mopane · Limpopo
Waterpoort · Tshipise
Thohoyandou
Shoshong · Sefare · Chadibe · Tom Burke · Baltmore · 2046 · Louis Trichardt · Shingwedzi · Mapai · Mepuze · Chigubo
Mahalapye · Bochum · Bandelierkop · Giyani
Lephepe · Ellisras · Marken · Duiwelskloof · Dinizza
Mookane · LIMPOPO · Pietersburg · Tzaneen · Phalaborwa · Mabalane · Massingir

MOZAMBIQUE

aken · Oliphants · Drift · Vaalwater · Potgietersrus · Lebowakgomo · Olifants · 1
pdiole · Mochudi · Naboomspruit · Penge · Satara · Maccaretane · Guija
ORONE · Thokweng · Thabazimbi · Roedtan · Burgersfort · Chokwe · Chiberto
nga · Ramotswa · Bela-Bela · Nylstroom · Marble Hall · Graskop · Skukuza · Magude · Xai-Xai
ye · Dwarsberg · Siyabuswa · Groblersdal · 22 · Lydenburg · Nelspruit · KaNyamazane · Manhica · Marracuene
athrine · Lobatse · Sun City · Soshanguve · Mamelodi · Middelburg · eMgwenya · eMjindini · Moamba · Matola · Cabo de
Zeerust · Swartruggens · Rustenburg · Brits · PRETORIA · Witbank · Komati · Bullendon · MBABANE · Santa Maria
Mmabatho · Koster · GAUTENG · Kempton Park · MPUMALANGA · Silobela · SWAZILAND · Bela Vista
Mafikeng · Johannesburg · Kathlehong · KwaZamokhule · Ermelo · Wesselton · Big Bend · Nhlangano
lichtenburg · Khutsong · Carletonville · Oikasenq · Vereeniging · Embalenhle · Vhal · Thandaukhama · Lavumisa · Makatini Flats
WEST · Sannieshof · Klerksdorp · Evaton · Vanderbijlpark · Standerton · Wakkerstroom · Mondlo · Libhombo
reyville · Joubertont · Tumahole · Sasolburg · Sakhile · Vukuzakhe · Paulpietersburg · Hlabisa
Letsopa · Kgotsong · Vaal Dam · Namahadi · Newcastle · Vryheid · Rhehokwa · St Lucia Estuary
legeng · Tswelelang · Viljoenkroon · Petrus Steyn · Madanheni · Osizweni · Nongweni · Empangeni
melong · Bloemhof · Maokeng · Kroonstad · Reitz · Ezenzeleni · Ladysmith · Mondi · Richards Bay
Hertzogville · Thabong · Welkom · Bohlokong · Harrismith · Dundee · Nqwegwe · Eshkhawini
Phahameng · Maslo · Matwabeng · Bethlehem · Steadville · Ezakheni · Umhlali · Gundumbili · 2
OF · Virginia · Phuthaditjhaba · Ladysmith · Nqwegwe · Stanger
FREE STATE · Meqheleng · Butha-Buthe · Estcourt · Wembesi · Ngwelezana · KwaDukuza
emfontein · Hlohlowane · Teyateyaneng · Hlotse · Mokhotlong · Eshkhawini
sburg · Mangaung · MASERU · Roma · KWAZULU-NATAL
Riet · Wepener · Thaba-Nchu · Pietermaritzburg · Verulam
enburg · LESOTHO · 3095 · Thaba Putsoa · Pinetown · KwaMashu
ntein · Mafeteng · Qacha's · Timeville · Umlazi · Durban
Trompsburg · Mohale's · Hoek · Moyeni · Ixopo · Isipingo · Amanzimtoti
Springfontein · Zastron · Matatiele · Scottburgh
Lephoi · Alival North · Mount Fletcher · Khangweni · Port Shepstone
CA · Montertad · Dohathole · GRIQUALAND EAST · Kokstad · Gamalakhe · Margate
ayamnbunt · Mzamomhle · Nkululeko · Bendearg · Mount Frere · Flagstaff · South Sand Bluff
elburg · Nomonde · Masibambane · Dyoki · Dordrecht · Cala
Luxolweni · Clarkebury · Umtata · Port St Johns · 30°
ASTERN CAPE · Mlungisi · Queenstown · Elliotdale · Coffee Bay
lihlei · Cradock · Sada · Kati-Kati · Tsomo · Willowvale
erset · Groot Winterberg · 2571 · King William's · Bisho
East · Lingelethu · Town · Stutterheim · INDIAN · 3
Kwatinidubu · Zwelitsha · Beacon Bay
Great Fish Dam · Mdantsane · East London · OCEAN
Grahamstown
trug · Nkwenkwezi · Great Fish Point
nhaea · Alexandria
Kwanobuhle · Algoa Bay
Port Elizabeth
Cape · Recife

1:10M

Km · Miles
300 · 200
200 · 100
100
0 · 0

C · 30° · D

© Bartholomew Ltd

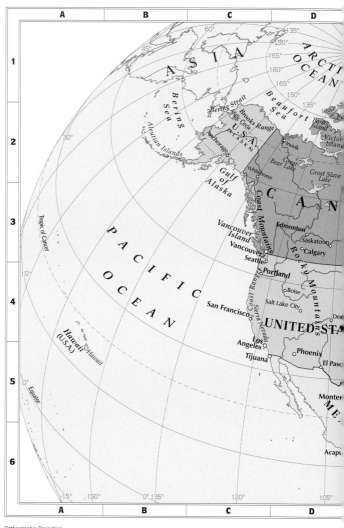

Orthographic Projection

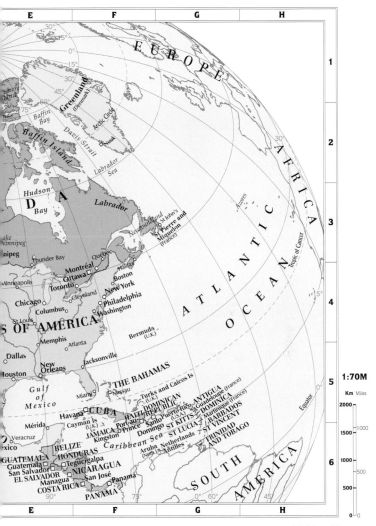

E   F   G   H

1

EUROPE

-30°
-15°
0°
15°
30°
45°
60°
75°

Greenland
(Denmark)

Baffin
Bay

Arctic Circle

Davis Strait

Baffin Island

Nuuk

2

30°

Labrador
Sea

A
FRICA

Hudson
Bay

D
A

Labrador

Newfoundland

St John's
St Pierre and
Miquelon
(France)

Azores

3

Tropic of Cancer

Lake
Winnipeg

Winnipeg

Thunder Bay

Québec

Halifax

Montréal
Ottawa

Boston

Minneapolis

Toronto

Cleveland

New York

Chicago

Columbus

Philadelphia

St Louis

Washington

A
TLANTIC

OCEAN

15°

4

S OF AMERICA

Memphis

Atlanta

Bermuda
(U.K.)

Dallas

Houston

New
Orleans

Jacksonville

THE BAHAMAS

Nassau

1:70M

5

Gulf
of
Mexico

Miami

Turks and Caicos Is
(U.K.)

Km   Miles

2000

Havana

CUBA

HAITI

DOMINICAN
REPUBLIC

Puerto Rico
(USA)

ANTIGUA
Guadeloupe (France)

Equator

0°

Cayman Is
(U.K.)

Port-au-

Santo

1500

1000

Mérida

JAMAICA

Kingston

Prince

Domingo

ST KITTS

DOMINICA

Martinique (France)

Veracruz

BELIZE

Caribbean Sea

ST LUCIA

BARBADOS

exico

HONDURAS

Aruba

Netherlands

ST VINCENT

1000

500

GUATEMALA

Tegucigalpa

(Neth.)

Antilles

TRINIDAD
AND TOBAGO

6

Guatemala

NICARAGUA

San Salvador

EL SALVADOR

Managua

San José

SOUTH

500

COSTA RICA

Panama

AMERICA

90°

PANAMA

75°

0°   60°   45°

0

0

E   F   G   H

© Bartholomew Ltd

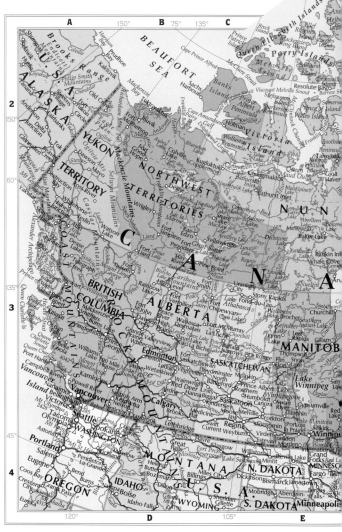

Lambert Azimuthal Equal Area Projection

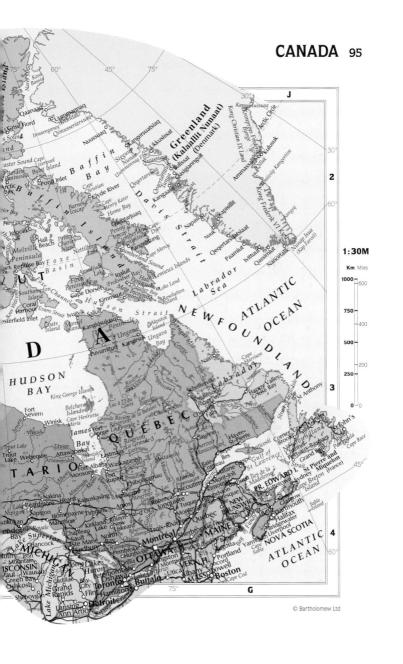

Lambert Azimuthal Equal Area Projection

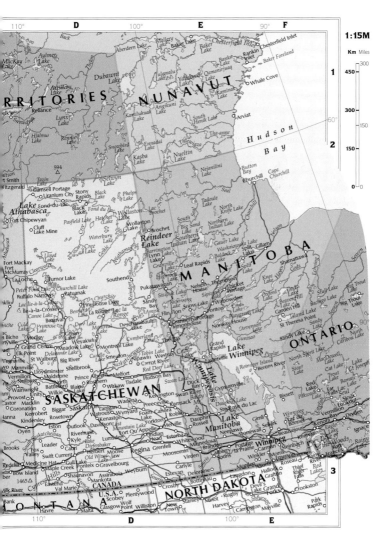

1:15M

Km Miles
┌ 300
450 ┤
│
300 ┤├ 150
│
150 ┤
│
0 ┴ 0

© Bartholomew Ltd

Lambert Azimuthal Equal Area Projection

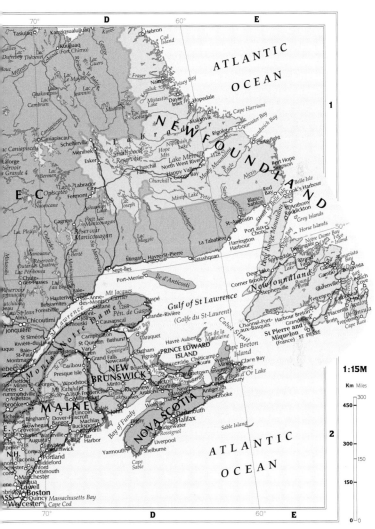

70°   D   60°   E

ATLANTIC OCEAN

Tasiujaq   Kangiqsualujjuaq   Korok   Hebron
euilles   Lac   Kuujjuaq   Cod Island
Dufreboy   Thévenet   (Fort Chimo)
Métres   Lac Kasoak   Rivière aux Feuilles   Fraser   Nain   Voisey Bay
louc   Lac   Koksoak   à la Baleine   Saluak   Hopedale
Lac   Ghakontpaul   Lac Jeannin
Lac   Cambrien   Mistinibi   Mastastiac Lake   Davis Inlet
Lac aux Goélands   Makkovik   Cape Harrison
lac Caniapiscau   Caniapiscau   Labrador   Nipishish Lake   Rigolet   Groswater Bay
Laforge Réservoir   Schefferville   Menihek   Smallwood   Hope Mts   Sandwich Bay
Grande 4   Esker   Reservoir   Lake Melville   1128   Cartwright
Lac   Berman   Churchill Falls   North West River   Goose Bay   Moly Mountains   Eagle   Port Hope Simpson
E   C   Opscoteo   Labrador   Fermont   Churchill   Happy Valley   Aegis   Red Bay   Cook's Harbour
Lac   Naocane   Ashuanipi Lake   Joseph   Minipi Lake   Petit Mecatina   Blanc-Sablon   Belle Isle
Gagnon   Petit Lac Manicouagan   St-Augustin   St Anthony   Roddickton
Lac Pletipi   Réservoir Manicouagan   Lac Magpie   Port au Choix   Gulf of Belle Isle   Grey Islands
Manouane   Berté   La Tabatière   Harrington Harbour   Horse Islands
Outardes Quatre   Réservoir   Mingan   Havre-St-Pierre   Natashquan   Springdale   Notre Dame Bay   Fogo Island
Lac Péribonca   Lac   au Brochu   Baie-   Sept-Îles   Île d'Anticosti   Deer Lake   Grand Falls   Gander   Bonavista Bay
des-Passes   Port-Menier   Corner Brook   Newfoundland   Gambo   Bonavista
Réservoir   Baie-   Mt Jacques   Cartier   Stephenville   Round Pond   Clarenville   Trinity Bay
Gouin   Betsiamites   Hauterive   des-Monts   1268   Gulf of St Lawrence   Burgeo   Come by Chance   Carbonear
Jonquière   Chicoutimi   Mont-   Matane   Gaspé   (Golfe du St-Laurent)   Channel-Port-   Harbour Breton   Marystown   Conception Bay
St Siméon   Campbellton   Grande-Rivière   aux-Basques   St Pierre and   St JOHN'S   Placentia
Rivière-du-Loup   St Quentin   Chaleur Bay   Pén. de Gaspé   Miquelon   Ferryland   (Péninsula)
uque   Baie-   Bathurst   Paraquet   (France)   ST PIERRE   Burin   Freshwater   Trepassey
Montmagny   St-Paul   Caraquet   Îles de la Madeleine   Cape Race
ebec   Edmundston   Campbellton   Newcastle   Havre Aubert   PRINCE EDWARD
Newport   Caribou   Chatham   Tignish   ISLAND   Chéticamp
psburg   Berlin   Presque Isle   Grand Lake   Summerside   Charlottetown   Inverness   Sydney   Clare Bay
rrières   St-Georges   Mt Katahdin   Woodstock   NEW   Minto   Moncton   Springhill   Glasgow   Bras d'Or Lake   Sydney
rummondville   1606   Fredericton   BRUNSWICK   Riverview   Amherst   Antigonish
Asbestos   Magog   Willington   Oromocto   Sussex   Truro   Sherbrooke
rbrooke   MAINE   Lincoln   NOVA SCOTIA
Richmond   Bingham   Dover-Foxcroft   Calais   Dartmouth
E.   Newport   Skowhegan   St John   Digby   Halifax
Groveton   Waterville   Bangor   Machias   Bay of Fundy   Bridgewater
nsburyPort   Asbestos   Augusta   Bucksport   Lake Rossignol
eton   1918   Lewiston   Brunswick   Bar Harbor   Liverpool   Sable Island
tpelier   Conway   Portland   Shelburne
N.H.   Laconia   Olddeford   Yarmouth
ochester   Berlin   Sanford   Cape
cord   Portsmouth   Sable   ATLANTIC
ene   Manchester
nbridge   Nashua   OCEAN
SSI   Lowell
   Quincy   Massachusetts Bay
Worcester   Boston   Cape Cod

70°   D   60°   E

1:15M

Km   Miles
        ⌐300
450⌐
        ⌐150
300⌐
150⌐
        ⌐0
0⌐

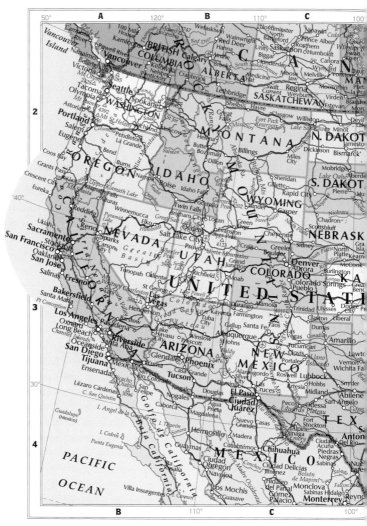

Lambert Azimuthal Equal Area Projection

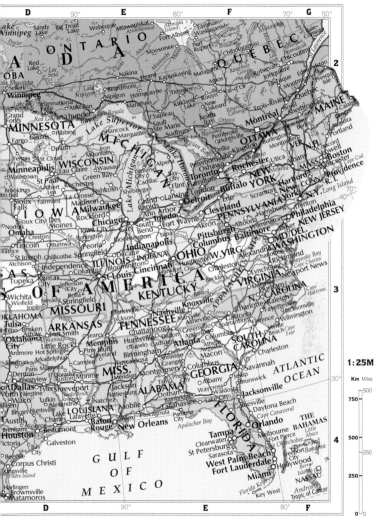

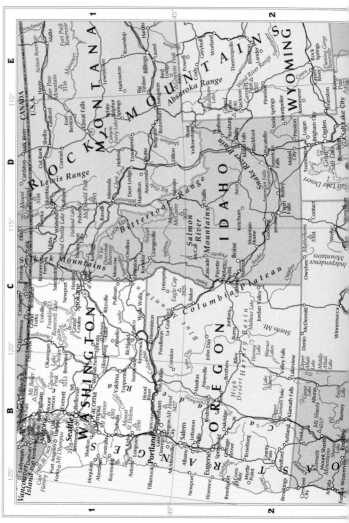

Lambert Azimuthal Equal Area Projection

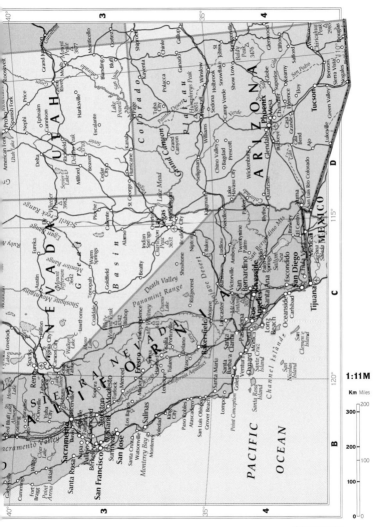

1:11M

Km Miles

© Bartholomew Ltd

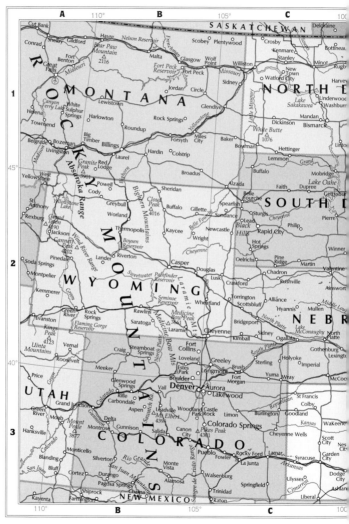

Lambert Azimuthal Equal Area Projection

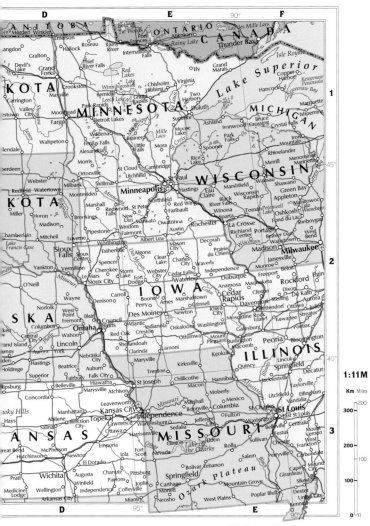

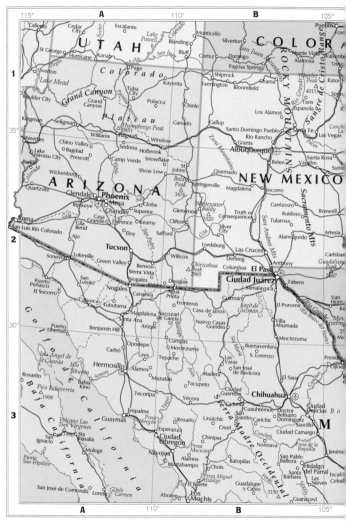

Lambert Azimuthal Equal Area Projection

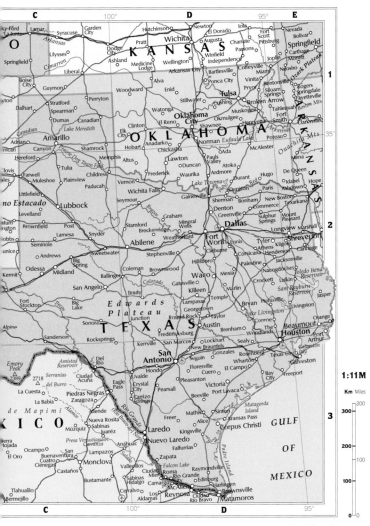

1:11M

Km Miles
— 200
300 —
— 100
200 —
100 —
0 — 0

Lambert Azimuthal Equal Area Projection

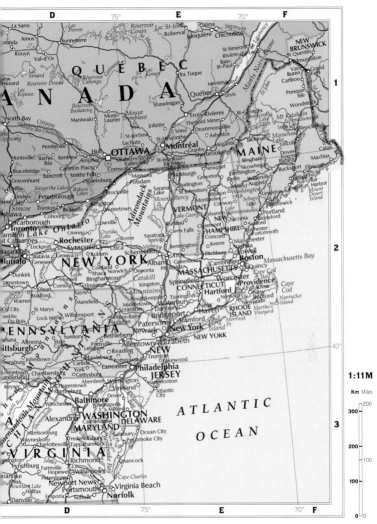

1:11M

Km Miles

300 — 200

200 — 100

100 —

0 — 0

© Bartholomew Ltd

110

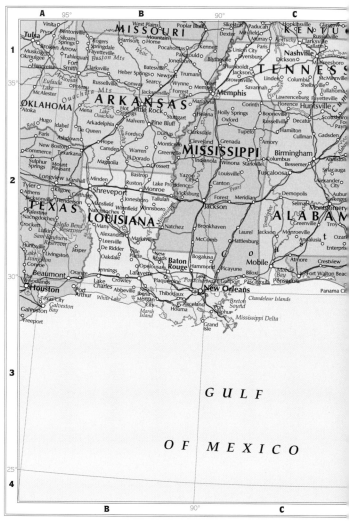

Lambert Azimuthal Equal Area Projection

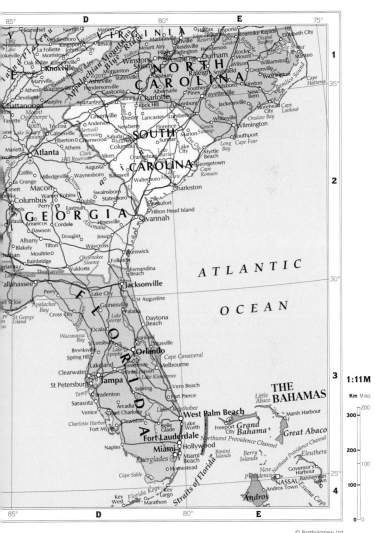

A 110° **B**

Tijuana · Mexicali
Ensenada
San Luis · Río Colorado
El Golfo · de Sta Clara
San Vicente · Picacho del Diablo 3096 · San Felipe · El Socorro
Vicente Guerrero · San Quintín
Cedros · Rosario
San Fernando

Ajo · Tucson · Willcox · Lordsburg · NEW MEXICO · Hobbs · Seminole · Lam
ARIZONA · Chiricahua Peak 2985 · Deming · Las Cruces · Guadalupe Peak 2667 · Eunice · Andrews · Spring · Midland
Green Valley · Sierra Vista · Benson · Bisbee · Columbus · El Paso · Ciudad Juárez · Fabens · San Lavaca · Pecos · UNITEI
Nogales · Nogales · Douglas · Agua Prieta · Lago de Guzmán · Fort Stockton · Big Lake
Tubutama · Cananea · Fronteras · Guzmán · El Porvenir · Van Horn · Mt Livermore 2554 · Alpine
Caborca · Santa Ana · Magdalena de García · Nacozari · Casa de Janos · Villa Ahumada · Marfa · Presidio
Benjamín Hill · Arizpe · Nuevo Casas Grandes · Moctezuma · Emory Peak · Amista Reservo
Opodepe · Cumpas · Buenaventura · Ojinaga · Serranía del Burs 2718 · La Cuest
Puerto Libertad · Carbó · Moctezuma · Tepache · Las Varas · Madera · La Babia

Golfo de California

L. Ángel de la Guarda
Bahía · Rosarito
Sebastián Vizcaíno · Pico de la Cerbería 1908 · Bahía · Kino
Guerrero Negro · Punta Eugenia · Bahía Tortugas · Vizcaíno
Pta San Hipólito

Tiburón · Hermosillo · San José de Bavicora · Chihuahua · La Junta · Ciudad Delicias
Tecoripa · Yécora · Cuauhtémoc · Saucillo · Bolsón
Empalme · Psa Obregón · Uruáchic · Carichic · Doctor B. · Domínguez · Ciudad Camargo · Sierra Mojada · Ocampo
Vol. Las Tres Vírgenes · Guaymas · Rosario · Esperanza · Crom · Nonoava · Presa de la Boquilla · Jiménez · El Oro · Buenaventura
Santa Rosalía · Ciudad Obregón · Navojoa · Chinipas · Batopilas · San Pablo · Ballezo · Hidalgo del Parral · Escalón · Monclova
Mulegé · Huatabampo · Álamos · El Fuerte · Presa M. Hidalgo · Guadalupe y Calvo · Barbara · Las Nieves · Ceballos · Castaño
Verde · Choix · 3150

San José de Comondú · Loreto · Isla Carmen · Ahome · Los Mochis · Guasave · Guanaceví · Indé · Bermejillo · Tlahualilo · San Pedro · de las Colonias
Villa Insurgentes · Villa Constitución · Topolobampo · Guamúchil · Mocorito · Topia · Tepehuanes · Mapimí · Torreón · Matamoros · Parras · Viesca · Gener
Bahía Magdalena · Isla Santa Margarita · Puerto Cortés · La Paz · Isla Espíritu Santo · Isla Cerralvo · San Pedro · San José · Navolato · Culiacán · Santiago · Nuevo · Ideal · Nazas · Nazas · Cepe
Pichilingue · El Dorado · Costa · Papasquiaro · Guadalupe Victoria · Miguel · Concepción
Todos Santos · San Lucas · San José del Cabo · Santiago · La Cruz · Cosalá · Co Huehueto 3150 · Durango · Villa Unión · Auza · Camach
Picacho del Diablo 2165 · Villa Union · Sombrerete · Río Grande · Cañitas de Felipe Pescad
Mazatlán · Rosario · San Alto 3559 · Fresnillo · Villa de Cos

MEXIC O
Escuinapa · Jerez · Salinas
Teacapán · Acaponeta · Zacatecas
Tecuala · Nayar · Mezquitic · Villanueva
Tuxpán · Ruíz · Colotlán · Aguascalientes
Santiago Ixcuintla · San Martín de Bolaños · Calvillo · Jalpa · 2985
Tepic · Teul de o · Yahualica · Encarnac · León
Islas Marías · Compostela · C. Ortega · Ixtlán · Tequila · Tepatitlán · Silao
Las Varas · Puerto Vallarta · Bahía de Banderas · Ameca · Guadalajara · La Piedad · Irapuato
Cabo Corrientes · Tomatlán · Cocula · Zacoalco · Lago de Chapala · Sahuayo · Zamora · Hidalgo
Autlán · Sayula · Ciudad Guzmán · Zacapu · Pátzcuar
Nevado de Colima 4339 · Colima 3859 · Uruapan
Cihuatlán · Manzanillo · Tecomán · Tepalcatepec · Apatzingán
Islas Revillagigedo (Mexico) · Isla San Benedicto · Armería · Coalcomán · Aguililla · Sierra Infernillo
Isla Socorro · Arteaga

PACIFIC

OCEAN

Lázaro Cárdenas
Zihuatanejo
Petatla

A 110° **B**

2

3

30°

20°

114

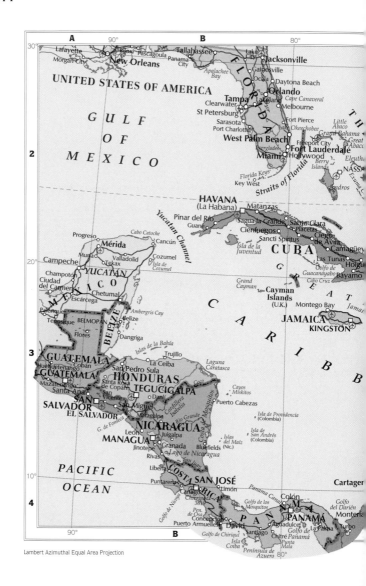

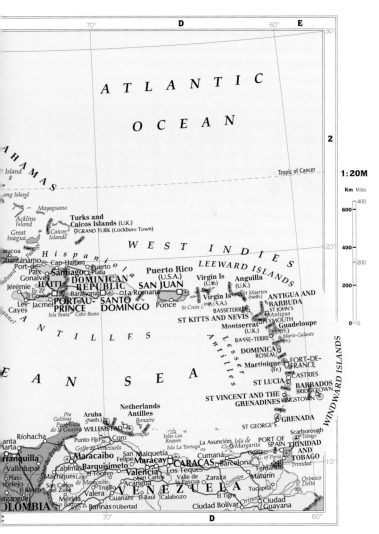

ATLANTIC

OCEAN

2

Tropic of Cancer

1:20M

Km   Miles
┌ 400
600 ┤
     ├ 200
400 ┤
     ├ 200
200 ┤
     ├
0 ┴ 0

70°   **D**   60°   **E**
30°

Island
ong Island

*B
A
H
A
M
A
S*

Mayaguana

*Acklins
Island*
*Great
Inagua*   *Caicos
Islands*

Turks and
Caicos Islands (U.K.)
☐GRAND TURK (Cockburn Town)

W E S T   I N D I E S

aracoa
uantánamo   *Hispaniola*

L E E W A R D   I S L A N D S

Port-de-   *Cap-Haïtien*   *Puerto
Paix*   *Plata*
Gonaïves   **HAITI**   **DOMINICAN**
Jérémie   **REPUBLIC**
             *Ile de
             (Gon.)*   *Barahona*
Les   *Jacmel*   **PORT-AU-**   **SANTO**
Cayes   **PRINCE**   **DOMINGO**
             Isla Beata   *Cabo Beata*

Puerto Rico
(U.S.A.)
SAN JUAN
Ponce

Virgin Is
(U.K.)
Virgin Is
(U.S.A.)
St Croix I.

Anguilla
(U.K.)

*St Maarten
(Neth.)*
Antigua   **ANTIGUA AND
BARBUDA**
ST JOHN'S

BASSETERRE
ST KITTS AND NEVIS
Montserrat   **PLYMOUTH**
(U.K.)   Guadeloupe
BASSE-TERRE   (Fr.)
              Marie-Galante
              (Fr.)

DOMINICA
ROSEAU
Martinique   **FORT-DE-**
(Fr.)   **FRANCE**
        ST LUCIA ☐**CASTRIES**

ST VINCENT AND THE   BARBADOS
GRENADINES KINGSTOWN ☐**BRIDGETOWN**

*A
N
T
I
L
L
E
S*

*Lesser
Antilles*

ST GEORGE'S ☐**GRENADA**

*W
I
N
D
W
A
R
D
I
S
L
A
N
D
S*

E A N   S E A

Netherlands
Antilles
Bonaire
Aruba
(Neth.)
☐WILLEMSTAD
Curaçao

*Islas Los
Roques*
Isla La Tortuga

*Isla de
Margarita*
La Asunción   PORT OF
SPAIN

Scarborough
Tobago
**TRINIDAD
AND
TOBAGO**
Trinidad

*Pta
Gallinas*
*Peninsula
de la Guajira*
Ríohacha
anta
arta

Punto Fijo
Coro
Golfo de Venezuela

G. of Paria
*San
Fernando*

10°

Maracaibo
ranquilla
Valledupar
Cabimas   Barquisimeto
Plato   *Machiques*   *Lago
de Maracaibo*
celejo   *San Carlos
del Zulia*
El Banco   *Trujillo*
gangue   *Mérida*   *Valera*
OLOMBIA   *Pico Bolívar
5007*   *Barinas*

San Maiquetía
Felipe   **Maracay** ☐
El Tocuyo   **Valencia**
San Carlos
Acarigua
VENEZUELA
Guanare
El Baúl   *Calabozo*

Cumaná
Barcelona

Los Teques
CARACAS
*Valle de
la Pascua*
Zaraza   *Guárico*
El Tigre
Ciudad Bolívar   *Orinoco*

Maturín
Tucupita
*Orinoco
Delta*
*Ciudad
Guayana*

San Libertad

70°   **D**   60°

© Bartholomew Ltd

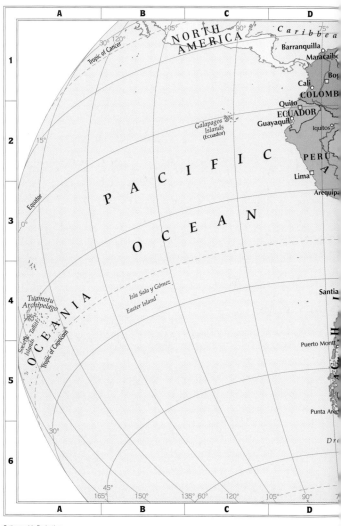

	A	B	C	D

NORTH AMERICA

Caribbea

Barranquilla
Maracaibo

Cali
Bo
COLOMB
Quito
ECUADOR
Guayaquil
Iquitos

Galapagos Islands (Ecuador)

PERU
Lima
Arequipa

PACIFIC

OCEAN

Tropic of Cancer

Equator

Isla Sala y Gómez
Easter Island

Tuamotu Archipelago

Society Islands
Tahiti

OCEANIA

Tropic of Capricorn

Santia

Puerto Montt

Punta Are

Dr

30°

45°
165°   150°   135° 60°   120°   105°   90°   7

Orthographic Projection

1:70M

Km Miles

2000 —

1500 —
        — 1000

1000 —
        — 500

500 —

0 — 0

Pta Gallinas
Ríohacha
Santa Marta   Golfo de Venezuela   Coro
Cartagena   Barranquilla Maracaibo   Maiquetía   CARACAS
Golfo del Darién   Sincelejo   Cabimas San Felipe   Los Teques
Valledupar   Machiques   Valera Acarigua   Zaraza
Monteria   El Banco   Lago de Maracaibo   Guanare   Valle de la Pascua
la Palma   Turbo   Mérida   Barinas   El Baúl   Calabozo
Pamplona   Pico Bolívar   San Fernando
Bucaramanga   Cúcuta   5007   de Apure   Ciudad Bolívar
Quibdó   Socorro   San Cristóbal   Arauca   Ciudad Guayana
Medellín   Sierra Nevada   VENEZUELA   El Callao
del Cocuy   Puerto Carreño   La Paragua
Tunja   5493   Yopal   La Gran Sabana
Quibdó   Pereira   Manizales   Bisinaca   Puerto Nuevo
Armenia   Ibagué   BOGOTÁ   Puerto Ayacucho   Mt Roraima
Cali   Palmira   Villavicencio   Guaviare   2811
Popayán   COLOMBIA   San José del Guaviare   Orinoco
Neiva
Tumaco   Florencia   Mitú   Pico da Neblina
Pasto   Mocoa   3014   Uaupés
Esmeraldas   Ipiales   Lérida   Tapuruçuara
Ibarra   Puerto Leguizamo   Negro   Barcelos
QUITO   Napo   Uarini
Manta   ECUADOR   Cabo   El Encanto   La Pedrera   Maraã
Portoviejo   Ambato   Pantoja   Fonte Boa   Manacapuru
Riobamba   Rio   Tonantins   Santo Antônio   Manaus
Alausí   Tigre   Curaray   do Içá   Coari   Iracoatiara
Guayaquil   Santa Clara   Amazonas   Beruri   Borba
Isla Puná   Gualaceo   Iquitos   Leticia   Tabatinga
Cuenca   Benjamim Constant   Coari
Tumbes   Machala   Barranca   Carauari   Novo Aripuanã
Talara   Loja   Lagunas   Requena   Tapauá   Manicoré
Sullana   Piura   Yurimaguas   Eirunepé   Lábrea   Barra do São Manuel
Catacaos   Jaén   Tarapoto   Envira   Humaitá
Chiclayo   Riola   Cruzeiro do Sul   Boca do Acre   Porto Velho
Cajamarca   Contamana   Tarauacá   Feijó   Sena Madureira   Ariquemes
Trujillo   Otuzco   Pucallpa   Rio Branco   Abunã
Chimbote   Porto Acre   Jaru   Pimenta Bueno
Huaraz   Huánuco   Puerto Portillo   Xapuri   Guayaramerín   Serra dos Parecis
Huarmey   Cerro   Atalaya   Alerta   Cobija   Riberalta   Vilhena
Barranca   de Pasco   Río de las Piedras   Mategua
La Merced   Huancayo   Exaltación   Puerto Alegre
Huacho   Ayacucho   Machupicchu   Puerto Maldonado
Callao   San Vicente   Cusco (CUZCO)   Mato Grosso
LIMA   de Cañete   Abancay   Sandia   Santa Ana   Trinidad   Loreto   Pontes-e-Lacerda
Chincha Alta   Yanacocha   Ayaviri   San Borja   Ascensión   Porto Esperidião
Pisco   Ica   Coracora   Nudo   Juliaca   Lago Titicaca   San Pedro
Nazca   Coropuna   6425   LA PAZ   BOLIVIA
PACIFIC   Chala   Chuquibamba   Arequipa   Montero   El Cerro
OCEAN   Camaná   Moquegua   Cochabamba   Warnes   Santa Cruz
Mollendo   Oruro   Huanuni   Grande   Bañados del Izozog
Ilo   Tacna   Corque   Cabezas   Tucavaca

Lambert Azimuthal Equal Area Projection

ATLANTIC

OCEAN

1 : 25M

Km Miles

750 — 500

500 — 250

Equator 0°

250 —

0 — 0

C 50° **D** 40° **E**

10°

1

0°

2

GEORGETOWN
New
Amsterdam PARAMARIBO
Nieuw
Nickerie St-Laurent-du-Maroni
Professor van
Blommestein Mer
SURINAME Kourou CAYENNE
French
Guiana Oyapoque
Pontoetoe

Lourenço Calçoene
Serra Tumucumaque Amapá Ilha de Maracá

Porto Macapá Mouths of the Amazon
Arere Santana Cabo
Mazagão Chaves Anaguarinho
Oriximiná Óbidos Almeirim Ilha de Marajó Baía de Marajó
rucara Breves Salinópolis Bragança
Parintins Monte Portelo Belém Viseu
Urucurituba Alegre Cametá Castanhal
Santarém Altamira Açará Curupuru São Luís
Itaituba Tucuruí Pinheiro Parnaíba Camocim
areacanga Viana Itapicuru
Bacabal Mirim Luzilândia
Maraba Pedreiras Codó Tianguá Sobral Fortaleza
Araras São Imperatriz Grajaú Caxias Timon Campo Maior Canindé Aracati
Manuelzinho Félix Tocantinópolis Barra Codó Pres. Dutra Buriti Bravo Teresina Quixadá de Calcanhar
Porto Franco do Corda Palmeirais Crateús Sousa Macau Touros
Araguaína Balsas Jerumenha Floriano Piros Iguatu Mossoró Natal
Conceição Carolina Uruçuí Oeiras Crato Campina João
do Araguaia Canto do Buriti Paulistana Juazeiro Grande Pessoa
B R A Z I L Santa Maria Pedro São Raimundo Nonato do Norte Salgueiro Olinda
das Barreiras Afonso Floresta Caruaru Recife
Porto Petrolina Garanhuns Maceió
Ilha do Nacional Juazeiro Paulo Afonso Arapiraca
Bananal São Félix Dianópolis Corrente Senhor do Bonfim Afonso Monte Santo
Porto Natividade Xique Jacobina Aracaju
Artur Barreiras Irecê Xique Senhor Estância
Porangatu Cavalcante Botirama Feira de
Uruaçu Correntina Santana Santa
Rosário Oeste Niquelândia Posse Bom Jesus Sto Antônio Alagoinhas
Cuiabá Barra do Formosa da Lapa Itaberaba de Jesus Salvador
Garcas BRASÍLIA Brumado Guanambi Itabuna Ubaitaba
Rondonópolis Ipora Goiás Anápolis Unaí Januária Vitória da Jequié Ilhéus
Alto Garças Goiânia Arinos Espinosa Conquista Itapetinga Una
Rio Verde Montes Claros Salinas Almenara Porto Seguro
Jataí Itumbiara Paraúna Jequitaí Teófilo Alcobaça
Rio Verde de Mato Grosso Araguari de Minas Otóni

Serra Tumucumaque
Serra do Cachimbo
Serra do Roncador
Serra do Caiapó
Serra Geral de Goiás
Chapada Diamantina
Serra do Espinhaço
Ponta

C 50° **D** 40° **E**

10°

3

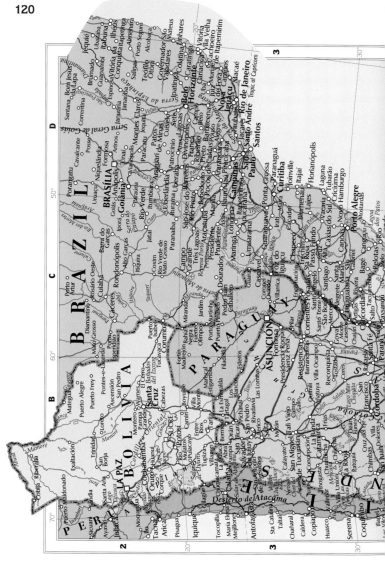

Lambert Azimuthal Equal Area Projection

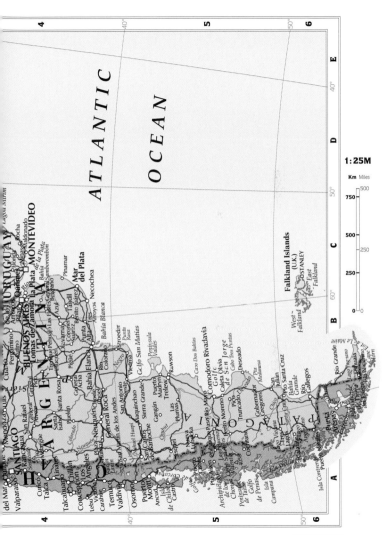

1:25M

Km Miles
500

750

500
250

250

0 0

© Bartholomew Ltd

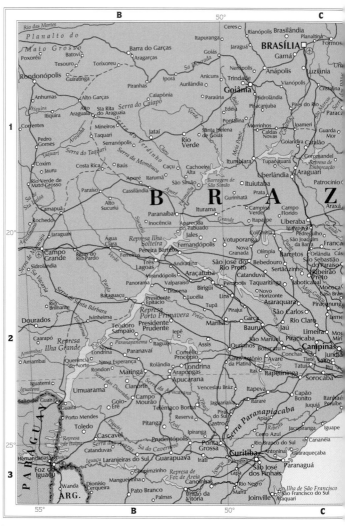

B   50°   C

Rio das Mortes
Planalto do   Ceres ○   ○Rianópolis Brasilândia
Mato Grosso   ○Planaltina
Poxoréu ○   Barra do Garças Jaraguá○   **BRASÍLIA**□ ○Formos
       Batoví○   Goiás○   Gamá
○Tesouro   Torixoreu○ Aragarças○   Sa Dourada
Rondonópolis○   Guiratinga○   ○Iporá   Nerópolis○ ○Anápolis   Luziânia○
Anhumas○   Piranhas○   Anicuns○ Trindade○   Una○
○Itiquira   Alto Garças○   ○Caiapônia Aurilândia○   **Goiânia**   Vianópolis○
○Correntes Alto Sta Rita Serra do Caiapó   ○Paraúna   ○Edéia Hidrolândia○   Cristalina○
         Araguaia do Araguaia   Piracanjuba○ Pires do Rio○   ○Paraca
Pedro○   ○Mineiros   ○Jataí   Santa Helena Pontalina○   ○Ipameri Guarda○
Gomes○ Arrialá ○Taquari   de Goiás Morrinhos○ Caldas○   ○Mor
○Coxim   Serra do Taquari Serranópolis○   **Rio**   ○   Novas   Goiandira○ Catalão○
○Jauru   ○Baús   Serra da Mombuca **Verde** Itumbiara○ Tupaciguara○ Coromandel○
Rio Verde de○   Costa Rica○   Caçu○ Cachoeira   Represa de
Mato Grosso   Paraíso○   Itarumã○   Alta   Uberlândia○ ○Araguari Embocação
○Camapuã   Cassilândia○ São Simão○ ○Ituiutaba   Patrocínio○
○Rochedo   **B R A** Curinhatã○   ○Araxá   **Z**
○Jaraguá   Alto○   Ituiama○ Campina○
Campo○   Sucuriú   Paranaíba○   Verde○   Campo   Uberaba○
Grande   Inocência○ Aparecida○ Prata○   Florido○
              Água○   do Tabuado Jales○   Colômbia○   Pedregulho○
Sidrolândia○ Clara Represa Ilha   Fernandópolis○ Votuporanga○ São Joaquim○ Franca○
         Ribas do○ Solteira   Nova○   Olímpia○ da Barra Orlândia○ Cás
         Rio Pardo Pereira Barreto○ Andradina○ Granada○ Barretos○ São Sebastião○ Ribeirão
○Dourados Três○   Ferreiros○   **São José do** Bebedouro○ Sertãozinho○ do Paraíso Preto○
              Lagoas Mirandópolis○ Araçatuba○ **Rio Preto** Catanduva○ Taquaritinga○ Jaboticabal○ Moenca○
         Panorama○ Valparaíso○ Birigüi○ Penápolis○ Novo○ Araraquara○ Piracanunga○
○Batagaçu   Dracena○ Lucélia○ Tupã○ Lins○ Horizonte ○São Carlos Rio Claro○
              Presidente○ Garça○   Pirajú○   Limeira○
Caarapó○   Represa   Epitácio Represa Marília○ Bauru○ Jaú○   Piracicaba○ Campinas
○Ivinheima Porto Primavera Feixa○   São Manuel○   Conchas○ Jundiaí
Teodoro○ Presidente○ Ourinhos○ Avaré○   Tietê○ Itu
Sampaio Prudente Iepê○ Assis○ Santo○ Tatuí○ Sorocaba
Nova○ Paranavaí○ Rolândia○ Cornélio○ Antônio○ Itapetininga
○Arirambá Londrina Nova Esperança○ Procópio da Platina Itapeva○
Iguatemi○ Rondon○ Maringá○ Apucarana○ Venceslau Bráz○ Itararé○ Capão○
Umuarama○ Cianorte○ Serra da Apucarana Jaguariaíva○ Bonito Itanhaé
Golo○ Campo○ Telêmaco Borba○ Apiaí○ Juquiá○ Ponbe
Guaíra○ Erê Mourão Reserva○ Castro○ Serra Paranapiacaba Jacupiranga○ Iguape
Porto Mendes○ Pitanga○ Ipiranga○   Ribeira○ Cananéia
Toledo○ Cascavel○ Prudentópolis○ Ponta○ Rio Branco do Sul○ Cananéia
Catanduvas○ Guarapuava○ Grossa Antonina○ Guaraqueçaba○
Iguaçu○ Laranjeiras do Sul○ Irati○ Palmeira○ **Curitiba** São José○ Paranaguá
Foz do○ Chopimzinho○ Lapa○ dos Pinhais○
Iguaçu Manguerinha○ Represa de Canoinhas○ Rio Negro○
○Wanda Dionísio○ Foz de Areia União da○ Mafra○ Ilha de São Francisco
ARG. Cerqueira Pato Branco○ Vitória Joinville○ São Francisco do Sul
Palmas○ Araquari○

55°   B   50°   C

Lambert Azimuthal Equal Area Projection

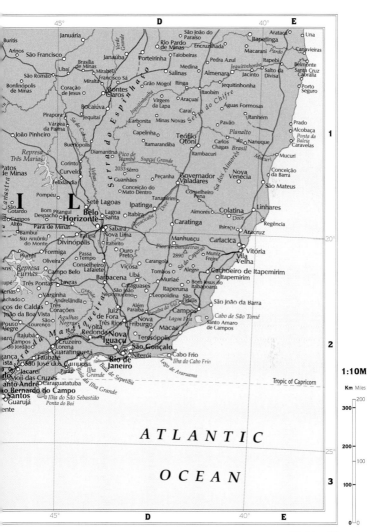

ATLANTIC

OCEAN

1:10M

Km Miles

© Bartholomew Ltd

124

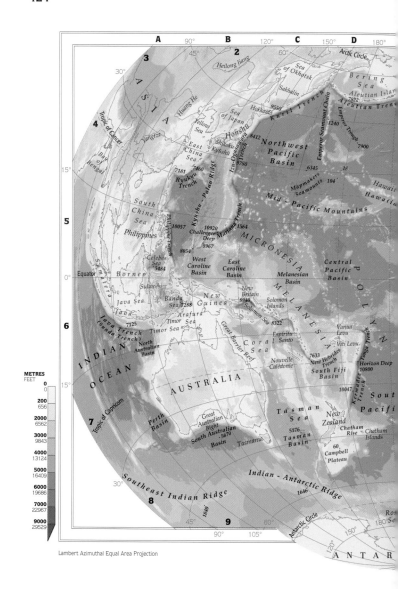

Lambert Azimuthal Equal Area Projection

METRES
FEET

METRES	FEET
0	0
200	656
2000	6562
3000	9843
4000	13124
5000	16409
6000	19686
7000	22967
9000	29529

A 90° B 120° C 150° D 180°

ASIA

Arctic Circle
45°
30°
Heilong Jiang
60°
Sea of Okhotsk
Bering Sea
Aleutian Islands
7822
Aleutian Trench
Tropic of Cancer
Huang He
Hokkaido
9550
Sakhalin
Kuril Trench
1240
Emperor Seamount Chain
Emperor Trough
7900
Yangtze
Yellow Sea
Sea of Japan
Honshu
Shikoku
8412
Northwest Pacific Basin
6345
18
Bay of Bengal
East China Sea
Kyushu
Izu-Ogasawara Trench
9780
Mapmakers Seamounts
104
Hawai
15°
7181
7460
Ryukyu Trench
Kyushu - Palau Ridge
Mid - Pacific Mountains
Hawaiia
South China Sea
Philippines
Philippine Trench
10057
Challenger Deep
10920
Mariana Trench
1564
MICRONESIA
8967
Central Pacific Basin
Equator
Sumatra
Borneo
Celebes Sea
5484
8054
West Caroline Basin
East Caroline Basin
Melanesian Basin
0°
P
O
Java Sea
Sulawesi
Banda Sea
7288
New Guinea
New Britain
8940
Solomon Islands
Solomon Sea
8322
L
Y
Java
7125
Timor Sea
Arafura Sea
Great Barrier Reef
MELANESIA
Vanua Levu
N
Java Trench (Sunda Trench)
Timor Sea
North Australian Basin
Coral Sea
Espiritu Santo
Viti Levu
E
S
I
A
INDIAN OCEAN
Nouvelle Calédonie
New Hebrides Trench
7633
South Fiji Basin
Horizon Deep
10800
Tonga Trench
15°
AUSTRALIA
10047
Sout
Paci
Tropic of Capricorn
Perth Basin
Great Australian Bight
Tasman Sea
New Zealand
Tasman Basin
5176
Chatham Rise
Chatham Islands
7
South Australian Basin
5670
Tasmania
60
Campbell Plateau
30°
Southeast Indian Ridge
Indian - Antarctic Ridge
1646
8
1840
9
90° 105°
Antarctic Circle
Ross Se
150°
180°
120°
A N T A R

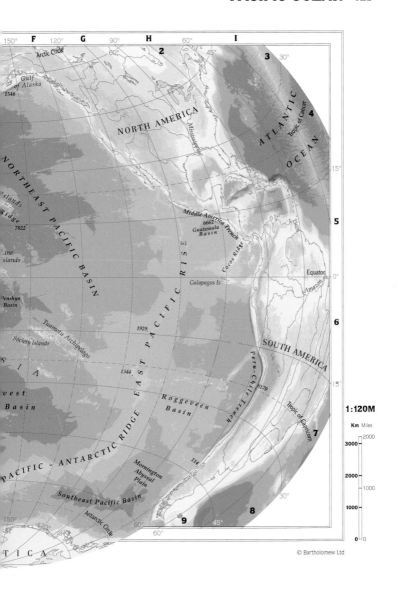

150° **F** 120° **G** 90° **H** 60° **I**

Arctic Circle **2** 45° **3** 30°

Gulf
of Alaska
1546

NORTH AMERICA

ATLANTIC **4** Tropic of Cancer

OCEAN 15°

NORTHEAST PACIFIC BASIN

slands
Ridge
7022

Middle America Trench
6662
Guatemala **5**
Basin

Cocos Ridge

ine
slands

Equator 0°

enrhyn
Basin

Galapagos Is

Amazon

EAST PACIFIC RISE

6

Tuamotu Archipelago

1929

SOUTH AMERICA

Society Islands

1344

Peru-Chile Trench

S I A

Roggeveen
Basin

3170

west
Basin

Tropic of Capricorn 15°

1:120M

PACIFIC - ANTARCTIC RIDGE

114

Mornington
Abyssal
Plain

7

Km Miles

3000 2000

Southeast Pacific Basin

2000

Antarctic Circle

30°

1000

8

1000

150° 120° 60°

9 45°

0 0

T I C A

© Bartholomew Ltd

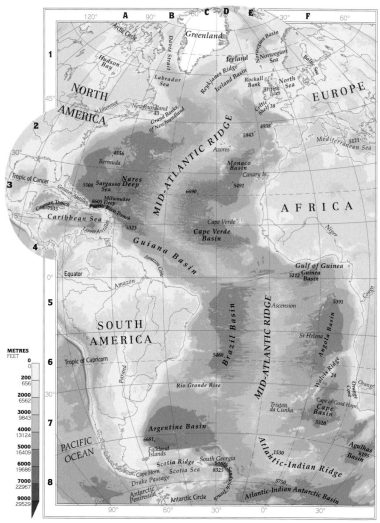

METRES
FEET

0	0
200	656
2000	6562
3000	9843
4000	13124
5000	16409
6000	19686
7000	22967
9000	29529

Lambert Azimuthal Equal Area Projection

© Bartholomew Ltd

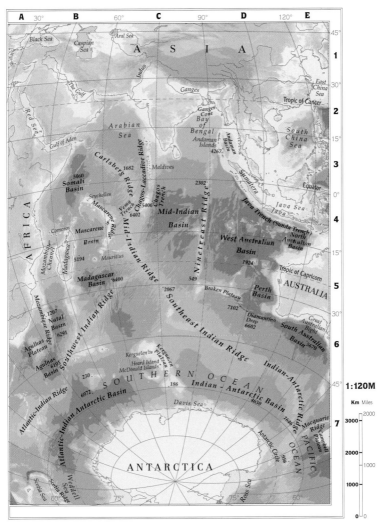

Lambert Azimuthal Equal Area Projection

© Bartholomew Ltd

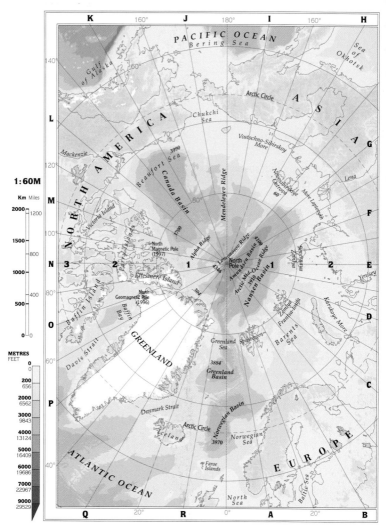

1 : 60M

Km Miles
2000 — 1200
1500 — 800
1000 — 400
500 — 0
0 — 0

METRES
FEET
0
0
200
656
2000
6562
3000
9843
4000
13124
5000
16409
6000
19686
7000
22967
9000
29529

Polar Stereographic Projection

© Bartholomew Ltd

NATIONAL STATISTICS
130-145

GEOGRAPHICAL INFORMATION
146-159

COUNTRY	AREA		POPULATION	CAPITAL
	sq km	sq mls		
AFGHANISTAN	652 225	251 825	21 354 000	Kābul
ALBANIA	28 748	11 100	3 119 000	Tirana (Tiranë)
ALGERIA	2 381 741	919 595	30 081 000	Algiers (Alger)
American Samoa	197	76	63 000	Fagatogo
ANDORRA	465	180	72 000	Andorra la Vella
ANGOLA	1 246 700	481 354	12 092 000	Luanda
Anguilla (U.K.)	155	60	8 000	The Valley
ANTIGUA AND BARBUDA	442	171	67 000	St John's
ARGENTINA	2 766 889	1 068 302	36 123 000	Buenos Aires
ARMENIA	29 800	11 506	3 536 000	Yerevan (Erevan)
Aruba (Netherlands)	193	75	94 000	Oranjestad
AUSTRALIA	7 682 395	2 966 189	18 520 000	Canberra
AUSTRIA	83 855	32 377	8 140 000	Vienna (Wien)
AZERBAIJAN	86 600	33 436	7 669 000	Baku (Bakı)
Azores (Portugal)	2 300	888	243 600	Ponta Delgada
THE BAHAMAS	13 939	5 382	296 000	Nassau
BAHRAIN	691	267	595 000	Manama
BANGLADESH	143 998	55 598	124 774 000	Dhaka (Dacca)
BARBADOS	430	166	268 000	Bridgetown
BELARUS	207 600	80 155	10 315 000	Minsk
BELGIUM	30 520	11 784	10 141 000	Brussels (Bruxelles)
BELIZE	22 965	8 867	230 000	Belmopan
BENIN	112 620	43 483	5 781 000	Porto-Novo
Bermuda (U.K.)	54	21	64 000	Hamilton
BHUTAN	46 620	18 000	2 004 000	Thimphu
BOLIVIA	1 098 581	424 164	7 957 000	La Paz/Sucre
BOSNIA-HERZEGOVINA	51 130	19 741	3 675 000	Sarajevo
BOTSWANA	581 370	224 468	1 570 000	Gaborone
BRAZIL	8 547 379	3 300 161	165 851 000	Brasília

LANGUAGES	RELIGIONS	CURRENCY
Dari, Pushtu, Uzbek	Muslim	Afghani
Albanian	Muslim, Orthodox, Roman Catholic	Lek
Arabic, French, Berber	Muslim	Dinar
Samoan, English	Protestant, Roman Catholic	US dollar
Catalan, French, Spanish	Roman Catholic	Euro
Portuguese, local languages	Roman Catholic, trad. beliefs, Protestant	Kwanza
English	Protestant, Roman Catholic	E. Carib. dollar
English, Creole	Protestant, Roman Catholic	E. Carib. dollar
Spanish, Amerindian languages	Roman Catholic	Peso
Armenian, Azeri, Russian	Orthodox, Roman Catholic, Muslim	Dram
Dutch, Papiamento	Roman Catholic, Protestant	Florin
English, Italian, Greek	Protestant, Roman Catholic, Aboriginal beliefs	Dollar
German	Roman Catholic	Euro
Azeri, Armenian, Russian	Muslim	Manat
Portuguese	Roman Catholic, Protestant	Euro
English, Creole, French Creole	Protestant, Roman Catholic	Dollar
Arabic, English	Muslim, Christian	Dinar
Bengali, Bihari, Hindi, English, local languages	Muslim, Hindu	Taka
English, Creole	Protestant, Roman Catholic	Dollar
Belorussian, Russian, Ukrainian	Orthodox, Roman Catholic	Rouble
Flemish, Walloon, German, Italian	Roman Catholic, Protestant	Euro
English, Creole, Spanish, Mayan	Roman Catholic, Protestant, Hindu	Dollar
French, local languages	Trad. beliefs, Roman Catholic	CFA franc
English	Protestant, Roman Catholic	Dollar
Dzongkha, Nepali	Buddhist, Hindu, Muslim	Ngultrum, Indian rupee
Spanish, Quechua, Aymara	Roman Catholic	Boliviano
Bosnian, Serbian, Croatian	Muslim, Orthodox, Roman Catholic, Protestant	Marka
English, Setswana, local languages	Trad. beliefs, Protestant, Roman Catholic	Pula
Portuguese, Amerindian languages	Roman Catholic	Real

COUNTRY	AREA		POPULATION	CAPITAL
	sq km	sq mls		
BRUNEI	5 765	2 226	315 000	Bandar Seri Begawan
BULGARIA	110 994	42 855	8 336 000	Sofia (Sofiya)
BURKINA	274 200	105 869	11 305 000	Ouagadougou
BURUNDI	27 835	10 747	6 457 000	Bujumbura
CAMBODIA	181 000	69 884	10 716 000	Phnum Pénh
CAMEROON	475 442	183 569	14 305 000	Yaoundé
CANADA	9 970 610	3 849 674	30 563 000	Ottawa
Canary Islands (Spain)	7 447	2 875	1 606 522	Santa Cruz de Tenerife
CAPE VERDE	4 033	1 557	408 000	Praia
Cayman Islands (U.K.)	259	100	36 000	George Town
CENTRAL AFRICAN REPUBLIC	622 436	240 324	3 485 000	Bangui
CHAD	1 284 000	495 755	7 270 000	Ndjamena
CHILE	756 945	292 258	14 824 000	Santiago
CHINA	9 584 492	3 700 593	1 262 817 000	Beijing (Peking)
Christmas Island (Austr.)	135	52	2 195	The Settlement
Cocos Islands (Austr.)	14	5	637	Home Island
COLOMBIA	1 141 748	440 831	40 803 000	Bogotá
COMOROS	1 862	719	658 000	Moroni
CONGO	342 000	132 047	2 785 000	Brazzaville
CONGO, DEMOCRATIC REPUBLIC OF	2 345 410	905 568	49 139 000	Kinshasa
Cook Islands (N.Z.)	293	113	19 000	Avarua
COSTA RICA	51 100	19 730	3 841 000	San José
CÔTE D'IVOIRE	322 463	124 504	14 292 000	Yamoussoukro
CROATIA	56 538	21 829	4 481 000	Zagreb
CUBA	110 860	42 803	11 116 000	Havana (La Habana)
CYPRUS	9 251	3 572	771 000	Nicosia (Lefkosia)
CZECH REPUBLIC	78 864	30 450	10 282 000	Prague (Praha)
DENMARK	43 075	16 631	5 270 000	Copenhagen
DJIBOUTI	23 200	8 958	623 000	Djibouti

LANGUAGES	RELIGIONS	CURRENCY
Malay, English, Chinese	Muslim, Buddhist, Christian	Dollar (Ringgit)
Bulgarian	Orthodox, Muslim	Lev
French, Voltaic languages	Trad. beliefs, Muslim, Roman Catholic	CFA franc
Kirundi, French	Roman Catholic, Protestant	Franc
Khmer, Vietnamese	Buddhist, Muslim	Riel
French, English, local languages	Trad. beliefs, Roman Catholic, Muslim, Protestant	CFA franc
English, French, Amerindian languages, Inuktitut	Roman Catholic, Protestant	Dollar
Spanish	Roman Catholic	Euro
Portuguese, Portuguese Creole	Roman Catholic	Escudo
English	Protestant, Roman Catholic	Dollar
French, Sango, local languages	Protestant, Roman Catholic, Trad. beliefs	CFA franc
Arabic, French, local languages	Muslim, Trad. beliefs, Roman Catholic	CFA franc
Spanish, Amerindian languages	Roman Catholic	Peso
Chinese, regional languages	Confucian, Taoist, Buddhist	Yuan
English	Buddhist, Muslim, Protestant, Roman Catholic	Austr. dollar
English	Muslim, Christian	Austr. dollar
Spanish, Amerindian languages	Roman Catholic	Peso
Comorian, French, Arabic	Muslim	Franc
French, Kongo, Monokutuba, local languages	Roman Catholic, Protestant	CFA franc
French, Lingala, Swahili, Kongo, local languages	Roman Catholic, Protestant	Franc
English, Maori	Protestant, Roman Catholic	Dollar
Spanish	Roman Catholic, Protestant	Colón
French, Akan, local languages	Trad. beliefs, Muslim, Roman Catholic	CFA franc
Croatian, Serbian	Roman Catholic, Orthodox, Muslim	Kuna
Spanish	Roman Catholic, Protestant	Peso
Greek, Turkish, English	Greek Orthodox, Muslim	Pound
Czech, Moravian, Slovak	Roman Catholic, Protestant	Koruna
Danish	Protestant, Roman Catholic	Krone
Somali, French, Arabic, Issa, Afar	Muslim	Franc

COUNTRY	AREA		POPULATION	CAPITAL
	sq km	sq mls		
DOMINICA	750	290	71 000	Roseau
DOMINICAN REPUBLIC	48 442	18 704	8 232 000	Santo Domingo
EAST TIMOR	14 874	5 743	750 000	Dili
ECUADOR	272 045	105 037	12 175 000	Quito
EGYPT	1 000 250	386 199	65 978 000	Cairo (El Qâhira)
EL SALVADOR	21 041	8 124	6 032 000	San Salvador
EQUATORIAL GUINEA	28 051	10 831	431 000	Malabo
ERITREA	117 400	45 328	3 577 000	Asmara
ESTONIA	45 200	17 452	1 429 000	Tallinn
ETHIOPIA	1 133 880	437 794	59 649 000	Addis Ababa (Ādīs Ābeba)
Falkland Islands (U.K.)	12 170	4 699	2 000	Stanley
Faroe Islands (Denmark)	1 399	540	43 000	Tórshavn (Thorshavn)
FIJI	18 330	7 077	796 000	Suva
FINLAND	338 145	130 559	5 154 000	Helsinki (Helsingfor
FRANCE	543 965	210 026	58 683 000	Paris
French Guiana	90 000	34 749	167 000	Cayenne
French Polynesia	3 265	1 261	227 000	Papeete
GABON	267 667	103 347	1 167 000	Libreville
THE GAMBIA	11 295	4 361	1 229 000	Banjul
GAZA	363	140	1 036 000	Gaza
GEORGIA	69 700	26 911	5 059 000	T'bilisi
GERMANY	357 028	137 849	82 133 000	Berlin
GHANA	238 537	92 100	19 162 000	Accra
Gibraltar (U.K.)	0.7	3	25 000	Gibraltar
GREECE	131 957	50 949	10 600 000	Athens (Athina)
Greenland (Denmark)	2 175 600	840 004	56 000	Nuuk (Godthåb)
GRENADA	378	146	93 000	St George's
Guadeloupe (France)	1 780	687	443 000	Basse-Terre
Guam (U.S.A.)	541	209	161 000	Agana
GUATEMALA	108 890	42 043	10 801 000	Guatemala
Guernsey (U.K.)	78	30	64 555	St Peter Port

LANGUAGES	RELIGIONS	CURRENCY
English, French Creole	Roman Catholic, Protestant	E. Carib. dollar
Spanish, French Creole	Roman Catholic, Protestant	Peso
Portuguese, Tetun, English	Roman Catholic	US Dollar
Spanish, Amerindian languages	Roman Catholic	Sucre
Arabic, French	Muslim, Coptic Christian	Pound
Spanish	Roman Catholic, Protestant	Colón
Spanish, Fang	Roman Catholic	CFA franc
Tigrinya, Tigre	Muslim, Coptic Christian	Nakfa
Estonian, Russian	Protestant, Orthodox	Kroon
Amharic, Oromo, local languages	Ethiopian Orthodox, Muslim, Trad. beliefs	Birr
English	Protestant, Roman Catholic	Pound
Danish, Faroese	Protestant	Danish krone
English, Fijian, Hindi	Christian, Hindu, Muslim	Dollar
Finnish, Swedish	Protestant, Orthodox	Euro
French, Arabic	Roman Catholic, Protestant, Muslim	Euro
French, Creole	Roman Catholic, Protestant	Euro
French, Polynesian languages	Protestant, Roman Catholic	Pacific franc
French, Fang, local languages	Roman Catholic, Protestant	CFA franc
English, Malinke, Fulani	Muslim	Dalasi
Arabic	Muslim	
Georgian, Russian, Armenian	Orthodox, Muslim	Lari
German, Turkish	Protestant, Roman Catholic	Euro
English, Hausa, Akan, local languages	Protestant, Roman Catholic, Muslim, Trad. beliefs	Cedi
English, Spanish	Roman Catholic, Protestant	Pound
Greek, Macedonian	Greek Orthodox	Euro
Greenlandic, Danish	Protestant	Danish krone
English, Creole	Roman Catholic, Protestant	E. Carib. dollar
French, French Creole	Roman Catholic	Euro
Chamorro, English	Roman Catholic	US dollar
Spanish, Mayan languages	Roman Catholic, Protestant	Quetzal
English, French	Protestant, Roman Catholic	Pound

COUNTRY	AREA		POPULATION	CAPITAL
	sq km	sq mls		
GUINEA	245 857	94 926	7 337 000	Conakry
GUINEA-BISSAU	36 125	13 948	1 161 000	Bissau
GUYANA	214 969	83 000	850 000	Georgetown
HAITI	27 750	10 714	7 952 000	Port-au-Prince
HONDURAS	112 088	43 277	6 147 000	Tegucigalpa
HUNGARY	93 030	35 919	10 116 000	Budapest
ICELAND	102 820	39 699	276 000	Reykjavík
INDIA	3 065 027	1 183 414	982 223 000	New Delhi
INDONESIA	1 919 445	741 102	206 338 000	Jakarta
IRAN	1 648 000	636 296	65 758 000	Tehrän
IRAQ	438 317	169 235	21 800 000	Baghdäd
IRELAND, REPUBLIC OF	70 282	27 136	3 681 000	Dublin
Isle of Man (U.K.)	572	221	77 000	Douglas
ISRAEL	20 770	8 019	5 984 000	Jerusalem
ITALY	301 245	116 311	57 369 000	Rome (Roma)
JAMAICA	10 991	4 244	2 538 000	Kingston
JAPAN	377 727	145 841	126 281 000	Tökyö
Jersey (U.K.)	116	45	89 136	St Helier
JORDAN	89 206	34 443	6 304 000	Ammän
KAZAKHSTAN	2 717 300	1 049 155	16 319 000	Astana (Akmola)
KENYA	582 646	224 961	29 008 000	Nairobi
KIRIBATI	717	277	81 000	Bairiki
KUWAIT	17 818	6 880	1 811 000	Kuwait (Al Kuwayt)
KYRGYZSTAN	198 500	76 641	4 643 000	Bishkek (Frunze)
LAOS	236 800	91 429	5 163 000	Vientiane (Viangchan)
LATVIA	63 700	24 595	2 424 000	Rīga
LEBANON	10 452	4 036	3 191 000	Beirut (Beyrouth)
LESOTHO	30 355	11 720	2 062 000	Maseru
LIBERIA	111 369	43 000	2 666 000	Monrovia
LIBYA	1 759 540	679 362	5 339 000	Tripoli (Ţarābulus)
LIECHTENSTEIN	160	62	32 000	Vaduz

LANGUAGES	RELIGIONS	CURRENCY
French, Fulani, local languages	Muslim	Franc
Portuguese, Creole, local languages	Trad. beliefs, Muslim	Peso
English, Creole, Amerindian languages	Protestant, Hindu, Roman Catholic, Muslim	Dollar
French, Creole	Roman Catholic, Protestant	Gourde
Spanish, Amerindian languages	Roman Catholic, Protestant	Lempira
Hungarian	Roman Catholic, Protestant	Forint
Icelandic	Protestant, Roman Catholic	Króna
Hindi, English, regional languages	Hindu, Muslim, Sikh, Christian	Rupee
Bahasa Indonesian, Dutch, local languages	Muslim, Protestant, Roman Catholic	Rupiah
Farsi, Azeri, Kurdish	Muslim, Baha'i	Rial
Arabic, Kurdish, Turkmen	Muslim	Dinar
English, Irish	Roman Catholic, Protestant	Euro
English	Protestant, Roman Catholic	Pound
Hebrew, Arabic, Yiddish, English	Jewish, Muslim, Christian	Shekel
Italian	Roman Catholic	Euro
English, Creole	Protestant, Roman Catholic	Dollar
Japanese	Shintoist, Buddhist	Yen
English, French	Protestant, Roman Catholic	Pound
Arabic	Muslim	Dinar
Kazakh, Russian	Muslim, Orthodox, Protestant	Tenge
Swahili, English, local languages	Roman Catholic, Protestant, Trad. beliefs	Shilling
Kiribati, English	Roman Catholic, Protestant	Austr. dollar
Arabic	Muslim, Christian	Dinar
Kirghiz, Russian, Uzbek	Muslim, Orthodox	Som
Lao, local languages	Buddhist, Trad. beliefs	Kip
Latvian, Russian	Protestant, Roman Catholic, Orthodox	Lat
Arabic, French, Armenian	Muslim, Protestant, Roman Catholic	Pound
Sesotho, English, Zulu	Roman Catholic, Protestant	Loti
English, Creole, local languages	Muslim, Christian	Dollar
Arabic, Berber	Muslim	Dinar
German	Roman Catholic, Protestant	Swiss franc

COUNTRY	AREA		POPULATION	CAPITAL
	sq km	sq mls		
LITHUANIA	65 200	25 174	3 694 000	Vilnius
LUXEMBOURG	2 586	998	422 000	Luxembourg
MACEDONIA (F.Y.R.O.M.)	25 713	9 928	1 999 000	Skopje
MADAGASCAR	587 041	226 658	15 057 000	Antananarivo
Madeira (Portugal)	779	301	259 000	Funchal
MALAWI	118 484	45 747	10 346 000	Lilongwe
MALAYSIA	332 965	128 559	21 410 000	Kuala Lumpur
MALDIVES	298	115	271 000	Male
MALI	1 240 140	478 821	10 694 000	Bamako
MALTA	316	122	384 000	Valletta
MARSHALL ISLANDS	181	70	60 000	Dalap-Uliga-Darrit
Martinique (France)	1 079	417	389 000	Fort-de-France
MAURITANIA	1 030 700	397 955	2 529 000	Nouakchott
MAURITIUS	2 040	788	1 141 000	Port Louis
Mayotte (France)	373	144	144 944	Dzaoudzi
MEXICO	1 972 545	761 604	95 831 000	México (Mexico City)
MICRONESIA, FEDERATED STATES OF	701	271	114 000	Palikir
MOLDOVA	33 700	13 012	4 378 000	Chişinău (Kishnev)
MONACO	2	1	33 000	Monaco-Ville
MONGOLIA	1 565 000	604 250	2 579 000	Ulaanbaatar (Ulan Bator)
Montserrat (U.K.)	100	39	11 000	Plymouth
MOROCCO	446 550	172 414	27 377 000	Rabat
MOZAMBIQUE	799 380	308 642	18 880 000	Maputo
MYANMAR (BURMA)	676 577	261 228	44 497 000	Yangôn (Rangoon)
NAMIBIA	824 292	318 261	1 660 000	Windhoek
NAURU	21	8	11 000	Yaren
NEPAL	147 181	56 827	22 847 000	Kathmandu
NETHERLANDS	41 526	16 033	15 678 000	Amsterdam/The Hagu

LANGUAGES	RELIGIONS	CURRENCY
Lithuanian, Russian, Polish	Roman Catholic, Protestant, Orthodox	Litas
Luxembourgian, German, French	Roman Catholic, Protestant	Euro
Macedonian, Albanian	Orthodox, Muslim, Roman Catholic	Denar
Malagasy, French	Trad. beliefs, Roman Catholic, Protestant	Franc
Portuguese	Roman Catholic, Protestant	Euro
English, local languages	Protestant, Roman Catholic, Muslim Trad. beliefs	Kwacha
Malay, English, Chinese, Tamil, local languages	Muslim, Buddhist, Roman Catholic, Christian, Trad. beliefs	Dollar (Ringgit)
Maldivian	Muslim	Rufiyaa
French, local languages	Muslim, Trad. beliefs	CFA franc
Maltese, English	Roman Catholic	Lira
Marshallese, English	Protestant, Roman Catholic	US dollar
French, French Creole	Roman Catholic	Euro
Arabic, French, local languages	Muslim	Ouguiya
English	Hindu, Roman Catholic, Muslim	Rupee
Mahorian (Swahili), French	Muslim, Roman Catholic	Euro
Spanish, Amerindian languages	Roman Catholic	Peso
English, Trukese, Pohnpeian, local languages	Protestant, Roman Catholic	US dollar
Romanian, Russian, Ukrainian	Moldovan Orthodox	Leu
French, Monegasque, Italian	Roman Catholic	Euro
Mongolian, Kazakh, local languages	Buddhist, Muslim, Trad. beliefs	Tugrik
English	Protestant, Roman Catholic	E. Carib. dollar
Arabic, Berber, French, Spanish	Muslim	Dirham
Portuguese, Makua, Tsonga, local languages	Trad. beliefs, Roman Catholic, Muslim	Metical
Burmese, Shan, Karen, local languages	Buddhist, Muslim, Protestant	Kyat
English, Afrikaans, Ovambo, local languages	Protestant, Roman Catholic	Dollar
Nauruan, Kiribati, English	Protestant, Roman Catholic	Austr. dollar
Nepali, English, local languages,	Hindu, Buddhist	Rupee
Dutch	Roman Catholic, Protestant	Euro

COUNTRY	AREA		POPULATION	CAPITAL
	sq km	sq mls		
Netherlands Antilles	800	309	213 000	Willemstad
New Caledonia (France)	19 058	7 358	206 000	Nouméa
NEW ZEALAND	270 534	104 454	3 796 000	Wellington
NICARAGUA	130 000	50 193	4 807 000	Managua
NIGER	1 267 000	489 191	10 078 000	Niamey
NIGERIA	923 768	356 669	106 409 000	Abuja
Niue (N.Z.)	258	100	2 000	Alofi
Norfolk Island (Austr.)	35	14	2 000	Kingston
Northern Mariana Islands (U.S.A.)	477	184	70 000	Saipan
NORTH KOREA	120 538	46 540	23 348 000	P'yŏngyang
NORWAY	323 878	125 050	4 419 000	Oslo
OMAN	309 500	119 499	2 382 000	Muscat (Masqaṭ)
PAKISTAN	803 940	310 403	148 166 000	Islamabad
PALAU	497	192	19 000	Koror
PANAMA	77 082	29 762	2 767 000	Panamá (Panama City
PAPUA NEW GUINEA	462 840	178 704	4 600 000	Port Moresby
PARAGUAY	406 752	157 048	5 222 000	Asunción
PERU	1 285 216	496 225	24 797 000	Lima
PHILIPPINES	300 000	115 831	72 944 000	Manila
Pitcairn Islands (U.K.)	45	17	46	Adamstown
POLAND	312 683	120 728	38 718 000	Warsaw (Warszawa)
PORTUGAL	88 940	34 340	9 869 000	Lisbon (Lisboa)
Puerto Rico (U.S.A.)	9 104	3 515	3 810 000	San Juan
QATAR	11 437	4 416	579 000	Doha (Ad Dawḥah)
Réunion (France)	2 551	985	682 000	St-Denis
ROMANIA	237 500	91 699	22 474 000	Bucharest (Bucureşti)
RUSSIAN FEDERATION	17 075 400	6 592 849	147 434 000	Moscow (Moskva
RWANDA	26 338	10 169	6 604 000	Kigali
St Helena and Dependencies (U.K.)	121	47	5 644	Jamestown

LANGUAGES	RELIGIONS	CURRENCY
Dutch, Papiamento	Roman Catholic, Protestant	Guilder
French, local languages	Roman Catholic, Protestant	Pacific franc
English, Maori	Protestant, Roman Catholic	Dollar
Spanish, Amerindian languages	Roman Catholic, Protestant	Córdoba
French, Hausa, local languages	Muslim, Trad. beliefs	CFA franc
English, Creole, local languages	Muslim, Protestant, Roman Catholic, Trad. beliefs	Naira
English, Polynesian	Protestant, Roman Catholic	NZ dollar
English	Protestant, Roman Catholic	Austr. dollar
Engllish, Chamorro, Tagalog	Roman Catholic, Protestant	US dollar
Korean	Trad. beliefs, Chondoist, Buddhist, Confucian, Taoist	Won
Norwegian	Protestant, Roman Catholic	Krone
Arabic, Baluchi, Farsi	Muslim	Rial
Urdu, Punjabi, Sindhi, Pushtu, English	Muslim, Christian, Hindu	Rupee
Palauan, English	Roman Catholic, Protestant	US dollar
Spanish, English Creole, Amerindian languages	Roman Catholic	Balboa
English, Papuan languages	Protestant, Roman Catholic, Trad. beliefs	Kina
Spanish, Guarani	Roman Catholic	Guaraní
Spanish, Qechua, Aymara	Roman Catholic	Sol
English, Filipino, local languages	Roman Catholic, Agilipayan, Muslim	Peso
English	Protestant	Dollar
Polish, German	Roman Catholic, Orthodox	Złoty
Portuguese	Roman Catholic, Protestant	Euro
Spanish, English	Roman Catholic, Protestant	US dollar
Arabic, Indian languages	Muslim, Christian	Riyal
French	Roman Catholic	Euro
Romanian, Hungarian	Orthodox	Leu
Russian, Tatar, local languages	Orthodox, Muslim, other Christian, Jewish	Rouble
Kinyarwanda, French, English	Roman Catholic, Trad. beliefs	Franc
English	Protestant, Roman Catholic	Pound

COUNTRY	AREA		POPULATION	CAPITAL
	sq km	sq mls		
ST KITTS AND NEVIS	261	101	39 000	Basseterre
ST LUCIA	616	238	150 000	Castries
St Pierre and Miquelon (France)	242	93	7 000	St-Pierre
ST VINCENT AND THE GRENADINES	389	150	112 000	Kingstown
SAMOA	2 831	1 093	174 000	Apia
SAN MARINO	61	24	26 000	San Marino
SÃO TOMÉ AND PRÍNCIPE	964	372	141 000	São Tomé
SAUDI ARABIA	2 200 000	849 425	20 181 000	Riyadh (Ar Riyāḍ)
SENEGAL	196 720	75 954	9 003 000	Dakar
SEYCHELLES	455	176	76 000	Victoria
SIERRA LEONE	71 740	27 699	4 568 000	Freetown
SINGAPORE	639	247	3 476 000	Singapore
SLOVAKIA	49 035	18 933	5 377 000	Bratislava
SLOVENIA	20 251	7 819	1 993 000	Ljubljana
SOLOMON ISLANDS	28 370	10 954	417 000	Honiara
SOMALIA	637 657	246 201	9 237 000	Muqdisho (Mogadisl
SOUTH AFRICA, REPUBLIC OF	1 219 090	470 693	39 357 000	Pretoria/Cape Town
SOUTH KOREA	99 274	38 330	46 109 000	Seoul (Sŏul)
SPAIN	504 782	194 897	39 628 000	Madrid
SRI LANKA	65 610	25 332	18 455 000	Colombo
SUDAN	2 505 813	967 500	28 292 000	Khartoum
SURINAME	163 820	63 251	414 000	Paramaribo
Svalbard (Norway)	61 229	23 641	2 591	Longyearbyen
SWAZILAND	17 364	6 704	952 000	Mbabane
SWEDEN	449 964	173 732	8 875 000	Stockholm
SWITZERLAND	41 293	15 943	7 299 000	Bern (Berne)
SYRIA	185 180	71 498	15 333 000	Damascus (Dimashq
TAIWAN	36 179	13 969	21 908 135	T'aipei
TAJIKISTAN	143 100	55 251	6 015 000	Dushanbe

LANGUAGES	RELIGIONS	CURRENCY
English, Creole	Protestant, Roman Catholic	E. Carib. dollar
English, French Creole	Roman Catholic, Protestant	E. Carib. dollar
French	Roman Catholic	Euro
English, Creole	Protestant, Roman Catholic	E. Carib. dollar
Samoan, English	Protestant, Roman Catholic	Tala
Italian	Roman Catholic	Euro
Portuguese	Roman Catholic	Dobra
Arabic	Muslim	Riyal
French, Wolof, local languages	Muslim	CFA franc
Seychellois, English	Roman Catholic, Protestant	Rupee
English, Creole	Trad. beliefs, Muslim	Leone
Chinese, English, Malay	Buddhist, Taoist, Muslim, Christian	Dollar
Slovak, Hungarian, Czech	Roman Catholic, Protestant	Koruna
Slovene	Roman Catholic, Protestant	Tôlar
English, Solomon Islands Pidgin, local languages	Protestant, Roman Catholic	Dollar
Somali, Arabic	Muslim	Shilling
Afrikaans, English, local languages	Protestant, Roman Catholic	Rand
Korean	Buddhist, Protestant, Roman Catholic	Won
Spanish, Catalan, Galician, Basque	Roman Catholic	Euro
Sinhalese, Tamil, English	Buddhist, Hindu, Muslim	Rupee
Arabic, local languages	Muslim, Trad. beliefs	Dinar
Dutch, Surinamese, English	Hindu, Roman Catholic, Protestant, Muslim	Guilder
Norwegian	Protestant, Roman Catholic	Krone
Swazi, English	Protestant, Roman Catholic, Trad. beliefs	Emalangeni
Swedish	Protestant, Roman Catholic	Krona
German, French, Italian	Roman Catholic, Protestant	Franc
Arabic, Kurdish	Muslim, Christian	Pound
Chinese, local languages	Buddhist, Taoist, Confucian	Dollar
Tajik, Uzbek, Russian	Muslim	Rouble

COUNTRY	AREA		POPULATION	CAPITAL
	sq km	sq mls		
TANZANIA	945 087	364 900	32 102 000	Dodoma
THAILAND	513 115	198 115	60 300 000	Bangkok (Krung The
TOGO	56 785	21 925	4 397 000	Lomé
Tokelau (N.Z.)	10	4	1 000	none
TONGA	748	289	98 000	Nuku'alofa
TRINIDAD AND TOBAGO	5 130	1 981	1 283 000	Port of Spain
TUNISIA	164 150	63 379	9 335 000	Tunis
TURKEY	779 452	300 948	64 479 000	Ankara
TURKMENISTAN	488 100	188 456	4 309 000	Ashgabat (Ashkhabac
Turks and Caicos Islands (U.K.)	430	166	16 000	Grand Turk (Cockburn Town)
TUVALU	25	10	11 000	Vaiaku
UGANDA	241 038	93 065	20 554 000	Kampala
UKRAINE	603 700	233 090	50 861 000	Kiev (Kyiv)
UNITED ARAB EMIRATES	83 600	32 278	2 377 453	Abu Dhabi (Abū Ẓabī
UNITED KINGDOM	244 082	94 241	58 649 000	London
UNITED STATES OF AMERICA	9 809 378	3 787 422	274 028 000	Washington
URUGUAY	176 215	68 037	3 289 000	Montevideo
UZBEKISTAN	447 400	172 742	23 574 000	Tashkent
VANUATU	12 190	4 707	182 000	Port Vila
VATICAN CITY	0.5	0.2	480	Vatican City
VENEZUELA	912 050	352 144	23 242 000	Caracas
VIETNAM	329 565	127 246	77 562 000	Ha Nôi (Hanoi)
Virgin Islands (U.K.)	153	59	20 000	Road Town
Virgin Islands (U.S.A.)	352	136	94 000	Charlotte Amalie
Wallis and Futuna Islands (France)	274	106	14 000	Mata-Utu
WESTERN SAHARA	266 000	102 703	275 000	Laâyoune
YEMEN	527 968	203 850	16 887 000	Şan'ä'
YUGOSLAVIA	102 173	39 449	10 635 000	Belgrade (Beograd)
ZAMBIA	752 614	290 586	8 781 000	Lusaka
ZIMBABWE	390 759	150 873	11 377 000	Harare

LANGUAGES	RELIGIONS	CURRENCY
Swahili, English, local languages	Christian, Muslin, Trad. beliefs	Shilling
Thai, Lao, Chinese, Malay	Buddhist, Muslim	Baht
French, local languages	Trad. beliefs, Roman Catholic, Muslim	CFA franc
English, Tokelauan	Protestant, Roman Catholic	NZ dollar
Tongan, English	Protestant, Roman Catholic, Mormon	Pa'anga
English, Creole, Hindi	Roman Catholic, Hindu, Protestant	Dollar
Arabic, French	Muslim	Dinar
Turkish, Kurdish	Muslim	Lira
Turkmen, Russian	Muslim	Manat
English	Protestant	US dollar
Tuvaluan, English	Protestant	Dollar
English, Swahili, local languages	Roman Catholic, Protestant	Shilling
Ukrainian, Russian	Orthodox, Roman Catholic	Hryvnia
Arabic, Hindu, Urdu, Farsi	Muslim, Christian	Dirham
English	Protestant, Roman Catholic, Muslim	Pound
English, Spanish, Amerindian languages	Protestant, Roman Catholic	Dollar
Spanish	Roman Catholic, Protestant	Peso
Uzbek, Russian, Tajik	Muslim, Orthodox	Som
English, Creole	Protestant, Roman Catholic	Vatu
Italian	Roman Catholic	Euro
Spanish, Amerindian languages	Roman Catholic	Bolívar
Vietnamese, Thai, local languages	Buddhist, Roman Catholic	Dong
English	Protestant. Roman Catholic	US dollar
English, Spanish	Protestant, Roman Catholic	US dollar
French, Polynesian	Roman Catholic	Pacific franc
Arabic	Muslim	Dirham
Arabic	Muslim	Dinar, Rial
Serbian, Albanian	Serbian and Montenegrin Orthodox, Muslim	Dinar
English, local languages	Christian, Trad. beliefs	Kwacha
English, Shona, Ndebele	Protestant, Roman Catholic, Trad. beliefs	Dollar

ISLANDS

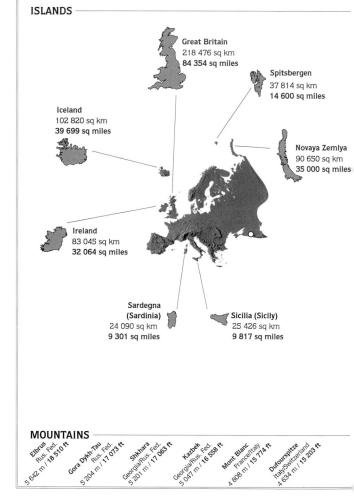

Great Britain
218 476 sq km
84 354 sq miles

Spitsbergen
37 814 sq km
14 600 sq miles

Iceland
102 820 sq km
39 699 sq miles

Novaya Zemlya
90 650 sq km
35 000 sq miles

Ireland
83 045 sq km
32 064 sq miles

**Sardegna
(Sardinia)**
24 090 sq km
9 301 sq miles

Sicilia (Sicily)
25 426 sq km
9 817 sq miles

MOUNTAINS

Elbrus
Rus. Fed.
5 642 m / **18 510 ft**

Gora Dykh-Tau
Rus. Fed.
5 204 m / **17 073 ft**

Shkhara
Georgia/Rus. Fed.
5 201 m / **17 063 ft**

Kazbek
Georgia/Rus. Fed.
5 047 m / **16 558 ft**

Mont Blanc
France/Italy
4 808 m / **15 774 ft**

Dufourspitze
Italy/Switzerland
4 634 m / **15 203 ft**

LAKES

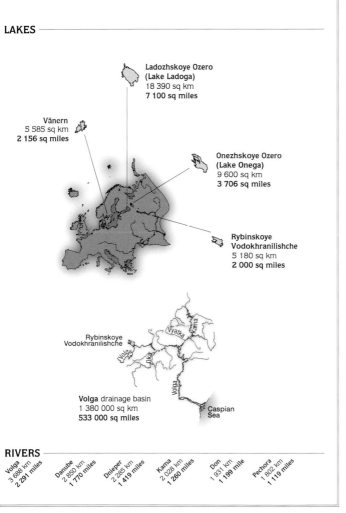

**Ladozhskoye Ozero
(Lake Ladoga)**
18 390 sq km
7 100 sq miles

Vänern
5 585 sq km
2 156 sq miles

**Onezhskoye Ozero
(Lake Onega)**
9 600 sq km
3 706 sq miles

**Rybinskoye
Vodokhranilishche**
5 180 sq km
2 000 sq miles

Rybinskoye
Vodokhranilishche

Nyatka

Kama

Volga

Oka

Volga

Volga drainage basin
1 380 000 sq km
533 000 sq miles

Caspian
Sea

RIVERS

Volga
3 688 km
2 291 miles

Danube
2 850 km
1 770 miles

Dnieper
2 285 km
1 419 miles

Kama
2 028 km
1 260 miles

Don
1 931 km
1 199 mile

Pechora
1 802 km
1 119 miles

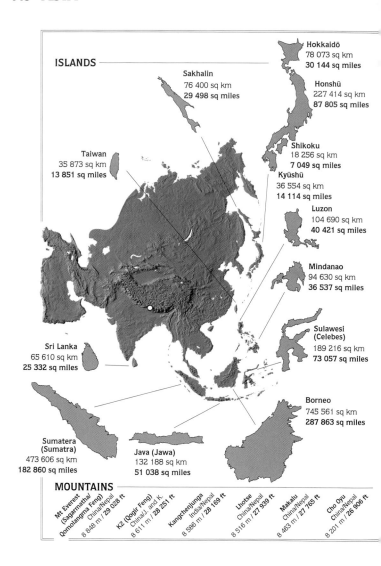

ISLANDS

Hokkaidō
78 073 sq km
30 144 sq miles

Sakhalin
76 400 sq km
29 498 sq miles

Honshū
227 414 sq km
87 805 sq miles

Taiwan
35 873 sq km
13 851 sq miles

Shikoku
18 256 sq km
7 049 sq miles

Kyūshū
36 554 sq km
14 114 sq miles

Luzon
104 690 sq km
40 421 sq miles

Mindanao
94 630 sq km
36 537 sq miles

Sulawesi
(Celebes)
189 216 sq km
73 057 sq miles

Sri Lanka
65 610 sq km
25 332 sq miles

Borneo
745 561 sq km
287 863 sq miles

Sumatera
(Sumatra)
473 606 sq km
182 860 sq miles

Java (Jawa)
132 188 sq km
51 038 sq miles

MOUNTAINS

Mt Everest
(Sagarmatha/
Qomolangma Feng)
China/Nepal
8 848 m / **29 028 ft**

K2 (Qogir Feng)
China/J. and K.
8 611 m / **28 251 ft**

Kangchenjunga
India/Nepal
8 586 m / **28 169 ft**

Lhotse
China/Nepal
8 516 m / **27 939 ft**

Makalu
China/Nepal
8 463 m / **27 765 ft**

Cho Oyu
China/Nepal
8 201 m / **26 906 ft**

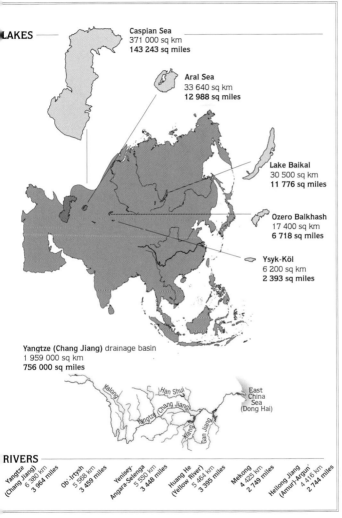

LAKES

Caspian Sea
371 000 sq km
143 243 sq miles

Aral Sea
33 640 sq km
12 988 sq miles

Lake Baikal
30 500 sq km
11 776 sq miles

Ozero Balkhash
17 400 sq km
6 718 sq miles

Ysyk-Köl
6 200 sq km
2 393 sq miles

Yangtze (Chang Jiang) drainage basin
1 959 000 sq km
756 000 sq miles

Yalong
Han Shui
Yangtze (Chang Jiang)
Min Jiang
Gan Jiang

East
China
Sea
(Dong Hai)

RIVERS

Yangtze
(Chang Jiang)
6 380 km
3 964 miles

Ob'-Irtysh
5 568 km
3 459 miles

Yenisey-
Angara-Selenga
5 550 km
3 448 miles

Huang He
(Yellow River)
5 464 km
3 395 miles

Mekong
4 425 km
2 749 miles

Heilong Jiang
(Amur)-Argun'
4 416 km
2 744 miles

© Bartholomew Ltd

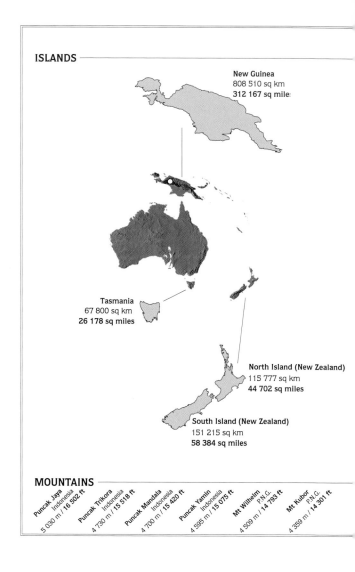

ISLANDS

New Guinea
808 510 sq km
312 167 sq mile:

Tasmania
67 800 sq km
26 178 sq miles

North Island (New Zealand)
115 777 sq km
44 702 sq miles

South Island (New Zealand)
151 215 sq km
58 384 sq miles

MOUNTAINS

Puncak Jaya
Indonesia
5 030 m / **16 502 ft**

Puncak Trikora
Indonesia
4 730 m / **15 518 ft**

Puncak Mandala
Indonesia
4 700 m / **15 420 ft**

Puncak Yamin
Indonesia
4 595 m / **15 075 ft**

Mt Wilhelm
P.N.G.
4 509 m / **14 793 ft**

Mt Kubor
P.N.G.
4 359 m / **14 301 ft**

LAKES

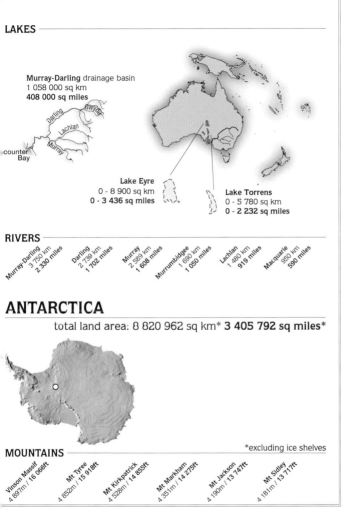

Murray-Darling drainage basin
1 058 000 sq km
408 000 sq miles

Darling
Gwydir
Lachlan
Murray

counter
Bay

Lake Eyre
0 - 8 900 sq km
0 - 3 436 sq miles

Lake Torrens
0 - 5 780 sq km
0 - 2 232 sq miles

RIVERS

Murray-Darling
3 750 km
2 330 miles

Darling
2 738 km
1 702 miles

Murray
2 589 km
1 608 miles

Murrumbidgee
1 690 km
1 050 miles

Lachlan
1 480 km
919 miles

Macquarie
950 km
590 miles

ANTARCTICA

total land area: 8 820 962 sq km* **3 405 792 sq miles***

*excluding ice shelves

MOUNTAINS

Vinson Massif
4 897m / 16 066ft

Mt Tyree
4 852m / 15 918ft

Mt Kirkpatrick
4 528m / 14 855ft

Mt Markham
4 351m / 14 275ft

Mt Jackson
4 190m / 13 747ft

Mt Sidley
4 181m / 13 717ft

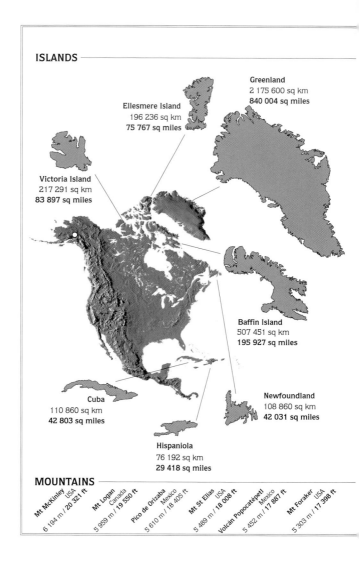

ISLANDS

Greenland
2 175 600 sq km
840 004 sq miles

Ellesmere Island
196 236 sq km
75 767 sq miles

Victoria Island
217 291 sq km
83 897 sq miles

Baffin Island
507 451 sq km
195 927 sq miles

Cuba
110 860 sq km
42 803 sq miles

Newfoundland
108 860 sq km
42 031 sq miles

Hispaniola
76 192 sq km
29 418 sq miles

MOUNTAINS

Mt McKinley
USA
6 194 m / **20 321 ft**

Mt Logan
Canada
5 959 m / **19 550 ft**

Pico de Orizaba
Mexico
5 610 m / **18 405 ft**

Mt St Elias
USA
5 489 m / **18 008 ft**

Volcán Popocatépetl
Mexico
5 452 m / **17 887 ft**

Mt Foraker
USA
5 303 m / **17 398 ft**

LAKES

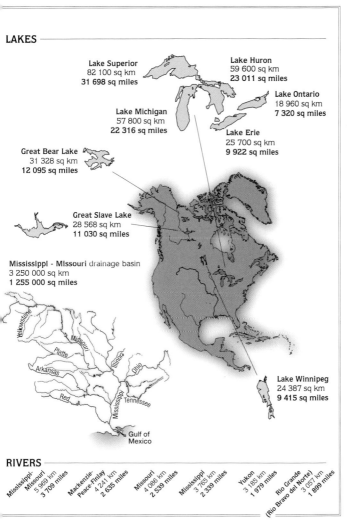

Lake Superior
82 100 sq km
31 698 sq miles

Lake Huron
59 600 sq km
23 011 sq miles

Lake Ontario
18 960 sq km
7 320 sq miles

Lake Michigan
57 800 sq km
22 316 sq miles

Lake Erie
25 700 sq km
9 922 sq miles

Great Bear Lake
31 328 sq km
12 095 sq miles

Great Slave Lake
28 568 sq km
11 030 sq miles

Mississippi - Missouri drainage basin
3 250 000 sq km
1 255 000 sq miles

Yellowstone
Missouri
Platte
Illinois
Arkansas
Ohio
Red
Mississippi
Tennessee
Gulf of
Mexico

Lake Winnipeg
24 387 sq km
9 415 sq miles

RIVERS

Mississippi - Missouri 5 969 km **3 709 miles**

Mackenzie - Peace-Finlay 4 241 km **2 635 miles**

Missouri 4 086 km **2 539 miles**

Mississippi 3 765 km **2 339 miles**

Yukon 3 185 km **1 979 miles**

Rio Grande (Rio Bravo del Norte) 3 057 km **1 899 miles**

ISLANDS

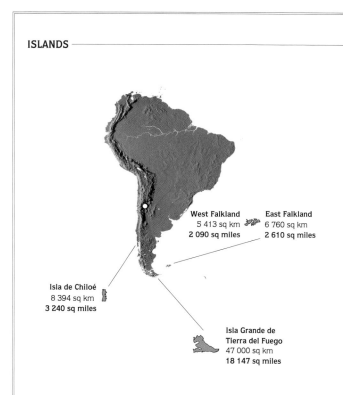

West Falkland
5 413 sq km
2 090 sq miles

East Falkland
6 760 sq km
2 610 sq miles

Isla de Chiloé
8 394 sq km
3 240 sq miles

Isla Grande de
Tierra del Fuego
47 000 sq km
18 147 sq miles

MOUNTAINS

Cerro
Aconcagua
Argentina
6 960 m / 22 834 ft

Nevado Ojos del
Salado
Argentina/Chile
6 908 m / 22 664 ft

Cerro Bonete
Argentina
6 872 m / 22 546 ft

Cerro Pissis
Argentina
6 858 m / 22 500 ft

Cerro Tupungato
Argentina/Chile
6 800 m / 22 309 ft

Cerro Mercedario
Argentina
6 770 m / 22 211 ft

LAKES

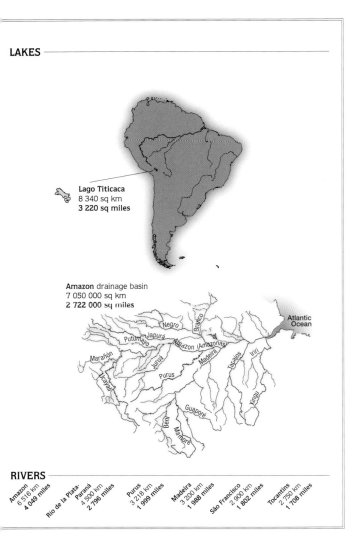

Lago Titicaca
8 340 sq km
3 220 sq miles

Amazon drainage basin
7 050 000 sq km
2 722 000 sq miles

Negro
Branco
Japurá
Putumayo
Amazon (Amazonas)
Marañón
Madeira
Iriri
Ucayali
Juruá
Tapajós
Purus
Xingu
Guaporé
Beni
Mamoré

Atlantic
Ocean

RIVERS

Amazon
6 516 km
4 049 miles

Rio de la Plata-
Paraná
4 500 km
2 796 miles

Purus
3 218 km
1 999 miles

Madeira
3 200 km
1 988 miles

São Francisco
2 900 km
1 802 miles

Tocantins
2 750 km
1 708 miles

ISLANDS

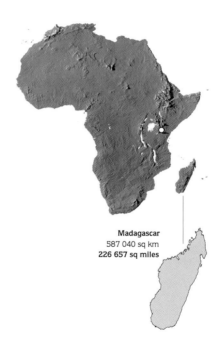

Madagascar
587 040 sq km
226 657 sq miles

MOUNTAINS

Kilimanjaro
Tanzania
5 895 m / **19 340 ft**

Kirinyaga
(Mt Kenya)
Kenya
5 199 m / **17 057 ft**

Margherita Peak
(Mt Stanley)
Dem. Rep. Congo/Uganda
5 110m / **16 765ft**

Meru
Tanzania
4 565 m / **14 977 ft**

Ras Dashen
Ethiopia
4 533 m / **14 872 ft**

Mt Karisimbi
Rwanda
4 510 m / **14 796 ft**

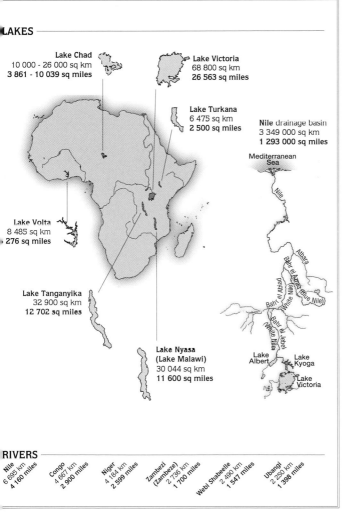

LAKES

Lake Chad
10 000 - 26 000 sq km
3 861 - 10 039 sq miles

Lake Victoria
68 800 sq km
26 563 sq miles

Lake Turkana
6 475 sq km
2 500 sq miles

Nile drainage basin
3 349 000 sq km
1 293 000 sq miles

Mediterranean
Sea

Nile

Atbara

Bahr el Azraq (Blue Nile)

White Nile

Bahr el Jebel (White Nile)

Bahr el Abiad

Lake Volta
8 485 sq km
276 sq miles

Lake Tanganyika
32 900 sq km
12 702 sq miles

**Lake Nyasa
(Lake Malawi)**
30 044 sq km
11 600 sq miles

Lake
Albert

Lake
Kyoga

Lake
Victoria

RIVERS

Nile
6 695 km
4 160 miles

Congo
4 667 km
2 900 miles

Niger
4 184 km
2 599 miles

**Zambezi
(Zambeze)** km
2 736
1 700 miles

Webi Shabeelle km
2 490
1 547 miles

Ubangi km
2 250
1 398 miles

© Bartholomew Ltd

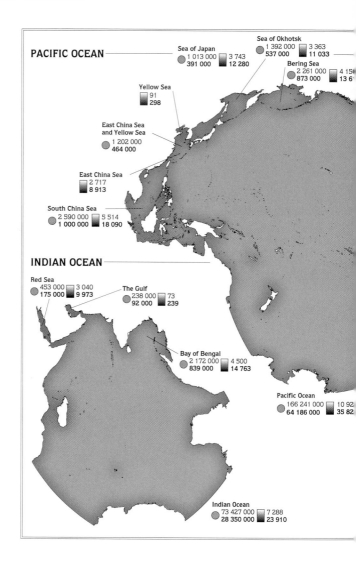

PACIFIC OCEAN

Sea of Japan
1 013 000 3 743
391 000 12 280

Sea of Okhotsk
1 392 000 3 363
537 000 11 033

Bering Sea
2 261 000 4 15●
873 000 13 6

Yellow Sea
91
298

East China Sea
and Yellow Sea
1 202 000
464 000

East China Sea
2 717
8 913

South China Sea
2 590 000 5 514
1 000 000 18 090

INDIAN OCEAN

Red Sea
453 000 3 040
175 000 9 973

The Gulf
238 000 73
92 000 239

Bay of Bengal
2 172 000 4 500
839 000 14 763

Pacific Ocean
166 241 000 10 92
64 186 000 35 82

Indian Ocean
73 427 000 7 288
28 350 000 23 910

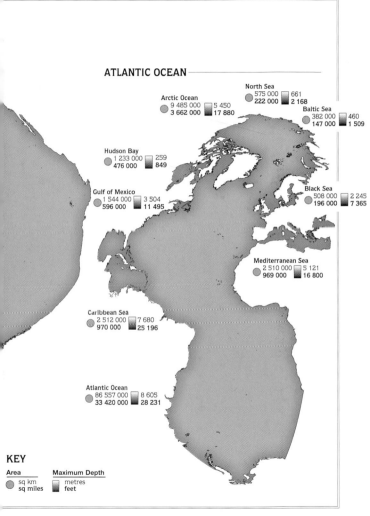

ATLANTIC OCEAN

North Sea
575 000 661
222 000 2 168

Arctic Ocean
9 485 000 5 450
3 662 000 17 880

Baltic Sea
382 000 460
147 000 1 509

Hudson Bay
1 233 000 259
476 000 849

Gulf of Mexico
1 544 000 3 504
596 000 11 495

Black Sea
508 000 2 245
196 000 7 365

Mediterranean Sea
2 510 000 5 121
969 000 16 800

Caribbean Sea
2 512 000 7 680
970 000 25 196

Atlantic Ocean
86 557 000 8 605
33 420 000 28 231

KEY

Area
sq km
sq miles

Maximum Depth
metres
feet

© Bartholomew Ltd

The index includes all names shown on the maps in the Atlas of the World. Names are referenced by page number and by a grid reference. The grid reference correlates to the alphanumeric values which appear within each map frame. Each entry also includes the country or geographical area in which the feature is located. Entries relating to names appearing on insets are indicated by a small box symbol: ▫, followed by a grid reference if the inset has its own alphanumeric values.

Name forms are as they appear on the maps, with additional alternative names or name forms included as cross-references which refer the user to the entry for the map form of the name. Names beginning with Mc or Mac are alphabetized exactly as they appear. The terms Saint, Sainte, etc. are abbreviated as St, Ste, etc. but alphabetized as if in the full form.

Names of physical features beginning with generic, geographical terms are permuted – the descriptive term is placed after the main part of the name. For example, Lake Superior is indexed as Superior, Lake; Mount Everest as Everest, Mount. This policy is applied to all languages.

Entries, other than those for towns and cities, include a descriptor indicating the type of geographical feature. Descriptors are not included where the type of feature is implicit in the name itself.

Administrative divisions are included to differentiate entries of the same name and feature type within the one country. In such cases, duplicate names are alphabetized in order of administrative division. Additional qualifiers are also included for names within selected geographical areas.

INDEX ABBREVIATIONS

admin. div.	administrative division	for.	forest	Pol.	Poland
Afgh.	Afghanistan	g.	gulf	Port.	Portugal
Alg.	Algeria	Ger.	Germany	prov.	province
Arg.	Argentina	Guat.	Guatemala	reg.	region
Austr.	Australia	hd	headland	Rep.	Republic
aut. reg.	autonomous region	Hond.	Honduras	Rus. Fed.	Russian Federation
aut. rep.	autonomous republic	imp. l.	impermanent lake		
		Indon.	Indonesia	S.	South
Azer.	Azerbaijan	isth.	isthmus	Switz.	Switzerland
Bangl.	Bangladesh	Kazakh.	Kazakhstan	Tajik.	Tajikistan
Bol.	Bolivia	Kyrg.	Kyrgyzstan	Tanz.	Tanzania
Bos.-Herz.	Bosnia Herzegovina	lag.	lagoon	terr.	territory
Bulg.	Bulgaria	Lith.	Lithuania	Thai.	Thailand
Can.	Canada	Lux.	Luxembourg	Trin. and Tob.	Trinidad and Tobago
C.A.R.	Central African Republic	Madag.	Madagascar		
		Maur.	Mauritania	Turkm.	Turkmenistan
Col.	Colombia	Mex.	Mexico	U.A.E.	United Arab Emirates
Czech Rep.	Czech Republic	Moz.	Mozambique		
Dem. Rep.	Democratic	mun.	municipality	U.K.	United Kingdom
Congo	Republic of Congo	N.	North	Ukr.	Ukraine
depr.	depression	Neth.	Netherlands	Uru.	Uruguay
des.	desert	Nic.	Nicaragua	U.S.A.	United States of America
Dom. Rep.	Dominican Republic	N.Z.	New Zealand		
		Pak.	Pakistan	Uzbek.	Uzbekistan
esc.	escarpment	Para.	Paraguay	val.	valley
est.	estuary	Phil.	Philippines	Venez.	Venezuela
Eth.	Ethiopia	plat.	plateau	Yugo.	Yugoslavia
Fin.	Finland	P.N.G.	Papua New Guinea		

A

68 C2 **Aachen** Ger.
68 B2 **Aalst** Belgium
68 B2 **Aarschot** Belgium
36 C2 **Aba** China
83 C4 **Aba** Nigeria
49 C2 **Ābādān** Iran
49 D2 **Abādeh** Iran
82 B1 **Abadla** Alg.
83 C4 **Abakaliki** Nigeria
51 H3 **Abakan** Rus. Fed.
118 A3 **Abancay** Peru
49 D2 **Abarqū** Iran
34 D2 **Abashiri** Japan
85 B4 **Ābaya Hāyk'** l. Eth.
　Ābay Wenz r. Eth./Sudan see
　　Blue Nile
50 G3 **Abaza** Rus. Fed.
76 A2 **Abbasanta** Sardinia Italy
72 C1 **Abbeville** France
110 B3 **Abbeville** U.S.A.
42 B1 **Abbottabad** Pak.
23 Q2 **Abbott Ice Shelf** Antarctica
83 E3 **Abéché** Chad
82 B4 **Abengourou** Côte d'Ivoire
61 E4 **Åbenrå** Denmark
82 C4 **Abeokuta** Nigeria
67 A2 **Aberaeron** U.K.
64 C2 **Aberchirder** U.K.
67 B3 **Aberdare** U.K.
67 A2 **Aberdaron** U.K.
90 B3 **Aberdeen** S. Africa
64 C2 **Aberdeen** U.K.
109 D3 **Aberdeen** MD U.S.A.
105 D1 **Aberdeen** SD U.S.A.
102 B1 **Aberdeen** WA U.S.A.
97 E1 **Aberdeen Lake** Can.
102 B2 **Abert, Lake** U.S.A.
67 A2 **Aberystwyth** U.K.
54 F2 **Abez'** Rus. Fed.
46 B3 **Abhā** Saudi Arabia
　Abiad, Bahr el r.
　　Sudan/Uganda see White Nile
82 B4 **Abidjan** Côte d'Ivoire
105 D3 **Abilene** KS U.S.A.
107 D2 **Abilene** TX U.S.A.
67 C3 **Abingdon** U.K.
59 D3 **Abinsk** Rus. Fed.
98 B2 **Abitibi, Lake** Can.
　Åbo Fin. see Turku
42 B1 **Abohar** India
82 C4 **Abomey** Benin
28 A1 **Abongabong, Gunung** mt.
　　Indon.
86 B2 **Abong Mbang** Cameroon
32 A2 **Aborlan** Phil.
83 D3 **Abou Déia** Chad
74 B2 **Abrantes** Port.
120 B3 **Abra Pampa** Arg.
104 A2 **Absaroka Range** mts U.S.A.
49 C1 **Abşeron Yarımadası** pen.
　　Azer.
46 B3 **Abū 'Arīsh** Saudi Arabia
47 C2 **Abu Dhabi** U.A.E.
84 B3 **Abu Hamed** Sudan
83 C4 **Abuja** Nigeria
49 C2 **Abū Kamāl** Syria
120 B1 **Abunã** r. Brazil
118 B2 **Abunã** Brazil
42 B2 **Abu Road** India
84 B2 **Abu Simbel** Egypt
85 A3 **Abu Zabad** Sudan
　Abū Zabī U.A.E. see
　　Abu Dhabi
85 A4 **Abyei** Sudan
113 B2 **Acambaro** Mex.
74 B1 **A Cañiza** Spain

112 B2 **Acaponeta** Mex.
113 C3 **Acapulco** Mex.
119 D2 **Acará** Brazil
118 B1 **Acarigua** Venez.
113 C3 **Acatlan** Mex.
113 C3 **Acayucán** Mex.
82 B4 **Accra** Ghana
66 B2 **Accrington** U.K.
42 B2 **Achalpur** India
65 A2 **Achill Island** Rep. of Ireland
69 D1 **Achim** Ger.
64 B2 **Achnasheen** U.K.
59 D2 **Achuyevo** Rus. Fed.
79 C3 **Acipayam** Turkey
77 C3 **Acireale** Sicily Italy
115 C2 **Acklins Island** Bahamas
121 B4 **Aconcagua, Cerro** mt. Arg.
74 B1 **A Coruña** Spain
76 A2 **Acqui Terme** Italy
71 D2 **Ács** Hungary
113 C2 **Actopán** Mex.
107 D2 **Ada** U.S.A.
47 C2 **Ada** Oman
　'Adan Yemen see Aden
48 B2 **Adana** Turkey
　Adapazari Turkey see
　　Sakarya
76 A1 **Adda** r. Italy
46 B2 **Ad Dafinah** Saudi Arabia
46 B2 **Ad Dahnā'** des. Saudi Arabia
46 B2 **Ad Dahnā'** des. Saudi Arabia
82 A2 **Ad Dakhla** Western Sahara
47 C2 **Ad Dammām** Saudi Arabia
46 A2 **Ad Dār al Ḥamrā'**
　　Saudi Arabia
46 B3 **Ad Darb** Saudi Arabia
46 B2 **Ad Dawādimī** Saudi Arabia
46 B2 **Ad Dawḩah** Qatar see Doha
46 B2 **Ad Dilam** Saudi Arabia
84 C2 **Ad Dir'iyah** Saudi Arabia
85 B4 **Addis Ababa** Eth.
49 C2 **Ad Dīwānīyah** Iraq
20 A2 **Adelaide** Austr.
18 C1 **Adelaide River** Austr.
69 D2 **Adelebsen** Ger.
23 J2 **Adélie Land** Antarctica
85 C3 **Aden** Yemen
85 C3 **Aden, Gulf of**
　　Somalia/Yemen
68 C2 **Adenau** Ger.
47 C2 **Adh Dhayd** U.A.E.
27 C3 **Adi** i. Indon.
46 A3 **Adī Ārk'ay** Eth.
84 B3 **Ādīgrat** Eth.
43 B3 **Adilabad** India
109 E2 **Adirondack Mountains**
　　U.S.A.
　Ādīs Ābeba Eth. see
　　Addis Ababa
85 B4 **Ādīs Alem** Eth.
78 C1 **Adjud** Romania
18 B1 **Admiralty Gulf** Austr.
96 A2 **Admiralty Island** U.S.A.
72 B3 **Adour** r. France
74 C2 **Adra** Spain
82 B2 **Adrar** Alg.
108 C2 **Adrian** MI U.S.A.
107 C1 **Adrian** TX U.S.A.
76 B2 **Adriatic Sea** Europe
84 B3 **Ādwa** Eth.
51 K2 **Adycha** r. Rus. Fed.
59 D2 **Adygeysk** Rus. Fed.
82 B4 **Adzopé** Côte d'Ivoire
79 B3 **Aegean Sea** Greece/Turkey
69 D1 **Aerzen** Ger.
74 B1 **A Estrada** Spain
84 B3 **Afabet** Eritrea
44 C3 **Afghanistan** country Asia
46 B3 **'Afīf** Saudi Arabia
48 B2 **Afyon** Turkey

83 C3 **Agadez** Niger
82 B1 **Agadir** Morocco
45 D2 **Agadyr'** Kazakh.
42 B2 **Agar** India
43 D2 **Agartala** India
49 C2 **Ağdam** Azer.
73 C3 **Agde** France
72 C3 **Agen** France
90 A2 **Aggeneys** S. Africa
79 C3 **Agia Vervara** Greece
79 B3 **Agios Dimitrios** Greece
79 C3 **Agios Efstratios** i. Greece
79 C3 **Agios Nikolaos** Greece
78 B1 **Agnita** Romania
43 B2 **Agra** India
49 C2 **Ağrı** Turkey
76 B3 **Agrigento** Sicily Italy
79 B3 **Agrinio** Greece
77 B2 **Agropoli** Italy
122 B2 **Água Clara** Brazil
114 B4 **Aguadulce** Panama
112 B2 **Aguanaval** r. Mex.
112 B1 **Agua Prieta** Mex.
112 B2 **Aguascalientes** Mex.
123 D1 **Águas Formosas** Brazil
74 B1 **Agueda** Port.
74 C1 **Aguilar de Campóo** Spain
75 C2 **Águilas** Spain
112 B3 **Aguililla** Mex.
90 B3 **Agulhas, Cape** S. Africa
123 D2 **Agulhas Negras** mt. Brazil
79 C2 **Ağva** Turkey
49 C2 **Ahar** Iran
68 C1 **Ahaus** Ger.
49 C2 **Ahlat** Turkey
68 C2 **Ahlen** Ger.
42 B2 **Ahmadabad** India
41 B3 **Ahmadnagar** India
42 B2 **Ahmadpur East** Pak.
42 B1 **Ahmadpur Sial** Pak.
112 B2 **Ahome** Mex.
47 C2 **Ahram** Iran
69 E1 **Ahrensburg** Ger.
72 C2 **Ahun** France
49 C2 **Ahvāz** Iran
90 A2 **Ai-Ais** Namibia
48 B2 **Aigialousa** Cyprus
79 B3 **Aigio** Greece
111 D2 **Aiken** U.S.A.
123 D1 **Aimorés** Brazil
123 D1 **Aimorés, Serra dos** hills
　　Brazil
82 B2 **'Aïn Ben Tili** Maur.
75 D2 **Aïn Defla** Alg.
82 B1 **Aïn Sefra** Alg.
104 D2 **Ainsworth** U.S.A.
　Aintab Turkey see Gaziante...
75 D2 **Aïn Taya** Alg.
75 D2 **Aïn Tédélès** Alg.
28 A1 **Airbangis** Indon.
96 C2 **Airdrie** Can.
72 B3 **Aire-sur-l'Adour** France
69 E3 **Aisch** r. Ger.
96 A1 **Aishihik Lake** Can.
68 A3 **Aisne** r. France
27 D3 **Aitape** P.N.G.
78 B1 **Aiud** Romania
73 D3 **Aix-en-Provence** France
73 D2 **Aix-les-Bains** France
30 A1 **Aizawl** India
56 C2 **Aizkraukle** Latvia
35 C3 **Aizu-wakamatsu** Japan
73 D3 **Ajaccio** Corsica France
83 E1 **Ajdābiyā** Libya
42 B2 **Ajmer** India
106 A2 **Ajo** U.S.A.
55 E3 **Akbulak** Rus. Fed.
48 B2 **Akçakale** Turkey
48 B2 **Akdağmadeni** Turkey
56 A2 **Åkersberga** Sweden

86 C2 **Aketi** Dem. Rep. Congo
55 D4 **Akhalk'alak'i** Georgia
47 C2 **Akhḍar, Jabal** *mts* Oman
79 C3 **Akhisar** Turkey
55 D4 **Akhtubinsk** Rus. Fed.
98 B1 **Akimiski Island** Can.
34 D3 **Akita** Japan
82 A3 **Akjoujt** Maur.
45 D1 **Akkol'** Kazakh.
56 B2 **Akmenrags** *pt* Latvia
Akmola Kazakh. *see* Astana
85 B4 **Akobo** Sudan
42 B2 **Akola** India
46 A3 **Akordat** Eritrea
95 G2 **Akpatok Island** Can.
60 □A3 **Akranes** Iceland
79 B2 **Akrathos, Akra** *pt* Greece
108 C2 **Akron** U.S.A.
43 B1 **Aksai Chin** *terr.* Asia
48 B2 **Aksaray** Turkey
44 B1 **Aksay** Kazakh.
59 D2 **Aksay** Rus. Fed.
48 B2 **Akşehir** Turkey
44 C2 **Akshiganak** Kazakh.
43 E2 **Aksu** China
46 A3 **Āksum** Eth.
44 B2 **Aktau** Kazakh.
45 D2 **Aktogay** Kazakh.
56 C3 **Aktsyabrski** Belarus
44 B1 **Aktyubinsk** Kazakh.
83 C4 **Akure** Nigeria
60 □B2 **Akureyri** Iceland
Akyab Myanmar *see* Sittwe
110 C2 **Alabama** *r.* U.S.A.
110 C2 **Alabama** *state* U.S.A.
79 C3 **Alaçatı** Turkey
40 O1 **Alağir** Rus. Fed.
119 E3 **Alagoinhas** Brazil
75 C1 **Alagón** Spain
47 B2 **Al Aḥmadī** Kuwait
45 E2 **Alakol', Ozero** *salt l.* Kazakh.
60 J2 **Alakurtti** Rus. Fed.
46 B3 **Al 'Alayyah** Saudi Arabia
49 C2 **Al 'Amādīyah** Iraq
103 C3 **Alamo** U.S.A.
106 B2 **Alamogordo** U.S.A.
112 A2 **Alamos** *Sonora* Mex.
112 B2 **Alamos** *Sonora* Mex.
112 B2 **Alamos** *r.* Mex.
104 B3 **Alamosa** U.S.A.
61 G3 **Åland** *is* Fin.
48 B2 **Alanya** Turkey
48 B3 **Al 'Aqabah** Jordan
46 B2 **Al 'Aqīq** Saudi Arabia
75 C2 **Alarcón, Embalse de** *resr* Spain
46 B2 **Al Arṭāwīyah** Saudi Arabia
29 C2 **Alas** Indon.
79 C3 **Alaşehir** Turkey
96 A2 **Alaska** *state* U.S.A.
92 C2 **Alaska, Gulf of** U.S.A.
49 C2 **Älät** Azer.
55 D3 **Alatyr'** Rus. Fed.
118 A2 **Alausí** Ecuador
61 H3 **Alavus** Fin.
20 B2 **Alawoona** Austr.
76 A2 **Alba** Italy
75 C2 **Albacete** Spain
78 B1 **Alba Iulia** Romania
77 C2 **Albania** *country* Europe
18 A3 **Albany** Austr.
98 B1 **Albany** *r.* Can.
111 D2 **Albany** *GA* U.S.A.
109 E2 **Albany** *NY* U.S.A.
102 B2 **Albany** *OR* U.S.A.
Al Başrah Iraq *see* Basra
19 D1 **Albatross Bay** Austr.
83 E1 **Al Bayḍā'** Libya
46 B3 **Al Bayḍā'** Yemen
111 D1 **Albemarle** U.S.A.

111 E1 **Albemarle Sound** *sea chan.* U.S.A.
76 A2 **Albenga** Italy
19 C2 **Alberga** *watercourse* Austr.
87 D2 **Albert, Lake** Dem. Rep.Congo/Uganda
96 C2 **Alberta** *prov.* Can.
68 B2 **Albert Kanaal** *canal* Belgium
105 E2 **Albert Lea** U.S.A.
72 C3 **Albi** France
46 A2 **Al Bi'r** Saudi Arabia
46 B3 **Al Birk** Saudi Arabia
46 B2 **Al Biyāḍh** *reg.* Saudi Arabia
61 E4 **Ålborg** Denmark
49 C2 **Alborz, Reshteh-ye** *mts* Iran
74 B2 **Albufeira** Port.
106 B1 **Albuquerque** U.S.A.
47 C2 **Al Buraymī** Oman
21 C3 **Albury** Austr.
74 B2 **Alcácer do Sal** Port.
74 C1 **Alcalá de Henares** Spain
74 C2 **Alcalá la Real** Spain
76 B3 **Alcamo** *Sicily* Italy
75 C1 **Alcañiz** Spain
74 B2 **Alcántara** Spain
74 C2 **Alcaraz** Spain
74 C2 **Alcaraz, Sierra de** *mts* Spain
74 C2 **Alcaudete** Spain
74 C2 **Alcázar de San Juan** Spain
59 D2 **Alchevs'k** Ukr.
123 E1 **Alcobaça** Brazil
75 C1 **Alcora** Spain
75 C2 **Alcoy** Spain
75 D2 **Alcúdia** Spain
110 C2 **Aldama** Mex.
51 J2 **Aldan** Rus. Fed.
51 J2 **Aldan** *r.* Rus. Fed.
63 C4 **Alderney** *i.* Channel Is
82 A3 **Aleg** Maur.
123 D2 **Alegre** Brazil
120 C3 **Alegrete** Brazil
51 K3 **Aleksandrovsk-Sakhalinskiy** Rus. Fed.
59 D1 **Alekseyevka** *Belgorodskaya Oblast'* Rus. Fed.
59 D1 **Alekseyevka** *Belgorodskaya Oblast'* Rus. Fed.
57 E3 **Aleksin** Rus. Fed.
77 D2 **Aleksinac** Yugo.
86 B3 **Alèmbé** Gabon
123 D2 **Além Paraíba** Brazil
61 F3 **Ålen** Norway
72 C2 **Alençon** France
48 B2 **Aleppo** Syria
118 A3 **Alerta** Peru
96 B2 **Alert Bay** Can.
73 C3 **Alès** France
78 B1 **Aleşd** Romania
76 A2 **Alessandria** Italy
61 E3 **Ålesund** Norway
92 B2 **Aleutian Islands** U.S.A.
51 L3 **Alevina, Mys** *c.* Rus. Fed.
96 A2 **Alexander Archipelago** *is* U.S.A.
90 A2 **Alexander Bay** S. Africa
110 C2 **Alexander City** U.S.A.
23 O2 **Alexander Island** Antarctica
21 C3 **Alexandra** Austr.
22 A3 **Alexandra** N.Z.
79 B2 **Alexandreia** Greece
Alexandretta Turkey *see* İskenderun
84 A1 **Alexandria** Egypt
78 C2 **Alexandria** Romania
91 C3 **Alexandria** S. Africa
110 B2 **Alexandria** *LA* U.S.A.
105 D1 **Alexandria** *MN* U.S.A.
109 D3 **Alexandria** *VA* U.S.A.
20 A3 **Alexandrina, Lake** Austr.

79 C2 **Alexandroupoli** Greece
99 E1 **Alexis** *r.* Can.
96 B2 **Alexis Creek** Can.
45 E1 **Aleysk** Rus. Fed.
75 C1 **Alfaro** Spain
49 C3 **Al Fāw** Iraq
69 D2 **Alfeld (Leine)** Ger.
123 C2 **Alfenas** Brazil
Al Furāt *r.* Iraq/Syria *see* Euphrates
74 B2 **Algeciras** Spain
75 C2 **Algemesí** Spain
46 A3 **Algena** Eritrea
Alger Alg. *see* **Algiers**
82 C1 **Algeria** *country* Africa
47 C3 **Al Ghaydah** Yemen
76 A2 **Alghero** *Sardinia* Italy
47 B3 **Al Ghwaybiyah** Saudi Arabia
83 C1 **Algiers** Alg.
91 C3 **Algoa Bay** S. Africa
105 E2 **Algona** U.S.A.
49 C2 **Al Ḥadīthah** Iraq
47 C2 **Al Ḥajar al Gharbī** *mts* Oman
83 D2 **Al Ḥamādah al Ḥamrā'** *plat.* Libya
75 C2 **Alhama de Murcia** Spain
46 B2 **Al Ḥanākīyah** Saudi Arabia
49 C2 **Al Ḥasakah** Syria
49 C2 **Al Ḥayy** Iraq
46 B3 **Al Ḥazm al-Jawf** Yemen
47 C3 **Al Ḥibāk** *des.* Saudi Arabia
49 C2 **Al Ḥillah** Iraq
46 B2 **Al Ḥillah** Saudi Arabia
47 B2 **Al Ḥinnāh** Saudi Arabia
46 B3 **Al Ḥudaydah** Yemen
47 B2 **Al Ḥufūf** Saudi Arabia
83 D2 **Al Hulayq al Kabir** *hills* Libya
47 C2 **'Alīābād** Iran
79 C3 **Aliağa** Turkey
79 B2 **Aliakmonas** *r.* Greece
75 C2 **Alicante** Spain
107 D3 **Alice** U.S.A.
77 C3 **Alice, Punta** *pt* Italy
19 C2 **Alice Springs** Austr.
43 B2 **Aligarh** India
49 C2 **Alīgūdarz** Iran
37 E1 **Alihe** China
86 B3 **Alima** *r.* Congo
79 C3 **Aliova** *r.* Turkey
85 C3 **Ali Sabieh** Djibouti
91 C3 **Aliwal North** S. Africa
83 E2 **Al Jaghbūb** Libya
46 B2 **Al Jahrah** Kuwait
47 C2 **Al Jamalīyah** Qatar
46 A2 **Al Jawf** Saudi Arabia
83 D1 **Al Jawsh** Libya
74 B2 **Aljezur** Port.
47 B2 **Al Jubayl** Saudi Arabia
46 B2 **Al Junaynah** Saudi Arabia
74 B2 **Aljustrel** Port.
46 B2 **Al Kahfah** Saudi Arabia
47 C2 **Al Kāmil** Oman
48 B2 **Al Karak** Jordan
47 C2 **Al Khābūrah** Oman
46 B2 **Al Khamāsīn** Saudi Arabia
47 C2 **Al Khaṣab** Oman
46 B3 **Al Khawkhah** Yemen
47 C2 **Al Khawr** Qatar
83 E2 **Al Khufrah** Libya
83 D1 **Al Khums** Libya
47 B2 **Al Khunn** Saudi Arabia
47 C2 **Al Kir'ānah** Qatar
68 B1 **Alkmaar** Neth.
49 C2 **Al Kūt** Iraq
Al Kuwayt Kuwait *see* Kuwait
48 B2 **Al Lādhiqīyah** Syria
43 C2 **Allahabad** India
51 K2 **Allakh-Yun'** Rus. Fed.

30 A2 **Allanmyo** Myanmar
109 D2 **Allegheny** r. U.S.A.
108 C3 **Allegheny Mountains** U.S.A.
65 B1 **Allen, Lough** l.
       Rep. of Ireland
113 B2 **Allende** Coahuila Mex.
113 B2 **Allende** Nuevo León Mex.
109 D2 **Allentown** U.S.A.
41 B4 **Alleppey** India
69 D1 **Aller** r. Ger.
104 C2 **Alliance** NE U.S.A.
108 C2 **Alliance** OH U.S.A.
46 B2 **Al Lith** Saudi Arabia
64 C2 **Alloa** U.K.
99 C2 **Alma** Can.
       Alma-Ata Kazakh. see
       Almaty
74 B2 **Almada** Port.
74 C2 **Almadén** Spain
       Al Madīnah Saudi Arabia see
       Medina
84 B1 **Al Mafraq** Jordan
46 B3 **Al Maḥwīt** Yemen
46 B2 **Al Majma'ah** Saudi Arabia
103 B2 **Almanor, Lake** U.S.A.
75 C2 **Almansa** Spain
47 C2 **Al Mariyyah** U.A.E.
83 E1 **Al Marj** Libya
45 D2 **Almaty** Kazakh.
49 C2 **Al Mawṣil** Iraq
74 C1 **Almazán** Spain
119 C2 **Almeirim** Brazil
68 C1 **Almelo** Neth.
123 D1 **Almenara** Brazil
74 B1 **Almendra, Embalse de** resr
       Spain
74 B2 **Almendralejo** Spain
74 C2 **Almería** Spain
74 C2 **Almería, Golfo de** b. Spain
55 E3 **Al'met'yevsk** Rus. Fed.
46 B2 **Al Mindak** Saudi Arabia
47 C2 **Al Mish'āb** Saudi Arabia
74 B2 **Almodôvar** Port.
74 B2 **Almonte** Spain
43 B2 **Almora** India
47 B2 **Al Mubarrez** Saudi Arabia
47 C2 **Al Mudaibī** Oman
48 B3 **Al Mudawwarah** Jordan
47 B3 **Al Mukallā** Yemen
46 B3 **Al Mukhā** Yemen
74 C2 **Almuñécar** Spain
46 A2 **Al Muwayliḥ** Saudi Arabia
79 B3 **Almyros** Greece
64 B2 **Alness** U.K.
66 C1 **Alnwick** U.K.
79 B3 **Alonnisos** i. Greece
27 C3 **Alor** i. Indon.
28 B1 **Alor Setar** Malaysia
       Alost Belgium see Aalst
54 C2 **Alozero** Rus. Fed.
108 C1 **Alpena** U.S.A.
107 C2 **Alpine** U.S.A.
52 D5 **Alps** mts Europe
47 B3 **Al Qa'āmīyāt** reg.
       Saudi Arabia
83 D1 **Al Qaddāḥiyah** Libya
46 B2 **Al Qā'iyah** Saudi Arabia
48 C2 **Al Qāmishlī** Syria
48 B2 **Al Qaryatayn** Syria
47 B3 **Al Qaṭn** Yemen
48 B2 **Al Qunayṭirah** Syria
46 B3 **Al Qunfidhah** Saudi Arabia
46 B2 **Al Quwayʻīyah** Saudi Arabia
69 D2 **Alsfeld** Ger.
60 H2 **Alta** Norway
60 H2 **Altaelva** r. Norway
36 B1 **Altai Mountains** Asia
111 D2 **Altamaha** r. U.S.A.
119 C2 **Altamira** Brazil

77 C2 **Altamura** Italy
36 B1 **Altay** China
36 C1 **Altay** Mongolia
73 D2 **Altdorf** Switz.
75 C2 **Altea** Spain
69 F2 **Altenburg** Ger.
68 C2 **Altenkirchen (Westerwald)**
       Ger.
79 C3 **Altınoluk** Turkey
79 D3 **Altıntaş** Turkey
120 B2 **Altiplano** plain Bol.
70 C2 **Altmühl** r. Ger.
75 C1 **Alto del Moncayo** mt. Spain
122 B1 **Alto Garças** Brazil
89 C2 **Alto Molócuè** Moz.
97 E3 **Altona** Can.
109 D2 **Altoona** U.S.A.
122 B1 **Alto Sucuriú** Brazil
70 C2 **Altötting** Ger.
36 B2 **Altun Shan** mts China
102 B2 **Alturas** U.S.A.
107 D2 **Altus** U.S.A.
67 C2 **Alūksne** Latvia
46 B2 **Al 'Ulā** Saudi Arabia
83 D1 **Al 'Uqaylah** Libya
59 C3 **Alushta** Ukr.
107 D1 **Alva** U.S.A.
113 C3 **Alvarado** Mex.
61 F3 **Älvdalen** Sweden
61 F3 **Älvdalen** val. Sweden
60 H2 **Älvsbyn** Sweden
46 A2 **Al Wajh** Saudi Arabia
42 B2 **Alwar** India
49 C2 **Al Widyān** plat.
       Iraq/Saudi Arabia
       Alxa Youqi China see
       Ehen Hudag
       Alxa Zuoqi China see
       Bayan Hot
19 C1 **Alyangula** Austr.
56 B3 **Alytus** Lith.
104 C1 **Alzada** U.S.A.
68 D3 **Alzey** Ger.
18 C2 **Amadeus, Lake** salt flat
       Austr.
95 G2 **Amadjuak Lake** Can.
74 B2 **Amadora** Port.
46 B2 **Amā'ir** Saudi Arabia
61 F4 **Åmål** Sweden
79 B3 **Amaliada** Greece
27 D3 **Amamapare** Indon.
122 A2 **Amambaí** Brazil
122 B2 **Amambaí** r. Brazil
37 E3 **Amami-Ō-shima** i. Japan
37 E3 **Amami-shotō** is Japan
45 C1 **Amangel'dy** Kazakh.
77 C3 **Amantea** Italy
91 D3 **Amanzimtoti** S. Africa
119 C1 **Amapá** Brazil
74 B2 **Amareleja** Port.
107 C1 **Amarillo** U.S.A.
76 B2 **Amaro, Monte** mt. Italy
48 B1 **Amasya** Turkey
118 C2 **Amazon** r. S. America
119 D1 **Amazon, Mouths of the**
       Brazil
       Amazonas r. S. America see
       Amazon
42 B1 **Ambala** India
89 D3 **Ambalavao** Madag.
89 D2 **Ambanja** Madag.
118 A2 **Ambato** Ecuador
89 D3 **Ambato Boeny** Madag.
89 D3 **Ambato Finandrahana**
       Madag.
89 D2 **Ambatolampy** Madag.
89 D2 **Ambatondrazaka** Madag.
69 E3 **Amberg** Ger.
114 B3 **Ambergris Cay** i. Belize
43 C2 **Ambikapur** India

89 D2 **Ambilobe** Madag.
66 B1 **Ambleside** U.K.
89 D3 **Amboasary** Madag.
89 D3 **Ambohimahasoa** Madag.
27 C3 **Ambon** Indon.
27 C3 **Ambon** i. Indon.
89 D3 **Ambositra** Madag.
89 D3 **Ambovombe** Madag.
103 C4 **Amboy** U.S.A.
88 A1 **Ambriz** Angola
36 C2 **Amdo** China
113 B2 **Amealco** Mex.
112 B2 **Ameca** Mex.
68 B1 **Ameland** i. Neth.
102 D2 **American Falls** U.S.A.
102 D2 **American Falls Reservoir**
       U.S.A.
103 D2 **American Fork** U.S.A.
17 G4 **American Samoa** terr.
       S. Pacific Ocean
111 D2 **Americus** U.S.A.
68 B1 **Amersfoort** Neth.
23 F2 **Amery Ice Shelf** Antarctica
105 E2 **Ames** U.S.A.
79 B3 **Amfissa** Greece
51 J2 **Amga** Rus. Fed.
34 C1 **Amgu** Rus. Fed.
83 C2 **Amguid** Alg.
51 K3 **Amgun'** r. Rus. Fed.
99 D2 **Amherst** Can.
72 C2 **Amiens** France
41 B3 **Amindivi Islands** India
90 A1 **Aminuis** Namibia
42 A2 **Amir Chah** Pak.
97 D2 **Amisk Lake** Can.
107 C3 **Amistad Reservoir**
       Mex./U.S.A.
66 A2 **Amlwch** U.K.
48 B2 **'Ammān** Jordan
95 I2 **Ammassalik** Greenland
46 B3 **Am Nābiyah** Yemen
49 D2 **Amol** Iran
79 C3 **Amorgos** i. Greece
98 C2 **Amos** Can.
       Amoy China see Xiamen
123 C2 **Amparo** Brazil
75 D1 **Amposta** Spain
43 B2 **Amravati** India
42 B1 **Amritsar** India
68 B1 **Amstelveen** Neth.
68 B1 **Amsterdam** Neth.
71 C2 **Amstetten** Austria
83 E3 **Am Timan** Chad
32 B1 **Amudar'ya** r. Asia
94 E1 **Amund Ringnes Island** Can.
94 C2 **Amundsen Gulf** Can.
23 M2 **Amundsen Sea** Antarctica
29 C2 **Amuntai** Indon.
       Amur r. China/Rus. Fed. see
       Heilong Jiang
46 A3 **'Amur, Wadi** watercourse
       Sudan
51 I2 **Anabar** r. Rus. Fed.
51 I2 **Anabarskiy Zaliv** b.
       Rus. Fed.
102 D1 **Anaconda** U.S.A.
107 D1 **Anadarko** U.S.A.
48 B1 **Anadolu Dağları** mts Turkey
51 N2 **Anadyr'** r. Rus. Fed.
49 C2 **'Ānah** Iraq
113 B2 **Anáhuac** Mex.
28 B1 **Anambas, Kepulauan** is
       Indon.
105 E2 **Anamosa** U.S.A.
48 B2 **Anamur** Turkey
35 B4 **Anan** Japan
41 B3 **Anantapur** India
42 B1 **Anantnag**
       Jammu and Kashmir

58 B2 **Anan'yiv** Ukr.
59 D3 **Anapa** Rus. Fed.
122 C1 **Anápolis** Brazil
120 B3 **Añatuya** Arg.
33 B2 **Anbyon** N. Korea
72 B2 **Ancenis** France
76 B2 **Ancona** Italy
121 A5 **Ancud** Chile
Anda China see Daqing
61 E3 **Åndalsnes** Norway
110 C2 **Andalusia** U.S.A.
43 D3 **Andaman Islands** India
31 A2 **Andaman Sea** Indian Ocean
89 □D2 **Andapa** Madag.
68 B2 **Andelst** Neth.
60 G2 **Andenes** Norway
68 B2 **Andenne** Belgium
68 B2 **Anderlecht** Belgium
94 C2 **Anderson** r. Can.
94 B2 **Anderson** AK U.S.A.
108 B2 **Anderson** IN U.S.A.
111 D2 **Anderson** SC U.S.A.
89 □D2 **Andes** mts S. America
89 □D2 **Andilamena** Madag.
89 □D2 **Andilanatoby** Madag.
45 D2 **Andizhan** Uzbek.
89 □D2 **Andoany** Madag.
Andong China see Dandong
33 B2 **Andong** S. Korea
75 D1 **Andorra** country Europe
75 D1 **Andorra la Vella** Andorra
67 C3 **Andover** U.K.
122 B2 **Andradina** Brazil
57 D2 **Andreapol'** Rus. Fed.
123 D2 **Andrelândia** Brazil
117 C2 **Andrews** U.S.A.
77 C2 **Andria** Italy
89 □D3 **Androka** Madag.
114 C2 **Andros** i. Bahamas
79 B3 **Andros** i. Greece
111 E4 **Andros Town** Bahamas
41 B3 **Āndrott** i. India
58 B1 **Andrushivka** Ukr.
60 G2 **Andselv** Norway
74 C2 **Andújar** Spain
88 A2 **Andulo** Angola
82 C3 **Anéfis** Mali
83 D3 **Aney** Niger
51 H3 **Angara** r. Rus. Fed.
37 C1 **Angarsk** Rus. Fed.
61 G3 **Ånge** Sweden
112 A2 **Ángel de la Guarda, Isla** i. Mex.
32 B1 **Angeles** Phil.
110 D1 **Angel Falls** waterfall Venez.
61 F4 **Ängelholm** Sweden
60 G3 **Ångermanälven** r. Sweden
72 B2 **Angers** France
97 E1 **Angikuni Lake** l. Can.
66 A2 **Anglesey** i. U.K.
89 C2 **Angoche** Moz.
47 C2 **Angohrān** Iran
88 A2 **Angola** country Africa
108 C2 **Angola** U.S.A.
96 A2 **Angoon** U.S.A.
72 C2 **Angoulême** France
45 D2 **Angren** Uzbek.
115 D3 **Anguilla** terr. West Indies
61 F4 **Anholt** i. Denmark
39 B3 **Anhua** China
39 B3 **Anhui** prov. China
122 B1 **Anhumas** Brazil
122 C1 **Anicuns** Brazil
34 D1 **Aniva, Mys** c. Rus. Fed.
33 B2 **Anju** N. Korea
38 A2 **Ankang** China
48 B2 **Ankara** Turkey
38 B2 **Anlu** China
59 E1 **Anna** Rus. Fed.
83 C1 **Annaba** Alg.

69 F2 **Annaberg-Buchholtz** Ger.
46 B2 **An Nafūd** des. Saudi Arabia
49 C2 **An Najaf** Iraq
64 C3 **Annan** U.K.
109 D3 **Annapolis** U.S.A.
43 C2 **Annapurna I** mt. Jammu and Kashmir/Nepal
108 C2 **Ann Arbor** U.S.A.
118 C1 **Anna Regina** Guyana
49 C2 **An Nāşiriyah** Iraq
73 D2 **Annecy** France
46 B3 **An Nimāş** Saudi Arabia
30 B1 **Anning** China
110 C2 **Anniston** U.S.A.
73 C2 **Annonay** France
47 B2 **An Nu'ayriyah** Saudi Arabia
89 □D2 **Anorontany, Tanjona** hd Madag.
79 C3 **Ano Viannos** Greece
39 B3 **Anpu** China
38 B2 **Anqing** China
70 C2 **Ansbach** Ger.
38 C1 **Anshan** China
39 A3 **Anshun** China
82 C3 **Ansongo** Mali
118 A3 **Antabamba** Peru
48 B2 **Antakya** Turkey
89 □D2 **Antalaha** Madag.
48 B2 **Antalya** Turkey
48 B2 **Antalya Körfezi** g. Turkey
89 □D2 **Antananarivo** Madag.
23 Q3 **Antarctic Peninsula** Antarctica
64 B2 **An Teallach** mt. U.K.
74 B2 **Antequera** Spain
106 B2 **Anthony** U.S.A.
82 B2 **Anti Atlas** mts Morocco
73 D3 **Antibes** France
99 D2 **Anticosti, Île d'** i. Can.
99 D2 **Antigonish** Can.
115 D3 **Antigua** i. Antigua
115 D3 **Antigua and Barbuda** country West Indies
113 C2 **Antiguo-Morelos** Mex.
79 B3 **Antikythira** i. Greece
Antioch Turkey see Antakya
120 A3 **Antofagasta** Chile
122 C3 **Antonina** Brazil
65 C1 **Antrim** U.K.
65 C1 **Antrim Hills** U.K.
89 □D2 **Antsalova** Madag.
89 □D2 **Antsirabe** Madag.
89 □D2 **Antsirañana** Madag.
89 □D2 **Antsohihy** Madag.
68 B2 **Antwerpen** Belgium
An Uaimh Rep. of Ireland see Navan
43 C2 **Anugul** India
42 B2 **Anupgarh** India
41 C4 **Anuradhapura** Sri Lanka
Anvers Belgium see Antwerpen
36 C2 **Anxi** China
19 C3 **Anxious Bay** Austr.
38 B2 **Anyang** China
33 B2 **Anyang** S. Korea
76 B2 **Anzio** Italy
34 D2 **Aomori** Japan
Aoraki mt. N.Z. see Cook, Mount
76 A1 **Aosta** Italy
111 D3 **Apalachee Bay** U.S.A.
118 B2 **Apaporis** r. Col.
122 B2 **Aparecida do Tabuado** Brazil
32 B1 **Aparri** Phil.
54 C2 **Apatity** Rus. Fed.
112 B3 **Apatzingán** Mex.
68 B1 **Apeldoorn** Neth.
68 C1 **Apen** Ger.

122 C2 **Apiaí** Brazil
32 B2 **Apo, Mount** vol. Phil.
69 E2 **Apolda** Ger.
20 B3 **Apollo Bay** Austr.
111 D3 **Apopka, Lake** U.S.A.
122 B2 **Aporé** Brazil
122 B1 **Aporé** r. Brazil
48 B2 **Apostolos Andreas, Cape** Cyprus
101 E3 **Appalachian Mountains** U.S.A.
76 A2 **Aqaba, Gulf of** Asia
21 D2 **Appin** Austr.
108 B2 **Appleton** U.S.A.
76 B2 **Aprilia** Italy
59 D3 **Apsheronsk** Rus. Fed.
122 B2 **Apucarana** Brazil
122 B2 **Apucarana, Serra da** hills Brazil
46 A2 **Aqaba, Gulf of** Asia
122 A1 **Aquidauana** r. Brazil
43 C2 **Ara** India
85 A4 **Arab, Bahr el** watercourse Sudan
24 B4 **Arabian Sea** Indian Ocean
119 E3 **Aracaju** Brazil
119 E2 **Aracati** Brazil
122 B2 **Araçatuba** Brazil
123 D1 **Aracruz** Brazil
123 D1 **Araçuaí** Brazil
78 B1 **Arad** Romania
83 E3 **Arada** Chad
124 C6 **Arafura Sea** Austr./Indon.
122 B1 **Aragarças** Brazil
75 C1 **Aragón** r. Spain
119 D2 **Araguaia** r. Brazil
119 D2 **Araguaína** Brazil
122 C1 **Araguari** Brazil
35 C3 **Arai** Japan
83 C2 **Arak** Alg.
49 C2 **Arāk** Iran
30 A1 **Arakan Yoma** mts Myanmar
49 C1 **Araks** r. Armenia/Turkey
44 C2 **Aral Sea** salt l. Kazakh./Uzbek.
44 C2 **Aral'sk** Kazakh.
Aral'skoye More salt l. Kazakh./Uzbek. see Aral Sea
74 C1 **Aranda de Duero** Spain
77 D2 **Arandelovac** Yugo.
65 B1 **Aran Island** Rep. of Ireland
65 B2 **Aran Islands** Rep. of Ireland
74 C1 **Aranjuez** Spain
90 A1 **Aranos** Namibia
107 D3 **Aransas Pass** U.S.A.
35 B4 **Arao** Japan
82 B3 **Araouane** Mali
119 E2 **Arapiraca** Brazil
122 B2 **Arapongas** Brazil
122 C3 **Araquari** Brazil
46 B1 **'Ar'ar** Saudi Arabia
122 C2 **Araraquara** Brazil
119 C2 **Araras** Brazil
122 B3 **Araras, Serra das** mts Brazil
20 B3 **Ararat** Austr.
123 D2 **Araruama, Lago de** lag. Brazil
123 E1 **Arataca** Brazil
Aratürük China see Yiwu
118 A1 **Arauca** Col.
122 C1 **Araxá** Brazil
49 C2 **Arbīl** Iraq
64 C2 **Arbroath** U.K.
42 A2 **Arbu Lut, Dasht-e** des. Afgh.
72 B3 **Arcachon** France
111 D3 **Arcadia** U.S.A.
102 B2 **Arcata** U.S.A.
113 B3 **Arcelia** Mex.
54 C2 **Archangel** Rus. Fed.
19 D1 **Archer** r. Austr.

102 D2 **Arco** U.S.A.
74 B2 **Arcos de la Frontera** Spain
95 F2 **Arctic Bay** Can.
128 **Arctic Ocean**
94 C2 **Arctic Red** *r.* Can.
49 C2 **Ardabīl** Iran
49 C1 **Ardahan** Turkey
61 E3 **Årdalstangen** Norway
49 D2 **Ardestān** Iran
21 C2 **Ardlethan** Austr.
107 D2 **Ardmore** U.S.A.
64 A2 **Ardnamurchan, Point of** U.K.
20 A2 **Ardrossan** Austr.
64 B3 **Ardrossan** U.K.
103 B3 **Arena, Point** U.S.A.
61 E4 **Arendal** Norway
69 E1 **Arendsee (Altmark)** Ger.
118 A3 **Arequipa** Peru
119 C2 **Arere** Brazil
74 C1 **Arévalo** Spain
76 B2 **Arezzo** Italy
72 B2 **Argentan** France
121 C3 **Argentina** *country* S. America
121 A6 **Argentino, Lago** *l.* Arg.
72 C2 **Argenton-sur-Creuse** France
78 C2 **Argeş** *r.* Romania
42 A1 **Arghandab** *r.* Afgh.
79 B3 **Argolikos Kolpos** *b.* Greece
79 B3 **Argos** Greece
79 B3 **Argostoli** Greece
75 C1 **Arguís** Spain
37 E1 **Argun'** *r.* China/Rus. Fed.
18 B1 **Argyle, Lake** Austr.
61 F4 **Århus** Denmark
90 A2 **Ariamsvlei** Namibia
120 A2 **Arica** Chile
64 A2 **Arinagour** U.K.
123 C1 **Arinos** Brazil
118 C3 **Aripuanã** Brazil
118 B2 **Aripuanã** *r.* Brazil
118 B2 **Ariquemes** Brazil
122 B1 **Ariranhã** *r.* Brazil
106 A2 **Arizona** *state* U.S.A.
112 A1 **Arizpe** Mex.
46 B2 **'Arjah** Saudi Arabia
60 G2 **Arjeplog** Sweden
110 B2 **Arkadelphia** U.S.A.
45 C1 **Arkalyk** Kazakh.
110 B2 **Arkansas** *r.* U.S.A.
110 B1 **Arkansas** *state* U.S.A.
105 D3 **Arkansas City** U.S.A.
 Arkhangel'sk Rus. Fed. *see* Archangel
65 C2 **Arklow** Rep. of Ireland
70 C1 **Arkona, Kap** *c.* Ger.
50 G1 **Arkticheskogo Instituta, Ostrova** *is* Rus. Fed.
73 C3 **Arles** France
83 C3 **Arlit** Niger
68 B3 **Arlon** Belgium
65 C1 **Armagh** U.K.
84 B2 **Armant** Egypt
49 C1 **Armavir** Rus. Fed.
49 C1 **Armenia** *country* Asia
118 A1 **Armenia** Col.
112 B3 **Armeria** Mex.
21 D2 **Armidale** Austr.
98 B1 **Armstrong** Can.
48 B1 **Armyans'k** Ukr.
48 B2 **Arnaoutis, Cape** Cyprus
68 B2 **Arnhem** Neth.
19 C1 **Arnhem, Cape** Austr.
19 C1 **Arnhem Bay** Austr.
19 C1 **Arnhem Land** *reg.* Austr.
76 B2 **Arno** *r.* Italy
20 A2 **Arno Bay** Austr.
98 C2 **Arnprior** Can.

68 D2 **Arnsberg** Ger.
69 E2 **Arnstadt** Ger.
90 A2 **Aroab** Namibia
69 D2 **Arolsen** Ger.
46 A3 **Aroma** Sudan
76 A1 **Arona** Italy
112 B2 **Aros** *r.* Mex.
49 C2 **Ar Ramādī** Iraq
64 B3 **Arran** *i.* U.K.
48 B2 **Ar Raqqah** Syria
72 C1 **Arras** France
46 B2 **Ar-Rass** Saudi Arabia
113 C3 **Arriagá** Mex.
47 C2 **Ar Rimāl** *reg.* Saudi Arabia
 Ar Riyāḍ Saudi Arabia *see* Riyadh
113 C2 **Arroyo Seco** Mex.
47 C2 **Ar Rustāq** Oman
48 C2 **Ar Ruṭbah** Iraq
49 D3 **Arsenajān** Iran
34 B2 **Arsen'yev** Rus. Fed.
79 B3 **Arta** Greece
112 B3 **Arteaga** Mex.
34 B2 **Artem** Rus. Fed.
59 D2 **Artemivs'k** Ukr.
72 C2 **Artenay** France
106 C2 **Artesia** U.S.A.
19 E2 **Arthur Point** Austr.
22 B2 **Arthur's Pass** N.Z.
120 C4 **Artigas** Uru.
97 D1 **Artillery Lake** Can.
58 B2 **Artsyz** Ukr.
45 D3 **Artux** China
49 C1 **Artvin** Turkey
27 C3 **Aru, Kepulauan** *is* Indon.
87 D2 **Arua** Uganda
115 D3 **Aruba** *terr.* West Indies
87 D3 **Arusha** Tanz.
37 C1 **Arvayheer** Mongolia
97 E1 **Arviat** Can.
60 G2 **Arvidsjaur** Sweden
61 F4 **Arvika** Sweden
55 D3 **Arzamas** Rus. Fed.
75 C2 **Arzew** Alg.
68 C2 **Arzfeld** Ger.
69 F2 **Aš** Czech Rep.
83 C4 **Asaba** Nigeria
34 D2 **Asahi-dake** *vol.* Japan
34 D2 **Asahikawa** Japan
46 B3 **Āsalē** *l.* Eth.
43 C2 **Asansol** India
99 C2 **Asbestos** Can.
77 C2 **Ascea** Italy
120 B2 **Ascensión** Bol.
80 C4 **Ascension** *i.* S. Atlantic Ocean
69 D3 **Aschaffenburg** Ger.
68 C2 **Ascheberg** Ger.
69 E2 **Aschersleben** Ger.
76 B2 **Ascoli Piceno** Italy
60 G3 **Åsele** Sweden
78 B2 **Asenovgrad** Bulg.
18 A2 **Ashburton** *watercourse* Austr.
22 B2 **Ashburton** N.Z.
110 B2 **Ashdown** U.S.A.
111 D1 **Asheville** U.S.A.
21 D1 **Ashford** Austr.
67 D3 **Ashford** U.K.
44 B3 **Ashgabat** Turkm.
65 C3 **Ashington** U.K.
35 B4 **Ashizuri-misaki** *pt* Japan
 Ashkhabad Turkm. *see* Ashgabat
104 D3 **Ashland** *KS* U.S.A.
108 C3 **Ashland** *KY* U.S.A.
108 C2 **Ashland** *OH* U.S.A.
102 B2 **Ashland** *OR* U.S.A.
108 A1 **Ashland** *WI* U.S.A.
56 C3 **Ashmyany** Belarus

46 B3 **Ash Sharawrah** Saudi Arabia
49 C2 **Ash Sharqāṭ** Iraq
49 C2 **Ash Shaṭrah** Iraq
47 B3 **Ash Shiḥr** Yemen
47 C2 **Ash Shināş** Oman
46 B2 **Ash Shu'bah** Saudi Arabia
46 B2 **Ash Shumlūl** Saudi Arabia
108 C2 **Ashtabula** U.S.A.
99 D1 **Ashuanipi Lake** Can.
74 B2 **Asilah** Morocco
76 A2 **Asinara, Golfo dell'** *b.* Sardinia Italy
50 G3 **Asino** Rus. Fed.
56 C3 **Asipovichy** Belarus
46 B2 **'Asīr** *reg.* Saudi Arabia
61 F4 **Askim** Norway
36 C1 **Askiz** Rus. Fed.
84 B3 **Asmara** Eritrea
61 F4 **Åsnen** *l.* Sweden
84 B2 **Asoteriba, Jebel** *mt.* Sudan
71 D2 **Aspang-Markt** Austria
104 B3 **Aspen** U.S.A.
22 A2 **Aspiring, Mount** N.Z.
85 C3 **Assab** Eritrea
46 B2 **As Salamiyah** Saudi Arabia
49 C2 **As Samāwah** Iraq
47 C2 **Aş Şanām** *reg.* Saudi Arabia
83 E2 **Aş Sarīr** *reg.* Libya
68 C1 **Assen** Neth.
68 B2 **Assesse** Belgium
83 D1 **As Sidrah** Libya
97 D3 **Assiniboia** Can.
96 C2 **Assiniboine, Mount** Can.
122 B2 **Assis** Brazil
46 B2 **Aş Şubayḩīyah** Kuwait
49 C2 **As Sulaymānīyah** Iraq
46 B2 **As Sulayyil** Saudi Arabia
46 B2 **As Sūq** Saudi Arabia
48 B2 **As Suwaydā'** Syria
47 C2 **As Suwayq** Oman
79 B3 **Astakos** Greece
45 D1 **Astana** Kazakh.
49 C2 **Āstārā** Iran
76 A2 **Asti** Italy
42 B1 **Astor** Jammu and Kashmir
74 B1 **Astorga** Spain
102 B1 **Astoria** U.S.A.
55 D4 **Astrakhan'** Rus. Fed.
56 C3 **Astravyets** Belarus
79 C3 **Astypalaia** *i.* Greece
120 C3 **Asunción** Para.
84 B2 **Aswān** Egypt
84 B2 **Asyūt** Egypt
120 B3 **Atacama, Desierto de** *des.* Chile
120 B3 **Atacama, Salar de** *salt flat* Chile
82 C4 **Atakpamé** Togo
79 B3 **Atalanti** Greece
118 A3 **Atalaya** Peru
46 B3 **'Ataq** Yemen
82 A2 **Atâr** Maur.
103 B3 **Atascadero** U.S.A.
45 D2 **Atasu** Kazakh.
84 B3 **Atbara** Sudan
84 B3 **Atbara** *r.* Sudan
45 C1 **Atbasar** Kazakh.
105 D3 **Atchison** U.S.A.
76 B2 **Aterno** *r.* Italy
76 B2 **Atessa** Italy
68 A2 **Ath** Belgium
96 C2 **Athabasca** Can.
97 C2 **Athabasca** *r.* Can.
97 D2 **Athabasca, Lake** Can.
79 B3 **Athens** Greece
111 D2 **Athens** *GA* U.S.A.
108 C3 **Athens** *OH* U.S.A.
111 D1 **Athens** *TN* U.S.A.
107 D2 **Athens** *TX* U.S.A.

Athina Greece *see* **Athens**
65 C2 **Athlone** Rep. of Ireland
79 B2 **Athos** *mt.* Greece
65 C2 **Athy** Rep. of Ireland
83 D3 **Ati** Chad
98 A2 **Atikokan** Can.
55 D3 **Atkarsk** Rus. Fed.
111 D2 **Atlanta** U.S.A.
105 D2 **Atlantic** U.S.A.
109 E3 **Atlantic City** U.S.A.
126 **Atlantic Ocean**
90 A3 **Atlantis** S. Africa
82 B1 **Atlas Mountains** *mts* Africa
82 C1 **Atlas Saharien** *mts* Alg.
96 A2 **Atlin** Can.
96 A2 **Atlin Lake** Can.
110 C2 **Atmore** U.S.A.
107 D2 **Atoka** U.S.A.
43 C2 **Atrai** *r.* India
46 B2 **Aṭ Ṭā'if** Saudi Arabia
31 B2 **Attapu** Laos
79 C3 **Attavyros** *mt.* Greece
98 B1 **Attawapiskat** Can.
98 B1 **Attawapiskat** *r.* Can.
98 B1 **Attawapiskat Lake** Can.
68 C2 **Attendorn** Ger.
46 B3 **At Turbah** Yemen
44 B2 **Atyrau** Kazakh.
73 C3 **Aubenas** France
94 C2 **Aubry Lake** Can.
110 C2 **Auburn** *AL* U.S.A.
103 B3 **Auburn** *CA* U.S.A.
105 D2 **Auburn** *NE* U.S.A.
109 D2 **Auburn** *NY* U.S.A.
72 C2 **Aubusson** France
72 C3 **Auch** France
22 B1 **Auckland** N.Z.
69 F2 **Aue** Ger.
70 C2 **Augsburg** Ger.
77 C3 **Augusta** *Sicily* Italy
111 D2 **Augusta** *GA* U.S.A.
105 D3 **Augusta** *KS* U.S.A.
109 F2 **Augusta** *ME* U.S.A.
18 A2 **Augustus, Mount** Austr.
68 A2 **Aulnoye-Aymeries** France
90 B2 **Auob** *watercourse*
         Namibia/S. Africa
42 B3 **Aurangābād** India
68 C1 **Aurich** Ger.
122 B1 **Aurilândia** Brazil
72 C3 **Aurillac** France
104 C3 **Aurora** *CO* U.S.A.
108 B2 **Aurora** *IL* U.S.A.
105 D2 **Aurora** *NE* U.S.A.
90 A2 **Aus** Namibia
105 E2 **Austin** *MN* U.S.A.
103 C3 **Austin** *NV* U.S.A.
107 D2 **Austin** *TX* U.S.A.
18 B2 **Australia** *country* Oceania
21 C3 **Australian Capital Territory**
         admin. div. Austr.
70 C2 **Austria** *country* Europe
112 B3 **Autlán** Mex.
72 C3 **Autun** France
73 C2 **Auxerre** France
73 D2 **Auxonne** France
73 C2 **Avallon** France
99 E2 **Avalon Peninsula** Can.
122 C2 **Avaré** Brazil
59 D2 **Avdiyivka** Ukr.
74 B1 **Aveiro** Port.
77 B2 **Avellino** Italy
68 A2 **Avesnes-sur-Helpe** France
61 G3 **Avesta** Sweden
76 B2 **Avezzano** Italy
64 C2 **Aviemore** U.K.
77 C2 **Avigliano** Italy
73 C3 **Avignon** France
74 C1 **Ávila** Spain
74 B1 **Avilés** Spain

77 C3 **Avola** *Sicily* Italy
67 C3 **Avon** *r.* England U.K.
67 C3 **Avon** *r.* England U.K.
72 B2 **Avranches** France
22 B1 **Awanui** N.Z.
85 C4 **Āwash** Eth.
85 C3 **Āwash** *r.* Eth.
83 D2 **Awbārī** Libya
85 C4 **Aw Dheegle** Somalia
64 B2 **Awe, Loch** *l.* U.K.
85 A4 **Aweil** Sudan
94 E1 **Axel Heiberg Island** Can.
82 B4 **Axim** Ghana
118 A3 **Ayacucho** Peru
45 E2 **Ayagoz** Kazakh.
36 B2 **Ayakkum Hu** *salt l.* China
74 B2 **Ayamonte** Spain
51 K3 **Ayan** Rus. Fed.
118 A3 **Ayaviri** Peru
44 A2 **Aybas** Kazakh.
59 D2 **Aydar** *r.* Ukr.
45 C2 **Aydarkul', Ozero** *l.* Uzbek.
79 C3 **Aydın** Turkey
45 C2 **Ayeat, Gora** *hill* Kazakh.
18 C2 **Ayers Rock** *hill* Austr.
67 C3 **Aylesbury** U.K.
74 C1 **Ayllón** Spain
97 I1 **Aylmer Lake** Can.
85 B4 **Ayod** Sudan
51 M2 **Ayon, Ostrov** *i.* Rus. Fed.
82 B3 **'Ayoûn el 'Atroûs** Maur.
19 D1 **Ayr** Austr.
64 B3 **Ayr** U.K.
66 A1 **Ayre, Point of** Isle of Man
44 C2 **Ayteke Bi** Kazakh.
78 C2 **Aytos** Bulg.
113 C3 **Ayutla** Mex.
31 B2 **Ayutthaya** Thai.
79 C3 **Ayvacık** Turkey
79 C3 **Ayvalık** Turkey
82 C3 **Azaouagh, Vallée de**
         watercourse Mali/Niger
         Azbine *mts* Niger *see*
         L'Aïr, Massif de
49 C1 **Azerbaijan** *country* Asia
54 D2 **Azopol'ye** Rus. Fed.
52 A5 **Azores** *aut. reg.*
         N. Atlantic Ocean
59 D2 **Azov** Rus. Fed.
59 D2 **Azov, Sea of** Rus. Fed./Ukr.
         Azraq, Baḥr el *r.* Eth./Sudan
         see Blue Nile
74 B2 **Azuaga** Spain
114 B4 **Azuero, Península de** *pen.*
         Panama
121 C4 **Azul** Arg.
48 B2 **Az Zarqā'** Jordan
46 B3 **Az Zaydīyah** Yemen
82 C2 **Azzel Matti, Sebkha**
         salt pan Alg.
46 B2 **Az Zilfī** Saudi Arabia
46 B3 **Az Zuqur** *i.* Yemen

B

85 C4 **Baardheere** Somalia
45 C3 **Bābā, Kūh-e** *mts* Afgh.
78 C2 **Babadag** Romania
79 C2 **Babaeski** Turkey
85 C3 **Bāb al Mandab** *str.*
         Africa/Asia
29 C2 **Babana** Indon.
27 C3 **Babar** *i.* Indon.
87 D3 **Babati** Tanz.
57 E2 **Babayevo** Rus. Fed.
96 B2 **Babine** *r.* Can.
96 B2 **Babine Lake** Can.

27 C3 **Babo** Indon.
49 D2 **Bābol** Iran
90 A3 **Baboon Point** S. Africa
56 C3 **Babruysk** Belarus
32 B1 **Babuyan** *i.* Phil.
32 B1 **Babuyan Islands** Phil.
119 D2 **Bacabal** Brazil
27 C3 **Bacan** *i.* Indon.
78 C1 **Bacău** Romania
20 B3 **Bacchus Marsh** Austr.
45 D3 **Bachu** China
97 I1 **Back** *r.* Can.
77 C1 **Bačka Palanka** Yugo.
30 B1 **Bac Lac** Vietnam
31 B3 **Bac Liêu** Vietnam
32 B1 **Bacolod** Phil.
98 C1 **Bacqueville, Lac** *l.* Can.
74 B2 **Badajoz** Spain
30 A1 **Badarpur** India
69 E2 **Bad Berka** Ger.
69 D2 **Bad Berleburg** Ger.
69 E1 **Bad Bevensen** Ger.
68 C2 **Bad Ems** Ger.
71 D2 **Baden** Austria
70 B2 **Baden-Baden** Ger.
69 E2 **Bad Harzburg** Ger.
69 D2 **Bad Hersfeld** Ger.
70 C2 **Bad Hofgastein** Austria
69 D2 **Bad Homburg vor der Höhe**
         Ger.
42 A2 **Badin** Pak.
48 B2 **Bādiyat ash Shām** *des.* Asia
69 E2 **Bad Kissingen** Ger.
68 C3 **Bad Kreuznach** Ger.
69 E2 **Bad Lauterberg im Harz**
         Ger.
69 D2 **Bad Lippspringe** Ger.
69 D3 **Bad Mergentheim** Ger.
69 D2 **Bad Nauheim** Ger.
68 C2 **Bad Neuenahr-Ahrweiler**
         Ger.
69 E2 **Bad Neustadt an der Saale**
         Ger.
69 E1 **Bad Oldesloe** Ger.
69 D2 **Bad Pyrmont** Ger.
46 A2 **Badr Ḥunayn** Saudi Arabia
69 D1 **Bad Salzdetfurth** Ger.
69 E2 **Bad Salzungen** Ger.
70 C1 **Bad Schwartau** Ger.
69 E1 **Bad Segeberg** Ger.
41 C4 **Badulla** Sri Lanka
68 D1 **Bad Zwischenahn** Ger.
74 C2 **Baeza** Spain
82 A3 **Bafatá** Guinea-Bissau
128 Q2 **Baffin Bay** *sea*
         Can./Greenland
95 K2 **Baffin Island** Can.
86 B2 **Bafia** Cameroon
82 A3 **Bafing** *r.* Guinea/Mali
82 A3 **Bafoulabé** Mali
86 B2 **Bafoussam** Cameroon
44 B3 **Bāfq** Iran
48 B1 **Bafra** Turkey
47 C2 **Bāft** Iran
87 C2 **Bafwasende**
         Dem. Rep. Congo
87 D3 **Bagamoyo** Tanz.
28 B1 **Bagan Datuk** Malaysia
88 B2 **Bagani** Namibia
28 B1 **Bagansiapiapi** Indon.
106 A2 **Bagdad** U.S.A.
120 C4 **Bagé** Brazil
49 C2 **Baghdad** Iraq
45 C3 **Baghlān** Afgh.
72 C3 **Bagnères-de-Luchon**
         France
56 B3 **Bagrationovsk** Rus. Fed.
         Bagrax China *see* Bohu
32 B1 **Baguio** Phil.
83 C3 **Bagzane, Monts** *mts* Niger

Bahamas *country*
West Indies *see*
The Bahamas
43 C2 **Baharampur** India
84 A2 **Bahariya Oasis** Egypt
28 B1 **Bahau** Malaysia
40 B2 **Bahawalnagar** Pak.
42 B2 **Bahawalpur** Pak.
121 B4 **Bahía Blanca** Arg.
112 A2 **Bahía Kino** Mex.
120 C3 **Bahía Negra** Para.
112 A2 **Bahía Tortugas** Mex.
85 B3 **Bahir Dar** Eth.
43 C2 **Bahraich** India
47 C2 **Bahrain** *country* Asia
47 D2 **Bāhū Kālāt** Iran
78 B1 **Baia Mare** Romania
37 E1 **Baicheng** China
99 D2 **Baie-Comeau** Can.
Baie-du-Poste Can. *see*
Mistissini
99 C2 **Baie-St-Paul** Can.
33 B1 **Baihe** China
37 D1 **Baikal, Lake** Rus. Fed.
78 B2 **Băileşti** Romania
36 C2 **Baima** China
43 C2 **Bairang** China
111 D2 **Bainbridge** U.S.A.
Bairin Youqi China *see*
Daban
21 C3 **Bairnsdale** Austr.
33 B1 **Baishan** *Jilin* China
33 B1 **Baishan** *Jilin* China
38 A2 **Baiyin** China
84 B3 **Baiyuda Desert** Sudan
71 D2 **Baja** Hungary
112 A1 **Baja California** *pen.* Mex.
46 B3 **Bājil** Yemen
82 A3 **Bakel** Senegal
103 C3 **Baker** *CA* U.S.A.
104 C1 **Baker** *MT* U.S.A.
102 C2 **Baker** *OR* U.S.A.
102 B1 **Baker, Mount** *vol.* U.S.A.
97 E1 **Baker Foreland** *hd* Can.
97 E1 **Baker Lake** Can.
97 E1 **Baker Lake** *l.* Can.
103 C3 **Bakersfield** U.S.A.
59 C2 **Bakhchysaray** Ukr.
44 B3 **Bakherden** Turkm.
59 C1 **Bakhmut** Ukr.
Bākhtarān Iran *see*
Kermānshāh
Bakı Azer. *see* **Baku**
79 C2 **Bakırköy** Turkey
60 □C2 **Bakkaflói** *b.* Iceland
86 C2 **Bakouma** C.A.R.
49 C1 **Baku** Azer.
32 A2 **Balabac** Phil.
32 A2 **Balabac** *i.* Phil.
32 A2 **Balabac Strait** Malaysia/Phil.
29 C2 **Balaiberkuak** Indon.
20 A2 **Balaklava** Austr.
59 C3 **Balaklava** Ukr.
59 D2 **Balakliya** Ukr.
55 D3 **Balakovo** Rus. Fed.
44 C3 **Bālā Morghāb** Afgh.
113 C3 **Balancán** Mex.
79 C3 **Balan Dağı** *hill* Turkey
32 B1 **Balanga** Phil.
43 C2 **Balāngīr** India
55 D3 **Balashov** Rus. Fed.
71 D2 **Balaton** *l.* Hungary
71 D2 **Balatonboglár** Hungary
118 C2 **Balbina, Represa de** *resr*
Brazil
65 C2 **Balbriggan** Rep. of Ireland
20 A2 **Balcanoona** Austr.
78 C2 **Balchik** Bulg.
22 A3 **Balclutha** N.Z.
97 E2 **Baldock Lake** Can.

97 D2 **Baldy Mountain** Can.
106 B2 **Baldy Peak** U.S.A.
Baleares, Islas *is* Spain *see*
Balearic Islands
75 D2 **Balearic Islands** *is* Spain
123 E1 **Baleia, Ponta da** *pt* Brazil
43 C2 **Bāleshwar** India
29 C2 **Bali** *i.* Indon.
28 A1 **Balige** Indon.
43 C2 **Baliguda** India
79 C3 **Balıkesir** Turkey
29 C2 **Balikpapan** Indon.
29 C2 **Bali Sea** Indon.
78 B2 **Balkan Mountains**
Bulg./Yugo.
45 C2 **Balkhash** Kazakh.
45 D2 **Balkhash, Ozero** *l.* Kazakh.
18 B3 **Balladonia** Austr.
65 B2 **Ballaghaderreen**
Rep. of Ireland
60 G2 **Ballangen** Norway
20 B3 **Ballarat** Austr.
18 B2 **Ballard, Lake** *salt flat* Austr.
64 C2 **Ballater** U.K.
82 B3 **Ballé** Mali
21 D1 **Ballina** Austr.
65 B1 **Ballina** Rep. of Ireland
65 B2 **Ballinasloe** Rep. of Ireland
107 D2 **Ballinger** U.S.A.
65 B2 **Ballinrobe** Rep. of Ireland
65 B1 **Ballycastle** Rep. of Ireland
65 C1 **Ballycastle** U.K.
65 C1 **Ballyclare** U.K.
65 C1 **Ballycastle** U.K.
65 B1 **Ballymena** U.K.
65 C1 **Ballymoney** U.K.
65 D1 **Ballynahinch** U.K.
65 B1 **Ballyshannon** Rep. of Ireland
63 B2 **Ballyvoy** U.K.
19 D2 **Balonne** *r.* Austr.
42 B2 **Balotra** India
43 C2 **Balrampur** India
20 B2 **Balranald** Austr.
78 B2 **Balş** Romania
119 D2 **Balsas** Brazil
113 C3 **Balsas** Mex.
58 B2 **Balta** Ukr.
58 B2 **Bălţi** Moldova
61 G4 **Baltic Sea** *g.* Europe
48 B2 **Baltīm** Egypt
91 C1 **Baltimore** S. Africa
109 D3 **Baltimore** U.S.A.
56 A3 **Baltiysk** Rus. Fed.
30 A1 **Balu** India
56 C2 **Balvi** Latvia
45 D2 **Balykchy** Kyrg.
55 E4 **Balykshi** Kazakh.
47 C2 **Bam** Iran
19 D1 **Bamaga** Austr.
98 A1 **Bamaji Lake** Can.
82 B3 **Bamako** Mali
86 C2 **Bambari** C.A.R.
69 E3 **Bamberg** Ger.
87 C2 **Bambili** Dem. Rep. Congo
87 C2 **Bambouti** C.A.R.
123 C2 **Bambuí** Brazil
86 B2 **Bamenda** Cameroon
42 A1 **Bāmīān** Afgh.
120 B2 **Bañados del Izozog** *swamp*
Bol.
87 C2 **Banalia** Dem. Rep. Congo
119 C3 **Bananal, Ilha do** *i.* Brazil
42 B2 **Banas** *r.* India
79 C3 **Banaz** Turkey
30 B2 **Ban Ban** Laos
65 C1 **Banbridge** U.K.
67 C2 **Banbury** U.K.
98 C2 **Bancroft** Can.
87 C2 **Banda** Dem. Rep. Congo

43 C2 **Banda** India
27 C3 **Banda, Kepulauan** *is* Indon.
28 A1 **Banda Aceh** Indon.
47 C2 **Bandar-e 'Abbās** Iran
49 C2 **Bandar-e Anzalī** Iran
47 C2 **Bandar-e Chārak** Iran
49 C2 **Bandar-e Emām Khomeynī**
Iran
47 C2 **Bandar-e Lengeh** Iran
47 C2 **Bandar-e Maqām** Iran
29 C1 **Bandar Seri Begawan**
Brunei
27 C3 **Banda Sea** Indon.
123 D2 **Bandeiras, Pico de** *mt.*
Brazil
91 C1 **Bandelierkop** S. Africa
112 B2 **Banderas, Bahía de** *b.* Mex.
82 B3 **Bandiagara** Mali
79 C2 **Bandırma** Turkey
65 B3 **Bandon** Rep. of Ireland
86 B3 **Bandundu** Dem. Rep. Congo
29 B2 **Bandung** Indon.
96 C2 **Banff** Can.
64 C2 **Banff** U.K.
82 B3 **Banfora** Burkina
32 B2 **Banga** Phil.
41 B3 **Bangalore** India
86 C2 **Bangassou** C.A.R.
27 C3 **Banggai** Indon.
27 C3 **Banggai, Kepulauan** *is*
Indon.
29 C1 **Banggi** *i. Sabah* Malaysia
83 E1 **Banghāzī** Libya
28 B2 **Bangka** *i.* Indon.
29 C2 **Bangkalan** Indon.
28 B1 **Bangkinang** Indon.
28 B2 **Bangko** Indon.
31 B2 **Bangkok** Thai.
43 C2 **Bangladesh** *country* Asia
65 D1 **Bangor** *Northern Ireland* U.K.
66 A2 **Bangor** *Wales* U.K.
109 F2 **Bangor** U.S.A.
31 A2 **Bang Saphan Yai** Thai.
32 B1 **Bangued** Phil.
86 B2 **Bangui** C.A.R.
89 B2 **Bangweulu, Lake** Zambia
30 B1 **Ban Houayxay** Laos
83 D1 **Banī Walīd** Libya
48 B2 **Bāniyās** Syria
77 C2 **Banja Luka** Bos.-Herz.
29 C2 **Banjarmasin** Indon.
82 A3 **Banjul** Gambia
96 A2 **Banks Island** *B.C.* Can.
94 C2 **Banks Island** *N.W.T.* Can.
97 E1 **Banks Lake** *l.* Can.
22 B2 **Banks Peninsula** N.Z.
43 C2 **Bankura** India
30 A1 **Banmauk** Myanmar
30 B2 **Ban Mouang** Laos
65 C1 **Bann** *r.* U.K.
30 B2 **Ban Napè** Laos
31 A3 **Ban Na San** Thai.
111 E4 **Bannerman Town** Bahamas
42 B1 **Bannu** Pak.
42 B2 **Banswara** India
31 A3 **Ban Tha Kham** Thai.
30 A2 **Ban Tha Song Yang** Thai.
31 B2 **Ban Tôp** Laos
65 B3 **Bantry** Rep. of Ireland
65 B3 **Bantry Bay** Rep. of Ireland
86 B2 **Banyo** Cameroon
75 D1 **Banyoles** Spain
29 C2 **Banyuwangi** Indon.
Bao'an China *see* **Shenzhen**
37 D2 **Baochang** China
38 B2 **Baoding** China
38 A2 **Baoji** China
31 B2 **Bao Lôc** Vietnam
34 B1 **Baoqing** China
30 A1 **Baoshan** China

38 B1 **Baotou** China
49 C2 **Ba'qūbah** Iraq
77 C2 **Bar** Yugo.
85 C4 **Baraawe** Somalia
115 C2 **Baracoa** Cuba
21 C2 **Baradine** Austr.
115 C3 **Barahona** Dom. Rep.
84 B3 **Baraka** *watercourse*
   Eritrea/Sudan
29 C1 **Baram** *r. Sarawak* Malaysia
56 C3 **Baranavichy** Belarus
58 B1 **Baranivka** Ukr.
96 A2 **Baranof Island** U.S.A.
27 C3 **Barat Daya, Kepulauan** *is*
   Indon.
123 D2 **Barbacena** Brazil
115 E3 **Barbados** *country*
   West Indies
75 D1 **Barbastro** Spain
72 B2 **Barbezieux-St-Hilaire**
   France
19 D2 **Barcaldine** Austr.
75 D1 **Barcelona** Spain
118 C2 **Barcelona** Venez.
73 D3 **Barcelonnette** France
118 B2 **Barcelos** Brazil
   Barcoo Creek *watercourse*
   Austr. *see* **Cooper Creek**
71 D2 **Barcs** Hungary
43 C3 **Barddhamān** India
71 E2 **Bardejov** Slovakia
47 C2 **Bardsīr** Iran
43 B2 **Bareilly** India
128 B2 **Barents Sea** Arctic Ocean
46 A3 **Barentu** Eritrea
43 C2 **Barh** India
109 F2 **Bar Harbor** U.S.A.
77 D2 **Bari** Italy
42 B1 **Barīkōt** Afgh.
118 A1 **Barinas** Venez.
43 C2 **Baripada** India
43 D2 **Barisal** Bangl.
28 B2 **Barisan, Pegunungan** *mts*
   Indon.
29 C2 **Barito** *r.* Indon.
47 C2 **Barkā** Oman
56 C2 **Barkava** Latvia
19 C1 **Barkly Tableland** *reg.* Austr.
36 C2 **Barkol** China
78 C1 **Bârlad** Romania
73 D2 **Bar-le-Duc** France
18 A2 **Barlee, Lake** *salt flat* Austr.
77 C2 **Barletta** Italy
21 C2 **Barmedman** Austr.
42 B2 **Barmer** India
67 A2 **Barmouth** U.K.
69 D1 **Barmstedt** Ger.
66 C1 **Barnard Castle** U.K.
21 D2 **Barnato** Austr.
50 G3 **Barnaul** Rus. Fed.
95 G2 **Barnes Icecap** Can.
68 B1 **Barneveld** Neth.
66 C2 **Barnsley** U.K.
67 A3 **Barnstaple** U.K.
111 D2 **Barnwell** U.S.A.
   Baroda India *see* **Vadodara**
118 B1 **Barquisimeto** Venez.
64 A2 **Barra** *i.* U.K.
21 D2 **Barraba** Austr.
119 D2 **Barra do Corda** Brazil
122 B1 **Barra do Garças** Brazil
118 C2 **Barra do São Manuel** Brazil
118 A3 **Barranca** *Lima* Peru
118 A2 **Barranca** *Loreto* Peru
120 C3 **Barranqueras** Arg.
118 A1 **Barranquilla** Col.
119 D3 **Barreiras** Brazil
122 C2 **Barretos** Brazil
98 C2 **Barrie** Can.
96 B2 **Barrière** Can.

20 B2 **Barrier Range** *hills* Austr.
21 D2 **Barrington, Mount** Austr.
97 D2 **Barrington Lake** Can.
21 C1 **Barringun** Austr.
65 C2 **Barrow** *r.* Rep. of Ireland
19 C2 **Barrow Creek** Austr.
66 B1 **Barrow-in-Furness** U.K.
18 A2 **Barrow Island** Austr.
94 E2 **Barrow Strait** Can.
67 B3 **Barry** U.K.
98 C2 **Barrys Bay** Can.
42 B2 **Barsalpur** India
103 C4 **Barstow** U.S.A.
73 C2 **Bar-sur-Aube** France
48 B1 **Bartın** Turkey
19 D1 **Bartle Frere, Mount** Austr.
107 D1 **Bartlesville** U.S.A.
71 E1 **Bartoszyce** Pol.
29 C2 **Barung** *i.* Indon.
37 D1 **Baruun Urt** Mongolia
59 D2 **Barvinkove** Ukr.
21 C2 **Barwon** *r.* Austr.
56 C3 **Barysaw** Belarus
78 C2 **Basarabi** Romania
73 D2 **Basel** Switz.
59 C2 **Bashtanka** Ukr.
32 B2 **Basilan** *i.* Phil.
67 D3 **Basildon** U.K.
67 C3 **Basingstoke** U.K.
49 C2 **Başkale** Turkey
98 C1 **Baskatong, Réservoir**
   resr Can.
   Basle Switz. *see* **Basel**
86 C2 **Basoko** Dem. Rep. Congo
49 C2 **Basra** Iraq
96 C2 **Bassano** Can.
82 C4 **Bassar** Togo
91 A2 **Bassein** Myanmar
115 D3 **Basse-Terre** Guadeloupe
115 D3 **Basseterre**
   St Kitts and Nevis
82 B3 **Bassikounou** Maur.
19 D3 **Bass Strait** Austr.
47 C2 **Bastak** Iran
69 E2 **Bastheim** Ger.
43 C2 **Basti** India
73 D3 **Bastia** *Corsica* France
72 B2 **Bastogne** Belgium
110 B2 **Bastrop** U.S.A.
   Basuo China *see* **Dongfang**
86 A2 **Bata** Equat. Guinea
51 J2 **Batagay** Rus. Fed.
122 B2 **Bataguaçu** Brazil
74 B2 **Batalha** Port.
39 C3 **Batan** *i.* Phil.
86 B2 **Batangafo** C.A.R.
32 B1 **Batangas** Phil.
28 B2 **Batanghari** *r.* Indon.
39 C3 **Batan Islands** Phil.
109 D2 **Batavia** U.S.A.
59 D2 **Bataysk** Rus. Fed.
98 B2 **Batchawana Mountain** Can.
18 C1 **Batchelor** Austr.
31 B2 **Bătdâmbâng** Cambodia
21 D3 **Batemans Bay** Austr.
110 B1 **Batesville** U.S.A.
57 D2 **Batetskiy** Rus. Fed.
67 B3 **Bath** U.K.
42 B1 **Bathinda** India
21 C2 **Bathurst** Austr.
99 D2 **Bathurst** Can.
94 C2 **Bathurst Inlet** Can.
94 C2 **Bathurst Inlet** *inlet* Can.
18 C1 **Bathurst Island** Austr.
94 E1 **Bathurst Island** Can.
46 B1 **Bāṭin, Wādī al** *watercourse*
   Asia
49 C2 **Batman** Turkey
83 C1 **Batna** Alg.
110 B2 **Baton Rouge** U.S.A.

112 B2 **Batopilas** Mex.
86 B2 **Batouri** Cameroon
122 B1 **Batovi** Brazil
60 I1 **Båtsfjord** Norway
41 C4 **Batticaloa** Sri Lanka
77 B2 **Battipaglia** Italy
97 D2 **Battle** *r.* Can.
108 B2 **Battle Creek** U.S.A.
103 C2 **Battle Mountain** U.S.A.
42 B1 **Battura Glacier**
   Jammu and Kashmir
85 B4 **Batu** *mt.* Eth.
28 A1 **Batu, Pulau-pulau** *is* Indon.
49 C1 **Bat'umi** Georgia
28 B1 **Batu Pahat** Malaysia
28 B1 **Baubau** Indon.
83 C3 **Bauchi** Nigeria
72 B2 **Baugé** France
73 D2 **Baume-les-Dames** France
122 C2 **Bauru** Brazil
122 B1 **Baús** Brazil
56 B2 **Bauska** Latvia
70 C1 **Bautzen** Ger.
112 B2 **Bavispe** *r.* Mex.
55 E3 **Bavly** Rus. Fed.
30 A1 **Bawdwin** Myanmar
29 C2 **Bawean** *i.* Indon.
84 A2 **Bawku** Ghana
82 B3 **Bawku** Ghana
114 C2 **Bayamo** Cuba
   Bayan Gol China *see*
   Dengkou
36 C1 **Bayanhongor** Mongolia
38 A2 **Bayan Hot** China
32 B2 **Bayawan** Phil.
48 C1 **Bayburt** Turkey
108 C2 **Bay City** *MI* U.S.A.
107 D3 **Bay City** *TX* U.S.A.
54 F2 **Baydaratskaya Guba** *b.*
   Rus. Fed.
85 C4 **Baydhabo** Somalia
49 C2 **Bayjī** Iraq
   Baykal, Ozero *l.* Rus. Fed.
   see **Baikal, Lake**
51 I3 **Baykal'skiy Khrebet** *mts*
   Rus. Fed.
44 C2 **Baykonur** Kazakh.
55 E3 **Baymak** Rus. Fed.
32 B1 **Bayombong** Phil.
72 B3 **Bayonne** France
79 C3 **Bayramiç** Turkey
69 E3 **Bayreuth** Ger.
40 B3 **Bayt al Faqīh** Yemen
74 C2 **Baza** Spain
74 C2 **Baza, Sierra de** *mts* Spain
44 A2 **Bazardyuzi, Gora** *mt.*
   Azer./Rus. Fed.
72 B3 **Bazas** France
42 A2 **Bazdar** Pak.
38 A2 **Bazhong** China
62 B1 **Bazmān** Iran
47 D2 **Bazmān, Kūh-e** *mt.* Iran
67 D3 **Beachy Head** *hd* U.K.
91 C3 **Beacon Bay** S. Africa
18 B1 **Beagle Gulf** Austr.
89 □D2 **Bealanana** Madag.
98 B1 **Beardmore** Can.
50 C2 **Bear Island** *i.* Arctic Ocean
102 E1 **Bear Paw Mountain** U.S.A.
115 C3 **Beata, Cabo** *c.* Dom. Rep.
115 C3 **Beata, Isla** *i.* Dom. Rep.
105 D2 **Beatrice** U.S.A.
103 C3 **Beatty** U.S.A.
21 D1 **Beaudesert** Austr.
20 B3 **Beaufort** Austr.
29 C1 **Beaufort** *Sabah* Malaysia
111 D2 **Beaufort** U.S.A.
128 L2 **Beaufort Sea** Can./U.S.A.
90 B3 **Beaufort West** S. Africa
64 B2 **Beauly** *r.* U.K.

75 D2 **Berrouaghia** Alg.
114 C2 **Berry Islands** Bahamas
68 C1 **Bersenbrück** Ger.
58 B2 **Bershad'** Ukr.
99 D1 **Bertë, Lac** *l.* Can.
86 B2 **Bertoua** Cameroon
118 B2 **Beruri** Brazil
66 B1 **Berwick-upon-Tweed** U.K.
59 C2 **Beryslav** Ukr.
89 □D2 **Besalampy** Madag.
73 D2 **Besançon** France
97 D2 **Besnard Lake** Can.
110 C2 **Bessemer** U.S.A.
44 B2 **Besshoky, Gora** *hill* Kazakh.
74 B1 **Betanzos** Spain
86 B2 **Bétaré Oya** Cameroon
90 A2 **Bethanie** Namibia
91 C2 **Bethlehem** S. Africa
109 D2 **Bethlehem** U.S.A.
89 □D3 **Betioky** Madag.
45 D2 **Betpak-Dala** *plain* Kazakh.
89 □D3 **Betroka** Madag.
99 D2 **Betsiamites** Can.
89 □D2 **Betsiboka** *r.* Madag.
105 E2 **Bettendorf** U.S.A.
43 C2 **Bettiah** India
43 B2 **Betul** India
43 B2 **Betwa** *r.* India
66 B2 **Betws-y-coed** U.K.
66 C2 **Beverley** U.K.
69 D2 **Beverungen** Ger.
68 B1 **Beverwijk** Neth.
67 D3 **Bexhill** U.K.
79 C2 **Beykoz** Turkey
82 B4 **Beyla** Guinea
44 B2 **Beyneu** Kazakh.
48 B1 **Beypazarı** Turkey
     Beyrouth Lebanon *see* Beirut
48 B2 **Beyşehir** Turkey
48 B2 **Beyşehir Gölü** *l.* Turkey
59 D2 **Beysug** *r.* Rus. Fed.
56 C2 **Bezhanitsy** Rus. Fed.
57 E2 **Bezhetsk** Rus. Fed.
73 C3 **Béziers** France
43 C2 **Bhadrakh** India
41 B3 **Bhadravati** India
43 C2 **Bhagalpur** India
42 A2 **Bhairi Hol** *mt.* Pak.
42 B1 **Bhakkar** Pak.
30 A1 **Bhamo** Myanmar
43 C3 **Bhanjanagar** India
42 B2 **Bharatpur** India
42 B2 **Bharuch** India
43 C3 **Bhawanipatna** India
91 C1 **Bhekuzulu** S. Africa
42 B2 **Bhilwara** India
41 B3 **Bhima** *r.* India
42 B2 **Bhiwani** India
91 C3 **Bhown**d S. Africa
42 B2 **Bhopal** India
43 C2 **Bhubaneshwar** India
42 A2 **Bhuj** India
30 A2 **Bhumiphol Dam** Thai.
42 B2 **Bhusawal** India
43 D2 **Bhutan** *country* Asia
30 D2 **Bia, Phou** *mt.* Laos
27 D3 **Biak** Indon.
27 D3 **Biak** *i.* Indon.
71 E1 **Biała Podlaska** Pol.
71 D1 **Białogard** Pol.
71 E1 **Białystok** Pol.
77 C3 **Bianco** Italy
72 B3 **Biarritz** France
73 D2 **Biasca** Switz.
34 D2 **Bibai** Japan
88 A2 **Bibala** Angola
70 B2 **Biberach an der Riß** Ger.
83 C4 **Bida** Nigeria
109 E2 **Biddeford** U.S.A.

67 A3 **Bideford** U.K.
67 A3 **Bideford Bay** U.K.
69 D2 **Biedenkopf** Ger.
73 D2 **Biel** Switz.
69 D1 **Bielefeld** Ger.
76 A1 **Biella** Italy
71 D2 **Bielsko-Biała** Pol.
31 B2 **Biên Hoa** Vietnam
98 C1 **Bienville, Lac** *l.* Can.
68 B3 **Bièvre** Belgium
86 B3 **Bifoun** Gabon
79 C2 **Biga** Turkey
91 D2 **Big Bend** Swaziland
97 D2 **Biggar** Can.
64 C3 **Biggar** U.K.
102 D1 **Big Hole** *r.* U.S.A.
104 B1 **Bighorn** *r.* U.S.A.
104 B2 **Bighorn Mountains** U.S.A.
107 C2 **Big Lake** U.S.A.
108 B2 **Big Rapids** U.S.A.
97 D2 **Big River** Can.
97 E2 **Big Sand Lake** Can.
105 D2 **Big Sioux** *r.* U.S.A.
107 C2 **Big Spring** U.S.A.
102 E1 **Big Timber** U.S.A.
98 B1 **Big Trout Lake** Can.
98 A1 **Big Trout Lake** *l.* Can.
77 C2 **Bihać** Bos.-Herz.
43 C2 **Bihar Sharif** India
78 B1 **Bihor, Vârful** *mt.* Romania
82 A3 **Bijagós, Arquipélago dos** *is*
     Guinea-Bissau
49 C2 **Bījār** Iran
77 C2 **Bijeljina** Bos.-Herz.
77 C2 **Bijelo Polje** Yugo.
39 A3 **Bijie** China
42 B2 **Bikaner** India
37 E1 **Bikin** Rus. Fed.
86 B3 **Bikoro** Dem. Rep. Congo
47 C2 **Bilād Banī Bū 'Alī** Oman
43 C2 **Bilaspur** India
58 C2 **Bila Tserkva** Ukr.
31 A2 **Bilauktaung Range** *mts*
     Myanmar/Thai.
74 C1 **Bilbao** Spain
79 C2 **Bilecik** Turkey
71 E1 **Biłgoraj** Pol.
58 C2 **Bilhorod-Dnistrovs'kyy** Ukr.
87 C2 **Bili** Dem. Rep. Congo
51 M2 **Bilibino** Rus. Fed.
102 E1 **Billings** U.S.A.
67 B3 **Bill of Portland** *hd* U.K.
83 D3 **Bilma** Niger
19 E2 **Biloela** Austr.
59 C2 **Bilohirs'k** Ukr.
58 B1 **Bilohir"ya** Ukr.
59 C1 **Bilopillya** Ukr.
59 D2 **Bilovods'k** Ukr.
110 C2 **Biloxi** U.S.A.
19 C2 **Bilpa Morea Claypan**
     salt flat Austr.
69 E2 **Bilshausen** Ger.
83 E3 **Biltine** Chad
58 C2 **Bilyayivka** Ukr.
111 E3 **Bimini Islands** Bahamas
43 B2 **Bina-Etawa** India
27 C3 **Binaija, Gunung** *mt.* Indon.
86 B3 **Bindu** Dem. Rep. Congo
89 C2 **Bindura** Zimbabwe
75 D1 **Binefar** Spain
21 D1 **Bingara** Austr.
68 C3 **Bingen am Rhein** Ger.
109 F1 **Bingham** U.S.A.
109 D2 **Binghamton** U.S.A.
49 C2 **Bingöl** Turkey
28 A1 **Binjai** Indon.
28 B2 **Bintuan** Indon.
29 C1 **Bintulu** *Sarawak* Malaysia
38 B2 **Binzhou** China
86 A2 **Bioco** *i.* Equat. Guinea

77 C2 **Biograd na Moru** Croatia
86 C1 **Birao** C.A.R.
43 C2 **Biratnagar** Nepal
96 C2 **Birch Mountains** Can.
68 B1 **Birdaard** Neth.
19 C2 **Birdsville** Austr.
48 B2 **Birecik** Turkey
28 A1 **Bireun** Indon.
43 C2 **Birganj** Nepal
85 B3 **Birhan** *mt.* Eth.
122 B2 **Birigüi** Brazil
44 B3 **Birjand** Iran
66 B2 **Birkenhead** U.K.
67 C2 **Birmingham** U.K.
110 C2 **Birmingham** U.S.A.
82 A2 **Bīr Mogreïn** Maur.
83 C3 **Birnin-Kebbi** Nigeria
83 C3 **Birnin Konni** Niger
37 E1 **Birobidzhan** Rus. Fed.
65 C2 **Birr** Rep. of Ireland
64 C1 **Birsay** U.K.
46 A2 **Bīr Shalatein** Egypt
55 B2 **Biržai** Lith.
43 B2 **Bisalpur** India
106 B2 **Bisbee** U.S.A.
72 A2 **Biscay, Bay of** *sea*
     France/Spain
70 C2 **Bischofshofen** Austria
98 B2 **Biscotasi Lake** Can.
45 D2 **Bishkek** Kyrg.
91 C3 **Bisho** S. Africa
103 C3 **Bishop** U.S.A.
37 E1 **Bishui** China
118 B1 **Bisinaca** Col.
83 C1 **Biskra** Alg.
104 C1 **Bismarck** U.S.A.
73 D2 **Bissa, Djebel** *mt.* Alg.
82 A3 **Bissau** Guinea-Bissau
97 E2 **Bissett** Can.
96 C2 **Bistcho Lake** Can.
78 B1 **Bistriţa** Romania
78 C1 **Bistriţa** *r.* Romania
68 C3 **Bitburg** Ger.
73 D2 **Bitche** France
83 D3 **Bitkine** Chad
77 D2 **Bitola** Macedonia
77 C2 **Bitonto** Italy
90 A3 **Bitterfontein** S. Africa
102 D1 **Bitterroot** *r.* U.S.A.
102 C1 **Bitterroot Range** *mts* U.S.A.▮
59 D1 **Bityug** *r.* Rus. Fed.
83 D3 **Biu** Nigeria
35 C3 **Biwa-ko** *l.* Japan
36 B1 **Biysk** Rus. Fed.
83 C1 **Bizerte** Tunisia
60 □A2 **Bjargtangar** *hd* Iceland
60 G3 **Bjästa** Sweden
60 G2 **Bjerkvik** Norway
     Björneborg Fin. *see* Pori
     Bjørnøya *i.* Arctic Ocean *see*
     Bear Island
82 B3 **Bla** Mali
105 E3 **Black** *r.* U.S.A.
19 D2 **Blackall** Austr.
66 B2 **Blackburn** U.K.
102 D2 **Blackfoot** U.S.A.
104 C2 **Black Hills** U.S.A.
64 B2 **Black Isle** *pen.* U.K.
97 D2 **Black Lake** Can.
97 D2 **Black Lake** *l.* Can.
67 B3 **Black Mountains** U.K.
66 B2 **Blackpool** U.K.
     Black River *r.* Vietnam *see*
     Đa, Sông
108 A2 **Black River Falls** U.S.A.
108 C3 **Blacksburg** U.S.A.
48 B1 **Black Sea** Asia/Europe
65 A1 **Blacksod Bay** Rep. of Irela
65 C2 **Blackstairs Mountains**
     Rep. of Ireland

82 B4 **Black Volta** *r.* Africa
65 C2 **Blackwater** *r.* Rep. of Ireland
96 B1 **Blackwater Lake** *l.* Can.
18 A3 **Blackwood** *r.* Austr.
44 A2 **Blagodarnyy** Rus. Fed.
78 B2 **Blagoevgrad** Bulg.
37 E1 **Blagoveshchensk** Rus. Fed.
97 D2 **Blaine Lake** Can.
105 D2 **Blair** U.S.A.
64 C2 **Blair Atholl** U.K.
64 C2 **Blairgowrie** U.K.
111 D2 **Blakely** U.S.A.
121 B4 **Blanca, Bahía** *b.* Arg.
20 A1 **Blanche, Lake** *salt flat* Austr.
120 B2 **Blanco** *r.* Bol.
99 E1 **Blanc-Sablon** Can.
60 □A2 **Blanda** *r.* Iceland
67 B3 **Blandford Forum** U.K.
103 E3 **Blanding** U.S.A.
75 D1 **Blanes** Spain
28 A1 **Blangkejeren** Indon.
68 C2 **Blankenheim** Ger.
68 C2 **Blankenrath** Ger.
71 D2 **Blansko** Czech Rep.
89 C2 **Blantyre** Malawi
66 C1 **Blaydon** U.K.
21 C2 **Blayney** Austr.
22 B2 **Blenheim** N.Z.
83 C1 **Blida** Alg.
98 B2 **Blind River** Can.
91 C1 **Bloemfontein** S. Africa
91 C2 **Bloemhof** S. Africa
91 C2 **Bloemhof Dam** S. Africa
60 □A2 **Blönduós** Iceland
65 B1 **Bloody Foreland** *pt*
      Rep. of Ireland
106 B1 **Bloomfield** U.S.A.
108 B2 **Bloomington** *Il.* U.S.A.
108 B3 **Bloomington** *In.* U.S.A.
108 C3 **Bluefield** U.S.A.
114 B3 **Bluefields** Nic.
21 C2 **Blue Mountains** Austr.
102 C1 **Blue Mountains** U.S.A.
84 B3 **Blue Nile** *r.* Eth./Sudan
94 D2 **Bluenose Lake** Can.
108 C3 **Blue Ridge** *mts* U.S.A.
65 B1 **Blue Stack Mountains**
      Rep. of Ireland
22 A3 **Bluff** N.Z.
103 E3 **Bluff** U.S.A.
120 D3 **Blumenau** Brazil
20 A2 **Blyth** Austr.
66 C1 **Blyth** U.K.
103 D4 **Blythe** U.S.A.
110 C1 **Blytheville** U.S.A.
82 A4 **Bo** Sierra Leone
119 D2 **Boa Esperança, Açude** *resr*
      Brazil
118 B1 **Boa Vista** Brazil
21 C2 **Bobadah** Austr.
89 B3 **Bobai** China
39 □D2 **Boabomby, Tanjona** *c.* Madag.
82 B3 **Bobo-Dioulasso** Burkina
57 F3 **Bobrov** Rus. Fed.
59 C1 **Bobrovytsya** Ukr.
59 C2 **Bobrynets'** Ukr.
89 □D3 **Boby** *mt.* Madag.
118 B2 **Boca do Acre** Brazil
123 C1 **Bocaiúva** Brazil
86 B2 **Bocaranga** C.A.R.
71 E2 **Bochnia** Pol.
68 C2 **Bocholt** Ger.
68 C2 **Bochum** Ger.
91 C1 **Bochum** S. Africa
69 E1 **Bockenem** Ger.
86 B2 **Boda** C.A.R.
51 I3 **Bodaybo** Rus. Fed.
83 D3 **Bodélé** *reg.* Chad
60 H2 **Boden** Sweden

67 A3 **Bodmin** U.K.
67 A3 **Bodmin Moor** *moorland* U.K.
60 F2 **Bodø** Norway
79 C3 **Bodrum** Turkey
86 C3 **Boende** Dem. Rep. Congo
110 C2 **Bogalusa** U.S.A.
82 B3 **Bogandé** Burkina
36 B2 **Bogda Shan** *mts* China
21 D1 **Boggabilla** Austr.
65 B2 **Boggeragh Mountains**
      Rep. of Ireland
68 B3 **Bogny-sur-Meuse** France
65 C2 **Bog of Allen** *reg.*
      Rep. of Ireland
21 C3 **Bogong, Mount** Austr.
28 B2 **Bogor** Indon.
57 E3 **Bogoroditsk** Rus. Fed.
118 A1 **Bogotá** Col.
50 G3 **Bogotol** Rus. Fed.
51 H3 **Boguchany** Rus. Fed.
59 E2 **Boguchar** Rus. Fed.
38 B2 **Bo Hai** *g.* China
68 A3 **Bohain-en-Vermandois**
      France
38 B2 **Bohai Wan** *b.* China
91 C2 **Bohlokong** S. Africa
70 C2 **Böhmer Wald** *mts* Ger.
59 D1 **Bohodukhiv** Ukr.
32 B2 **Bohol** *i.* Phil.
32 B2 **Bohol Sea** Phil.
36 B2 **Bohu** China
123 C2 **Boi, Ponta do** *pt* Brazil
122 B1 **Bois** *r.* Brazil
94 C2 **Bois, Lac des** *l.* Can.
102 C2 **Boise** U.S.A.
107 C1 **Boise City** U.S.A.
91 C2 **Boitumelong** S. Africa
69 F1 **Boizenburg** Ger.
44 B3 **Bojnūrd** Iran
86 B3 **Bokatola** Dem. Rep. Congo
82 A3 **Boké** Guinea
86 C3 **Bokele** Dem. Rep. Congo
61 E4 **Boknafjorden** *sea chan.*
      Norway
83 D3 **Bokoro** Chad
31 A2 **Bokpyin** Myanmar
57 D2 **Boksitogorsk** Rus. Fed.
90 B2 **Bokspits** S. Africa
82 A3 **Bolama** Guinea-Bissau
72 C2 **Bolbec** France
45 E2 **Bule** China
86 B3 **Boleko** Dem. Rep. Congo
82 B3 **Bolgatanga** Ghana
58 B2 **Bolhrad** Ukr.
34 B1 **Boli** China
78 C2 **Bolintin-Vale** Romania
105 E3 **Bolivar** U.S.A.
118 A1 **Bolívar, Pico** *mt.* Venez.
120 B2 **Bolivia** *country* S. America
57 E3 **Bolkhov** Rus. Fed.
73 C3 **Bollène** France
61 G3 **Bollnäs** Sweden
21 C1 **Bollon** Austr.
69 E2 **Bollstedt** Ger.
86 B3 **Bolobo** Dem. Rep. Congo
76 B2 **Bologna** Italy
57 D2 **Bologovo** Rus. Fed.
57 D2 **Bologoye** Rus. Fed.
86 B2 **Bolomba** Dem. Rep. Congo
31 B2 **Bolovens, Phoup
** Laos
51 H1 **Bol'shevik, Ostrov** *i.*
      Rus. Fed.
54 E2 **Bol'shezemel'skaya Tundra**
      lowland Rus. Fed.
51 L2 **Bol'shoy Aluy** *r.* Rus. Fed.
34 B2 **Bol'shoy Kamen'** Rus. Fed.
      Bol'shoy Kavkaz *mts*
      Asia/Europe *see* Caucasus

51 K2 **Bol'shoy Lyakhovskiy,**
      Ostrov *i.* Rus. Fed.
68 B1 **Bolsward** Neth.
66 B2 **Bolton** U.K.
48 B1 **Bolu** Turkey
60 □A2 **Bolungarvík** Iceland
76 B1 **Bolzano** Italy
86 B3 **Boma** Dem. Rep. Congo
21 D2 **Bomaderry** Austr.
21 C3 **Bombala** Austr.
      Bombay India *see* **Mumbai**
123 C1 **Bom Despacho** Brazil
43 D2 **Bomdila** India
119 D3 **Bom Jesus da Lapa** Brazil
123 D2 **Bom Jesus do Itabapoana**
      Brazil
83 D1 **Bon, Cap** *c.* Tunisia
115 D3 **Bonaire** *i.* Neth. Antilles
18 B1 **Bonaparte Archipelago**
      is Austr.
99 E2 **Bonavista** Can.
99 E2 **Bonavista Bay** Can.
86 C3 **Bondo** Dem. Rep. Congo
82 B4 **Bondoukou** Côte d'Ivoire
26 C3 **Bonerate, Kepulauan**
      is Indon.
123 C1 **Bonfinópolis de Minas**
      Brazil
85 B4 **Bonga** Eth.
43 D2 **Bongaigaon** India
86 C2 **Bongandanga**
      Dem. Rep. Congo
86 C2 **Bongo, Massif des** *mts*
      C.A.R.
83 D3 **Bongor** Chad
82 B4 **Bongouanou** Côte d'Ivoire
31 B2 **Bông Son** Vietnam
107 D2 **Bonham** U.S.A.
73 D3 **Bonifacio** *Corsica* France
76 A2 **Bonifacio, Strait of**
      France/Italy
68 C2 **Bonn** Ger.
102 C1 **Bonners Ferry** U.S.A.
18 A3 **Bonnie Rock** Austr.
97 C2 **Bonnyville** Can.
76 A2 **Bonorva** *Sardinia* Italy
29 C1 **Bontang** Indon.
32 B1 **Bontoc** Phil.
28 B3 **Bontosunggu** Indon.
91 C3 **Bontrug** S. Africa
20 B2 **Booligal** Austr.
21 C1 **Boomi** Austr.
21 D1 **Boonah** Austr.
105 E2 **Boone** U.S.A.
110 C2 **Booneville** U.S.A.
105 E3 **Boonville** U.S.A.
21 C2 **Boorowa** Austr.
94 F2 **Boothia, Gulf of** Can.
94 E2 **Boothia Peninsula** Can.
68 A2 **Boppard** Ger.
85 B3 **Bor** Sudan
48 B2 **Bor** Turkey
77 D2 **Bor** Yugo.
61 F4 **Borås** Sweden
47 C2 **Borāzjān** Iran
118 C2 **Borba** Brazil
72 B3 **Bordeaux** France
95 F2 **Borden Peninsula** Can.
20 B3 **Bordertown** Austr.
75 D2 **Bordj Bou Arréridj** Alg.
75 D2 **Bordj Bounaama** Alg.
83 C1 **Bordj Messaouda** Alg.
83 C2 **Bordj Omer Driss** Alg.
62 B1 **Borðoy** *i.* Faroe Is.
60 □A3 **Borgarnes** Iceland
76 A1 **Borgosesia** Italy
55 D3 **Borisoglebsk** Rus. Fed.
57 E2 **Borisoglebskiy** Rus. Fed.
59 D1 **Borisovka** Rus. Fed.
68 C2 **Borken** Ger.

60 G2   **Borkenes** Norway
68 C1   **Borkum** Ger.
68 C1   **Borkum** i. Ger.
61 G3   **Borlänge** Sweden
69 F2   **Borna** Ger.
29 C1   **Borneo** i. Asia
61 F4   **Bornholm** i. Denmark
79 C3   **Bornova** Turkey
58 B1   **Borodyanka** Ukr.
57 D2   **Borovichi** Rus. Fed.
57 E2   **Borovsk** Rus. Fed.
19 C1   **Borroloola** Austr.
78 B1   **Borşa** Romania
58 B2   **Borshchiv** Ukr.
37 D1   **Borshchovochnyy Khrebet** mts Rus. Fed.
69 E1   **Börßum** Ger.
         Bortala China see **Bole**
49 C2   **Borūjerd** Iran
58 A2   **Boryslav** Ukr.
58 C1   **Boryspil'** Ukr.
59 C1   **Borzna** Ukr.
37 D1   **Borzya** Rus. Fed.
77 C1   **Bosanska Dubica** Bos.-Herz.
77 C1   **Bosanska Gradiška** Bos.-Herz.
77 C2   **Bosanska Krupa** Bos.-Herz.
77 C1   **Bosanski Novi** Bos.-Herz.
77 C2   **Bosanski Grahovo** Bos.-Herz.
39 A3   **Bose** China
91 C2   **Boshof** S. Africa
77 C2   **Bosnia-Herzegovina** country Europe
86 B2   **Bosobolo** Dem. Rep. Congo
78 C2   **Bosporus** str. Turkey
86 B2   **Bossangoa** C.A.R.
86 B2   **Bossembélé** C.A.R.
36 B2   **Bosten Hu** l. China
66 C2   **Boston** U.K.
109 E2 **Boston** U.S.A.
110 B1 **Boston Mountains** U.S.A.
21 C2   **Botany Bay** Austr.
78 B2   **Botev** mt. Bulg.
61 G3   **Bothnia, Gulf of** Fin./Sweden
78 C1   **Botoşani** Romania
91 C2   **Botshabelo** S. Africa
88 B3   **Botswana** country Africa
77 C3   **Botte Donato, Monte** mt. Italy
104 C1 **Bottineau** U.S.A.
68 C2   **Bottrop** Ger.
122 C2 **Botucatu** Brazil
82 B4   **Bouaké** Côte d'Ivoire
86 B3   **Bouar** C.A.R.
82 B1   **Bouârfa** Morocco
90 D2   **Bouctouche** Can.
75 E2   **Bougaa** Alg.
82 B3   **Bougouni** Mali
68 B3   **Bouillon** Belgium
75 D2   **Bouira** Alg.
82 A2   **Boujdour** Western Sahara
104 B2 **Boulder** U.S.A.
103 D3 **Boulder City** U.S.A.
19 C2   **Boulia** Austr.
72 C2   **Boulogne-Billancourt** France
67 D3   **Boulogne-sur-Mer** France
86 B3   **Boumango** Gabon
86 B2   **Boumba** r. Cameroon
75 D2   **Boumerdes** Alg.
82 B4   **Bouna** Côte d'Ivoire
82 B4   **Boundiali** Côte d'Ivoire
102 D2 **Bountiful** U.S.A.
82 B3   **Bourem** Mali
72 C2   **Bourganeuf** France
73 D2   **Bourg-en-Bresse** France
72 C2   **Bourges** France
21 C2   **Bourke** Austr.

67 C3   **Bournemouth** U.K.
83 C1   **Bou Saâda** Alg.
83 D3   **Bousso** Chad
82 A3   **Boutilimit** Maur.
97 C3   **Bow** r. Can.
19 D2   **Bowen** Austr.
97 C3   **Bow Island** Can.
108 B3 **Bowling Green** KY U.S.A.
108 C2 **Bowling Green** OH U.S.A.
104 C1 **Bowman** U.S.A.
69 D3   **Boxberg** Ger.
68 B2   **Boxtel** Neth.
48 B1   **Boyabat** Turkey
39 B3   **Boyang** China
65 B2   **Boyle** Rep. of Ireland
65 C2   **Boyne** r. Rep. of Ireland
104 B2 **Boysen Reservoir** U.S.A.
120 B3 **Boyuibe** Bol.
79 C3   **Bozburun** Turkey
79 C3   **Bozcaada** i. Turkey
79 C3   **Bozdağ** mt. Turkey
79 C3   **Boz Dağları** mts Turkey
79 C3   **Bozdoğan** Turkey
102 D1 **Bozeman** U.S.A.
86 B2   **Bozoum** C.A.R.
79 D3   **Bozüyük** Turkey
77 C2   **Brač** i. Croatia
98 C2   **Bracebridge** Can.
99 D2   **Brachet, Lac au** l. Can.
67 C3   **Bracknell** U.K.
77 C2   **Bradano** r. Italy
111 D3 **Bradenton** U.S.A.
66 C2   **Bradford** U.K.
109 D2 **Bradford** U.S.A.
107 D2 **Brady** U.S.A.
64 C2   **Braemar** U.K.
74 B1   **Braga** Port.
119 D2 **Bragança** Brazil
74 B1   **Bragança** Port.
123 C2 **Bragança Paulista** Brazil
57 D3   **Brahin** Belarus
41 C3   **Brahmapur** India
30 A1   **Brahmaputra** r. China/India
78 C1   **Brăila** Romania
105 E1 **Brainerd** U.S.A.
67 D3   **Braintree** U.K.
68 B2   **Braives** Belgium
69 D1   **Brake (Unterweser)** Ger.
68 D1   **Bramsche** Ger.
118 B2 **Branco** r. Brazil
69 F1   **Brandenburg** Ger.
97 E3   **Brandon** Can.
65 A2   **Brandon Mountain** Rep. of Ireland
90 B3   **Brandvlei** S. Africa
71 D1   **Braniewo** Pol.
98 B2   **Brantford** Can.
99 D2   **Bras d'Or Lake** Can.
123 D1 **Brasil, Planalto do** plat. Brazil
122 C1 **Brasilândia** Brazil
122 C1 **Brasília** Brazil
123 D1 **Brasília de Minas** Brazil
56 C2   **Braslaw** Belarus
78 C1   **Braşov** Romania
71 D2   **Bratislava** Slovakia
51 H3   **Bratsk** Rus. Fed.
69 E1   **Braunau am Inn** Austria
60 □A2 **Brautarholt** Iceland
         Bravo del Norte, Río r. Mex./U.S.A. see **Rio Grande**
103 C4 **Brawley** U.S.A.
65 C2   **Bray** Rep. of Ireland
118 C2 **Brazil** country S. America
107 D3 **Brazos** r. U.S.A.
86 B3   **Brazzaville** Congo
77 C2   **Brčko** Bos.-Herz.
64 C2   **Brechin** U.K.
68 B2   **Brecht** Belgium

107 D2 **Breckenridge** U.S.A.
71 D2   **Břeclav** Czech Rep.
67 B3   **Brecon** U.K.
67 B3   **Brecon Beacons** reg. U.K.
68 B2   **Breda** Neth.
90 B3   **Bredasdorp** S. Africa
70 B2   **Bregenz** Austria
60 H1   **Breivikbotn** Norway
60 E3   **Brekstad** Norway
69 D1   **Bremen** Ger.
69 D1   **Bremerhaven** Ger.
102 B1 **Bremerton** U.S.A.
69 D1   **Bremervörde** Ger.
107 D2 **Brenham** U.S.A.
76 B1   **Brennero** Italy
70 C2   **Brenner Pass** Austria/Italy
67 D3   **Brentwood** U.K.
76 B1   **Brescia** Italy
76 B1   **Bressanone** Italy
64 □   **Bressay** i. U.K.
72 B2   **Bressuire** France
56 B3   **Brest** Belarus
72 B2   **Brest** France
110 C3 **Breton Sound** b. U.S.A.
119 C2 **Breves** Brazil
21 C1   **Brewarrina** Austr.
102 C1 **Brewster** U.S.A.
57 E2   **Breytovo** Rus. Fed.
77 C1   **Brezovo Polje** hill Croatia
86 C2   **Bria** C.A.R.
73 D3   **Briançon** France
58 B2   **Briceni** Moldova
67 B3   **Bridgend** U.K.
109 E2 **Bridgeport** CT U.S.A.
104 C2 **Bridgeport** NE U.S.A.
115 E3 **Bridgetown** Barbados
99 D2   **Bridgewater** Can.
67 B3   **Bridgwater** U.K.
66 C1   **Bridlington** U.K.
66 C1   **Bridlington Bay** U.K.
73 D2   **Brig** Switz.
102 D2 **Brigham City** U.S.A.
22 B3   **Brighton** N.Z.
67 C3   **Brighton** U.K.
73 D3   **Brignoles** France
69 D2   **Brilon** Ger.
77 C2   **Brindisi** Italy
21 D1   **Brisbane** Austr.
67 B3   **Bristol** U.K.
111 D1 **Bristol** U.S.A.
67 A3   **Bristol Channel** est. U.K.
96 B2   **British Columbia** prov. Can.
24 C6   **British Indian Ocean Territory** terr. Indian Ocean
91 C2   **Brits** S. Africa
90 B3   **Britstown** S. Africa
72 C2   **Brive-la-Gaillarde** France
74 C1   **Briviesca** Spain
71 D2   **Brno** Czech Rep.
111 D2 **Broad** r. U.S.A.
98 C1   **Broadback** r. Can.
64 A1   **Broad Bay** U.K.
64 B3   **Broad Law** hill U.K.
104 B1 **Broadus** U.S.A.
97 D2   **Brochet** Can.
97 D2   **Brochet, Lac** l. Can.
69 E1   **Bröckel** Ger.
94 D1   **Brock Island** Can.
98 C2   **Brockville** Can.
95 F2   **Brodeur Peninsula** Can.
64 B3   **Brodick** U.K.
71 D1   **Brodnica** Pol.
58 B1   **Brody** Ukr.
107 D1 **Broken Arrow** U.S.A.
105 D2 **Broken Bow** U.S.A.
20 B2   **Broken Hill** Austr.
67 B2   **Bromsgrove** U.K.
61 E4   **Brønderslev** Denmark
60 F2   **Brønnøysund** Norway
32 A2   **Brooke's Point** Phil.

68 B2 **Beaumont** Belgium
22 A3 **Beaumont** N.Z.
107 E2 **Beaumont** U.S.A.
73 C2 **Beaune** France
68 B2 **Beauraing** Belgium
97 E2 **Beauséjour** Can.
72 C2 **Beauvais** France
97 D2 **Beauval** Can.
97 D2 **Beaver** r. Can.
103 D3 **Beaver** U.S.A.
94 B2 **Beaver Creek** Can.
108 B2 **Beaver Dam** U.S.A.
97 E2 **Beaver Hill Lake** Can.
108 B1 **Beaver Island** U.S.A.
96 C2 **Beaverlodge** Can.
42 B2 **Beawar** India
122 C2 **Bebedouro** Brazil
69 D2 **Bebra** Ger.
74 B1 **Becerreá** Spain
82 B1 **Béchar** Alg.
108 C3 **Beckley** U.S.A.
85 B4 **Bedelē** Eth.
67 C2 **Bedford** U.K.
83 C2 **Bedford** U.S.A.
68 C1 **Bedum** Neth.
21 D2 **Beecroft Peninsula** Austr.
69 F1 **Beelitz** Ger.
21 C1 **Beenleigh** Austr.
48 B2 **Be'ér Sheva'** Israel
107 D3 **Beeville** U.S.A.
21 C3 **Bega** Austr.
75 D1 **Begur, Cap de** c. Spain
49 D2 **Behshahr** Iran
37 E1 **Bei'an** China
39 A3 **Beihai** China
38 B2 **Beijing** China
68 C1 **Beilen** Neth.
64 B3 **Beinn an Oir** hill U.K.
64 A2 **Beinn Mhòr** hill U.K.
89 C2 **Beira** Moz.
48 B2 **Beirut** Lebanon
91 C1 **Beitbridge** Zimbabwe
74 B2 **Beja** Port.
83 C1 **Bejaïa** Alg.
74 B1 **Béjar** Spain
42 A2 **Beji** r. Pak.
44 B2 **Bekdash** Turkm.
71 E2 **Békés** Hungary
71 E2 **Békéscsaba** Hungary
89 □D3 **Bekily** Madag.
42 A2 **Bela** Pak.
91 C1 **Bela-Bela** S. Africa
86 B2 **Bélabo** Cameroon
77 D2 **Bela Crkva** Yugo.
29 C1 **Belaga** Sarawak Malaysia
29 C1 **Delangiran** Indon.
56 C3 **Belarus** country Europe
    Belau country
    N. Pacific Ocean see **Palau**
91 D2 **Bela Vista** Moz.
28 A1 **Belawan** Indon.
51 M2 **Belaya** r. Rus. Fed.
71 D1 **Belchatów** Pol.
96 C1 **Belcher Islands** Can.
85 C4 **Beledweyne** Somalia
119 D2 **Belém** Brazil
106 B2 **Belen** U.S.A.
57 D2 **Belev** Rus. Fed.
65 D1 **Belfast** U.K.
109 F2 **Belfast** U.S.A.
73 D2 **Belfort** France
41 B3 **Belgaum** India
68 B2 **Belgium** country Europe
59 D1 **Belgorod** Rus. Fed.
102 D1 **Belgrade** U.S.A.
77 D2 **Belgrade** Yugo.
83 D4 **Beli** Nigeria
28 B2 **Belinyu** Indon.
29 B2 **Belitung** i. Indon.
114 B3 **Belize** Belize

114 B3 **Belize** country
    Central America
51 K1 **Bel'kovskiy, Ostrov** i.
    Rus. Fed.
96 B2 **Bella Bella** Can.
72 C2 **Bellac** France
96 B2 **Bella Coola** Can.
21 C1 **Bellata** Austr.
104 C2 **Belle Fourche** U.S.A.
104 C2 **Belle Fourche** r. U.S.A.
111 D3 **Belle Glade** U.S.A.
72 B2 **Belle-Île** i. France
99 E1 **Belle Isle** i. Can.
99 E1 **Belle Isle, Strait of** Can.
98 C2 **Belleville** Can.
108 B3 **Belleville** IL U.S.A.
105 D3 **Belleville** KS U.S.A.
102 B1 **Bellevue** U.S.A.
102 B1 **Bellingham** U.S.A.
23 O2 **Bellingshausen Sea**
    Antarctica
73 D2 **Bellinzona** Switz.
76 D1 **Belluno** Italy
90 A3 **Bellville** S. Africa
123 E1 **Belmonte** Brazil
114 B3 **Belmopan** Belize
65 B1 **Belmullet** Rep. of Ireland
37 E1 **Belogorsk** Rus. Fed.
89 □D3 **Beloha** Madag.
123 D1 **Belo Horizonte** Brazil
108 B2 **Beloit** U.S.A.
54 C2 **Belomorsk** Rus. Fed.
59 D3 **Belorechensk** Rus. Fed.
55 E3 **Beloretsk** Rus. Fed.
    Belorussia country Europe
    see **Belarus**
54 F2 **Beloyarskiy** Rus. Fed.
54 C2 **Beloye, Ozero** l. Rus. Fed.
    Beloye More sea Rus. Fed.
    see **White Sea**
54 C2 **Belozersk** Rus. Fed.
45 E2 **Belukha, Gora** mt.
    Kazakh./Rus. Fed.
54 D2 **Belush'ye** Rus. Fed.
57 D2 **Belyy** Rus. Fed.
50 F2 **Belyy, Ostrov** i. Rus. Fed.
69 F1 **Belzig** Ger.
105 E1 **Bemidji** U.S.A.
86 C3 **Bena Dibele**
    Dem. Rep. Congo
21 C3 **Benalla** Austr.
74 B1 **Benavente** Spain
64 A2 **Benbecula** i. U.K.
102 B2 **Bend** U.S.A.
91 C3 **Bendearg** mt. S. Africa
20 B3 **Bendigo** Austr.
89 C2 **Bene** Moz.
70 C2 **Benešov** Czech Rep.
77 B2 **Benevento** Italy
127 C2 **Bengal, Bay of** sea
    Indian Ocean
38 B2 **Bengbu** China
29 B1 **Bengkayang** Indon.
28 B2 **Bengkulu** Indon.
88 A2 **Benguela** Angola
64 B1 **Ben Hope** hill U.K.
120 B2 **Beni** r. Bol.
87 C2 **Beni** Dem. Rep. Congo
82 B1 **Beni-Abbès** Alg.
75 C2 **Benidorm** Spain
82 B1 **Beni Mellal** Morocco
82 C4 **Benin** country Africa
82 C4 **Benin, Bight of** g. Africa
83 C4 **Benin City** Nigeria
84 B2 **Beni Suef** Egypt
121 C4 **Benito Juárez** Arg.
118 B2 **Benjamin Constant** Brazil
112 A1 **Benjamín Hill** Mex.
27 C3 **Benjina** Indon.
64 B2 **Ben Lawers** mt. U.K.

64 B2 **Ben Lomond** hill U.K.
64 C2 **Ben Macdui** mt. U.K.
64 A2 **Ben More** hill U.K.
22 B2 **Benmore, Lake** N.Z.
64 B1 **Ben More Assynt** hill U.K.
96 A2 **Bennett** Can.
51 K1 **Bennetta, Ostrov** i.
    Rus. Fed.
64 B2 **Ben Nevis** mt. U.K.
109 E2 **Bennington** U.S.A.
91 C2 **Benoni** S. Africa
69 D3 **Bensheim** Ger.
106 A2 **Benson** U.S.A.
26 C3 **Benteng** Indon.
108 B2 **Benton Harbor** U.S.A.
110 B1 **Bentonville** U.S.A.
83 C4 **Benue** r. Nigeria
65 B1 **Benwee Head** hd
    Rep. of Ireland
64 B2 **Ben Wyvis** mt. U.K.
38 C1 **Benxi** China
    Beograd Yugo. see **Belgrade**
43 C2 **Beohari** India
35 B4 **Beppu** Japan
77 C2 **Berane** Yugo.
77 C2 **Berat** Albania
27 C3 **Berau, Teluk** b. Indon.
84 B3 **Berber** Sudan
85 C3 **Berbera** Somalia
86 B2 **Berbérati** C.A.R.
72 C1 **Berck** France
59 D2 **Berdyans'k** Ukr.
58 B2 **Berdychiv** Ukr.
58 A2 **Berehove** Ukr.
27 D3 **Bereina** P.N.G.
46 A2 **Berenice** Egypt
97 E2 **Berens River** Can.
58 B2 **Berezhany** Ukr.
58 C2 **Berezivka** Ukr.
58 B1 **Berezne** Ukr.
54 D2 **Bereznik** Rus. Fed.
54 E3 **Berezniki** Rus. Fed.
54 F2 **Berezovo** Rus. Fed.
75 D1 **Berga** Spain
79 C3 **Bergama** Turkey
76 A1 **Bergamo** Italy
70 C1 **Bergen** Mecklenburg-
    Vorpommern Ger.
69 D1 **Bergen** Niedersachsen Ger.
61 E3 **Bergen** Norway
68 B2 **Bergen op Zoom** Neth.
72 C3 **Bergerac** France
68 C2 **Bergheim (Erft)** Ger.
68 C2 **Bergisch Gladbach** Ger.
90 A1 **Bergland** Namibia
60 H2 **Bergsviken** Sweden
51 M3 **Beringa, Ostrov** i. Rus. Fed.
68 B2 **Beringen** Belgium
92 B1 **Bering Sea** N. Pacific Ocean
51 N2 **Bering Strait**
    Can./U.S.A.
103 B3 **Berkeley** U.S.A.
68 B1 **Berkhout** Neth.
23 O2 **Berkner Island** Antarctica
78 B2 **Berkovitsa** Bulg.
60 I1 **Berlevåg** Norway
69 F1 **Berlin** Ger.
109 E2 **Berlin** U.S.A.
69 E2 **Berlingerode** Ger.
21 D3 **Bermagui** Austr.
112 B2 **Bermejillo** Mex.
120 B3 **Bermejo** Bol.
93 F4 **Bermuda** terr.
    N. Atlantic Ocean
73 D2 **Bern** Switz.
69 E2 **Bernburg (Saale)** Ger.
95 F2 **Bernier Bay** Can.
68 C3 **Bernkastel-Kues** Ger.
89 □D3 **Beroroha** Madag.
20 B2 **Berri** Austr.

110 B2 **Brookhaven** U.S.A.
102 B2 **Brookings** OR U.S.A.
105 D2 **Brookings** SD U.S.A.
97 C2 **Brooks** Can.
94 B2 **Brooks Range** mts U.S.A.
111 D3 **Brooksville** U.S.A.
64 B2 **Broom, Loch** inlet U.K.
18 B1 **Broome** Austr.
102 B2 **Brothers** U.S.A.
 Broughton Island Can. see
 Qikiqtarjuaq
58 C1 **Brovary** Ukr.
107 C2 **Brownfield** U.S.A.
96 C3 **Browning** U.S.A.
110 C1 **Brownsville** TN U.S.A.
107 D3 **Brownsville** TX U.S.A.
107 D2 **Brownwood** U.S.A.
60 □A2 **Brú** Iceland
72 C1 **Bruay-la-Bussière** France
108 B1 **Bruce Crossing** U.S.A.
71 D2 **Bruck an der Mur** Austria
68 A2 **Bruges** Belgium
 Brugge Belgium see **Bruges**
96 C2 **Brûlé** Can.
119 D3 **Brumado** Brazil
61 F3 **Brumunddal** Norway
29 C1 **Brunei** country Asia
70 C2 **Brunico** Italy
69 D1 **Brunsbüttel** Ger.
111 D2 **Brunswick** GA U.S.A.
109 F2 **Brunswick** ME U.S.A.
21 D1 **Brunswick Head** Austr.
104 C2 **Brush** U.S.A.
68 B2 **Brussels** Belgium
 Bruxelles Belgium see
 Brussels
107 D2 **Bryan** U.S.A.
57 D3 **Bryansk** Rus. Fed.
59 D2 **Bryn'kovskaya** Rus. Fed.
59 D2 **Bryukhovetskaya** Rus. Fed.
71 D1 **Brzeg** Pol.
82 A3 **Buba** Guinea-Bissau
48 B2 **Bucak** Turkey
118 A1 **Bucaramanga** Col.
21 C3 **Buchan** Austr.
82 A4 **Buchanan** Liberia
78 C2 **Bucharest** Romania
69 D1 **Bucholz in der Nordheide**
 Ger.
78 C1 **Bucin, Pasul** pass Romania
69 D1 **Bückeburg** Ger.
106 A2 **Buckeye** U.S.A.
64 C2 **Buckhaven** U.K.
64 C2 **Buckie** U.K.
19 C1 **Buckingham Bay** Austr.
19 D2 **Buckland Tableland** reg.
 Austr.
20 A2 **Buckleboo** Austr.
109 F2 **Bucksport** U.S.A.
 Bucureşti Romania see
 Bucharest
57 D3 **Buda-Kashalyova** Belarus
71 D2 **Budapest** Hungary
43 B2 **Budaun** India
76 A2 **Buddusò** Sardinia Italy
67 A3 **Bude** U.K.
55 D4 **Budennovsk** Rus. Fed.
57 D2 **Budogoshch'** Rus. Fed.
76 A2 **Budoni** Sardinia Italy
86 A2 **Buea** Cameroon
112 B2 **Buenaventura** Mex.
74 C1 **Buendia, Embalse de** resr
 Spain
123 D1 **Buenópolis** Brazil
121 C4 **Buenos Aires** Arg.
121 A5 **Buenos Aires, Lago** l.
 Arg./Chile
109 E2 **Buffalo** NY U.S.A.
104 C1 **Buffalo** SD U.S.A.
104 B2 **Buffalo** WY U.S.A.

97 D2 **Buffalo Narrows** Can.
90 A2 **Buffels** watercourse S. Africa
78 C2 **Buftea** Romania
71 E1 **Bug** r. Pol.
29 C2 **Bugel, Tanjung** pt Indon.
77 C2 **Bugojno** Bos.-Herz.
32 A2 **Bugsuk** i. Phil.
55 E3 **Buguruslan** Rus. Fed.
78 C1 **Buhuşi** Romania
67 B2 **Builth Wells** U.K.
37 D1 **Buir Nur** l. Mongolia
88 A3 **Buitepos** Namibia
77 D2 **Bujanovac** Yugo.
87 C3 **Bujumbura** Burundi
37 D1 **Bukachacha** Rus. Fed.
87 C3 **Bukavu** Dem. Rep. Congo
44 C3 **Bukhara** Uzbek.
28 B2 **Bukittinggi** Indon.
87 D3 **Bukoba** Tanz.
21 D2 **Bulahdelal** Austr.
89 B3 **Bulawayo** Zimbabwe
79 C3 **Buldan** Turkey
91 D2 **Bulembu** Swaziland
37 C1 **Bulgan** Mongolia
78 C2 **Bulgaria** country Europe
22 B2 **Buller** r. N.Z.
20 B1 **Bulloo Downs** Austr.
90 A1 **Büllsport** Namibia
26 C3 **Bulukumba** Indon.
86 B3 **Bulungu** Dem. Rep. Congo
86 C2 **Bumba** Dem. Rep. Congo
30 A1 **Bumhkang** Myanmar
86 B3 **Buna** Dem. Rep. Congo
18 A3 **Bunbury** Austr.
65 C1 **Buncrana** Rep. of Ireland
87 D3 **Bunda** Tanz.
19 E2 **Bundaberg** Austr.
21 D2 **Bundarra** Austr.
42 B2 **Bundi** India
65 B1 **Bundoran** Rep. of Ireland
21 C3 **Bungendore** Austr.
35 B4 **Bungo-suidō** sea chan.
 Japan
87 D2 **Bunia** Dem. Rep. Congo
86 C3 **Bunianga** Dem. Rep. Congo
31 B2 **Buôn Mê Thuôt** Vietnam
87 D3 **Bura** Kenya
43 C1 **Burang** China
85 C4 **Burao** Somalia
46 B2 **Buraydah** Saudi Arabia
68 D2 **Burbach** Ger.
48 B2 **Burdur** Turkey
85 B3 **Burē** Eth.
67 D2 **Bure** r. U.K.
78 C2 **Burgas** Bulg.
69 E1 **Burg bei Magdeburg** Ger.
69 E1 **Burgdorf** Niedersachsen Ger.
69 E1 **Burgdorf** Niedersachsen Ger.
69 E2 **Burgeo** Can.
91 D1 **Burgersfort** S. Africa
68 A2 **Burgh-Haamstede** Neth.
113 C2 **Burgos** Mex.
74 C1 **Burgos** Spain
79 C3 **Burhaniye** Turkey
42 B2 **Burhanpur** India
69 D1 **Burhave (Butjadingen)** Ger.
99 E2 **Burin** Can.
119 D2 **Buriti Bravo** Brazil
123 C1 **Buritis** Brazil
19 C1 **Burketown** Austr.
82 B3 **Burkina** country Africa
102 D2 **Burley** U.S.A.
104 C3 **Burlington** CO U.S.A.
105 E2 **Burlington** IA U.S.A.
111 E1 **Burlington** NC U.S.A.
109 E2 **Burlington** VT U.S.A.
 Burma country Asia see
 Myanmar
102 B2 **Burney** U.S.A.
19 D4 **Burnie** Austr.

66 B2 **Burnley** U.K.
102 C2 **Burns** U.S.A.
96 B2 **Burns Lake** Can.
45 E2 **Burqin** China
20 A2 **Burra** Austr.
77 D2 **Burrel** Albania
65 B2 **Burren** reg. Rep. of Ireland
21 C2 **Burrendong Reservoir**
 Austr.
21 C2 **Burren Junction** Austr.
75 C2 **Burriana** Spain
21 C2 **Burrinjuck Reservoir** Austr.
112 B2 **Burro, Serranías del** mts
 Mex.
79 C2 **Bursa** Turkey
84 B2 **Bûr Safâga** Egypt
 Bûr Sa'îd Egypt see
 Port Said
98 C1 **Burton, Lac** l. Can.
65 B1 **Burtonport** Rep. of Ireland
67 C2 **Burton upon Trent** U.K.
27 C3 **Buru** i. Indon.
87 D3 **Burundi** country Africa
87 C3 **Bururi** Burundi
59 C1 **Buryn'** Ukr.
44 B2 **Burynshyk** Kazakh.
67 D2 **Bury St Edmunds** U.K.
86 C3 **Busanga** Dem. Rep. Congo
47 C2 **Büshehr** Iran
87 D3 **Bushenyi** Uganda
86 C2 **Businga** Dem. Rep. Congo
18 A3 **Busselton** Austr.
107 C3 **Bustamante** Mex.
32 A1 **Busuanga** Phil.
86 C2 **Buta** Dem. Rep. Congo
87 C3 **Butare** Rwanda
91 C2 **Butha Buthe** Lesotho
108 D2 **Butler** U.S.A.
27 C3 **Buton** i. Indon.
102 D1 **Butte** U.S.A.
28 B1 **Butterworth** Malaysia
64 A1 **Butt of Lewis** hd U.K.
97 E2 **Button Bay** Can.
32 B2 **Butuan** Phil.
59 E1 **Buturlinovka** Rus. Fed.
43 C2 **Butwal** Nepal
69 D1 **Butzbach** Ger.
85 C4 **Buulobarde** Somalia
85 C5 **Buur Gaabo** Somalia
85 C4 **Buurhabaka** Somalia
69 D1 **Buxtehude** Ger.
57 F2 **Buy** Rus. Fed.
79 C3 **Buynaksk** Rus. Fed.
78 C1 **Buzău** Romania
89 C2 **Búzi** Moz.
55 E3 **Buzuluk** Rus. Fed.
56 C3 **Byala** Bulg.
56 C3 **Byalynichy** Belarus
56 D3 **Byarezina** r. Belarus
56 B3 **Byaroza** Belarus
71 D1 **Bydgoszcz** Pol.
56 C3 **Byerazino** Belarus
56 C2 **Byeshankovichy** Belarus
57 D3 **Bykhaw** Belarus
95 F2 **Bylot Island** Can.
21 C2 **Byrock** Austr.
21 D1 **Byron Bay** Austr.
51 J2 **Bytantay** r. Rus. Fed.
71 D1 **Bytom** Pol.
71 D1 **Bytów** Pol.

C

122 B2 **Caarapó** Brazil
32 B1 **Cabanatuan** Phil.
85 C3 **Cabdul Qaadir** Somalia

74 B2 **Cabeza del Buey** Spain
120 B2 **Cabezas** Bol.
118 A1 **Cabimas** Venez.
88 A1 **Cabinda** Angola
86 B3 **Cabinda** prov. Angola
123 D2 **Cabo Frio** Brazil
123 D2 **Cabo Frio, Ilha do** i. Brazil
98 C2 **Cabonga, Réservoir** resr Can.
19 E2 **Caboolture** Austr.
118 A2 **Cabo Pantoja** Peru
112 A1 **Caborca** Mex.
99 D2 **Cabot Strait** Can.
123 D1 **Cabral, Serra do** mts Brazil
75 D2 **Cabrera** i. Spain
97 D2 **Cabri** Can.
75 C2 **Cabriel** r. Spain
120 C3 **Caçador** Brazil
77 D2 **Čačak** Yugo.
76 A2 **Caccia, Capo c.** Sardinia Italy
119 C3 **Cáceres** Brazil
74 B2 **Cáceres** Spain
96 B2 **Cache Creek** Can.
82 A3 **Cacheu** Guinea-Bissau
119 C2 **Cachimbo, Serra do** hills Brazil
122 B1 **Cachoeira Alta** Brazil
123 D2 **Cachoeiro de Itapemirim** Brazil
82 A3 **Cacine** Guinea-Bissau
88 A2 **Cacolo** Angola
122 B1 **Caçu** Brazil
71 D2 **Čadca** Slovakia
69 D1 **Cadenberge** Ger.
113 B2 **Cadereyta** Mex.
108 B2 **Cadillac** U.S.A.
74 B2 **Cádiz** Spain
74 B2 **Cádiz, Golfo de g.** Spain
96 C2 **Cadotte Lake** Can.
72 B2 **Caen** France
66 A2 **Caernarfon** U.K.
66 A2 **Caernarfon Bay** U.K.
120 B3 **Cafayate** Arg.
32 B2 **Cagayan de Oro** Phil.
76 B2 **Cagli** Italy
76 A3 **Cagliari** Sardinia Italy
76 A3 **Cagliari, Golfo di b.** Sardinia Italy
65 B3 **Caha Mountains** Rep. of Ireland
65 A3 **Cahermore** Rep. of Ireland
65 A3 **Cahersiveen** Rep. of Ireland
65 C2 **Cahir** Rep. of Ireland
89 C2 **Cahora Bassa, Lago de** resr Moz.
65 C3 **Cahore Point** Rep. of Ireland
72 C3 **Cahors** France
58 B2 **Cahul** Moldova
89 C2 **Caia** Moz.
119 C3 **Caiabis, Serra dos** hills Brazil
88 B2 **Caianda** Angola
122 B1 **Caiapó, Serra do** mts Brazil
122 B1 **Caiapônia** Brazil
115 C2 **Caicos Islands** Turks and Caicos Is
64 C2 **Cairngorm Mountains** U.K.
66 A1 **Cairnryan** U.K.
19 D1 **Cairns** Austr.
84 B1 **Cairo** Egypt
66 C2 **Caistor** U.K.
88 A2 **Caiundo** Angola
118 A2 **Cajamarca** Peru
77 C1 **Čakovec** Croatia
91 C3 **Cala** S. Africa
118 B1 **Calabozo** Venez.
78 B2 **Calafat** Romania
121 A6 **Calafate** Arg.
75 C1 **Calahorra** Spain
72 C1 **Calais** France

109 F1 **Calais** U.S.A.
120 B3 **Calama** Chile
32 A1 **Calamian Group** is Phil.
75 C1 **Calamocha** Spain
88 A1 **Calandula** Angola
28 A1 **Calang** Indon.
83 E1 **Calanscio Sand Sea** des. Libya
32 B1 **Calapan** Phil.
78 C2 **Călăraşi** Romania
75 C1 **Calatayud** Spain
32 B1 **Calayan** i. Phil.
32 B1 **Calbayog** Phil.
119 E2 **Calcanhar, Ponta do** pt Brazil
119 C1 **Calçoene** Brazil
      Calcutta India see Kolkata
74 B2 **Caldas da Rainha** Port.
122 C1 **Caldas Novas** Brazil
120 A3 **Caldera** Chile
102 C2 **Caldwell** U.S.A.
91 C3 **Caledon** r. Lesotho/S. Africa
90 A3 **Caledon** S. Africa
121 B5 **Caleta Olivia** Arg.
66 A1 **Calf of Man** i. Isle of Man
96 C2 **Calgary** Can.
118 A1 **Cali** Col.
41 B3 **Calicut** India
103 D3 **Caliente** U.S.A.
103 B2 **California state** U.S.A.
112 A1 **California, Golfo de g.** Mex.
103 B3 **California Aqueduct** canal U.S.A.
90 B3 **Calitzdorp** S. Africa
113 C2 **Qalkini** Mex.
20 B1 **Callabonna, Lake** salt flat Austr.
64 B2 **Callander** U.K.
118 A3 **Callao** Peru
76 B3 **Caltagirone** Sicily Italy
76 B3 **Caltanissetta** Sicily Italy
88 A2 **Caluquembe** Angola
85 D3 **Caluula** Somalia
73 D3 **Calvi** Corsica France
75 D2 **Calvià** Spain
112 B2 **Calvillo** Mex.
90 A3 **Calvinia** S. Africa
77 C2 **Calvo, Monte** mt. Italy
112 B2 **Camacho** Mex.
88 A2 **Camacupa** Angola
114 C2 **Camagüey** Cuba
118 A3 **Camana** Peru
122 B1 **Camapuã** Brazil
113 C2 **Camargo** Mex.
31 B3 **Ca Mau** Vietnam
31 B2 **Cambodia** country Asia
67 A3 **Camborne** U.K.
73 C1 **Cambrai** France
67 B2 **Cambrian Mountains** U.K.
22 C1 **Cambridge** N.Z.
67 D2 **Cambridge** U.K.
109 E2 **Cambridge** MA U.S.A.
109 D3 **Cambridge** MD U.S.A.
105 E1 **Cambridge** MN U.S.A.
108 C2 **Cambridge** OH U.S.A.
99 D1 **Cambrien, Lac** l. Can.
21 D3 **Camden** Austr.
110 B2 **Camden** AR U.S.A.
109 F2 **Camden** ME U.S.A.
86 B2 **Cameroon** country Africa
119 D2 **Cametá** Brazil
32 B1 **Camiguin** i. Phil.
120 B3 **Camiri** Bol.
119 D2 **Camocim** Brazil
19 C1 **Camooweal** Austr.
31 A3 **Camorta** i. India
121 A5 **Campana, Isla** i. Chile
90 B2 **Campbell** S. Africa
22 B2 **Campbell, Cape** N.Z.
96 B2 **Campbell River** Can.

108 B3 **Campbellsville** U.S.A.
99 D2 **Campbellton** Can.
64 B3 **Campbeltown** U.K.
113 C3 **Campeche** Mex.
113 C3 **Campeche, Bahía de** g. Mex.
20 B3 **Camperdown** Austr.
78 C1 **Câmpina** Romania
119 E2 **Campina Grande** Brazil
122 C2 **Campinas** Brazil
122 C1 **Campina Verde** Brazil
76 B2 **Campobasso** Italy
123 C2 **Campo Belo** Brazil
122 C1 **Campo Florido** Brazil
120 B3 **Campo Gallo** Arg.
122 B2 **Campo Grande** Brazil
119 D2 **Campo Maior** Brazil
74 B2 **Campo Maior** Port.
122 B2 **Campo Mourão** Brazil
123 D2 **Campos** Brazil
123 C1 **Campos Altos** Brazil
123 C2 **Campos do Jordão** Brazil
78 C1 **Câmpulung** Romania
106 A2 **Camp Verde** U.S.A.
31 B2 **Cam Ranh** Vietnam
96 C2 **Camrose** Can.
97 D2 **Camsell Portage** Can.
79 C2 **Çan** Turkey
94 F3 **Canada** country N. America
107 C1 **Canadian** U.S.A.
107 D1 **Canadian** r. U.S.A.
79 C2 **Çanakkale** Turkey
112 A1 **Cananea** Mex.
122 C2 **Cananéia** Brazil
      Canarias, Islas terr. N. Atlantic Ocean see Canary Islands
82 A2 **Canary Islands** terr. N. Atlantic Ocean
123 C1 **Canastra, Serra da** mts Brazil
112 B2 **Canatlán** Mex.
111 D3 **Canaveral, Cape** U.S.A.
123 E1 **Canavieiras** Brazil
21 C3 **Canberra** Austr.
113 C2 **Cancún** Mex.
79 C3 **Çandarlı** Turkey
113 C3 **Candelaria** Mex.
97 D2 **Candle Lake** l. Can.
88 A2 **Cangamba** Angola
74 B1 **Cangas del Narcea** Spain
120 C4 **Canguçu** Brazil
38 B2 **Cangzhou** China
99 D1 **Caniapiscau** Can.
99 D1 **Caniapiscau** r. Can.
99 C1 **Caniapiscau, Lac** l. Can.
76 B3 **Canicattì** Sicily Italy
119 E2 **Canindé** Brazil
112 B2 **Cañitas de Felipe Pescador** Mex.
48 B1 **Çankırı** Turkey
96 C2 **Canmore** Can.
64 A2 **Canna** i. U.K.
41 B3 **Cannanore** India
73 D3 **Cannes** France
67 B2 **Cannock** U.K.
21 C3 **Cann River** Austr.
120 C3 **Canoas** Brazil
97 D2 **Canoe Lake** l. Can.
122 B3 **Canoinhas** Brazil
104 B3 **Canon City** U.S.A.
97 D2 **Canora** Can.
21 C2 **Canowindra** Austr.
74 B1 **Cantabrian Sea** sea Spain
74 C1 **Cantábrica, Cordillera** mts Spain
67 D3 **Canterbury** U.K.
22 B2 **Canterbury Bight** b. N.Z.
22 B2 **Canterbury Plains** N.Z.
31 B2 **Cân Thơ** Vietnam
119 D2 **Canto do Buriti** Brazil

Canton China *see* Guangzhou
110 C2 Canton *MS* U.S.A.
108 C2 Canton *OH* U.S.A.
107 C1 Canyon U.S.A.
102 D1 Canyon Ferry Lake U.S.A.
30 B1 Cao Băng Vietnam
122 C2 Capão Bonito Brazil
123 D2 Caparaó, Serra de *mts* Brazil
19 D4 Cape Barren Island Austr.
20 A3 Cape Borda Austr.
99 D2 Cape Breton Island Can.
82 B4 Cape Coast Ghana
109 E2 Cape Cod Bay U.S.A.
95 F2 Cape Dorset Can.
111 E2 Cape Fear *r.* U.S.A.
105 F3 Cape Girardeau U.S.A.
123 D1 Capelinha Brazil
68 B2 Capelle aan de IJssel Neth.
88 A1 Capenda-Camulemba Angola
90 A3 Cape Town S. Africa
80 B2 Cape Verde *country* N. Atlantic Ocean
19 D1 Cape York Peninsula Austr.
115 C3 Cap-Haïtien Haiti
119 D2 Capim *r.* Brazil
77 C2 Čapljina Bos.-Herz.
77 B3 Capo d'Orlando *Sicily* Italy
76 A2 Capraia, Isola di *i.* Italy
76 A2 Caprara, Punta *pt* Sardinia Italy
76 B2 Capri, Isola di *i.* Italy
88 B2 Caprivi Strip *reg.* Namibia
118 B2 Caquetá *r.* Col.
78 B2 Caracal Romania
118 B1 Caracas Venez.
119 D2 Caracol Brazil
123 C2 Caraguatatuba Brazil
121 A4 Carahue Chile
123 D1 Caraí Brazil
123 D2 Carangola Brazil
78 B1 Caransebeş Romania
99 D2 Caraquet Can.
114 B3 Caratasca, Laguna *lag.* Hond.
123 D1 Caratinga Brazil
118 B2 Carauari Brazil
75 C2 Caravaca de la Cruz Spain
123 E1 Caravelas Brazil
97 E3 Carberry Can.
112 A2 Carbó Mex.
76 A3 Carbonara, Capo *c.* Sardinia Italy
104 B3 Carbondale *CO* U.S.A.
108 B3 Carbondale *IL* U.S.A.
99 E2 Carbonear Can.
123 D1 Carbonita Brazil
75 C2 Carcaixent Spain
72 C3 Carcassonne France
96 A1 Carcross Can.
113 C3 Cárdenas Mex.
67 B3 Cardiff U.K.
67 A2 Cardigan U.K.
67 A2 Cardigan Bay U.K.
96 C3 Cardston Can.
78 B1 Carei Romania
72 B2 Carentan France
18 B2 Carey, Lake *salt flat* Austr.
123 D2 Cariacica Brazil
114 B3 Caribbean Sea N. Atlantic Ocean
109 F1 Caribou U.S.A.
98 B1 Caribou Lake Can.
96 C2 Caribou Mountains Can.
112 B2 Carichic Mex.
68 B3 Carignan France
21 C2 Carinda Austr.
75 C1 Cariñena Spain

98 C2 Carleton Place Can.
91 C2 Carletonville S. Africa
65 C1 Carlingford Lough *inlet* Rep. of Ireland/U.K.
66 B1 Carlisle U.K.
109 D2 Carlisle U.S.A.
123 D1 Carlos Chagas Brazil
65 C2 Carlow Rep. of Ireland
103 C4 Carlsbad *CA* U.S.A.
106 C2 Carlsbad *NM* U.S.A.
97 D3 Carlyle Can.
96 A1 Carmacks Can.
97 E3 Carman Can.
67 A3 Carmarthen U.K.
67 A3 Carmarthen Bay U.K.
72 C3 Carmaux France
113 C3 Carmelita Guat.
112 A2 Carmen, Isla *i.* Mex.
72 B2 Carnac France
90 B3 Carnarvon S. Africa
65 C1 Carndonagh Rep. of Ireland
18 B2 Carnegie, Lake *salt flat* Austr.
64 B2 Carn Eighe *mt.* U.K.
31 A3 Car Nicobar *i.* India
86 B2 Carnot C.A.R.
20 A2 Carnot, Cape Austr.
65 C2 Carnsore Point Rep. of Ireland
119 D2 Carolina Brazil
27 D2 Caroline Islands N. Pacific Ocean
71 D2 Carpathian Mountains Europe
78 B1 Carpaţii Meridionali *mts* Romania
19 C1 Carpentaria, Gulf of Austr.
73 D3 Carpentras France
65 B3 Carrantuohill *mt.* Rep. of Ireland
73 E3 Carrara Italy
65 C2 Carrickmacross Rep. of Ireland
65 B2 Carrick-on-Shannon Rep. of Ireland
65 C2 Carrick-on-Suir Rep. of Ireland
105 D1 Carrington U.S.A.
107 D3 Carrizo Springs U.S.A.
106 B2 Carrizozo U.S.A.
105 E2 Carroll U.S.A.
111 C2 Carrollton U.S.A.
97 D2 Carrot River Can.
103 C3 Carson City U.S.A.
118 A1 Cartagena Col.
75 C2 Cartagena Spain
114 B4 Cartago Costa Rica
105 E3 Carthage *MO* U.S.A.
107 E2 Carthage *TX* U.S.A.
99 E1 Cartwright Can.
119 E2 Caruarú Brazil
82 B1 Casablanca Morocco
122 B2 Casa Branca Brazil
112 B1 Casa de Janos Mex.
106 A2 Casa Grande U.S.A.
76 A1 Casale Monferrato Italy
77 C2 Casarano Italy
102 C2 Cascade U.S.A.
102 B2 Cascade Range *mts* Can./U.S.A.
74 B2 Cascais Port.
122 B2 Cascavel Brazil
76 B2 Caserta Italy
85 D3 Caseyr, Raas *c.* Somalia
65 C2 Cashel Rep. of Ireland
21 D1 Casino Austr.
75 C1 Caspe Spain
104 B2 Casper U.S.A.
49 C1 Caspian Sea Asia/Europe
122 C2 Cássia Brazil

96 B2 Cassiar Can.
96 A2 Cassiar Mountains Can.
122 B1 Cassilândia Brazil
76 B2 Cassino Italy
64 B2 Cassley *r.* U.K.
119 D2 Castanhal Brazil
120 B4 Castaño *r.* Arg.
112 B2 Castaños Mex.
72 C3 Casteljaloux France
75 C2 Castelló de la Plana Spain
74 B2 Castelo Branco Port.
76 B3 Castelvetrano *Sicily* Italy
20 B3 Casterton Austr.
76 B2 Castiglione della Pescaia Italy
65 B2 Castlebar Rep. of Ireland
64 A2 Castlebay U.K.
65 C1 Castleblayney Rep. of Ireland
65 C1 Castlederg U.K.
64 C3 Castle Douglas U.K.
96 C3 Castlegar Can.
65 B2 Castleisland Rep. of Ireland
20 B3 Castlemaine Austr.
65 B2 Castlerea Rep. of Ireland
21 C2 Castlereagh *r.* Austr.
104 C3 Castle Rock U.S.A.
97 C2 Castor Can.
72 C3 Castres France
115 D3 Castries St Lucia
122 C2 Castro Brazil
121 A5 Castro Chile
74 B2 Castro Verde Port.
77 C3 Castrovillari Italy
118 A2 Catacaos Peru
123 D2 Cataguases Brazil
120 B3 Catamarca Arg.
32 B1 Catanduanes *i.* Phil.
122 C2 Catanduva Brazil
122 B3 Catanduvas Brazil
77 C3 Catania *Sicily* Italy
77 C3 Catanzaro Italy
32 B1 Catarman Phil.
32 B1 Catbalogan Phil.
113 C3 Catemaco Mex.
115 C2 Cat Island Bahamas
98 A1 Cat Lake *l.* Can.
113 D2 Catoche, Cabo *c.* Mex.
109 E2 Catskill Mountains U.S.A.
32 B2 Cauayan Phil.
118 A1 Cauca *r.* Col.
119 E2 Caucaia Brazil
49 C1 Caucasus *mts* Asia/Europe
68 A2 Caudry France
77 C3 Caulonia Italy
99 D2 Causapscal Can.
73 D3 Cavaillon France
119 D3 Cavalcante Brazil
65 C2 Cavan Rep. of Ireland
122 B3 Cavernoso, Serra do *mts* Brazil
119 D2 Caxias Brazil
120 C3 Caxias do Sul Brazil
88 A1 Caxito Angola
119 C1 Cayenne Fr. Guiana
114 B3 Cayman Islands *terr.* West Indies
85 C4 Caynabo Somalia
120 A2 Cazombo Angola
112 B2 Ceballos Mex.
32 B1 Cebu Phil.
32 B1 Cebu *i.* Phil.
76 B2 Cecina Italy
105 F2 Cedar *r.* U.S.A.
103 D3 Cedar City U.S.A.
105 E2 Cedar Falls U.S.A.
97 D2 Cedar Lake *l.* Can.

105 E2 Cedar Rapids U.S.A.
112 A2 Cedros, Isla i. Mex.
19 C3 Ceduna Austr.
85 C4 Ceeldheere Somalia
85 C3 Ceerigaabo Somalia
76 B3 Cefalù Sicily Italy
113 B2 Celaya Mex.
Celebes i. Indon. see Sulawesi
124 B5 Celebes Sea Indon./Phil.
113 C2 Celestún Mex.
69 E1 Celle Ger.
63 B3 Celtic Sea Rep. of Ireland/U.K.
27 D3 Cenderawasih, Teluk b. Indon.
118 A1 Central, Cordillera mts Col.
118 A3 Central, Cordillera mts Peru
32 B1 Central, Cordillera mts Phil.
86 C2 Central African Republic country Africa
42 A2 Central Brahui Range mts Pak.
105 D2 Central City U.S.A.
108 B3 Centralia IL U.S.A.
102 B1 Centralia WA U.S.A.
42 A2 Central Makran Range mts Pak.
27 D3 Central Range mts P.N.G.
Central Siberian Plateau Rus. Fed. see Sredne-Sibirskoye Ploskogor'ye
Cephalonia i. Greece see Kefallonia
120 B3 Ceres Arg.
122 C1 Ceres Brazil
90 A3 Ceres S. Africa
72 C3 Céret France
74 C1 Cerezo de Abajo Spain
77 C2 Cerignola Italy
78 C2 Cernavodă Romania
113 C2 Cerralvo Mex.
112 B2 Cerralvo, Isla i. Mex.
113 B2 Cerritos Mex.
122 C2 Cerro Azul Brazil
113 C2 Cerro Azul Mex.
118 A3 Cerro de Pasco Peru
73 D3 Cervione Corsica France
74 B1 Cervo Spain
76 B2 Cesena Italy
56 C2 Cēsis Latvia
70 C2 České Budějovice Czech Rep.
69 F3 Český Les mts Czech Rep./Ger.
79 C3 Çeşme Turkey
21 D2 Cessnock Austr.
77 C2 Cetinje Yugo.
77 C3 Cetraro Italy
74 B2 Ceuta N. Africa
73 C3 Cévennes mts France
Ceylon country Asia see Sri Lanka
47 D2 Chābahār Iran
43 C1 Chabyêr Caka salt l. China
118 A2 Chachapoyas Peru
57 D3 Chachersk Belarus
31 B2 Chachoengsao Thai.
83 D3 Chad country Africa
83 D3 Chad, Lake Africa
37 C1 Chadaasan Mongolia
104 C2 Chadron U.S.A.
33 B2 Chaeryŏng N. Korea
42 A2 Chagai Pak.
45 C3 Chaghcharān Afgh.
57 E2 Chagoda Rus. Fed.
44 B2 Chagyl Turkm.
43 C2 Chāībāsa India

31 B2 Chainat Thai.
31 B2 Chaiyaphum Thai.
120 C4 Chajarí Arg.
99 D1 Chakonipau, Lake Can.
118 A3 Chala Peru
42 A1 Chalap Dalan mts Afgh.
99 D2 Chaleur Bay inlet Can.
42 B2 Chalisgaon India
79 C3 Chalki i. Greece
79 B3 Chalkida Greece
72 B2 Challans France
102 D2 Challis U.S.A.
73 C2 Châlons-en-Champagne France
73 C2 Chalon-sur-Saône France
106 B1 Chama U.S.A.
89 C2 Chama Zambia
42 A1 Chaman Pak.
42 B1 Chamba India
42 B2 Chambal r. India
105 D2 Chamberlain U.S.A.
109 D3 Chambersburg U.S.A.
73 D2 Chambéry France
89 C2 Chambeshi Zambia
108 B2 Champaign U.S.A.
109 E2 Champlain, Lake Can./U.S.A.
113 C3 Champotón Mex.
120 A3 Chañaral Chile
94 B2 Chandalar r. U.S.A.
110 C3 Chandeleur Islands U.S.A.
42 B1 Chandigarh India
106 A2 Chandler U.S.A.
43 B3 Chandrapur India
31 B2 Chang, Ko i. Thai.
Chang'an China see Rong'an
89 C3 Changane r. Moz.
89 C2 Changara Moz.
33 B1 Changbai China
33 B1 Changbai Shan mts China/N. Korea
37 E2 Changchun China
39 B3 Changde China
33 B2 Ch'angdo N. Korea
33 C3 Changhua Taiwan
33 B3 Changhŭng S. Korea
Chang Jiang r. China see Yangtze
33 B1 Changjin N. Korea
33 B1 Changjin-gang r N. Korea
39 B3 Changsha China
33 B2 Changsŏng S. Korea
39 B3 Changting China
33 B3 Ch'angwŏn S. Korea
38 B2 Changyuan China
38 B2 Changzhou China
79 B3 Chania Greece
63 C4 Channel Islands Europe
103 C4 Channel Islands U.S.A.
99 E2 Channel-Port-aux-Basques Can.
31 B2 Chanthaburi Thai.
72 C2 Chantilly France
105 D3 Chanute U.S.A.
50 G3 Chany, Ozero salt l. Rus. Fed.
39 B3 Chaoyang China
Chaoyang China see Huinan
39 B3 Chaozhou China
112 B2 Chapala, Laguna de l. Mex.
44 B1 Chapayevo Kazakh.
120 C3 Chapecó Brazil
111 E1 Chapel Hill U.S.A.
98 B2 Chapleau Can.
57 E3 Chaplygin Rus. Fed.
59 C2 Chaplynka Ukr.
113 C2 Charcas Mex.
67 B3 Chard U.K.
44 C3 Chardzhev Turkm.

72 B2 Charente r. France
45 C2 Chārīkār Afgh.
54 E2 Charkayuvom Rus. Fed.
68 B2 Charleroi Belgium
109 D3 Charles, Cape U.S.A.
105 E2 Charles City U.S.A.
108 B3 Charleston IL U.S.A.
111 E2 Charleston SC U.S.A.
108 C3 Charleston WV U.S.A.
103 C3 Charleston Peak U.S.A.
19 D2 Charleville Austr.
73 C2 Charleville-Mézières France
111 D1 Charlotte U.S.A.
111 D3 Charlotte Harbor b. U.S.A.
109 D3 Charlottesville U.S.A.
99 D2 Charlottetown Can.
20 B3 Charlton Austr.
98 C1 Charlton Island Can.
19 D2 Charters Towers Austr.
72 C2 Chartres France
96 C2 Chase Can.
56 C3 Chashniki Belarus
22 A3 Chaslands Mistake c. N.Z.
33 B1 Chasŏng N. Korea
72 B2 Chassiron, Pointe de pt France
72 B2 Châteaubriant France
72 C2 Château-du-Loir France
72 C2 Châteaudun France
72 B2 Châteaulin France
73 D3 Châteauneuf-les-Martigues France
72 C2 Châteauneuf-sur-Loire France
73 C2 Château-Thierry France
96 C2 Chateh Can.
68 B2 Châtelet Belgium
72 C2 Châtellerault France
99 D2 Chatham N.B. Can.
108 C2 Chatham Ont. Can.
73 C2 Châtillon-sur-Seine France
111 D2 Chattahoochee r. U.S.A.
111 C1 Chattanooga U.S.A.
31 B2 Châu Đôc Vietnam
30 A1 Chauk Myanmar
73 D2 Chaumont France
72 C2 Chauny France
119 D2 Chaves Brazil
74 B1 Chaves Port.
98 C1 Chavigny, Lac l. Can.
57 D3 Chavusy Belarus
57 E2 Chayevo Rus. Fed.
54 E3 Chaykovskiy Rus. Fed.
70 C1 Cheb Czech Rep.
53 D3 Cheboksary Rus. Fed.
108 C1 Cheboygan U.S.A.
33 B2 Chech'ŏn S. Korea
30 A2 Cheduba Island Myanmar
82 B2 Chegga Maur.
102 B1 Chehalis U.S.A.
33 B3 Cheju S. Korea
33 B3 Cheju-do i. S. Korea
33 B3 Cheju-haehyŏp sea chan. S. Korea
57 E2 Chekhov Rus. Fed.
102 B1 Chelan, Lake U.S.A.
49 D2 Cheleken Turkm.
75 D2 Chélif, Oued r. Alg.
44 B2 Chelkar Kazakh.
71 E1 Chełm Pol.
67 D3 Chelmer r. U.K.
71 D1 Chełmno Pol.
67 D3 Chelmsford U.K.
67 B3 Cheltenham U.K.
55 F3 Chelyabinsk Rus. Fed.
69 F2 Chemnitz Ger.
82 B2 Chenachane Alg.
38 B1 Chengde China
38 A2 Chengdu China
39 B4 Chengmai China

Chengshou China see
Yingshan
38 A2 **Chengxian** China
Chengyang China see Juxian
Chennai India see Madras
39 B3 **Chenzhou** China
67 B3 **Chepstow** U.K.
72 B2 **Cherbourg** France
57 E3 **Cheremisinovo** Rus. Fed.
37 C1 **Cheremkhovo** Rus. Fed.
57 E2 **Cherepovets** Rus. Fed.
59 C2 **Cherkasy** Ukr.
55 D4 **Cherkessk** Rus. Fed.
59 C1 **Chernihiv** Ukr.
59 D2 **Chernivka** Ukr.
58 B2 **Chernivtsi** Ukr.
58 B1 **Chernyakhiv** Ukr.
56 B3 **Chernyakhovsk** Rus. Fed.
57 E3 **Chernyanka** Rus. Fed.
51 I2 **Chernyshevskiy** Rus. Fed.
105 D2 **Cherokee** U.S.A.
51 K2 **Cherskogo, Khrebet** mts
Rus. Fed.
59 E2 **Chertkovo** Rus. Fed.
58 A1 **Chervonohrad** Ukr.
56 C3 **Chervyen'** Belarus
57 D3 **Cherykaw** Belarus
109 D3 **Chesapeake Bay** U.S.A.
54 D2 **Cheshskaya Guba** b.
Rus. Fed.
66 B2 **Chester** U.K.
108 B3 **Chester** IL U.S.A.
111 D2 **Chester** SC U.S.A.
66 C2 **Chesterfield** U.K.
97 E1 **Chesterfield Inlet** Can.
97 E1 **Chesterfield Inlet** inlet Can.
109 F1 **Chesuncook Lake** U.S.A.
99 D2 **Chéticamp** Can.
113 D3 **Chetumal** Mex.
96 B2 **Chetwynd** Can.
66 B1 **Cheviot Hills** U.K.
104 C2 **Cheyenne** U.S.A.
104 C2 **Cheyenne** r. U.S.A.
104 C3 **Cheyenne Wells** U.S.A.
43 C2 **Chhapra** India
43 B2 **Chhatarpur** India
39 C3 **Chiai** Taiwan
30 A2 **Chiang Dao** Thai.
30 A2 **Chiang Mai** Thai.
30 A2 **Chiang Rai** Thai.
76 A1 **Chiavenno** Italy
89 C3 **Chiboma** Moz.
98 C2 **Chibougamau** Can.
91 D1 **Chibuto** Moz.
43 D1 **Chibuzhang Hu** l. China
108 B2 **Chicago** U.S.A.
96 A2 **Chichagof Island** U.S.A.
67 C2 **Chichester** U.K.
18 A2 **Chichester Range**
mts Austr.
107 D1 **Chickasha** U.S.A.
118 A2 **Chiclayo** Peru
121 B5 **Chico** r. Arg.
103 B3 **Chico** U.S.A.
99 C2 **Chicoutimi** Can.
76 B2 **Chieti** Italy
37 D2 **Chifeng** China
123 D1 **Chifre, Serra do** mts Brazil
45 D2 **Chiganak** Kazakh.
113 C3 **Chignahuapán** Mex.
89 C3 **Chigubo** Moz.
112 B2 **Chihuahua** Mex.
56 C2 **Chikhachevo** Rus. Fed.
35 C3 **Chikuma-gawa** r. Japan
96 B2 **Chilanko** r. Can.
42 B1 **Chilas** Jammu and Kashmir
107 C2 **Childress** U.S.A.
121 A4 **Chile** country S. America
120 B3 **Chilecito** Arg.
43 C3 **Chilika Lake** India

89 B2 **Chililabombwe** Zambia
96 B2 **Chilko** r. Can.
96 B2 **Chilko Lake** Can.
121 A4 **Chillán** Chile
105 E3 **Chillicothe** MO U.S.A.
108 C3 **Chillicothe** OH U.S.A.
96 B3 **Chilliwack** Can.
121 A5 **Chiloé, Isla de** i. Chile
113 C3 **Chilpancingo** Mex.
21 C3 **Chiltern** Austr.
39 C3 **Chilung** Taiwan
87 D3 **Chimala** Tanz.
120 B4 **Chimbas** Arg.
55 E4 **Chimbay** Uzbek.
118 A2 **Chimborazo** mt. Ecuador
118 A2 **Chimbote** Peru
Chimkent Kazakh. see
Shymkent
89 C2 **Chimoio** Moz.
45 C3 **Chimtargha, Qullai** mt. Tajik.
36 B2 **China** country Asia
113 C2 **China** Mex.
118 A3 **Chincha Alta** Peru
96 C2 **Chinchaga** r. Can.
113 D3 **Chinchorro, Banco**
sea feature Mex.
89 C2 **Chinde** Moz.
33 B3 **Chindo** S. Korea
33 B3 **Chin-do** i. S. Korea
36 C2 **Chindu** China
30 A1 **Chindwin** r. Myanmar
33 A2 **Chinghwa** N. Korea
88 B2 **Chingola** Zambia
88 A2 **Chinguar** Angola
33 B2 **Chinhae** S. Korea
89 C2 **Chinhoyi** Zimbabwe
42 B1 **Chiniot** Pak.
112 B3 **Chinipas** Mex.
33 B2 **Chinju** S. Korea
86 C2 **Chinko** r. C.A.R.
106 B1 **Chinle** U.S.A.
39 B3 **Chinmen** Taiwan
35 C3 **Chino** Japan
72 C2 **Chinon** France
106 A2 **Chino Valley** U.S.A.
89 C2 **Chinsali** Zambia
76 B1 **Chioggia** Italy
79 C3 **Chios** Greece
79 C3 **Chios** i. Greece
89 C2 **Chipata** Zambia
88 A2 **Chipindo** Angola
89 C3 **Chipinge** Zimbabwe
41 B3 **Chiplun** India
67 B3 **Chippenham** U.K.
67 C3 **Chipping Norton** U.K.
45 C2 **Chirchik** Uzbek.
89 C3 **Chiredzi** Zimbabwe
106 B2 **Chiricahua Peak** U.S.A.
114 B4 **Chiriquí, Golfo de** b.
Panama
33 B2 **Chiri-san** mt. S. Korea
114 B4 **Chirripo** mt. Costa Rica
89 B2 **Chirundu** Zimbabwe
105 E1 **Chisholm** U.S.A.
58 C1 **Chişinău** Moldova
55 E3 **Chistopol'** Rus. Fed.
37 D1 **Chita** Rus. Fed.
88 A2 **Chitado** Angola
89 C2 **Chitambo** Zambia
88 B1 **Chitato** Angola
89 C1 **Chitipa** Malawi
41 B3 **Chitradurga** India
42 B1 **Chitral** Pak.
114 B4 **Chitré** Panama
43 D2 **Chittagong** Bangl.
42 B2 **Chittaurgarh** India
89 C2 **Chitungwiza** Zimbabwe
88 B2 **Chiume** Angola
89 C2 **Chivhu** Zimbabwe
121 B4 **Choele Choel** Arg.

112 B2 **Choix** Mex.
71 D1 **Chojnice** Pol.
85 B3 **Ch'ok'ē Mountains** Eth.
51 K2 **Chokurdakh** Rus. Fed.
89 C3 **Chókwé** Moz.
72 B2 **Cholet** France
70 C1 **Chomutov** Czech Rep.
51 I2 **Chona** r. Rus. Fed.
33 B2 **Ch'ŏnan** S. Korea
118 A2 **Chone** Ecuador
33 B1 **Ch'ŏngjin** N. Korea
33 B2 **Chŏngju** N. Korea
33 B2 **Chŏngp'yŏng** N. Korea
38 A3 **Chongqing** China
38 A2 **Chongqing** mun. China
39 A3 **Chongzuo** China
33 B2 **Chŏnju** S. Korea
122 B3 **Chopimzinho** Brazil
66 B2 **Chorley** U.K.
59 C2 **Chornomors'ke** Ukr.
58 B2 **Chortkiv** Ukr.
33 B2 **Ch'ŏrwŏn** S. Korea
33 B1 **Ch'osan** N. Korea
35 D3 **Chōshi** Japan
71 D1 **Choszczno** Pol.
82 A2 **Choûm** Maur.
37 D1 **Choybalsan** Mongolia
37 D1 **Choyr** Mongolia
22 B2 **Christchurch** N.Z.
67 C3 **Christchurch** U.K.
95 G2 **Christian, Cape** Can.
91 C2 **Christiana** S. Africa
22 A2 **Christina, Mount** N.Z.
16 B4 **Christmas Island** terr.
Indian Ocean
79 C3 **Chrysi** i. Greece
121 B5 **Chubut** r. Arg.
58 B1 **Chudniv** Ukr.
57 D2 **Chudovo** Rus. Fed.
Chudskoye Ozero l.
Estonia/Rus. Fed. see
Peipus, Lake
94 B2 **Chugach Mountains** U.S.A.
35 B4 **Chūgoku-sanchi** mts Japan
34 B2 **Chuguyevka** Rus. Fed.
59 D2 **Chuhuyiv** Ukr.
128 J3 **Chukchi Sea**
Rus. Fed./U.S.A.
51 N2 **Chukotskiy Poluostrov** pen.
Rus. Fed.
103 C4 **Chula Vista** U.S.A.
50 G3 **Chulym** Rus. Fed.
120 B3 **Chumbicha** Arg.
51 K3 **Chumikan** Rus. Fed.
31 A2 **Chumphon** Thai.
33 B2 **Ch'unch'ŏn** S. Korea
Chungking China see
Chongqing
42 B3 **Churu** India
51 H2 **Chunya** r. Rus. Fed.
118 A3 **Chuquibamba** Peru
120 B3 **Chuquicamata** Chile
73 D2 **Chur** Switz.
30 A1 **Churachandpur** India
97 E2 **Churchill** Can.
97 E2 **Churchill** r. Man. Can.
99 D1 **Churchill** r. Nfld. Can.
97 E2 **Churchill, Cape** Can.
99 D1 **Churchill Falls** Can.
97 D2 **Churchill Lake** Can.
42 B2 **Churu** India
99 C2 **Chute-des-Passes** Can.
30 B1 **Chuxiong** China
58 B2 **Ciadâr-Lunga** Moldova
29 B2 **Ciamis** Indon.
28 B2 **Cianjur** Indon.
122 B2 **Cianorte** Brazil
71 E1 **Ciechanów** Pol.
114 C2 **Ciego de Ávila** Cuba
114 B2 **Cienfuegos** Cuba
75 C2 **Cieza** Spain

74 C2 **Cigüela** r. Spain
48 B2 **Cihanbeyli** Turkey
112 B3 **Cihuatlán** Mex.
74 C2 **Cijara, Embalse de** resr
 Spain
29 B2 **Cilacap** Indon.
107 C1 **Cimarron** r. U.S.A.
58 B2 **Cimişlia** Moldova
76 B2 **Cimone, Monte** mt. Italy
108 C3 **Cincinnati** U.S.A.
79 C3 **Çine** Turkey
68 B2 **Ciney** Belgium
113 C3 **Cintalapa** Mex.
94 B2 **Circle** AK U.S.A.
104 B1 **Circle** MT U.S.A.
26 B3 **Cirebon** Indon.
67 C3 **Cirencester** U.K.
76 A1 **Ciriè** Italy
77 C3 **Cirò Marina** Italy
77 C2 **Čitluk** Bos.-Herz.
90 A3 **Citrusdal** S. Africa
113 B2 **Ciudad Acuña** Mex.
113 B3 **Ciudad Altamirano** Mex.
118 B1 **Ciudad Bolívar** Venez.
112 B2 **Ciudad Camargo** Mex.
113 C3 **Ciudad del Carmen** Mex.
112 B2 **Ciudad Delicias** Mex.
113 C2 **Ciudad de Valles** Mex.
118 B1 **Ciudad Guayana** Venez.
106 B3 **Ciudad Guerrero** Mex.
112 B3 **Ciudad Guzmán** Mex.
113 C3 **Ciudad Hidalgo** Mex.
113 C3 **Ciudad Ixtepec** Mex.
112 B1 **Ciudad Juárez** Mex.
113 C2 **Ciudad Mante** Mex.
113 C2 **Ciudad Mier** Mex.
112 B2 **Ciudad Obregón** Mex.
74 C2 **Ciudad Real** Spain
113 C2 **Ciudad Río Bravo** Mex.
74 B1 **Ciudad Rodrigo** Spain
113 C2 **Ciudad Victoria** Mex.
75 D1 **Ciutadella de Menorca**
 Spain
79 D1 **Cıvan Dağ** mt. Turkey
76 B1 **Cividale del Friuli** Italy
76 B2 **Civitanova Marche** Italy
76 D2 **Civitavecchia** Italy
72 C2 **Civray** France
79 C3 **Çivril** Turkey
38 C2 **Cixi** China
67 D3 **Clacton-on-Sea** U.K.
96 C2 **Claire, Lake** Can.
73 C2 **Clamecy** France
90 A3 **Clanwilliam** S. Africa
20 A2 **Clare** Austr.
65 A2 **Clare Island** Rep. of Ireland
109 E2 **Claremont** U.S.A.
65 B2 **Claremorris** Rep. of Ireland
22 B2 **Clarence** N.Z.
99 E2 **Clarenville** Can.
96 C2 **Claresholm** Can.
105 D2 **Clarinda** U.S.A.
91 C3 **Clarkebury** S. Africa
102 C1 **Clark Fork** r. U.S.A.
111 D2 **Clark Hill Reservoir** U.S.A.
108 C3 **Clarksburg** U.S.A.
110 B2 **Clarksdale** U.S.A.
110 B1 **Clarksville** AR U.S.A.
110 C1 **Clarksville** TN U.S.A.
122 B1 **Claro** r. Brazil
107 C1 **Clayton** U.S.A.
65 B3 **Clear, Cape** Rep. of Ireland
105 E2 **Clear Lake** U.S.A.
103 B3 **Clear Lake** l. U.S.A.
96 C2 **Clearwater** Can.
97 C2 **Clearwater** r. Can.
111 D3 **Clearwater** U.S.A.
102 C1 **Clearwater** r. U.S.A.
107 D2 **Cleburne** U.S.A.
19 D2 **Clermont** Austr.

73 C2 **Clermont-Ferrand** France
20 A2 **Cleve** Austr.
110 B2 **Cleveland** MS U.S.A.
108 C2 **Cleveland** OH U.S.A.
111 D1 **Cleveland** TN U.S.A.
102 D1 **Cleveland, Mount** U.S.A.
111 D3 **Clewiston** U.S.A.
65 A2 **Clifden** Rep. of Ireland
21 D1 **Clifton** Austr.
106 B2 **Clifton** U.S.A.
96 B2 **Clinton** Can.
105 E2 **Clinton** IA U.S.A.
105 E3 **Clinton** MO U.S.A.
107 D1 **Clinton** OK U.S.A.
64 A2 **Clisham** hill U.K.
66 B2 **Clitheroe** U.K.
65 B3 **Clonakilty** Rep. of Ireland
19 D2 **Cloncurry** Austr.
65 C1 **Clones** Rep. of Ireland
65 C2 **Clonmel** Rep. of Ireland
68 D1 **Cloppenburg** Ger.
104 B2 **Cloud Peak** U.S.A.
107 C2 **Clovis** U.S.A.
97 D2 **Cluff Lake Mine** Can.
78 B1 **Cluj-Napoca** Romania
19 C2 **Cluny** Austr.
72 D2 **Cluses** France
22 A3 **Clutha** r. N.Z.
64 B3 **Clyde** r. U.K.
64 B3 **Clyde, Firth of** est. U.K.
64 B3 **Clydebank** U.K.
95 G2 **Clyde River** Can.
112 B3 **Coalcomán** Mex.
103 C3 **Coaldale** U.S.A.
96 B2 **Coal River** Can.
118 B2 **Coari** Brazil
118 D2 **Coari** r. Brazil
110 B2 **Coastal Plain** U.S.A.
96 B2 **Coast Mountains** Can.
103 B2 **Coast Ranges** mts U.S.A.
64 B3 **Coatbridge** U.K.
95 F2 **Coats Island** Can.
23 R2 **Coats Land** reg. Antarctica
113 C3 **Coatzacoalcos** Mex.
114 A3 **Cobán** Guat.
21 C2 **Cobar** Austr.
65 B3 **Cóbh** Rep. of Ireland
120 B2 **Cobija** Bol.
109 D2 **Cobourg** Can.
18 C1 **Cobourg Peninsula** Austr.
21 C3 **Cobram** Austr.
69 E2 **Coburg** Ger.
120 B2 **Cochabamba** Bol.
68 C2 **Cochem** Ger.
41 B4 **Cochin** India
96 C3 **Cochrane** Alta Can.
98 B2 **Cochrane** Ont. Can.
121 A5 **Cochrane** Chile
20 B2 **Cockburn** Austr.
   Cockburn Town Turks and
   Caicos Is. see **Grand Turk**
66 B1 **Cockermouth** U.K.
90 B3 **Cockscomb** mt. S. Africa
114 B3 **Coco** r. Hond./Nic.
16 A4 **Cocos Islands** terr.
   Indian Ocean
112 B2 **Cocula** Mex.
118 A1 **Cocuy, Sierra Nevada del**
   mt. Col.
109 E2 **Cod, Cape** U.S.A.
76 B2 **Codigoro** Italy
99 D1 **Cod Island** Can.
119 D2 **Codó** Brazil
104 B2 **Cody** U.S.A.
19 D1 **Coen** Austr.
68 C2 **Coesfeld** Ger.
102 C1 **Coeur d'Alene** U.S.A.
91 C3 **Coffee Bay** S. Africa
105 D3 **Coffeyville** U.S.A.
21 D2 **Coffs Harbour** Austr.

72 B2 **Cognac** France
86 A2 **Cogo** Equat. Guinea
20 B3 **Cohuna** Austr.
114 B4 **Coiba, Isla** i. Panama
121 A5 **Coihaique** Chile
41 B3 **Coimbatore** India
74 B1 **Coimbra** Port.
20 B3 **Colac** Austr.
123 D1 **Colatina** Brazil
104 C3 **Colby** U.S.A.
67 D3 **Colchester** U.K.
97 C2 **Cold Lake** l. Can.
64 C3 **Coldstream** U.K.
107 D2 **Coleman** U.S.A.
20 B3 **Coleraine** Austr.
65 C1 **Coleraine** U.K.
91 C3 **Colesberg** S. Africa
112 B3 **Colima** Mex.
112 B3 **Colima, Nevado de** vol. Mex.
64 A2 **Coll** i. U.K.
21 C1 **Collarenebri** Austr.
18 B1 **Collier Bay** Austr.
22 B2 **Collingwood** N.Z.
65 B1 **Collooney** Rep. of Ireland
73 D2 **Colmar** France
68 C2 **Cologne** Ger.
122 C2 **Colômbia** Brazil
118 A1 **Colombia** country S. America
41 B4 **Colombo** Sri Lanka
72 C3 **Colomiers** France
120 C4 **Colón** Arg.
114 C4 **Colón** Panama
77 C3 **Colonna, Capo** c. Italy
64 A2 **Colonsay** i. U.K.
121 B4 **Colorado** r. Arg.
106 A2 **Colorado** r. Mex./U.S.A.
107 D3 **Colorado** r. U.S.A.
104 B3 **Colorado** state U.S.A.
103 B3 **Colorado Plateau** U.S.A.
104 C3 **Colorado Springs** U.S.A.
112 B3 **Colotlán** Mex.
104 B1 **Colstrip** U.S.A.
105 E3 **Columbia** MO U.S.A.
111 D2 **Columbia** SC U.S.A.
110 C1 **Columbia** TN U.S.A.
102 B1 **Columbia** r. U.S.A.
96 C2 **Columbia, Mount** Can.
102 D1 **Columbia Falls** U.S.A.
96 B2 **Columbia Mountains** Can.
102 C1 **Columbia Plateau** U.S.A.
111 D2 **Columbus** GA U.S.A.
108 B3 **Columbus** IN U.S.A.
110 C2 **Columbus** MS U.S.A.
105 D2 **Columbus** NE U.S.A.
106 B2 **Columbus** NM U.S.A.
108 C3 **Columbus** OH U.S.A.
102 C1 **Colville** U.S.A.
94 A2 **Colville** r. U.S.A.
94 C2 **Colville Lake** Can.
66 B2 **Colwyn Bay** U.K.
76 B2 **Comacchio** Italy
113 C3 **Comalcalco** Mex.
78 C1 **Comăneşti** Romania
98 C1 **Comencho, Lac** l. Can.
65 C2 **Comeragh Mountains**
   Rep. of Ireland
43 D2 **Comilla** Bangl.
76 A2 **Comino, Capo** c. Sardinia
   Italy
113 C3 **Comitán de Domínguez**
   Mex.
72 C2 **Commentry** France
107 D2 **Commerce** U.S.A.
95 F2 **Committee Bay** Can.
76 A1 **Como** Italy
76 A1 **Como, Lago di** l. Italy
121 B5 **Comodoro Rivadavia** Arg.
89 D2 **Comoros** country Africa
72 C2 **Compiègne** France
112 B2 **Compostela** Mex.

58 B2 **Comrat** Moldova
82 A4 **Conakry** Guinea
123 E1 **Conceição da Barra** Brazil
119 D2 **Conceição do Araguaia** Brazil
123 D1 **Conceição do Mato Dentro** Brazil
120 B3 **Concepción** Arg.
121 A4 **Concepción** Chile
112 B2 **Concepción** Mex.
114 B4 **Concepción** Panama
103 B4 **Conception, Point** U.S.A.
122 C2 **Conchas** Brazil
106 C1 **Conchas Lake** U.S.A.
112 B2 **Conchos** r. Chihuahua Mex.
113 C2 **Conchos** r. Nuevo León/ Tamaulipas Mex.
103 B3 **Concord** CA U.S.A.
109 E2 **Concord** NH U.S.A.
120 C4 **Concordia** Arg.
90 A2 **Concordia** S. Africa
105 D3 **Concordia** U.S.A.
21 C2 **Condobolin** Austr.
72 C3 **Condom** France
102 B1 **Condon** U.S.A.
76 B1 **Conegliano** Italy
72 C2 **Conflans** France
86 B3 **Congo** country Africa
86 B3 **Congo** r. Congo/ Dem. Rep. Congo
86 C3 **Congo, Democratic Republic of** country Africa
97 C2 **Conklin** Can.
65 B1 **Conn, Lough** l. Rep. of Ireland
65 B2 **Connaught** reg. Rep. of Ireland
109 E2 **Connecticut** r. U.S.A.
109 E2 **Connecticut** state U.S.A.
65 B2 **Connemara** reg. Rep. of Ireland
102 D1 **Conrad** U.S.A.
107 D2 **Conroe** U.S.A.
123 D2 **Conselheiro Lafaiete** Brazil
123 D1 **Conselheiro Pena** Brazil
66 C1 **Consett** U.K.
31 B3 **Côn Son** i. Vietnam
78 C2 **Constanța** Romania
74 B2 **Constantina** Spain
83 C1 **Constantine** Alg.
102 D2 **Contact** U.S.A.
118 A2 **Contamana** Peru
121 A6 **Contreras, Isla** i. Chile
94 D2 **Contwoyto Lake** Can.
110 B1 **Conway** AR U.S.A.
109 E2 **Conway** NH U.S.A.
19 C2 **Coober Pedy** Austr.
22 B2 **Cook, Mount** mt. N.Z.
111 C1 **Cookeville** U.S.A.
17 G4 **Cook Islands** S. Pacific Ocean
99 E1 **Cook's Harbour** Can.
65 C1 **Cookstown** U.K.
22 B2 **Cook Strait** N.Z.
19 D1 **Cooktown** Austr.
21 C2 **Coolabah** Austr.
21 C2 **Coolamon** Austr.
21 D1 **Coolangatta** Austr.
18 B3 **Coolgardie** Austr.
21 C3 **Cooma** Austr.
20 B2 **Coombah** Austr.
21 C2 **Coonabarabran** Austr.
20 A3 **Coonalpyn** Austr.
21 C2 **Coonamble** Austr.
20 A1 **Cooper Creek** watercourse Austr.
102 B2 **Coos Bay** U.S.A.
21 C2 **Cootamundra** Austr.
113 C3 **Copainalá** Mex.
113 C3 **Copala** Mex.

61 F4 **Copenhagen** Denmark
77 C2 **Copertino** Italy
120 A3 **Copiapó** Chile
108 B1 **Copper Harbor** U.S.A.
       Coppermine Can. see Kugluktuk
94 D2 **Coppermine** r. Can.
90 B2 **Copperton** S. Africa
120 A3 **Coquimbo** Chile
78 B2 **Corabia** Romania
123 D1 **Coração de Jesus** Brazil
118 A3 **Coracora** Peru
21 D1 **Coraki** Austr.
18 A2 **Coral Bay** Austr.
95 F2 **Coral Harbour** Can.
124 D7 **Coral Sea** S. Pacific Ocean
20 B3 **Corangamite, Lake** Austr.
67 C2 **Corby** U.K.
121 A5 **Corcovado, Golfo de** sea chan. Chile
111 D2 **Cordele** U.S.A.
32 B1 **Cordilleras Range** mts Phil.
120 B4 **Córdoba** Arg.
113 C3 **Córdoba** Mex.
74 C2 **Córdoba** Spain
121 B4 **Córdoba, Sierras de** mts Arg.
79 A3 **Corfu** i. Greece
74 B2 **Coria** Spain
110 C2 **Corinth** U.S.A.
123 D1 **Corinto** Brazil
65 B3 **Cork** Rep. of Ireland
79 C2 **Çorlu** Turkey
122 B2 **Cornélio Procópio** Brazil
99 E2 **Corner Brook** Can.
21 C3 **Corner Inlet** b. Austr.
103 B3 **Corning** CA U.S.A.
109 D2 **Corning** NY U.S.A.
       Corn Islands is Nic. see Maíz, Islas del
76 B2 **Corno, Monte** mt. Italy
98 C2 **Cornwall** Can.
94 E1 **Cornwallis Island** Can.
118 B1 **Coro** Venez.
122 C1 **Coromandel** Brazil
22 C1 **Coromandel Peninsula** N.Z.
97 C2 **Coronation** Can.
94 D2 **Coronation Gulf** Can.
120 C3 **Coronel Oviedo** Para.
121 B4 **Coronel Suárez** Arg.
77 D2 **Çorovodë** Albania
107 D3 **Corpus Christi** U.S.A.
120 B2 **Corque** Bol.
119 D3 **Corrente** Brazil
122 B1 **Correntes** Brazil
119 D3 **Correntina** Brazil
65 B2 **Corrib, Lough** l. Rep. of Ireland
120 C3 **Corrientes** Arg.
112 B2 **Corrientes, Cabo** c. Mex.
21 C3 **Corryong** Austr.
       Corse i. France see Corsica
73 D3 **Corse, Cap** c. Corsica France
73 D3 **Corsica** i. France
107 D2 **Corsicana** U.S.A.
73 D3 **Corte** Corsica France
74 B2 **Cortegana** Spain
104 B3 **Cortez** U.S.A.
76 B1 **Cortina d'Ampezzo** Italy
109 D2 **Cortland** U.S.A.
76 B2 **Cortona** Italy
       Çoruh Turkey see Artvin
48 B1 **Çorum** Turkey
122 C1 **Corumbá** Brazil
122 C1 **Corumbá** r. Brazil
102 B2 **Corvallis** U.S.A.
66 B2 **Corwen** U.K.
112 B2 **Cosalá** Mex.
113 C3 **Cosamaloapan** Mex.

77 C3 **Cosenza** Italy
73 C2 **Cosne-Cours-sur-Loire** France
75 C2 **Costa Blanca** coastal area Spain
75 D1 **Costa Brava** coastal area Spain
74 B2 **Costa del Sol** coastal area Spain
114 B3 **Costa de Mosquitos** coastal area Nic.
122 B1 **Costa Rica** Brazil
114 B3 **Costa Rica** country Central America
112 B2 **Costa Rica** Mex.
78 B2 **Costești** Romania
32 B2 **Cotabato** Phil.
82 B4 **Côte d'Ivoire** country Africa
118 A2 **Cotopaxi, Volcán** vol. Ecuador
67 B3 **Cotswold Hills** U.K.
102 B2 **Cottage Grove** U.S.A.
70 C1 **Cottbus** Ger.
20 A3 **Coüedic, Cape de** Austr.
105 D2 **Council Bluffs** U.S.A.
102 B1 **Cowlitz** r. U.S.A.
56 B2 **Courland Lagoon** b. Lith./Rus. Fed.
96 B3 **Courtenay** Can.
72 B2 **Coutances** France
72 B2 **Coutras** France
68 B2 **Couvin** Belgium
67 C2 **Coventry** U.K.
108 C3 **Covington** U.S.A.
18 B3 **Cowan, Lake** salt flat Austr.
64 C2 **Cowdenbeath** U.K.
21 C3 **Cowes** Austr.
21 C2 **Cowra** Austr.
122 B1 **Coxim** Brazil
43 D2 **Cox's Bazar** Bangl.
113 B3 **Coyuca de Benitez** Mex.
113 C2 **Cozumel** Mex.
113 D2 **Cozumel, Isla de** i. Mex.
91 C3 **Cradock** S. Africa
104 B2 **Craig** U.S.A.
70 C2 **Crailsheim** Ger.
78 B2 **Craiova** Romania
97 D2 **Cranberry Portage** Can.
21 C3 **Cranbourne** Austr.
96 C3 **Cranbrook** Can.
119 D2 **Crateús** Brazil
119 E2 **Crato** Brazil
104 C2 **Crawford** U.S.A.
108 B2 **Crawfordsville** U.S.A.
67 C3 **Crawley** U.K.
102 D1 **Crazy Mountains** U.S.A.
97 C2 **Cree** r. Can.
112 B2 **Creel** Mex.
97 D2 **Cree Lake** Can.
68 B1 **Creil** Neth.
73 D2 **Crema** Italy
76 B1 **Cremona** Italy
76 B2 **Cres** i. Croatia
102 B2 **Crescent City** U.S.A.
96 C3 **Creston** Can.
105 E2 **Creston** U.S.A.
110 C2 **Crestview** U.S.A.
79 B3 **Crete** i. Greece
75 D1 **Creus, Cap de** c. Spain
66 B2 **Crewe** U.K.
64 B2 **Crianlarich** U.K.
120 D3 **Criciúma** Brazil
64 C2 **Crieff** U.K.
76 B1 **Crikvenica** Croatia
59 C2 **Crimea** pen. Ukr.
69 F2 **Crimmitschau** Ger.
122 C1 **Cristalina** Brazil
69 E1 **Crivitz** Ger.
       Crna Gora aut. rep. Yugo. see Montenegro

77 D2 **Crni Vrh** *mt.* Yugo.
77 C1 **Črnomelj** Slovenia
65 B2 **Croagh Patrick** *hill*
　　　Rep. of Ireland
77 C1 **Croatia** *country* Europe
29 C1 **Crocker, Banjaran** *mts*
　　　Malaysia
107 D2 **Crockett** U.S.A.
27 C3 **Croker Island** Austr.
67 D2 **Cromer** U.K.
22 A3 **Cromwell** N.Z.
105 D1 **Crookston** U.S.A.
21 C2 **Crookwell** Austr.
104 C1 **Crosby** U.S.A.
111 D3 **Cross City** U.S.A.
110 B2 **Crossett** U.S.A.
66 B1 **Cross Fell** *hill* U.K.
97 E2 **Cross Lake** *l.* Can.
111 C1 **Crossville** U.S.A.
77 C3 **Crotone** Italy
67 D3 **Crowborough** U.K.
110 B2 **Crowley** U.S.A.
96 C3 **Crowsnest Pass** Can.
114 C2 **Cruz, Cabo** *c.* Cuba
120 C3 **Cruz Alta** Brazil
120 B4 **Cruz del Eje** Arg.
123 D2 **Cruzeiro** Brazil
118 A2 **Cruzeiro do Sul** Brazil
20 A2 **Crystal Brook** Austr.
107 D3 **Crystal City** U.S.A.
108 B3 **Crystal Falls** U.S.A.
71 E2 **Csongrád** Hungary
88 B2 **Cuando** *r.* Angola/Zambia
88 A2 **Cuangar** Angola
88 B2 **Cuango** *r.* Angola/
　　　Dem. Rep. Congo
88 A1 **Cuanza** *r.* Angola
107 C3 **Cuatro Ciénegas** Mex.
112 B2 **Cuauhtémoc** Mex.
113 C3 **Cuautla** Mex.
114 B2 **Cuba** *country* West Indies
88 A2 **Cubal** Angola
88 B2 **Cubango** *r.* Angola/Namibia
118 A1 **Cúcuta** Col.
41 B3 **Cuddalore** India
43 B3 **Cuddapah** India
74 C1 **Cuéllar** Spain
88 A2 **Cuemba** Angola
118 A2 **Cuenca** Ecuador
75 C1 **Cuenca** Spain
75 C1 **Cuenca, Serranía de** *mts*
　　　Spain
113 C3 **Cuernavaca** Mex.
107 D3 **Cuero** U.S.A.
119 C3 **Cuiabá** Brazil
119 C3 **Cuiabá** *r.* Brazil
64 A2 **Cuillin Sound** *sea chan.* U.K.
88 A1 **Cuilo** Angola
88 B2 **Cuito** *r.* Angola
88 A2 **Cuito Cuanavale** Angola
28 B1 **Cukai** Malaysia
21 C3 **Culcairn** Austr.
21 C1 **Culgoa** Austr.
112 B2 **Culiacán** Mex.
32 A1 **Culion** *i.* Phil.
75 C2 **Cullera** Spain
110 C2 **Cullman** U.S.A.
65 C1 **Cullybackey** U.K.
119 C3 **Culuene** *r.* Brazil
118 B1 **Cumaná** Venez.
109 D3 **Cumberland** U.S.A.
108 B3 **Cumberland** *r.* U.S.A.
97 D2 **Cumberland Lake** Can.
95 G2 **Cumberland Peninsula** Can.
110 C1 **Cumberland Plateau** U.S.A.
95 G2 **Cumberland Sound**
　　　sea chan. Can.
64 C3 **Cumbernauld** U.K.
103 B3 **Cummings** U.S.A.
64 B3 **Cumnock** U.K.

112 B1 **Cumpas** Mex.
113 C3 **Cunduacán** Mex.
88 A2 **Cunene** *r.* Angola
76 A2 **Cuneo** Italy
21 C1 **Cunnamulla** Austr.
76 A1 **Cuorgnè** Italy
64 C2 **Cupar** U.K.
115 D3 **Curaçao** *i.* Neth. Antilles
118 A2 **Curaray** *r.* Ecuador
121 A4 **Curicó** Chile
122 C3 **Curitiba** Brazil
20 A2 **Curnamona** Austr.
19 D3 **Currie** Austr.
19 E2 **Curtis Island** Austr.
119 C2 **Curuá** *r.* Brazil
28 B2 **Curup** Indon.
119 D2 **Cururupu** Brazil
123 D1 **Curvelo** Brazil
118 A3 **Cusco** Peru
107 D1 **Cushing** U.S.A.
102 D1 **Cut Bank** U.S.A.
43 C2 **Cuttack** India
69 D1 **Cuxhaven** Ger.
32 B1 **Cuyo Islands** Phil.
　　　Cuzco Peru *see* **Cusco**
87 C3 **Cyangugu** Rwanda
79 B3 **Cyclades** *is* Greece
97 C3 **Cypress Hills** Can.
48 B2 **Cyprus** *country* Asia
70 C2 **Czech Republic** *country*
　　　Europe
71 D1 **Czersk** Pol.
71 D1 **Częstochowa** Pol.

D

30 B1 **Đa, Sông** *r.* Vietnam
37 D2 **Daban** China
82 A3 **Dabola** Guinea
　　　Dacca Bangl. *see* **Dhaka**
70 C2 **Dachau** Ger.
38 A2 **Dachuan** China
42 A2 **Dadu** Pak.
32 B1 **Daet** Phil.
82 A3 **Dagana** Senegal
32 B1 **Dagupan** Phil.
42 B3 **Dahanu** India
37 D2 **Da Hinggan Ling** *mts* China
84 C3 **Dahlak Archipelago** *is*
　　　Eritrea
68 C2 **Dahlem** Ger.
28 B2 **Daik** Indon.
74 C2 **Daimiel** Spain
19 C2 **Dajarra** Austr.
82 A3 **Dakar** Senegal
85 C4 **Daketa Shet'** *watercourse*
　　　Eth.
84 A2 **Dakhla Oasis** Egypt
31 A3 **Dakoank** India
56 C3 **Dakol'ka** *r.* Belarus
77 D2 **Đakovica** Yugo.
77 C1 **Đakovo** Croatia
88 B2 **Dala** Angola
36 C2 **Dalain Hob** China
61 G3 **Dalälven** *r.* Sweden
79 C3 **Dalaman** Turkey
79 C3 **Dalaman** *r.* Turkey
37 C2 **Dalandzadgad** Mongolia
31 B2 **Đa Lat** Vietnam
42 A2 **Dalbandin** Pak.
64 C3 **Dalbeattie** U.K.
19 E2 **Dalby** Austr.
111 C1 **Dale Hollow Lake** U.S.A.
21 C3 **Dalgety** Austr.
107 C1 **Dalhart** U.S.A.
99 D2 **Dalhousie** Can.
30 B1 **Dali** China

38 C2 **Dalian** China
64 C3 **Dalkeith** U.K.
107 D2 **Dallas** U.S.A.
96 A2 **Dall Island** U.S.A.
77 C2 **Dalmacija** *reg.* Croatia
34 C2 **Dal'negorsk** Rus. Fed.
34 B1 **Dal'nerechensk** Rus. Fed.
82 B4 **Daloa** Côte d'Ivoire
19 D2 **Dalrymple, Mount** Austr.
60 □A3 **Dalsmynni** Iceland
43 C2 **Daltenganj** India
111 D2 **Dalton** U.S.A.
28 B1 **Daludalu** Indon.
60 □B2 **Dalvík** Iceland
18 C1 **Daly** *r.* Austr.
19 C1 **Daly Waters** Austr.
42 B2 **Damān** India
48 B2 **Damanhûr** Egypt
27 C3 **Damar** *i.* Indon.
48 B2 **Damascus** Syria
83 D3 **Damaturu** Nigeria
44 B3 **Dāmāvand, Qolleh-ye** *mt.*
　　　Iran
49 D2 **Damghan** Iran
69 D1 **Damme** Ger.
43 B2 **Damoh** India
82 B4 **Damongo** Ghana
27 C3 **Dampir, Selat** *sea chan.*
　　　Indon.
43 D1 **Damxung** China
82 B4 **Danané** Côte d'Ivoire
31 B2 **Đa Nẵng** Vietnam
109 E2 **Danbury** U.S.A.
33 A1 **Dandong** China
114 B3 **Dangriga** Belize
38 B2 **Dangshan** China
57 F2 **Danilov** Rus. Fed.
57 F2 **Danilovskaya**
　　　Vozvyshennost' *hills*
　　　Rus. Fed.
38 B2 **Danjiangkou** China
57 E3 **Dankov** Rus. Fed.
114 B3 **Danlí** Hond.
69 E1 **Dannenberg (Elbe)** Ger.
22 C2 **Dannevirke** N.Z.
30 B2 **Dan Sai** Thai.
　　　Dantu China *see* **Zhenjiang**
78 A1 **Danube** *r.* Europe
108 B2 **Danville** IL U.S.A.
108 C3 **Danville** KY U.S.A.
109 D3 **Danville** VA U.S.A.
39 A4 **Danzhou** China
39 D3 **Daoxian** China
82 C3 **Dapaong** Togo
36 C2 **Da Qaidam Zhen** China
37 E1 **Daqing** China
48 B2 **Dar'ā** Syria
47 C2 **Dārāb** Iran
84 D1 **Daraj** Libya
49 D2 **Dārān** Iran
31 B2 **Đa Rằng, Sông** *r.* Vietnam
43 C2 **Darbhanga** India
87 D3 **Dar es Salaam** Tanz.
42 B1 **Dargai** Pak.
22 B1 **Dargaville** N.Z.
21 C3 **Dargo** Austr.
37 D1 **Darhan** Mongolia
118 A1 **Darién, Golfo del** *g.* Col.
43 C2 **Dārjiling** India
36 C2 **Darlag** China
20 B2 **Darling** *r.* Austr.
21 C1 **Darling Downs** *hills* Austr.
18 A3 **Darling Range** *hills* Austr.
66 C1 **Darlington** U.K.
21 C2 **Darlington Point** Austr.
71 D1 **Darłowo** Pol.
69 D3 **Darmstadt** Ger.
83 E1 **Darnah** Libya
20 B2 **Darnick** Austr.
75 C1 **Daroca** Spain

67 D3   **Dartford** U.K.
67 A3   **Dartmoor** *hills* U.K.
99 D2   **Dartmouth** Can.
67 B3   **Dartmouth** U.K.
65 B1   **Darty Mountains**
        Rep. of Ireland
27 D3   **Daru** P.N.G.
18 C1   **Darwin** Austr.
44 B2   **Dashkhovuz** Turkm.
42 A2   **Dasht** *r.* Pak.
29 C1   **Datadian** Indon.
79 C3   **Datça** Turkey
38 B1   **Datong** China
32 B2   **Datu Piang** Phil.
42 B1   **Daud Khel** Pak.
56 B2   **Daugava** *r.* Latvia
56 C2   **Daugavpils** Latvia
68 C2   **Daun** Ger.
97 D2   **Dauphin** Can.
97 E2   **Dauphin Lake** Can.
41 B3   **Davangere** India
32 B2   **Davao** Phil.
32 B2   **Davao Gulf** Phil.
105 E2 **Davenport** U.S.A.
67 C2   **Daventry** U.K.
91 C2   **Daveyton** S. Africa
114 B4 **David** Panama
97 D2   **Davidson** Can.
94 E3   **Davidson Lake** Can.
103 B3 **Davis** U.S.A.
99 D1   **Davis Inlet** Can.
127 F3 **Davis Sea** Antarctica
128 P3 **Davis Strait** Can./Greenland
73 D2   **Davos** Switz.
47 C3   **Dawqah** Oman
94 B2   **Dawson** Can.
111 D2 **Dawson** U.S.A.
96 B2   **Dawson Creek** Can.
96 B2   **Dawsons Landing** Can.
36 C2   **Dawu** China
        Dawukou China *see*
        Shizuishan
72 B3   **Dax** France
34 C2   **Daxue Shan** *mts* China
39 B3   **Dayong** China
48 C2   **Dayr az Zawr** Syria
108 C3 **Dayton** U.S.A.
111 D3 **Daytona Beach** U.S.A.
90 B3   **De Aar** S. Africa
39 B3   **De'an** China
120 B4 **Deán Funes** Arg.
96 B2   **Dease Lake** Can.
94 D2   **Dease Strait** Can.
103 C3 **Death Valley** *depr.* U.S.A.
72 C2   **Deauville** France
29 C1   **Debak** *Sarawak* Malaysia
77 D2   **Debar** Macedonia
71 E2   **Debrecen** Hungary
85 B3   **Debre Markos** Eth.
85 B3   **Debre Tabor** Eth.
85 B4   **Debre Zeyit** Eth.
110 C2 **Decatur** *AL* U.S.A.
108 B3 **Decatur** *IL* U.S.A.
41 B3   **Deccan** *plat.* India
70 C1   **Děčín** Czech Rep.
105 E2 **Decorah** U.S.A.
55 C2   **Dedovichi** Rus. Fed.
89 C2   **Dedza** Malawi
66 B2   **Dee** *r. England/Wales* U.K.
64 C2   **Dee** *r. Scotland* U.K.
21 D1   **Deepwater** Austr.
99 E2   **Deer Lake** Can.
102 D1 **Deer Lodge** U.S.A.
108 C2 **Defiance** U.S.A.
36 C2   **Dêgê** China
85 C4   **Degeh Bur** Eth.
70 C2   **Deggendorf** Ger.
59 E2   **Degtevo** Rus. Fed.
43 B1   **Dehra Dun** India

43 C2   **Dehri** India
37 E2   **Dehui** China
68 A2   **Deinze** Belgium
78 B1   **Dej** Romania
108 B2 **De Kalb** U.S.A.
46 A3   **Dekemhare** Eritrea
86 C3   **Dekese** Dem. Rep. Congo
103 C3 **Delano** U.S.A.
103 D3 **Delano Peak** U.S.A.
42 A1   **Delārām** Afgh.
91 C2   **Delareyville** S. Africa
97 D2   **Delaronde Lake** Can.
108 C2 **Delaware** U.S.A.
109 D3 **Delaware** *r.* U.S.A.
109 D3 **Delaware** *state* U.S.A.
109 D3 **Delaware Bay** U.S.A.
21 C3   **Delegate** Austr.
73 D2   **Delémont** Switz.
68 B1   **Delft** Neth.
68 C1   **Delfzijl** Neth.
89 D2   **Delgado, Cabo** *c.* Moz.
43 B2   **Delhi** India
28 B2   **Deli** *i.* Indon.
94 C2   **Déline** Can.
69 F2   **Delitzsch** Ger.
75 D2   **Dellys** Alg.
69 D1   **Delmenhorst** Ger.
77 B1   **Delnice** Croatia
51 L1   **De-Longa, Ostrova** *is*
        Rus. Fed.
79 B3   **Delphi** Greece
107 C3 **Del Rio** U.S.A.
103 D3 **Delta** *CO* U.S.A.
103 D3 **Delta** *UT* U.S.A.
94 B2   **Delta Junction** U.S.A.
77 D3   **Delvinë** Albania
86 C3   **Demba** Dem. Rep. Congo
85 B4   **Dembî Dolo** Eth.
57 D2   **Demidov** Rus. Fed.
106 B2 **Deming** U.S.A.
79 C3   **Demirci** Turkey
78 C2   **Demirköy** Turkey
70 C1   **Demmin** Ger.
110 C2 **Demopolis** U.S.A.
28 B2   **Dempo, Gunung** *vol.* Indon.
57 D2   **Demyansk** Rus. Fed.
90 B3   **De Naawte** S. Africa
85 C3   **Denakil** *reg.* Eritrea/Eth.
68 B1   **Den Burg** Neth.
68 B2   **Dendermonde** Belgium
38 A1   **Dengkou** China
38 B2   **Dengzhou** China
        Den Haag Neth. *see*
        The Hague
18 A2   **Denham** Austr.
68 B1   **Den Helder** Neth.
20 B3   **Deniliquin** Austr.
102 C2 **Denio** U.S.A.
105 D2 **Denison** *IA* U.S.A.
107 D2 **Denison** *TX* U.S.A.
79 C3   **Denizli** Turkey
21 C3   **Denman** Austr.
18 A3   **Denmark** Austr.
61 F4   **Denmark** *country* Europe
128 Q3 **Denmark Strait**
        Greenland/Iceland
29 C2   **Denpasar** Indon.
107 D2 **Denton** U.S.A.
18 A3   **D'Entrecasteaux, Point**
        Austr.
104 B3 **Denver** U.S.A.
43 C2   **Deogarh** *Orissa* India
42 B2   **Deogarh** *Rajasthan* India
43 C2   **Deoghar** India
51 K2   **Deputatskiy** Rus. Fed.
36 C3   **Dêqên** China
110 B2 **De Queen** U.S.A.
42 A2   **Dera Bugti** Pak.
42 B1   **Dera Ghazi Khan** Pak.

42 B1   **Dera Ismail Khan** Pak.
55 D4   **Derbent** Rus. Fed.
18 B1   **Derby** Austr.
67 C2   **Derby** U.K.
65 B2   **Derg, Lough** *l.*
        Rep. of Ireland
59 D1   **Derhachi** Ukr.
110 B3 **De Ridder** U.S.A.
59 D2   **Derkul** *r.* Rus. Fed./Ukr.
84 B3   **Derudeb** Sudan
90 B3   **De Rust** S. Africa
77 C2   **Derventa** Bos.-Herz.
66 C2   **Derwent** *r.* U.K.
66 B1   **Derwent Water** *l.* U.K.
45 C1   **Derzhavinsk** Kazakh.
120 B2 **Desaguadero** *r.* Bol.
97 D2   **Deschambault Lake** Can.
102 B1 **Deschutes** *r.* U.S.A.
85 B3   **Desē** Eth.
121 B5 **Deseado** Arg.
121 B5 **Deseado** *r.* Arg.
105 E2 **Des Moines** U.S.A.
105 E2 **Des Moines** *r.* U.S.A.
59 C1   **Desna** *r.* Rus. Fed./Ukr.
57 D3   **Desnogorsk** Rus. Fed.
69 F2   **Dessau** Ger.
94 B2   **Destruction Bay** Can.
96 C1   **Detah** Can.
69 D2   **Detmold** Ger.
108 C2 **Detroit** U.S.A.
105 D1 **Detroit Lakes** U.S.A.
68 C2   **Deurne** Neth.
78 B1   **Deva** Romania
68 C1   **Deventer** Neth.
64 C2   **Deveron** *r.* U.K.
71 D2   **Devět Skal** *hill* Czech Rep.
105 D1 **Devil's Lake** U.S.A.
96 A2   **Devil's Paw** *mt.* U.S.A.
67 C3   **Devizes** U.K.
42 B2   **Devli** India
78 C2   **Devnya** Bulg.
96 C2   **Devon** Can.
94 E1   **Devon Island** Can.
19 D4   **Devonport** Austr.
42 B2   **Dewas** India
27 D3   **Deyang** China
38 A2   **Deyong, Tanjung** *pt* Indon.
49 C2   **Dezfūl** Iran
38 B2   **Dezhou** China
47 C2   **Dhahran** Saudi Arabia
43 D2   **Dhaka** Bangl.
46 B3   **Dhamār** Yemen
43 C2   **Dhamtari** India
43 C2   **Dhanbad** India
43 C2   **Dhankuta** Nepal
43 C2   **Dharmanagar** India
43 C2   **Dharmjaygarh** India
41 B3   **Dhārwād** India
42 B2   **Dhasa** India
46 B3   **Dhubāb** Yemen
42 B2   **Dhule** India
112 A1 **Diablo, Picacho del**
        mt. Mex.
19 C2   **Diamantina** *watercourse*
        Austr.
123 D1 **Diamantina** Brazil
119 D3 **Diamantina, Chapada** *plat.*
        Brazil
119 C3 **Diamantino** Brazil
82 B4   **Dianra** Côte d'Ivoire
82 C3   **Diapaga** Burkina
47 C2   **Dibā al Ḩiṣn** U.A.E.
86 C3   **Dibaya** Dem. Rep. Congo
30 A1   **Dibrugarh** India
104 C1 **Dickinson** U.S.A.
110 C1 **Dickson** U.S.A.
        Dicle *r.* Turkey *see* Tigris

73 D3 **Die** France
97 D2 **Diefenbaker, Lake** Can.
82 B3 **Diéma** Mali
30 B2 **Diên Châu** Vietnam
69 D1 **Diepholz** Ger.
72 C2 **Dieppe** France
83 D3 **Diffa** Niger
99 D2 **Digby** Can.
73 D3 **Digne-les-Bains** France
73 C2 **Digoin** France
32 B2 **Digos** Phil.
27 D3 **Digul** r. Indon.
　　 Dihang r. China/India see
　　 Brahmaputra
73 C2 **Dijon** France
85 C3 **Dikhil** Djibouti
79 C3 **Dikili** Turkey
68 A2 **Diksmuide** Belgium
83 D3 **Dikwa** Nigeria
85 B4 **Dīla** Eth.
27 C3 **Dili** East Timor
69 D2 **Dillenburg** Ger.
102 D1 **Dillon** U.S.A.
86 C4 **Dilolo** Dem. Rep. Congo
30 A1 **Dimapur** India
　　 Dimashq Syria see
　　 Damascus
20 B3 **Dimboola** Austr.
78 C2 **Dimitrovgrad** Bulg.
55 D3 **Dimitrovgrad** Rus. Fed.
32 B1 **Dinagat** i. Phil.
72 B2 **Dinan** France
68 B2 **Dinant** Belgium
79 D3 **Dinar** Turkey
49 D2 **Dīnār, Kūh-e** mt. Iran
41 B3 **Dindigul** India
91 D1 **Dindiza** Moz.
69 E2 **Dingelstädt** Ger.
65 A2 **Dingle** Rep. of Ireland
65 A2 **Dingle Bay** Rep. of Ireland
64 B2 **Dingwall** U.K.
38 A2 **Dingxi** China
43 C2 **Dinngyê** China
122 B3 **Dionísio Cerqueira** Brazil
82 A3 **Diourbel** Senegal
32 B2 **Dipolog** Phil.
42 B1 **Dir** Pak.
19 D1 **Direction, Cape** Austr.
85 C4 **Dirē Dawa** Eth.
88 B2 **Dirico** Angola
18 A2 **Dirk Hartog Island** Austr.
21 C1 **Dirranbandi** Austr.
46 B3 **Dirs** Saudi Arabia
18 B2 **Disappointment, Lake**
　　 salt flat Austr.
20 B3 **Discovery Bay** b. Austr.
111 E1 **Dismal Swamp** U.S.A.
67 D2 **Diss** U.K.
76 B3 **Dittaino** r. Sicily Italy
42 B2 **Diu** India
123 D2 **Divinópolis** Brazil
55 D4 **Divnoye** Rus. Fed.
82 B4 **Divo** Côte d'Ivoire
48 B2 **Divriği** Turkey
108 B2 **Dixon** U.S.A.
96 A2 **Dixon Entrance** sea chan.
　　 Can./U.S.A.
48 C2 **Diyarbakır** Turkey
42 A2 **Diz** Pak.
83 D2 **Djado** Niger
83 D2 **Djado, Plateau du** Niger
86 B3 **Djambala** Congo
83 C2 **Djanet** Alg.
83 C1 **Djelfa** Alg.
87 C2 **Djéma** C.A.R.
82 B3 **Djenné** Mali
82 B3 **Djibo** Burkina
85 C3 **Djibouti** country Africa
85 C3 **Djibouti** Djibouti
82 C4 **Djougou** Benin

60 □C3 **Djúpivogur** Iceland
59 E1 **Dmitriyevka** Rus. Fed.
57 E3 **Dmitriyev-L'govskiy**
　　 Rus. Fed.
57 E2 **Dmitrov** Rus. Fed.
　　 Dnepr r. Rus. Fed. see
　　 Dnieper
57 D3 **Dnieper** r. Europe
　　 Dnipro r. Ukr. see **Dnieper**
59 C2 **Dniprodzerzhyns'k** Ukr.
59 D2 **Dnipropetrovs'k** Ukr.
59 C2 **Dniprorudne** Ukr.
58 B2 **Dnister** r. Ukr.
56 C2 **Dno** Rus. Fed.
83 D4 **Doba** Chad
56 B2 **Dobele** Latvia
69 F2 **Döbeln** Ger.
27 C3 **Doberai, Jazirah** pen.
　　 Indon.
27 C3 **Dobo** Indon.
77 C2 **Doboj** Bos.-Herz.
78 C2 **Dobrich** Bulg.
57 F3 **Dobrinka** Rus. Fed.
57 E3 **Dobroye** Rus. Fed.
57 D3 **Dobrush** Belarus
123 E1 **Doce** r. Brazil
113 B2 **Doctor Arroyo** Mex.
112 B2 **Doctor Belisario**
　　 Domínguez Mex.
79 C3 **Dodecanese** is Greece
　　 Dodekanisos is Greece see
　　 Dodecanese
104 C3 **Dodge City** U.S.A.
87 D3 **Dodoma** Tanz.
68 C2 **Doetinchem** Neth.
27 C3 **Dofa** Indon.
43 C1 **Dogai Coring** salt l. China
96 B2 **Dog Creek** Can.
35 B3 **Dōgo** i. Japan
83 C3 **Dogondoutchi** Niger
49 C2 **Doğubeyazıt** Turkey
47 C2 **Doha** Qatar
30 A2 **Doi Saket** Thai.
68 B1 **Dokkum** Neth.
56 C3 **Dokshytsy** Belarus
59 D2 **Dokuchayevs'k** Ukr.
27 D3 **Dolak, Pulau** i. Indon.
57 D2 **Dolbeau** Can.
72 B2 **Dol-de-Bretagne** France
73 D2 **Dole** France
67 B2 **Dolgellau** U.K.
57 E3 **Dolgorukovo** Rus. Fed.
57 E3 **Dolgoye** Rus. Fed.
76 B1 **Dolomites** mts Italy
85 C4 **Dolo Odo** Eth.
94 D2 **Dolphin and Union Strait**
　　 Can.
58 A2 **Dolyna** Ukr.
70 C2 **Domažlice** Czech Rep.
61 E3 **Dombås** Norway
71 D2 **Dombóvár** Hungary
96 B2 **Dome Creek** Can.
115 D3 **Dominica** country
　　 West Indies
115 D3 **Dominican Republic** country
　　 West Indies
57 E2 **Domodedovo** Rus. Fed.
79 B3 **Domokos** Greece
29 C2 **Dompu** Indon.
57 E3 **Don** r. Rus. Fed.
64 C2 **Don** r. U.K.
65 D1 **Donaghadee** U.K.
20 B3 **Donald** Austr.
　　 Donau r. Austria/Ger. see
　　 Danube
70 C2 **Donauwörth** Ger.
74 B2 **Don Benito** Spain
66 C2 **Doncaster** U.K.
88 A1 **Dondo** Angola
89 C2 **Dondo** Moz.

41 C4 **Dondra Head** hd Sri Lanka
65 B1 **Donegal** Rep. of Ireland
65 B1 **Donegal Bay** Rep. of Ireland
59 D2 **Donets'k** Ukr.
59 D2 **Donets'kyy Kryazh** hills
　　 Rus. Fed./Ukr.
18 A2 **Dongara** Austr.
30 B1 **Dongchuan** China
39 A4 **Dongfang** China
34 B1 **Dongfanghong** China
26 B3 **Donggala** Indon.
33 A2 **Donggang** China
30 B2 **Đông Ha** Vietnam
　　 Dong Hai sea N. Pacific
　　 Ocean see **East China Sea**
30 B2 **Đông Hôi** Vietnam
86 B3 **Dongou** Congo
31 B2 **Dong Phraya Fai** mts Thai.
39 B3 **Dongshan** China
38 B2 **Dongsheng** China
38 C2 **Dongtai** China
39 B3 **Dongting Hu** l. China
　　 Dong Ujimqin Qi China see
　　 Uliastai
38 B2 **Dongying** China
22 B1 **Donnellys Crossing** N.Z.
75 C1 **Donostia-San Sebastián**
　　 Spain
85 C4 **Dooxo Nugaaleed** val.
　　 Somalia
67 B3 **Dorchester** U.K.
90 A1 **Dordabis** Namibia
72 B2 **Dordogne** r. France
68 B2 **Dordrecht** Neth.
91 C3 **Dordrecht** S. Africa
97 D2 **Doré Lake** l. Can.
69 D1 **Dorfmark** Ger.
82 B3 **Dori** Burkina
90 A3 **Doring** r. S. Africa
64 B2 **Dornoch** U.K.
64 B2 **Dornoch Firth** est. U.K.
57 D3 **Dorogobuzh** Rus. Fed.
58 B2 **Dorohoi** Romania
36 C1 **Döröö Nuur** salt l.
　　 Mongolia
60 G3 **Dorotea** Sweden
18 A2 **Dorre Island** Austr.
21 D2 **Dorrigo** Austr.
86 B2 **Dorsale Camerounaise**
　　 slope Cameroon/Nigeria
68 C2 **Dortmund** Ger.
68 C2 **Dortmund-Ems-Kanal**
　　 canal Ger.
121 B5 **Dos Bahías, Cabo** c. Arg.
69 F1 **Dosse** r. Ger.
82 C3 **Dosso** Niger
111 C2 **Dothan** U.S.A.
69 D1 **Dötlingen** Ger.
73 C1 **Douai** France
86 A2 **Douala** Cameroon
72 B2 **Douarnenez** France
82 B3 **Douentza** Mali
66 A1 **Douglas** Isle of Man
90 B2 **Douglas** S. Africa
96 A2 **Douglas** AK U.S.A.
106 B2 **Douglas** AZ U.S.A.
111 D2 **Douglas** GA U.S.A.
104 B2 **Douglas** WY U.S.A.
72 C1 **Doullens** France
122 B1 **Dourada, Serra** hills Brazil
122 B2 **Dourados** Brazil
122 B2 **Dourados, Serra dos** hills
　　 Brazil
74 B1 **Douro** r. Port.
67 D3 **Dover** U.K.
109 D3 **Dover** U.S.A.
63 D3 **Dover, Strait of** France/U.K.
109 F1 **Dover-Foxcroft** U.S.A.
47 C2 **Dowlatābād** Būshehr Iran
47 C2 **Dowlatābād** Kermān Iran

65 D1 **Downpatrick** U.K.
45 C3 **Dowshi** Afgh.
35 B3 **Dōzen** *is* Japan
98 C2 **Dozois, Réservoir** *resr* Can.
122 B2 **Dracena** Brazil
68 C1 **Drachten** Neth.
78 B2 **Drăgăneşti-Olt** Romania
78 B2 **Drăgăşani** Romania
56 C3 **Drahichyn** Belarus
91 C2 **Drakensberg** *mts* Lesotho/S. Africa
91 C2 **Drakensberg** *mts* S. Africa
126 B8 **Drake Passage** S. Atlantic Ocean
79 B2 **Drama** Greece
61 F4 **Drammen** Norway
77 C1 **Drava** *r.* Europe
96 C2 **Drayton Valley** Can.
69 D2 **Dreieich** Ger.
79 B3 **Drepano, Akra** *pt* Greece
70 C1 **Dresden** Ger.
72 C2 **Dreux** France
68 B1 **Driemond** Neth.
77 C2 **Drina** *r.* Bos.-Herz./Yugo.
77 C2 **Drniš** Croatia
78 B2 **Drobeta-Turnu Severin** Romania
69 D1 **Drochtersen** Ger.
65 C2 **Drogheda** Rep. of Ireland
58 A2 **Drohobych** Ukr.
65 C1 **Dromore** U.K.
42 B1 **Drosh** Pak.
21 C3 **Drouin** Austr.
96 C2 **Drumheller** Can.
108 C1 **Drummond Island** U.S.A.
99 C2 **Drummondville** Can.
56 B3 **Druskininkai** Lith.
59 D2 **Druzhkivka** Ukr.
56 D2 **Druzhnaya Gorka** Rus. Fed.
98 A2 **Dryden** Can.
18 B1 **Drysdale** *r.* Austr.
46 A2 **Dubā** Saudi Arabia
47 C2 **Dubai** U.A.E.
97 D1 **Dubawnt Lake** Can.
       Dubayy U.A.E. *see* Dubai
46 A2 **Dubbagh, Jabal ad** *mt.* Saudi Arabia
21 C2 **Dubbo** Austr.
65 C2 **Dublin** Rep. of Ireland
111 D2 **Dublin** U.S.A.
58 B1 **Dubno** Ukr.
109 D2 **Du Bois** U.S.A.
82 A4 **Dubréka** Guinea
77 C2 **Dubrovnik** Croatia
58 B1 **Dubrovytsya** Ukr.
57 D3 **Dubrowna** Belarus
105 E2 **Dubuque** U.S.A.
97 D2 **Duck Bay** Can.
31 B2 **Đuc Trong** Vietnam
69 E2 **Duderstadt** Ger.
50 G2 **Dudinka** Rus. Fed.
67 B2 **Dudley** U.K.
74 B1 **Duero** *r.* Spain
64 C2 **Dufftown** U.K.
99 C1 **Dufreboy, Lac** *l.* Can.
77 C2 **Dugi Rat** Croatia
68 C2 **Duisburg** Ger.
91 D1 **Duiwelskloof** S. Africa
91 C3 **Dukathole** S. Africa
47 C2 **Dukhān** Qatar
57 D2 **Dukhovshchina** Rus. Fed.
       Dukou China *see* Panzhihua
56 C2 **Dūkštas** Lith.
36 C2 **Dulan** China
120 B4 **Dulce** *r.* Arg.
68 C2 **Dülmen** Ger.
78 B2 **Dulovo** Bulg.
105 E1 **Duluth** U.S.A.
32 B2 **Dumaguete** Phil.

28 B1 **Dumai** Indon.
32 B1 **Dumaran** *i.* Phil.
110 B2 **Dumas** *AR* U.S.A.
107 C1 **Dumas** *TX* U.S.A.
64 B3 **Dumbarton** U.K.
71 D2 **Ďumbier** *mt.* Slovakia
64 C3 **Dumfries** U.K.
23 J3 **Dumont d'Urville Sea** Antarctica
84 B1 **Dumyât** Egypt
       Duna *r.* Hungary *see* Danube
       Dunaj *r.* Slovakia *see* Danube
71 D2 **Dunakeszi** Hungary
       Dunărea *r.* Romania *see* Danube
78 C1 **Dunării, Delta** Romania
71 D2 **Dunaújváros** Hungary
       Dunav *r.* Yugo. *see* Danube
58 B2 **Dunayivtsi** Ukr.
64 C2 **Dunbar** U.K.
64 C1 **Dunbeath** U.K.
96 B3 **Duncan** Can.
107 D2 **Duncan** U.S.A.
64 C1 **Duncansby Head** *hd* U.K.
65 C1 **Dundalk** Rep. of Ireland
65 C2 **Dundalk Bay** Rep. of Ireland
       Dundas Greenland *see* Uummannaq
91 C2 **Dundee** S. Africa
64 C2 **Dundee** U.K.
65 D1 **Drundrum Bay** U.K.
22 B3 **Dunedin** N.Z.
64 C2 **Dunfermline** U.K.
65 C1 **Dungannon** U.K.
42 B2 **Dungarpur** India
65 C2 **Dungarvan** Rep. of Ireland
67 D3 **Dungeness** *hd* U.K.
65 C1 **Dungiven** U.K.
21 D2 **Dungog** Austr.
87 C2 **Dungu** Dem. Rep. Congo
28 B1 **Dungun** Malaysia
84 B2 **Dunqunab** Sudan
37 E2 **Dunhua** China
36 C2 **Dunhuang** China
       Dunkerque France *see* Dunkirk
72 C1 **Dunkirk** France
109 D2 **Dunkirk** U.S.A.
65 C2 **Dún Laoghaire** Rep. of Ireland
65 D1 **Dunmurry** U.K.
64 C1 **Dunnet Head** *hd* U.K.
64 C3 **Duns** U.K.
67 C3 **Dunstable** U.K.
78 B2 **Dupnitsa** Bulg.
104 C1 **Dupree** U.S.A.
18 B1 **Durack** *r.* Austr.
112 B2 **Durango** Mex.
74 C1 **Durango** Spain
104 B3 **Durango** U.S.A.
107 D2 **Durant** U.S.A.
121 C4 **Durazno** Uru.
91 D2 **Durban** S. Africa
72 C3 **Durban-Corbières** France
90 A3 **Durbanville** S. Africa
68 B2 **Durbuy** Belgium
68 C2 **Düren** Ger.
111 E1 **Durham** U.S.A.
28 B1 **Duri** Indon.
77 C2 **Durmitor** *mt.* Yugo.
64 B1 **Durness** U.K.
77 C2 **Durrës** Albania
65 A3 **Dursey Island** Rep. of Ireland
79 C3 **Dursunbey** Turkey
27 D3 **D'Urville, Tanjung** *pt* Indon.
22 B2 **D'Urville Island** N.Z.
39 A3 **Dushan** China
45 C2 **Dushanbe** Tajik.

68 C2 **Düsseldorf** Ger.
39 A3 **Duyun** China
59 D2 **Dvorichna** Ukr.
42 A2 **Dwarka** India
91 C1 **Dwarsberg** S. Africa
102 C1 **Dworshak Reservoir** U.S.A.
57 D3 **Dyat'kovo** Rus. Fed.
64 C2 **Dyce** U.K.
95 G2 **Dyer, Cape** Can.
110 C1 **Dyersburg** U.S.A.
71 D2 **Dyje** *r.* Austria/Czech Rep.
71 D1 **Dylewska Góra** *hill* Pol.
59 D2 **Dymytrov** Ukr.
91 C3 **Dyoki** S. Africa
55 E3 **Dyurtyuli** Rus. Fed.
37 D2 **Dzamïn Üüd** Mongolia
       Dzhambul Kazakh. *see* Taraz
49 D1 **Dzhanga** Turkm.
44 B2 **Dzhangala** Kazakh.
59 C2 **Dzhankoy** Ukr.
55 D4 **Dzhanybek** Kazakh.
45 C2 **Dzhizak** Uzbek.
59 D3 **Dzhubga** Rus. Fed.
51 K3 **Dzhugdzhur, Khrebet** *mts* Rus. Fed.
       Dzhungarskiy Alatau, Khrebet *mts* China/Kazakh.
44 C2 **Dzhusaly** Kazakh.
71 E1 **Działdowo** Pol.
37 D1 **Dzuunmod** Mongolia
56 C3 **Dzyarzhynsk** Belarus
56 C3 **Dzyatlavichy** Belarus

E

99 E1 **Eagle** *r.* Can.
102 C1 **Eagle Cap** *mt.* U.S.A.
98 A2 **Eagle Lake** *l.* Can.
102 B2 **Eagle Lake** *l.* U.S.A.
107 C3 **Eagle Pass** U.S.A.
94 B2 **Eagle Plain** Can.
98 A1 **Ear Falls** Can.
67 D3 **Eastbourne** U.K.
124 C3 **East China Sea** N. Pacific Ocean
22 B1 **East Coast Bays** N.Z.
67 D2 **East Dereham** U.K.
97 D3 **Eastend** Can.
116 B4 **Easter Island** *i.* S. Pacific Ocean
91 C3 **Eastern Cape** *prov.* S. Africa
84 B2 **Eastern Desert** Egypt
41 B3 **Eastern Ghats** *mts* India
97 E2 **Easterville** Can.
121 C6 **East Falkland** *i.* Falkland Is.
68 C1 **East Frisian Islands** *is* Ger.
64 B3 **East Kilbride** U.K.
67 C3 **Eastleigh** U.K.
108 C2 **East Liverpool** U.S.A.
91 C3 **East London** S. Africa
98 C1 **Eastmain** Can.
98 C1 **Eastmain** *r.* Can.
111 D2 **Eastman** U.S.A.
108 A3 **East St Louis** U.S.A.
       East Siberian Sea Rus. Fed. *see* Vostochno-Sibirskoye More
27 C3 **East Timor** *country* Asia
108 A2 **Eau Claire** U.S.A.
27 D2 **Eauripik** *atoll* Micronesia
113 C2 **Ebano** Mex.
67 B3 **Ebbw Vale** U.K.
70 C1 **Eberswalde-Finow** Ger.
77 C2 **Eboli** Italy
86 B2 **Ebolowa** Cameroon
75 D1 **Ebro** *r.* Spain
75 C1 **Echarri-Aranaz** Spain
82 C1 **Ech Chélif** Alg.

112 A2 **Echeverria, Pico** *mt.* Mex.
97 E2 **Echoing** *r.* Can.
68 C3 **Echternach** Lux.
20 B3 **Echuca** Austr.
74 B2 **Écija** Spain
70 B1 **Eckernförde** Ger.
95 F2 **Eclipse Sound** *sea chan.* Can.
118 A2 **Ecuador** *country* S. America
84 C3 **Ed** Eritrea
85 A3 **Ed Da'ein** Sudan
85 B3 **Ed Damazin** Sudan
84 B3 **Ed Damer** Sudan
84 B3 **Ed Debba** Sudan
84 B3 **Ed Dueim** Sudan
19 D4 **Eddystone Point** Austr.
68 B1 **Ede** Neth.
86 B2 **Edéa** Cameroon
122 C1 **Edéia** Brazil
21 C3 **Eden** Austr.
65 E4 **Eden** *r.* U.K.
91 C2 **Edenburg** S. Africa
65 C2 **Edenderry** Rep. of Ireland
20 B3 **Edenhope** Austr.
79 B2 **Edessa** Greece
50 C1 **Edgeøya** *i.* Svalbard
107 D3 **Edinburg** U.S.A.
64 C3 **Edinburgh** U.K.
78 C2 **Edirne** Turkey
96 C2 **Edmonton** Can.
99 D2 **Edmundston** Can.
79 C3 **Edremit** Turkey
79 C3 **Edremit Körfezi** *b.* Turkey
62 C2 **Edson** Can.
07 C3 **Edward, Lake** Dem. Rep Congo/Uganda
107 C2 **Edwards Plateau** *TX* U.S.A.
68 C1 **Eenrum** Neth.
108 B3 **Effingham** U.S.A.
103 C3 **Egan Range** *mts* U.S.A.
71 E2 **Eger** Hungary
61 E4 **Egersund** Norway
60 ☐C2 **Egilsstaðir** Iceland
48 B2 **Eğirdir** Turkey
48 B2 **Eğirdir Gölü** *l.* Turkey
72 C2 **Égletons** France
22 B1 **Egmont, Mt** *vol.* N.Z.
51 M2 **Egvekinot** Rus. Fed.
84 B2 **Egypt** *country* Africa
36 C2 **Ehen Hudag** China
68 C1 **Eibergen** Neth.
68 C2 **Eifel** *hills* Ger.
64 A2 **Eigg** *i.* U.K.
41 B4 **Eight Degree Channel** India/Maldives
18 B1 **Eighty Mile Beach** Austr.
69 F2 **Eilenburg** Ger.
69 D2 **Einbeck** Ger.
68 B2 **Eindhoven** Neth.
118 B2 **Eirunepé** Brazil
88 B2 **Eiseb** *watercourse* Namibia
69 E2 **Eisenach** Ger.
70 C1 **Eisenhüttenstadt** Ger.
71 D2 **Eisenstadt** Austria
69 E2 **Eisleben Lutherstadt** Ger.
75 C2 **Eivissa** Spain
Eivissa *i.* Spain *see* **Ibiza**
75 C1 **Ejea de los Caballeros** Spain
89 ☐D3 **Ejeda** Madag.
Ejin Qi China *see* **Dalain Hob**
61 H4 **Ekenäs** Fin.
45 D1 **Ekibastuz** Kazakh.
60 J2 **Ekostrovskaya Imandra, Ozero** *l.* Rus. Fed.
61 F4 **Eksjö** Sweden
90 A2 **Eksteenfontein** S. Africa
61 F4 **Ekwan** *r.* Can.
30 A2 **Ela** Myanmar
48 A2 **El 'Amirîya** Egypt

91 C2 **Elandsdoorn** S. Africa
48 B2 **El 'Arîsh** Egypt
79 B3 **Elassona** Greece
48 B3 **Elat** Israel
48 B2 **Elazığ** Turkey
76 B2 **Elba, Isola d'** *i.* Italy
118 A1 **El Banco** Col.
77 D2 **Elbasan** Albania
118 B1 **El Baúl** Venez.
82 C1 **El Bayadh** Alg.
69 D1 **Elbe** *r.* Ger.
104 B3 **Elbert, Mount** U.S.A.
111 D2 **Elberton** U.S.A.
72 C2 **Elbeuf** France
48 B2 **Elbistan** Turkey
71 D1 **Elbląg** Pol.
55 D4 **Elbrus** *mt.* Rus. Fed.
Elburz Mountains Iran *see* **Alborz, Reshteh-ye**
118 B1 **El Callao** Venez.
107 D3 **El Campo** U.S.A.
103 C4 **El Centro** U.S.A.
120 B2 **El Cerro** Bol.
75 C2 **Elche** Spain
75 C2 **Elda** Spain
105 E3 **Eldon** U.S.A.
112 B2 **El Dorado** Mex.
110 B2 **El Dorado** *AR* U.S.A.
105 D3 **El Dorado** *KS* U.S.A.
82 B2 **El Eglab** *plat.* Alg.
74 C2 **El Ejido** Spain
57 E2 **Elektrostal'** Rus. Fed.
118 A2 **El Encanto** Col.
114 C2 **Eleuthera** *i.* Bahamas
85 A3 **El Fasher** Sudan
112 B2 **El Fuerte** Mex.
85 A3 **El Geneina** Sudan
84 B3 **El Geteina** Sudan
64 C2 **Elgin** U.K.
108 B2 **Elgin** U.S.A.
84 B2 **El Gîza** Egypt
83 C1 **El Goléa** Alg.
112 A1 **El Golfo de Santa Clara** Mex.
87 D2 **Elgon, Mount** Uganda
48 A2 **El Hammâm** Egypt
82 A2 **El Hammâmi** *reg.* Maur.
82 A2 **El Hierro** *i.* Canary Is
113 C2 **El Higo** Mex.
82 C2 **El Homr** Alg.
El Iskandarîya Egypt *see* **Alexandria**
55 D4 **Elista** Rus. Fed.
109 E2 **Elizabeth** U.S.A.
111 C1 **Elizabeth City** U.S.A.
108 B3 **Elizabethtown** U.S.A.
82 B1 **El Jadida** Morocco
71 E1 **Ełk** Pol.
107 D1 **Elk City** U.S.A.
96 C2 **Elkford** Can.
84 B2 **El Khârga** Egypt
108 B2 **Elkhart** U.S.A.
El Khartum Sudan *see* **Khartoum**
78 C2 **Elkhovo** Bulg.
108 D3 **Elkins** U.S.A.
96 C3 **Elko** Can.
102 C2 **Elko** U.S.A.
97 C2 **Elk Point** Can.
94 E1 **Ellef Ringnes Island** Can.
105 D1 **Ellendale** U.S.A.
102 B1 **Ellensburg** U.S.A.
22 B2 **Ellesmere, Lake** N.Z.
95 F1 **Ellesmere Island** Can.
66 B2 **Ellesmere Port** U.K.
23 O2 **Ellesworth Mountains** Antarctica
94 E2 **Ellice** *r.* Can.
Ellice Islands *country* S. Pacific Ocean *see* **Tuvalu**

91 C3 **Elliotdale** S. Africa
91 C1 **Ellisras** S. Africa
64 C2 **Ellon** U.K.
109 F2 **Ellsworth** U.S.A.
79 C3 **Elmalı** Turkey
48 B2 **El Mansûra** Egypt
83 C1 **El Meghaïer** Alg.
84 B2 **El Minya** Egypt
109 D2 **Elmira** U.S.A.
75 C2 **El Moral** Spain
69 D1 **Elmshorn** Ger.
85 A3 **El Muglad** Sudan
32 A1 **El Nido** Phil.
85 B3 **El Obeid** Sudan
112 B2 **El Oro** Mex.
83 C1 **El Oued** Alg.
106 A2 **Eloy** U.S.A.
106 B2 **El Paso** U.S.A.
112 B1 **El Porvenír** Mex.
75 D1 **El Prat de Llobregat** Spain
El Qâhira Egypt *see* **Cairo**
107 D1 **El Reno** U.S.A.
113 B2 **El Salado** Mex.
112 B2 **El Salto** Mex.
114 B3 **El Salvador** *country* Central America
113 B2 **El Salvador** Mex.
106 B3 **El Sauz** Mex.
112 A1 **El Socorro** Mex.
El Suweis Egypt *see* **Suez**
113 C2 **El Temascal** Mex.
118 B1 **El Tigre** Venez.
115 D4 **El Tocuyo** Venez.
84 B2 **El Tûr** Egypt
El Uqsur Egypt *see* **Luxor**
56 C2 **Elva** Estonia
74 B2 **Elvas** Port.
61 E3 **Elverum** Norway
87 E2 **El Wak** Kenya
67 D2 **Ely** U.K.
105 E1 **Ely** *MN* U.S.A.
103 D3 **Ely** *NV* U.S.A.
49 D2 **Emāmrūd** Iran
61 G4 **Emån** *r.* Sweden
44 B2 **Emba** Kazakh.
44 B2 **Emba** *r.* Kazakh.
91 C2 **Embalenhle** S. Africa
122 C1 **Emborcação, Represa de** *resr* Brazil
87 D3 **Embu** Kenya
68 C1 **Emden** Ger.
19 D2 **Emerald** Austr.
97 E3 **Emerson** Can.
79 C3 **Emet** Turkey
91 C2 **eMgwenya** S. Africa
91 C2 **eMijindini** S. Africa
83 D3 **Emi Koussi** *mt.* Chad
78 C2 **Emine, Nos** *pt* Bulg.
48 B2 **Emirdağ** Turkey
56 B2 **Emmaste** Estonia
68 B1 **Emmeloord** Neth.
68 C2 **Emmelshausen** Ger.
68 C1 **Emmen** Neth.
107 C3 **Emory Peak** U.S.A.
112 A2 **Empalme** Mex.
91 D2 **Empangeni** S. Africa
76 B2 **Empoli** Italy
105 D3 **Emporia** *KS* U.S.A.
109 D3 **Emporia** *VA* U.S.A.
68 C1 **Ems** *r.* Ger.
68 C1 **Emsdetten** Ger.
91 C3 **Emzinoni** S. Africa
27 D3 **Enarotali** Indon.
112 B2 **Encarnación** Mex.
120 C3 **Encarnación** Para.
123 D1 **Encruzilhada** Brazil
28 B1 **Endau** Malaysia
26 C3 **Endeh** Indon.
94 A2 **Endicott Mountains** U.S.A.
59 C2 **Enerhodar** Ukr.

55 D3 Engel's Rus. Fed.
28 B2 Enggano *i.* Indon.
66 C2 England *admin. div.* U.K.
98 A1 English *r.* Can.
63 C4 English Channel
       France/U.K.
107 D1 Enid U.S.A.
68 B1 Enkhuizen Neth.
61 G4 Enköping Sweden
76 B3 Enna *Sicily* Italy
97 D1 Ennadai Lake Can.
85 A3 En Nahud Sudan
83 E3 Ennedi, Massif *mts* Chad
21 C1 Enngonia Austr.
65 B2 Ennis Rep. of Ireland
107 D2 Ennis U.S.A.
65 C2 Enniscorthy Rep. of Ireland
65 C1 Enniskillen U.K.
65 B2 Ennistymon Rep. of Ireland
70 C2 Enns *r.* Austria
60 H2 Enontekiö Fin.
21 C1 Ensay Austr.
68 C1 Enschede Neth.
112 A1 Ensenada Mex.
38 A2 Enshi China
96 C1 Enterprise China
110 C2 Enterprise *AL* U.S.A.
102 C1 Enterprise *OR* U.S.A.
120 B3 Entre Rios Bol.
74 B2 Entroncamento Port.
83 C4 Enugu Nigeria
118 A2 Envira Brazil
103 D3 Ephraim U.S.A.
102 C1 Ephrata U.S.A.
73 D2 Épinal France
67 C3 Epsom U.K.
86 A2 Equatorial Guinea *country*
       Africa
69 F3 Erbendorf Ger.
68 C3 Erbeskopf *hill* Ger.
49 C2 Erciş Turkey
33 B1 Erdao Jiang *r.* China
79 C2 Erdek Turkey
48 B2 Erdemli Turkey
120 C3 Erechim Brazil
37 D1 Ereentsav Mongolia
48 B2 Ereğli *Konya* Turkey
48 B1 Ereğli *Zonguldak* Turkey
37 D2 Erenhot China
69 E2 Erevan Armenia *see* Yerevan
       Erfurt Ger.
48 B2 Ergani Turkey
82 B2 'Erg Chech *des.* Alg./Mali
83 D3 Erg du Ténéré *des.* Niger
79 C2 Ergene *r.* Turkey
108 C2 Erie U.S.A.
108 C2 Erie, Lake Can./U.S.A.
34 D2 Erimo-misaki *c.* Japan
84 B3 Eritrea *country* Africa
69 E3 Erlangen Ger.
18 C2 Erldunda Austr.
91 C3 Ermelo S. Africa
48 B2 Ermenek Turkey
79 B3 Ermoupoli Greece
41 B4 Ernakulam India
41 B3 Erode India
68 B2 Erp Neth.
82 B1 Er Rachidia Morocco
85 B3 Er Rahad Sudan
65 B1 Errigal *hill* Rep. of Ireland
65 A1 Erris Head *hd* Rep. of Ireland
77 D2 Erseka Albania
59 E1 Ertil' Rus. Fed.
69 D2 Erwitte Ger.
69 F2 Erzgebirge *mts*
       Czech Rep./Ger.
48 B2 Erzincan Turkey
49 C2 Erzurum Turkey
61 E4 Esbjerg Denmark
103 D3 Escalante U.S.A.

112 B2 Escalón Mex.
108 B1 Escanaba U.S.A.
113 C3 Escárcega Mex.
75 C1 Escatrón Spain
68 A2 Escaut *r.* Belgium
69 E1 Eschede Ger.
68 B3 Esch-sur-Alzette Lux.
69 E2 Eschwege Ger.
68 C2 Eschweiler Ger.
103 C4 Escondido U.S.A.
112 B2 Escuinapa Mex.
79 C3 Eşen Turkey
49 D2 Eşfahān Iran
91 D2 Esikhawini S. Africa
66 B1 Esk *r.* U.K.
99 D1 Esker Can.
60 □C2 Eskifjörður Iceland
61 G4 Eskilstuna Sweden
       Eskimo Point Can. *see*
       Arviat
48 B2 Eskişehir Turkey
49 C2 Eslāmābād-e Gharb Iran
79 C3 Esler Dağı *mt.* Turkey
79 C3 Eşme Turkey
118 A1 Esmeraldas Ecuador
47 D2 Espakeh Iran
72 C3 Espalion France
98 B2 Espanola Can.
106 B1 Espanola U.S.A.
18 B3 Esperance Austr.
112 B2 Esperanza Mex.
74 B2 Espichel, Cabo *c.* Port.
123 D1 Espinhaço, Serra do *mts*
       Brazil
119 D3 Espinosa Brazil
112 A2 Espíritu Santo, Isla *i.* Mex.
61 H3 Espoo Fin.
121 A5 Esquel Arg.
82 B1 Essaouira Morocco
82 A2 Es Semara Western Sahara
68 C2 Essen Ger.
118 C1 Essequibo *r.* Guyana
51 L3 Esso Rus. Fed.
47 C2 Eşţahbān Iran
119 E3 Estância Brazil
91 C2 Estcourt S. Africa
75 C1 Estella Spain
74 B2 Estepona Spain
74 C1 Esteras de Medinaceli
       Spain
97 D2 Esterhazy Can.
120 B3 Esteros Para.
104 B2 Estes Park U.S.A.
97 D3 Estevan Can.
105 E2 Estherville U.S.A.
97 D2 Eston Can.
56 C2 Estonia *country* Europe
74 B1 Estrela, Serra da *mts* Port.
74 B2 Estremoz Port.
20 A1 Étadunna Austr.
72 C2 Étampes France
72 C1 Étaples France
43 B2 Etawah India
91 D2 eThandakukhanya S. Africa
85 B4 Ethiopia *country* Africa
77 C3 Etna, Monte *vol. Sicily* Italy
96 A2 Etolin Island *i.* U.S.A.
88 A2 Etosha Pan *salt pan* Namibia
68 C3 Ettelbruck Lux.
68 B2 Etten-Leur Neth.
67 D3 Eu France
21 C2 Euabalong Austr.
       Euboea *i.* Greece *see* Evvoia
18 B3 Eucla Austr.
111 C2 Eufaula U.S.A.
107 D1 Eufaula Lake *resr* U.S.A.
102 B2 Eugene U.S.A.
112 A2 Eugenia, Punta *pt* Mex.
21 C1 Eulo Austr.
21 C2 Eumungerie Austr.

107 C2 Eunice U.S.A.
48 C2 Euphrates *r.* Asia
102 B2 Eureka *CA* U.S.A.
102 C1 Eureka *MT* U.S.A.
103 C3 Eureka *NV* U.S.A.
20 B2 Euriowie Austr.
21 C3 Euroa Austr.
74 B2 Europa Point Gibraltar
96 B2 Eutsuk Lake Can.
98 C1 Evans, Lac *l.* Can.
21 D1 Evans Head Austr.
95 F2 Evans Strait Can.
104 A2 Evanston U.S.A.
108 B3 Evansville U.S.A.
91 C2 Evaton S. Africa
47 C2 Evaz Iran
51 L2 Evensk Rus. Fed.
18 C2 Everard Range *hills* Austr.
43 C2 Everest, Mount China/Nep.
102 B1 Everett U.S.A.
68 A2 Evergem Belgium
111 D3 Everglades *swamp* U.S.A.
86 B2 Evinayong Equat. Guinea
61 E4 Evje Norway
74 B2 Évora Port.
72 C2 Évreux France
79 C3 Evros *r.* Greece/Turkey
79 B3 Evrotas *r.* Greece
48 B2 Evrychou Cyprus
79 B3 Evvoia *i.* Greece
87 E2 Ewaso Ngiro *r.* Kenya
120 B2 Exaltación Bol.
67 B3 Exe *r.* U.K.
67 B3 Exeter U.K.
67 B3 Exmoor *hills* U.K.
67 B3 Exmouth U.K.
18 A2 Exmouth Gulf Austr.
114 C2 Exuma Cays *is* Bahamas
59 D2 Eya *r.* Rus. Fed.
85 C4 Eyl Somalia
20 A1 Eyre, Lake *salt flat* Austr.
19 C3 Eyre Peninsula Austr.
62 B1 Eysturoy *i.* Faroe Is
91 D2 Ezakheni S. Africa
91 C2 Ezenzeleni S. Africa
38 B2 Ezhou China
54 E2 Ezhva Rus. Fed.
79 C3 Ezine Turkey

F

106 B2 Fabens U.S.A.
76 B2 Fabriano Italy
83 D3 Fachi Niger
82 C3 Fada-Ngourma Burkina
76 B2 Faenza Italy
27 C3 Fafanlap Indon.
78 B1 Făgăraş Romania
61 E3 Fagernes Norway
61 G4 Fagersta Sweden
121 B6 Fagnano, Lago *l.* Arg./Chile
82 B3 Faguibine, Lac *l.* Mali
60 □B3 Fagurhólsmýri Iceland
94 B2 Fairbanks U.S.A.
105 D2 Fairbury U.S.A.
103 B3 Fairfield U.S.A.
64 □ Fair Isle *i.* U.K.
105 E2 Fairmont *MN* U.S.A.
108 C3 Fairmont *WV* U.S.A.
96 C2 Fairview Can.
27 D2 Fais *i.* Micronesia
42 B1 Faisalabad Pak.
104 C1 Faith U.S.A.
43 C2 Faizabad India
27 C3 Fakfak Indon.
33 A1 Faku China
82 A4 Falaba Sierra Leone

107 D3 **Falcon Lake** *l.* Mex./U.S.A.
107 D3 **Falfurrias** U.S.A.
96 C2 **Falher** Can.
69 F2 **Falkenberg** Ger.
61 F4 **Falkenberg** Sweden
69 F1 **Falkensee** Ger.
64 C3 **Falkirk** U.K.
121 C6 **Falkland Islands** *terr.*
S. Atlantic Ocean
61 F4 **Falköping** Sweden
103 C3 **Fallon** U.S.A.
109 E2 **Fall River** U.S.A.
105 D2 **Falls City** U.S.A.
67 A3 **Falmouth** U.K.
90 A3 **False Bay** S. Africa
61 F4 **Falster** *i.* Denmark
78 C1 **Fălticeni** Romania
61 G3 **Falun** Sweden
39 A3 **Fangchenggang** China
39 C3 **Fangshan** Taiwan
37 E1 **Fangzheng** China
76 B2 **Fano** Italy
30 B1 **Fan Si Pan** *mt.* Vietnam
87 C2 **Faradje** Dem. Rep. Congo
89 □D3 **Farafangana** Madag.
89 □D3 **Farafra Oasis** Egypt
44 C3 **Farāh** Afgh.
82 A3 **Faranah** Guinea
46 B3 **Farasān, Jazāʾir** *is*
Saudi Arabia
22 B2 **Farewell, Cape** N.Z.
105 D1 **Fargo** U.S.A.
105 E2 **Faribault** U.S.A.
109 E2 **Farmington** *ME* U.S.A.
106 B1 **Farmington** *NM* U.S.A.
109 □3 **Farmville** U.S.A.
67 C3 **Farnborough** U.K.
96 C2 **Farnham, Mount** Can.
96 A1 **Faro** Can.
74 B2 **Faro** Port.
56 A2 **Fårö** *i.* Sweden
62 B1 **Faroe Islands** *terr.*
N. Atlantic Ocean
47 C2 **Farrāshband** Iran
Farvel, Kap *c.* Greenland *see*
Nunap Isua
107 C2 **Farwell** U.S.A.
47 C2 **Fāryāb** Iran
47 C2 **Fasā** Iran
77 C2 **Fasano** Italy
58 B1 **Fastiv** Ukr.
43 B2 **Fatehgarh** India
43 C2 **Fatehpur** India
60 G2 **Fauske** Norway
60 □A3 **Faxaflói** *b.* Iceland
60 G3 **Faxälven** *r.* Sweden
83 D3 **Faya** Chad
110 B1 **Fayetteville** *AR* U.S.A.
111 E1 **Fayetteville** *NC* U.S.A.
110 C1 **Fayetteville** *TN* U.S.A.
42 B1 **Fazilka** India
82 A2 **Fdérik** Maur.
111 E2 **Fear, Cape** U.S.A.
22 C2 **Featherston** N.Z.
72 C2 **Fécamp** France
16 D2 **Federated States of**
Micronesia *country*
N. Pacific Ocean
70 C1 **Fehmarn** *i.* Ger.
69 F1 **Fehrbellin** Ger.
123 D2 **Feia, Lagoa** *lag.* Brazil
118 A2 **Feijó** Brazil
22 C2 **Feilding** N.Z.
119 E3 **Feira de Santana** Brazil
75 D2 **Felanitx** Spain
113 D3 **Felipe C. Puerto** Mex.
123 D1 **Felixlândia** Brazil
67 D3 **Felixstowe** U.K.
69 D2 **Felsberg** Ger.
76 B1 **Feltre** Italy

61 F3 **Femunden** *l.* Norway
39 B3 **Fengcheng** *Jiangxi* China
33 A1 **Fengcheng** *Liaoning* China
30 A1 **Fengqing** China
38 B2 **Fengxian** China
Fengxing China *see*
Lincang
39 C3 **Fengyüan** Taiwan
38 B1 **Fengzhen** China
73 D3 **Feno, Capo di** *c.* Corsica
France
89 □D2 **Fenoarivo Atsinanana**
Madag.
59 D2 **Feodosiya** Ukr.
76 A3 **Fer, Cap de** *c.* Alg.
45 D2 **Fergana** Uzbek.
105 D1 **Fergus Falls** U.S.A.
82 B4 **Ferkessédougou**
Côte d'Ivoire
76 B2 **Fermo** Italy
99 D1 **Fermont** Can.
74 B1 **Fermoselle** Spain
65 B2 **Fermoy** Rep. of Ireland
111 D2 **Fernandina Beach** U.S.A.
122 B2 **Fernandópolis** Brazil
96 C3 **Fernie** Can.
76 B2 **Ferrara** Italy
122 B2 **Ferreiros** Brazil
76 A2 **Ferro, Capo** *c. Sardinia* Italy
74 B1 **Ferrol** Spain
68 B1 **Ferwerd** Neth.
82 B1 **Fès** Morocco
86 B3 **Feshi** Dem. Rep. Congo
105 E3 **Festus** U.S.A.
79 C3 **Fethiye** Turkey
64 □ **Fetlar** *i.* U.K.
98 C1 **Feuilles, Rivière aux** *r.* Can.
45 D3 **Feyẕābād** Afgh.
Fez Morocco *see* Fès
89 □D3 **Fianarantsoa** Madag.
85 B4 **Fichē** Eth.
77 C2 **Fier** Albania
64 C2 **Fife Ness** *pt* U.K.
72 C3 **Figeac** France
74 B1 **Figueira da Foz** Port.
75 D1 **Figueres** Spain
82 B1 **Figuig** Morocco
17 F4 **Fiji** *country* S. Pacific Ocean
120 B3 **Filadélfia** Para.
23 Q2 **Filchner Ice Shelf** Antarctica
66 C1 **Filey** U.K.
79 B3 **Filippiada** Greece
61 F4 **Filipstad** Sweden
64 C2 **Findhorn** *r.* U.K.
109 C2 **Findlay** U.S.A.
19 D1 **Fingal** Austr.
109 D2 **Finger Lakes** U.S.A.
60 I3 **Finland** *country* Europe
61 H4 **Finland, Gulf of** Europe
96 B2 **Finlay** *r.* Can.
21 C3 **Finley** Austr.
69 E2 **Finne** *ridge* Ger.
60 H2 **Finnmarksvidda** *reg.* Norway
60 G2 **Finnsnes** Norway
61 G4 **Finspång** Sweden
64 A2 **Fionnphort** U.K.
Fırat *r.* Turkey *see* Euphrates
Firenze Italy *see* Florence
73 C2 **Firminy** France
43 B2 **Firozabad** India
42 B1 **Firozpur** India
47 C2 **Fīrūzābād** Iran
90 A2 **Fish** *watercourse* Namibia
90 B3 **Fish** *r.* S. Africa
67 A3 **Fishguard** U.K.
73 C2 **Fismes** France
74 B1 **Fisterra, Cabo** *c.* Spain
109 E2 **Fitchburg** U.S.A.
97 C2 **Fitzgerald** Can.
18 B1 **Fitzroy Crossing** Austr.

76 B2 **Fivizzano** Italy
87 C3 **Fizi** Dem. Rep. Congo
60 G3 **Fjällsjöälven** *r.* Sweden
91 C3 **Flagstaff** S. Africa
106 A1 **Flagstaff** U.S.A.
98 C1 **Flaherty Island** Can.
66 C1 **Flamborough Head** *hd* U.K.
69 F1 **Fläming** *hills* Ger.
104 B2 **Flaming Gorge Reservoir**
U.S.A.
102 D1 **Flathead** *r.* U.S.A.
102 D1 **Flathead Lake** U.S.A.
19 D1 **Flattery, Cape** Austr.
102 B1 **Flattery, Cape** U.S.A.
66 B2 **Fleetwood** U.K.
61 E4 **Flekkefjord** Norway
70 B1 **Flensburg** Ger.
72 B2 **Flers** France
19 D1 **Flinders** *r.* Austr.
18 A3 **Flinders Bay** Austr.
19 D3 **Flinders Island** Austr.
20 A2 **Flinders Ranges** *mts* Austr.
97 D2 **Flin Flon** Can.
108 C2 **Flint** U.S.A.
75 D1 **Florac** France
110 C2 **Florence** Italy
110 C2 **Florence** *AL* U.S.A.
106 A2 **Florence** *AZ* U.S.A.
102 B2 **Florence** *OR* U.S.A.
111 E2 **Florence** *SC* U.S.A.
118 A1 **Florencia** Col.
114 B3 **Flores** Guat.
26 C3 **Flores** *i.* Indon.
26 B3 **Flores Sea** Indon.
119 E2 **Floresta** Brazil
107 D3 **Floresville** U.S.A.
118 DE **Floriana** Brazil
120 C3 **Florianópolis** Brazil
121 C4 **Florida** Uru.
111 D2 **Florida** *state* U.S.A.
111 D4 **Florida, Straits of**
Bahamas/U.S.A.
111 D4 **Florida Keys** *is* U.S.A.
79 B2 **Florina** Greece
61 E3 **Florø** Norway
97 D2 **Foam Lake** Can.
77 C2 **Foča** Bos.-Herz.
78 B1 **Focşani** Romania
39 B3 **Fogang** China
77 C2 **Foggia** Italy
99 E2 **Fogo Island** Can.
72 C3 **Foix** France
57 D2 **Fokino** Rus. Fed.
98 B2 **Foleyet** Can.
76 B2 **Foligno** Italy
67 D3 **Folkestone** U.K.
111 D2 **Folkston** U.S.A.
76 B2 **Follonica** Italy
97 D2 **Fond-du-Lac** Can.
97 D2 **Fond du Lac** *r.* Can.
108 B2 **Fond du Lac** U.S.A.
74 B1 **Fondevila** Spain
76 B2 **Fondi** Italy
114 B3 **Fonseca, Golfo de** *b.*
Central America
118 B2 **Fonte Boa** Brazil
72 B2 **Fontenay-le-Comte** France
60 □C2 **Fontur** *pt* Iceland
21 C2 **Forbes** Austr.
69 E3 **Forchheim** Ger.
61 E3 **Forde** Norway
21 C1 **Forde Bridge** Austr.
110 B2 **Fordyce** U.S.A.
110 C2 **Forest** U.S.A.
21 C3 **Forest Hill** Austr.
99 D2 **Forestville** Can.
64 C2 **Forfar** U.K.
102 B1 **Forks** U.S.A.
76 B2 **Forlì** Italy
75 D2 **Formentera** *i.* Spain

75 D2 **Formentor, Cap de** c. Spain
123 C2 **Formiga** Brazil
120 C3 **Formosa** Arg.
Formosa country Asia see Taiwan
122 C1 **Formosa** Brazil
64 C1 **Forres** U.K.
18 B3 **Forrest** Austr.
110 B1 **Forrest City** U.S.A.
19 D1 **Forsayth** Austr.
61 H3 **Forssa** Fin.
21 D2 **Forster** Austr.
104 B1 **Forsyth** U.S.A.
42 B2 **Fort Abbas** Pak.
98 B1 **Fort Albany** Can.
119 E2 **Fortaleza** Brazil
96 C2 **Fort Assiniboine** Can.
64 B2 **Fort Augustus** U.K.
102 D1 **Fort Benton** U.S.A.
103 B3 **Fort Bragg** U.S.A.
Fort Chimo Can. see Kuujjuaq
97 C2 **Fort Chipewyan** Can.
104 B2 **Fort Collins** U.S.A.
115 D3 **Fort-de-France** Martinique
105 E2 **Fort Dodge** U.S.A.
98 A2 **Fort Frances** Can.
Fort Franklin Can. see Déline
98 C1 **Fort George** Can.
94 C2 **Fort Good Hope** Can.
64 C2 **Forth** r. U.K.
64 C2 **Forth, Firth of** est. U.K.
120 C3 **Fortín Madrejón** Para.
111 D3 **Fort Lauderdale** U.S.A.
96 B1 **Fort Liard** Can.
97 C2 **Fort Mackay** Can.
97 C2 **Fort McMurray** Can.
94 C2 **Fort McPherson** Can.
104 C2 **Fort Morgan** U.S.A.
111 D3 **Fort Myers** U.S.A.
96 B1 **Fort Nelson** Can.
96 B2 **Fort Nelson** r. Can.
110 C2 **Fort Payne** U.S.A.
104 B1 **Fort Peck** U.S.A.
104 B1 **Fort Peck Reservoir** U.S.A.
111 D3 **Fort Pierce** U.S.A.
96 C1 **Fort Providence** Can.
97 D2 **Fort Qu'Appelle** Can.
96 C1 **Fort Resolution** Can.
98 C1 **Fort Rupert** Can.
96 B2 **Fort St James** Can.
96 B2 **Fort St John** Can.
96 C2 **Fort Saskatchewan** Can.
105 E3 **Fort Scott** U.S.A.
98 C1 **Fort Severn** Can.
44 B2 **Fort-Shevchenko** Kazakh.
96 B1 **Fort Simpson** Can.
97 C1 **Fort Smith** Can.
110 B1 **Fort Smith** U.S.A.
107 C2 **Fort Stockton** U.S.A.
106 C2 **Fort Sumner** U.S.A.
96 C2 **Fort Vermilion** Can.
110 C2 **Fort Walton Beach** U.S.A.
108 B2 **Fort Wayne** U.S.A.
64 B2 **Fort William** U.K.
107 D2 **Fort Worth** U.S.A.
94 B2 **Fort Yukon** U.S.A.
39 B3 **Foshan** China
60 F3 **Fosna** pen. Norway
61 E3 **Fosnavåg** Norway
60 □B3 **Foss** Iceland
60 □A2 **Fossá** Iceland
76 A2 **Fossano** Italy
21 C3 **Foster** Austr.
72 B2 **Fougères** France
64 □ **Foula** i. U.K.
79 C3 **Fournoi** i. Greece
82 A3 **Fouta Djallon** reg. Guinea
22 A3 **Foveaux Strait** N.Z.

104 C3 **Fowler** U.S.A.
18 C3 **Fowlers Bay** Austr.
96 C3 **Fox Creek** Can.
95 F2 **Foxe Basin** g. Can.
95 F2 **Foxe Channel** Can.
95 F2 **Foxe Peninsula** Can.
22 B2 **Fox Glacier** N.Z.
96 C2 **Fox Lake** Can.
96 A1 **Fox Mountain** Can.
22 C2 **Foxton** N.Z.
97 D2 **Fox Valley** Can.
65 C1 **Foyle, Lough** b. Rep. of Ireland/U.K.
122 B3 **Foz de Areia, Represa de** resr Brazil
88 A2 **Foz do Cunene** Angola
122 B3 **Foz do Iguaçu** Brazil
75 D1 **Fraga** Spain
122 C2 **Franca** Brazil
77 C2 **Francavilla Fontana** Italy
72 C2 **France** country Europe
86 B3 **Franceville** Gabon
105 D2 **Francis Case, Lake** U.S.A.
123 D1 **Francisco Sá** Brazil
88 B3 **Francistown** Botswana
96 B2 **François Lake** Can.
69 D2 **Frankenberg (Eder)** Ger.
69 D3 **Frankenthal (Pfalz)** Ger.
69 E2 **Frankenwald** mts Ger.
108 C3 **Frankfort** U.S.A.
69 D2 **Frankfurt am Main** Ger.
70 C1 **Frankfurt an der Oder** Ger.
69 E3 **Fränkische Schweiz** reg. Ger.
109 D2 **Franklin** U.S.A.
94 C2 **Franklin Bay** Can.
102 C1 **Franklin D. Roosevelt Lake** U.S.A.
96 B1 **Franklin Mountains** Can.
94 E2 **Franklin Strait** Can.
22 B2 **Franz Josef Glacier** N.Z.
Franz Josef Land is Rus. Fed. see Zemlya Frantsa-Iosifa
76 A3 **Frasca, Capo della** c. Sardinia Italy
96 B3 **Fraser** r. B.C. Can.
99 D1 **Fraser** r. Nfld. Can.
90 B3 **Fraserburg** S. Africa
64 C2 **Fraserburgh** U.K.
98 B2 **Fraserdale** Can.
19 E2 **Fraser Island** Austr.
96 B2 **Fraser Lake** Can.
121 C4 **Fray Bentos** Uru.
61 E4 **Fredericia** Denmark
107 D2 **Frederick** U.S.A.
107 D2 **Fredericksburg** TX U.S.A.
109 D3 **Fredericksburg** VA U.S.A.
96 A2 **Frederick Sound** sea chan. U.S.A.
99 D2 **Fredericton** Can.
61 F4 **Frederikshavn** Denmark
Frederikshamn Fin. see Hamina
61 F4 **Fredrikstad** Norway
108 B2 **Freeport** IL U.S.A.
107 D3 **Freeport** TX U.S.A.
114 C2 **Freeport City** Bahamas
107 D3 **Freer** U.S.A.
91 C2 **Free State** prov. S. Africa
82 A4 **Freetown** Sierra Leone
74 B2 **Fregenal de la Sierra** Spain
72 B2 **Fréhel, Cap** c. France
70 B2 **Freiburg im Breisgau** Ger.
70 C2 **Freising** Ger.
70 C2 **Freistadt** Austria
73 D3 **Fréjus** France
18 A3 **Fremantle** Austr.
105 D2 **Fremont** NE U.S.A.
108 C2 **Fremont** OH U.S.A.
119 C1 **French Guiana** terr. S. America

102 E1 **Frenchman** r. U.S.A.
17 H5 **French Polynesia** terr. S. Pacific Ocean
112 B2 **Fresnillo** Mex.
103 C3 **Fresno** U.S.A.
75 D2 **Freu, Cap des** c. Spain
73 D2 **Freyming-Merlebach** France
82 A3 **Fria** Guinea
120 B3 **Frías** Arg.
70 B2 **Friedrichshafen** Ger.
69 F1 **Friesack** Ger.
68 C1 **Friesoythe** Ger.
Frobisher Bay Can. see Iqaluit
95 G2 **Frobisher Bay** b. Can.
69 F2 **Frohburg** Ger.
55 D4 **Frolovo** Rus. Fed.
20 A2 **Frome, Lake** salt flat Austr.
20 A2 **Frome Downs** Austr.
68 C2 **Fröndenberg** Ger.
113 C3 **Frontera** Mex.
112 B1 **Fronteras** Mex.
76 B2 **Frosinone** Italy
60 E3 **Frøya** i. Norway
Frunze Kyrg. see **Bishkek**
73 D2 **Frutigen** Switz.
71 D2 **Frýdek-Místek** Czech Rep.
39 B3 **Fu'an** China
74 C1 **Fuenlabrada** Spain
120 C3 **Fuerte Olimpo** Para.
82 A2 **Fuerteventura** i. Canary Is
32 B1 **Fuga** i. Phil.
47 C2 **Fujairah** U.A.E.
35 C3 **Fuji** Japan
39 B3 **Fujian** prov. China
35 C3 **Fujinomiya** Japan
35 C3 **Fuji-san** vol. Japan
35 C3 **Fukui** Japan
35 B4 **Fukuoka** Japan
35 D3 **Fukushima** Japan
69 D2 **Fulda** Ger.
69 D2 **Fulda** r. Ger.
38 A3 **Fuling** China
105 E3 **Fulton** U.S.A.
73 C2 **Fumay** France
82 A1 **Funchal** Madeira
74 B1 **Fundão** Port.
99 D2 **Fundy, Bay of** g. Can.
38 B2 **Funing** Jiangsu China
39 A3 **Funing** Yunnan China
83 C3 **Funtua** Nigeria
47 C2 **Fürgun, Küh-e** mt. Iran
57 F2 **Furmanov** Rus. Fed.
123 C2 **Furnas, Represa** resr Brazil
19 D4 **Furneaux Group** is Austr.
68 C1 **Fürstenau** Ger.
69 E3 **Fürth** Ger.
34 D3 **Furukawa** Japan
95 F2 **Fury and Hecla Strait** Can.
33 A1 **Fushun** China
33 B1 **Fusong** China
47 C2 **Fuwayriţ** Qatar
38 B2 **Fuyang** China
37 E1 **Fuyu** China
36 B1 **Fuyun** China
39 B3 **Fuzhou** China
Fuzhou China see **Linchuan**
61 F4 **Fyn** i. Denmark
F.Y.R.O.M. country Europe see **Macedonia**

G

85 C4 **Gaalkacyo** Somalia
88 A2 **Gabela** Angola
83 D1 **Gabès** Tunisia
83 D1 **Gabès, Golfe de** g. Tunisia

86 B3 **Gabon** *country* Africa
91 C1 **Gaborone** Botswana
78 C2 **Gabrovo** Bulg.
82 A3 **Gabú** Guinea-Bissau
41 B3 **Gadag** India
69 E1 **Gadebusch** Ger.
110 C3 **Gadsden** U.S.A.
78 C2 **Găeşti** Romania
76 B2 **Gaeta** Italy
111 D1 **Gaffney** U.S.A.
83 C1 **Gafsa** Tunisia
57 E2 **Gagarin** Rus. Fed.
82 B4 **Gagnoa** Côte d'Ivoire
99 D1 **Gagnon** Can.
49 C1 **Gagra** Georgia
90 A2 **Gaiab** *watercourse* Namibia
72 C3 **Gaillac** France
111 D3 **Gainesville** *FL* U.S.A.
111 D3 **Gainesville** *GA* U.S.A.
107 D2 **Gainesville** *TX* U.S.A.
66 C2 **Gainsborough** U.K.
20 A2 **Gairdner, Lake**
    salt flat Austr.
64 B2 **Gairloch** U.K.
65 B2 **Galana** *r.* Kenya
71 D2 **Galanta** Slovakia
116 C2 **Galapagos Islands** *is*
    Pacific Ocean
64 C3 **Galashiels** U.K.
78 C1 **Galaţi** Romania
61 E3 **Galdhøpiggen** *mt.* Norway
113 B2 **Galeana** Mex.
96 C2 **Galena** U.S.A.
96 C2 **Galena Bay** Can.
108 A2 **Galesburg** U.S.A.
90 B2 **Galeshewe** S. Africa
54 D3 **Galich** Rus. Fed.
84 D1 **Galilee, Sea of** Israel
110 C1 **Gallatin** U.S.A.
41 C4 **Galle** Sri Lanka
118 A1 **Gallinas, Punta** *pt* Col.
77 C2 **Gallipoli** Italy
    Gallipoli Turkey *see* Gelibolu
60 H2 **Gällivare** Sweden
106 B1 **Gallup** U.S.A.
82 A2 **Galtat Zemmour**
    Western Sahara
65 B2 **Galtymore** *hill* Rep. of Ireland
107 E3 **Galveston** U.S.A.
107 E3 **Galveston Bay** U.S.A.
65 B2 **Galway** Rep. of Ireland
65 B2 **Galway Bay** Rep. of Ireland
122 C1 **Gamá** Brazil
91 B3 **Gamalakhe** S. Africa
    Gambia *country* Africa *see*
    The Gambia
20 A3 **Gambier Islands** Austr.
99 E2 **Gambo** Can.
88 B3 **Gamboma** Congo
106 B1 **Ganado** U.S.A.
49 D3 **Ganäveh** Iran
49 C1 **Gäncä** Azer.
    Gand Belgium *see* Gent
29 C2 **Gandadiwata, Bukit** *mt.*
    Indon.
86 C3 **Gandajika** Dem. Rep. Congo
99 E2 **Gander** Can.
99 E2 **Gander** *r.* Can.
69 D1 **Ganderkesee** Ger.
75 D1 **Gandesa** Spain
42 B2 **Gāndhīdhām** India
42 B2 **Gandhinagar** India
42 B2 **Gāndhī Sāgar** *resr* India
75 C2 **Gandía** Spain
    Ganga *r.* Bangl./India *see*
    Ganges
121 B5 **Gángán** Arg.
42 B2 **Ganganagar** India
36 C2 **Gangca** China
43 C1 **Gangdisê Shan** *mts* China
43 D2 **Ganges** *r.* Bangl./India

73 C3 **Ganges** France
43 C2 **Ganges, Mouths of the**
    Bangl./India
43 C2 **Gangtok** India
73 C2 **Gannat** France
104 B2 **Gannett Peak** U.S.A.
90 A3 **Gansbaai** S. Africa
38 A1 **Gansu** *prov.* China
39 B3 **Ganzhou** China
82 B3 **Gao** Mali
82 A3 **Gaoual** Guinea
38 B2 **Gaoyou** China
38 B2 **Gaoyou Hu** *l.* China
73 D3 **Gap** France
75 C2 **Gap Carbon** *hd* Alg.
43 C1 **Gar** China
21 C1 **Garah** Austr.
119 E2 **Garanhuns** Brazil
103 B2 **Garberville** U.S.A.
69 D1 **Garbsen** Ger.
122 C2 **Garça** Brazil
76 B1 **Garda, Lago di** *l.* Italy
69 E1 **Gardelegen** Ger.
104 C3 **Garden City** U.S.A.
97 E2 **Garden Hill** Can.
45 C3 **Gardēz** Afgh.
56 B2 **Gargždai** Lith.
43 C2 **Garhchiroli** India
91 C3 **Gariep Dam** *resr* S. Africa
90 A3 **Garies** S. Africa
87 D3 **Garissa** Kenya
70 C2 **Garmisch-Partenkirchen**
    Ger.
45 D3 **Garmo, Qullai** *mt.* Tajik.
20 B2 **Garnpung Lake** *imp. l.* Austr.
72 B3 **Garonne** *r.* France
89 C4 **Garoowe** Somalia
42 B2 **Garoth** India
86 B2 **Garoua** Cameroon
64 B2 **Garry** *r.* U.K.
94 E2 **Garry Lake** Can.
87 E3 **Garsen** Kenya
29 B2 **Garut** Indon.
108 B2 **Gary** U.S.A.
113 B2 **Garza García** Mex.
36 C2 **Garzê** China
72 B3 **Gascony, Gulf of** *g.*
    France/Spain
18 A2 **Gascoyne** *r.* Austr.
83 D3 **Gashua** Nigeria
99 D2 **Gaspé** Can.
99 D2 **Gaspé, Péninsule de**
    pen. Can.
111 E1 **Gaston, Lake** U.S.A.
111 D1 **Gastonia** U.S.A.
75 C2 **Gata, Cabo de** *c.* Spain
56 C2 **Gatchina** Rus. Fed.
66 C1 **Gateshead** U.K.
107 D2 **Gatesville** U.S.A.
98 C2 **Gatineau** *r.* Can.
21 D1 **Gatton** Austr.
97 E2 **Gauer Lake** Can.
61 E4 **Gausta** *mt.* Norway
91 C2 **Gauteng** *prov.* S. Africa
47 C2 **Gāvbandī** Iran
79 B3 **Gavdos** *i.* Greece
61 G3 **Gävle** Sweden
57 F2 **Gavrilov Posad** Rus. Fed.
57 E2 **Gavrilov-Yam** Rus. Fed.
30 A1 **Gawai** Myanmar
20 A2 **Gawler** Austr.
20 A2 **Gawler Ranges** *hills* Austr.
43 C2 **Gaya** India
82 C3 **Gaya** Niger
108 C1 **Gaylord** U.S.A.
54 E2 **Gayny** Rus. Fed.
84 B1 **Gaza** *terr.* Asia
48 B2 **Gaza** Gaza
44 C2 **Gaz-Achak** Turkm.
44 B3 **Gazandzhyk** Turkm.

48 B2 **Gaziantep** Turkey
82 B4 **Gbarnga** Liberia
71 D1 **Gdańsk** Pol.
56 A3 **Gdańsk, Gulf of**
    Pol./Rus. Fed.
56 C2 **Gdov** Rus. Fed.
71 D1 **Gdynia** Pol.
84 B3 **Gedaref** Sudan
69 D2 **Gedern** Ger.
79 C3 **Gediz** *r.* Turkey
70 C1 **Gedser** Denmark
69 D2 **Geel** Belgium
20 B3 **Geelong** Austr.
69 E1 **Geesthacht** Ger.
43 C1 **Gê'gyai** China
97 D2 **Geikie** *r.* Can.
61 E3 **Geilo** Norway
30 B1 **Gejiu** China
76 B3 **Gela** *Sicily* Italy
59 D1 **Gelendzhik** Rus. Fed.
79 C2 **Gelibolu** Turkey
68 C2 **Gelsenkirchen** Ger.
86 B2 **Gemena** Dem. Rep. Congo
79 C2 **Gemlik** Turkey
85 C4 **Genalē Wenz** *r.* Eth.
121 B4 **General Acha** Arg.
121 B3 **General Alvear** Arg.
121 C4 **General Belgrano** Arg.
112 B2 **General Cepeda** Mex.
121 B4 **General Pico** Arg.
121 B4 **General Roca** Arg.
32 B2 **General Santos** Phil.
109 D2 **Genesee** *r.* U.S.A.
109 D2 **Geneseo** U.S.A.
    Geneva Switz. *see* Genève
100 D2 **Geneva** U.S.A.
    Geneva, Lake France/Switz.
    see Léman, Lac
73 D2 **Genève** Switz.
74 B2 **Genil** *r.* Spain
68 B2 **Genk** Belgium
76 A2 **Genoa** Italy
    Genoa Italy *see* Genoa
68 A2 **Gent** Belgium
69 F1 **Genthin** Ger.
18 A3 **Geographe Bay** Austr.
99 D1 **George** *r.* Can.
90 B3 **George** S. Africa
111 D3 **George, Lake** *FL* U.S.A.
109 E2 **George, Lake** *NY* U.S.A.
82 A3 **Georgetown** Gambia
119 C1 **Georgetown** Guyana
28 B1 **George Town** Malaysia
111 E2 **Georgetown** *SC* U.S.A.
107 D2 **Georgetown** *TX* U.S.A.
23 I2 **George V Land** *reg.*
    Antarctica
49 C1 **Georgia** *country* Asia
111 D2 **Georgia** *state* U.S.A.
98 B2 **Georgian Bay** Can.
19 C2 **Georgina** *watercourse* Austr.
45 E2 **Georgiyevka** Kazakh.
55 D4 **Georgiyevsk** Rus. Fed.
69 F2 **Gera** Ger.
119 D3 **Geral de Goiás, Serra** *hills*
    Brazil
22 B2 **Geraldine** N.Z.
18 A2 **Geraldton** Austr.
48 B1 **Gerede** Turkey
42 A1 **Gereshk** Afgh.
103 C2 **Gerlach** U.S.A.
71 E2 **Gerlachovský štít** *mt.*
    Slovakia
70 C1 **Germany** *country* Europe
68 C2 **Gerolstein** Ger.
69 E3 **Gerolzhofen** Ger.
69 D2 **Gersfeld (Rhön)** Ger.
43 C1 **Gêrzê** China
109 D2 **Gettysburg** *PA* U.S.A.
104 D1 **Gettysburg** *SD* U.S.A.

77 D2 **Gevgelija** Macedonia
74 C1 **Gexto** Spain
79 C3 **Geyikli** Turkey
90 B2 **Ghaap Plateau** S. Africa
83 C1 **Ghadāmis** Libya
43 C2 **Ghaghara** *r.* India
82 B4 **Ghana** *country* Africa
88 B3 **Ghanzi** Botswana
83 C1 **Ghardaïa** Alg.
83 D1 **Gharyān** Libya
43 C2 **Ghatal** India
43 C2 **Ghazipur** India
45 C3 **Ghazni** Afgh.
         Ghent Belgium *see* **Gent**
78 B1 **Gherla** Romania
73 D3 **Ghisonaccia** *Corsica* France
42 B2 **Ghotāru** India
42 A2 **Ghotki** Pak.
59 E3 **Giaginskaya** Rus. Fed.
65 C1 **Giant's Causeway** *lava field*
         U.K.
29 C2 **Gianyar** Indon.
77 C3 **Giarre** *Sicily* Italy
76 A1 **Giaveno** Italy
90 A2 **Gibeon** Namibia
74 B2 **Gibraltar** *terr.* Europe
74 B2 **Gibraltar, Strait of**
         Morocco/Spain
18 B2 **Gibson Desert** Austr.
36 C1 **Gichgeniyn Nuruu** *mts*
         Mongolia
85 B4 **Gīdolē** Eth.
72 C2 **Gien** France
69 D2 **Gießen** Ger.
69 E1 **Gifhorn** Ger.
96 C2 **Gift Lake** Can.
35 C3 **Gifu** Japan
64 B3 **Gigha** *i.* U.K.
74 B1 **Gijón** Spain
106 A2 **Gila** *r.* U.S.A.
106 A2 **Gila Bend** U.S.A.
19 D1 **Gilbert** *r.* Austr.
         Gilbert Islands *country*
         Pacific Ocean *see* **Kiribati**
102 D1 **Gildford** U.S.A.
84 A2 **Gilf Kebir Plateau** Egypt
21 C2 **Gilgandra** Austr.
42 B1 **Gilgit** Jammu and Kashmir
42 B1 **Gilgit** *r.* Jammu and Kashmir
21 C2 **Gilgunnia** Austr.
97 E2 **Gillam** Can.
104 B2 **Gillette** U.S.A.
67 D3 **Gillingham** U.K.
97 E2 **Gimli** Can.
85 C4 **Ginir** Eth.
77 C2 **Ginosa** Italy
21 C3 **Gippsland** *reg.* Austr.
42 A2 **Girdar Dhor** *r.* Pak.
48 B1 **Giresun** Turkey
75 D1 **Girona** Spain
64 B3 **Girvan** U.K.
22 C1 **Gisborne** N.Z.
61 F4 **Gislaved** Sweden
87 C3 **Gitarama** Rwanda
76 B2 **Giulianova** Italy
78 C2 **Giurgiu** Romania
78 C1 **Giuvala, Pasul** *pass*
         Romania
73 C2 **Givors** France
91 D1 **Giyani** S. Africa
48 B3 **Giza Pyramids** Egypt
77 D2 **Gjirokastër** Albania
94 E2 **Gjoa Haven** Can.
61 F3 **Gjøvik** Norway
99 E2 **Glace Bay** Can.
102 B1 **Glacier Peak** *vol.* U.S.A.
19 E2 **Gladstone** Austr.
60 □A2 **Gláma** *mts* Iceland
77 C2 **Glamoč** Bos.-Herz.
68 C3 **Glan** *r.* Ger.

65 B2 **Glanaruddery Mountains**
         Rep. of Ireland
64 B3 **Glasgow** U.K.
108 B3 **Glasgow** *KY* U.S.A.
104 B1 **Glasgow** *MT* U.S.A.
67 B3 **Glastonbury** U.K.
69 F2 **Glauchau** Ger.
54 E3 **Glazov** Rus. Fed.
57 E3 **Glazunovka** Rus. Fed.
64 B2 **Glen Coe** *val.* U.K.
106 A2 **Glendale** U.S.A.
21 D2 **Glen Davis** Austr.
104 C1 **Glendive** U.S.A.
20 B3 **Glenelg** *r.* Austr.
21 D1 **Glen Innes** Austr.
94 B2 **Glennallen** U.S.A.
64 C2 **Glenrothes** U.K.
109 E2 **Glens Falls** U.S.A.
64 C2 **Glen Shee** *val.* U.K.
65 B1 **Glenties** Rep. of Ireland
106 B2 **Glenwood** U.S.A.
104 B3 **Glenwood Springs** U.S.A.
71 D1 **Gliwice** Pol.
106 A2 **Globe** U.S.A.
71 D1 **Głogów** Pol.
60 F2 **Glomfjord** Norway
61 F4 **Glomma** *r.* Norway
21 D2 **Gloucester** Austr.
67 B3 **Gloucester** U.K.
69 F1 **Glöwen** Ger.
45 E1 **Glubokoye** Kazakh.
69 D1 **Glückstadt** Ger.
71 C2 **Gmünd** Austria
70 C2 **Gmunden** Austria
69 D1 **Gnarrenburg** Ger.
71 D1 **Gniezno** Pol.
77 D2 **Gnjilane** Yugo.
43 D2 **Goalpara** India
64 B3 **Goat Fell** *hill* U.K.
85 C4 **Goba** Eth.
88 A3 **Gobabis** Namibia
121 A5 **Gobernador Gregores** Arg.
37 D2 **Gobi** *des.* China/Mongolia
68 C2 **Goch** Ger.
90 A1 **Gochas** Namibia
43 B3 **Godavari** *r.* India
41 C3 **Godavari, Mouths of the**
         India
98 B2 **Goderich** Can.
42 B2 **Godhra** India
97 E2 **Gods** *r.* Can.
97 E2 **Gods Lake** *l.* Can.
         Godwin-Austen, Mount
         China/Jammu and Kashmir
         see **K2**
98 C2 **Goéland, Lac au** *l.* Can.
99 D1 **Goélands, Lac aux** *l.* Can.
68 A2 **Goes** Neth.
122 C1 **Goiandira** Brazil
122 C1 **Goiânia** Brazil
122 B1 **Goiás** Brazil
122 B2 **Goio-Erê** Brazil
79 C2 **Gökçeada** *i.* Turkey
79 C3 **Gökçedağ** Turkey
89 B2 **Gokwe** Zimbabwe
61 E3 **Gol** Norway
30 A1 **Golaghat** India
79 C2 **Gölcük** Turkey
71 E1 **Goldap** Pol.
69 F1 **Goldberg** Ger.
21 D1 **Gold Coast** Austr.
82 B4 **Gold Coast** *coastal area*
         Ghana
96 C2 **Golden** Can.
22 C2 **Golden Bay** N.Z.
96 B3 **Golden Hinde** *mt.* Can.
65 B2 **Golden Vale** *lowland*
         Rep. of Ireland
103 C3 **Goldfield** U.S.A.
96 B3 **Gold River** Can.

111 E1 **Goldsboro** U.S.A.
103 C4 **Goleta** U.S.A.
36 C2 **Golmud** China
49 D2 **Golpāyegān** Iran
64 C2 **Golspie** U.K.
87 C3 **Goma** Dem. Rep. Congo
43 C2 **Gomati** *r.* India
83 D3 **Gombe** Nigeria
83 D3 **Gombi** Nigeria
         Gomel' Belarus *see* **Homyel'**
112 B2 **Gómez Palacio** Mex.
115 C3 **Gonaïves** Haiti
49 D2 **Gonbad-e Kavus** Iran
85 B3 **Gonder** Eth.
43 C2 **Gondia** India
79 C2 **Gönen** Turkey
83 D4 **Gongola** *r.* Nigeria
21 C2 **Gongolgon** Austr.
113 C2 **Gonzáles** Mex.
107 D3 **Gonzales** U.S.A.
90 A3 **Good Hope, Cape of**
         S. Africa
102 D2 **Gooding** U.S.A.
104 C3 **Goodland** U.S.A.
21 C1 **Goodooga** Austr.
66 C2 **Goole** U.K.
21 C2 **Goolgowi** Austr.
20 A3 **Goolwa** Austr.
21 D1 **Goondiwindi** Austr.
102 B2 **Goose Lake** U.S.A.
70 B2 **Göppingen** Ger.
43 C2 **Gorakhpur** India
77 C2 **Goražde** Bos.-Herz.
79 C3 **Gördes** Turkey
57 D3 **Gordeyevka** Rus. Fed.
19 D4 **Gordon, Lake** Austr.
83 D4 **Goré** Chad
85 B4 **Gorē** Eth.
22 A3 **Gore** N.Z.
65 C2 **Gorey** Rep. of Ireland
49 D2 **Gorgān** Iran
49 C1 **Gori** Georgia
76 B1 **Gorizia** Italy
         Gor'kiy Rus. Fed. *see*
         Nizhniy Novgorod
71 E2 **Gorlice** Pol.
71 C1 **Görlitz** Ger.
77 D2 **Gornji Milanovac** Yugo.
77 C2 **Gornji Vakuf** Bos.-Herz.
45 E1 **Gorno-Altaysk** Rus. Fed.
78 C2 **Gornotrakiyska Nizina**
         lowland Bulg.
45 E1 **Gornyak** Rus. Fed.
27 D3 **Goroka** P.N.G.
82 B3 **Gorom Gorom** Burkina
27 C2 **Gorontalo** Indon.
57 E3 **Gorshechnoye** Rus. Fed.
65 B2 **Gorumna Island**
         Rep. of Ireland
59 D3 **Goryachiy Klyuch** Rus. Fed
71 D1 **Gorzów Wielkopolski** Pol.
21 D2 **Gosford** Austr.
34 D2 **Goshogawara** Japan
69 E2 **Goslar** Ger.
77 C2 **Gospić** Croatia
67 C3 **Gosport** U.K.
77 D2 **Gostivar** Macedonia
         Göteborg Sweden *see*
         Gothenburg
69 E2 **Gotha** Ger.
61 F4 **Gothenburg** Sweden
104 C2 **Gothenburg** U.S.A.
61 G4 **Gotland** *i.* Sweden
79 B2 **Gotse Delchev** Bulg.
61 G4 **Gotska Sandön** *i.* Sweden
35 B4 **Götsu** Japan
69 D2 **Göttingen** Ger.
96 B2 **Gott Peak** Can.
68 B1 **Gouda** Neth.
82 A3 **Goudiri** Senegal

83 D3	Goudoumaria Niger	
98 C2	Gouin, Réservoir *resr* Can.	
21 C2	Goulburn Austr.	
21 B3	Goulburn *r. N.S.W.* Austr.	
21 B3	Goulburn *r. Vic.* Austr.	
82 B3	Goundam Mali	
75 D2	Gouraya Alg.	
72 C3	Gourdon France	
83 D3	Gouré Niger	
90 B3	Gourits *r.* S. Africa	
82 B3	Gourma-Rharous Mali	
21 C3	Gourock Range *mts* Austr.	
123 D1	Governador Valadares Brazil	
111 E3	Governor's Harbour Bahamas	
36 C2	Govĭ Altayn Nuruu *mts* Mongolia	
43 C2	Govind Ballash Pant Sāgar *resr* India	
67 A3	Gower *pen.* U.K.	
120 C3	Goya Arg.	
49 C1	Göyçay Azer.	
43 C1	Gozha Co *salt l.* China	
90 B3	Graaf-Reinet S. Africa	
69 E1	Grabow Ger.	
77 C2	Gračac Croatia	
55 E3	Grachevka Rus. Fed.	
69 F2	Gräfenhainichen Ger.	
21 D1	Grafton Austr.	
105 D1	Grafton U.S.A.	
107 D2	Graham U.S.A.	
96 A2	Graham Island Can.	
23 P3	Graham Land *reg.* Antarctica	
91 C3	Grahamstown S. Africa	
119 D2	Grajaú Brazil	
79 B2	Grammos *mt.* Greece	
64 B2	Grampian Mountains U.K.	
114 B3	Granada Nic.	
74 C2	Granada Spain	
109 E1	Granby Can.	
82 A2	Gran Canaria *i.* Canary Is	
120 B3	Gran Chaco *reg.* Arg./Para.	
104 C1	Grand *r.* U.S.A.	
114 C2	Grand Bahama *i.* Bahamas	
99 E2	Grand Bank Can.	
126 C2	Grand Banks of Newfoundland *sea feature* N. Atlantic Ocean	
106 A1	Grand Canyon U.S.A.	
106 A1	Grand Canyon *gorge* U.S.A.	
114 B3	Grand Cayman *i.* Cayman Is	
97 C2	Grand Centre Can.	
102 C1	Grand Coulee U.S.A.	
120 B2	Grande *r.* Bol.	
122 B2	Grande *r.* Brazil	
121 B6	Grande, Bahía *b.* Arg.	
123 D2	Grande, Ilha *i.* Brazil	
96 C2	Grande Cache Can.	
89 D2	Grande Comore *i.* Comoros	
96 C2	Grande Prairie Can.	
83 D3	Grand Erg de Bilma *des.* Niger	
82 B1	Grand Erg Occidental *des.* Alg.	
83 C2	Grand Erg Oriental *des.* Alg.	
99 D2	Grande-Rivière Can.	
98 C1	Grande Rivière de la Baleine *r.* Can.	
120 B4	Grandes, Salinas *salt marsh* Arg.	
99 D2	Grand Falls *N.B.* Can.	
99 E2	Grand Falls *Nfld.* Can.	
96 C3	Grand Forks Can.	
105 D1	Grand Forks U.S.A.	
96 C1	Grandin, Lac *l.* Can.	
105 D2	Grand Island U.S.A.	
110 B3	Grand Isle U.S.A.	
104 B3	Grand Junction U.S.A.	
82 B4	Grand-Lahou Côte d'Ivoire	
99 D2	Grand Lake *l. N.B.* Can.	
99 E2	Grand Lake *l. Nfld.* Can.	
105 E1	Grand Marais U.S.A.	
74 B2	Grândola Port.	
97 E2	Grand Rapids Can.	
108 B2	Grand Rapids *MI* U.S.A.	
105 E1	Grand Rapids *MN* U.S.A.	
104 A2	Grand Teton *mt.* U.S.A.	
115 C2	Grand Turk Turks and Caicos Is	
102 C1	Grangeville U.S.A.	
96 B2	Granisle Can.	
102 E1	Granite Peak U.S.A.	
76 B3	Granitola, Capo *c.* Sicily Italy	
61 F4	Gränna Sweden	
69 F1	Gransee Ger.	
67 C2	Grantham U.K.	
64 C2	Grantown-on-Spey U.K.	
106 B1	Grants U.S.A.	
102 B2	Grants Pass U.S.A.	
72 B2	Granville France	
97 D2	Granville Lake Can.	
123 D1	Grão Mogol Brazil	
91 D1	Graskop S. Africa	
73 D3	Grasse France	
75 D1	Graus Spain	
60 F2	Gravdal Norway	
72 B2	Grave, Pointe de *pt* France	
97 D3	Gravelbourg Can.	
98 C2	Gravenhurst Can.	
21 D1	Gravesend Austr.	
67 D3	Gravesend U.K.	
73 D2	Gray France	
71 D2	Graz Austria	
114 C2	Great Abaco *i.* Bahamas	
18 B3	Great Australian Bight *g.* Austr.	
22 C1	Great Barrier Island N.Z.	
19 D1	Great Barrier Reef Austr.	
103 C3	Great Basin U.S.A.	
94 D2	Great Bear Lake Can.	
105 D3	Great Bend U.S.A.	
31 A2	Great Coco Island Cocos Is	
21 B3	Great Dividing Range *mts* Austr.	
114 B2	Greater Antilles *is* Caribbean Sea	
102 D1	Great Falls U.S.A.	
91 C3	Great Fish *r.* S. Africa	
91 C3	Great Fish Point S. Africa	
115 C2	Great Inagua *i.* Bahamas	
90 B3	Great Karoo *plat.* S. Africa	
91 C3	Great Kei *r.* S. Africa	
67 B2	Great Malvern U.K.	
31 A3	Great Nicobar *i.* India	
67 D2	Great Ouse *r.* U.K.	
87 D3	Great Rift Valley Africa	
87 D3	Great Ruaha *r.* Tanz.	
102 D2	Great Salt Lake U.S.A.	
103 D2	Great Salt Lake Desert U.S.A.	
84 A2	Great Sand Sea *des.* Egypt/Libya	
18 B2	Great Sandy Desert Austr.	
96 C1	Great Slave Lake Can.	
111 D1	Great Smoky Mountains U.S.A.	
18 B2	Great Victoria Desert Austr.	
38 B1	Great Wall China	
67 D2	Great Yarmouth U.K.	
75 C1	Gredos, Sierra de *mts* Spain	
79 B3	Greece *country* Europe	
104 C2	Greeley U.S.A.	
50 F1	Greem-Bell, Ostrov *i.* Rus. Fed.	
108 B3	Green *r. KY* U.S.A.	
104 B3	Green *r. WY* U.S.A.	
108 B2	Green Bay U.S.A.	
108 B1	Green Bay *b.* U.S.A.	
108 C3	Greenbrier *r.* U.S.A.	
108 B3	Greencastle U.S.A.	
111 D1	Greeneville U.S.A.	
109 E2	Greenfield U.S.A.	
97 D2	Green Lake Can.	
95 I2	Greenland *terr.* N. America	
128 R2	Greenland Sea Greenland/Svalbard	
64 B3	Greenock U.K.	
103 D3	Green River *UT* U.S.A.	
104 B2	Green River *WY* U.S.A.	
108 B3	Greensburg *IN* U.S.A.	
109 D2	Greensburg *PA* U.S.A.	
111 E2	Green Swamp U.S.A.	
108 A2	Greenup U.S.A.	
82 B4	Greenville Liberia	
110 C2	Greenville *AL* U.S.A.	
110 B2	Greenville *MS* U.S.A.	
111 E1	Greenville *NC* U.S.A.	
111 D2	Greenville *SC* U.S.A.	
107 D2	Greenville *TX* U.S.A.	
21 D2	Greenwell Point Austr.	
111 D2	Greenwood U.S.A.	
18 B2	Gregory, Lake *salt flat* Austr.	
19 D1	Gregory Range *hills* Austr.	
70 C1	Greifswald Ger.	
69 F2	Greiz Ger.	
61 F4	Grenå Denmark	
110 C2	Grenada U.S.A.	
115 D3	Grenada *country* West Indies	
72 C3	Grenade France	
21 C2	Grenfell Austr.	
97 D2	Grenfell Can.	
73 D2	Grenoble France	
19 D1	Grenville, Cape Austr.	
102 B1	Gresham U.S.A.	
68 C1	Greven Ger.	
79 B2	Grevena Greece	
68 D1	Grevenbroich Ger.	
69 E1	Grevesmühlen Ger.	
104 B2	Greybull U.S.A.	
96 A1	Grey Hunter Peak Can.	
99 E1	Grey Islands Can.	
22 B2	Greymouth N.Z.	
20 B1	Grey Range *hills* Austr.	
65 C2	Greystones Rep. of Ireland	
111 D2	Griffin U.S.A.	
21 C2	Griffith Austr.	
69 F2	Grimma Ger.	
70 C1	Grimmen Ger.	
66 C2	Grimsby U.K.	
96 C2	Grimshaw Can.	
60 □B2	Grímsstaðir Iceland	
61 E4	Grimstad Norway	
105 E2	Grinnell U.S.A.	
91 C3	Griqualand East *reg.* S. Africa	
90 B2	Griqualand West *reg.* S. Africa	
95 F1	Grise Fiord Can.	
64 C1	Gritley U.K.	
91 C2	Groblersdal S. Africa	
90 B2	Groblershoop S. Africa	
	Grodno Belarus *see* Hrodna	
72 B2	Groix, Île de *i.* France	
68 C1	Gronau (Westfalen) Ger.	
60 F3	Grong Norway	
68 C1	Groningen Neth.	
90 B2	Grootdrink S. Africa	
19 C1	Groote Eylandt *i.* Austr.	
88 A2	Grootfontein Namibia	
90 A2	Groot Karas Berg *plat.* Namibia	
90 B3	Groot Swartberge *mts* S. Africa	
91 C3	Groot Winterberg *mt.* S. Africa	
69 D2	Großenlüder Ger.	
70 C2	Großer Rachel *mt.* Ger.	
71 C2	Grosser Speikkogel *mt.* Austria	

76 B2 **Grosseto** Italy
69 D3 **Groß-Gerau** Ger.
70 C2 **Großglockner** *mt.* Austria
68 C1 **Groß-Hesepe** Ger.
69 E2 **Großlohra** Ger.
90 A1 **Gross Ums** Namibia
99 E1 **Groswater Bay** Can.
98 B2 **Groundhog** *r.* Can.
103 B3 **Grover Beach** U.S.A.
109 E2 **Groveton** U.S.A.
55 D4 **Groznyy** Rus. Fed.
77 C1 **Grubišno Polje** Croatia
71 D1 **Grudziądz** Pol.
90 A2 **Grünau** Namibia
60 □A3 **Grundarfjörður** Iceland
57 E3 **Gryazi** Rus. Fed.
57 F2 **Gryazovets** Rus. Fed.
71 D1 **Gryfice** Pol.
70 C1 **Gryfino** Pol.
114 C2 **Guacanayabo, Golfo de** *b.*
Cuba
112 B2 **Guadalajara** Mex.
75 C1 **Guadalope** *r.* Spain
74 B2 **Guadalquivir** *r.* Spain
100 B4 **Guadalupe** *i.* Mex.
74 B2 **Guadalupe, Sierra de** *mts*
Spain
106 C2 **Guadalupe Peak** U.S.A.
112 B2 **Guadalupe Victoria** Mex.
112 B2 **Guadalupe y Calvo** Mex.
74 C1 **Guadarrama, Sierra de** *mts*
Spain
115 D3 **Guadeloupe** *terr.* West Indies
74 B2 **Guadiana** *r.* Port./Spain
74 C2 **Guadix** Spain
122 B2 **Guaíra** Brazil
115 C3 **Guajira, Península de la**
pen. Col.
118 A2 **Gualaceo** Ecuador
27 D2 **Guam** *terr.* N. Pacific Ocean
112 B2 **Guamúchil** Mex.
112 B2 **Guanacevi** Mex.
119 D3 **Guanambi** Brazil
118 B1 **Guanare** Venez.
114 B2 **Guane** Cuba
38 A2 **Guang'an** China
39 B3 **Guangchang** China
39 B3 **Guangdong** *prov.* China
39 A3 **Guangxi** *aut. reg.* China
38 A2 **Guangyuan** China
39 B3 **Guangzhou** China
123 D1 **Guanhães** Brazil
115 D4 **Guanipa** *r.* Venez.
39 A3 **Guanling** China
33 A1 **Guanshui** China
    Guansuo China *see* Guanling
115 C2 **Guantánamo** Cuba
118 B3 **Guaporé** *r.* Bol./Brazil
122 B3 **Guarapuava** Brazil
122 C3 **Guaraqueçaba** Brazil
123 C2 **Guaratinguetá** Brazil
74 B1 **Guarda** Port.
122 C1 **Guarda Mor** Brazil
74 C1 **Guardo** Spain
123 C2 **Guarujá** Brazil
112 B2 **Guasave** Mex.
114 A3 **Guatemala** *country*
Central America
114 A3 **Guatemala** Guat.
118 B1 **Guaviare** *r.* Col.
123 C2 **Guaxupé** Brazil
118 A2 **Guayaquil** Ecuador
118 B3 **Guayaramerín** Bol.
112 A2 **Guaymas** Mex.
85 B3 **Guba** Eth.
54 E1 **Guba Dolgaya** Rus. Fed.
57 E3 **Gubkin** Rus. Fed.
83 C1 **Guelma** Alg.
82 A2 **Guelmine** Morocco
98 B2 **Guelph** Can.

113 C2 **Guémez** Mex.
72 C2 **Guéret** France
63 C4 **Guernsey** *terr.* Channel Is
112 A2 **Guerrero Negro** Mex.
99 D1 **Guers, Lac** *l.* Can.
38 B2 **Guichi** China
86 B2 **Guider** Cameroon
76 B2 **Guidonia-Montecelio** Italy
39 A3 **Guigang** China
68 A3 **Guignicourt** France
91 D1 **Guija** Moz.
67 C3 **Guildford** U.K.
39 B3 **Guilin** China
98 C1 **Guillaume-Delisle, Lac**
l. Can.
74 B1 **Guimarães** Port.
82 A3 **Guinea** *country* Africa
80 D3 **Guinea, Gulf of** Africa
82 A3 **Guinea-Bissau** *country*
Africa
72 B2 **Guingamp** France
72 B2 **Guipavas** France
122 B1 **Guiratinga** Brazil
118 B1 **Güiria** Venez.
68 A3 **Guise** France
39 A3 **Guiyang** China
39 A3 **Guizhou** *prov.* China
42 A1 **Gujranwala** Pak.
42 B1 **Gujrat** Pak.
59 D2 **Gukovo** Rus. Fed.
44 B2 **Gulabie** Uzbek.
21 C2 **Gulargambone** Austr.
41 B3 **Gulbarga** India
56 C2 **Gulbene** Latvia
110 C2 **Gulfport** U.S.A.
37 E1 **Gulian** China
45 C2 **Gulistan** Uzbek.
    Gulja China *see* Yining
97 D2 **Gull Lake** Can.
79 C3 **Güllük** Turkey
87 D2 **Gulu** Uganda
88 B2 **Gumare** Botswana
44 B3 **Gumdag** Turkm.
43 C2 **Gumla** India
68 C2 **Gummersbach** Ger.
42 B2 **Guna** India
21 C3 **Gundagai** Austr.
79 C3 **Güney** Turkey
86 B3 **Gungu** Dem. Rep. Congo
97 E2 **Gunisao** *r.* Can.
21 D2 **Gunnedah** Austr.
104 B3 **Gunnison** CO U.S.A.
103 D3 **Gunnison** UT U.S.A.
104 B3 **Gunnison** *r.* U.S.A.
41 B3 **Guntakal** India
110 C2 **Guntersville** U.S.A.
41 C3 **Guntur** India
28 A1 **Gunungsitoli** Indon.
28 A1 **Gunungtua** Indon.
70 C2 **Günzburg** Ger.
70 C2 **Gunzenhausen** Ger.
42 B2 **Gurgaon** India
119 D2 **Gurgueia** *r.* Brazil
118 B1 **Guri, Embalse de**
resr Venez.
122 C1 **Gurinhatã** Brazil
119 D2 **Gurupi** *r.* Brazil
42 B2 **Guru Sikhar** *mt.* India
    Gur'yev Kazakh. *see* Atyrau
83 C3 **Gusau** Nigeria
33 A2 **Gusev** Rus. Fed.
42 A1 **Gushgy** Turkm.
38 B2 **Gushi** China
51 I3 **Gusinoozersk** Rus. Fed.
57 F2 **Gus'-Khrustal'nyy** Rus. Fed.
76 A3 **Guspini** *Sardinia* Italy
96 A2 **Gustavus** U.S.A.
69 F1 **Güstrow** Ger.
69 D2 **Gütersloh** Ger.
89 C2 **Gutu** Zimbabwe
43 D2 **Guwahati** India

118 C1 **Guyana** *country* S. America
    Guyi China *see* Sanjiang
107 C1 **Guymon** U.S.A.
21 D2 **Guyra** Austr.
38 A2 **Guyuan** China
112 B1 **Guzmán** Mex.
112 B1 **Guzmán, Lago de** *l.* Mex.
42 A2 **Gwadar** Pak.
43 B2 **Gwalior** India
89 B3 **Gwanda** Zimbabwe
65 B1 **Gweebarra Bay**
Rep. of Ireland
65 B1 **Gweedore** Rep. of Ireland
89 B2 **Gweru** Zimbabwe
83 D3 **Gwoza** Nigeria
21 D2 **Gwydir** *r.* Austr.
43 C2 **Gyangzê** China
43 C1 **Gyaring Co** *l.* China
36 C2 **Gyaring Hu** *l.* China
54 G1 **Gydanskiy Poluostrov** *pen.*
Rus. Fed.
    Gyêgu China *see* Yushu
19 E2 **Gympie** Austr.
71 D2 **Gyöngyös** Hungary
71 D2 **Győr** Hungary
97 E2 **Gypsumville** Can.
71 E2 **Gyula** Hungary
49 C1 **Gyumri** Armenia
44 B3 **Gyzylarbat** Turkm.

H

56 B2 **Haapsalu** Estonia
68 B1 **Haarlem** Neth.
69 C2 **Haarstrang** *ridge* Ger.
22 A2 **Haast** N.Z.
46 B3 **Habbān** Yemen
49 C2 **Ḥabbānīyah, Hawr al** *l.* Iraq
35 C4 **Hachijō-jima** *i.* Japan
34 D2 **Hachinohe** Japan
89 C3 **Hacufera** Moz.
47 C2 **Ḥadd, Ra's al** *pt* Oman
64 C3 **Haddington** U.K.
83 D3 **Hadejia** Nigeria
61 E4 **Haderslev** Denmark
59 C1 **Hadyach** Ukr.
33 B2 **Haeju** N. Korea
33 B2 **Haeju-man** *b.* N. Korea
33 B3 **Haenam** S. Korea
46 B2 **Ḥafar al Bāṭin** Saudi Arabia
30 A1 **Hāflong** India
60 □A3 **Hafnarfjörður** Iceland
46 A3 **Hagar Nish Plateau** Eritrea
68 C2 **Hagen** Ger.
69 E1 **Hagenow** Ger.
96 B2 **Hagensborg** Can.
109 D3 **Hagerstown** U.S.A.
61 F3 **Hagfors** Sweden
35 B4 **Hagi** Japan
30 B1 **Ha Giang** Vietnam
65 B2 **Hag's Head** *hd*
Rep. of Ireland
84 B1 **Ha** Tanz.
30 B1 **Hai Dương** Vietnam
39 B3 **Haifeng** China
39 B3 **Haikou** China
46 B2 **Hā'il** Saudi Arabia
37 D1 **Hailar** China
60 H2 **Hailuoto** *i.* Fin.
37 D3 **Hainan** *i.* China
39 A4 **Hainan** *prov.* China
96 A2 **Haines** U.S.A.
96 A1 **Haines Junction** Can.
69 E2 **Hainich** *ridge* Ger.
69 E2 **Hainleite** *ridge* Ger.
30 B1 **Hai Phong** Vietnam
115 C3 **Haiti** *country* West Indies

84 B3 **Haiya** Sudan
71 E2 **Hajdúböszörmény** Hungary
46 B3 **Ḥajjah** Yemen
47 C2 **Ḥājjīābād** Iran
30 A1 **Haka** Myanmar
49 C2 **Hakkâri** Turkey
34 D2 **Hakodate** Japan
        Halab Syria *see* Aleppo
46 B2 **Ḥalabān** Saudi Arabia
49 C2 **Halabja** Iraq
84 B2 **Halaib** Sudan
46 A2 **Halaib Triangle** *terr.*
        Egypt/Sudan
47 C3 **Ḥalāniyāt, Juzur al** *is* Oman
46 A2 **Ḥālat 'Ammār** Saudi Arabia
36 C1 **Halban** Mongolia
69 E2 **Halberstadt** Ger.
32 B1 **Halcon, Mount** Phil.
61 F4 **Halden** Norway
69 E1 **Haldensleben** Ger.
43 B2 **Haldwani** India
47 C2 **Ḥāleh** Iran
22 A3 **Halfmoon Bay** N.Z.
99 D2 **Halifax** Can.
66 C2 **Halifax** U.K.
109 D3 **Halifax** U.S.A.
33 B3 **Halla-san** *mt.* S. Korea
95 F2 **Hall Beach** Can.
68 B2 **Halle** Belgium
70 C2 **Hallein** Austria
69 E2 **Halle (Saale)** Ger.
105 D1 **Hallock** U.S.A.
95 G2 **Hall Peninsula** Can.
18 B1 **Halls Creek** Austr.
27 C2 **Halmahera** *i.* Indon.
61 F4 **Halmstad** Sweden
33 D4 **Hamada** Japan
49 C2 **Hamadān** Iran
48 B2 **Ḥamāh** Syria
35 C4 **Hamamatsu** Japan
61 F3 **Hamar** Norway
84 B2 **Hamāta, Gebel** *mt.* Egypt
41 C4 **Hambantota** Sri Lanka
69 D1 **Hamburg** Ger.
46 A2 **Ḥamḍ, Wādī al** *watercourse*
        Saudi Arabia
46 B3 **Ḥamdah** Saudi Arabia
61 H3 **Hämeenlinna** Fin.
69 D1 **Hameln** Ger.
18 A2 **Hamersley Range** *mts* Austr.
33 B2 **Hamhŭng** N. Korea
36 C2 **Hami** China
84 B2 **Hamid** Sudan
20 B3 **Hamilton** Austr.
98 C2 **Hamilton** Can.
22 C1 **Hamilton** N.Z.
64 B3 **Hamilton** U.K.
110 C2 **Hamilton** AL U.S.A.
102 D1 **Hamilton** MT U.S.A.
108 C2 **Hamilton** OH U.S.A.
61 I3 **Hamina** Fin.
68 C2 **Hamm** Ger.
82 B2 **Hammada du Drâa** *plat.* Alg.
49 C2 **Ḥammār, Hawr al** *imp. l.* Iraq
69 D2 **Hammelburg** Ger.
60 G3 **Hammerdal** Sweden
60 H1 **Hammerfest** Norway
110 B2 **Hammond** U.S.A.
109 E3 **Hammonton** U.S.A.
47 C2 **Hāmūn-e Jaz Mūriān**
        salt marsh Iran
42 A2 **Hamun-i-Lora** *dry lake* Pak.
42 A2 **Hamun-i-Mashkel**
        salt flat Pak.
46 A2 **Ḥanak** Saudi Arabia
34 D3 **Hanamaki** Japan
69 D2 **Hanau** Ger.
38 B2 **Hancheng** China
108 B1 **Hancock** U.S.A.
38 B2 **Handan** China

103 C3 **Hanford** U.S.A.
36 C1 **Hangayn Nuruu** *mts*
        Mongolia
        Hanggin Houqi China *see*
        Xamba
38 C2 **Hangö** Fin. *see* Hanko
38 C2 **Hangzhou** China
        Hangzhou Wan *b.* China
        Hanjia China *see* Pengshui
        Hanjiang China *see*
        Yangzhou
61 H4 **Hanko** Fin.
103 D3 **Hanksville** U.S.A.
22 B2 **Hanmer Springs** N.Z.
97 C2 **Hanna** Can.
105 E3 **Hannibal** U.S.A.
69 D1 **Hannover** Ger.
69 D2 **Hannoversch Münden** Ger.
61 F4 **Hanöbukten** *b.* Sweden
30 B1 **Ha Nôi** Vietnam
        Hanoi Vietnam *see* Ha Nôi
98 B2 **Hanover** Can.
90 B3 **Hanover** S. Africa
61 E4 **Hanstholm** Denmark
56 C3 **Hantsavichy** Belarus
43 C2 **Hanumana** India
42 B2 **Hanumangarh** India
38 A2 **Hanzhong** China
60 H2 **Haparanda** Sweden
68 B2 **Hapert** Neth.
99 D1 **Happy Valley-Goose Bay**
        Can.
46 A2 **Ḥaql** Saudi Arabia
47 B2 **Ḥaraḍh** Saudi Arabia
56 C2 **Haradok** Belarus
46 B3 **Ḥarajā** Saudi Arabia
99 C2 **Harare** Zimbabwe
47 C3 **Ḥarāsīs, Jiddat al** *des.*
        Oman
37 D1 **Har-Ayrag** Mongolia
37 E1 **Harbin** China
99 E2 **Harbour Breton** Can.
42 B2 **Harda Khās** India
68 C1 **Hardenberg** Neth.
68 B1 **Harderwijk** Neth.
90 A3 **Hardeveld** *mts* S. Africa
102 C1 **Hardin** U.S.A.
96 C1 **Hardisty Lake** Can.
68 C1 **Haren (Ems)** Ger.
85 C4 **Hārer** Eth.
85 C4 **Hargeysa** Somalia
78 C1 **Harghita-Mădăraş, Vârful**
        mt. Romania
36 C2 **Har Hu** *l.* China
42 B1 **Haripur** Pak.
42 A1 **Hari Rud** *r.* Afgh./Iran
68 B1 **Harlingen** Neth.
107 D3 **Harlingen** U.S.A.
67 D3 **Harlow** U.K.
102 E1 **Harlowton** U.S.A.
102 C2 **Harney Basin** U.S.A.
102 C2 **Harney Lake** U.S.A.
61 G3 **Härnösand** Sweden
37 E1 **Har Nur** China
        Har Nuur *l.* Mongolia
82 B4 **Harper** Liberia
69 D1 **Harpstedt** Ger.
98 C1 **Harricanaw** *r.* Can.
21 D2 **Harrington** Austr.
99 E1 **Harrington Harbour** Can.
64 A2 **Harris, Sound of** *sea chan.*
        U.K.
108 B3 **Harrisburg** IL U.S.A.
109 D2 **Harrisburg** PA U.S.A.
91 C2 **Harrismith** S. Africa
110 B1 **Harrison** U.S.A.
99 E1 **Harrison, Cape** Can.
94 A2 **Harrison Bay** U.S.A.
109 D3 **Harrisonburg** U.S.A.
105 E3 **Harrisonville** U.S.A.

66 C2 **Harrogate** U.K.
78 C2 **Hârşova** Romania
60 G2 **Harstad** Norway
90 B2 **Hartbees** *watercourse*
        S. Africa
71 D2 **Hartberg** Austria
109 E2 **Hartford** U.S.A.
67 A3 **Hartland Point** U.K.
66 C1 **Hartlepool** U.K.
96 B2 **Hartley Bay** Can.
91 B2 **Harts** *r.* S. Africa
111 D2 **Hartwell Reservoir** U.S.A.
36 C1 **Har Us Nuur** *l.* Mongolia
104 C1 **Harvey** U.S.A.
67 D3 **Harwich** U.K.
69 E2 **Harz** *hills* Ger.
41 B3 **Hassan** India
68 B2 **Hasselt** Belgium
83 C1 **Hassi Messaoud** Alg.
61 F4 **Hässleholm** Sweden
68 B2 **Hastière-Lavaux** Belgium
21 C3 **Hastings** Austr.
22 C1 **Hastings** N.Z.
67 D3 **Hastings** U.K.
105 E2 **Hastings** MN U.S.A.
105 D2 **Hastings** NE U.S.A.
        Hatay Turkey *see* Antakya
97 C2 **Hatchet Lake** Can.
20 B2 **Hatfield** Austr.
36 C1 **Hatgal** Mongolia
30 B2 **Ha Tinh** Vietnam
111 E1 **Hatteras, Cape** U.S.A.
110 C2 **Hattiesburg** U.S.A.
68 C2 **Hattingen** Ger.
31 B3 **Hat Yai** Thai.
85 C4 **Haud** *reg.* Eth.
61 E4 **Haugesund** Norway
61 E4 **Haukeligrend** Norway
60 I2 **Haukipudas** Fin.
22 C1 **Hauraki Gulf** N.Z.
82 B1 **Haut Atlas** *mts* Morocco
98 C2 **Hauterive** Can.
82 B1 **Hauts Plateaux** *plat.* Alg.
114 B2 **Havana** Cuba
67 C3 **Havant** U.K.
69 E1 **Havel** *r.* Ger.
69 F1 **Havelberg** Ger.
22 B2 **Havelock** N.Z.
22 C1 **Havelock North** N.Z.
67 A3 **Haverfordwest** U.K.
71 D2 **Havlíčkův Brod** Czech Rep.
60 H1 **Havøysund** Norway
79 C3 **Havran** Turkey
102 E1 **Havre** U.S.A.
99 D2 **Havre Aubert** Can.
99 D1 **Havre-St-Pierre** Can.
92 A5 **Hawaiian Islands**
        N. Pacific Ocean
66 B2 **Hawarden** U.K.
22 A2 **Hawea, Lake** N.Z.
22 B1 **Hawera** N.Z.
66 B1 **Hawes** U.K.
64 C3 **Hawick** U.K.
22 C1 **Hawke Bay** N.Z.
20 A2 **Hawker** Austr.
20 B1 **Hawkers Gate** Austr.
103 C3 **Hawthorne** U.S.A.
20 B2 **Hay** Austr.
96 C1 **Hay** *r.* Can.
102 C1 **Hayden** U.S.A.
97 E2 **Hayes** *r.* Man. Can.
94 E2 **Hayes** *r.* Nunavut Can.
47 C3 **Haymā'** Oman
79 C2 **Hayrabolu** Turkey
96 C1 **Hay River** Can.
105 D3 **Hays** U.S.A.
46 B3 **Hays** Yemen
58 B2 **Haysyn** Ukr.
67 C3 **Haywards Heath** U.K.
42 A1 **Hazarajat** *reg.* Afgh.

108 C3 **Hazard** U.S.A.
43 C2 **Hazāribāg** India
43 C2 **Hazaribagh Range** mts India
96 B2 **Hazelton** Can.
109 D2 **Hazleton** U.S.A.
21 C3 **Healesville** Austr.
98 B2 **Hearst** Can.
38 B2 **Hebei** prov. China
21 C1 **Hebel** Austr.
110 B1 **Heber Springs** U.S.A.
38 B2 **Hebi** China
99 D1 **Hebron** Can.
96 A2 **Hecate Strait** Can.
39 A3 **Hechi** China
61 F3 **Hede** Sweden
68 B1 **Heerenveen** Neth.
68 B1 **Heerhugowaard** Neth.
68 B2 **Heerlen** Neth.
48 B2 **Hefa** Israel
38 B2 **Hefei** China
38 B3 **Hefeng** China
37 E1 **Hegang** China
70 B1 **Heide** Ger.
90 A1 **Heide** Namibia
70 B2 **Heidelberg** Ger.
90 B3 **Heidelberg** S. Africa
70 B2 **Heilbronn** Ger.
37 E1 **Heilong Jiang** r.
     China/Rus. Fed.
61 I3 **Heinola** Fin.
60 F3 **Helagsfjället** mt. Sweden
110 B2 **Helena** AR U.S.A.
102 D1 **Helena** MT U.S.A.
64 D1 **Helensburgh** U.K.
70 B1 **Helgoland** i. Ger.
70 B1 **Helgoländer Bucht** b. Ger.
     Helixi China see Ningguo
60 □A3 **Hella** Iceland
68 B2 **Hellevoetsluis** Neth.
75 C2 **Hellín** Spain
44 C3 **Helmand** r. Afgh.
68 B1 **Helmbrechts** Ger.
90 A2 **Helmeringhausen** Namibia
68 B2 **Helmond** Neth.
64 C1 **Helmsdale** U.K.
64 C1 **Helmsdale** r. U.K.
69 E1 **Helmstedt** Ger.
33 B1 **Helong** China
61 F4 **Helsingborg** Sweden
     Helsingfors Fin. see Helsinki
61 F4 **Helsingør** Denmark
61 H3 **Helsinki** Fin.
65 C2 **Helvick Head** hd
     Rep. of Ireland
67 C3 **Hemel Hempstead** U.K.
69 D1 **Hemmoor** Ger.
60 F2 **Hemnesberget** Norway
38 B2 **Henan** prov. China
108 B3 **Henderson** KY U.S.A.
111 E1 **Henderson** NC U.S.A.
103 D3 **Henderson** NV U.S.A.
107 E2 **Henderson** TX U.S.A.
111 D1 **Hendersonville** U.S.A.
67 C3 **Hendon** U.K.
30 A1 **Hengduan Shan** mts China
68 C1 **Hengelo** Neth.
     Hengnan China see
     Hengyang
38 B2 **Hengshui** China
39 A3 **Hengxian** China
39 B3 **Hengyang** China
     Hengzhou China see
     Hengxian
59 C2 **Heniches'k** Ukr.
68 C2 **Hennef (Sieg)** Ger.
98 B1 **Henrietta Maria, Cape** Can.
107 D1 **Henryetta** U.S.A.
95 G2 **Henry Kater, Cape** Can.
69 D1 **Henstedt-Ulzburg** Ger.
88 A3 **Hentiesbaai** Namibia

30 A2 **Henzada** Myanmar
39 A3 **Hepu** China
44 C3 **Herāt** Afgh.
97 D2 **Herbert** Can.
69 D2 **Herbstein** Ger.
67 B2 **Hereford** U.K.
107 C2 **Hereford** U.S.A.
69 D1 **Herford** Ger.
68 C2 **Herkenbosch** Neth.
64 □ **Herma Ness** hd U.K.
90 A3 **Hermanus** S. Africa
21 C2 **Hermidale** Austr.
102 C1 **Hermiston** U.S.A.
27 D3 **Hermit Islands** P.N.G.
112 A2 **Hermosillo** Mex.
122 B3 **Hernandarias** Para.
68 C2 **Herne** Ger.
61 E4 **Herning** Denmark
91 C2 **Hertzogville** S. Africa
19 E2 **Hervey Bay** b. Austr.
69 F2 **Herzberg** Ger.
69 E3 **Herzogenaurach** Ger.
39 A3 **Heshan** China
96 A1 **Hess** r. Can.
69 D2 **Hessisch Lichtenau** Ger.
104 C1 **Hettinger** U.S.A.
69 E2 **Hettstedt** Ger.
66 B1 **Hexham** U.K.
39 B3 **Hexian** China
39 B3 **Heyuan** China
20 B3 **Heywood** Austr.
38 B2 **Heze** China
105 D3 **Hiawatha** U.S.A.
105 E1 **Hibbing** U.S.A.
22 C1 **Hicks Bay** N.Z.
34 D2 **Hidaka-sanmyaku** mts
     Japan
113 C2 **Hidalgo** Mex.
112 B2 **Hidalgo del Parral** Mex.
122 C1 **Hidrolândia** Brazil
     High Atlas mts Morocco see
     Haut Atlas
102 B2 **High Desert** U.S.A.
96 C2 **High Level** Can.
111 E1 **High Point** U.S.A.
96 C2 **High Prairie** Can.
96 C2 **High River** Can.
97 D2 **Highrock Lake** Can.
67 B3 **High Wycombe** U.K.
56 B2 **Hiiumaa** i. Estonia
46 A2 **Hijaz** reg. Saudi Arabia
22 C1 **Hikurangi** mt. N.Z.
69 E2 **Hildburghausen** Ger.
69 E2 **Hilders** Ger.
69 D1 **Hildesheim** Ger.
68 C2 **Hillesheim** Ger.
108 C3 **Hillsboro** OH U.S.A.
107 D2 **Hillsboro** TX U.S.A.
21 C1 **Hillston** Austr.
111 D2 **Hilton Head Island** U.S.A.
68 B1 **Hilversum** Neth.
36 B2 **Himalaya** mts Asia
35 B4 **Himeji** Japan
91 C2 **Himeville** S. Africa
48 B2 **Ḥimş** Syria
19 D1 **Hinchinbrook Island** Austr.
42 A1 **Hindu Kush** mts Afgh./Pak.
111 D2 **Hinesville** U.S.A.
43 B2 **Hinganghat** India
49 C2 **Hınıs** Turkey
60 G2 **Hinnøya** i. Norway
74 B2 **Hinojosa del Duque** Spain
96 C2 **Hinton** Can.
43 C2 **Hīrākud Reservoir** India
35 C3 **Hirosaki** Japan
35 B4 **Hiroshima** Japan
69 E3 **Hirschaid** Ger.
69 E2 **Hirschberg** Ger.
73 C2 **Hirson** France

61 E4 **Hirtshals** Denmark
42 B2 **Hisar** India
115 C2 **Hispaniola** i. Caribbean Sea
49 C2 **Hīt** Iraq
35 D3 **Hitachi** Japan
35 D3 **Hitachinaka** Japan
60 E3 **Hitra** i. Norway
61 G4 **Hjälmaren** l. Sweden
97 D1 **Hjalmar Lake** Can.
61 F4 **Hjerring** Denmark
91 D2 **Hlabisa** S. Africa
60 □B2 **Hlíð** Iceland
59 C2 **Hlobyne** Ukr.
91 C2 **Hlohlowane** S. Africa
91 C2 **Hlotse** Lesotho
59 C1 **Hlukhiv** Ukr.
56 C2 **Hlybokaye** Belarus
84 C4 **Ho** Ghana
90 A1 **Hoachanas** Namibia
19 D4 **Hobart** Austr.
107 D1 **Hobart** U.S.A.
107 C2 **Hobbs** U.S.A.
61 E4 **Hobro** Denmark
85 C4 **Hobyo** Somalia
31 B2 **Hồ Chí Minh** Vietnam
82 B3 **Hồd** reg. Maur.
71 E2 **Hódmezővásárhely** Hungary
68 B2 **Hoek van Holland** Neth.
33 B2 **Hoeyang** N. Korea
69 E2 **Hof** Ger.
69 E2 **Hofheim in Unterfranken**
     Ger.
60 □B3 **Höfn** Austurland Iceland
60 □A2 **Höfn** Vestfirðir Iceland
60 □B3 **Hofsjökull** ice cap Iceland
35 B4 **Hōfu** Japan
83 C2 **Hoggar** plat. Alg.
61 G4 **Högsby** Sweden
68 C2 **Hohe Rhön** mts Ger.
68 C2 **Hohe Venn** moorland
     Belgium
43 C1 **Hoh Xil Shan** mts China
31 B2 **Hội An** Vietnam
30 A1 **Hojai** India
22 B2 **Hokitika** N.Z.
34 D2 **Hokkaidō** i. Japan
96 B2 **Holberg** Can.
106 A2 **Holbrook** U.S.A.
105 D2 **Holdrege** U.S.A.
114 C2 **Holguín** Cuba
60 □B2 **Hóll** Iceland
     Holland country Europe see
     Netherlands
108 B2 **Holland** U.S.A.
68 B1 **Hollum** Neth.
110 C2 **Holly Springs** U.S.A.
111 D3 **Hollywood** U.S.A.
60 F2 **Holm** Norway
94 D2 **Holman** Can.
60 H3 **Holmsund** Sweden
90 A2 **Holoog** Namibia
61 E4 **Holstebro** Denmark
111 D1 **Holston** r. U.S.A.
66 A2 **Holyhead** U.K.
66 C1 **Holy Island** England U.K.
66 A2 **Holy Island** Wales U.K.
104 C2 **Holyoke** U.S.A.
69 D2 **Holzminden** Ger.
30 A1 **Homalin** Myanmar
69 D2 **Homberg (Efze)** Ger.
82 B3 **Hombori** Mali
95 D2 **Home Bay** Can.
111 D3 **Homestead** U.S.A.
60 F3 **Hommelvik** Norway
57 D2 **Homyel'** Belarus
90 A3 **Hondeklipbaai** S. Africa
113 D3 **Hondo** r. Belize/Mex.
107 D3 **Hondo** U.S.A.
114 B3 **Honduras** country
     Central America

61 F3 **Hønefoss** Norway
103 B2 **Honey Lake** U.S.A.
72 C2 **Honfleur** France
30 B1 **Hồng Gai** Vietnam
38 B3 **Honghu** China
39 A3 **Hongjiang** China
37 D3 **Hong Kong** China
39 B3 **Hong Kong** *special admin. reg.* China
33 B1 **Hongwŏn** N. Korea
38 B2 **Hongze Hu** *l.* China
34 D3 **Honjō** Japan
60 I1 **Honningsvåg** Norway
35 B3 **Honshū** *i.* Japan
102 B1 **Hood, Mount** *vol.* U.S.A.
18 A3 **Hood Point** Austr.
102 B1 **Hood River** U.S.A.
68 C1 **Hoogeveen** Neth.
68 C1 **Hoogezand-Sappemeer** Neth.
68 C2 **Hoog-Keppel** Neth.
  Hook of Holland Neth. *see* Hoek van Holland
96 A2 **Hoonah** U.S.A.
68 B1 **Hoorn** Neth.
96 B3 **Hope** Can.
110 B2 **Hope** U.S.A.
51 N2 **Hope, Point** U.S.A.
99 D1 **Hopedale** Can.
21 D1 **Hope Mountains** Can.
20 B3 **Hopetoun** Austr.
90 B2 **Hopetown** S. Africa
109 D3 **Hopewell** U.S.A.
98 C1 **Hopewell Islands** Can.
18 B2 **Hopkins, Lake** *salt flat* Austr.
108 B3 **Hopkinsville** U.S.A.
102 B1 **Hoquiam** U.S.A.
49 C1 **Horasan** Turkey
61 F4 **Hörby** Sweden
57 D3 **Horki** Belarus
59 D2 **Horlivka** Ukr.
47 D2 **Hormak** Iran
47 D2 **Hormuz, Strait of** Iran/Oman
71 D2 **Horn** Austria
60 □A2 **Horn** *c.* Iceland
121 B6 **Horn, Cape** *c.* Chile
109 D2 **Hornell** U.S.A.
98 B2 **Hornepayne** Can.
66 C2 **Hornsea** U.K.
58 C1 **Horodenka** Ukr.
59 C1 **Horodnya** Ukr.
58 B2 **Horodok** *Khmel'nyts'ka Oblast'* Ukr.
58 A1 **Horodok** *L'vivs'ka Oblast'* Ukr.
  Horqin Youyi Qianqi China *see* Ulanhot
99 E1 **Horse Islands** Can.
20 B3 **Horsham** Austr.
94 C2 **Horton** *r.* Can.
85 B4 **Hosa'ina** Eth.
42 A2 **Hoshab** Pak.
42 B1 **Hoshiarpur** India
45 E3 **Hotan** China
90 B2 **Hotazel** S. Africa
110 B2 **Hot Springs** *AR* U.S.A.
104 C2 **Hot Springs** *SD* U.S.A.
96 C1 **Hottah Lake** Can.
68 B2 **Houffalize** Belgium
38 B2 **Houma** China
110 B3 **Houma** U.S.A.
96 B2 **Houston** Can.
107 D3 **Houston** U.S.A.
90 B2 **Houwater** S. Africa
36 C1 **Hovd** Mongolia
36 C1 **Hove** U.K.
36 C1 **Hövsgöl Nuur** *l.* Mongolia
36 C2 **Hövüün** Mongolia
84 A3 **Howar, Wadi** *watercourse* Sudan

21 C3 **Howe, Cape** Austr.
21 C3 **Howlong** Austr.
69 D2 **Höxter** Ger.
64 C1 **Hoy** *i.* U.K.
61 E3 **Høyanger** Norway
70 C1 **Hoyerswerda** Ger.
71 D1 **Hradec Králové** Czech Rep.
77 C2 **Hrasnica** Bos.-Herz.
59 C1 **Hrebinka** Ukr.
56 B3 **Hrodna** Belarus
30 A1 **Hsi-hseng** Myanmar
39 C3 **Hsinchu** Taiwan
39 C3 **Hsinying** Taiwan
30 A1 **Hsipaw** Myanmar
38 A2 **Huachi** China
118 A3 **Huacho** Peru
37 D2 **Huade** China
33 B1 **Huadian** China
38 B2 **Huaibei** China
39 A3 **Huaihua** China
38 B2 **Huainan** China
38 B2 **Huaiyang** China
38 B2 **Huaiyin** China
113 C3 **Huajuápan de León** Mex.
27 C3 **Huaki** Indon.
39 C3 **Hualien** Taiwan
118 A3 **Huallaga** *r.* Peru
88 A2 **Huambo** Angola
118 A3 **Huancayo** Peru
  Huangcaoba China *see* Xingyi
38 B2 **Huangchuan** China
  Huang Hai *sea see* Yellow Sea
38 B2 **Huang He** *r.* China
39 A4 **Huanglu** China
38 B3 **Huangshan** China
38 B2 **Huangshi** China
38 A2 **Huangtu Gaoyuan** *plat.* China
39 C3 **Huangyan** China
33 B1 **Huanren** China
118 A2 **Huánuco** Peru
120 B2 **Huanuni** Bol.
118 A2 **Huaráz** Peru
118 A3 **Huarmey** Peru
120 A3 **Huasco** Chile
120 A3 **Huasco** *r.* Chile
112 B2 **Huatabampo** Mex.
113 C3 **Huatusco** Mex.
39 A3 **Huayuan** China
38 B2 **Hubei** *prov.* China
41 D3 **Hubli** India
112 B2 **Huehuetenango** Guat.
112 B2 **Huehueto, Cerro** *mt.* Mex.
113 C2 **Huejutla** Mex.
74 B2 **Huelva** Spain
75 C2 **Huércal-Overa** Spain
75 C1 **Huesca** Spain
74 C2 **Huéscar** Spain
18 B3 **Hughes** Austr.
107 D2 **Hugo** U.S.A.
38 B1 **Huhhot** China
90 B2 **Huhudi** S. Africa
90 A2 **Huib-Hoch Plateau** Namibia
39 B3 **Huichang** China
33 B1 **Huich'ŏn** N. Korea
39 B3 **Huilai** China

88 A2 **Huila Plateau** Angola
30 B1 **Huili** China
33 B1 **Huinan** China
61 H3 **Huittinen** Fin.
113 C3 **Huixtla** Mex.
  Huiyang China *see* **Huizhou**
30 B1 **Huize** China
39 B3 **Huizhou** China
37 C1 **Hujirt** Mongolia
46 B2 **Hujr** Saudi Arabia
90 B1 **Hukuntsi** Botswana
46 B2 **Hulayfah** Saudi Arabia
34 B1 **Hulin** China
98 C2 **Hull** Can.
  Hulun China *see* **Hailar**
37 D1 **Hulun Nur** *l.* China
59 D2 **Hulyaypole** Ukr.
37 E1 **Huma** China
118 B2 **Humaitá** Brazil
90 D3 **Humansdorp** S. Africa
66 C2 **Humber** *est.* U.K.
94 D3 **Humboldt** Can.
110 C1 **Humboldt** U.S.A.
103 C2 **Humboldt** *r.* U.S.A.
71 E2 **Humenné** Slovakia
21 C3 **Hume Reservoir** Austr.
106 A1 **Humphreys Peak** U.S.A.
33 A1 **Hun** *r.* China
60 □A2 **Húnaflói** *b.* Iceland
39 B3 **Hunan** *prov.* China
33 C1 **Hunchun** China
78 B1 **Hunedoara** Romania
69 D2 **Hünfeld** Ger.
71 C2 **Hungary** *country* Europe
20 B1 **Hungerford** Austr.
33 B2 **Hŭngnam** N. Korea
67 D2 **Hunstanton** U.K.
69 D1 **Hunte** *r.* Ger.
19 D4 **Hunter Islands** Austr.
67 C2 **Huntingdon** U.K.
108 B2 **Huntington** *IN* U.S.A.
108 C3 **Huntington** *WV* U.S.A.
22 C1 **Huntly** N.Z.
64 C2 **Huntly** U.K.
98 C2 **Huntsville** Can.
110 C2 **Huntsville** *AL* U.S.A.
107 D2 **Huntsville** *TX* U.S.A.
27 D3 **Huon Peninsula** P.N.G.
38 B2 **Huozhou** China
84 B2 **Hurghada** Egypt
105 D2 **Huron** U.S.A.
108 C2 **Huron, Lake** Can./U.S.A.
103 D3 **Hurricane** U.S.A.
60 □B2 **Húsavík** Iceland
78 C1 **Huşi** Romania
48 A2 **Huslia** U.S.A.
46 B3 **Husn Al 'Abr** Yemen
70 B1 **Husum** Ger.
37 C1 **Hutag** Mongolia
28 A1 **Hutanopan** Indon.
105 D3 **Hutchinson** U.S.A.
38 C2 **Huzhou** China
60 □C3 **Hvalnes** Iceland
60 □B3 **Hvannadalshnúkur** *vol.* Iceland
77 C2 **Hvar** *i.* Croatia
88 B2 **Hwange** Zimbabwe
104 C2 **Hyannis** U.S.A.
36 C1 **Hyargas Nuur** *salt l.* Mongolia
18 A3 **Hyden** Austr.
41 B3 **Hyderabad** India
42 A2 **Hyderabad** Pak.
73 D3 **Hyères** France
73 D3 **Hyères, Îles d'** *is* France
33 B1 **Hyesan** N. Korea
96 B2 **Hyland Post** Can.
35 B3 **Hyōno-sen** *mt.* Japan
67 D3 **Hythe** U.K.
61 H3 **Hyvinkää** Fin.

I

118 B2 **Iaco** r. Brazil
78 C2 **Ialomiţa** r. Romania
78 C1 **Ianca** Romania
78 C1 **Iaşi** Romania
32 A1 **Iba** Phil.
83 C4 **Ibadan** Nigeria
118 A1 **Ibagué** Col.
118 A1 **Ibarra** Ecuador
46 B3 **Ibb** Yemen
68 C1 **Ibbenbüren** Ger.
83 C4 **Ibi** Nigeria
123 C1 **Ibiá** Brazil
123 D1 **Ibiraçu** Brazil
75 D2 **Ibiza** i. Spain
119 D3 **Ibotirama** Brazil
47 C2 **Ibrā'** Oman
47 C2 **Ibri** Oman
118 A3 **Ica** Peru
48 B2 **İçel** Turkey
60 ☐A3 **Iceland** country Europe
34 D3 **Ichinoseki** Japan
59 C1 **Ichnya** Ukr.
33 C2 **Ich'ŏn** N. Korea
107 E2 **Idabel** U.S.A.
102 C2 **Idaho** state U.S.A.
102 D2 **Idaho Falls** U.S.A.
68 C3 **Idar-Oberstein** Ger.
84 B2 **Idfu** Egypt
83 D2 **Idhān Awbārī** des. Libya
83 D2 **Idhān Murzūq** des. Libya
86 B3 **Idiofa** Dem. Rep. Congo
48 B2 **Idlib** Syria
122 B2 **Iepê** Brazil
68 A2 **Ieper** Belgium
87 D3 **Ifakara** Tanz.
89 ☐D3 **Ifanadiana** Madag.
83 C4 **Ife** Nigeria
82 C3 **Ifôghas, Adrar des** hills Mali
29 C1 **Igan** Sarawak Malaysia
122 C2 **Igarapava** Brazil
54 E3 **Igarka** Rus. Fed.
42 B3 **Igatpuri** India
49 C2 **Iğdır** Turkey
76 A3 **Iglesias** Sardinia Italy
95 F2 **Igloolik** Can.
      Igluligaarjuk Can. see
      Chesterfield Inlet
98 A2 **Ignace** Can.
56 C2 **Ignalina** Lith.
78 C2 **İğneada** Turkey
79 B3 **Igoumenitsa** Greece
54 E3 **Igra** Rus. Fed.
54 F2 **Igrim** Rus. Fed.
122 B3 **Iguaçu** r. Brazil
122 B3 **Iguaçu Falls** Arg./Brazil
113 C3 **Iguala** Mex.
75 D1 **Igualada** Spain
122 C2 **Iguape** Brazil
122 B2 **Iguatemi** Brazil
122 B2 **Iguatemi** r. Brazil
119 E2 **Iguatu** Brazil
86 A3 **Iguéla** Gabon
87 D3 **Igunga** Tanz.
37 D2 **Ihbulag** Mongolia
89 ☐D3 **Ihosy** Madag.
60 I3 **Iisalmi** Fin.
83 C4 **Ijebu-Ode** Nigeria
68 B1 **IJmuiden** Neth.
68 B1 **IJssel** r. Neth.
68 B1 **IJsselmeer** l. Neth.
91 C2 **Ikageng** S. Africa
79 C3 **Ikaria** i. Greece
86 C3 **Ikela** Dem. Rep. Congo
78 B2 **Ikhtiman** Bulg.
35 A4 **Iki** i. Japan
89 ☐D3 **Ikongo** Madag.

33 B2 **Iksan** S. Korea
32 B1 **Ilagan** Phil.
49 C2 **Īlām** Iran
43 C2 **Ilam** Nepal
71 D1 **Iława** Pol.
47 C2 **Ilazārān, Kūh-e** mt. Iran
97 D2 **Île-à-la-Crosse** Can.
97 D2 **Île-à-la-Crosse, Lac** l. Can.
86 C3 **Ilebo** Dem. Rep. Congo
87 D2 **Ileret** Kenya
67 D3 **Ilford** U.K.
67 A3 **Ilfracombe** U.K.
123 D2 **Ilha Grande, Baía da** b.
      Brazil
122 B2 **Ilha Grande, Represa** resr
      Brazil
122 B2 **Ilha Solteira, Represa** resr
      Brazil
74 B1 **Ílhavo** Port.
119 E3 **Ilhéus** Brazil
32 B2 **Iligan** Phil.
120 A4 **Illapel** Chile
58 C2 **Illichivs'k** Ukr.
108 A3 **Illinois** r. U.S.A.
108 B3 **Illinois** state U.S.A.
58 B2 **Illintsi** Ukr.
83 C2 **Illizi** Alg.
57 D2 **Il'men', Ozero** l. Rus. Fed.
69 E2 **Ilmenau** Ger.
118 A3 **Ilo** Peru
60 J3 **Ilomantsi** Fin.
83 C4 **Ilorin** Nigeria
21 D1 **Iluka** Austr.
95 H2 **Ilulissat** Greenland
35 A4 **Imari** Japan
85 C4 **Īmī** Eth.
76 B2 **Imola** Italy
119 D2 **Imperatriz** Brazil
104 C2 **Imperial** U.S.A.
86 B2 **Impfondo** Congo
30 A1 **Imphal** India
72 C2 **İmroz** Turkey
118 B3 **Inambari** r. Peru
83 C2 **In Aménas** Alg.
27 C3 **Inanwatan** Indon.
60 I2 **Inari** Fin.
60 I2 **Inarijärvi** l. Fin.
35 D3 **Inawashiro-ko** l. Japan
48 B1 **İnce Burun** pt Turkey
33 B2 **Inch'ŏn** S. Korea
91 D2 **Incomati** r. Moz.
46 A3 **Inda Silasē** Eth.
112 B2 **Indé** Mex.
103 C1 **Independence** CA U.S.A.
105 E2 **Independence** IA U.S.A.
105 D3 **Independence** KS U.S.A.
105 E3 **Independence** MO U.S.A.
102 C2 **Independence Mountains**
      U.S.A.
44 B2 **Inderborskiy** Kazakh.
40 D2 **India** country Asia
109 D2 **Indiana** U.S.A.
108 B2 **Indiana** state U.S.A.
108 B3 **Indianapolis** U.S.A.
97 D2 **Indian Head** Can.
127 **Indian Ocean**
105 E2 **Indianola** IA U.S.A.
110 B2 **Indianola** MS U.S.A.
103 C3 **Indian Springs** U.S.A.
54 D2 **Indiga** Rus. Fed.
51 K2 **Indigirka** r. Rus. Fed.
77 D1 **Indija** Yugo.
103 C4 **Indio** U.S.A.
26 B3 **Indonesia** country Asia
42 B2 **Indore** India
29 B2 **Indramayu, Tanjung**
      pt Indon.
72 C2 **Indre** r. France
42 A2 **Indus** r. China/Pak.

42 A2 **Indus, Mouths of the** Pak.
48 B1 **İnebolu** Turkey
79 C2 **İnegöl** Turkey
112 B3 **Infiernillo, Presa** resr Mex.
21 D1 **Inglewood** Austr.
70 C2 **Ingolstadt** Ger.
43 C2 **Ingrāj Bāzār** India
91 D2 **Inhaca** Moz.
89 C3 **Inhambane** Moz.
65 A2 **Inishbofin** i. Rep. of Ireland
65 B2 **Inishmore** i. Rep. of Ireland
65 C1 **Inishowen** pen.
      Rep. of Ireland
22 B2 **Inland Kaikoura Range**
      mts N.Z.
70 C2 **Inn** r. Europe
95 G1 **Innaanganeq** c. Greenland
      Inner Mongolia aut. reg.
      China see **Nei Mongol**
      Zizhiqu
64 B2 **Inner Sound** sea chan. U.K.
19 D1 **Innisfail** Austr.
70 C2 **Innsbruck** Austria
122 B1 **Inocência** Brazil
86 B3 **Inongo** Dem. Rep. Congo
71 D1 **Inowrocław** Pol.
82 C2 **In Salah** Alg.
30 A2 **Insein** Myanmar
54 F2 **Inta** Rus. Fed.
105 E1 **International Falls** U.S.A.
98 C1 **Inukjuak** Can.
94 C2 **Inuvik** Can.
64 B2 **Inveraray** U.K.
22 A3 **Invercargill** N.Z.
21 D1 **Inverell** Austr.
64 B2 **Invergordon** U.K.
96 C2 **Invermere** Can.
99 D2 **Inverness** Can.
64 B2 **Inverness** U.K.
64 C2 **Inverurie** U.K.
20 A3 **Investigator Strait** Austr.
45 E1 **Inya** Rus. Fed.
87 D3 **Inyonga** Tanz.
55 D3 **Inza** Rus. Fed.
79 B3 **Ioannina** Greece
105 D3 **Iola** U.S.A.
64 A2 **Iona** i. U.K.
79 B3 **Ionian Islands** Greece
77 C3 **Ionian Sea** Greece/Italy
      Ionioi Nisoi is Greece see
      Ionian Islands
79 C3 **Ios** i. Greece
105 E2 **Iowa** state U.S.A.
105 E2 **Iowa City** U.S.A.
122 C1 **Ipameri** Brazil
123 D1 **Ipatinga** Brazil
49 C1 **Ipatovo** Rus. Fed.
91 C2 **Ipelegeng** S. Africa
118 A1 **Ipiales** Col.
122 B3 **Ipiranga** Brazil
28 B1 **Ipoh** Malaysia
122 B1 **Iporá** Brazil
86 C2 **Ippy** C.A.R.
79 C2 **Ipsala** Turkey
21 D1 **Ipswich** Austr.
67 D2 **Ipswich** U.K.
95 G2 **Iqaluit** Can.
120 A3 **Iquique** Chile
118 A2 **Iquitos** Peru
79 C3 **Irakleio** Greece
      Iraklion Greece see
      Irakleio
44 B3 **Iran** country Asia
29 C1 **Iran, Pegunungan**
      mts Indon.
47 D2 **Īrānshahr** Iran
112 B2 **Irapuato** Mex.
49 C2 **Iraq** country Asia
122 B3 **Irati** Brazil
48 B2 **Irbid** Jordan

54 F3 Irbit Rus. Fed.
119 D3 Irecê Brazil
65 C2 Ireland, Republic of country Europe
86 C3 Irema Dem. Rep. Congo
44 C2 Irgiz Kazakh.
82 B3 Irígui reg. Mali/Maur.
87 D3 Iringa Tanz.
119 C2 Iriri r. Brazil
63 B3 Irish Sea Rep. of Ireland/U.K.
37 C1 Irkutsk Rus. Fed.
20 A2 Iron Knob Austr.
108 B1 Iron Mountain U.S.A.
108 A1 Ironwood U.S.A.
32 B1 Irosin Phil.
35 C4 Irō-zaki pt Japan
58 C1 Irpin' Ukr.
30 A2 Irrawaddy r. Myanmar
31 A2 Irrawaddy, Mouths of the Myanmar
54 F2 Irtysh r. Kazakh./Rus. Fed.
75 C1 Irún Spain
64 B3 Irvine U.K.
32 B2 Isabela Phil.
114 B3 Isabelia, Cordillera mts Nic.
60 □A2 Ísafjörður Iceland
35 B4 Isahaya Japan
73 E2 Isar r. Ger.
64 □ Isbister U.K.
76 B2 Ischia, Isola d' i. Italy
35 C4 Ise Japan
86 C2 Isengi Dem. Rep. Congo
69 D1 Iserlohn Ger.
69 D1 Isernhagen Ger.
35 C4 Ise-wan b. Japan
82 C4 Iseyin Nigeria
Isfahan Iran see Eşfahān
34 D2 Ishikari-wan b. Japan
45 D1 Ishim r. Kazakh./Rus. Fed.
34 D3 Ishinomaki Japan
35 D3 Ishioka Japan
108 B1 Ishpeming U.S.A.
79 C2 Işıklar Dağı mts Turkey
79 C3 Işıklı Turkey
91 D2 Isipingo S. Africa
87 C2 Isiro Dem. Rep. Congo
48 B2 İskenderun Turkey
50 G3 İskitim Rus. Fed.
78 B2 Iskūr r. Bulg.
96 A2 Iskut r. Can.
42 B1 Islamabad Pak.
20 A2 Island Lagoon salt flat Austr.
97 E2 Island Lake l. Can.
22 B1 Islands, Bay of N.Z.
64 A3 Islay i. U.K.
66 A1 Isle of Man i. Irish Sea
84 B1 Ismā'īlīya Egypt
77 C3 Isola di Capo Rizzuto Italy
78 C2 Isperikh Bulg.
48 B2 Israel country Asia
73 C2 Issoire France
79 C2 İstanbul Turkey
İstanbul Boğazı str. Turkey see Bosporus
79 B3 Istiaia Greece
76 B1 Istra pen. Croatia
73 C3 Istres France
119 D3 Itaberaba Brazil
123 D1 Itabira Brazil
123 D1 Itabirito Brazil
119 E3 Itabuna Brazil
118 C2 Itacoatiara Brazil
122 B2 Itaguajé Brazil
122 B2 Itaí Brazil
122 B3 Itaipu, Represa de resr Brazil

119 C2 Itaituba Brazil
120 D3 Itajaí Brazil
123 C2 Itajubá Brazil
76 B2 Italy country Europe
123 D1 Itamarandiba Brazil
123 D1 Itambacuri Brazil
123 D1 Itambé, Pico de mt. Brazil
30 A1 Itanagar India
122 C2 Itanhaém Brazil
123 D1 Itanhém Brazil
123 D1 Itaobím Brazil
122 C1 Itapajipe Brazil
123 E1 Itapebi Brazil
123 D2 Itapemirim Brazil
123 D2 Itaperuna Brazil
123 D1 Itapetinga Brazil
122 C2 Itapetininga Brazil
122 C2 Itapeva Brazil
119 E2 Itapicuru r. Brazil
119 D2 Itapicuru Mirim Brazil
122 C1 Itapuranga Brazil
122 C2 Itararé Brazil
43 B2 Itarsi India
122 B1 Itarumã Brazil
123 D2 Itaúna Brazil
39 C3 Itbayat i. Phil.
109 D2 Ithaca U.S.A.
69 D1 Ith Hils ridge Ger.
86 C2 Itimbiri r. Dem. Rep. Congo
123 D1 Itinga Brazil
122 B1 Itiquira Brazil
122 A1 Itiquira r. Brazil
35 C4 Itō Japan
122 C2 Itu Brazil
118 A2 Ituí r. Brazil
122 C1 Ituiutaba Brazil
87 C3 Itula Dem. Rep. Congo
122 C1 Itumbiara Brazil
122 B1 Iturama Brazil
69 D1 Itzehoe Ger.
51 N2 Iul'tin Rus. Fed.
122 B2 Ivaí r. Brazil
60 I2 Ivalo Fin.
56 C3 Ivanava Belarus
20 B2 Ivanhoe Austr.
58 B1 Ivankiv Ukr.
58 A2 Ivano-Frankivs'k Ukr.
57 F2 Ivanovo Rus. Fed.
56 C3 Ivatsevichy Belarus
79 C2 Ivaylovgrad Bulg.
54 F2 Ivdel' Rus. Fed.
122 B2 Ivinheima Brazil
122 B2 Ivinheima r. Brazil
95 H2 Ivittuut Greenland
Ivory Coast country Africa see Côte d'Ivoire
76 A1 Ivrea Italy
79 C3 İvrindi Turkey
95 F2 Ivujivik Can.
35 D3 Iwaki Japan
35 B4 Iwakuni Japan
34 D2 Iwamizawa Japan
34 D2 Iwanai Japan
56 C3 Iwye Belarus
91 D3 Ixopo S. Africa
112 B2 Ixtlán Mex.
113 D2 Izamal Mex.
49 C1 Izberbash Rus. Fed.
54 E3 Izhevsk Rus. Fed.
54 E2 Izhma Rus. Fed.
57 E3 Izmalkovo Rus. Fed.
58 B2 Izmayil Ukr.
79 C3 İzmir Turkey
79 C2 İznik Gölü l. Turkey
113 C3 Izúcar de Matamoros Mex.
35 B3 Izumo Japan
58 B1 Izyaslav Ukr.
59 D2 Izyum Ukr.

J

Jabal, Bahr el r. Sudan/Uganda see White Nile
74 C2 Jabalón r. Spain
43 B2 Jabalpur India
18 C1 Jabiru Austr.
77 C2 Jablanica Bos.-Herz.
119 E2 Jaboatão Brazil
122 C2 Jaboticabal Brazil
75 C1 Jaca Spain
113 C2 Jacala Mex.
119 C2 Jacareacanga Brazil
123 C2 Jacareí Brazil
123 D1 Jacinto Brazil
109 E1 Jackman U.S.A.
110 C2 Jackson AL U.S.A.
108 C2 Jackson MI U.S.A.
110 B2 Jackson MS U.S.A.
110 C1 Jackson TN U.S.A.
104 A2 Jackson WY U.S.A.
22 A2 Jackson Head pt N.Z.
110 B2 Jacksonville AR U.S.A.
111 D2 Jacksonville FL U.S.A.
108 A3 Jacksonville IL U.S.A.
111 E2 Jacksonville NC U.S.A.
107 D2 Jacksonville TX U.S.A.
115 C3 Jacmel Haiti
42 A2 Jacobabad Pak.
119 D3 Jacobina Brazil
99 D2 Jacques Cartier, Mont mt. Can.
119 D2 Jacunda Brazil
122 C2 Jacupiranga Brazil
77 C2 Jadovnik mt. Bos.-Herz.
118 A2 Jaén Peru
74 C2 Jaén Spain
20 A3 Jaffa, Cape Austr.
41 B4 Jaffna Sri Lanka
41 C3 Jagdalpur India
91 C2 Jagersfontein S. Africa
47 C2 Jaghīn Iran
122 C2 Jaguariaíva Brazil
47 C2 Jahrom Iran
42 B2 Jaipur India
42 B2 Jaisalmer India
43 C2 Jajarkot Nepal
77 C2 Jajce Bos.-Herz.
28 B2 Jakarta Indon.
96 A1 Jakes Corner Can.
60 G2 Jäkkvik Sweden
60 H3 Jakobstad Fin.
45 D3 Jalālābād Afgh.
45 C2 Jalal-Abad Kyrg.
42 B1 Jalandhar India
113 C3 Jalapa Enríquez Mex.
122 B2 Jales Brazil
42 B2 Jalgaon India
83 D4 Jalingo Nigeria
42 B3 Jalna India
112 B2 Jalpa Mex.
43 C2 Jalpaiguri India
113 C2 Jalpan Mex.
83 E2 Jālū Libya
114 C3 Jamaica country West Indies
114 C3 Jamaica Channel Haiti/Jamaica
43 C2 Jamalpur Bangl.
28 B2 Jambi Indon.
105 D2 James r. ND/SD U.S.A.
109 D3 James r. VA U.S.A.
98 B1 James Bay Can.
20 A2 Jamestown Austr.
105 D1 Jamestown ND U.S.A.
109 D2 Jamestown NY U.S.A.
42 B1 Jammu Jammu and Kashmir
42 B1 Jammu and Kashmir terr. Asia

42 B2 **Jamnagar** India
61 I3 **Jämsä** Fin.
43 C2 **Jamshedpur** India
43 C2 **Jamuna** r. Bangl.
43 C2 **Janakpur** Nepal
123 D1 **Janaúba** Brazil
49 D2 **Jandaq** Iran
108 B2 **Janesville** U.S.A.
52 C2 **Jan Mayen** i. Arctic Ocean
90 B3 **Jansenville** S. Africa
123 D1 **Januária** Brazil
42 B2 **Jaora** India
35 B4 **Japan** country Asia
124 C3 **Japan, Sea of**
        N. Pacific Ocean
118 B2 **Japurá** r. Brazil
122 C1 **Jaraguá** Brazil
122 B2 **Jaraguari** Brazil
120 C3 **Jardim** Brazil
37 D1 **Jargalant** Mongolia
71 D1 **Jarocin** Pol.
71 E1 **Jarosław** Pol.
60 F3 **Järpen** Sweden
38 A2 **Jartai** China
118 B3 **Jaru** Brazil
        Jarud China see **Lubei**
47 C2 **Jäsk** Iran
71 E2 **Jasło** Pol.
96 C2 **Jasper** Can.
108 B3 **Jasper** IN U.S.A.
107 E2 **Jasper** TX U.S.A.
71 D2 **Jastrzębie-Zdrój** Pol.
71 D2 **Jászberény** Hungary
122 B1 **Jataí** Brazil
42 A2 **Jati** Pak.
122 C2 **Jaú** Brazil
118 B2 **Jaú** r. Brazil
113 C2 **Jaumave** Mex.
43 C2 **Jaunpur** India
122 B1 **Jauru** Brazil
29 B2 **Java** i. Indon.
37 D1 **Javarthushuu** Mongolia
127 D4 **Java Sea** Indon.
        Jawa i. Indon. see **Java**
85 C4 **Jawhar** Somalia
71 D1 **Jawor** Pol.
71 D1 **Jaworzno** Pol.
27 D3 **Jaya, Puncak** mt. Indon.
27 D3 **Jayapura** Indon.
96 B1 **Jean Marie River** Can.
99 D1 **Jeannin, Lac** l. Can.
84 A3 **Jebel Abyad Plateau** Sudan
64 C3 **Jedburgh** U.K.
46 A2 **Jeddah** Saudi Arabia
69 E1 **Jeetze** r. Ger.
103 C3 **Jefferson, Mount** U.S.A.
105 E3 **Jefferson City** U.S.A.
56 C2 **Jēkabpils** Latvia
71 D1 **Jelenia Góra** Pol.
56 B2 **Jelgava** Latvia
29 C2 **Jember** Indon.
69 E2 **Jena** Ger.
48 B2 **Jenīn** West Bank
110 B2 **Jennings** U.S.A.
119 D3 **Jequié** Brazil
123 D1 **Jequitaí** Brazil
123 D1 **Jequitinhonha** Brazil
123 E1 **Jequitinhonha** r. Brazil
115 C3 **Jérémie** Haiti
112 B2 **Jerez** Mex.
74 B2 **Jerez de la Frontera** Spain
77 D3 **Jergucat** Albania
83 C1 **Jerid, Chott el** salt l.
        Tunisia
102 D2 **Jerome** U.S.A.
63 C4 **Jersey** terr. Channel Is
119 D2 **Jerumenha** Brazil
48 B2 **Jerusalem** Israel/West Bank
21 D3 **Jervis Bay Territory**
        admin. div. Austr.

76 B1 **Jesenice** Slovenia
76 B2 **Jesi** Italy
69 F2 **Jessen** Ger.
43 C2 **Jessore** Bangl.
111 D2 **Jesup** U.S.A.
113 C3 **Jesús Carranza** Mex.
42 B2 **Jhalawar** India
42 B1 **Jhang** Pak.
43 B2 **Jhansi** India
43 C2 **Jharsuguda** India
42 B1 **Jhelum** Pak.
38 C2 **Jiading** China
37 E1 **Jiamusi** China
39 B3 **Ji'an** Jiangxi China
33 B1 **Ji'an** Jilin China
30 A1 **Jianchuan** China
        Jiandaoyu China see **Zigui**
38 B2 **Jiangsu** prov. China
39 B3 **Jiangxi** prov. China
38 A2 **Jiangyou** China
38 B3 **Jianli** China
39 B3 **Jianyang** Fujian China
38 A2 **Jianyang** Sichuan China
38 B2 **Jiaohe** China
38 C2 **Jiaozhou** China
38 B2 **Jiaozuo** China
38 C2 **Jiaxing** China
36 C2 **Jiayuguan** China
        Jiddah Saudi Arabia see
        Jeddah
60 G2 **Jiehkkevarri** mt. Norway
38 B2 **Jiexiu** China
36 C2 **Jigzhi** China
71 D2 **Jihlava** Czech Rep.
85 C4 **Jijiga** Eth.
85 C4 **Jilib** Somalia
37 E2 **Jilin** China
33 B1 **Jilin** prov. China
33 A1 **Jilin Handa Ling** mts China
85 B4 **Jīma** Eth.
112 B2 **Jiménez** Chihuahua Mex.
113 C2 **Jiménez** Tamaulipas Mex.
38 B2 **Jinan** China
38 B2 **Jincheng** China
21 C3 **Jindabyne** Austr.
71 D2 **Jindřichův Hradec**
        Czech Rep.
39 B3 **Jingdezhen** China
39 B3 **Jinggangshan** China
30 B1 **Jinghong** China
38 B2 **Jingmen** China
38 A2 **Jingning** China
38 B2 **Jingsha** China
38 A2 **Jingtai** China
39 A3 **Jingxi** China
33 B1 **Jingyu** China
38 A2 **Jingyuan** China
38 B2 **Jingzhou** China
39 B3 **Jinhua** China
38 B1 **Jining** Nei Mongol China
38 B2 **Jining** Shandong China
87 D2 **Jinja** Uganda
85 B4 **Jinka** Eth.
114 B3 **Jinotepe** Nic.
39 A3 **Jinping** China
        Jinsha Jiang r. China see
        Yangtze
38 B3 **Jinshi** China
38 C1 **Jinzhou** China
118 B2 **Jiparaná** r. Brazil
47 C2 **Jiroft** Iran
39 A3 **Jishou** China
78 B2 **Jiu** r. Romania
38 A2 **Jiuding Shan** mt. China
38 B3 **Jiujiang** China
34 B1 **Jixi** China
46 B3 **Jīzān** Saudi Arabia
119 E2 **João Pessoa** Brazil
123 C1 **João Pinheiro** Brazil
42 B2 **Jodhpur** India

60 I3 **Joensuu** Fin.
35 C3 **Jōetsu** Japan
89 C3 **Jofane** Moz.
56 C2 **Jõgeva** Estonia
91 C2 **Johannesburg** S. Africa
102 C2 **John Day** U.S.A.
102 B1 **John Day** r. U.S.A.
96 C2 **John d'Or Prairie** Can.
111 E1 **John H. Kerr Reservoir**
        U.S.A.
64 C1 **John o'Groats** U.K.
111 D1 **Johnson City** U.S.A.
96 A1 **Johnson's Crossing** Can.
17 G2 **Johnston Atoll**
        N. Pacific Ocean
64 B3 **Johnstone** U.K.
109 D2 **Johnstown** U.S.A.
28 B1 **Johor Bahru** Malaysia
56 C2 **Jõhvi** Estonia
122 C3 **Joinville** Brazil
73 D2 **Joinville** France
62 A2 **Jokkmokk** Sweden
60 □B2 **Jökulsá á Fjöllum** r. Iceland
108 B2 **Joliet** U.S.A.
98 C2 **Joliette** Can.
32 B2 **Jolo** Phil.
32 B2 **Jolo** i. Phil.
29 C2 **Jombang** Indon.
43 C2 **Jomsom** Nepal
56 B2 **Jonava** Lith.
110 B1 **Jonesboro** AR U.S.A.
110 B2 **Jonesboro** LA U.S.A.
95 F1 **Jones Sound** sea chan. Can.
61 F4 **Jönköping** Sweden
99 C2 **Jonquière** Can.
113 C3 **Jonuta** Mex.
105 E3 **Joplin** U.S.A.
48 B2 **Jordan** country Asia
48 B2 **Jordan** r. Asia
104 B1 **Jordan** U.S.A.
102 C2 **Jordan Valley** U.S.A.
30 A1 **Jorhat** India
61 E4 **Jørpeland** Norway
83 C4 **Jos** Nigeria
113 C3 **José Cardel** Mex.
99 D1 **Joseph, Lac** l. Can.
18 B1 **Joseph Bonaparte Gulf**
        Austr.
83 C4 **Jos Plateau** Nigeria
61 E3 **Jotunheimen** mts Norway
90 B3 **Joubertina** S. Africa
91 C2 **Jouberton** S. Africa
61 I3 **Joutseno** Fin.
102 B1 **Juan de Fuca Strait**
        Can./U.S.A.
        Juanshui China see
        Tongcheng
113 B2 **Juaréz** Mex.
119 D2 **Juàzeiro** Brazil
119 E2 **Juàzeiro do Norte** Brazil
85 B4 **Juba** Sudan
85 C5 **Jubba** r. Somalia
46 B2 **Jubbah** Saudi Arabia
75 C2 **Júcar** r. Spain
113 C3 **Juchitán** Mex.
70 C2 **Judenburg** Austria
69 D2 **Jühnde** Ger.
114 B3 **Juigalpa** Nic.
68 C1 **Juist** i. Ger.
123 D2 **Juiz de Fora** Brazil
118 A3 **Juliaca** Peru
43 C2 **Jumla** Nepal
42 B2 **Junagadh** India
107 D2 **Junction** U.S.A.
105 D3 **Junction City** U.S.A.
122 C2 **Jundiaí** Brazil
96 A2 **Juneau** U.S.A.
21 C2 **Junee** Austr.
73 D2 **Jungfrau** mt. Switz.
109 D2 **Juniata** r. U.S.A.

60 G3 **Junsele** Sweden
102 C2 **Juntura** U.S.A.
122 C2 **Juquiá** Brazil
85 A4 **Jur** r. Sudan
73 D2 **Jura** mts France/Switz.
64 B2 **Jura** i. U.K.
64 B3 **Jura, Sound of** sea chan.
U.K.
56 B2 **Jurbarkas** Lith.
56 B2 **Jūrmala** Latvia
118 B2 **Juruá** r. Brazil
118 C2 **Juruena** r. Brazil
118 B2 **Jutaí** r. Brazil
69 F2 **Jüterbog** Ger.
38 B2 **Juxian** China
47 C2 **Jūyom** Iran
90 B1 **Jwaneng** Botswana
61 I3 **Jyväskylä** Fin.

K

42 B1 **K2** mt. China/
Jammu and Kashmir
87 C3 **Kabalo** Dem. Rep. Congo
87 C3 **Kabare** Dem. Rep. Congo
98 B2 **Kabinakagami Lake** Can.
86 C3 **Kabinda** Dem. Rep. Congo
86 B2 **Kabo** C.A.R.
88 B2 **Kabompo** Zambia
87 C3 **Kabongo** Dem. Rep. Congo
45 C3 **Kābul** Afgh.
32 B2 **Kaburuang** i. Indon.
89 B2 **Kabwe** Zambia
42 A2 **Kachchh, Gulf of** India
51 I3 **Kachug** Rus. Fed.
49 C1 **Kaçkar Dağı** mt. Turkey
79 C2 **Kadıköy** Turkey
82 B3 **Kadiolo** Mali
41 B3 **Kadmat** i. India
89 B2 **Kadoma** Zimbabwe
31 A2 **Kadonkani** Myanmar
85 A3 **Kadugli** Sudan
83 C3 **Kaduna** Nigeria
57 E2 **Kaduy** Rus. Fed.
54 E2 **Kadzherom** Rus. Fed.
82 A3 **Kaédi** Maur.
86 B1 **Kaélé** Cameroon
82 A3 **Kaffrine** Senegal
79 B3 **Kafireas, Akra** pt Greece
89 B2 **Kafue** Zambia
89 B2 **Kafue** r. Zambia
86 B2 **Kaga Bandoro** C.A.R.
59 E2 **Kagal'nitskaya** Rus. Fed.
35 B4 **Kagoshima** Japan
58 C2 **Kaharlyk** Ukr.
29 C2 **Kahayan** r. Indon.
86 C3 **Kahemba** Dem. Rep. Congo
69 E2 **Kahla** Ger.
47 C2 **Kahnūj** Iran
60 H2 **Kahperusvaarat** mts Fin.
48 B2 **Kahramanmaraş** Turkey
47 C2 **Kahūrak** Iran
27 C3 **Kai, Kepulauan** is Indon.
83 C4 **Kaiama** Nigeria
22 B2 **Kaiapoi** N.Z.
27 C3 **Kai Besar** i. Indon.
22 B2 **Kaimanawa Mountains** N.Z.
35 C4 **Kainan** Japan

83 C3 **Kainji Reservoir** Nigeria
22 B1 **Kaipara Harbour** N.Z.
42 B2 **Kairana** India
83 D1 **Kairouan** Tunisia
22 B1 **Kaitaia** N.Z.
22 C1 **Kaitawa** N.Z.
  Kaitong China see Tongyu
27 C3 **Kaiwatu** Indon.
33 A1 **Kaiyuan** Liaoning China
30 B1 **Kaiyuan** Yunnan China
60 I3 **Kajaani** Fin.
19 D2 **Kajabbi** Austr.
90 B2 **Kakamas** S. Africa
87 D2 **Kakamega** Kenya
59 C2 **Kakhovka** Ukr.
59 C2 **Kakhovs'ke**
  Vodoskhovyshche resr Ukr.
41 C3 **Kākināda** India
96 C1 **Kakisa** Can.
87 C3 **Kakoswa** Dem. Rep. Congo
94 B2 **Kaktovik** U.S.A.
  Kalaallit Nunaat terr.
N. America see Greenland
27 C3 **Kalabahi** Indon.
88 B2 **Kalabo** Zambia
59 E1 **Kalach** Rus. Fed.
87 D2 **Kalacha Dida** Kenya
30 A1 **Kaladan** r. India/Myanmar
88 B3 **Kalahari Desert** Africa
60 H3 **Kalajoki** Fin.
79 B3 **Kalamaria** Greece
79 B3 **Kalamata** Greece
108 B2 **Kalamazoo** U.S.A.
79 B3 **Kalampaka** Greece
59 C2 **Kalanchak** Ukr.
31 B2 **Kalasin** Thai.
47 C2 **Kalāt** Iran
42 A2 **Kalat** Pak.
18 A2 **Kalbarri** Austr.
79 C3 **Kale** Turkey
48 B1 **Kalecik** Turkey
86 C3 **Kalema** Dem. Rep. Congo
87 C3 **Kalémié** Dem. Rep. Congo
30 A1 **Kalemyo** Myanmar
  Kalgan China see
Zhangjiakou
18 B3 **Kalgoorlie** Austr.
77 C2 **Kali** Croatia
78 C2 **Kaliakra, Nos** pt Bulg.
87 C3 **Kalima** Dem. Rep. Congo
29 C2 **Kalimantan** reg. Indon.
56 B3 **Kaliningrad** Rus. Fed.
59 D2 **Kalininskaya** Rus. Fed.
56 C3 **Kalinkavichy** Belarus
102 D1 **Kalispell** U.S.A.
71 D1 **Kalisz** Pol.
59 E2 **Kalitva** r. Rus. Fed.
60 H2 **Kalix** Sweden
60 H2 **Kalixälven** r. Sweden
79 C3 **Kalkan** Turkey
88 A3 **Kalkfeld** Namibia
60 I3 **Kallavesi** l. Fin.
61 G4 **Kallsjön** l. Sweden
61 G4 **Kalmar** Sweden
61 G4 **Kalmarsund** sea chan.
Sweden
88 B2 **Kalomo** Zambia
96 B2 **Kalone Peak** Can.
43 B1 **Kalpa** India
41 B3 **Kalpeni** i. India
43 B2 **Kalpi** India
69 D1 **Kaltenkirchen** Ger.
57 E3 **Kaluga** Rus. Fed.
61 F4 **Kalundborg** Denmark
58 A2 **Kalush** Ukr.
57 E2 **Kalyazin** Rus. Fed.
79 C3 **Kalymnos** i. Greece
87 C3 **Kama** Dem. Rep. Congo
30 A2 **Kama** Myanmar
54 E3 **Kama** r. Rus. Fed.

34 D3 **Kamaishi** Japan
48 B2 **Kaman** Turkey
88 A2 **Kamanjab** Namibia
46 B3 **Kamarān** i. Yemen
42 A2 **Kamarod** Pak.
18 B3 **Kambalda** Austr.
87 C4 **Kambove** Dem. Rep. Congo
78 C2 **Kamchiya** r. Bulg.
78 B2 **Kamenitsa** mt. Bulg.
76 B2 **Kamenjak, Rt** pt Croatia
44 B1 **Kamenka** Kazakh.
59 D1 **Kamenka** Rus. Fed.
59 E2 **Kamenolomni** Rus. Fed.
51 M2 **Kamenskoye** Rus. Fed.
59 E2 **Kamensk-Shakhtinskiy**
Rus. Fed.
54 F3 **Kamensk-Ural'skiy**
Rus. Fed.
90 A3 **Kamiesberge** mts S. Africa
90 A3 **Kamieskroon** S. Africa
97 D1 **Kamilukuak Lake** l. Can.
87 C3 **Kamina** Dem. Rep. Congo
97 E1 **Kaminak Lake** Can.
58 A1 **Kamin'-Kashyrs'kyy** Ukr.
96 B2 **Kamloops** Can.
86 C3 **Kamonia** Dem. Rep. Congo
87 D2 **Kampala** Uganda
28 B1 **Kampar** r. Indon.
28 B1 **Kampar** Malaysia
68 B1 **Kampen** Neth.
87 C3 **Kampene** Dem. Rep. Congo
31 A2 **Kamphaeng Phet** Thai.
31 B2 **Kâmpóng Cham** Cambodia
31 B2 **Kâmpóng Chhnăng**
Cambodia
  Kâmpóng Saôm Cambodia
see Sihanoukville
31 B2 **Kâmpóng Spoe** Cambodia
31 B2 **Kâmpôt** Cambodia
97 D2 **Kamsack** Can.
54 E3 **Kamskoye**
  Vodokhranilishche resr
Rus. Fed.
85 C4 **Kamsuuma** Somalia
58 B2 **Kam"yanets'-Podil's'kyy**
Ukr.
58 A1 **Kam"yanka-Buz'ka** Ukr.
56 B3 **Kamyanyets** Belarus
59 D2 **Kamyshevatskaya** Rus. Fed.
55 D3 **Kamyshin** Rus. Fed.
103 D3 **Kanab** U.S.A.
86 C3 **Kananga** Dem. Rep. Congo
55 D3 **Kanash** Rus. Fed.
108 C3 **Kanawha** r. U.S.A.
35 C3 **Kanazawa** Japan
30 A1 **Kanbalu** Myanmar
31 A2 **Kanchanaburi** Thai.
41 B3 **Kanchipuram** India
45 C3 **Kandahār** Afgh.
54 C2 **Kandalaksha** Rus. Fed.
29 C2 **Kandangan** Indon.
42 A2 **Kandhkot** Pak.
82 C3 **Kandi** Benin
42 B2 **Kandla** India
21 C2 **Kandos** Austr.
89 □D2**Kandreho** Madag.
73 C3 **Kandy** Sri Lanka
44 B2 **Kandyagash** Kazakh.
95 G1 **Kane Bassin** b. Greenland
59 D2 **Kanevskaya** Rus. Fed.
90 B1 **Kang** Botswana
95 H2 **Kangaatsiaq** Greenland
82 B3 **Kangaba** Mali
48 B2 **Kangal** Turkey
47 C2 **Kangān** Iran
28 B1 **Kangar** Malaysia
20 A3 **Kangaroo Island** Austr.
43 C2 **Kangchenjunga** mt.
India/Nepal
33 B2 **Kangdong** N. Korea

29 C2 **Kangean, Kepulauan** *is* Indon.
95 I2 **Kangeq** c. Greenland
95 I2 **Kangerlussuaq** *inlet* Greenland
95 H2 **Kangerlussuaq** *inlet* Greenland
95 H2 **Kangersuatsiaq** Greenland
33 B1 **Kanggye** N. Korea
99 D1 **Kangiqsualujjuaq** Can.
95 G2 **Kangiqsujuaq** Can.
95 G2 **Kangirsuk** Can.
43 C2 **Kangmar** China
33 B2 **Kangnŭng** S. Korea
33 A1 **Kangping** China
40 D2 **Kangto** *mt.* China/India
30 A1 **Kani** Myanmar
54 D2 **Kanin, Poluostrov** *pen.* Rus. Fed.
54 D2 **Kanin Nos** Rus. Fed.
59 C2 **Kaniv** Ukr.
61 H3 **Kankaanpää** Fin.
108 B2 **Kankakee** U.S.A.
82 B3 **Kankan** Guinea
43 C2 **Kanker** India
Kannur India *see* **Cannanore**
83 C3 **Kano** Nigeria
90 B3 **Kanonkop** *pt* S. Africa
35 B4 **Kanoya** Japan
43 C2 **Kanpur** India
104 C3 **Kansas** *r.* U.S.A.
105 D3 **Kansas** *state* U.S.A.
105 E3 **Kansas City** U.S.A.
51 H3 **Kansk** Rus. Fed.
82 C3 **Kantchari** Burkina
59 D2 **Kantemirovka** Rus. Fed.
65 B2 **Kanturk** Rep. of Ireland
91 D2 **KaNyamazane** S. Africa
91 C1 **Kanye** Botswana
39 C3 **Kaohsiung** Taiwan
88 A2 **Kaokoveld** *plat.* Namibia
82 A3 **Kaolack** Senegal
88 B2 **Kaoma** Zambia
86 C3 **Kapanga** Dem. Rep. Congo
45 D2 **Kapchagay** Kazakh.
45 D2 **Kapchagayskoye Vodokhranilishche** *resr* Kazakh.
68 B2 **Kapellen** Belgium
89 B2 **Kapiri Mposhi** Zambia
95 H2 **Kapisillit** Greenland
98 B1 **Kapiskau** *r.* Can.
29 C1 **Kapit** *Sarawak* Malaysia
31 A3 **Kapoe** Thai.
85 B4 **Kapoeta** Sudan
71 D2 **Kaposvár** Hungary
29 B2 **Kapuas** *r.* Indon.
20 A2 **Kapunda** Austr.
98 B2 **Kapuskasing** Can.
71 D2 **Kapuvár** Hungary
56 C3 **Kapyl'** Belarus
82 C4 **Kara** Togo
79 C3 **Kara Ada** *i.* Turkey
44 B2 **Kara-Bogaz Gol, Zaliv** *b.* Turkm.
44 B2 **Karabogazkel'** Turkm.
48 B1 **Karabük** Turkey
44 C2 **Karabutak** Kazakh.
78 C2 **Karacaköy** Turkey
57 D3 **Karachev** Rus. Fed.
42 A2 **Karachi** Pak.
Kara Deniz *sea* Asia/Europe *see* **Black Sea**
45 D2 **Karaganda** Kazakh.
45 D2 **Karagayly** Kazakh.
51 L3 **Karaginskiy Zaliv** *b.* Rus. Fed.
49 D2 **Karaj** Iran
44 B2 **Karakalpakiya** Kazakh.
32 B2 **Karakelong** *i.* Indon.

45 D2 **Kara-Köl** Kyrg.
45 D2 **Karakol** Kyrg.
42 B1 **Karakoram** *mts* Asia
44 B2 **Karakum, Peski** *des.* Kazakh.
Karakum Desert Turkm. *see* **Karakumy, Peski**
44 C3 **Karakumy, Peski** *des.* Turkm.
48 B2 **Karaman** Turkey
45 E2 **Karamay** China
22 B2 **Karamea** N.Z.
22 B2 **Karamea Bight** *b.* N.Z.
48 B2 **Karapınar** Turkey
90 A2 **Karasburg** Namibia
54 F1 **Kara Sea** *sea* Rus. Fed.
60 I2 **Karasjok** Norway
50 G3 **Karasuk** Rus. Fed.
45 D2 **Karatau** Kazakh.
45 C2 **Karatau, Khrebet** *mts* Kazakh.
54 F2 **Karataykha** Rus. Fed.
35 A4 **Karatsu** Japan
28 B2 **Karawang** Indon.
49 C2 **Karbalā'** Iraq
71 E2 **Karcag** Hungary
79 B3 **Karditsa** Greece
56 B2 **Kärdla** Estonia
90 B3 **Kareeberge** *mts* S. Africa
43 B2 **Kareli** India
42 B1 **Kargil** Jammu and Kashmir
89 B2 **Kariba** Zimbabwe
89 B2 **Kariba, Lake** *resr* Zambia/Zimbabwe
29 B2 **Karimata, Pulau-pulau** *is* Indon.
29 B2 **Karimata, Selat** *str.* Indon.
43 B3 **Karimnagar** India
29 C2 **Karimunjawa, Pulau-pulau** *is* Indon.
59 C2 **Karkinits'ka Zatoka** *g.* Ukr.
59 D2 **Karlivka** Ukr.
77 C1 **Karlovac** Croatia
70 C1 **Karlovy Vary** Czech Rep.
61 F4 **Karlshamn** Sweden
61 G4 **Karlskrona** Sweden
70 B2 **Karlsruhe** Ger.
61 F4 **Karlstad** Sweden
69 D3 **Karlstadt** Ger.
57 D3 **Karma** Belarus
61 E4 **Karmøy** *i.* Norway
42 B2 **Karnafuli Reservoir** Bangl.
42 B2 **Karnal** India
78 C2 **Karnobat** Bulg.
42 A2 **Karodi** Pak.
89 B2 **Karoi** Zimbabwe
89 C1 **Karonga** Malawi
84 B3 **Karora** Eritrea
79 C3 **Karpathos** *i.* Greece
79 B3 **Karpenisi** Greece
54 D2 **Karpogory** Rus. Fed.
18 A2 **Karratha** Austr.
49 C1 **Kars** Turkey
55 C2 **Kārsava** Latvia
45 C3 **Karshi** Uzbek.
54 E2 **Karskiye Vorota, Proliv** *str.* Rus. Fed.
Karskoye More *sea* Rus. Fed. *see* **Kara Sea**
69 E1 **Karstädt** Ger.
79 C2 **Kartal** Turkey
55 F3 **Kartaly** Rus. Fed.
41 B3 **Karwar** India
51 I3 **Karymskoye** Rus. Fed.
79 B3 **Karystos** Greece
48 A2 **Kaş** Turkey
98 B1 **Kasabonika Lake** Can.
86 C3 **Kasaji** Dem. Rep. Congo
89 C2 **Kasama** Zambia
88 B2 **Kasane** Botswana

86 B3 **Kasangulu** Dem. Rep. Con
41 B3 **Kasaragod** India
97 D1 **Kasba Lake** Can.
88 B2 **Kasempa** Zambia
87 C4 **Kasenga** Dem. Rep. Congo
87 C3 **Kasese** Dem. Rep. Congo
87 D2 **Kasese** Uganda
49 D2 **Kāshān** Iran
Kashgar China *see* **Kashi**
45 D3 **Kashi** China
35 D3 **Kashima-nada** *b.* Japan
57 E2 **Kashin** Rus. Fed.
57 E3 **Kashira** Rus. Fed.
57 E3 **Kashirskoye** Rus. Fed.
35 C3 **Kashiwazaki** Japan
44 B3 **Kāshmar** Iran
42 A2 **Kashmor** Pak.
87 C3 **Kashyukulu** Dem. Rep. Congo
55 D3 **Kasimov** Rus. Fed.
61 H3 **Kaskinen** Fin.
87 C3 **Kasongo** Dem. Rep. Congo
86 B3 **Kasongo-Lunda** Dem. Rep. Congo
79 C3 **Kasos** *i.* Greece
Kaspiyskoye More *sea* Asia/Europe *see* **Caspian S**
84 B3 **Kassala** Sudan
69 D2 **Kassel** Ger.
48 B1 **Kastamonu** Turkey
79 B3 **Kastelli** Greece
79 B2 **Kastoria** Greece
57 D3 **Kastsyukovichy** Belarus
87 D3 **Kasulu** Tanz.
89 C2 **Kasungu** Malawi
109 F1 **Katahdin, Mount** U.S.A.
86 C3 **Katako-Kombe** Dem. Rep. Congo
18 A3 **Katanning** Austr.
31 A3 **Katchall** *i.* India
79 B2 **Katerini** Greece
96 A2 **Kate's Needle** *mt.* Can./U.S.A.
89 C2 **Katete** Zambia
30 A1 **Katha** Myanmar
46 A2 **Katherîna, Gebel** *mt.* Egyp
18 C1 **Katherine** *r.* Austr.
42 B2 **Kathiawar** *pen.* India
91 C2 **Kathlehong** S. Africa
43 C2 **Kathmandu** Nepal
90 B2 **Kathu** S. Africa
42 B1 **Kathua** Jammu and Kashm
82 B3 **Kati** Mali
43 C2 **Katihar** India
22 C1 **Katikati** N.Z.
91 C3 **Kati-Kati** S. Africa
88 B2 **Katima Mulilo** Namibia
79 B3 **Kato Achaïa** Greece
21 D2 **Katoomba** Austr.
71 D1 **Katowice** Pol.
61 G4 **Katrineholm** Sweden
83 C3 **Katsina** Nigeria
83 C4 **Katsina-Ala** Nigeria
45 C3 **Kattakurgan** Uzbek.
61 F4 **Kattegat** *str.* Denmark/Sweden
68 B1 **Katwijk aan Zee** Neth.
61 H3 **Kauhajoki** Fin.
56 B3 **Kaunas** Lith.
83 C3 **Kaura-Namoda** Nigeria
60 H2 **Kautokeino** Norway
79 B2 **Kavala** Greece
34 C2 **Kavalerovo** Rus. Fed.
41 C3 **Kavali** India
41 B4 **Kavaratti** *i.* India
78 C2 **Kavarna** Bulg.
49 D2 **Kavīr, Dasht-e** *des.* Iran
35 C3 **Kawagoe** Japan
22 B1 **Kawakawa** N.Z.
35 C3 **Kawanishi** Japan

98 C2 **Kawartha Lakes** Can.
35 C3 **Kawasaki** Japan
22 C1 **Kawerau** N.Z.
31 A2 **Kawkareik** Myanmar
30 A1 **Kawlin** Myanmar
31 A2 **Kawmapyin** Myanmar
31 A2 **Kawthaung** Myanmar
45 D3 **Kaxgar He** r. China
82 B3 **Kaya** Burkina
29 C1 **Kayan** r. Indon.
104 B2 **Kaycee** U.S.A.
106 A1 **Kayenta** U.S.A.
82 A3 **Kayes** Mali
45 D2 **Kaynar** Kazakh.
48 B2 **Kayseri** Turkey
45 D1 **Kazakhskiy**
         Melkosopochnik plain
         Kazakh.
49 D1 **Kazakhskiy Zaliv** b. Kazakh.
44 E2 **Kazakhstan** country Asia
55 D3 **Kazan'** Rus. Fed.
48 A1 **Kazanlŭk** Bulg.
44 A2 **Kazbek** mt.
         Georgia/Rus. Fed.
49 D3 **Kāzerūn** Iran
71 E2 **Kazincbarcika** Hungary
54 F2 **Kazymskiy Mys** Rus. Fed.
79 B3 **Kea** i. Greece
65 C1 **Keady** U.K.
105 D2 **Kearney** U.S.A.
106 A2 **Kearny** U.S.A.
84 A3 **Kebkabiya** Sudan
60 G2 **Kebnekaise** mt. Sweden
85 C4 **K'ebrī Dehar** Eth.
29 B2 **Kebumen** Indon.
96 B2 **Kechika** r. Can.
71 D2 **Kecskemét** Hungary
66 C1 **Kėdainiai** Lith.
82 A3 **Kédougou** Senegal
71 D1 **Kędzierzyn-Koźle** Pol.
96 A1 **Keele** r. Can.
96 A1 **Keele Peak** Can.
109 E2 **Keene** U.S.A.
90 A2 **Keetmanshoop** Namibia
97 E3 **Keewatin** Can.
79 B3 **Kefallonia** i. Greece
27 C3 **Kefamenanu** Indon.
60 □A3 **Keflavík** Iceland
45 D2 **Kegen** Kazakh.
96 C2 **Keg River** Can.
30 A1 **Kehsi Mansam** Myanmar
66 C2 **Keighley** U.K.
55 B2 **Keila** Estonia
90 B2 **Keimoes** S. Africa
60 I3 **Keitele** i. Fin.
20 B3 **Keith** Austr.
71 E2 **Kékes** mt. Hungary
28 B1 **Kelang** Malaysia
60 J2 **Keles-Uayv, Gora** hill
         Rus. Fed.
70 C2 **Kelheim** Ger.
48 B1 **Kelkit** r. Turkey
96 B1 **Keller Lake** l. Can.
102 C1 **Kellogg** U.S.A.
60 I2 **Kelloselkä** Fin.
65 C2 **Kells** Rep. of Ireland
55 B2 **Kelmė** Lith.
83 D4 **Kelo** Chad
96 C3 **Kelowna** Can.
64 C3 **Kelso** U.K.
102 B1 **Kelso** U.S.A.
28 B1 **Keluang** Malaysia
97 D2 **Kelvington** Can.
54 C2 **Kem'** Rus. Fed.
96 B2 **Kemano** Can.
79 C3 **Kemer** Turkey
54 G3 **Kemerovo** Rus. Fed.
60 H2 **Kemi** Fin.
60 I2 **Kemijärvi** Fin.
60 I2 **Kemijoki** r. Fin.

104 A2 **Kemmerer** U.S.A.
60 I3 **Kempele** Fin.
21 D2 **Kempsey** Austr.
98 C2 **Kempt, Lac** l. Can.
70 C2 **Kempten (Allgäu)** Ger.
91 C2 **Kempton Park** S. Africa
29 C2 **Kemujan** i. Indon.
99 C2 **Kenaston** Can.
66 B1 **Kendal** U.K.
27 C3 **Kendari** Indon.
29 C2 **Kendawangan** Indon.
83 D3 **Kendégué** Chad
43 C2 **Kendujhargarh** India
82 A4 **Kenema** Sierra Leone
86 B3 **Kenge** Dem. Rep. Congo
30 A1 **Kengtung** Myanmar
90 B2 **Kenhardt** S. Africa
82 B1 **Kénitra** Morocco
65 B3 **Kenmare** Rep. of Ireland
104 C1 **Kenmare** U.S.A.
65 A3 **Kenmare River** inlet
         Rep. of Ireland
68 C3 **Kenn** Ger.
105 E3 **Kennett** U.S.A.
102 C1 **Kennewick** U.S.A.
97 E3 **Kenora** Can.
108 B2 **Kenosha** U.S.A.
106 C2 **Kent** U.K.
45 C2 **Kentau** Kazakh.
108 B3 **Kentucky** r. U.S.A.
108 C3 **Kentucky** state U.S.A.
108 B3 **Kentucky Lake** U.S.A.
87 D2 **Kenya** country Africa
         Kenya, Mount Kenya see
         Kirinyaga
105 E2 **Keokuk** U.S.A.
79 C3 **Kepsut** Turkey
20 B3 **Kerang** Austr.
59 D2 **Kerch** Ukr.
27 D3 **Kerema** P.N.G.
96 C3 **Keremeos** Can.
84 B3 **Keren** Eritrea
49 C2 **Kerend** Iran
127 C7 **Kerguelen Plateau**
         sea feature Indian Ocean
87 D3 **Kericho** Kenya
22 B1 **Kerikeri** N.Z.
28 B2 **Kerinci, Gunung** vol. Indon.
45 C3 **Kerki** Turkm.
79 A3 **Kerkyra** Greece
         Kerkyra i. Greece see Corfu
84 B3 **Kerma** Sudan
47 C1 **Kermān** Iran
49 C2 **Kermānshāh** Iran
107 C2 **Kermit** U.S.A.
103 C3 **Kern** r. U.S.A.
68 C2 **Kerpen** Ger.
97 D2 **Kerrobert** Can.
107 D2 **Kerrville** U.S.A.
48 B2 **Keryneia** Cyprus
98 B1 **Kesagami Lake** Can.
79 C2 **Keşan** Turkey
34 D3 **Kesennuma** Japan
42 B2 **Keshod** India
68 C2 **Kessel** Neth.
66 B1 **Keswick** U.K.
71 D2 **Keszthely** Hungary
50 G3 **Ket'** r. Rus. Fed.
29 C2 **Ketapang** Indon.
96 A2 **Ketchikan** U.S.A.
102 D2 **Ketchum** U.S.A.
67 C2 **Kettering** U.K.
68 C2 **Kevelaer** Ger.
108 B2 **Kewanee** U.S.A.
108 B1 **Keweenaw Bay** b. U.S.A.
108 B1 **Keweenaw Peninsula** U.S.A.
111 D3 **Key Largo** U.S.A.
109 D3 **Keyser** U.S.A.
111 D4 **Key West** U.S.A.

91 C2 **Kgotsong** S. Africa
37 E1 **Khabarovsk** Rus. Fed.
48 B1 **Khadyzhensk** Rus. Fed.
30 A1 **Khagrachari** Bangl.
42 A2 **Khairpur** Pak.
90 B1 **Khakhea** Botswana
36 C1 **Khamar-Daban, Khrebet**
         mts Rus. Fed.
42 B2 **Khambhat** India
41 B3 **Khambhat, Gulf of** India
42 B2 **Khamgaon** India
46 B3 **Khamir** Yemen
46 B3 **Khamis Mushayţ**
         Saudi Arabia
45 C3 **Khānābād** Afgh.
42 B2 **Khandwa** India
51 K2 **Khandyga** Rus. Fed.
42 B1 **Khanewal** Pak.
34 B2 **Khanka, Lake**
         China/Rus. Fed.
42 B2 **Khanpur** Pak.
45 D2 **Khantau** Kazakh.
51 H2 **Khantayskoye, Ozero** l.
         Rus. Fed.
54 F2 **Khanty-Mansiysk** Rus. Fed.
31 A3 **Khao Chum Thong** Thai.
31 A2 **Khao Laem Reservoir** Thai.
55 D4 **Kharabali** Rus. Fed.
43 C2 **Kharagpur** India
47 C2 **Khārān** r. Iran
59 D2 **Kharkiv** Ukr.
         Khar'kov Ukr. see Kharkiv
78 C2 **Kharmanli** Bulg.
54 D3 **Kharovsk** Rus. Fed.
84 B3 **Khartoum** Sudan
55 D4 **Khasav'yurt** Rus. Fed.
47 D2 **Khāsh** Iran
46 A3 **Khashm el Ģirba** Sudan
46 A3 **Khashm el Girba Dam**
         Sudan
42 D2 **Khāsi Hills** India
78 C2 **Khaskovo** Bulg.
91 C3 **Khayamnandi** S. Africa
45 C2 **Khayatbashi, Gora** mt.
         Uzbek.
46 A2 **Khaybar** Saudi Arabia
90 A3 **Khayelitsha** S. Africa
30 B2 **Khê Bo** Vietnam
75 D2 **Khemis Miliana** Alg.
31 B2 **Khommarot** Thai.
83 C1 **Khenchela** Alg.
49 D3 **Kherāmeh** Iran
59 C2 **Kherson** Ukr.
51 H2 **Kheta** r. Rus. Fed.
37 D1 **Khilok** Rus. Fed.
57 E2 **Khimki** Rus. Fed.
57 E3 **Khlevnoye** Rus. Fed.
58 B2 **Khmel'nyts'kyy** Ukr.
44 B1 **Khobda** Kazakh.
44 B1 **Khodzheyli** Uzbek.
57 E3 **Khokhol'skiy** Rus. Fed.
42 A2 **Khokhropar** Pak.
57 D2 **Kholm** Rus. Fed.
57 D2 **Kholm-Zhirkovskiy**
         Rus. Fed.
47 C2 **Khonj** Iran
31 B2 **Khon Kaen** Thai.
30 A1 **Khonsa** India
51 K2 **Khonuu** Rus. Fed.
54 E2 **Khoreyver** Rus. Fed.
37 D1 **Khorinsk** Rus. Fed.
59 C2 **Khorol** Ukr.
49 C2 **Khorramābād** Iran
49 C2 **Khorramshahr** Iran
45 D3 **Khorugh** Tajik.
44 B1 **Khromtau** Kazakh.
58 B2 **Khrystynivka** Ukr.
45 C2 **Khŭjand** Tajik.

31 B2 **Khu Khan** Thai.
46 A2 **Khulays** Saudi Arabia
43 C2 **Khulna** Bangl.
49 D2 **Khunsar** Iran
47 B2 **Khurays** Saudi Arabia
42 B1 **Khushab** Pak.
58 A2 **Khust** Ukr.
91 C2 **Khutsong** S. Africa
42 A2 **Khuzdar** Pak.
47 C2 **Khvormūj** Iran
49 C2 **Khvoy** Iran
57 D2 **Khvoynaya** Rus. Fed.
45 D3 **Khyber Pass** Afgh./Pak.
21 D2 **Kiama** Austr.
87 C3 **Kiambi** Dem. Rep. Congo
87 D3 **Kibiti** Tanz.
77 D2 **Kičevo** Macedonia
82 C3 **Kidal** Mali
67 B2 **Kidderminster** U.K.
82 A3 **Kidira** Senegal
22 C1 **Kidnappers, Cape** N.Z.
70 C1 **Kiel** Ger.
71 E1 **Kielce** Pol.
66 B1 **Kielder Water** *resr* U.K.
58 C1 **Kiev** Ukr.
82 A3 **Kiffa** Maur.
87 D3 **Kigali** Rwanda
87 C3 **Kigoma** Tanz.
56 B2 **Kihnu** *i.* Estonia
60 I2 **Kiiminki** Fin.
35 B4 **Kii-suidō** *sea chan.* Japan
77 D1 **Kikinda** Yugo.
87 C3 **Kikondja** Dem. Rep. Congo
27 D3 **Kikori** P.N.G.
27 D3 **Kikori** *r.* P.N.G.
86 B3 **Kikwit** Dem. Rep. Congo
33 B1 **Kilchu** N. Korea
86 B3 **Kilembe** Dem. Rep. Congo
107 E2 **Kilgore** U.S.A.
87 D3 **Kilimanjaro** *vol.* Tanz.
48 B2 **Kılıs** Turkey
58 B2 **Kiliya** Ukr.
65 B2 **Kilkee** Rep. of Ireland
65 D1 **Kilkeel** U.K.
65 C2 **Kilkenny** Rep. of Ireland
79 B2 **Kilkis** Greece
65 B1 **Killala Bay** Rep. of Ireland
65 B2 **Killaloe** Rep. of Ireland
97 C2 **Killam** Can.
65 B2 **Killarney** Rep. of Ireland
107 D2 **Killeen** U.S.A.
64 B2 **Killin** U.K.
65 B1 **Killybegs** Rep. of Ireland
64 B3 **Kilmarnock** U.K.
21 B3 **Kilmore** Austr.
87 D3 **Kilosa** Tanz.
65 B2 **Kilrush** Rep. of Ireland
87 C3 **Kilwa** Dem. Rep. Congo
87 D3 **Kilwa Masoko** Tanz.
87 D3 **Kimambi** Tanz.
20 A2 **Kimba** Austr.
104 C2 **Kimball** U.S.A.
96 C3 **Kimberley** Can.
90 B2 **Kimberley** S. Africa
18 B1 **Kimberley Plateau** Austr.
33 B1 **Kimch'aek** N. Korea
33 B2 **Kimch'ŏn** S. Korea
95 G2 **Kimmirut** Can.
57 E3 **Kimovsk** Rus. Fed.
86 B3 **Kimpese** Dem. Rep. Congo
57 E2 **Kimry** Rus. Fed.
29 C1 **Kinabalu, Gunung** *mt.* Sabah
    Malaysia
96 C2 **Kinbasket Lake** Can.
98 B2 **Kincardine** Can.
30 A1 **Kinda** Myanmar
87 C3 **Kinda** Dem. Rep. Congo
66 C2 **Kinder Scout** *hill* U.K.
97 D2 **Kindersley** Can.
82 A3 **Kindia** Guinea

87 C3 **Kindu** Dem. Rep. Congo
54 D3 **Kineshma** Rus. Fed.
19 E2 **Kingaroy** Austr.
103 B3 **King City** U.S.A.
98 C1 **King George Islands** Can.
56 C2 **Kingisepp** Rus. Fed.
19 D3 **King Island** Austr.
18 B1 **King Leopold Ranges** *hills*
    Austr.
106 A1 **Kingman** U.S.A.
103 B3 **Kings** *r.* U.S.A.
20 A3 **Kingscote** Austr.
67 D2 **King's Lynn** U.K.
18 B1 **King Sound** *b.* Austr.
102 D2 **Kings Peak** U.S.A.
111 D1 **Kingsport** U.S.A.
98 C2 **Kingston** Can.
114 C3 **Kingston** Jamaica
109 E2 **Kingston** U.S.A.
20 A3 **Kingston South East** Austr.
66 C2 **Kingston upon Hull** U.K.
115 D3 **Kingstown** St Vincent
107 D3 **Kingsville** U.S.A.
67 B3 **Kingswood** U.K.
64 B2 **Kingussie** U.K.
94 E2 **King William Island** Can.
91 C3 **King William's Town**
    S. Africa
35 D3 **Kinka-san** *i.* Japan
61 F4 **Kinna** Sweden
65 B3 **Kinsale** Rep. of Ireland
86 B3 **Kinshasa** Dem. Rep. Congo
111 E1 **Kinston** U.S.A.
56 B2 **Kintai** Lith.
82 B4 **Kintampo** Ghana
64 B3 **Kintyre** *pen.* U.K.
98 C2 **Kipawa, Lac** *l.* Can.
51 I3 **Kirensk** Rus. Fed.
57 E3 **Kireyevsk** Rus. Fed.
    Kirghizia *country* Asia *see*
    Kyrgyzstan
17 G3 **Kiribati** *country*
    Pacific Ocean
48 B2 **Kırıkkale** Turkey
57 E2 **Kirillov** Rus. Fed.
    Kirin China *see* **Jilin**
87 D3 **Kirinyaga** *mt.* Kenya
57 D3 **Kirishi** Rus. Fed.
79 C3 **Kırkağaç** Turkey
64 C2 **Kirkcaldy** U.K.
64 B3 **Kirkcudbright** U.K.
60 J2 **Kirkenes** Norway
98 B2 **Kirkland Lake** Can.
105 E2 **Kirksville** U.S.A.
49 C2 **Kirkūk** Iraq
64 C1 **Kirkwall** U.K.
57 D3 **Kirov** *Kaluzhskaya Oblast'*
    Rus. Fed.
54 D3 **Kirov** Rus. Fed.
    Kirovabad Azer. *see* **Gäncä**
54 E3 **Kirovo-Chepetsk** Rus. Fed.
59 C2 **Kirovohrad** Ukr.
54 C2 **Kirovsk** Rus. Fed.
59 D2 **Kirovs'ke** Ukr.
64 C2 **Kirriemuir** U.K.
54 E3 **Kirs** Rus. Fed.
42 A2 **Kirthar Range** *mts* Pak.
60 H2 **Kiruna** Sweden
35 C3 **Kiryū** Japan
57 E2 **Kirzhach** Rus. Fed.
87 C2 **Kisangani** Dem. Rep. Congo
86 B3 **Kisantu** Dem. Rep. Congo
28 A1 **Kisaran** Indon.
50 G3 **Kiselevsk** Rus. Fed.
43 C2 **Kishanganj** India
    Kishinev Moldova *see*
    Chişinău
45 D1 **Kishkenekol'** Kazakh.
42 B1 **Kishtwar**
    Jammu and Kashmir

83 C4 **Kisi** Nigeria
87 D3 **Kisii** Kenya
71 D2 **Kiskunfélegyháza** Hungary
71 D2 **Kiskunhalas** Hungary
55 D4 **Kislovodsk** Rus. Fed.
85 C5 **Kismaayo** Somalia
87 C3 **Kisoro** Uganda
88 A4 **Kissidougou** Guinea
111 D3 **Kissimmee** U.S.A.
111 D3 **Kissimmee, Lake** U.S.A.
97 C2 **Kississing Lake** Can.
87 D3 **Kisumu** Kenya
82 B3 **Kita** Mali
34 D3 **Kitakami** Japan
34 D3 **Kitakami-gawa** *r.* Japan
35 B4 **Kita-Kyūshū** Japan
87 D2 **Kitale** Kenya
34 D2 **Kitami** Japan
98 B2 **Kitchener** Can.
61 J3 **Kitee** Fin.
87 D2 **Kitgum** Uganda
96 B2 **Kitimat** Can.
86 B3 **Kitona** Dem. Rep. Congo
87 D3 **Kitunda** Tanz.
96 B2 **Kitwanga** Can.
87 C4 **Kitwe** Zambia
69 E3 **Kitzingen** Ger.
60 I3 **Kiuruvesi** Fin.
87 C3 **Kivu, Lake**
    Dem. Rep. Congo/Rwanda
78 C2 **Kıyıköy** Turkey
54 E3 **Kizel** Rus. Fed.
79 C3 **Kızılca Dağ** *mt.* Turkey
55 D4 **Kizlyar** Rus. Fed.
60 I1 **Kjøllefjord** Norway
60 G2 **Kjøpsvik** Norway
70 C1 **Kladno** Czech Rep.
70 C2 **Klagenfurt** Austria
56 B2 **Klaipėda** Lith.
62 A3 **Klaksvík** Faroe Is
102 B2 **Klamath** *r.* U.S.A.
102 B2 **Klamath Falls** U.S.A.
102 B2 **Klamath Mountains** U.S.A.
70 C2 **Klatovy** Czech Rep.
90 A3 **Klawer** S. Africa
96 A2 **Klawock** U.S.A.
96 B2 **Kleena Kleene** Can.
90 B2 **Kleinbegin** S. Africa
90 A2 **Kleinsee** S. Africa
91 C2 **Klerksdorp** S. Africa
57 D3 **Kletnya** Rus. Fed.
68 C2 **Kleve** Ger.
57 D3 **Klimavichy** Belarus
57 D3 **Klimovo** Rus. Fed.
57 E2 **Klimovsk** Rus. Fed.
57 E2 **Klin** Rus. Fed.
69 F2 **Klínovec** *mt.* Czech Rep.
61 G4 **Klintehamn** Sweden
57 D3 **Klintsy** Rus. Fed.
77 C2 **Ključ** Bos.-Herz.
71 D1 **Kłodzko** Pol.
68 C1 **Kloosterhaar** Neth.
71 D2 **Klosterneuburg** Austria
69 E1 **Klötze (Altmark)** Ger.
71 D1 **Kluczbork** Pol.
96 A2 **Klukwan** U.S.A.
42 A2 **Klupro** Pak.
56 C3 **Klyetsk** Belarus
66 C1 **Knaresborough** U.K.
61 F3 **Knästen** *hill* Sweden
97 E2 **Knee Lake** Can.
69 E1 **Knesebeck** Ger.
69 E3 **Knetzgau** Ger.
77 C2 **Knin** Croatia
71 C2 **Knittelfeld** Austria
77 D2 **Knjaževac** Yugo.
68 A2 **Knokke-Heist** Belgium
111 D1 **Knoxville** U.S.A.
90 B3 **Knysna** S. Africa
35 C4 **Kōbe** Japan

København Denmark *see* Copenhagen
68 C2 **Koblenz** Ger.
27 C3 **Kobroör** *i.* Indon.
56 B3 **Kobryn** Belarus
79 C2 **Kocasu** *r.* Turkey
77 D2 **Kočani** Macedonia
43 C3 **Koch Bihār** India
Kochi India *see* Cochin
35 B4 **Kōchi** Japan
55 D4 **Kochubey** Rus. Fed.
43 C2 **Kodarma** India
85 B4 **Kodok** Sudan
58 B2 **Kodyma** Ukr.
79 C2 **Kodzhaele** *mt.* Bulg./Greece
90 A2 **Koës** Namibia
90 C2 **Koffiefontein** S. Africa
82 B4 **Koforidua** Ghana
35 C3 **Kōfu** Japan
99 D1 **Kogaluk** *r.* Can.
42 B1 **Kohat** Pak.
30 A1 **Kohima** India
56 C2 **Kohtla-Järve** Estonia
45 D2 **Kokand** Uzbek.
60 H3 **Kokkola** Fin.
45 C2 **Kokpekti** Kazakh.
45 C1 **Kokshetau** Kazakh.
99 D1 **Koksoak** *r.* Can.
91 C3 **Kokstad** S. Africa
Koktokay China *see* Fuyun
26 C3 **Kolaka** Indon.
54 C2 **Kola Peninsula** *pen.* Rus. Fed.
60 H2 **Kolari** Fin.
82 A3 **Kolda** Senegal
61 E4 **Kolding** Denmark
75 D2 **Koléa** Alg.
54 D2 **Kolguyev, Ostrov** *i.* Rus. Fed.
41 B3 **Kolhapur** India
56 B2 **Kolkasrags** *pt* Latvia
Kollam India *see* Quilon
Köln Ger. *see* Cologne
43 C2 **Kolkata** India
71 D1 **Kołobrzeg** Pol.
82 B3 **Kolokani** Mali
57 E2 **Kolomna** Rus. Fed.
58 B2 **Kolomyya** Rus. Fed.
90 B2 **Kolonkwane** Botswana
50 G3 **Kolpashevo** Rus. Fed.
57 E3 **Kolpny** Rus. Fed.
Kol'skiy Poluostrov *pen.* Rus. Fed. *see* Kola Peninsula
46 B2 **Koluli** Eritrea
87 C4 **Kolwezi** Dem. Rep. Congo
51 L2 **Kolyma** *r.* Rus. Fed.
51 L2 **Kolymskaya Nizmennost'** *lowland* Rus. Fed.
51 M2 **Kolymskiy, Khrebet** *mts* Rus. Fed.
35 C3 **Komaki** Japan
51 M3 **Komandorskiye Ostrova** *is* Rus. Fed.
71 D2 **Komárno** Slovakia
91 D2 **Komati** *r.* Swaziland
35 C3 **Komatsu** Japan
87 C3 **Kombe** Dem. Rep. Congo
58 C2 **Kominternivs'ke** Ukr.
77 C2 **Komiža** Croatia
71 D2 **Komló** Hungary
86 B3 **Komono** Congo
79 C2 **Komotini** Greece
90 B3 **Komsberg** *mts* S. Africa
45 C1 **Komsomolets** Kazakh.
51 H1 **Komsomolets, Ostrov** *i.* Rus. Fed.
57 F2 **Komsomol'sk** Rus. Fed.
59 C2 **Komsomol's'k** Ukr.

55 D4 **Komsomol'skiy** Rus. Fed.
37 E1 **Komsomol'sk-na-Amure** Rus. Fed.
57 E2 **Konakovo** Rus. Fed.
43 C3 **Kondagaon** India
54 F2 **Kondinskoye** Rus. Fed.
87 D3 **Kondoa** Tanz.
54 C2 **Kondopoga** Rus. Fed.
57 E3 **Kondrovo** Rus. Fed.
95 I2 **Kong Christian IX Land** *reg.* Greenland
95 I2 **Kong Frederik VI Kyst** *coastal area* Greenland
33 B2 **Kongju** S. Korea
87 C3 **Kongolo** Dem. Rep. Congo
61 E4 **Kongsberg** Norway
61 F3 **Kongsvinger** Norway
45 D3 **Kongur Shan** *mt.* China
68 C2 **Königswinter** Ger.
71 D1 **Konin** Pol.
77 C2 **Konjic** Bos.-Herz.
90 A2 **Konkiep** *watercourse* Namibia
59 C1 **Konotop** Ukr.
70 B2 **Konstanz** Ger.
83 C3 **Kontagora** Nigeria
31 B2 **Kon Tum** Vietnam
31 B2 **Kontum, Plateau du** Vietnam
48 B2 **Konya** Turkey
68 C3 **Konz** Ger.
54 E3 **Konzhakovskiy Kamen', Gora** *mt.* Rus. Fed.
102 C1 **Kooskia** U.S.A.
96 C3 **Kootenay Lake** Can.
90 B3 **Kootjieskolk** S. Africa
60 ☐B2 **Kópasker** Iceland
76 B1 **Koper** Slovenia
61 G4 **Kopparberg** Sweden
77 C1 **Koprivnica** Croatia
57 F3 **Korablino** Rus. Fed.
41 C3 **Koraput** India
69 D2 **Korbach** Ger.
77 D2 **Korçë** Albania
77 C2 **Korčula** Croatia
77 C2 **Korčula** *i.* Croatia
33 B1 **Korea, North** *country* Asia
33 B2 **Korea, South** *country* Asia
38 C2 **Korea Bay** *g.* China/N. Korea
33 B3 **Korea Strait** Japan/S. Korea
59 D2 **Korenovsk** Rus. Fed.
58 B1 **Korets'** Ukr.
79 C2 **Körfez** Turkey
82 B4 **Korhogo** Côte d'Ivoire
79 B3 **Korinthiakos Kolpos** *sea chan.* Greece
79 B3 **Korinthos** Greece
71 D2 **Köris-hegy** *hill* Hungary
77 D2 **Koritnik** *mt.* Albania
35 D3 **Kōriyama** Japan
48 B2 **Korkuteli** Turkey
38 B2 **Korla** China
71 D2 **Körmend** Hungary
82 B3 **Koro** Mali
99 D1 **Koroc** *r.* Can.
59 D1 **Korocha** Rus. Fed.
87 D3 **Korogwe** Tanz.
27 C2 **Koror** Palau
58 B1 **Korosten'** Ukr.
58 B1 **Korostyshiv** Ukr.
83 D3 **Koro Toro** Chad
59 C2 **Korsun'-Shevchenkivs'kyy** Ukr.
71 E1 **Korsze** Pol.
68 A2 **Kortrijk** Belgium
51 L3 **Koryakskaya, Sopka** *vol.* Rus. Fed.
51 M2 **Koryakskiy Khrebet** *mts* Rus. Fed.
54 D2 **Koryazhma** Rus. Fed.

33 B2 **Koryŏng** S. Korea
59 C1 **Koryukivka** Ukr.
79 C3 **Kos** Greece
79 C3 **Kos** *i.* Greece
33 B2 **Kosan** N. Korea
71 D1 **Kościan** Pol.
21 C3 **Kosciuszko, Mount** Austr.
36 B1 **Kosh-Agach** Rus. Fed.
71 E2 **Košice** Slovakia
60 H2 **Koskullskulle** Sweden
33 B2 **Kosŏng** N. Korea
77 D2 **Kosovo** *prov.* Yugo.
77 D2 **Kosovska Mitrovica** Yugo.
82 B4 **Kossou, Lac de** *l.* Côte d'Ivoire
44 C1 **Kostanay** Kazakh.
78 B2 **Kostenets** Bulg.
91 C2 **Koster** S. Africa
85 B3 **Kosti** Sudan
54 C2 **Kostomuksha** Rus. Fed.
58 B1 **Kostopil'** Ukr.
57 F2 **Kostroma** Rus. Fed.
57 F2 **Kostroma** *r.* Rus. Fed.
70 C1 **Kostrzyn** Pol.
71 D1 **Koszalin** Pol.
71 D2 **Kőszeg** Hungary
42 B2 **Kota** India
28 B2 **Kotaagung** Indon.
29 C2 **Kotabaru** Indon.
29 C1 **Kota Belud** *Sabah* Malaysia
28 B1 **Kota Bharu** Malaysia
28 B2 **Kotabumi** Indon.
29 C1 **Kota Kinabalu** *Sabah* Malaysia
29 C1 **Kota Samarahan** *Sarawak* Malaysia
54 D3 **Kotel'nich** Rus. Fed.
55 D4 **Kotel'nikovo** Rus. Fed.
51 K1 **Kotel'nyy, Ostrov** *i.* Rus. Fed.
69 E2 **Köthen (Anhalt)** Ger.
61 I3 **Kotka** Fin.
54 D2 **Kotlas** Rus. Fed.
77 C2 **Kotor Varoš** Bos.-Herz.
55 D3 **Kotovo** Rus. Fed.
58 B2 **Kotovs'k** Ukr.
51 H2 **Kotuy** *r.* Rus. Fed.
68 A2 **Koudekerke** Neth.
82 D3 **Koudougou** Burkina
90 B3 **Kougaberge** *mts* S. Africa
86 B3 **Koulamoutou** Gabon
82 B3 **Koulikoro** Mali
82 A3 **Koundâra** Guinea
119 C1 **Kourou** Fr. Guiana
82 B3 **Kouroussa** Guinea
83 D3 **Kousséri** Cameroon
82 B3 **Koutiala** Mali
61 I3 **Kouvola** Fin.
60 J2 **Kovdor** Rus. Fed.
58 A1 **Kovel'** Ukr.
57 F2 **Kovrov** Rus. Fed.
22 B2 **Kowhitirangi** N.Z.
39 B3 **Kowloon** China
79 C3 **Köyceğiz** Turkey
54 D2 **Koyda** Rus. Fed.
94 A2 **Koyukuk** *r.* U.S.A.
79 B2 **Kozani** Greece
58 C1 **Kozelets'** Ukr.
57 E3 **Kozel'sk** Rus. Fed.
Kozhikode India *see* Calicut
58 B2 **Kozyatyn** Ukr.
31 A3 **Krabi** Thai.
31 A2 **Kra Buri** Thai.
31 B2 **Krâchéh** Cambodia
61 E4 **Kragerø** Norway
68 B1 **Kraggenburg** Neth.
77 D2 **Kragujevac** Yugo.
28 B2 **Krakatau** *i.* Indon.
71 D1 **Kraków** Pol.

59 D2 **Kramators'k** Ukr.
61 G3 **Kramfors** Sweden
79 B3 **Kranidi** Greece
54 E1 **Krasino** Rus. Fed.
56 C2 **Krāslava** Latvia
69 F2 **Kraslice** Czech Rep.
57 D3 **Krasnapollye** Belarus
57 D3 **Krasnaya Gora** Rus. Fed.
55 D3 **Krasnoarmeysk** Rus. Fed.
59 D2 **Krasnoarmiys'k** Ukr.
54 D2 **Krasnoborsk** Rus. Fed.
59 D2 **Krasnodar** Rus. Fed.
59 D2 **Krasnodon** Ukr.
56 C2 **Krasnogorodskoye** Rus. Fed.
59 D1 **Krasnogvardeyskoye** Rus. Fed.
59 D2 **Krasnohrad** Ukr.
59 C2 **Krasnohvardiys'ke** Ukr.
54 E3 **Krasnokamsk** Rus. Fed.
57 D2 **Krasnomayskiy** Rus. Fed.
59 C2 **Krasnoperekops'k** Ukr.
55 D3 **Krasnoslobodsk** Rus. Fed.
54 E3 **Krasnoufimsk** Rus. Fed.
51 H3 **Krasnoyarsk** Rus. Fed.
57 F2 **Krasnoye-na-Volge** Rus. Fed.
57 D3 **Krasnyy** Rus. Fed.
57 E2 **Krasnyy Kholm** Rus. Fed.
55 C4 **Krasnyy Luch** Ukr.
59 E2 **Krasnyy Sulin** Rus. Fed.
58 B2 **Krasyliv** Ukr.
68 C2 **Krefeld** Ger.
59 C2 **Kremenchuk** Ukr.
59 C2 **Kremenchuts'ka Vodoskhovyshche** *resr* Ukr.
71 D2 **Křemešník** *hill* Czech Rep.
59 D2 **Kreminna** Ukr.
71 D2 **Krems an der Donau** Austria
57 D2 **Kresttsy** Rus. Fed.
56 B2 **Kretinga** Lith.
68 C2 **Kreuzau** Ger.
68 C2 **Kreuztal** Ger.
86 A2 **Kribi** Cameroon
79 B3 **Krikellos** Greece
34 D1 **Kril'on, Mys** *c.* Rus. Fed.
41 C3 **Krishna** *r.* India
41 C3 **Krishna, Mouths of the** India
43 C2 **Krishnanagar** India
61 E4 **Kristiansand** Norway
61 F4 **Kristianstad** Sweden
60 E3 **Kristiansund** Norway
61 F4 **Kristinehamn** Sweden
Kríti *i.* Greece *see* Crete
Krivoy Rog Ukr. *see* Kryvyy Rih
77 C1 **Križevci** Croatia
76 B1 **Krk** *i.* Croatia
60 F3 **Krokom** Sweden
59 C1 **Krolevets'** Ukr.
69 E2 **Kronach** Ger.
31 B2 **Krŏng Kaôh Kŏng** Cambodia
95 I2 **Kronprins Frederik Bjerge** *nunataks* Greenland
91 C1 **Kroonstad** S. Africa
55 D4 **Kropotkin** Rus. Fed.
71 E2 **Krosno** Pol.
71 D1 **Krotoszyn** Pol.
28 B2 **Krui** Indon.
77 C2 **Krujë** Albania
79 C2 **Krumovgrad** Bulg.
Krung Thep Thai. *see* Bangkok
56 C3 **Krupki** Belarus
77 D2 **Kruševac** Yugo.
69 E2 **Krušné Hory** *mts* Czech Rep.
96 A2 **Kruzof Island** U.S.A.
57 D3 **Krychaw** Belarus
59 D3 **Krymsk** Rus. Fed.

79 C3 **Krytiko Pelagos** *sea* Greece
59 C2 **Kryvyy Rih** Ukr.
82 B2 **Ksabi** Alg.
75 D2 **Ksar el Boukhari** Alg.
82 B1 **Ksar el Kebir** Morocco
57 E3 **Kshenskiy** Rus. Fed.
46 B2 **Kū', Jabal al** *hill* Saudi Arabia
29 C1 **Kuala Belait** Brunei
28 B1 **Kuala Kerai** Malaysia
28 B1 **Kuala Lipis** Malaysia
28 B1 **Kuala Lumpur** Malaysia
29 C2 **Kualapembuang** Indon.
28 B1 **Kuala Terengganu** Malaysia
28 B2 **Kualatungal** Indon.
29 C1 **Kuamut** *Sabah* Malaysia
33 A1 **Kuandian** China
28 B1 **Kuantan** Malaysia
57 D2 **Kuban'** *r.* Rus. Fed.
57 E2 **Kubenskoye, Ozero** *l.* Rus. Fed.
78 C2 **Kubrat** Bulg.
29 C1 **Kubuang** Indon.
29 C1 **Kuching** *Sarawak* Malaysia
77 C2 **Kuçovë** Albania
29 C2 **Kudus** Indon.
70 C2 **Kufstein** Austria
94 D2 **Kugluktuk** Can.
60 I3 **Kuhmo** Fin.
47 C2 **Kūhrān, Kūh-e** *mt.* Iran
Kuitin China *see* Kuytun
88 A2 **Kuito** Angola
96 A2 **Kuiu Island** U.S.A.
60 I2 **Kuivaniemi** Fin.
33 B2 **Kujang** N. Korea
77 D2 **Kukës** Albania
79 C3 **Kula** Turkey
43 D2 **Kula Kangri** *mt.* Bhutan
44 B2 **Kulandy** Kazakh.
56 B2 **Kuldiga** Latvia
90 B1 **Kule** Botswana
69 E2 **Kulmbach** Ger.
45 C3 **Kŭlob** Tajik.
44 B2 **Kul'sary** Kazakh.
45 D1 **Kulunda** Rus. Fed.
95 I2 **Kulusuk** Greenland
35 C3 **Kumagaya** Japan
35 B4 **Kumamoto** Japan
77 D2 **Kumanovo** Macedonia
82 B4 **Kumasi** Ghana
86 A2 **Kumba** Cameroon
46 B2 **Kumdah** Saudi Arabia
55 E3 **Kumertau** Rus. Fed.
33 B2 **Kumi** S. Korea
61 G4 **Kumla** Sweden
85 D3 **Kumo** Nigeria
30 A1 **Kumon Range** *mts* Myanmar
30 B1 **Kumphawapi** Thai.
Kumul China *see* Hami
34 D2 **Kunashir, Ostrov** *i.* Rus. Fed.
29 C1 **Kundat** *Sabah* Malaysia
45 D2 **Kungei Alatau** *mts* Kazakh./Kyrg.
44 B2 **Kungrad** Uzbek.
61 F4 **Kungsbacka** Sweden
86 B2 **Kungu** Dem. Rep. Congo
54 E3 **Kungur** Rus. Fed.
30 A1 **Kunhing** Myanmar
45 D3 **Kunlun Shan** *mts* China
30 B1 **Kunming** China
33 B2 **Kunsan** S. Korea
18 B1 **Kununurra** Austr.
60 I3 **Kuopio** Fin.
77 C1 **Kupa** *r.* Croatia/Slovenia
27 C3 **Kupang** Indon.
56 B2 **Kupiškis** Lith.
79 C2 **Küplü** Turkey
96 A2 **Kupreanof Island** U.S.A.
59 D2 **Kup"yans'k** Ukr.
45 E2 **Kuqa** China

35 B4 **Kurashiki** Japan
35 B3 **Kurayoshi** Japan
57 E3 **Kurchatov** Rus. Fed.
78 C2 **Kürdzhali** Bulg.
35 B4 **Kure** Japan
56 B2 **Kuressaare** Estonia
54 F3 **Kurgan** Rus. Fed.
61 H3 **Kurikka** Fin.
124 C3 **Kuril Trench** *sea feature* N. Pacific Ocean
57 E3 **Kurkino** Rus. Fed.
85 B3 **Kurmuk** Sudan
41 B3 **Kurnool** India
35 D3 **Kuroiso** Japan
21 D2 **Kurri Kurri** Austr.
57 E3 **Kursk** Rus. Fed.
90 B2 **Kuruman** S. Africa
90 B2 **Kuruman** *watercourse* S. Africa
35 B4 **Kurume** Japan
51 I3 **Kurumkan** Rus. Fed.
41 C4 **Kurunegala** Sri Lanka
79 C3 **Kuşadası** Turkey
79 C3 **Kuşadası Körfezi** *b.* Turkey
79 C2 **Kuş Gölü** *l.* Turkey
59 D2 **Kushchevskaya** Rus. Fed.
34 D2 **Kushiro** Japan
44 C1 **Kushmurun** Kazakh.
43 C2 **Kushtia** Bangl.
34 D2 **Kussharo-ko** *l.* Japan
79 C3 **Kütahya** Turkey
49 C1 **K'ut'aisi** Georgia
77 C1 **Kutjevo** Croatia
71 D1 **Kutno** Pol.
86 B3 **Kutu** Dem. Rep. Congo
94 D2 **Kuujjua** *r.* Can.
99 D1 **Kuujjuaq** Can.
Kuujjuarapik Can. *see* Poste-de-la-Baleine
60 I2 **Kuusamo** Fin.
88 A2 **Kuvango** Angola
57 D2 **Kuvshinovo** Rus. Fed.
46 B2 **Kuwait** *country* Asia
47 B2 **Kuwait** Kuwait
Kuybyshev Rus. Fed. *see* Samara
59 D2 **Kuybysheve** Ukr.
55 D3 **Kuybyshevskoye Vodokhranilishche** *resr* Rus. Fed.
45 E2 **Kuytun** China
79 C3 **Kuyucak** Turkey
55 D3 **Kuznetsk** Rus. Fed.
58 B1 **Kuznetsovs'k** Ukr.
60 H1 **Kvaløund** Norway
91 C2 **KwaMashu** S. Africa
33 B2 **Kwangju** S. Korea
33 B1 **Kwanmo-bong** *mt.* N. Korea
91 C3 **Kwanobuhle** S. Africa
90 B3 **Kwanonzame** S. Africa
91 C3 **Kwatinidubu** S. Africa
91 C2 **KwaZamokuhle** S. Africa
91 D2 **Kwazulu-Natal** *prov.* S. Africa
89 B2 **Kwekwe** Zimbabwe
86 B3 **Kwenge** *r.* Dem. Rep. Congo
71 D1 **Kwidzyn** Pol.
86 B3 **Kwilu** *r.* Angola/Dem. Rep. Congo
27 C3 **Kwoka** *mt.* Indon.
21 C3 **Kyabram** Austr.
30 A2 **Kyaikto** Myanmar
37 D1 **Kyakhta** Rus. Fed.
20 A2 **Kyancutta** Austr.
30 A1 **Kyaukpadaung** Myanmar
30 A2 **Kyaukpyu** Myanmar
56 B3 **Kybartai** Lith.
30 A2 **Kyebogyi** Myanmar
30 A2 **Kyeintali** Myanmar
42 B1 **Kyelang** India

Kyiv Ukr. see Kiev
Kyklades is Greece see Cyclades
97 D2   Kyle Can.
64 B2   Kyle of Lochalsh U.K.
68 C3   Kyll r. Ger.
79 B3   Kyllini mt. Greece
79 B3   Kymi Greece
20 B3   Kyneton Austr.
87 D2   Kyoga, Lake Uganda
21 D1   Kyogle Austr.
33 B2   Kyŏngju S. Korea
35 C4   Kyōto Japan
79 B3   Kyparissia Greece
45 C1   Kypshak, Ozero salt l. Kazakh.
79 B3   Kyra Panagia i. Greece
45 D2   Kyrgyzstan country Asia
69 F1   Kyritz Ger.
00 H3   Kyrönjoki r. Fin.
54 E2   Kyrta Rus. Fed.
54 D2   Kyssa Rus. Fed.
79 B3   Kythira i. Greece
79 B3   Kythnos i. Greece
96 B2   Kyuquot Can.
35 A4   Kyūshū i. Japan
78 B2   Kyustendil Bulg.
58 C1   Kyyivs'ke Vodoskhovyshche resr Ukr.
60 H3   Kyyjärvi Fin.
36 C1   Kyzyl Rus. Fed.
44 C2   Kyzylkum Desert Kazakh./Uzbek.
45 C2   Kyzylorda Kazakh.

L

113 C3   La Angostura, Presa de resr Mex.
85 C4   Laascaanood Somalia
113 D3   La Ascensión, Bahía de b. Mex.
118 B1   La Asunción Venez.
82 A2   Laâyoune Western Sahara
55 D4   Laba r. Rus. Fed.
112 B2   La Babia Mex.
114 B3   La Bahía, Islas de is Hond.
99 D1   La Baleine, Rivière à r. Can.
120 D3   La Banda Arg.
72 B2   La Baule-Escoublac France
96 A1   Laberge, Lake Can.
97 C2   La Biche, Lac l. Can.
55 D4   Labinsk Rus. Fed.
32 B1   Labo Phil.
112 B2   La Boquilla, Presa de resr Mex.
72 B3   Labouheyre France
99 D1   Labrador reg. Can.
99 D1   Labrador City Can.
126 C1   Labrador Sea Can./Greenland
118 B2   Lábrea Brazil
29 C1   Labuan Malaysia
28 B1   Labuhanbilik Indon.
27 C3   Labuna Indon.
31 A2   Labutta Myanmar
54 F2   Labytnangi Rus. Fed.
77 C2   Laç Albania
74 B1   La Cabrera, Sierra de mts Spain
73 C2   La Capelle France
99 D1   Lac Bermen l. Can.
41 B3   Laccadive Islands India
97 C2   Lac du Bonnet Can.
114 B3   La Ceiba Hond.
21 B2   Lachlan r. Austr.

109 E1   Lachute Can.
73 D3   La Ciotat France
97 C2   Lac La Biche Can.
          Lac la Martre Can. see Wha Ti
96 C2   Lacombe Can.
113 C3   La Concordia Mex.
76 A3   Laconi Sardinia Italy
109 E2   Laconia U.S.A.
72 B2   La Coubre, Pointe de pt France
96 C2   La Crete Can.
108 A2   La Crosse U.S.A.
112 B2   La Cruz Mex.
112 B2   La Cuesta Mex.
43 B1   Ladakh Range mts India
74 C1   La Demanda, Sierra de mts Spain
90 B3   Ladismith S. Africa
47 D2   Lādīz Iran
54 C2   Ladoga, Lake Rus. Fed.
          Ladozhskoye Ozero l. Rus. Fed. see Ladoga, Lake
96 B3   Ladysmith Can.
91 C2   Ladysmith S. Africa
27 D3   Lae P.N.G.
30 B2   Lae Thai.
120 B3   La Esmeralda Bol.
61 F4   Læsø i. Denmark
111 C2   La Fayette U.S.A.
108 B2   Lafayette IN U.S.A.
110 B2   Lafayette LA U.S.A.
83 C4   Lafia Nigeria
72 B2   La Flèche France
111 D1   La Follette U.S.A.
90 C1   Laforge Can.
47 C2   Lāft Iran
76 A3   La Galite i. Tunisia
49 C1   Lagan' Rus. Fed.
86 B2   Lagdo, Lac de l. Cameroon
83 C1   Laghouat Alg.
123 D1   Lagoa Santa Brazil
82 A2   La Gomera i. Canary Is
115 C3   La Gonâve, Île de i. Haiti
82 C4   Lagos Nigeria
74 B2   Lagos Port.
102 C1   La Grande U.S.A.
98 C1   La Grande 2, Réservoir resr Can.
98 C1   La Grande 3, Réservoir resr Can.
99 C1   La Grande 4, Réservoir resr Can.
18 B1   Lagrange Austr.
111 C2   La Grange U.S.A.
118 B1   La Gran Sabana plat. Venez.
120 D3   Laguna Brazil
118 A2   Lagunas Peru
          La Habana Cuba see Havana
29 C1   Lahad Datu Sabah Malaysia
72 B2   La Hague, Cap de c. France
28 B2   Lahat Indon.
46 B3   Laḥij Yemen
49 C2   Lāhījān Iran
68 C2   Lahnstein Ger.
42 B1   Lahore Pak.
42 A2   Lahri Pak.
61 I3   Lahti Fin.
83 D4   Laï Chad
21 D1   Laidley Austr.
72 C2   L'Aigle France
90 B3   Laingsburg S. Africa
60 H2   Lainioälven r. Sweden
83 C3   L'Aïr, Massif de mts Niger
64 B1   Lairg U.K.
76 B1   Laives Italy
38 B2   Laiwu China
38 B2   Laiyang China
38 B2   Laizhou China
38 B2   Laizhou Wan b. China

18 C1   Lajamanu Austr.
120 C3   Lajes Brazil
112 B2   La Junta Mex.
104 C3   La Junta U.S.A.
114 B2   La Juventud, Isla de i. Cuba
21 C2   Lake Cargelligo Austr.
21 D2   Lake Cathie Austr.
110 B2   Lake Charles U.S.A.
111 D2   Lake City FL U.S.A.
111 E2   Lake City SC U.S.A.
96 B3   Lake Cowichan Can.
106 A2   Lake Havasu City U.S.A.
111 D3   Lakeland U.S.A.
96 C2   Lake Louise Can.
102 B1   Lake Oswego U.S.A.
22 A2   Lake Paringa N.Z.
110 B2   Lake Providence U.S.A.
22 B2   Lake Pukaki N.Z.
21 C3   Lakes Entrance Austr.
102 B2   Lakeview U.S.A.
104 B3   Lakewood CO U.S.A.
109 E2   Lakewood NJ U.S.A.
111 D3   Lake Worth U.S.A.
42 A2   Lakhpat India
42 B1   Lakki Pak.
79 B3   Lakonikos Kolpos b. Greece
60 H1   Lakselv Norway
112 A2   La Laguna, Picacho de mt. Mex.
113 C3   La Libertad Guat.
74 B1   Lalín Spain
43 B2   Lalitpur India
97 D2   La Loche Can.
68 B2   La Louvière Belgium
76 A2   La Maddalena Sardinia Italy
99 D2   La Madeleine, Îles de is Can.
          La Manche str. France/U.K. see English Channel
104 C3   Lamar U.S.A.
47 C2   Lamard Iran
76 A3   La Marmora, Punta mt. Sardinia Italy
96 C1   La Martre, Lac l. Can.
86 B3   Lambaréné Gabon
90 A3   Lambert's Bay S. Africa
60 □A2   Lambeyri Iceland
74 B1   Lamego Port.
118 A3   La Merced Peru
20 B3   Lameroo Austr.
107 C2   Lamesa U.S.A.
79 B3   Lamia Greece
105 F2   Lamoni U.S.A.
30 A2   Lampang Thai.
107 D2   Lampasas U.S.A.
113 B2   Lampazos Mex.
67 A2   Lampeter U.K.
30 A2   Lamphun Thai.
87 E3   Lamu Kenya
75 D2   La Nao, Cabo de c. Spain
64 C3   Lanark U.K.
31 A2   Lanbi Kyun i. Myanmar
          Lancang Jiang r. China see Mekong
66 B1   Lancaster U.K.
103 C4   Lancaster CA U.S.A.
108 C3   Lancaster OH U.S.A.
109 D2   Lancaster PA U.S.A.
111 D2   Lancaster SC U.S.A.
95 F2   Lancaster Sound str. Can.
          Lanzhou China see Lanzhou
70 C2   Landeck Austria
104 B2   Lander U.S.A.
67 A3   Land's End pt U.K.
70 C2   Landshut Ger.
61 F4   Landskrona Sweden
111 C2   Lanett U.S.A.
90 B2   Langberg mts S. Africa
105 D1   Langdon U.S.A.

61 F4 **Langeland** *i.* Denmark
69 D1 **Langen** Ger.
68 C1 **Langeoog** Ger.
68 C1 **Langeoog** *i.* Ger.
69 D2 **Langgöns** Ger.
60 ☐A3 **Langjökull** *ice cap* Iceland
73 C3 **Langogne** France
72 B3 **Langon** France
73 D2 **Langres** France
28 A1 **Langsa** Indon.
30 B1 **Lang Son** Vietnam
69 D1 **Langwedel** Ger.
97 D2 **Lanigan** Can.
121 A4 **Lanín, Volcán** *vol.* Arg./Chile
49 C2 **Länkäran** Azer.
72 B2 **Lannion** France
108 C2 **Lansing** U.S.A.
39 B3 **Lanxi** China
85 B4 **Lanya** Sudan
82 A2 **Lanzarote** *i.* Canary Is
38 A2 **Lanzhou** China
32 B1 **Laoag** Phil.
30 B1 **Lao Cai** Vietnam
38 B2 **Laohekou** China
      Laojunmiao China *see*
      Yumen
33 B1 **Laoling** China
33 B1 **Lao Ling** *mts* China
73 C2 **Laon** France
30 B2 **Laos** *country* Asia
33 B1 **Laotougou** China
122 C3 **Lapa** Brazil
82 A2 **La Palma** *i.* Canary Is
114 C4 **La Palma** Panama
118 B1 **La Paragua** Venez.
120 B2 **La Paz** Bol.
112 A2 **La Paz** Mex.
118 B2 **La Pedrera** Col.
34 D1 **La Pérouse Strait**
      Japan/Rus. Fed.
113 C2 **La Pesca** Mex.
112 B2 **La Piedad** Mex.
121 C4 **La Plata** Arg.
121 C4 **La Plata, Río de** *sea chan.*
      Arg./Uru.
61 I3 **Lappeenranta** Fin.
60 G2 **Lappland** *reg.* Europe
79 C2 **Lâpseki** Turkey
51 J1 **Laptev Sea** Rus. Fed.
      Laptevykh, More *sea*
      Rus. Fed. *see* **Laptev Sea**
60 H3 **Lapua** Fin.
120 B3 **La Quiaca** Arg.
47 C2 **Lār** Iran
62 B1 **Larache** Morocco
104 B2 **Laramie** U.S.A.
104 B2 **Laramie Mountains** U.S.A.
122 B3 **Laranjeiras do Sul** Brazil
27 C3 **Larantuka** Indon.
27 C3 **Larat** *i.* Indon.
75 D2 **Larba** Alg.
68 B3 **L'Ardenne, Plateau de**
      Belgium
74 C1 **Laredo** Spain
107 D3 **Laredo** U.S.A.
64 B3 **Largs** U.K.
120 B3 **La Rioja** Arg.
79 B3 **Larisa** Greece
42 A2 **Larkana** Pak.
48 B2 **Larnaka** Cyprus
65 D1 **Larne** U.K.
68 B2 **La Roche-en-Ardenne**
      Belgium
72 B2 **La Rochelle** France
72 B2 **La Roche-sur-Yon** France
75 C2 **La Roda** Spain
115 D3 **La Romana** Dom. Rep.
97 D2 **La Ronge** Can.
97 D2 **La Ronge, Lac** *l.* Can.
18 C1 **Larrimah** Austr.

23 P3 **Larsen Ice Shelf** Antarctica
61 F4 **Larvik** Norway
98 C2 **La Sarre** Can.
106 B2 **Las Cruces** U.S.A.
121 C4 **Las Flores** Arg.
121 B4 **Las Heras** Arg.
30 A1 **Lashio** Myanmar
77 C3 **La Sila** *reg.* Italy
120 B3 **Las Lomitas** Arg.
112 B2 **Las Nieves** Mex.
82 A2 **Las Palmas de Gran**
      Canaria Canary Is
76 A2 **La Spezia** Italy
118 B3 **Las Piedras, Río de** *r.* Peru
121 B5 **Las Plumas** Arg.
97 D2 **Last Mountain Lake** Can.
120 B3 **Las Tórtolas, Cerro** *mt.*
      Chile
86 B3 **Lastoursville** Gabon
77 C2 **Lastovo** *i.* Croatia
112 A2 **Las Tres Vírgenes, Volcán**
      vol. Mex.
114 C2 **Las Tunas** Cuba
112 B2 **Las Varas** *Chihuahua* Mex.
112 B2 **Las Varas** *Nayarit* Mex.
106 B1 **Las Vegas** *NM* U.S.A.
103 C3 **Las Vegas** *NV* U.S.A.
99 E1 **La Tabatière** Can.
72 B2 **La Teste** France
76 B2 **Latina** Italy
115 D3 **La Tortuga, Isla** *i.* Venez.
32 B1 **La Trinidad** Phil.
57 E2 **Latskoye** Rus. Fed.
99 C2 **La Tuque** Can.
56 B2 **Latvia** *country* Europe
70 C1 **Lauchhammer** Ger.
69 E3 **Lauf an der Pegnitz** Ger.
73 D2 **Laufen** Switz.
19 D4 **Launceston** Austr.
67 A3 **Launceston** U.K.
30 A1 **Launggyaung** Myanmar
19 D1 **Laura** Austr.
110 C2 **Laurel** *MS* U.S.A.
102 E1 **Laurel** *MT* U.S.A.
77 C2 **Lauria** Italy
111 E2 **Laurinburg** U.S.A.
73 D2 **Lausanne** Switz.
29 C2 **Laut** *i.* Indon.
69 D2 **Lautersbach (Hessen)** Ger.
29 C2 **Laut Kecil, Kepulauan**
      is Indon.
68 C1 **Lauwersmeer** *l.* Neth.
72 B2 **Laval** France
18 B2 **Laverton** Austr.
123 D2 **Lavras** Brazil
91 D2 **Lavumisa** Swaziland
29 C1 **Lawas** *Sarawak* Malaysia
30 A1 **Lawksawk** Myanmar
82 B3 **Lawra** Ghana
105 D3 **Lawrence** U.S.A.
110 C1 **Lawrenceburg** U.S.A.
107 D2 **Lawton** U.S.A.
46 A2 **Lawz, Jabal al** *mt.*
      Saudi Arabia
61 F4 **Laxå** Sweden
77 D2 **Lazarevac** Yugo.
112 A1 **Lázaro Cárdenas** *Baja*
      California Norte Mex.
112 B3 **Lázaro Cárdenas**
      Michoacán Mex.
56 B3 **Lazdijai** Lith.
104 C2 **Lead** U.S.A.
104 B3 **Leadville** U.S.A.
      Leaf Bay Can. *see* **Tasiujaq**
97 D2 **Leaf Rapids** Can.
65 B2 **Leane, Lough** *l.*
      Rep. of Ireland
98 C1 **L'Eau Claire, Lac à** *l.* Can.
105 E3 **Leavenworth** U.S.A.

48 B2 **Lebanon** *country* Asia
105 E3 **Lebanon** *MO* U.S.A.
109 E2 **Lebanon** *NH* U.S.A.
102 B2 **Lebanon** *OR* U.S.A.
109 D2 **Lebanon** *PA* U.S.A.
57 E3 **Lebedyan'** Rus. Fed.
59 C1 **Lebedyn** Ukr.
72 C2 **Le Blanc** France
71 D1 **Lębork** Pol.
91 C1 **Lebowakgomo** S. Africa
74 B2 **Lebrija** Spain
121 A4 **Lebu** Chile
72 C3 **Le Bugue** France
77 C2 **Lecce** Italy
76 A1 **Lecco** Italy
70 C2 **Lech** *r.* Austria/Ger.
79 B3 **Lechaina** Greece
39 B3 **Lechang** China
70 B1 **Leck** Ger.
72 C3 **Lectoure** France
74 B1 **Ledesma** Spain
72 C2 **Le Dorat** France
96 C2 **Leduc** Can.
105 E1 **Leech Lake** U.S.A.
66 C2 **Leeds** U.K.
66 B2 **Leek** U.K.
68 C1 **Leer (Ostfriesland)** Ger.
111 D3 **Leesburg** U.S.A.
110 B2 **Leesville** U.S.A.
21 C2 **Leeton** Austr.
90 B3 **Leeu-Gamka** S. Africa
68 B1 **Leeuwarden** Neth.
18 A3 **Leeuwin, Cape** Austr.
115 D3 **Leeward Islands**
      Caribbean Sea
79 B3 **Lefkada** Greece
79 B3 **Lefkada** *i.* Greece
      Lefkosia Cyprus *see* **Nicosia**
32 B1 **Legaspi** Phil.
76 B1 **Legnago** Italy
71 D1 **Legnica** Pol.
43 B1 **Leh** Jammu and Kashmir
72 C2 **Le Havre** France
90 B1 **Lehututu** Botswana
42 B1 **Leiah** Pak.
71 D2 **Leibnitz** Austria
67 C2 **Leicester** U.K.
19 C1 **Leichhardt** *r.* Austr.
68 B1 **Leiden** Neth.
68 A2 **Leie** *r.* Belgium
20 A2 **Leigh Creek** Austr.
61 E3 **Leikanger** Norway
69 D1 **Leine** *r.* Ger.
65 C2 **Leinster** *reg.* Rep. of Ireland
69 F2 **Leipzig** Ger.
60 F2 **Leirangen** Norway
74 B2 **Leiria** Port.
61 E4 **Leirvik** Norway
65 C2 **Leixlip** Rep. of Ireland
39 B3 **Leiyang** China
39 B3 **Leizhou** China
39 A3 **Leizhou Bandao** *pen.* China
86 B3 **Lékana** Congo
68 B1 **Lelystad** Neth.
121 B6 **Le Maire, Estrecho de**
      sea chan. Arg.
73 D2 **Léman, Lac** *l.* France/Switz.
72 C2 **Le Mans** France
105 D2 **Le Mars** U.S.A.
122 C2 **Leme** Brazil
48 B2 **Lemesos** Cyprus
69 D1 **Lemförde** Ger.
95 G2 **Lemieux Islands** Can.
104 C1 **Lemmon** U.S.A.
103 C3 **Lemoore** U.S.A.
99 D1 **Le Moyne, Lac** *l.* Can.
30 A1 **Lemro** *r.* Myanmar
77 C2 **Le Murge** *hills* Italy
51 J2 **Lena** *r.* Rus. Fed.
68 C1 **Lengerich** Ger.

39 B3 **Lengshuijiang** China
39 B3 **Lengshuitan** China
59 D2 **Lenine** Ukr.
    Leningrad Rus. Fed. *see*
    St Petersburg
59 D2 **Leningradskaya** Rus. Fed.
45 D3 **Lenin Peak** Kyrg./Tajik.
    Leninsk Kazakh. *see*
    Baykonur
57 E3 **Leninskiy** Rus. Fed.
68 A2 **Lens** Belgium
72 C1 **Lens** France
51 I2 **Lensk** Rus. Fed.
71 D2 **Lenti** Hungary
77 C3 **Lentini** Sicily Italy
82 B3 **Léo** Burkina
71 D2 **Leoben** Austria
67 B2 **Leominster** U.K.
112 B2 **León** Mex.
114 B3 **León** Nic.
74 B1 **León** Spain
90 A1 **Leonardville** Namibia
18 B2 **Leonora** Austr.
123 D2 **Leopoldina** Brazil
91 C1 **Lephepe** Botswana
91 C3 **Lephoi** S. Africa
39 B3 **Leping** China
73 C2 **Le-Puy-en-Velay** France
118 A2 **Lérida** Col.
74 C1 **Lerma** Spain
79 C3 **Leros** i. Greece
98 F1 **Le Roy, Lac** l. Can.
61 F4 **Lerum** Sweden
64 □ **Lerwick** U.K.
79 C3 **Lesbos** i. Greece
115 C3 **Les Cayes** Haiti
37 C3 **Leshan** China
54 D2 **Leshukonskoye** Rus. Fed.
77 D2 **Leskovac** Yugo.
72 B2 **Lesneven** France
57 E2 **Lesnoye** Rus. Fed.
51 H3 **Lesosibirsk** Rus. Fed.
34 B1 **Lesotho** country Africa
34 B1 **Lesozavodsk** Rus. Fed.
72 B2 **Les Sables-d'Olonne** France
115 D3 **Lesser Antilles** is
    Caribbean Sea
96 C2 **Lesser Slave Lake** Can.
73 C3 **Les Vans** France
    Lesvos i. Greece *see* Lesbos
71 D1 **Leszno** Pol.
67 C3 **Letchworth** U.K.
96 C3 **Lethbridge** Can.
118 C1 **Lethem** Guyana
27 C3 **Leti, Kepulauan** is Indon.
119 B2 **Leticia** Col.
91 C1 **Letlhakeng** Botswana
72 C1 **Le Touquet-Paris-Plage**
    France
67 D3 **Le Tréport** France
31 A2 **Letsok-aw Kyun** i. Myanmar
91 C3 **Letsopa** S. Africa
65 C1 **Letterkenny** Rep. of Ireland
73 C3 **Leucate, Étang de** l. France
28 A1 **Leuser, Gunung** mt. Indon.
68 B2 **Leuven** Belgium
79 B3 **Levadeia** Greece
60 F3 **Levanger** Norway
107 C2 **Levelland** U.S.A.
18 B1 **Lévêque, Cape** Austr.
68 C2 **Leverkusen** Ger.
71 D2 **Levice** Slovakia
22 C2 **Levin** N.Z.
99 C2 **Lévis** Can.
57 E3 **Lev Tolstoy** Rus. Fed.
64 A1 **Lewis, Isle of** i. U.K.
108 C3 **Lewisburg** U.S.A.
102 D1 **Lewis Range** mts U.S.A.
102 C1 **Lewiston** ID U.S.A.

109 E2 **Lewiston** ME U.S.A.
102 E1 **Lewistown** U.S.A.
108 C3 **Lexington** KY U.S.A.
104 D2 **Lexington** NE U.S.A.
109 D3 **Lexington** VA U.S.A.
32 B1 **Leyte** i. Phil.
77 C2 **Lezhë** Albania
57 F2 **Lezhnevo** Rus. Fed.
57 E3 **L'gov** Rus. Fed.
43 C2 **Lhagoi Kangri** mt. China
43 D2 **Lhasa** China
43 C2 **Lhazê** China
28 A1 **Lhokseumawe** Indon.
35 B3 **Liancourt Rocks** i.
    N. Pacific Ocean
39 B3 **Lianhua** China
39 B3 **Lianjiang** China
38 C1 **Lianshan** China
38 B2 **Lianyungang** China
39 B3 **Lianzhou** China
33 A1 **Liao** r. China
38 B2 **Liaocheng** China
38 C1 **Liaodong Bandao** pen.
    China
38 C1 **Liaodong Wan** b. China
38 C1 **Liaoning** prov. China
33 A1 **Liaoyang** China
33 B1 **Liaoyuan** China
96 B1 **Liard** r. Can.
102 C1 **Libby** U.S.A.
86 B2 **Libenge** Dem. Rep. Congo
104 C3 **Liberal** U.S.A.
71 D1 **Liberec** Czech Rep.
82 B4 **Liberia** country Africa
114 B3 **Liberia** Costa Rica
118 B1 **Libertad** Venez.
68 B3 **Libin** Belgium
72 B3 **Libourne** France
86 A2 **Libreville** Gabon
83 D2 **Libya** country Africa
83 E2 **Libyan Desert** Egypt/Libya
84 A1 **Libyan Plateau** Egypt
76 B3 **Licata** Sicily Italy
    Licheng China see Lipu
89 C2 **Lichinga** Moz.
69 E2 **Lichte** Ger.
91 C2 **Lichtenburg** S. Africa
69 E2 **Lichtenfels** Ger.
56 C3 **Lida** Belarus
61 F4 **Lidköping** Sweden
18 C2 **Liebig, Mount** Austr.
73 D2 **Liechtenstein** country
    Europe
68 B2 **Liège** Belgium
60 J3 **Lieksa** Fin.
87 C2 **Lienart** Dem. Rep. Congo
70 C2 **Lienz** Austria
56 B2 **Liepāja** Latvia
70 C2 **Liezen** Austria
65 C2 **Liffey** r. Rep. of Ireland
65 C1 **Lifford** Rep. of Ireland
21 C1 **Lightning Ridge** Austr.
89 C2 **Ligonha** r. Moz.
73 D3 **Ligurian Sea** France/Italy
87 C4 **Likasi** Dem. Rep. Congo
96 B2 **Likely** Can.
57 E2 **Likhoslavl'** Rus. Fed.
29 B1 **Liku** Indon.
73 D3 **L'Île-Rousse** Corsica France
39 B3 **Liling** China
61 F4 **Lilla Edet** Sweden
68 B2 **Lille** Belgium
73 C1 **Lille** France
61 E4 **Lille Bælt** sea chan.
    Denmark
61 F3 **Lillehammer** Norway
61 F4 **Lillestrøm** Norway
96 B2 **Lillooet** Can.
89 C2 **Lilongwe** Malawi
32 B2 **Liloy** Phil.

118 A3 **Lima** Peru
108 C2 **Lima** U.S.A.
65 C1 **Limavady** U.K.
121 B4 **Limay** r. Arg.
69 F2 **Limbach-Oberfrohna** Ger.
56 B2 **Limbaži** Latvia
86 A2 **Limbe** Cameroon
68 D2 **Limburg an der Lahn** Ger.
90 B2 **Lime Acres** S. Africa
122 C2 **Limeira** Brazil
65 B2 **Limerick** Rep. of Ireland
61 E4 **Limfjorden** sea chan.
    Denmark
79 C3 **Limnos** i. Greece
72 C2 **Limoges** France
114 B3 **Limón** Costa Rica
104 C3 **Limon** U.S.A.
72 C3 **Limoux** France
89 C3 **Limpopo** r. S. Africa/
    Zimbabwe
91 C1 **Limpopo** prov. S. Africa
32 A1 **Linapacan** i. Phil.
121 A4 **Linares** Chile
113 C2 **Linares** Mex.
74 C2 **Linares** Spain
30 B1 **Lincang** China
39 B3 **Linchuan** China
66 C2 **Lincoln** U.K.
108 C2 **Lincoln** IL U.S.A.
109 F1 **Lincoln** ME U.S.A.
105 D2 **Lincoln** NE U.S.A.
119 C1 **Linden** Guyana
110 C1 **Linden** U.S.A.
87 C2 **Lindi** r. Dem. Rep. Congo
87 D3 **Lindi** Tanz.
    Lindisfarne i. U.K. *see*
    Holy Island
48 A2 **Lindos** Greece
109 D2 **Lindsay** Can.
38 B2 **Linfen** China
32 B1 **Lingayen** Phil.
38 B2 **Lingbao** China
91 C3 **Lingelethu** S. Africa
91 C3 **Lingelihle** S. Africa
68 C1 **Lingen (Ems)** Ger.
28 B2 **Lingga, Kepulauan** is Indon.
39 A3 **Lingshan** China
39 A4 **Lingshui** China
82 A3 **Linguère** Senegal
123 D1 **Linhares** Brazil
38 A1 **Linhe** China
61 G4 **Linköping** Sweden
34 B1 **Linkou** China
38 B2 **Linqing** China
122 C2 **Lins** Brazil
104 C1 **Linton** U.S.A.
37 D2 **Linxi** China
37 C2 **Linxia** China
38 B2 **Linyi** Shandong China
38 B2 **Linyi** Shandong China
70 C2 **Linying** China
70 C2 **Linz** Austria
73 C3 **Lion, Golfe du** g. France
77 B3 **Lipari** Italy
76 B3 **Lipari, Isole** is Italy
57 E3 **Lipetsk** Rus. Fed.
78 B1 **Lipova** Romania
69 D2 **Lippstadt** Ger.
39 B3 **Lipu** China
44 C1 **Lisakovsk** Kazakh.
86 C3 **Lisala** Dem. Rep. Congo
    Lisboa Port. *see* Lisbon
74 B2 **Lisbon** Port.
65 C1 **Lisburn** U.K.
65 B2 **Liscannor Bay**
    Rep. of Ireland
72 C2 **Lisieux** France
67 A3 **Liskeard** U.K.
57 E3 **Liski** Rus. Fed.
21 D1 **Lismore** Austr.

65 C1 **Lisnaskea** U.K.
65 B2 **Listowel** Rep. of Ireland
39 A3 **Litang** *Guangxi* China
36 C2 **Litang** *Sichuan* China
108 B3 **Litchfield** *IL* U.S.A.
105 E1 **Litchfield** *MN* U.S.A.
21 D2 **Lithgow** Austr.
79 B3 **Lithino, Akra** *pt* Greece
56 B2 **Lithuania** *country* Europe
70 C1 **Litoměřice** Czech Rep.
114 C2 **Little Abaco** *i.* Bahamas
41 D3 **Little Andaman** *i.* India
105 E1 **Little Falls** U.S.A.
107 C2 **Littlefield** U.S.A.
67 C3 **Littlehampton** U.K.
90 A2 **Little Karas Berg** *plat.*
           Namibia
90 B3 **Little Karoo** *plat.* S. Africa
64 A2 **Little Minch** *sea chan.* U.K.
104 C1 **Little Missouri** *r.* U.S.A.
31 A3 **Little Nicobar** *i.* India
110 B2 **Little Rock** U.S.A.
109 E2 **Littleton** U.S.A.
38 B2 **Liujiachang** China
39 A3 **Liuzhou** China
56 C2 **Līvāni** Latvia
18 B1 **Liveringa** Austr.
106 C2 **Livermore, Mount** U.S.A.
99 D2 **Liverpool** Can.
66 B2 **Liverpool** U.K.
95 F2 **Liverpool, Cape** Can.
21 C2 **Liverpool Range** *mts* Austr.
102 D1 **Livingston** *MT* U.S.A.
107 E2 **Livingston** *TX* U.S.A.
107 D2 **Livingston, Lake** U.S.A.
88 B2 **Livingstone** Zambia
77 C2 **Livno** Bos.-Herz.
57 E3 **Livny** Rus. Fed.
108 C2 **Livonia** U.S.A.
76 B2 **Livorno** Italy
87 D3 **Liwale** Tanz.
38 B2 **Liyang** China
67 A4 **Lizard Point** U.K.
76 B1 **Ljubljana** Slovenia
61 G3 **Ljungan** *r.* Sweden
61 F4 **Ljungby** Sweden
61 G3 **Ljusdal** Sweden
61 G3 **Ljusnan** *r.* Sweden
67 B3 **Llandeilo** U.K.
67 B3 **Llandovery** U.K.
67 B2 **Llandrindod Wells** U.K.
66 B2 **Llandudno** U.K.
67 A3 **Llanelli** U.K.
66 A2 **Llangefni** U.K.
107 C2 **Llano Estacado** *plain* U.S.A.
118 B1 **Llanos** *reg.* Col./Venez.
75 D1 **Lleida** Spain
67 A2 **Lleyn Peninsula** U.K.
75 C2 **Lliria** Spain
74 C1 **Llodio** Spain
96 B2 **Lloyd George, Mount** Can.
97 D2 **Lloyd Lake** Can.
97 C2 **Lloydminster** Can.
120 B3 **Llullaillaco, Volcán** *vol.* Chile
91 C2 **Lobatse** Botswana
88 A2 **Lobito** Angola
69 F1 **Loburg** Ger.
64 B2 **Lochaber** *mts* U.K.
72 C2 **Loches** France
64 B2 **Lochgilphead** U.K.
64 B1 **Lochinver** U.K.
64 A2 **Lochmaddy** U.K.
64 C2 **Lochnagar** *mt.* U.K.
20 A2 **Lock** Austr.
64 C2 **Lockerbie** U.K.
107 D3 **Lockhart** U.S.A.
109 D2 **Lock Haven** U.S.A.
109 D2 **Lockport** U.S.A.
31 B2 **Lộc Ninh** Vietnam
73 C3 **Lodève** France

54 C2 **Lodeynoye Pole** Rus. Fed.
60 F2 **Løding** Norway
87 D2 **Lodwar** Kenya
71 D1 **Łódź** Pol.
30 B2 **Loei** Thai.
90 A3 **Loeriesfontein** S. Africa
60 F2 **Lofoten** *is* Norway
102 D2 **Logan** U.S.A.
94 B2 **Logan, Mount** Can.
108 B2 **Logansport** U.S.A.
76 B1 **Logatec** Slovenia
74 C1 **Logroño** Spain
69 D1 **Löhne** Ger.
69 D1 **Lohne (Oldenburg)** Ger.
30 A2 **Loikaw** Myanmar
30 A2 **Loi Lan** *mt.* Myanmar/Thai.
72 B2 **Loire** *r.* France
118 A2 **Loja** Ecuador
74 C2 **Loja** Spain
60 I2 **Lokan tekojärvi** *l.* Fin.
68 B2 **Lokeren** Belgium
90 B1 **Lokgwabe** Botswana
87 D2 **Lokichar** Kenya
87 D2 **Lokichokio** Kenya
57 D2 **Loknya** Rus. Fed.
83 C4 **Lokoja** Nigeria
57 D3 **Lokot'** Rus. Fed.
56 C2 **Loksa** Estonia
95 G2 **Loks Land** *i.* Can.
61 F4 **Lolland** *i.* Denmark
87 D3 **Lollondo** Tanz.
90 B2 **Lolwane** S. Africa
79 B2 **Lom** Bulg.
61 E3 **Lom** Norway
87 C2 **Lomami** *r.* Dem. Rep. Congo
121 C4 **Lomas de Zamora** Arg.
29 C2 **Lombok** *i.* Indon.
29 C2 **Lombok, Selat** *sea chan.*
           Indon.
82 C4 **Lomé** Togo
86 C3 **Lomela** *r.* Dem. Rep. Congo
68 B2 **Lommel** Belgium
64 B2 **Lomond, Loch** *l.* U.K.
56 C2 **Lomonosov** Rus. Fed.
103 B4 **Lompoc** U.S.A.
31 B2 **Lom Sak** Thai.
71 E1 **Łomża** Pol.
98 B2 **London** Can.
67 C3 **London** U.K.
108 C3 **London** U.S.A.
65 C1 **Londonderry** U.K.
18 B1 **Londonderry, Cape** Austr.
122 B2 **Londrina** Brazil
51 M2 **Longa, Proliv** *sea chan.*
           Rus. Fed.
29 C1 **Long Akah** *Sarawak* Malaysia
111 E2 **Long Bay** *b.* U.S.A.
103 C4 **Long Beach** U.S.A.
65 C2 **Longford** Rep. of Ireland
29 C2 **Longiram** Indon.
115 C2 **Long Island** Bahamas
98 C1 **Long Island** Can.
27 D3 **Long Island** P.N.G.
109 E2 **Long Island** U.S.A.
98 B2 **Longlac** Can.
98 B2 **Long Lake** *l.* Can.
104 B2 **Longmont** U.S.A.
108 C2 **Long Point** *pt* Can.
39 B3 **Longquan** China
99 E2 **Long Range Mountains**
           Can.
19 D2 **Longreach** Austr.
67 D2 **Long Stratton** U.K.
66 B1 **Longtown** U.K.
73 D2 **Longuyon** France
107 E2 **Longview** *TX* U.S.A.
102 B1 **Longview** *WA* U.S.A.
38 A2 **Longxi** China
39 B3 **Longxi Shan** *mt.* China
31 B2 **Long Xuyên** Vietnam

39 B3 **Longyan** China
50 C1 **Longyearbyen** Svalbard
70 B2 **Lons-le-Saunier** France
111 E2 **Lookout, Cape** U.S.A.
65 B2 **Loop Head** *hd*
           Rep. of Ireland
31 B2 **Lop Buri** Thai.
32 B1 **Lopez** Phil.
36 C2 **Lop Nur** *salt l.* China
86 B2 **Lopori** *r.* Dem. Rep. Congo
74 B2 **Lora del Río** Spain
108 C2 **Lorain** U.S.A.
42 A1 **Loralai** Pak.
75 C2 **Lorca** Spain
106 B2 **Lordsburg** U.S.A.
123 C2 **Lorena** Brazil
120 B2 **Loreto** Bol.
112 A2 **Loreto** Mex.
72 B2 **Lorient** France
64 B2 **Lorn, Firth of** *est.* U.K.
20 B3 **Lorne** Austr.
106 B1 **Los Alamos** U.S.A.
107 D3 **Los Aldamas** Mex.
121 A4 **Los Ángeles** Chile
103 C4 **Los Angeles** U.S.A.
103 B3 **Los Banos** U.S.A.
120 B3 **Los Blancos** Arg.
121 A5 **Los Chonos, Archipiélago**
           is Chile
59 E1 **Losevo** Rus. Fed.
76 C2 **Lošinj** *i.* Croatia
112 B2 **Los Mochis** Mex.
114 B4 **Los Mosquitos, Golfo de**
           Panama
86 B2 **Losombo** Dem. Rep. Congo
115 D3 **Los Roques, Islas** *is* Vene
64 C2 **Lossiemouth** U.K.
118 B1 **Los Teques** Venez.
120 A4 **Los Vilos** Chile
72 C3 **Lot** *r.* France
64 C1 **Loth** U.K.
87 D2 **Lotikipi Plain** Kenya
86 C3 **Loto** Dem. Rep. Congo
57 E2 **Lotoshino** Rus. Fed.
30 B1 **Louang Namtha** Laos
30 B2 **Louangphrabang** Laos
86 B3 **Loubomo** Congo
72 B2 **Loudéac** France
39 B3 **Loudi** China
86 B3 **Loudima** Congo
82 A3 **Louga** Senegal
67 C2 **Loughborough** U.K.
65 B2 **Loughrea** Rep. of Ireland
73 D2 **Louhans** France
65 B2 **Louisburgh** Rep. of Ireland
91 C1 **Louis Trichardt** S. Africa
108 B3 **Louisville** *KY* U.S.A.
110 C2 **Louisville** *MS* U.S.A.
54 C2 **Loukhi** Rus. Fed.
98 C1 **Loups-Marins, Lacs des**
           lakes Can.
72 B3 **Lourdes** France
119 C1 **Lourenço** Brazil
74 B1 **Lousã** Port.
21 C2 **Louth** Austr.
66 C2 **Louth** U.K.
           Louvain Belgium *see* Leuve
57 D2 **Lovat'** *r.* Rus. Fed.
78 B2 **Lovech** Bulg.
104 B2 **Loveland** U.S.A.
103 C2 **Lovelock** U.S.A.
107 C2 **Lovington** U.S.A.
87 C3 **Lowa** Dem. Rep. Congo
109 E2 **Lowell** U.S.A.
96 C3 **Lower Arrow Lake** Can.
22 B2 **Lower Hutt** N.Z.
65 C1 **Lower Lough Erne** *l.* U.K.
96 B2 **Lower Post** Can.
67 D2 **Lowestoft** U.K.

71 D1 Łowicz Pol.
109 D2 Lowville U.S.A.
20 B2 Loxton Austr.
Loyang China see Luoyang
57 D3 Loyew Belarus
60 F2 Løypskardtinden *mt.*
Norway
77 C2 Loznica Yugo.
59 D2 Lozova Ukr.
88 B2 Luacano Angola
38 B2 Lu'an China
88 A1 Luanda Angola
89 C2 Luangwa *r.* Zambia
89 B2 Luanshya Zambia
74 B1 Luarca Spain
88 B2 Luau Angola
71 E1 Lubaczów Pol.
88 A2 Lubango Angola
87 C3 Lubao Dem. Rep. Congo
71 E1 Lubartów Pol.
69 D1 Lübbecke Ger.
107 C2 Lubbock U.S.A.
69 E1 Lübeck Ger.
37 E2 Lubei China
55 C3 Lubenka Kazakh.
71 D1 Lubin Pol.
71 E1 Lublin Pol.
59 C1 Lubny Ukr.
29 C1 Lubok Antu *Sarawak*
Malaysia
69 E1 Lübow Ger.
69 E1 Lübtheen Ger.
87 C3 Lubudi Dem. Rep. Congo
28 B2 Lubuklinggau Indon.
87 C4 Lubumbashi
Dem. Rep. Congo
88 B2 Lubungu Zambia
87 C3 Lubutu Dem. Rep. Congo
88 A1 Lucala Angola
65 C2 Lucan Rep. of Ireland
88 B1 Lucapa Angola
64 B3 Luce Bay U.K.
122 B2 Lucélia Brazil
32 B1 Lucena Phil.
74 C2 Lucena Spain
71 D2 Lučenec Slovakia
77 C2 Lucera Italy
Lucerne Switz. *see* Luzern
69 E1 Lüchow Ger.
88 A2 Lucira Angola
69 F1 Luckenwalde Ger.
90 B2 Luckhoff S. Africa
43 C2 Lucknow India
88 B2 Lucusse Angola
Lüda China *see* Dalian
68 C2 Lüdenscheid Ger.
69 E1 Lüder Ger.
88 A3 Lüderitz Namibia
42 B1 Ludhiana India
108 B2 Ludington U.S.A.
67 B2 Ludlow U.K.
103 C4 Ludlow U.S.A.
78 C2 Ludogorie *reg.* Bulg.
61 G3 Ludvika Sweden
70 B2 Ludwigsburg Ger.
69 F1 Ludwigsfelde Ger.
69 D3 Ludwigshafen am Rhein
Ger.
69 E1 Ludwigslust Ger.
56 C2 Ludza Latvia
86 C3 Luebo Dem. Rep. Congo
88 A2 Luena Angola
38 A2 Lüeyang China
39 B3 Lufeng China
107 E2 Lufkin U.S.A.
56 C2 Luga Rus. Fed.
56 C2 Luga *r.* Rus. Fed.
73 D2 Lugano Switz.
89 C2 Lugenda *r.* Moz.
74 B1 Lugo Spain

78 B1 Lugoj Romania
59 D2 Luhans'k Ukr.
87 D3 Luhombero Tanz.
58 B1 Luhyny Ukr.
88 B2 Luiana Angola
86 C3 Luilaka *r.* Dem. Rep. Congo
73 D2 Luino Italy
60 I2 Luiro *r.* Fin.
86 C3 Luiza Dem. Rep. Congo
38 B2 Lujiang China
77 C2 Lukavac Bos.-Herz.
86 B3 Lukenie *r.* Dem. Rep. Congo
106 A2 Lukeville U.S.A.
57 E3 Lukhovitsy Rus. Fed.
71 E1 Łuków Pol.
88 B2 Lukulu Zambia
60 H2 Luleå Sweden
60 H2 Luleälven *r.* Sweden
78 C2 Lüleburgaz Turkey
38 B2 Lüliang Shan *mts* China
29 C2 Lumajang Indon.
43 C1 Lumajangdong Co *salt l.*
China
88 B2 Lumbala Kaquengue Angola
88 B2 Lumbala N'guimbo Angola
111 E2 Lumberton U.S.A.
29 C1 Lumbis Indon.
74 B1 Lumbrales Spain
31 B2 Lumphǎt Cambodia
97 D2 Lumsden Can.
22 A3 Lumsden N.Z.
61 F4 Lund Sweden
89 C2 Lundazi Zambia
67 A3 Lundy Island U.K.
09 E1 Lüneburg Ger.
69 E1 Lüneburger Heide *reg.* Ger.
68 C2 Lünen Ger.
73 D2 Lunéville France
88 B2 Lunga *r.* Zambia
82 A4 Lungi Sierra Leone
30 A1 Lunglei India
65 C2 Lungnaquilla Mountain
Rep. of Ireland
88 B2 Lungwebungu *r.* Zambia
42 B2 Luni *r.* India
56 C3 Luninyets Belarus
82 A4 Lunsar Sierra Leone
45 E2 Luntai China
39 A3 Luodian China
39 B3 Luoding China
38 B2 Luohe China
38 B2 Luoyang China
39 A3 Lupanshui China
78 B1 Lupeni Romania
99 C2 Lupilichi Moz.
69 F2 Luppa Ger.
89 C2 Lúrio Moz.
89 D2 Lurio *r.* Moz.
89 B2 Lusaka Zambia
86 C3 Lusambo Dem. Rep. Congo
77 C2 Lushnjë Albania
104 C2 Lusk U.S.A.
44 B3 Lut, Dasht-e *des.* Iran
69 F2 Lutherstadt Wittenberg Ger.
67 C3 Luton U.K.
29 C1 Lutong *Sarawak* Malaysia
97 C1 Łutselk'e Can.
58 B1 Luts'k Ukr.
90 B2 Lutzputs S. Africa
90 A3 Lutzville S. Africa
85 C4 Luuq Somalia
105 D2 Luverne U.S.A.
87 C3 Luvua *r.* Dem. Rep. Congo
91 D1 Luvuvhu *r.* S. Africa
87 D2 Luwero Uganda
27 C3 Luwuk Indon.
68 C3 Luxembourg *country* Europe
68 C3 Luxembourg Lux.
73 D2 Luxeuil-les-Bains France

91 C3 Luxolweni S. Africa
84 B2 Luxor Egypt
68 B2 Luyksgestel Neth.
54 D2 Luza Rus. Fed.
73 D2 Luzern Switz.
39 A3 Luzhou China
122 C1 Luziânia Brazil
119 D2 Luziândia Brazil
32 B1 Luzon *i.* Phil.
39 C3 Luzon Strait Phil.
58 A2 L'viv Ukr.
L'vov Ukr. *see* L'viv
56 C3 Lyakhavichy Belarus
60 G3 Lycksele Sweden
91 D2 Lydenburg S. Africa
56 C3 Lyel'chytsy Belarus
56 C3 Lyepyel' Belarus
67 B3 Lyme Bay U.K.
109 D3 Lynchburg U.S.A.
97 D2 Lynn Lake Can.
97 D1 Lynn Lake Can.
73 C2 Lyon France
57 D2 Lyozna Belarus
54 E3 Lys'va Rus. Fed.
59 D2 Lysychans'k Ukr.
66 B2 Lytham St Anne's U.K.
56 C3 Lyuban' Belarus
57 E2 Lyubertsy Rus. Fed.
58 B1 Lyubeshiv Ukr.
57 F2 Lyubim Rus. Fed.
59 D2 Lyubotyn Ukr.
57 D2 Lyubytino Rus. Fed.
57 D3 Lyudinovo Rus. Fed.

M

48 B2 Ma'an Jordan
56 C2 Maardu Estonia
68 B2 Maas *r.* Neth.
68 B2 Maaseik Belgium
32 B1 Maasin Phil.
68 B2 Maastricht Neth.
89 C3 Mabalane Moz.
118 C1 Mabaruma Guyana
89 C3 Mabote Moz.
90 B2 Mabule Botswana
90 B1 Mabutsane Botswana
123 D2 Macaé Brazil
89 C2 Macaloge Moz.
94 E2 MacAlpine Lake Can.
119 C1 Macapá Brazil
118 A2 Macará Ecuador
123 D1 Macarani Brazil
29 C2 Macassar Strait Indon.
119 E2 Macau Brazil
39 B3 Macau *special admin. reg.*
China
89 C2 Maccaretane Moz.
66 B2 Macclesfield U.K.
18 B2 Macdonald, Lake
salt flat Austr.
18 C2 Macdonnell Ranges
mts Austr.
98 A1 MacDowell Lake Can.
74 B1 Macedo de Cavaleiros Port.
20 B3 Macedon *mt.* Austr.
77 D2 Macedonia *country* Europe
119 E2 Maceió Brazil
76 B2 Macerata Italy
20 A2 Macfarlane, Lake
salt flat Austr.
65 B3 Macgillycuddy's Reeks *mts*
Rep. of Ireland
42 A2 Mach Pak.
123 C2 Machado Brazil
89 C3 Machaila Moz.
87 D3 Machakos Kenya

118 A2 **Machala** Ecuador
89 C3 **Machanga** Moz.
38 B2 **Macheng** China
109 F2 **Machias** U.S.A.
118 A1 **Machiques** Venez.
118 A3 **Machupicchu** Peru
91 D2 **Macia** Moz.
78 C1 **Măcin** Romania
21 D1 **Macintyre** r. Austr.
19 D2 **Mackay** Austr.
18 B2 **Mackay, Lake** salt flat Austr.
97 C1 **MacKay Lake** Can.
96 B2 **Mackenzie** Can.
96 A1 **Mackenzie** r. Can.
94 B2 **Mackenzie Bay** Can.
94 D1 **Mackenzie King Island** Can.
96 A1 **Mackenzie Mountains** Can.
97 C2 **Macklin** Can.
21 D2 **Macksville** Austr.
21 D1 **Maclean** Austr.
18 A2 **Macleod, Lake** imp. l. Austr.
108 A2 **Macomb** U.S.A.
76 A2 **Macomer** Sardinia Italy
73 C2 **Mâcon** France
111 D2 **Macon** GA U.S.A.
105 E3 **Macon** MO U.S.A.
21 C2 **Macquarie** r. Austr.
21 C2 **Macquarie Marshes** Austr.
20 A1 **Macumba** watercourse Austr.
113 C3 **Macuspana** Mex.
112 B2 **Macuzari, Presa** resr Mex.
91 D2 **Madadeni** S. Africa
89 □D3 **Madagascar** country Africa
83 D2 **Madama** Niger
79 B2 **Madan** Bulg.
27 D3 **Madang** P.N.G.
118 D2 **Madeira** r. Brazil
82 A1 **Madeira** terr.
        N. Atlantic Ocean
112 B2 **Madera** Mex.
103 B3 **Madera** U.S.A.
41 B3 **Madgaon** India
86 B3 **Madingou** Congo
108 B3 **Madison** IN U.S.A.
105 D2 **Madison** SD U.S.A.
108 B3 **Madison** WI U.S.A.
108 C3 **Madison** WV U.S.A.
102 D1 **Madison** r. U.S.A.
108 B3 **Madisonville** U.S.A.
29 C2 **Madiun** Indon.
87 D2 **Mado Gashi** Kenya
36 C2 **Madoi** China
56 C2 **Madona** Latvia
46 A2 **Madrakah** Saudi Arabia
41 C3 **Madras** India
102 B2 **Madras** U.S.A.
113 C2 **Madre, Laguna** lag. Mex.
113 B3 **Madre del Sur, Sierra**
        mts Mex.
112 B2 **Madre Occidental, Sierra**
        mts Mex.
113 B2 **Madre Oriental, Sierra**
        mts Mex.
74 C1 **Madrid** Spain
74 C2 **Madridejos** Spain
29 C2 **Madura** i. Indon.
29 C2 **Madura, Selat** sea chan.
        Indon.
41 B4 **Madurai** India
35 C3 **Maebashi** Japan
30 A2 **Mae Hong Son** Thai.
30 A2 **Mae Sariang** Thai.
30 A2 **Mae Suai** Thai.
91 C2 **Mafeteng** Lesotho
91 C3 **Mafikeng** S. Africa
87 D3 **Mafinga** Tanz.
122 C3 **Mafra** Brazil
51 L3 **Magadan** Rus. Fed.

121 A6 **Magallanes, Estrecho de**
        sea chan. Chile
115 C4 **Magangue** Col.
112 A1 **Magdalena** Mex.
106 B2 **Magdalena** U.S.A.
112 A2 **Magdalena, Bahía** b. Mex.
69 E1 **Magdeburg** Ger.
65 C1 **Magherafelt** U.K.
55 E3 **Magnitogorsk** Rus. Fed.
110 B2 **Magnolia** U.S.A.
99 D1 **Magpie, Lac** l. Can.
82 A3 **Magta' Lahjar** Maur.
119 D2 **Maguarinho, Cabo** c. Brazil
91 D2 **Magude** Moz.
30 A1 **Magwe** Myanmar
49 C2 **Mahābād** Iran
42 B2 **Mahajan** India
89 □D2 **Mahajanga** Madag.
29 C2 **Makakam** r. Indon.
91 C1 **Mahalapye** Botswana
89 □D2 **Mahalevona** Madag.
43 C2 **Mahanadi** r. India
89 □D2 **Mahanoro** Madag.
31 B2 **Maha Sarakham** Thai.
89 □D2 **Mahavavy** r. Madag.
46 B2 **Mahd adh Dhahab**
        Saudi Arabia
118 C1 **Mahdia** Guyana
42 B2 **Mahesāna** India
42 B2 **Mahi** r. India
22 C1 **Mahia Peninsula** N.Z.
57 D3 **Mahilyow** Belarus
75 D2 **Mahón** Spain
42 B2 **Mahuva** India
78 C2 **Mahya Dağı** mt. Turkey
97 D2 **Maidstone** Can.
67 D3 **Maidstone** U.K.
83 D3 **Maiduguri** Nigeria
43 C2 **Mailani** India
69 D2 **Main** r. Ger.
86 B3 **Mai-Ndombe, Lac** l.
        Dem. Rep. Congo
69 E3 **Main-Donau-Kanal**
        canal Ger.
109 F1 **Maine** state U.S.A.
30 A1 **Maingkwan** Myanmar
64 C1 **Mainland** i. Scotland U.K.
64 □ **Mainland** i. Scotland U.K.
89 □D2 **Maintirano** Madag.
69 D2 **Mainz** Ger.
118 B1 **Maiquetía** Venez.
21 D2 **Maitland** N.S.W. Austr.
20 A2 **Maitland** S.A. Austr.
114 B3 **Maíz, Islas del** is Nic.
35 C3 **Maizuru** Japan
77 D2 **Majene** Indon.
29 C2 **Maja Jezercë** mt. Albania
        Majorca i. Spain see
        Mallorca
91 C2 **Majwemasweu** S. Africa
86 B3 **Makabana** Congo
26 B3 **Makale** Indon.
45 E2 **Makanchi** Kazakh.
77 C2 **Makarska** Croatia
        Makassar Indon. see
        Ujung Pandang
44 B2 **Makat** Kazakh.
91 D2 **Makatini Flats** lowland
        S. Africa
82 A4 **Makeni** Sierra Leone
88 B3 **Makgadikgadi** salt pan
        Botswana
55 D4 **Makhachkala** Rus. Fed.
44 B2 **Makhambet** Kazakh.
87 D3 **Makindu** Kenya
45 D1 **Makinsk** Kazakh.
59 D2 **Makiyivka** Ukr.
        Makkah Saudi Arabia see
        Mecca
99 E1 **Makkovik** Can.

71 E2 **Makó** Hungary
86 B2 **Makokou** Gabon
87 D3 **Makongolosi** Tanz.
90 B2 **Makopong** Botswana
47 D2 **Makran** reg. Iran/Pak.
57 E2 **Maksatikha** Rus. Fed.
49 C2 **Mākū** Iran
30 A1 **Makum** India
35 B4 **Makurazaki** Japan
83 C4 **Makurdi** Nigeria
60 G2 **Malå** Sweden
114 B4 **Mala, Punta** pt Panama
86 A2 **Malabo** Equat. Guinea
28 A1 **Malacca, Strait of**
        Indon./Malaysia
102 D2 **Malad City** U.S.A.
56 C3 **Maladzyechna** Belarus
74 C2 **Málaga** Spain
85 B4 **Malakal** Sudan
29 C2 **Malang** Indon.
88 A1 **Malanje** Angola
61 G4 **Mälaren** l. Sweden
121 B4 **Malargüe** Arg.
48 B2 **Malatya** Turkey
89 C2 **Malawi** country Africa
        Malawi, Lake Africa see
        Nyasa, Lake
57 D2 **Malaya Vishera** Rus. Fed.
32 B2 **Malaybalay** Phil.
49 C2 **Malāyer** Iran
28 B1 **Malaysia** country Asia
49 C2 **Malazgirt** Turkey
71 D1 **Malbork** Pol.
69 F1 **Malchin** Ger.
68 A2 **Maldegem** Belgium
24 C5 **Maldives** country
        Indian Ocean
121 C4 **Maldonado** Uru.
79 B3 **Maleas, Akra** pt Greece
71 D2 **Malé Karpaty** hills Slovakia
102 C2 **Malheur Lake** U.S.A.
82 B3 **Mali** country Africa
82 A3 **Mali** Guinea
26 C3 **Malili** Indon.
87 E3 **Malindi** Kenya
65 C1 **Malin Head** hd
        Rep. of Ireland
65 B1 **Malin More** Rep. of Ireland
79 B1 **Malkara** Turkey
56 C3 **Mal'kavichy** Belarus
78 C2 **Malko Tŭrnovo** Bulg.
21 C3 **Mallacoota** Austr.
21 C3 **Mallacoota Inlet** b. Austr.
64 B2 **Mallaig** U.K.
97 E1 **Mallery Lake** Can.
75 D2 **Mallorca** i. Spain
65 B2 **Mallow** Rep. of Ireland
60 H2 **Malmberget** Sweden
68 C2 **Malmédy** Belgium
90 A3 **Malmesbury** S. Africa
61 F4 **Malmö** Sweden
30 A1 **Malong** China
86 C4 **Malonga** Dem. Rep. Congo
61 E3 **Måløy** Norway
57 E2 **Maloyaroslavets** Rus. Fed.
57 E2 **Maloye Borisovo** Rus. Fed.
53 E6 **Malta** country Europe
56 C2 **Malta** Latvia
102 E1 **Malta** U.S.A.
90 A1 **Maltahöhe** Namibia
66 C1 **Malton** U.K.
27 C3 **Maluku** i. Indon.
61 F3 **Malung** Sweden
91 C2 **Maluti Mountains** Lesotho
41 B3 **Malvan** India
110 B2 **Malvern** U.S.A.
58 B1 **Malyn** Ukr.
51 L2 **Malyy Anyuy** r. Rus. Fed.
49 C1 **Malyy Kavkaz** mts Asia
51 K2 **Malyy Lyakhovskiy, Ostrov** i.

Rus. Fed.
91 C2 **Mamafubedu** S. Africa
87 C2 **Mambasa** Dem. Rep. Congo
86 B2 **Mambéré** r. C.A.R.
91 C2 **Mamelodi** S. Africa
118 B3 **Mamoré** r. Bol./Brazil
82 A3 **Mamou** Guinea
29 C2 **Mamuju** Indon.
82 B4 **Man** Côte d'Ivoire
118 B2 **Manacapuru** Brazil
75 D2 **Manacor** Spain
27 C2 **Manado** Indon.
114 B3 **Managua** Nic.
89 ☐D3 **Manakara** Madag.
46 B3 **Manākhah** Yemen
47 C2 **Manama** Bahrain
27 D3 **Manam Island** P.N.G.
89 ☐D3 **Mananara** r. Madag.
89 ☐D2 **Mananara Avaratra** Madag.
89 ☐D3 **Mananjary** Madag.
82 A3 **Manantali, Lac de** l. Mali
45 E2 **Manas Hu** l. China
27 C3 **Manatuto** East Timor
118 B2 **Manaus** Brazil
48 B2 **Manavgat** Turkey
66 B2 **Manchester** U.K.
109 E2 **Manchester** U.S.A.
89 ☐D3 **Mandabe** Madag.
61 E4 **Mandal** Norway
27 D3 **Mandala, Puncak** mt. Indon.
30 A1 **Mandalay** Myanmar
37 D1 **Mandalgovĭ** Mongolia
104 C1 **Mandan** U.S.A.
86 B1 **Mandara Mountains**
Cameroon/Nigeria
76 A3 **Mandas** Sardinia Italy
68 C2 **Manderscheid** Ger.
42 B1 **Mandi** India
82 B3 **Mandiana** Guinea
42 B1 **Mandi Burewala** Pak.
43 C2 **Mandla** India
89 ☐D2 **Mandritsara** Madag.
42 B2 **Mandsaur** India
18 A3 **Mandurah** Austr.
41 B3 **Mandya** India
76 B1 **Manerbio** Italy
58 B1 **Manevychi** Ukr.
77 C2 **Manfredonia** Italy
82 B3 **Manga** Burkina
86 B3 **Mangai** Dem. Rep. Congo
22 C1 **Mangakino** N.Z.
78 C2 **Mangalia** Romania
41 B3 **Mangalore** India
91 C2 **Mangaung** S. Africa
29 B2 **Manggar** Indon.
44 B2 **Mangistau** Kazakh.
36 C2 **Mangnai** China
89 C2 **Mangochi** Malawi
27 C3 **Mangole** i. Indon.
122 B3 **Mangueirinha** Brazil
37 E1 **Mangui** China
105 D3 **Manhattan** U.S.A.
89 C3 **Manhica** Moz.
123 D2 **Manhuaçu** Brazil
89 ☐D2 **Mania** r. Madag.
76 B1 **Maniago** Italy
118 B2 **Manicoré** Brazil
99 D2 **Manicouagan** r. Can.
99 D1 **Manicouagan, Réservoir**
resr Can.
47 C2 **Manīfah** Saudi Arabia
32 B1 **Manila** Phil.
21 D2 **Manilla** Austr.
79 C3 **Manisa** Turkey
108 B2 **Manistee** U.S.A.
97 C2 **Manitoba** prov. Can.
97 E2 **Manitoba, Lake** Can.
108 B1 **Manitou Islands** U.S.A.
98 B2 **Manitoulin Island** Can.
108 B2 **Manitowoc** U.S.A.

98 C2 **Maniwaki** Can.
118 A1 **Manizales** Col.
105 E2 **Mankato** U.S.A.
82 B4 **Mankono** Côte d'Ivoire
97 D3 **Mankota** Can.
41 C4 **Mankulam** Sri Lanka
42 B2 **Manmad** India
41 B4 **Mannar, Gulf of**
India/Sri Lanka
69 D3 **Mannheim** Ger.
96 C2 **Manning** Can.
20 A2 **Mannum** Austr.
97 C2 **Mannville** Can.
27 C3 **Manokwari** Indon.
87 C3 **Manono** Dem. Rep. Congo
31 A2 **Manoron** Myanmar
73 D3 **Manosque** France
99 C1 **Manouane, Lac** l. Can.
75 D1 **Manresa** Spain
89 B2 **Mansa** Zambia
95 F2 **Mansel Island** Can.
60 I2 **Mansel'kya** ridge
Fin./Rus. Fed.
21 C3 **Mansfield** Austr.
66 C2 **Mansfield** U.K.
110 B2 **Mansfield** LA U.S.A.
108 C2 **Mansfield** OH U.S.A.
109 D2 **Mansfield** PA U.S.A.
118 A2 **Manta** Ecuador
111 E1 **Manteo** U.S.A.
72 C2 **Mantes-la-Jolie** France
123 C2 **Mantiqueira, Serra da** mts
Brazil
76 B1 **Mantova** Italy
Mantua Italy see **Mantova**
119 C2 **Manuelzinho** Brazil
27 C3 **Manui** i. Indon.
22 B1 **Manukau** N.Z.
110 B2 **Many** U.S.A.
55 D4 **Manych-Gudilo, Ozero** l.
Rus. Fed.
87 D3 **Manyoni** Tanz.
74 C2 **Manzanares** Spain
112 B3 **Manzanillo** Mex.
37 D1 **Manzhouli** China
91 D2 **Manzini** Swaziland
83 D3 **Mao** Chad
27 D3 **Maoke, Pegunungan**
mts Indon.
91 C2 **Maokeng** S. Africa
33 A1 **Maokui Shan** mt. China
39 D3 **Maoming** China
89 C3 **Mapai** Moz.
43 C1 **Mapam Yumco** l. China
113 C3 **Mapastepec** Mex.
112 B2 **Mapimí** Mex.
112 B2 **Mapimí, Bolsón de** des. Mex.
32 A2 **Mapin** i. Phil.
89 C3 **Mapinhane** Moz.
97 D3 **Maple Creek** Can.
89 C3 **Maputo** Moz.
91 D2 **Maputo** r. Moz./S. Africa
43 C2 **Maquan He** r. China
88 A1 **Maquela do Zombo** Angola
121 B5 **Maquinchao** Arg.
105 E2 **Maquoketa** U.S.A.
118 B2 **Maraã** Brazil
119 D2 **Maraba** Brazil
119 C1 **Maracá, Ilha de** i. Brazil
118 A1 **Maracaibo** Venez.
118 A1 **Maracaibo, Lago de**
l. Venez.
122 A2 **Maracaju, Serra de** hills
Brazil
118 B1 **Maracay** Venez.
83 D2 **Marādah** Libya
83 C3 **Maradi** Niger
49 C2 **Marāgheh** Iran
119 D2 **Marajó, Baía de** est. Brazil
119 C2 **Marajó, Ilha de** i. Brazil

47 C2 **Marākī** Iran
87 D2 **Maralal** Kenya
18 C3 **Maralinga** Austr.
49 C2 **Marand** Iran
118 A2 **Marañón** r. Peru
98 B2 **Marathon** Can.
111 D4 **Marathon** U.S.A.
74 C2 **Marbella** Spain
18 A2 **Marble Bar** Austr.
91 C1 **Marble Hall** S. Africa
91 D3 **Marburg** S. Africa
69 D2 **Marburg an der Lahn** Ger.
67 D2 **March** U.K.
68 B2 **Marche-en-Famenne**
Belgium
74 B2 **Marchena** Spain
120 B4 **Mar Chiquita, Lago** l. Arg.
109 E2 **Marcy, Mount** U.S.A.
42 B1 **Mardan** Pak.
121 C4 **Mar del Plata** Arg.
49 C2 **Mardin** Turkey
64 B2 **Maree, Loch** l. U.K.
76 B3 **Marettimo, Isola** i. Sicily Italy
57 D2 **Marevo** Rus. Fed.
106 C2 **Marfa** U.S.A.
18 A3 **Margaret River** Austr.
115 D3 **Margarita, Isla de** i. Venez.
91 D3 **Margate** S. Africa
67 D3 **Margate** U.K.
87 C2 **Margherita Peak**
Dem. Rep. Congo/Uganda
44 C3 **Margo, Dasht-i** des. Afgh.
59 C2 **Marhanets'** Ukr.
30 A1 **Mari** Myanmar
120 B3 **María Elena** Chile
124 C5 **Mariana Trench** sea feature
N. Pacific Ocean
110 B2 **Marianna** AR U.S.A.
111 C2 **Marianna** FL U.S.A.
70 C2 **Mariánské Lázně** Czech Rep.
112 B2 **Marías, Islas** is Mex.
46 B3 **Ma'rib** Yemen
77 C1 **Maribor** Slovenia
85 A4 **Marīd** watercourse Sudan
23 M2 **Marie Byrd Land** reg.
Antarctica
115 D3 **Marie-Galante** i. Guadeloupe
61 G3 **Mariehamn** Fin.
90 A1 **Mariental** Namibia
61 F4 **Mariestad** Sweden
111 D2 **Marietta** GA U.S.A.
108 C3 **Marietta** OH U.S.A.
73 D3 **Marignane** France
51 K3 **Maríí, Mys** pt Rus. Fed.
56 B3 **Marijampolė** Lith.
122 C2 **Marília** Brazil
74 B1 **Marín** Spain
77 C3 **Marina di Gioiosa Ionica**
Italy
56 C3 **Mar"ina Horka** Belarus
108 B1 **Marinette** U.S.A.
122 B2 **Maringá** Brazil
74 B2 **Marinha Grande** Port.
108 B2 **Marion** IN U.S.A.
108 C2 **Marion** OH U.S.A.
111 E2 **Marion** SC U.S.A.
108 C3 **Marion** VA U.S.A.
111 D2 **Marion, Lake** U.S.A.
20 A3 **Marion Bay** Austr.
120 B3 **Mariscal Estigarribia** Para.
78 C2 **Maritsa** r. Bulg.
59 D2 **Mariupol'** Ukr.
85 C4 **Marka** Somalia
91 C1 **Marken** S. Africa
68 B1 **Markermeer** l. Neth.
51 I2 **Markha** r. Rus. Fed.
59 D2 **Markivka** Ukr.
110 B2 **Marksville** U.S.A.
69 D3 **Marktheidenfeld** Ger.
69 F2 **Marktredwitz** Ger.

68 C2 **Marl** Ger.
68 A3 **Marle** France
107 D2 **Marlin** U.S.A.
72 C3 **Marmande** France
79 C2 **Marmara Denizi** *g.* Turkey
79 C3 **Marmaris** Turkey
72 C2 **Marne-la-Vallée** France
89 □D2 **Maroantsetra** Madag.
69 E2 **Maroldsweisach** Ger.
89 □D2 **Maromokotro** *mt.* Madag.
89 C2 **Marondera** Zimbabwe
119 C1 **Maroni** *r.* Fr. Guiana
86 B1 **Maroua** Cameroon
89 □D2 **Marovoay** Madag.
108 B1 **Marquette** U.S.A.
85 A3 **Marra, Jebel** *mt.* Sudan
91 D2 **Marracuene** Moz.
82 B1 **Marrakech** Morocco
85 A3 **Marra Plateau** Sudan
20 A1 **Marree** Austr.
54 F2 **Marresale** Rus. Fed.
89 C2 **Marromeu** Moz.
89 C2 **Marrupa** Moz.
84 B2 **Marsa Alam** Egypt
83 D1 **Marsa al Burayqah** Libya
87 D2 **Marsabit** Kenya
76 B3 **Marsala** *Sicily* Italy
84 A1 **Marsa Matrûh** Egypt
69 D2 **Marsberg** Ger.
76 B2 **Marsciano** Italy
21 C2 **Marsden** Austr.
73 D3 **Marseille** France
105 D2 **Marshall** *MN* U.S.A.
105 E3 **Marshall** *MO* U.S.A.
107 E2 **Marshall** *TX* U.S.A.
17 E2 **Marshall Islands** country
       N. Pacific Ocean
105 E2 **Marshalltown** U.S.A.
108 A2 **Marshfield** U.S.A.
111 E3 **Marsh Harbour** Bahamas
110 B3 **Marsh Island** U.S.A.
56 A2 **Märsta** Sweden
31 A2 **Martaban, Gulf of** Myanmar
29 C2 **Martapura** *Kalimantan*
       Selatan Indon.
28 B2 **Martapura** *Sumatera* Indon.
109 E2 **Martha's Vineyard** *i.* U.S.A.
73 D2 **Martigny** Switz.
71 D2 **Martin** Slovakia
104 C2 **Martin** U.S.A.
113 C2 **Martínez** Mex.
115 D3 **Martinique** *terr.* West Indies
109 D3 **Martinsburg** U.S.A.
108 D3 **Martinsville** U.S.A.
22 C2 **Marton** N.Z.
75 D1 **Martorell** Spain
74 C2 **Martos** Spain
44 B1 **Martuk** Kazakh.
73 C3 **Marvejols** France
44 C3 **Mary** Turkm.
19 E2 **Maryborough** Austr.
90 B2 **Marydale** S. Africa
109 D3 **Maryland** *state* U.S.A.
105 D3 **Marysville** U.S.A.
105 E2 **Maryville** *MO* U.S.A.
111 D1 **Maryville** *TN* U.S.A.
87 D3 **Masai Steppe** *plain* Tanz.
87 D3 **Masaka** Uganda
33 B2 **Masan** S. Korea
87 D4 **Masasi** Tanz.
32 B1 **Masbate** Phil.
32 B1 **Masbate** *i.* Phil.
91 C2 **Maseru** Lesotho
44 B3 **Mashhad** Iran
91 C3 **Masibambane** S. Africa
47 C3 **Masilah, Wâdî al**
       watercourse Yemen
91 C2 **Masilo** S. Africa
87 D2 **Masindi** Uganda
47 C2 **Masîrah** *i.* Oman

47 C3 **Maşîrah, Gulf of** *b.* Oman
49 C2 **Masjed Soleymân** Iran
65 B2 **Mask, Lough** *l.*
       Rep. of Ireland
89 □E2 **Masoala, Tanjona** *c.* Madag.
105 E2 **Mason City** U.S.A.
       Masqaṭ Oman *see* **Muscat**
76 B2 **Massa** Italy
109 E2 **Massachusetts** *state* U.S.A.
109 E2 **Massachusetts Bay** U.S.A.
89 C3 **Massangena** Moz.
88 A1 **Massango** Angola
84 B3 **Massawa** Eritrea
109 E2 **Massena** U.S.A.
96 A2 **Masset** Can.
73 C2 **Massif Central** *mts* France
108 C2 **Massillon** U.S.A.
82 B3 **Massina** Mali
89 C3 **Massinga** Moz.
91 D1 **Massingir** Moz.
46 A2 **Mastâbah** Saudi Arabia
22 C2 **Masterton** N.Z.
42 A2 **Mastung** Pak.
46 A2 **Mastûrah** Saudi Arabia
56 B3 **Masty** Belarus
35 B4 **Masuda** Japan
       Masuku Gabon *see*
       Franceville
89 C3 **Masvingo** Zimbabwe
86 B3 **Matadi** Dem. Rep. Congo
114 B3 **Matagalpa** Nic.
98 C2 **Matagami** Can.
98 C2 **Matagami, Lac** *l.* Can.
107 D3 **Matagorda Island** U.S.A.
88 A2 **Matala** Angola
82 A3 **Matam** Senegal
112 B2 **Matamoros** *Coahuila* Mex.
113 C2 **Matamoros** *Tamaulipas* Mex.
87 D3 **Matandu** *r.* Tanz.
76 C2 **Matane** Can.
114 B2 **Matanzas** Cuba
41 C4 **Matara** Sri Lanka
29 C2 **Mataram** Indon.
18 C1 **Mataranka** Austr.
75 D1 **Mataró** Spain
91 C3 **Matatiele** S. Africa
22 A3 **Mataura** N.Z.
22 C1 **Matawai** N.Z.
120 B2 **Mategua** Bol.
113 B2 **Matehuala** Mex.
77 C2 **Matera** Italy
107 D3 **Mathis** U.S.A.
43 B2 **Mathura** India
32 B2 **Mati** Phil.
66 C2 **Matlock** U.K.
118 C3 **Mato Grosso** Brazil
122 B1 **Mato Grosso, Planalto do**
       plat. Brazil
91 D2 **Matola** Moz.
       Matou China *see* **Pingguo**
35 B3 **Matsue** Japan
34 D2 **Matsumae** Japan
35 C4 **Matsusaka** Japan
39 C3 **Matsu Tao** *i.* Taiwan
35 B4 **Matsuyama** Japan
98 B1 **Mattagami** *r.* Can.
73 D2 **Matterhorn** *mt.* Italy/Switz.
102 C2 **Matterhorn** *mt.* U.S.A.
108 B3 **Mattoon** U.S.A.
118 B1 **Maturín** Venez.
91 C2 **Matwabeng** S. Africa
68 A2 **Maubeuge** France
72 C3 **Maubourguet** France
108 C2 **Maumee** *r.* U.S.A.
88 B2 **Maun** Botswana
30 A1 **Maungdaw** Myanmar
18 C2 **Maurice, Lake** *salt flat* Austr.
82 A3 **Mauritania** *country* Africa
81 H6 **Mauritius** *country*
       Indian Ocean

46 B2 **Mâwân, Khashm** *hill*
       Saudi Arabia
86 B3 **Mawanga** Dem. Rep. Congo
39 B3 **Mawei** China
30 A1 **Mawkmai** Myanmar
30 A1 **Mawlaik** Myanmar
46 B2 **Mawqaq** Saudi Arabia
46 B3 **Mawza** Yemen
76 A3 **Maxia, Punta** *mt. Sardinia*
       Italy
51 J2 **Maya** *r.* Rus. Fed.
115 C2 **Mayaguana** *i.* Bahamas
64 B3 **Maybole** U.K.
72 B2 **Mayenne** France
72 B2 **Mayenne** *r.* France
96 C2 **Mayerthorpe** Can.
108 B3 **Mayfield** U.S.A.
55 D4 **Maykop** Rus. Fed.
94 B2 **Mayo** Can.
86 B3 **Mayoko** Congo
89 D2 **Mayotte** *terr.* Africa
51 J3 **Mayskiy** Rus. Fed.
108 C3 **Maysville** U.S.A.
86 B3 **Mayumba** Gabon
105 D1 **Mayville** U.S.A.
119 C2 **Mazagão** Brazil
72 C3 **Mazamet** France
45 D3 **Mazar** China
76 B3 **Mazara del Vallo** *Sicily* Italy
45 C3 **Mazâr-e Sharif** Afgh.
112 B2 **Mazatán** Mex.
114 A3 **Mazatenango** Guat.
112 B2 **Mazatlán** Mex.
56 B2 **Mažeikiai** Lith.
56 B2 **Mazirbe** Latvia
89 B3 **Mazunga** Zimbabwe
56 C3 **Mazyr** Belarus
91 D2 **Mbabane** Swaziland
86 B2 **Mbaïki** C.A.R.
89 C1 **Mbala** Zambia
87 D2 **Mbale** Uganda
86 B2 **Mbalmayo** Cameroon
86 B3 **Mbandaka** Dem. Rep. Congo
86 A2 **Mbanga** Cameroon
88 A1 **M'banza Congo** Angola
87 D3 **Mbeya** Tanz.
87 D4 **Mbinga** Tanz.
86 B2 **Mbomo** Congo
86 B2 **Mbouda** Cameroon
82 A3 **Mbour** Senegal
82 A3 **Mbout** Maur.
86 C3 **Mbuji-Mayi**
       Dem. Rep. Congo
87 D3 **Mbuyuni** Tanz.
107 D2 **McAlester** U.S.A.
107 D3 **McAllen** U.S.A.
96 B2 **McBride** Can.
102 C2 **McCall** U.S.A.
94 E2 **McClintock Channel** Can.
94 D2 **McClure Strait** Can.
110 B2 **McComb** U.S.A.
104 C2 **McConaughy, Lake** U.S.A.
104 C2 **McCook** U.S.A.
102 C2 **McDermitt** U.S.A.
102 D1 **McDonald Peak** U.S.A.
102 C1 **McGuire, Mount** U.S.A.
96 C2 **McLennan** Can.
96 B2 **McLeod Lake** Can.
102 B1 **McMinnville** U.S.A.
110 C1 **McMinnville** *TN* U.S.A.
105 D3 **McPherson** U.S.A.
91 C3 **Mdantsane** S. Africa
103 D3 **Mead, Lake** *resr* U.S.A.
97 D2 **Meadow Lake** Can.
108 C2 **Meadville** U.S.A.
34 D2 **Meaken-dake** *vol.* Japan
74 B1 **Mealhada** Port.
99 E1 **Mealy Mountains** Can.
96 C2 **Meander River** Can.
46 A2 **Mecca** Saudi Arabia

68 B2   **Mechelen** Belgium
68 B2   **Mechelen** Neth.
68 C2   **Mechernich** Ger.
68 C2   **Meckenheim** Ger.
74 B1   **Meda** Port.
28 A1   **Medan** Indon.
121 B5   **Medanosa, Punta** pt Arg.
41 C4   **Medawachchiya** Sri Lanka
75 D2   **Médéa** Alg.
118 A1   **Medellín** Col.
83 D1   **Medenine** Tunisia
102 B2   **Medford** U.S.A.
78 C2   **Medgidia** Romania
78 B1   **Mediaş** Romania
104 B2   **Medicine Bow Mountains** U.S.A.
104 B2   **Medicine Bow Peak** U.S.A.
97 C2   **Medicine Hat** Can.
105 D3   **Medicine Lodge** U.S.A.
123 D1   **Medina** Brazil
46 A2   **Medina** Saudi Arabia
74 C1   **Medinaceli** Spain
74 C1   **Medina del Campo** Spain
74 B1   **Medina de Rioseco** Spain
52 D6   **Mediterranean Sea**
97 C2   **Medley** Can.
55 E3   **Mednogorsk** Rus. Fed.
51 L2   **Medvezh'i, Ostrova** is Rus. Fed.
54 C2   **Medvezh'yegorsk** Rus. Fed.
18 A2   **Meekatharra** Austr.
104 B2   **Meeker** U.S.A.
43 B2   **Meerut** India
68 A2   **Meetkerke** Belgium
79 D3   **Megalopoli** Greece
99 C2   **Mégantic** Can.
43 C2   **Meghāsani** mt. India
48 A2   **Megisti** i. Greece
60 I1   **Mehamn** Norway
18 A2   **Meharry, Mount** Austr.
47 C2   **Mehrān** watercourse Iran
122 C1   **Meia Ponte** r. Brazil
86 B2   **Meiganga** Cameroon
33 B1   **Meihekou** China
        Meijiang China see Ningdu
30 A1   **Meiktila** Myanmar
69 E2   **Meiningen** Ger.
70 C1   **Meißen** Ger.
39 B3   **Meizhou** China
120 B3   **Mejicana** mt Arg
120 A3   **Mejillones** Chile
85 B3   **Mek'elē** Eth.
82 C2   **Mekerrhane, Sebkha** salt pan Alg.
82 B1   **Meknès** Morocco
31 B2   **Mekong** r. Asia
31 B3   **Mekong, Mouths of the** Vietnam
28 B1   **Melaka** Malaysia
21 B3   **Melbourne** Austr.
111 D3   **Melbourne** U.S.A.
76 A2   **Mele, Capo** c. Italy
99 C1   **Mélèzes, Rivière aux** r. Can.
83 D3   **Mélfi** Chad
77 C2   **Melfi** Italy
97 D2   **Melfort** Can.
60 F3   **Melhus** Norway
74 B1   **Melide** Spain
82 B1   **Melilla** N. Africa
59 D2   **Melitopol'** Ukr.
69 D1   **Melle** Ger.
61 F4   **Mellerud** Sweden
69 E2   **Mellrichstadt** Ger.
68 D1   **Mellum** i. Ger.
120 C4   **Melo** Uru.
83 C1   **Melrhir, Chott** salt l. Alg.
67 C2   **Melton Mowbray** U.K.
72 C2   **Melun** France
97 D2   **Melville** Can.
19 D1   **Melville, Cape** Austr.

99 E1   **Melville, Lake** Can.
18 C1   **Melville Island** Austr.
94 D1   **Melville Island** Can.
95 F2   **Melville Peninsula** Can.
70 C2   **Memmingen** Ger.
29 B1   **Mempawah** Indon.
48 B3   **Memphis** Egypt
110 B1   **Memphis** TN U.S.A.
107 C2   **Memphis** TX U.S.A.
59 C1   **Mena** Ukr.
110 B2   **Mena** U.S.A.
82 C3   **Ménaka** Mali
        Mènam Khong r. Laos/Thai. see Mekong
73 C3   **Mende** France
84 B3   **Mendefera** Eritrea
113 C2   **Méndez** Mex.
87 D2   **Mendi** Eth.
27 D3   **Mendi** P.N.G.
67 B3   **Mendip Hills** U.K.
121 B4   **Mendoza** Arg.
79 C3   **Menemen** Turkey
28 B2   **Menggala** Indon.
30 B1   **Mengzi** China
99 D1   **Menihek** Can.
20 B2   **Menindee** Austr.
20 B2   **Menindee Lake** Austr.
20 A3   **Meningie** Austr.
72 C2   **Mennecy** France
108 B1   **Menominee** U.S.A.
88 A2   **Menongue** Angola
75 D1   **Menorca** i. Spain
28 A2   **Mentawai, Kepulauan** is Indon.
28 B2   **Mentok** Indon.
18 B2   **Menzies** Austr.
68 C1   **Meppel** Neth.
68 C1   **Meppen** Ger.
91 D1   **Mepuze** Moz.
91 C2   **Meqheleng** S. Africa
76 B1   **Merano** Italy
27 D3   **Merauke** Indon.
20 B2   **Merbein** Austr.
103 B3   **Merced** U.S.A.
120 C3   **Mercedes** Arg.
95 G2   **Mercy, Cape** Can.
107 C1   **Meredith, Lake** U.S.A.
59 D2   **Merefa** Ukr.
84 A3   **Merga Oasis** Sudan
31 A2   **Mergui** Myanmar
31 A2   **Mergui Archipelago** is Myanmar
78 C2   **Meriç** r. Greece/Turkey
113 D2   **Mérida** Mex.
74 B2   **Mérida** Spain
118 A1   **Mérida** Venez.
110 C2   **Meridian** U.S.A.
21 C3   **Merimbula** Austr.
84 B3   **Merowe** Sudan
18 A3   **Merredin** Austr.
64 B3   **Merrick** hill U.K.
108 B1   **Merrill** U.S.A.
108 B2   **Merrillville** U.S.A.
96 B2   **Merritt** Can.
21 C2   **Merrygoen** Austr.
84 C3   **Mersa Fatma** Eritrea
68 C3   **Mersch** Lux.
69 E2   **Merseburg (Saale)** Ger.
66 B2   **Mersey** r. U.K.
28 B1   **Mersing** Malaysia
67 D3   **Mers-les-Bains** France
42 B2   **Merta** India
67 B3   **Merthyr Tydfil** U.K.
74 B2   **Mértola** Port.
87 D3   **Meru** vol. Tanz.
68 C3   **Merzig** Ger.
106 A2   **Mesa** U.S.A.
77 C2   **Mesagne** Italy
69 D2   **Meschede** Ger.
57 E3   **Meshchovsk** Rus. Fed.

59 E2   **Meshkovskaya** Rus. Fed.
79 B2   **Mesimeri** Greece
79 B3   **Mesolongi** Greece
89 D2   **Messalo** r. Moz.
77 C3   **Messina** Sicily Italy
91 D1   **Messina** S. Africa
77 C3   **Messina, Stretta di** str. Italy
79 B3   **Messiniakos Kolpos** b. Greece
78 B2   **Mesta** r. Bulg.
118 B1   **Meta** r. Col./Venez.
95 G2   **Meta Incognita Peninsula** Can.
120 B3   **Metán** Arg.
79 B3   **Methoni** Greece
77 C2   **Metković** Croatia
28 B2   **Metro** Indon.
85 B4   **Metu** Eth.
73 D2   **Metz** France
68 B2   **Meuse** r. Belgium/France
107 D2   **Mexia** U.S.A.
112 A1   **Mexicali** Mex.
112 A1   **Mexico** country Central America
113 C2   **México** Mex.
105 E3   **Mexico** U.S.A.
93 E5   **Mexico, Gulf of** Mex./U.S.A.
69 F1   **Meyenburg** Ger.
44 C3   **Meymaneh** Afgh.
54 D2   **Mezen'** Rus. Fed.
54 D2   **Mezen'** r. Rus. Fed.
54 E1   **Mezhdusharskiy, Ostrov** i. Rus. Fed.
71 E2   **Mezőtúr** Hungary
112 B2   **Mezquitic** Mex.
56 C2   **Mežvidi** Latvia
89 C2   **Mfuwe** Zambia
91 D2   **Mhlume** Swaziland
42 B2   **Mhow** India
113 C3   **Miahuatlán** Mex.
74 B2   **Miajadas** Spain
111 D3   **Miami** FL U.S.A.
107 E1   **Miami** OK U.S.A.
111 D3   **Miami Beach** U.S.A.
49 C2   **Miandowāb** Iran
89 □D2   **Miandrivazo** Madag.
49 C2   **Mīāneh** Iran
42 B1   **Mianwali** Pak.
38 A2   **Mianyang** China
80 □D2   **Miarinarivo** Madag.
55 F3   **Miass** Rus. Fed.
96 C2   **Mica Creek** Can.
71 E2   **Michalovce** Slovakia
108 B1   **Michigan** state U.S.A.
108 B2   **Michigan, Lake** U.S.A.
100 D2   **Michigan City** U.S.A.
98 B2   **Michipicoten Island** Can.
98 B2   **Michipicoten River** Can.
57 F3   **Michurinsk** Rus. Fed.
68 A2   **Middelburg** Neth.
91 C3   **Middelburg** E. Cape S. Africa
91 C3   **Middelburg** Mpumalanga S. Africa
68 B2   **Middelharnis** Neth.
102 B2   **Middle Alkali Lake** U.S.A.
41 D3   **Middle Andaman** i. India
104 D2   **Middle Loup** r. U.S.A.
108 C3   **Middlesboro** U.S.A.
66 C1   **Middlesbrough** U.K.
109 E2   **Middletown** NY U.S.A.
108 C3   **Middletown** OH U.S.A.
46 B3   **Mīdī** Yemen
98 C2   **Midland** Can.
108 C2   **Midland** MI U.S.A.
107 C2   **Midland** TX U.S.A.
65 B3   **Midleton** Rep. of Ireland
62 B1   **Miðvágur** Faroe Is
77 D2   **Midzhur** mt. Bulg./Yugo.
71 E1   **Mielec** Pol.
78 C1   **Miercurea-Ciuc** Romania

74 B1 **Mieres** Spain
69 E1 **Mieste** Ger.
113 C3 **Miguel Alemán, Presa** resr Mex.
112 B2 **Miguel Auza** Mex.
112 B2 **Miguel Hidalgo, Presa** resr Mex.
31 A2 **Migyaunglaung** Myanmar
57 E3 **Mikhaylov** Rus. Fed.
        Mikhaylovgrad Bulg. see Montana
34 B2 **Mikhaylovka** Rus. Fed.
45 D1 **Mikhaylovskiy** Rus. Fed.
61 I3 **Mikkeli** Fin.
54 E2 **Mikun'** Rus. Fed.
35 C3 **Mikuni-sanmyaku** mts Japan
76 A1 **Milan** Italy
89 C2 **Milange** Moz.
        Milano Italy see Milan
79 C3 **Milas** Turkey
105 D1 **Milbank** U.S.A.
67 D2 **Mildenhall** U.K.
20 B2 **Mildura** Austr.
30 B1 **Mile** China
104 B1 **Miles City** U.S.A.
109 D3 **Milford** DE U.S.A.
103 D3 **Milford** UT U.S.A.
67 A3 **Milford Haven** U.K.
22 A2 **Milford Sound** N.Z.
75 D2 **Miliana** Alg.
84 B3 **Milk, Wādī al** watercourse Sudan
51 L3 **Milk'ovo** Rus. Fed.
97 C2 **Milk River** Can.
73 C3 **Millau** France
111 D2 **Milledgeville** U.S.A.
105 E1 **Mille Lacs** lakes U.S.A.
98 A1 **Mille Lacs, Lac des** l. Can.
105 D2 **Miller** U.S.A.
59 E2 **Millerovo** Rus. Fed.
20 A2 **Millers Creek** Austr.
20 B3 **Millicent** Austr.
109 F1 **Millinocket** U.S.A.
21 D1 **Millmerran** Austr.
66 B1 **Millom** U.K.
96 C1 **Mills Lake** l. Can.
79 B3 **Milos** i. Greece
57 E3 **Miloslavskoye** Rus. Fed.
59 E2 **Milove** Ukr.
20 B1 **Milparinka** Austr.
22 A3 **Milton** N.Z.
67 C2 **Milton Keynes** U.K.
108 B2 **Milwaukee** U.S.A.
72 B3 **Mimizan** France
86 B3 **Mimongo** Gabon
47 C2 **Mīnāb** Iran
26 C2 **Minahasa, Semenanjung** pen. Indon.
47 C2 **Mina Jebel Ali** U.A.E.
28 B1 **Minas** Indon.
121 C4 **Minas** Uru.
123 D1 **Minas Novas** Brazil
113 C3 **Minatitlán** Mex.
30 A1 **Minbu** Myanmar
32 B2 **Mindanao** i. Phil.
69 D1 **Minden** Ger.
110 B2 **Minden** LA U.S.A.
105 D2 **Minden** NE U.S.A.
32 B1 **Mindoro** i. Phil.
32 A1 **Mindoro Strait** Phil.
86 B3 **Mindouli** Congo
67 B3 **Minehead** U.K.
122 B1 **Mineiros** Brazil
107 D2 **Mineral Wells** U.S.A.
45 E3 **Minfeng** China
87 C4 **Minga** Dem. Rep. Congo
49 C1 **Mingäçevir** Azer.
99 D1 **Mingan** Can.
20 B2 **Mingary** Austr.
38 B2 **Mingguang** China

30 A1 **Mingin** Myanmar
75 C2 **Minglanilla** Spain
87 D4 **Mingoyo** Tanz.
37 E1 **Mingshui** China
39 B3 **Mingxi** China
41 B4 **Minicoy** i. India
18 A2 **Minilya** Austr.
99 D1 **Minipi Lake** Can.
98 A1 **Miniss Lake** Can.
83 C4 **Minna** Nigeria
105 E2 **Minneapolis** U.S.A.
97 E2 **Minnedosa** Can.
105 E2 **Minnesota** r. U.S.A.
105 E1 **Minnesota** state U.S.A.
74 B1 **Miño** r. Port./Spain
        Minorca i. Spain see Menorca
104 C1 **Minot** U.S.A.
56 C3 **Minsk** Belarus
71 E1 **Mińsk Mazowiecki** Pol.
99 D2 **Minto** Can.
98 C1 **Minto, Lac** l. Can.
38 A2 **Minxian** China
123 D1 **Mirabela** Brazil
123 D1 **Miralta** Brazil
79 C3 **Mirampelou, Kolpos** b. Greece
120 C3 **Miranda** Brazil
120 C2 **Miranda** r. Brazil
74 C1 **Miranda de Ebro** Spain
74 B1 **Mirandela** Port.
122 B2 **Mirandópolis** Brazil
47 C3 **Mirbāţ** Oman
29 C1 **Miri** Sarawak Malaysia
121 C4 **Mirim, Lagoa** l. Brazil
47 D2 **Mīrjāveh** Iran
69 F1 **Mirnyy** Rus. Fed.
42 A2 **Mirpur Khas** Pak.
79 B3 **Mirtoö Pelagos** sea Greece
33 B2 **Miryang** S. Korea
43 C2 **Mirzapur** India
34 B1 **Mishan** China
114 B3 **Miskitos, Cayos** is Nic.
71 E2 **Miskolc** Hungary
27 C3 **Misoöl** i. Indon.
83 D1 **Mişrātah** Libya
98 B1 **Missinaibi** r. Can.
98 B2 **Missinaibi Lake** Can.
96 B3 **Mission** Can.
98 B1 **Missisa Lake** Can.
110 C3 **Mississippi** r. U.S.A.
110 C2 **Mississippi** state U.S.A.
110 C3 **Mississippi Delta** U.S.A.
102 D1 **Missoula** U.S.A.
105 E3 **Missouri** r. U.S.A.
105 E3 **Missouri** state U.S.A.
99 C2 **Mistassibi** r. Can.
98 C1 **Mistassini, Lac** l. Can.
99 C1 **Mistastin Lake** Can.
71 D2 **Mistelbach** Austria
99 D1 **Mistinibi, Lac** l. Can.
98 C1 **Mistissini** Can.
19 D2 **Mitchell** Austr.
19 D1 **Mitchell** r. Austr.
105 D2 **Mitchell** U.S.A.
65 B2 **Mitchelstown** Rep. of Ireland
42 A2 **Mithi** Pak.
35 D3 **Mito** Japan
87 D3 **Mitole** Tanz.
21 D2 **Mittagong** Austr.
69 E2 **Mittelhausen** Ger.
69 D1 **Mittellandkanal** canal Ger.
69 F3 **Mitterteich** Ger.
118 A1 **Mitú** Col.
87 C4 **Mitumba, Chaîne des** mts Dem. Rep. Congo
87 C3 **Mitumba, Monts** mts Dem. Rep. Congo
86 B2 **Mitzic** Gabon

46 B2 **Miyah, Wādī al** watercourse Saudi Arabia
35 C4 **Miyake-jima** i. Japan
34 D3 **Miyako** Japan
35 B4 **Miyakonojō** Japan
44 B2 **Miyaly** Kazakh.
        Miyang China see Mile
35 B4 **Miyazaki** Japan
83 D1 **Mizdah** Libya
65 B3 **Mizen Head** hd Rep. of Ireland
58 A2 **Mizhhir"ya** Ukr.
61 G4 **Mjölby** Sweden
61 F3 **Mjøsa** l. Norway
87 D3 **Mkomazi** Tanz.
71 C1 **Mladá Boleslav** Czech Rep.
77 D2 **Mladenovac** Yugo.
71 E1 **Mława** Pol.
91 C3 **Mlungisi** S. Africa
58 B1 **Mlyniv** Ukr.
91 C2 **Mmabatho** S. Africa
91 C2 **Mmathethe** Botswana
103 E3 **Moab** U.S.A.
91 D2 **Moamba** Moz.
87 C3 **Moba** Dem. Rep. Congo
86 C2 **Mobayi-Mbongo** Dem. Rep. Congo
105 E3 **Moberly** U.S.A.
110 C2 **Mobile** U.S.A.
110 C2 **Mobile Bay** U.S.A.
104 C1 **Mobridge** U.S.A.
89 D2 **Moçambique** Moz.
30 B1 **Mộc Châu** Vietnam
91 C1 **Mochudi** Botswana
89 D2 **Mocímboa da Praia** Moz.
118 A1 **Mocoa** Col.
122 C2 **Mococa** Brazil
112 B2 **Mocorito** Mex.
112 B1 **Moctezuma** Chihuahua Mex.
112 B2 **Moctezuma** San Luis Potosí Mex.
112 B2 **Moctezuma** Sonora Mex.
89 C2 **Mocuba** Moz.
73 D2 **Modane** France
90 B2 **Modder** r. S. Africa
76 B2 **Modena** Italy
103 B3 **Modesto** U.S.A.
21 C3 **Moe** Austr.
68 C2 **Moers** Ger.
64 C3 **Moffat** U.K.
        Mogadishu Somalia see Muqdisho
91 C1 **Mogalakwena** r. S. Africa
30 A1 **Mogaung** Myanmar
        Mogilev Belarus see Mahilyow
122 C2 **Mogi-Mirim** Brazil
51 I3 **Mogocha** Rus. Fed.
30 A1 **Mogok** Myanmar
71 D2 **Mohács** Hungary
91 C3 **Mohale's Hoek** Lesotho
75 D2 **Mohammadia** Alg.
109 E2 **Mohawk** r. U.S.A.
87 D3 **Mohoro** Tanz.
58 B2 **Mohyliv Podil's'kyy** Ukr.
78 C1 **Moineşti** Romania
60 F2 **Mo i Rana** Norway
72 C3 **Moissac** France
103 C3 **Mojave** U.S.A.
103 C3 **Mojave Desert** U.S.A.
30 B1 **Mojiang** China
123 C2 **Moji das Cruzes** Brazil
122 C2 **Moji-Guaçu** r. Brazil
22 B1 **Mokau** N.Z.
91 C2 **Mokhotlong** Lesotho
33 B3 **Mokp'o** S. Korea
113 C2 **Molango** Mex.
        Moldavia country Europe see Moldova

60 E3 **Molde** Norway
58 B2 **Moldova** country Europe
78 B1 **Moldoveanu, Vârful** mt. Romania
58 B2 **Moldovei Centrale, Podişul** plat. Moldova
91 C1 **Molepolole** Botswana
56 C2 **Molétai** Lith.
77 C2 **Molfetta** Italy
75 C1 **Molina de Aragón** Spain
118 A3 **Mollendo** Peru
21 C2 **Molong** Austr.
90 B2 **Molopo** watercourse Botswana/S. Africa
86 B2 **Moloundou** Cameroon
Moluccas is Indon. see Maluku
27 C3 **Molucca Sea** Indon.
20 B2 **Momba** Austr.
87 D3 **Mombasa** Kenya
122 B1 **Mombuca, Serra da** hills Brazil
61 F4 **Møn** i. Denmark
73 D3 **Monaco** country Europe
64 B2 **Monadhliath Mountains** U.K.
65 C1 **Monaghan** Rep. of Ireland
57 D3 **Monastyrshchina** Rus. Fed.
58 B2 **Monastyryshche** Ukr.
34 D2 **Monbetsu** Japan
76 A1 **Moncalieri** Italy
54 C2 **Monchegorsk** Rus. Fed.
68 C2 **Mönchengladbach** Ger.
112 B2 **Monclova** Mex.
99 D2 **Moncton** Can.
74 B1 **Mondego** r. Port.
91 D2 **Mondlo** S. Africa
76 A2 **Mondovì** Italy
79 B3 **Monemvasia** Greece
34 D1 **Moneron, Ostrov** i. Rus. Fed.
105 E3 **Monett** U.S.A.
76 B1 **Monfalcone** Italy
74 B1 **Monforte** Spain
30 B1 **Mông Cai** Vietnam
30 B1 **Mong Lin** Myanmar
36 C1 **Mongolia** country Asia
30 A1 **Mong Pawk** Myanmar
30 A1 **Mong Ping** Myanmar
88 B2 **Mongu** Zambia
103 C3 **Monitor Range** mts U.S.A.
82 C4 **Mono** r. Togo
103 D3 **Mono Lake** U.S.A.
77 C2 **Monopoli** Italy
75 C1 **Monreal del Campo** Spain
110 B2 **Monroe** LA U.S.A.
109 B2 **Monroe** WI U.S.A.
110 C2 **Monroeville** U.S.A.
82 A4 **Monrovia** Liberia
67 A4 **Mons** Belgium
68 A2 **Mons** Belgium
90 B3 **Montagu** S. Africa
77 C3 **Montalto** mt. Italy
78 B2 **Montana** Bulg.
102 E1 **Montana** state U.S.A.
72 C2 **Montargis** France
72 C3 **Montauban** France
109 E2 **Montauk Point** U.S.A.
91 C2 **Mont-aux-Sources** mt. Lesotho
73 C2 **Montbard** France
73 D2 **Mont Blanc** mt. France/Italy
72 C3 **Montbrison** France
72 B3 **Montcornet** France
72 B3 **Mont-de-Marsan** France
72 C2 **Montdidier** France
119 C2 **Monte Alegre** Brazil
73 D3 **Monte-Carlo** Monaco
120 C4 **Monte Caseros** Arg.
114 C3 **Montego Bay** Jamaica
73 C3 **Montélimar** France
77 C2 **Montella** Italy

113 C2 **Montemorelos** Mex.
72 B2 **Montendre** France
77 C2 **Montenegro** aut. rep. Yugo.
89 C2 **Montepuez** Moz.
76 B2 **Montepulciano** Italy
103 B3 **Monterey** U.S.A.
103 B3 **Monterey Bay** U.S.A.
118 A1 **Montería** Col.
120 B2 **Montero** Bol.
113 B2 **Monterrey** Mex.
77 C2 **Montesano sulla Marcellana** Italy
77 C2 **Monte Sant'Angelo** Italy
119 E3 **Monte Santo** Brazil
76 A2 **Monte Santu, Capo di** c. Sardinia Italy
123 D1 **Montes Claros** Brazil
121 C4 **Montevideo** Uru.
105 D2 **Montevideo** U.S.A.
104 B3 **Monte Vista** U.S.A.
110 C2 **Montgomery** U.S.A.
73 D2 **Monthey** Switz.
110 B2 **Monticello** AR U.S.A.
103 E3 **Monticello** UT U.S.A.
72 C2 **Montignac** France
74 C2 **Montilla** Spain
99 D2 **Mont-Joli** Can.
98 C2 **Mont-Laurier** Can.
72 C2 **Montluçon** France
99 C2 **Montmagny** Can.
72 C2 **Montmorillon** France
19 E2 **Monto** Austr.
102 D2 **Montpelier** ID U.S.A.
109 E2 **Montpelier** VT U.S.A.
73 C3 **Montpellier** France
98 C2 **Montréal** Can.
97 D2 **Montreal Lake** Can.
97 D2 **Montreal Lake** l. Can.
67 D3 **Montreuil** France
73 D2 **Montreux** Switz.
64 C2 **Montrose** U.K.
104 B3 **Montrose** U.S.A.
115 D3 **Montserrat** terr. West Indies
30 A1 **Monywa** Myanmar
76 A1 **Monza** Italy
75 D1 **Monzón** Spain
91 C1 **Mookane** Botswana
21 D1 **Moonie** Austr.
21 C1 **Moonie** r. Austr.
20 A2 **Moonta** Austr.
18 A2 **Moore, Lake** salt flat Austr.
105 D1 **Moorhead** U.S.A.
21 C3 **Mooroopna** Austr.
90 A3 **Mooreesburg** S. Africa
98 B1 **Moose** r. Can.
99 B1 **Moose Factory** Can.
109 F1 **Moosehead Lake** U.S.A.
97 D2 **Moose Jaw** Can.
105 E1 **Moose Lake** U.S.A.
97 D2 **Moosomin** Can.
98 B1 **Moosonee** Can.
20 B2 **Mootwingee** Austr.
91 C1 **Mopane** S. Africa
82 B3 **Mopti** Mali
118 A3 **Moquegua** Peru
61 F3 **Mora** Sweden
105 E1 **Mora** U.S.A.
43 B2 **Moradabad** India
□D2 **Moramanga** Madag.
71 D2 **Morava** r. Europe
64 B2 **Moray Firth** b. U.K.
68 C3 **Morbach** Ger.
42 B2 **Morbi** India
72 B3 **Morcenx** France
37 E1 **Mordaga** China
97 E3 **Morden** Can.
59 E1 **Mordovo** Rus. Fed.
66 B1 **Morecambe** U.K.
66 B1 **Morecambe Bay** U.K.
21 C1 **Moree** Austr.

27 D3 **Morehead** P.N.G.
108 C3 **Morehead** U.S.A.
111 E2 **Morehead City** U.S.A.
113 B3 **Morelia** Mex.
75 C1 **Morella** Spain
74 B2 **Morena, Sierra** mts Spain
78 C2 **Moreni** Romania
96 A2 **Moresby, Mount** Can.
96 A2 **Moresby Island** Can.
110 B3 **Morgan City** U.S.A.
111 D1 **Morganton** U.S.A.
108 D3 **Morgantown** U.S.A.
73 D2 **Morges** Switz.
34 C2 **Mori** Japan
96 B2 **Morice Lake** Can.
34 D3 **Morioka** Japan
21 D2 **Morisset** Austr.
72 B2 **Morlaix** France
19 C1 **Mornington Island** Austr.
27 D3 **Morobe** P.N.G.
82 B1 **Morocco** country Africa
87 D3 **Morogoro** Tanz.
32 B2 **Moro Gulf** Phil.
90 B2 **Morokweng** S. Africa
□D3 **Morombe** Madag.
36 C1 **Mörön** Mongolia
□D3 **Morondava** Madag.
89 C2 **Moroni** Comoros
27 C2 **Morotai** i. Indon.
87 D2 **Moroto** Uganda
66 C1 **Morpeth** U.K.
122 C1 **Morrinhos** Brazil
97 E3 **Morris** Can.
105 D1 **Morris** U.S.A.
111 D1 **Morristown** U.S.A.
55 D3 **Morshanka** Rus. Fed.
122 B1 **Mortes, Rio das** r. Brazil
20 B3 **Mortlake** Austr.
21 D3 **Moruya** Austr.
64 B2 **Morvern** reg. U.K.
21 D3 **Morwell** Austr.
70 B2 **Mosbach** Ger.
57 E2 **Moscow** Rus. Fed.
102 C1 **Moscow** U.S.A.
68 C2 **Mosel** r. Ger.
102 C1 **Moses Lake** U.S.A.
□A3 **Mosfellsbær** Iceland
22 B3 **Mosgiel** N.Z.
57 D2 **Moshenskoye** Rus. Fed.
87 D3 **Moshi** Tanz.
60 F2 **Mosjøen** Norway
Moskva Rus. Fed. see Moscow
71 D2 **Mosonmagyaróvár** Hungary
61 F4 **Moss** Norway
90 B3 **Mossel Bay** S. Africa
90 B3 **Mossel Bay** b. S. Africa
86 B3 **Mossendjo** Congo
20 B2 **Mossgiel** Austr.
19 D1 **Mossman** Austr.
119 D2 **Mossoró** Brazil
21 D2 **Moss Vale** Austr.
70 C1 **Most** Czech Rep.
82 C1 **Mostaganem** Alg.
77 C2 **Mostar** Bos.-Herz.
120 C4 **Mostardas** Brazil
61 G4 **Motala** Sweden
64 C3 **Motherwell** U.K.
75 C2 **Motilla del Palancar** Spain
90 B1 **Motokwe** Botswana
74 C2 **Motril** Spain
78 B2 **Motru** Romania
113 D2 **Motul** Mex.
79 C3 **Moudros** Greece
86 B3 **Mouila** Gabon
20 B3 **Moulamein** Austr.
73 C2 **Moulins** France
31 A2 **Moulmein** Myanmar
111 D2 **Moultrie** U.S.A.

111 E2 **Moultrie, Lake** U.S.A.
108 B3 **Mound City** U.S.A.
83 D4 **Moundou** Chad
105 E3 **Mountain Grove** U.S.A.
110 B1 **Mountain Home** *AR* U.S.A.
102 C2 **Mountain Home** *ID* U.S.A.
111 D1 **Mount Airy** U.S.A.
20 A1 **Mount Barker** Austr.
21 C3 **Mount Beauty** Austr.
89 C2 **Mount Darwin** Zimbabwe
109 F2 **Mount Desert Island** U.S.A.
91 C3 **Mount Fletcher** S. Africa
91 C3 **Mount Frere** S. Africa
20 B3 **Mount Gambier** Austr.
27 D3 **Mount Hagen** P.N.G.
21 C2 **Mount Hope** Austr.
19 C2 **Mount Isa** Austr.
18 A2 **Mount Magnet** Austr.
20 A2 **Mount Manara** Austr.
22 C1 **Mount Maunganui** N.Z.
105 E2 **Mount Pleasant** *IA* U.S.A.
108 C2 **Mount Pleasant** *MI* U.S.A.
107 E2 **Mount Pleasant** *TX* U.S.A.
67 A3 **Mount's Bay** U.K.
102 B2 **Mount Shasta** U.S.A.
108 B3 **Mount Vernon** *IL* U.S.A.
108 C2 **Mount Vernon** *OH* U.S.A.
102 B1 **Mount Vernon** *WA* U.S.A.
19 D2 **Moura** Austr.
83 E3 **Mourdi, Dépression du**
        depr. Chad
65 C1 **Mourne Mountains** U.K.
68 A2 **Mouscron** Belgium
83 D3 **Moussoro** Chad
26 C2 **Moutong** Indon.
83 C2 **Mouydir, Monts du** *plat.* Alg.
91 C2 **Mouzon** France
65 B1 **Moy** r. Rep. of Ireland
85 B4 **Moyale** Eth.
91 C3 **Moyeni** Lesotho
45 D2 **Moyynty** Kazakh.
89 C3 **Mozambique** *country* Africa
81 G5 **Mozambique Channel** Africa
57 E2 **Mozhaysk** Rus. Fed.
87 D3 **Mpanda** Tanz.
89 C2 **Mpika** Zambia
89 C1 **Mporokoso** Zambia
91 C2 **Mpumalanga** *prov.* S. Africa
56 C2 **Mshinskaya** Rus. Fed.
75 D2 **M'Sila** Alg.
57 D2 **Msta** r. Rus. Fed.
57 D2 **Mstinskiy Most** Rus. Fed.
57 D3 **Mstsislaw** Belarus
57 E3 **Mtsensk** Rus. Fed.
87 E4 **Mtwara** Tanz.
86 B3 **Muanda** Dem. Rep. Congo
30 B2 **Muang Khammouan** Laos
31 B2 **Muang Khôngz** Laos
30 B1 **Muang Ngoy** Laos
30 B2 **Muang Pakbeng** Laos
30 B2 **Muang Pakxan** Laos
30 B1 **Muang Sing** Laos
30 B2 **Muang Vangviang** Laos
30 B2 **Muang Xaignabouri** Laos
28 B1 **Muar** Malaysia
28 B2 **Muarabungo** Indon.
28 B2 **Muaradua** Indon.
29 C2 **Muaralaung** Indon.
28 A2 **Muarasiberut** Indon.
28 B2 **Muaratembesi** Indon.
29 C2 **Muarateweh** Indon.
87 D2 **Mubende** Uganda
83 D3 **Mubi** Nigeria
88 B2 **Muconda** Angola
123 E1 **Mucuri** Brazil
123 E1 **Mucuri** r. Brazil
34 A2 **Mudanjiang** China
34 A1 **Mudan Jiang** r. China
79 C2 **Mudanya** Turkey
69 E1 **Müden (Örtze)** Ger.

21 C2 **Mudgee** Austr.
31 A2 **Mudon** Myanmar
48 B1 **Mudurnu** Turkey
89 C2 **Mueda** Moz.
89 B2 **Mufulira** Zambia
88 B2 **Mufumbwe** Zambia
79 C3 **Muğla** Turkey
84 B2 **Muhammad Qol** Sudan
69 F2 **Mühlberg** Ger.
69 E2 **Mühlhausen (Thüringen)**
        Ger.
31 B3 **Mui Ca Mau** *c.* Vietnam
65 C2 **Muine Bheag** Rep. of Ireland
89 C2 **Muite** Moz.
33 B2 **Muju** S. Korea
58 A2 **Mukacheve** Ukr.
29 C1 **Mukah** *Sarawak* Malaysia
31 B2 **Mukdahan** Thai.
18 A3 **Mukinbudin** Austr.
28 B2 **Mukomuko** Indon.
89 C2 **Mulanje, Mount** Malawi
69 F2 **Mulde** r. Ger.
112 A2 **Mulegé** Mex.
107 C2 **Muleshoe** U.S.A.
74 C2 **Mulhacén** *mt.* Spain
68 C2 **Mülheim an der Ruhr** Ger.
73 D2 **Mulhouse** France
34 B2 **Muling** China
34 B1 **Muling** r. China
64 B2 **Mull** i. U.K.
21 C2 **Mullaley** Austr.
104 C2 **Mullen** U.S.A.
29 C1 **Muller, Pegunungan**
        mts Indon.
18 A2 **Mullewa** Austr.
65 C2 **Mullingar** Rep. of Ireland
64 B3 **Mull of Galloway** *c.* U.K.
64 B2 **Mull of Kintyre** *hd* U.K.
64 A3 **Mull of Oa** *hd* U.K.
88 B2 **Mulobezi** Zambia
42 B1 **Multan** Pak.
41 B3 **Mumbai** India
88 B2 **Mumbwa** Zambia
113 D2 **Muna** Mex.
69 E2 **Münchberg** Ger.
        München Ger. *see* Munich
108 B2 **Muncie** U.S.A.
18 B3 **Mundrabilla** Austr.
86 C2 **Mungbere** Dem. Rep. Congo
43 C2 **Munger** India
20 A1 **Mungeranie** Austr.
21 C1 **Mungindi** Austr.
70 C2 **Munich** Ger.
123 D3 **Muniz Freire** Brazil
69 E1 **Münster** *Niedersachsen* Ger.
68 C2 **Münster** *Nordrhein-Westfalen*
        Ger.
65 B2 **Munster** *reg.* Rep. of Ireland
68 C2 **Münsterland** *reg.* Ger.
30 B1 **Muong Nhie** Vietnam
60 H2 **Muonio** Fin.
60 H2 **Muonioälven** r. Fin./Sweden
85 C4 **Muqdisho** Somalia
71 D2 **Mur** r. Austria
87 C3 **Muramvya** Burundi
87 D3 **Muranga** Kenya
49 C2 **Murat** r. Turkey
79 C2 **Muratlı** Turkey
18 A2 **Murchison** *watercourse*
        Austr.
75 C2 **Murcia** Spain
75 C2 **Mürefte** Turkey
78 B1 **Mureş** r. Romania
72 C3 **Muret** France
110 C1 **Murfreesboro** U.S.A.
45 D3 **Murghab** r. Afgh.
45 D3 **Murghob** Tajik.
123 D2 **Muriaé** Brazil
88 B1 **Muriege** Angola
69 F1 **Müritz** l. Ger.

54 C2 **Murmansk** Rus. Fed.
55 D3 **Murom** Rus. Fed.
34 D2 **Muroran** Japan
74 B1 **Muros** Spain
35 B4 **Muroto** Japan
35 B4 **Muroto-zaki** *pt* Japan
111 D1 **Murphy** U.S.A.
21 C1 **Murra Murra** Austr.
20 A3 **Murray** r. Austr.
96 B2 **Murray** r. Can.
108 B3 **Murray** U.S.A.
111 D2 **Murray, Lake** U.S.A.
20 A3 **Murray Bridge** Austr.
90 B3 **Murraysburg** S. Africa
20 B3 **Murrayville** Austr.
20 B2 **Murrumbidgee** r. Austr.
89 C2 **Murrupula** Moz.
21 D2 **Murrurundi** Austr.
77 C1 **Murska Sobota** Slovenia
22 C1 **Murupara** N.Z.
43 C2 **Murwara** India
21 D1 **Murwillumbah** Austr.
83 D2 **Murzūq** Libya
49 C2 **Muş** Turkey
78 B2 **Musala** *mt.* Bulg.
33 B1 **Musan** N. Korea
46 B3 **Musaymir** Yemen
47 C2 **Muscat** Oman
105 E2 **Muscatine** U.S.A.
18 C2 **Musgrave Ranges** *mts* Aus[tr.]
86 B3 **Mushie** Dem. Rep. Congo
28 B2 **Musi** r. Indon.
108 B2 **Muskegon** U.S.A.
107 D1 **Muskogee** U.S.A.
96 B2 **Muskwa** r. Can.
42 A1 **Muslimbagh** Pak.
46 A3 **Musmar** Sudan
87 D3 **Musoma** Tanz.
64 C3 **Musselburgh** U.K.
56 B2 **Mustjala** Estonia
21 D2 **Muswellbrook** Austr.
84 A2 **Mut** Egypt
89 C2 **Mutare** Zimbabwe
34 D2 **Mutsu** Japan
89 C2 **Mutuali** Moz.
60 I2 **Muurola** Fin.
38 A2 **Mu Us Shamo** *des.* China
88 A1 **Muxaluando** Angola
54 C2 **Muyezerskiy** Rus. Fed.
87 D3 **Muyinga** Burundi
44 B2 **Muynak** Uzbek.
42 B1 **Muzaffargarh** Pak.
43 C2 **Muzaffarpur** India
112 B2 **Múzquiz** Mex.
43 C1 **Muztag** *mt.* China
87 C3 **Mwanza** Dem. Rep. Congo
87 D3 **Mwanza** Tanz.
86 C3 **Mweka** Dem. Rep. Congo
89 B2 **Mwenda** Zambia
86 C3 **Mwene-Ditu**
        Dem. Rep. Congo
89 C3 **Mwenezi** Zimbabwe
87 C3 **Mweru, Lake**
        Dem. Rep. Congo/Zambia
86 C3 **Mwimba** Dem. Rep. Congo
88 B2 **Mwinilunga** Zambia
56 C3 **Myadzyel** Belarus
30 A2 **Myanaung** Myanmar
30 A1 **Myanmar** *country* Asia
31 A2 **Myaungmya** Myanmar
30 A1 **Myingyan** Myanmar
30 A1 **Myitkyina** Myanmar
59 C2 **Mykolayiv** Ukr.
79 C3 **Mykonos** Greece
79 C3 **Mykonos** *i.* Greece
54 E2 **Myla** Rus. Fed.
43 D2 **Mymensingh** Bangl.
30 A1 **Myohaung** Myanmar
33 B1 **Myŏnggan** N. Korea
56 C2 **Myory** Belarus

60 □B3 **Mýrdalsjökull** *ice cap*
Iceland
59 C2 **Myrhorod** Ukr.
58 C2 **Myronivka** Ukr.
111 E2 **Myrtle Beach** U.S.A.
21 C3 **Myrtleford** Austr.
102 B2 **Myrtle Point** U.S.A.
57 E2 **Myshkin** Rus. Fed.
71 C1 **Myślibórz** Pol.
41 B3 **Mysore** India
51 N2 **Mys Shmidta** Rus. Fed.
31 B2 **My Tho** Vietnam
79 C3 **Mytilini** Greece
57 E3 **Mytishchi** Rus. Fed.
91 C3 **Mzamomhle** S. Africa
89 C2 **Mzimba** Malawi
89 C2 **Mzuzu** Malawi

N

65 C2 **Naas** Rep. of Ireland
90 A2 **Nababeep** S. Africa
55 E1 **Naberezhnyye Chelny**
Rus. Fed.
27 D3 **Nabire** Indon.
48 B2 **Nãblus** West Bank
91 C1 **Naboomspruit** S. Africa
89 D1 **Nacala** Moz.
31 A2 **Nachuge** India
107 E2 **Nacogdoches** U.S.A.
112 B1 **Nacozari de García** Mex.
42 B2 **Nadiad** India
58 A2 **Nadvirna** Ukr.
54 C2 **Nadvoitsy** Rus. Fed.
54 G2 **Nadym** Rus. Fed.
61 F4 **Næstved** Denmark
79 B3 **Nafpaktos** Greece
79 B3 **Nafplio** Greece
83 D1 **Nafūsah, Jabal** *hills* Libya
46 B2 **Nafy** Saudi Arabia
32 B1 **Naga** Phil.
98 B1 **Nagagami** *r.* Can.
35 C3 **Nagano** Japan
35 C3 **Nagaoka** Japan
43 D2 **Nagaon** India
42 B1 **Nagar** India
42 B2 **Nagar Parkar** Pak.
35 A4 **Nagasaki** Japan
35 B4 **Nagato** Japan
42 B2 **Nagaur** India
41 B4 **Nagercoil** India
42 A2 **Nagha Kalat** Pak.
40 D2 **Nagina** India
35 C3 **Nagoya** Japan
43 B2 **Nagpur** India
36 C2 **Nagqu** China
71 D2 **Nagyatád** Hungary
71 D2 **Nagykanizsa** Hungary
96 B1 **Nahanni Butte** Can.
44 A3 **Nahāvand** Iran
69 E1 **Nahrendorf** Ger.
121 A5 **Nahuel Huapi, Lago** *l.* Arg.
99 D1 **Nain** Can.
49 D2 **Nā'īn** Iran
64 C2 **Nairn** U.K.
87 D3 **Nairobi** Kenya
87 D3 **Naivasha** Kenya
49 D2 **Najafābād** Iran
46 B2 **Najd** *reg.* Saudi Arabia
74 C1 **Nájera** Spain
33 C1 **Najin** N. Korea
46 B3 **Najrān** Saudi Arabia
Nakambé *watercourse*
Burkina/Ghana *see*
White Volta
35 C3 **Nakatsugawa** Japan
46 A3 **Nakfa** Eritrea

34 B2 **Nakhodka** Rus. Fed.
31 B2 **Nakhon Pathom** Thai.
31 B2 **Nakhon Ratchasima** Thai.
31 B2 **Nakhon Sawan** Thai.
31 A3 **Nakhon Si Thammarat** Thai.
98 B1 **Nakina** Can.
89 C1 **Nakonde** Zambia
61 F4 **Nakskov** Denmark
87 D3 **Nakuru** Kenya
96 C2 **Nakusp** Can.
43 D2 **Nalbari** India
55 D4 **Nal'chik** Rus. Fed.
83 D1 **Nālūt** Libya
91 C2 **Namahadi** S. Africa
45 D2 **Namangan** Uzbek.
90 A2 **Namaqualand** *reg.* Namibia
90 A2 **Namaqualand** *reg.* S. Africa
19 E2 **Nambour** Austr.
21 D2 **Nambucca Heads** Austr.
33 B2 **Namch'ŏn** N. Korea
31 A2 **Nam Chon Reservoir** Thai.
43 D1 **Nam Co** *salt l.* China
30 B1 **Nam Đinh** Vietnam
88 A3 **Namib Desert** Namibia
88 A2 **Namibe** Angola
88 A3 **Namibia** *country* Africa
40 D2 **Namjagbarwa Feng** *mt.*
China
27 C3 **Namlea** Indon.
21 C2 **Namoi** *r.* Austr.
102 C2 **Nampa** U.S.A.
82 B3 **Nampala** Mali
33 B2 **Namp'o** N. Korea
89 C2 **Nampula** Moz.
30 A1 **Namrup** India
30 A1 **Namsang** Myanmar
60 F3 **Namsos** Norway
31 A2 **Nam Tok** Thai.
51 J2 **Namtsy** Rus. Fed.
30 A1 **Namtu** Myanmar
68 B2 **Namur** Belgium
88 B2 **Namwala** Zambia
33 B2 **Namwŏn** S. Korea
30 A1 **Namya** R Myanmar
30 B2 **Nan** Thai.
96 B3 **Nanaimo** Can.
39 B3 **Nan'an** China
90 A1 **Nananib Plateau** Namibia
35 C3 **Nanao** Japan
30 B3 **Nanchang** *Jiangxi* China
39 B3 **Nanchang** *Jiangxi* China
38 A2 **Nanchong** China
31 A3 **Nancowry** *i.* India
73 D2 **Nancy** France
43 C1 **Nanda Devi** *mt.* India
09 A0 **Nandan** China
41 B3 **Nānded** India
42 B2 **Nandurbar** India
41 B3 **Nandyal** India
39 B3 **Nanfeng** China
86 B2 **Nanga Eboko** Cameroon
29 C2 **Nangahpinoh** Indon.
45 D3 **Nanga Parbat** *mt.*
Jammu and Kashmir
29 C2 **Nangatayap** Indon.
38 B2 **Nangong** China
87 D3 **Nangulangwa** Tanz.
38 C2 **Nanhui** China
38 B2 **Nanjing** China
Nanking China *see* **Nanjing**
88 A2 **Nankova** Angola
39 B3 **Nan Ling** *mts* China
39 A3 **Nanning** China
95 H2 **Nanortalik** Greenland
39 A3 **Nanpan Jiang** *r.* China
43 C2 **Nanpara** India
39 B3 **Nanping** China
37 E3 **Nansei-shotō** *is* Japan
72 B2 **Nantes** France
38 C2 **Nantong** China

109 F2 **Nantucket Island** U.S.A.
123 D1 **Nanuque** Brazil
32 B2 **Nanusa, Kepulauan**
is Indon.
39 B3 **Nanxiong** China
38 B2 **Nanyang** China
38 B2 **Nanzhang** China
99 C1 **Naococane, Lac** *l.* Can.
42 A2 **Naokot** Pak.
103 B3 **Napa** U.S.A.
94 D2 **Napaktulik Lake** Can.
95 H2 **Napasoq** Greenland
22 C1 **Napier** N.Z.
76 B2 **Naples** Italy
111 D3 **Naples** U.S.A.
118 A2 **Napo** *r.* Ecuador
Napoli Italy *see* **Naples**
82 B3 **Nara** Mali
61 I4 **Narach** Belarus
20 B3 **Naracoorte** Austr.
113 C2 **Naranjos** Mex.
31 B3 **Narathiwat** Thai.
73 C3 **Narbonne** France
31 A2 **Narcondam Island** India
95 G1 **Nares Strait** Can./Greenland
90 A1 **Narib** Namibia
55 D4 **Narimanov** Rus. Fed.
35 D3 **Narita** Japan
42 B3 **Narmada** *r.* India
42 B2 **Narnaul** India
76 B2 **Narni** Italy
58 B1 **Narodychi** Ukr.
57 E2 **Naro-Fominsk** Rus. Fed.
21 D3 **Narooma** Austr.
56 C3 **Narowlya** Belarus
21 C2 **Narrabri** Austr.
21 C2 **Narrandera** Austr.
21 C2 **Narromine** Austr.
56 C2 **Narva** Estonia
56 C2 **Narva Bay** Estonia/Rus. Fed.
60 G2 **Narvik** Norway
56 C2 **Narvskoye**
Vodokhranilishche *resr*
Estonia/Rus. Fed.
54 E2 **Nar'yan-Mar** Rus. Fed.
45 D2 **Naryn** Kyrg.
42 B2 **Nashik** India
109 E2 **Nashua** U.S.A.
110 C1 **Nashville** U.S.A.
85 B4 **Nāqir** Sudan
96 B4 **Nass** *r.* Can.
114 C2 **Nassau** Bahamas
84 B2 **Nasser, Lake** *resr* Egypt
61 F4 **Nässjö** Sweden
98 C1 **Nastapoca** *r.* Can.
90 O1 **Nastapoka Islands** Can.
88 B3 **Nata** Botswana
119 E2 **Natal** Brazil
99 D1 **Natashquan** Can.
99 D1 **Natashquan** *r.* Can.
110 B2 **Natchez** U.S.A.
110 B2 **Natchitoches** U.S.A.
21 C3 **Nathalia** Austr.
75 D1 **Nati, Punta** *pt* Spain
82 C3 **Natitingou** Benin
119 D3 **Natividade** Brazil
35 D3 **Natori** Japan
29 B1 **Natuna, Kepulauan** *is* Indon.
29 B1 **Natuna Besar** *i.* Indon.
88 A3 **Nauchas** Namibia
69 F1 **Nauen** Ger.
56 B2 **Naujoji Akmenė** Lith.
69 E2 **Naumburg (Saale)** Ger.
17 E3 **Nauru** *country*
S. Pacific Ocean
113 C2 **Nautla** Mex.
56 C3 **Navahrudak** Belarus
74 B2 **Navalmoral de la Mata**
Spain
74 B2 **Navalvillar de Pela** Spain

65 C2 Navan Rep. of Ireland
56 C2 Navapolatsk Belarus
51 M2 Navarin, Mys c. Rus. Fed.
121 B6 Navarino, Isla i. Chile
64 B1 Naver r. U.K.
57 D3 Navlya Rus. Fed.
78 C2 Năvodari Romania
45 C2 Navoi Uzbek.
112 B2 Navojoa Mex.
112 B2 Navolato Mex.
42 A2 Nawabshah Pak.
30 A1 Nawnghkio Myanmar
30 A1 Nawngleng Myanmar
49 C2 Naxçıvan Azer.
79 C3 Naxos i. Greece
112 B2 Nayar Mex.
34 D2 Nayoro Japan
48 B2 Nazareth Israel
112 B2 Nazas Mex.
112 B2 Nazas r. Mex.
118 A3 Nazca Peru
79 C3 Nazilli Turkey
85 B4 Nazrēt Eth.
47 C2 Nazwá Oman
89 B1 Nchelenge Zambia
90 B1 Ncojane Botswana
88 A1 N'dalatando Angola
86 C2 Ndélé C.A.R.
86 B3 Ndendé Gabon
83 D3 Ndjamena Chad
89 B2 Ndola Zambia
65 C1 Neagh, Lough l. U.K.
18 C2 Neale, Lake salt flat Austr.
79 B2 Nea Roda Greece
67 B3 Neath U.K.
21 C1 Nebine Creek r. Austr.
44 B3 Nebitdag Turkm.
118 B1 Neblina, Pico da mt. Brazil
57 D2 Nebolchi Rus. Fed.
104 C2 Nebraska state U.S.A.
105 D2 Nebraska City U.S.A.
76 B3 Nebrodi, Monti mts Sicily
    Italy
121 C4 Necochea Arg.
99 C1 Nedlouc, Lac l. Can.
103 D4 Needles U.S.A.
97 E2 Neepawa Can.
55 E3 Neftekamsk Rus. Fed.
50 F2 Nefteyugansk Rus. Fed.
88 A1 Negage Angola
85 B4 Negēlē Eth.
118 A2 Negra, Punta pt Peru
31 A2 Negrais, Cape Myanmar
121 B5 Negro r. Arg.
118 C2 Negro r. S. America
120 C4 Negro r. Uru.
74 B2 Negro, Cabo c. Morocco
32 B2 Negros i. Phil.
37 E1 Nehe China
38 A3 Neijiang China
97 D2 Neilburg Can.
38 A1 Nei Mongol Zizhiqu aut. reg.
    China
118 A1 Neiva Col.
97 E2 Nejanilini Lake Can.
85 B4 Nek'emtē Eth.
57 F2 Nekrasovskoye Rus. Fed.
57 D2 Nelidovo Rus. Fed.
41 B3 Nellore India
96 C3 Nelson Can.
97 E2 Nelson r. Can.
22 B2 Nelson N.Z.
20 B3 Nelson, Cape Austr.
21 D2 Nelson Bay Austr.
97 E2 Nelson House Can.
102 E1 Nelson Reservoir U.S.A.
91 D2 Nelspruit S. Africa
82 B3 Néma Maur.
56 B2 Neman Rus. Fed.
72 C2 Nemours France

34 D2 Nemuro Japan
58 B2 Nemyriv Ukr.
65 B2 Nenagh Rep. of Ireland
67 D2 Nene r. U.K.
37 E1 Nenjiang China
105 E3 Neosho U.S.A.
43 C2 Nepal country Asia
43 C2 Nepalganj Nepal
103 D3 Nephi U.S.A.
65 B1 Nephin hill Rep. of Ireland
65 B1 Nephin Beg Range hills
    Rep. of Ireland
99 D2 Nepisiguit r. Can.
87 C2 Nepoko r. Dem. Rep. Congo
72 C3 Nérac France
21 D1 Nerang Austr.
37 D1 Nerchinsk Rus. Fed.
57 F2 Nerekhta Rus. Fed.
77 C2 Neretva r. Bos.-Herz./Croatia
88 B2 Neriquinha Angola
56 B3 Neris r. Lith.
57 E2 Nerl' r. Rus. Fed.
54 F2 Nerokhi Rus. Fed.
122 C1 Nerópolis Brazil
51 J3 Neryungri Rus. Fed.
60 □C2 Neskaupstaður Iceland
64 B2 Ness, Loch l. U.K.
104 D3 Ness City U.S.A.
79 B2 Nestos r. Greece
68 B1 Netherlands country Europe
115 D3 Netherlands Antilles terr.
    West Indies
95 G2 Nettilling Lake Can.
69 F1 Neubrandenburg Ger.
73 D2 Neuchâtel Switz.
68 C2 Neuerburg Ger.
68 B3 Neufchâteau Belgium
73 D2 Neufchâteau France
72 C2 Neufchâtel-en-Bray France
67 D2 Neuhof Ger.
70 B1 Neumünster Ger.
70 B2 Neunkirchen Ger.
121 B4 Neuquén Arg.
121 B4 Neuquén r. Arg.
69 F1 Neuruppin Ger.
68 C2 Neuss Ger.
69 D1 Neustadt am Rübenberge
    Ger.
69 E3 Neustadt an der Aisch Ger.
69 F1 Neustrelitz Ger.
68 C2 Neuwied Ger.
105 E3 Nevada U.S.A.
103 C3 Nevada state U.S.A.
74 C2 Nevada, Sierra mts Spain
103 B2 Nevada, Sierra mts U.S.A.
56 C2 Nevel' Rus. Fed.
73 C2 Nevers France
21 C2 Nevertire Austr.
77 C2 Nevesinje Bos.-Herz.
55 D4 Nevinnomyssk Rus. Fed.
96 B2 Neya Austr.
108 B3 New Albany U.S.A.
119 C1 New Amsterdam Guyana
109 E2 Newark NJ U.S.A.
108 C2 Newark OH U.S.A.
66 C2 Newark-on-Trent U.K.
109 E2 New Bedford U.S.A.
111 E1 New Bern U.S.A.
111 D2 Newberry U.S.A.
107 E2 New Boston U.S.A.
107 D3 New Braunfels U.S.A.
65 C2 Newbridge Rep. of Ireland
99 D2 New Brunswick prov. Can.
67 C3 Newbury U.K.
17 E4 New Caledonia terr.
    S. Pacific Ocean
21 D2 Newcastle Austr.
99 D2 Newcastle Can.
91 C2 Newcastle S. Africa
65 D1 Newcastle U.K.

108 C2 New Castle U.S.A.
104 C2 Newcastle U.S.A.
66 B2 Newcastle-under-Lyme U.K.
66 C1 Newcastle upon Tyne U.K.
65 B2 Newcastle West
    Rep. of Ireland
42 B2 New Delhi India
96 C3 New Denver Can.
21 D2 New England Range
    mts Austr.
99 E2 Newfoundland i. Can.
99 E1 Newfoundland prov. Can.
99 D2 New Glasgow Can.
27 D3 New Guinea i. Indon./P.N.G.
109 E2 New Hampshire state U.S.A.
109 E2 New Haven U.S.A.
96 B2 New Hazelton Can.
    New Hebrides country
    S. Pacific Ocean see Vanuatu
110 B2 New Iberia U.S.A.
109 E3 New Jersey state U.S.A.
98 C2 New Liskeard Can.
18 A2 Newman Austr.
106 B2 New Mexico state U.S.A.
110 B3 New Orleans U.S.A.
108 C2 New Philadelphia U.S.A.
22 B1 New Plymouth N.Z.
67 C3 Newport England U.K.
67 B3 Newport Wales U.K.
110 B1 Newport AR U.S.A.
102 B2 Newport OR U.S.A.
109 E2 Newport RI U.S.A.
109 E2 Newport VT U.S.A.
102 C1 Newport WA U.S.A.
109 D3 Newport News U.S.A.
111 E3 New Providence i. Bahamas
67 A3 Newquay U.K.
110 B2 New Roads U.S.A.
65 C2 New Ross Rep. of Ireland
65 C1 Newry U.K.
    New Siberia Islands
    Rus. Fed. see
    Novosibirskiye Ostrova
20 B2 New South Wales
    state Austr.
105 D2 Newton IA U.S.A.
105 D3 Newton KS U.S.A.
67 B3 Newton Abbot U.K.
64 B3 Newton Stewart U.K.
65 B2 Newtown Rep. of Ireland
67 B2 Newtown U.K.
104 C1 New Town U.S.A.
65 D1 Newtownabbey U.K.
65 D1 Newtownards U.K.
64 C3 Newtown St Boswells U.K.
65 C1 Newtownstewart U.K.
105 E2 New Ulm U.S.A.
109 E2 New York U.S.A.
109 D2 New York state U.S.A.
22 B2 New Zealand country
    Oceania
47 C2 Neyrīz Iran
44 B3 Neyshābūr Iran
113 C3 Nezahualcóyotl, Presa
    resr Mex.
29 B1 Ngabang Indon.
43 C2 Ngamring China
43 C1 Ngangla Ringco salt l. China
45 E3 Nganglong Kangri mt. China
43 C1 Nganglong Kangri mts
    China
43 C1 Ngangzê Co salt l. China
30 A2 Ngao Thai.
86 B2 Ngaoundéré Cameroon
22 C1 Ngaruawahia N.Z.
30 A2 Ngathainggyaung Myanmar
86 B3 Ngo Congo
31 B2 Ngoc Linh mt. Vietnam
83 D4 Ngol Bembo Nigeria
36 C2 Ngoring Hu l. China

83 D3 **Ngourti** Niger
83 D3 **Nguigmi** Niger
27 D2 **Ngulu** atoll Micronesia
83 D3 **Nguru** Nigeria
91 D2 **Ngwelezana** S. Africa
89 C2 **Nhamalabué** Moz.
31 B2 **Nha Trang** Vietnam
20 B3 **Nhill** Austr.
91 D2 **Nhlangano** Swaziland
19 C1 **Nhulunbuy** Austr.
109 D2 **Niagara Falls** Can.
82 C3 **Niamey** Niger
87 C2 **Niangara** Dem. Rep. Congo
82 B3 **Niangay, Lac** l. Mali
28 A1 **Nias** i. Indon.
114 B3 **Nicaragua** country
   Central America
114 B3 **Nicaragua, Lago de** l. Nic.
73 D1 **Nice** France
41 D1 **Nicobar Islands** India
73 D3 **Nicosia** Cyprus
114 B4 **Nicoya, Golfo de** b.
   Costa Rica
56 B2 **Nida** Lith.
71 E1 **Nidzica** Pol.
70 B1 **Niebüll** Ger.
69 D2 **Niederaula** Ger.
86 B2 **Niefang** Equat. Guinea
69 F1 **Niemegk** Ger.
69 D1 **Nienburg (Weser)** Ger.
68 B1 **Nieuwe-Niedorp** Neth.
119 C1 **Nieuw Nickerie** Suriname
90 A3 **Nieuwoudtville** S. Africa
68 A2 **Nieuwpoort** Belgium
48 B2 **Niğde** Turkey
83 D3 **Niger** country Africa
83 C4 **Niger** r. Africa
83 C4 **Niger, Mouths of the** Nigeria
83 C4 **Nigeria** country Africa
98 B2 **Nighthawk Lake** Can.
79 B2 **Nigrita** Greece
35 C3 **Niigata** Japan
35 B4 **Niihama** Japan
35 C4 **Nii-jima** i. Japan
35 C3 **Niitsu** Japan
68 B2 **Nijmegen** Neth.
68 C1 **Nijverdal** Neth.
60 J2 **Nikel'** Rus. Fed.
50 C2 **Nikopol'** Ukr.
48 B1 **Niksar** Turkey
47 D2 **Nikshahr** Iran
77 C2 **Nikšić** Yugo.
84 B1 **Nile** r. Africa
108 B2 **Niles** U.S.A.
42 D2 **Nimach** India
73 C3 **Nîmes** France
21 C3 **Nimmitabel** Austr.
85 B4 **Nimule** Sudan
21 C1 **Nindigully** Austr.
41 B4 **Nine Degree Channel** India
21 C3 **Ninety Mile Beach** Austr.
22 B1 **Ninety Mile Beach** N.Z.
38 C3 **Ningbo** China
39 B3 **Ningde** China
39 B3 **Ningdu** China
39 C3 **Ningguo** China
38 C3 **Ninghai** China
   Ningjiang China see
   Songyuan
36 C2 **Ningjing Shan** mts China
38 A2 **Ningxia** aut. reg. China
38 B2 **Ningyang** China
30 B1 **Ninh Binh** Vietnam
31 B2 **Ninh Hoa** Vietnam
34 D2 **Ninohe** Japan
105 D2 **Niobrara** r. U.S.A.
82 B3 **Niono** Mali
82 B3 **Nioro** Mali
72 B2 **Niort** France

97 D2 **Nipawin** Can.
98 B2 **Nipigon** Can.
98 B2 **Nipigon, Lake** Can.
99 D1 **Nipishish Lake** Can.
98 C2 **Nipissing, Lake** Can.
103 C3 **Nipton** U.S.A.
119 D3 **Niquelândia** Brazil
41 B3 **Nirmal** India
77 D2 **Niš** Yugo.
77 D2 **Nišava** r. Yugo.
76 B3 **Niscemi** Sicily Italy
35 B4 **Nishino-omote** Japan
123 D2 **Niterói** Brazil
64 C3 **Nith** r. U.K.
71 D2 **Nitra** Slovakia
17 G4 **Niue** terr. S. Pacific Ocean
60 H3 **Nivala** Fin.
68 B2 **Nivelles** Belgium
41 B3 **Nizamabad** India
55 E3 **Nizhnekamsk** Rus. Fed.
51 H3 **Nizhneudinsk** Rus. Fed.
50 C2 **Nizhnevartovsk** Rus. Fed.
57 F3 **Nizhniy Kislyay** Rus. Fed.
55 D3 **Nizhniy Lomov** Rus. Fed.
55 D3 **Nizhniy Novgorod** Rus. Fed.
54 E2 **Nizhniy Odes** Rus. Fed.
54 E3 **Nizhniy Tagil** Rus. Fed.
51 G2 **Nizhnyaya Tunguska** r.
   Rus. Fed.
59 C1 **Nizhyn** Ukr.
87 D3 **Njinjo** Tanz.
87 D3 **Njombe** Tanz.
89 C2 **Nkhotakota** Malawi
86 A2 **Nkongsamba** Cameroon
91 C3 **Nkululeko** S. Africa
91 C3 **Nkwenkwezi** S. Africa
35 B4 **Nobeoka** Japan
20 B1 **Noccundra** Austr.
112 A1 **Nogales** Mex.
106 A2 **Nogales** U.S.A.
72 C2 **Nogent-le-Rotrou** France
57 E2 **Noginsk** Rus. Fed.
42 B2 **Nohar** India
68 C3 **Nohfelden** Ger.
72 B2 **Noirmoutier, Île de** i. France
72 B2 **Noirmoutier-en-l'Île** France
35 C4 **Nojima-zaki** c. Japan
42 B2 **Nokha** India
61 H3 **Nokia** Fin.
42 A2 **Nok Kundi** Pak.
86 B2 **Nola** C.A.R.
54 D3 **Nolinsk** Rus. Fed.
91 C3 **Nomonde** S. Africa
91 D2 **Nondweni** S. Africa
30 B2 **Nong Khai** Thai.
20 A2 **Nonning** Austr.
112 B2 **Nonoava** Mex.
33 B2 **Nonsan** S. Korea
31 B2 **Nonthaburi** Thai.
90 B3 **Nonzwakazi** S. Africa
45 C3 **Norak** Tajik.
98 C2 **Noranda** Can.
50 C1 **Nordaustlandet** i. Svalbard
96 C2 **Nordegg** Can.
68 C1 **Norden** Ger.
51 H3 **Nordenshel'da, Arkhipelag**
   is Rus. Fed.
68 C1 **Norderney** Ger.
68 C1 **Norderney** i. Ger.
69 E1 **Norderstedt** Ger.
61 E3 **Nordfjordeid** Norway
69 E2 **Nordhausen** Ger.
69 D1 **Nordholz** Ger.
68 C1 **Nordhorn** Ger.
60 I1 **Nordkapp** c. Norway
60 F3 **Nordli** Norway
70 C2 **Nördlingen** Ger.
60 G3 **Nordmaling** Sweden
62 B1 **Norðoyar** i. Faroe Is
65 C2 **Nore** r. Rep. of Ireland

105 D2 **Norfolk** NE U.S.A.
109 D3 **Norfolk** VA U.S.A.
17 E4 **Norfolk Island** terr.
   S. Pacific Ocean
61 E3 **Norheimsund** Norway
50 G2 **Noril'sk** Rus. Fed.
107 D1 **Norman** U.S.A.
   Normandes, Îles is Europe
   see Channel Islands
19 D1 **Normanton** Austr.
61 G4 **Norrköping** Sweden
61 G4 **Norrtälje** Sweden
18 B3 **Norseman** Austr.
60 G3 **Norsjö** Sweden
66 C1 **Northallerton** U.K.
18 A2 **Northampton** Austr.
67 C2 **Northampton** U.K.
41 D3 **North Andaman** i. India
97 D2 **North Battleford** Can.
00 C2 **North Bay** Can.
98 C1 **North Belcher Islands** Can.
64 C2 **North Berwick** U.K.
   North Cape Norway see
   Nordkapp
22 B3 **North Cape** c. N.Z.
98 A1 **North Caribou Lake** Can.
111 E1 **North Carolina** state U.S.A.
98 B2 **North Channel** lake channel
   Can.
64 A3 **North Channel** U.K.
96 B3 **North Cowichan** Can.
104 C1 **North Dakota** state U.S.A.
67 C3 **North Downs** hills U.K.
111 E3 **Northeast Providence**
   Channel Bahamas
69 D2 **Northeim** Ger.
90 A2 **Northern Cape** prov.
   S. Africa
97 E2 **Northern Indian Lake** Can.
65 C1 **Northern Ireland** prov. U.K.
16 D2 **Northern Mariana Islands**
   terr. N. Pacific Ocean
18 C1 **Northern Territory**
   admin. div. Austr.
64 C2 **North Esk** r. U.K.
105 E2 **Northfield** U.S.A.
67 D3 **North Foreland** c. U.K.
22 B1 **North Island** N.Z.
97 E2 **North Knife Lake** Can.
30 A1 **North Lakhimpur** India
104 C3 **North Platte** U.S.A.
104 C2 **North Platte** r. U.S.A.
64 C1 **North Ronaldsay** i. U.K.
62 D2 **North Sea** sea Europe
98 A1 **North Spirit Lake** l. Can.
21 D1 **North Stradbroke island**
   Austr.
22 B1 **North Taranaki Bight** b. N.Z.
98 C1 **North Twin Island** Can.
66 B1 **North Tyne** r. U.K.
64 A2 **North Uist** i. U.K.
99 D2 **Northumberland Strait** Can.
90 C2 **North West** prov. S. Africa
18 A2 **North West Cape** Austr.
111 E3 **Northwest Providence**
   Channel Bahamas
99 E1 **North West River** Can.
96 B1 **Northwest Territories**
   admin. div. Can.
66 C1 **North York Moors** moorland
   U.K.
108 C3 **Norton** U.S.A.
89 C2 **Norton** Zimbabwe
108 C2 **Norwalk** U.S.A.
61 F3 **Norway** country Europe
97 E2 **Norway House** Can.
128 A3 **Norwegian Sea**
   N. Atlantic Ocean
67 D2 **Norwich** U.K.
109 E2 **Norwich** CT U.S.A.

109 D2 Norwich NY U.S.A.
34 D2 Noshiro Japan
59 C1 Nosivka Ukr.
90 B2 Nosop watercourse Africa
54 E2 Nosovaya Rus. Fed.
47 C2 Noṣraṭābād Iran
       Nossob watercourse Africa
       see Nosop
89 □D2 Nosy Bé i. Madag.
89 □E2 Nosy Boraha i. Madag.
71 D1 Noteć r. Pol.
61 E4 Notodden Norway
35 C3 Noto-hantō pen. Japan
99 D2 Notre Dame, Monts
       mts Can.
99 E2 Notre Dame Bay Can.
98 C1 Nottaway r. Can.
67 C2 Nottingham U.K.
82 A2 Nouâdhibou Maur.
82 A3 Nouakchott Maur.
82 A3 Nouâmghâr Maur.
82 B3 Nouna Burkina
122 B2 Nova Esperança Brazil
123 D2 Nova Friburgo Brazil
77 C1 Nova Gradiška Croatia
122 C2 Nova Granada Brazil
123 D2 Nova Iguaçu Brazil
59 C2 Nova Kakhovka Ukr.
123 D1 Nova Lima Brazil
122 B2 Nova Londrina Brazil
59 C2 Nova Odesa Ukr.
118 B1 Nova Paraíso Brazil
99 D2 Nova Scotia prov. Can.
123 D1 Nova Venécia Brazil
51 K1 Novaya Sibir', Ostrov i.
       Rus. Fed.
54 E1 Novaya Zemlya is Rus. Fed.
71 D2 Nové Zámky Slovakia
59 C1 Novhorod-Sivers'kyy Ukr.
78 B2 Novi Iskŭr Bulg.
76 A2 Novi Ligure Italy
77 D2 Novi Pazar Yugo.
77 C1 Novi Sad Yugo.
55 D3 Novoanninskiy Rus. Fed.
118 B1 Novo Aripuanã Brazil
59 D2 Novoazovs'k Ukr.
59 E2 Novocherkassk Rus. Fed.
54 D2 Novodvinsk Rus. Fed.
120 C3 Novo Hamburgo Brazil
122 C2 Novo Horizonte Brazil
58 B1 Novohrad-Volyns'kyy Ukr.
71 D2 Novo Mesto Slovenia
59 D3 Novomikhaylovskiy
       Rus. Fed.
57 E3 Novomoskovsk Rus. Fed.
59 D2 Novomoskovs'k Ukr.
59 C2 Novomyrhorod Ukr.
59 C2 Novooleksiyivka Ukr.
59 D2 Novopskov Ukr.
59 D3 Novorossiysk Rus. Fed.
56 C2 Novorzhev Rus. Fed.
55 E3 Novosergiyevka Rus. Fed.
59 D2 Novoshakhtinsk Rus. Fed.
50 G3 Novosibirsk Rus. Fed.
51 K1 Novosibirskiye Ostrova is
       Rus. Fed.
57 E3 Novosil' Rus. Fed.
57 D2 Novosokol'niki Rus. Fed.
59 C2 Novotroyits'ke Ukr.
59 C2 Novoukrayinka Ukr.
58 A1 Novovolyns'k Ukr.
57 D3 Novozybkov Rus. Fed.
71 D2 Nový Jičín Czech Rep.
54 E2 Novyy Bor Rus. Fed.
59 D1 Novyy Oskol Rus. Fed.
54 G2 Novyy Port Rus. Fed.
50 G2 Novyy Urengoy Rus. Fed.
37 E1 Novyy Urgal Rus. Fed.
71 D1 Nowogard Pol.
21 D2 Nowra Austr.

49 D2 Now Shahr Iran
42 B1 Nowshera Pak.
71 E2 Nowy Sącz Pol.
71 E2 Nowy Targ Pol.
55 G2 Noyabr'sk Rus. Fed.
73 C2 Noyon France
89 C2 Nsanje Malawi
86 B3 Ntandembele
       Dem. Rep. Congo
87 D3 Ntungamo Uganda
47 C2 Nu'aym reg. Oman
84 B2 Nubian Desert Sudan
118 A3 Nudo Coropuna mt. Peru
97 E1 Nueltin Lake Can.
121 A5 Nueva Lubecka Arg.
113 B2 Nueva Rosita Mex.
112 B1 Nueva Casas Grandes
       Mex.
112 B2 Nuevo Ideal Mex.
113 C2 Nuevo Laredo Mex.
85 C4 Nugaal watercourse Somalia
73 C2 Nuits-St-Georges France
30 A1 Nu Jiang r. China
44 B2 Nukus Uzbek.
18 B2 Nullagine Austr.
18 B3 Nullarbor Plain Austr.
83 D4 Numan Nigeria
35 C3 Numazu Japan
61 E3 Numedal val. Norway
27 C3 Numfoor i. Indon.
21 C3 Numurkah Austr.
95 J3 Nunap Isua c. Greenland
97 E1 Nunavut admin. div. Can.
67 C2 Nuneaton U.K.
74 B1 Nuñomoral Spain
76 A2 Nuoro Sardinia Italy
46 B2 Nuqrah Saudi Arabia
20 A2 Nuriootpa Austr.
61 I3 Nurmes Fin.
69 E3 Nürnberg Ger.
30 A1 Nu Shan mts China
42 A2 Nushki Pak.
95 H2 Nuuk Greenland
95 H1 Nuussuaq Greenland
95 H1 Nuussuaq pen. Greenland
46 A2 Nuweiba el Muzeina Egypt
90 B3 Nuweveldberge mts
       S. Africa
54 F2 Nyagan' Rus. Fed.
43 D3 Nyainqêntanglha Feng mt.
       China
43 D2 Nyainqêntanglha Shan mts
       China
85 A3 Nyala Sudan
43 C2 Nyalam China
54 D2 Nyandoma Rus. Fed.
86 B3 Nyanga r. Gabon
89 C2 Nyanga Zimbabwe
89 C1 Nyasa, Lake Africa
61 F4 Nyborg Denmark
60 I1 Nyborg Norway
61 G4 Nybro Sweden
87 D3 Nyeri Kenya
43 C1 Nyima China
36 C3 Nyingchi China
71 E2 Nyíregyháza Hungary
61 F4 Nykøbing Denmark
61 G4 Nyköping Sweden
91 C1 Nylstroom S. Africa
21 C2 Nymagee Austr.
61 G4 Nynäshamn Sweden
21 C2 Nyngan Austr.
56 B3 Nyoman r. Belarus/Lith.
73 D3 Nyons France
54 E2 Nyrob Rus. Fed.
102 C2 Nyssa U.S.A.
87 C3 Nyunzu Dem. Rep. Congo
59 C2 Nyzhn'ohirs'kyy Ukr.
87 D3 Nzega Tanz.
82 B4 Nzérékoré Guinea

88 A1 N'zeto Angola

O

104 C2 Oahe, Lake U.S.A.
20 B2 Oakbank Austr.
110 B2 Oakdale U.S.A.
21 D1 Oakey Austr.
102 B1 Oak Harbor U.S.A.
108 C3 Oak Hill U.S.A.
103 B3 Oakland U.S.A.
18 B2 Oakover r. Austr.
102 B2 Oakridge U.S.A.
111 D1 Oak Ridge U.S.A.
22 B3 Oamaru N.Z.
32 B1 Oas Phil.
113 C3 Oaxaca Mex.
54 F2 Ob' r. Rus. Fed.
86 B2 Obala Cameroon
64 B2 Oban U.K.
74 B1 O Barco Spain
21 C2 Oberon Austr.
69 F3 Oberpfälzer Wald mts Ger.
69 F3 Oberviechtach Ger.
27 C3 Obi i. Indon.
119 C2 Óbidos Brazil
34 D2 Obihiro Japan
37 E1 Obluch'ye Rus. Fed.
57 E2 Obninsk Rus. Fed.
87 C2 Obo C.A.R.
85 C3 Obock Djibouti
86 B3 Obouya Congo
57 E3 Oboyan' Rus. Fed.
112 B2 Obregón, Presa resr Mex.
77 D2 Obrenovac Yugo.
55 E3 Obshchiy Syrt hills Rus. Fed.
54 G2 Obskaya Guba sea chan.
       Rus. Fed.
82 B4 Obuasi Ghana
58 C1 Obukhiv Ukr.
54 G2 Ob''yachevo Rus. Fed.
111 D3 Ocala U.S.A.
112 B2 Ocampo Mex.
74 C2 Ocaña Spain
118 A1 Occidental, Cordillera
       mts Col.
118 A3 Occidental, Cordillera mts
       Peru
109 D3 Ocean City U.S.A.
96 B2 Ocean Falls Can.
103 C4 Oceanside U.S.A.
59 C2 Ochakiv Ukr.
54 E3 Ocher Rus. Fed.
69 E3 Ochsenfurt Ger.
111 D2 Oconee r. U.S.A.
113 C3 Ocosingo Mex.
84 B2 Oda, Jebel mt. Sudan
34 D2 Ōdate Japan
35 C3 Odawara Japan
61 E3 Odda Norway
74 B2 Odemira Port.
79 C3 Ödemiş Turkey
61 F4 Odense Denmark
69 D3 Odenwald reg. Ger.
70 C1 Oderbucht b. Ger.
58 C2 Odesa Ukr.
107 C2 Odessa U.S.A.
82 B4 Odienné Côte d'Ivoire
71 D2 Odra r. Ger./Pol.
119 D2 Oeiras Brazil
68 D2 Oelde Ger.
104 C2 Oelrichs U.S.A.
69 F2 Oelsnitz Ger.
68 B1 Oenkerk Neth.
77 C2 Ofanto r. Italy
69 D2 Offenbach am Main Ger.
70 B2 Offenburg Ger.
85 C4 Ogadēn reg. Eth.
34 C3 Oga-hantō pen. Japan

35 C3 Ōgaki Japan
104 C2 Ogallala U.S.A.
83 C4 Ogbomoso Nigeria
102 D2 Ogden U.S.A.
109 D2 Ogdensburg U.S.A.
94 B2 Ogilvie r. Can.
94 B2 Ogilvie Mountains Can.
111 D2 Oglethorpe, Mount U.S.A.
98 B1 Ogoki r. Can.
98 B1 Ogoki Reservoir Can.
56 B2 Ogre Latvia
77 C1 Ogulin Croatia
108 B3 Ohio r. U.S.A.
108 C2 Ohio state U.S.A.
69 E2 Ohrdruf Ger.
77 D2 Ohrid Macedonia
119 C1 Oiapoque Brazil
109 D2 Oil City U.S.A.
68 A3 Oise r. France
35 B4 Ōita Japan
112 B2 Ojinaga Mex.
120 B3 Ojos del Salado, Nevado mt. Arg./Chile
57 F2 Oka r. Rus. Fed.
88 A3 Okahandja Namibia
88 A3 Okakarara Namibia
96 C3 Okanagan Falls Can.
96 C3 Okanagan Lake Can.
102 C1 Okanogan U.S.A.
102 C1 Okanogan r. U.S.A.
42 B1 Okara Pak.
88 B2 Okavango r. Botswana/Namibia
88 B2 Okavango Delta swamp Botswana
35 C3 Okaya Japan
35 B4 Okayama Japan
35 C4 Okazaki Japan
111 D3 Okeechobee, Lake U.S.A.
111 D2 Okefenokee Swamp U.S.A.
67 A3 Okehampton U.K.
42 A2 Okha India
51 K3 Okha Rus. Fed.
43 C2 Okhaldhunga Nepal
51 K3 Okhotka r. Rus. Fed.
51 K3 Okhotsk Rus. Fed.
124 C2 Okhotsk, Sea of Japan/Rus. Fed.
59 C1 Okhtyrka Ukr.
37 E3 Okinawa i. Japan
35 B3 Oki-shotō is Japan
107 D1 Oklahoma state U.S.A.
107 D1 Oklahoma City U.S.A.
107 D2 Okmulgee U.S.A.
46 A2 Oko, Wadi watercourse Sudan
86 B3 Okondja Gabon
96 C2 Okotoks Can.
57 D3 Okovskiy Les for. Rus. Fed.
86 B3 Okoyo Congo
60 H1 Øksfjord Norway
30 A2 Oktwin Myanmar
54 D2 Oktyabr'skiy Arkhangel'skaya Oblast' Rus. Fed.
51 L3 Oktyabr'skiy Kamchatskaya Oblast' Rus. Fed.
55 E3 Oktyabr'skiy Respublika Bashkortostan Rus. Fed.
54 F2 Oktyabr'skoye Rus. Fed.
51 H1 Oktyabr'skoy Revolyutsii, Ostrov i. Rus. Fed.
57 D2 Okulovka Rus. Fed.
34 C2 Okushiri-tō i. Japan
60 □A3 Ólafsvík Iceland
61 G4 Öland i. Sweden
121 B4 Olavarría Arg.
71 D1 Oława Pol.
76 A2 Olbia Sardinia Italy
94 B2 Old Crow Can.

69 D1 Oldenburg Ger.
70 C1 Oldenburg in Holstein Ger.
68 C1 Oldenzaal Neth.
65 B3 Old Head of Kinsale hd Rep. of Ireland
96 C2 Olds Can.
97 D2 Old Wives Lake Can.
109 D2 Olean U.S.A.
71 E1 Olecko Pol.
51 J2 Olekminsk Rus. Fed.
59 C2 Oleksandriya Ukr.
54 C2 Olenegorsk Rus. Fed.
51 I2 Olenek Rus. Fed.
51 I2 Olenek r. Rus. Fed.
57 D2 Olenino Rus. Fed.
58 B1 Olevs'k Ukr.
74 B2 Olhão Port.
90 A2 Olifants watercourse Namibia
91 D1 Olifants S. Africa
91 D1 Olifants r. Northern S. Africa
90 A3 Olifants r. W. Cape S. Africa
90 B2 Olifantshoek S. Africa
122 C2 Olímpia Brazil
119 E2 Olinda Brazil
91 C1 Oliphants Drift S. Africa
75 C2 Oliva Spain
123 D2 Oliveira Brazil
74 B2 Olivenza Spain
120 B3 Ollagüe Chile
118 A2 Olmos Peru
108 B3 Olney U.S.A.
71 D2 Olomouc Czech Rep.
32 B1 Olongapo Phil.
72 B3 Oloron-Ste-Marie France
75 D1 Olot Spain
37 D1 Olovyannaya Rus. Fed.
68 C2 Olpe Ger.
71 E1 Olsztyn Pol.
78 B2 Olt r. Romania
49 C1 Oltu Turkey
79 B3 Olympia Greece
102 B1 Olympia U.S.A.
79 B2 Olympus mt. Greece
102 B1 Olympus, Mount U.S.A.
51 M3 Olyutorskiy, Mys c. Rus. Fed.
65 C1 Omagh U.K.
105 D2 Omaha U.S.A.
47 C3 Oman country Asia
47 C2 Oman, Gulf of Asia
88 A3 Omaruru Namibia
88 B2 Omatako watercourse Namibia
84 B3 Omdurman Sudan
21 C3 Omeo Austr.
113 C3 Omotepee Mex.
46 A3 Om Hajēr Eritrea
96 B2 Omineca Mountains Can.
35 C3 Ōmiya Japan
68 C1 Ommen Neth.
51 L2 Omolon r. Rus. Fed.
68 B3 Omont France
50 F3 Omsk Rus. Fed.
51 L2 Omsukchan Rus. Fed.
78 C1 Omu, Vârful mt. Romania
35 A4 Ōmura Japan
109 D3 Onancock U.S.A.
108 C1 Onaping Lake Can.
99 C2 Onatchiway, Lac l. Can.
88 A2 Oncócua Angola
90 B3 Onderstedorings S. Africa
88 A2 Ondjiva Angola
54 C2 Onega Rus. Fed.
54 C2 Onega r. Rus. Fed.
54 C2 Onega, Lake l. Rus. Fed.
96 B2 One Hundred Mile House Can.
109 D2 Oneida Lake U.S.A.
105 D2 O'Neill U.S.A.
109 D2 Oneonta U.S.A.

78 C1 Oneşti Romania
      Onezhskoye, Ozero l. Rus. Fed. see Onega, Lake
90 B2 Ongers watercourse S. Africa
33 B2 Ongjin N. Korea
41 C3 Ongole India
89 □D3 Onilahy r. Madag.
83 C4 Onitsha Nigeria
90 A2 Onseepkans S. Africa
18 A2 Onslow Austr.
111 E2 Onslow Bay U.S.A.
98 A1 Ontario prov. Can.
102 C2 Ontario U.S.A.
109 D2 Ontario, Lake Can./U.S.A.
19 C2 Oodnadatta Austr.
      Oostende Belgium see Ostend
68 B2 Oosterhout Neth.
68 A2 Oosterschelde est. Neth.
68 B1 Oost-Vlieland Neth.
96 B2 Ootsa Lake Can.
96 B2 Ootsa Lake l. Can.
86 C3 Opala Dem. Rep. Congo
98 C1 Opataca, Lac l. Can.
71 D2 Opava Czech Rep.
111 C2 Opelika U.S.A.
110 B2 Opelousas U.S.A.
98 C1 Opinaca, Réservoir resr Can.
99 D1 Opiscotéo, Lac l. Can.
56 C2 Opochka Rus. Fed.
112 A2 Opodepe Mex.
71 D1 Opole Pol.
44 B2 Oporny Kazakh.
74 B1 Oporto Port.
22 C1 Opotiki N.Z.
61 E3 Oppdal Norway
22 B1 Opunake N.Z.
88 A2 Opuwo Namibia
78 B1 Oradea Romania
77 D2 Orahovac Yugo.
82 B1 Oran Alg.
120 B3 Orán Arg.
33 B1 Orang N. Korea
21 C2 Orange Austr.
73 C3 Orange France
90 A2 Orange r. Namibia/S. Africa
107 E2 Orange U.S.A.
111 D2 Orangeburg U.S.A.
108 C2 Orangeville Can.
69 F1 Oranienburg Ger.
90 A2 Oranjemund Namibia
88 B3 Orapa Botswana
78 B1 Orăştie Romania
76 B2 Orbetello Italy
21 C3 Orbost Austr.
10 B1 Ord, Mount Austr.
74 B1 Ordes Spain
48 B1 Ordu Turkey
      Ordzhonikidze Rus. Fed. see Vladikavkaz
59 C2 Ordzhonikidze Ukr.
61 G4 Örebro Sweden
102 B2 Oregon state U.S.A.
102 B1 Oregon City U.S.A.
55 D3 Orekhovo-Zuyevo Rus. Fed.
57 E3 Orel Rus. Fed.
51 K3 Orel', Ozero l. Rus. Fed.
103 D2 Orem U.S.A.
79 C3 Ören Turkey
55 E3 Orenburg Rus. Fed.
22 A3 Orepuki N.Z.
61 F4 Öresund str. Denmark/Sweden
67 D2 Orford Ness hd U.K.
79 C3 Orhaneli Turkey
79 C2 Orhangazi Turkey
51 I3 Orhon Gol r. Mongolia
120 B2 Oriental, Cordillera mts Bol.
118 A1 Oriental, Cordillera mts Col.
118 A3 Oriental, Cordillera mts Peru

75 C2 **Orihuela** Spain
59 D2 **Orikhiv** Ukr.
98 C2 **Orillia** Can.
118 B1 **Orinoco** r. Col./Venez.
118 B1 **Orinoco Delta** Venez.
61 H4 **Orissaare** Estonia
76 A3 **Oristano** Sardinia Italy
61 I3 **Orivesi** l. Fin.
119 C2 **Oriximiná** Brazil
113 C3 **Orizaba** Mex.
113 C3 **Orizaba, Pico de** vol. Mex.
60 E3 **Orkanger** Norway
61 F4 **Örkelljunga** Sweden
60 E3 **Orkla** r. Norway
64 C1 **Orkney Islands** is U.K.
122 C2 **Orlândia** Brazil
111 D3 **Orlando** U.S.A.
72 C2 **Orléans** France
42 A2 **Ormara** Pak.
32 B1 **Ormoc** Phil.
66 B2 **Ormskirk** U.K.
60 G3 **Örnsköldsvik** Sweden
82 B3 **Orodara** Burkina
102 C1 **Orofino** U.S.A.
        Oroqen Zizhiqi China see
        Alihe
32 B2 **Oroquieta** Phil.
76 A2 **Orosei** Sardinia Italy
76 A2 **Orosei, Golfo di** b. Sardinia
        Italy
71 E2 **Orosháza** Hungary
103 B3 **Oroville** U.S.A.
20 A2 **Orroroo** Austr.
57 D3 **Orsha** Belarus
55 E3 **Orsk** Rus. Fed.
61 E3 **Ørsta** Norway
74 B1 **Ortegal, Cabo** c. Spain
72 B3 **Orthez** France
74 B1 **Ortigueira** Spain
105 D1 **Ortonville** U.S.A.
51 J2 **Orulgan, Khrebet** mts
        Rus. Fed.
49 C2 **Orümîyeh, Daryächeh-ye**
        salt l. Iran
120 B2 **Oruro** Bol.
76 B2 **Orvieto** Italy
114 B4 **Osa, Península de** pen.
        Costa Rica
105 E3 **Osage** r. U.S.A.
35 C4 **Ōsaka** Japan
69 E1 **Oschersleben (Bode)** Ger.
76 A2 **Oschiri** Sardinia Italy
57 E3 **Oster** r. Rus. Fed.
45 D2 **Osh** Kyrg.
88 A2 **Oshakati** Namibia
98 C2 **Oshawa** Can.
34 C2 **Ō-shima** i. Japan
35 C4 **Ō-shima** i. Japan
108 B2 **Oshkosh** U.S.A.
49 C2 **Oshnovîyeh** Iran
83 C4 **Oshogbo** Nigeria
88 B3 **Oshwe** Dem. Rep. Congo
77 C1 **Osijek** Croatia
96 B2 **Osilinka** r. Can.
76 B2 **Osimo** Italy
91 D2 **Osizweni** S. Africa
105 E2 **Oskaloosa** U.S.A.
61 G4 **Oskarshamn** Sweden
57 E3 **Oskol** r. Rus. Fed.
61 F4 **Oslo** Norway
61 F4 **Oslofjorden** sea chan.
        Norway
48 B1 **Osmancık** Turkey
79 C2 **Osmaneli** Turkey
48 B2 **Osmaniye** Turkey
56 C2 **Os'mino** Rus. Fed.
68 D1 **Osnabrück** Ger.
121 A5 **Osorno** Chile
74 C1 **Osorno** Spain
96 C3 **Osoyoos** Can.

68 B2 **Oss** Neth.
19 D4 **Ossa, Mount** Austr.
51 L3 **Ossora** Rus. Fed.
57 D2 **Ostashkov** Rus. Fed.
69 D1 **Oste** r. Ger.
68 A2 **Ostend** Belgium
69 E1 **Osterburg (Altmark)** Ger.
61 F3 **Österdälven** l. Sweden
69 D1 **Osterholz-Scharmbeck** Ger.
69 E2 **Osterode am Harz** Ger.
60 F3 **Östersund** Sweden
        Ostfriesische Inseln is Ger.
        see **East Frisian Islands**
68 C1 **Ostfriesland** reg. Ger.
61 G3 **Östhammar** Sweden
71 D2 **Ostrava** Czech Rep.
71 D1 **Ostróda** Pol.
57 E3 **Ostrogozhsk** Rus. Fed.
71 E1 **Ostrołęka** Pol.
69 F2 **Ostrov** Czech Rep.
56 C2 **Ostrov** Rus. Fed.
71 E1 **Ostrowiec Świętokrzyski**
        Pol.
71 E1 **Ostrów Mazowiecka** Pol.
71 D1 **Ostrów Wielkopolski** Pol.
78 B2 **Osüm** r. Bulg.
35 B4 **Ōsumi-kaikyō** sea chan.
        Japan
35 B4 **Ōsumi-shotō** is Japan
74 B2 **Osuna** Spain
109 D2 **Oswego** U.S.A.
67 B2 **Oswestry** U.K.
35 C3 **Ōta** Japan
22 B3 **Otago Peninsula** N.Z.
22 C2 **Otaki** N.Z.
34 D2 **Otaru** Japan
88 A2 **Otavi** Namibia
102 C1 **Othello** U.S.A.
88 A3 **Otjiwarongo** Namibia
85 B3 **Otoro, Jebel** mt. Sudan
61 E4 **Otra** r. Norway
77 C2 **Otranto, Strait of**
        Albania/Italy
35 C3 **Ōtsu** Japan
61 E3 **Otta** Norway
98 C2 **Ottawa** Can.
98 C2 **Ottawa** r. Can.
108 B2 **Ottawa** IL U.S.A.
105 D3 **Ottawa** KS U.S.A.
98 B1 **Otter Rapids** Can.
68 B2 **Ottignies** Belgium
105 E2 **Ottumwa** U.S.A.
118 A2 **Otuzco** Peru
20 B3 **Otway, Cape** Austr.
110 B2 **Ouachita** r. U.S.A.
110 B2 **Ouachita, Lake** U.S.A.
110 B2 **Ouachita Mountains** U.S.A.
86 C2 **Ouadda** C.A.R.
83 D3 **Ouaddaï** reg. Chad
82 B3 **Ouagadougou** Burkina
82 B3 **Ouahigouya** Burkina
86 C2 **Ouanda-Djalié** C.A.R.
82 B2 **Ouarâne** reg. Maur.
83 C1 **Ouargla** Alg.
82 B1 **Ouarzazate** Morocco
68 A2 **Oudenaarde** Belgium
90 B3 **Oudtshoorn** S. Africa
75 D2 **Oued Tlélat** Alg.
72 A2 **Ouessant, Île d'** i. France
86 B2 **Ouésso** Congo
82 B1 **Oujda** Morocco
75 D2 **Ouled Farès** Alg.
60 I2 **Oulu** Fin.
60 I3 **Oulujärvi** l. Fin.
76 A1 **Oulx** Italy
83 D3 **Oum-Chalouba** Chad
83 D3 **Oum-Hadjer** Chad
83 E3 **Ounianga Kébir** Chad
68 B2 **Oupeye** Belgium

68 C3 **Our, Vallée de l'** val.
        Ger./Lux.
74 B1 **Ourense** Spain
122 C2 **Ourinhos** Brazil
123 D2 **Ouro Preto** Brazil
68 B2 **Ourthe** r. Belgium
66 C2 **Ouse** r. U.K.
        Outaouais, Rivière des r.
        Can. see **Ottawa**
99 D2 **Outardes** r. Can.
99 D1 **Outardes Quatre, Réservoi**
        resr Can.
64 A2 **Outer Hebrides** is U.K.
88 A3 **Outjo** Namibia
97 D2 **Outlook** Can.
60 I3 **Outokumpu** Fin.
20 B3 **Ouyen** Austr.
74 B1 **Ovar** Port.
60 H2 **Överkalix** Sweden
103 D3 **Overton** U.S.A.
60 H2 **Övertorneå** Sweden
74 B1 **Oviedo** Spain
61 E3 **Øvre Årdal** Norway
61 F3 **Øvre Rendal** Norway
58 B1 **Ovruch** Ukr.
86 B3 **Owando** Congo
35 C4 **Owase** Japan
105 E2 **Owatonna** U.S.A.
108 B3 **Owensboro** U.S.A.
103 C3 **Owens Lake** U.S.A.
98 B2 **Own Sound** Can.
83 C4 **Owerri** Nigeria
108 C2 **Owosso** U.S.A.
102 C2 **Owyhee** U.S.A.
102 C2 **Owyhee** r. U.S.A.
22 B2 **Oxford** N.Z.
67 C3 **Oxford** U.K.
110 C2 **Oxford** U.S.A.
97 E2 **Oxford Lake** Can.
20 B2 **Oxley** Austr.
        Ox Mountains
        Rep. of Ireland see
        Slieve Gamph
103 C4 **Oxnard** U.S.A.
35 C3 **Oyama** Japan
86 B2 **Oyem** Gabon
97 C2 **Oyen** Can.
73 D2 **Oyonnax** France
32 B2 **Ozamiz** Phil.
110 C2 **Ozark** U.S.A.
105 E3 **Ozark Plateau** U.S.A.
105 E3 **Ozarks, Lake of the** U.S.A.
51 L3 **Ozernovskiy** Rus. Fed.
56 B3 **Ozersk** Rus. Fed.
57 E3 **Ozery** Rus. Fed.
55 D3 **Ozinki** Rus. Fed.

P

95 H2 **Paamiut** Greenland
90 A3 **Paarl** S. Africa
71 D1 **Pabianice** Pol.
43 C2 **Pabna** Bangl.
42 A2 **Pab Range** mts Pak.
118 B1 **Pacaraima, Serra** mts Brazi
77 C3 **Pachino** Sicily Italy
113 C2 **Pachuca** Mex.
124 **Pacific Ocean**
71 D1 **Paczków** Pol.
28 B2 **Padang** Indon.
28 B2 **Padangpanjang** Indon.
28 A1 **Padangsidimpuan** Indon.
69 D2 **Paderborn** Ger.
        Padova Italy see **Padua**
107 D3 **Padre Island** U.S.A.
20 B3 **Padthaway** Austr.
76 B1 **Padua** Italy

108 B3 **Paducah** *KY* U.S.A.
107 C2 **Paducah** *TX* U.S.A.
33 B1 **Paegam** N. Korea
33 B1 **Paekdu-san** *mt.*
China/N. Korea
33 A2 **Paengnyŏng-do** *i.* S. Korea
22 C1 **Paeroa** N.Z.
48 B2 **Pafos** Cyprus
77 C2 **Pag** Croatia
32 B2 **Pagadian** Phil.
28 B2 **Pagai Selatan** *i.* Indon.
28 B2 **Pagai Utara** *i.* Indon.
27 D1 **Pagan** *i.* N. Mariana Is
29 C2 **Pagatan** Indon.
106 A1 **Page** U.S.A.
56 B2 **Pagėgiai** Lith.
104 B3 **Pagosa Springs** U.S.A.
56 C2 **Paide** Estonia
61 I3 **Päijänne** *l.* Fin.
43 C2 **Paikü Co** *l.* China
106 A1 **Painted Desert** U.S.A.
64 B3 **Paisley** U.K.
60 H2 **Pajala** Sweden
118 C1 **Pakaraima Mountains**
Guyana
42 A2 **Pakistan** *country* Asia
30 A1 **Pakokku** Myanmar
56 B2 **Pakruojis** Lith.
71 D2 **Paks** Hungary
98 A1 **Pakwash Lake** Can.
31 B2 **Paksé** Laos
83 D4 **Pala** Chad
28 B2 **Palabuhanratu, Teluk** *b.*
Indon.
79 C3 **Palaikastro** Greece
79 B3 **Palaiochora** Greece
90 B1 **Palamakoloi** Botswana
78 D1 **Palamós** Spain
51 L3 **Palana** Rus. Fed.
32 B1 **Palanan** Phil.
29 C2 **Palangkaraya** Indon.
42 B2 **Palanpur** India
88 B3 **Palapye** Botswana
51 L2 **Palatka** Rus. Fed.
111 D3 **Palatka** U.S.A.
27 C2 **Palau** *country*
N. Pacific Ocean
31 A2 **Palaw** Myanmar
32 A2 **Palawan** *i.* Phil.
61 H4 **Paldiski** Estonia
28 B2 **Palembang** Indon.
74 C1 **Palencia** Spain
113 C3 **Palenque** Mex.
107 D2 **Palestine** U.S.A.
30 A1 **Paletwa** Myanmar
42 B2 **Pali** India
77 C2 **Palinuro, Capo** *c.* Italy
79 B3 **Paliouri, Akra** *pt* Greece
68 B3 **Paliseul** Belgium
60 I3 **Paljakka** *hill* Fin.
56 C2 **Palkino** Rus. Fed.
41 B4 **Palk Strait** India/Sri Lanka
22 C2 **Palliser, Cape** N.Z.
74 B2 **Palma del Rio** Spain
75 D2 **Palma de Mallorca** Spain
122 B3 **Palmas** Brazil
82 B4 **Palmas, Cape** Liberia
122 C3 **Palmeira** Brazil
119 D2 **Palmeirais** Brazil
23 P2 **Palmer Land** *reg.*
Antarctica
22 C2 **Palmerston North** N.Z.
77 C3 **Palmi** Italy
113 C2 **Palmillas** Mex.
118 A1 **Palmira** Col.
103 C4 **Palm Springs** U.S.A.
17 G3 **Palmyra Atoll**
N. Pacific Ocean
85 B3 **Paloich** Sudan

113 C3 **Palomares** Mex.
75 C2 **Palos, Cabo de** *c.* Spain
60 I3 **Paltamo** Fin.
26 B3 **Palu** Indon.
51 M2 **Palyavaam** *r.* Rus. Fed.
72 C3 **Pamiers** France
45 D3 **Pamir** *mts* Asia
111 E1 **Pamlico Sound** *sea chan.*
U.S.A.
120 B2 **Pampa Grande** Bol.
121 B4 **Pampas** *reg.* Arg.
118 A1 **Pamplona** Col.
75 C1 **Pamplona** Spain
79 D2 **Pamukova** Turkey
28 B2 **Panaitan** *i.* Indon.
41 B3 **Panaji** India
114 B4 **Panama** *country*
Central America
114 C4 **Panamá** Panama
114 C4 **Panamá, Golfo de** *g.* Panama
114 C4 **Panama Canal** Panama
110 C2 **Panama City** U.S.A.
103 C3 **Panamint Range** *mts* U.S.A.
29 B1 **Panarik** Indon.
32 B1 **Panay** *i.* Phil.
77 D2 **Pančevo** Yugo.
32 B1 **Pandan** Phil.
43 C2 **Pandaria** India
41 B3 **Pandharpur** India
56 B2 **Panevėžys** Lith.
29 C2 **Pangkalanbuun** Indon.
28 A1 **Pangkalansusu** Indon.
28 B2 **Pangkalpinang** Indon.
95 G2 **Pangnirtung** Can.
54 G2 **Pangody** Rus. Fed.
57 F3 **Panino** Rus. Fed.
42 B2 **Panipat** India
42 A2 **Panjgur** Pak.
33 C1 **Pan Ling** *mts* China
43 C2 **Panna** India
18 A2 **Pannawonica** Austr.
122 B2 **Panorama** Brazil
33 B1 **Panshi** China
113 C2 **Pánuco** Mex.
39 A3 **Panxian** China
30 B1 **Panzhihua** China
77 C3 **Paola** Italy
31 B2 **Paôy Pêt** Cambodia
71 D2 **Pápa** Hungary
22 B1 **Papakura** N.Z.
113 C2 **Papantla** Mex.
68 C1 **Papenburg** Ger.
27 D3 **Papua, Gulf of** P.N.G.
27 D3 **Papua New Guinea** *country*
Oceania
30 A2 **Papun** Myanmar
18 A2 **Paraburdoo** Austr.
122 C1 **Paracatu** Brazil
123 C1 **Paracatu** *r.* Brazil
20 A2 **Parachilna** Austr.
118 D2 **Paracín** Yugo.
123 D1 **Pará de Minas** Brazil
103 B3 **Paradise** U.S.A.
119 B1 **Paragould** U.S.A.
119 C3 **Paraguai** *r.* Brazil
120 C3 **Paraguay** *r./para.*
120 C3 **Paraguay** *country*
S. America
123 D2 **Paraíba do Sul** *r.* Brazil
122 B1 **Paraíso** Brazil
113 C3 **Paraíso** Mex.
82 C4 **Parakou** Benin
119 C1 **Paramaribo** Suriname
51 L3 **Paramushir, Ostrov** *i.*
Rus. Fed.
120 B4 **Paraná** Arg.
122 A3 **Paraná** *r.* S. America
122 C3 **Paranaguá** Brazil
122 B1 **Paranaíba** Brazil
122 B2 **Paranaíba** *r.* Brazil

122 B2 **Paranapanema** *r.* Brazil
122 B2 **Paranapiacaba, Serra** *mts*
Brazil
122 B2 **Paranavaí** Brazil
22 B2 **Paraparaumu** N.Z.
123 D2 **Parati** Brazil
122 B1 **Paraúna** Brazil
73 C2 **Paray-le-Monial** France
41 B3 **Parbhani** India
69 E1 **Parchim** Ger.
123 E1 **Pardo** *r. Bahia* Brazil
122 B2 **Pardo** *r. Mato Grosso do Sul*
Brazil
122 C2 **Pardo** *r. São Paulo* Brazil
71 D1 **Pardubice** Czech Rep.
118 B3 **Parecis, Serra dos** *hills*
Brazil
98 C2 **Parent, Lac** *l.* Can.
26 B3 **Parepare** Indon.
57 D2 **Parfino** Rus. Fed.
79 B3 **Parga** Greece
77 C3 **Parghelia** Italy
115 D3 **Paria, Gulf of**
Trin. and Tob./Venez.
118 B1 **Parima, Serra** *mts* Brazil
119 C2 **Parintins** Brazil
72 C2 **Paris** France
110 C1 **Paris** *TN* U.S.A.
107 D2 **Paris** *TX* U.S.A.
61 H3 **Parkano** Fin.
106 A2 **Parker** U.S.A.
108 C3 **Parkersburg** U.S.A.
21 C2 **Parkes** Austr.
108 A1 **Park Falls** U.S.A.
105 D1 **Park Rapids** U.S.A.
76 B2 **Parma** Italy
119 D2 **Parnaíba** Brazil
119 D2 **Parnaíba** *r.* Brazil
79 B3 **Parnassos** *mt.* Greece
22 B2 **Parnassus** N.Z.
79 B3 **Parnon** *mts* Greece
56 B2 **Pärnu** Estonia
33 B2 **P'aro-ho** *l.* S. Korea
20 B2 **Paroo** *watercourse* Austr.
44 C3 **Paropamisus** *mts* Afgh.
79 C3 **Paros** *i.* Greece
112 B2 **Parras** Mex.
94 C2 **Parry, Cape** Can.
94 D1 **Parry Islands** Can.
98 B2 **Parry Sound** Can.
105 D3 **Parsons** U.S.A.
69 F2 **Partenstein** Ger.
72 B2 **Parthenay** France
65 B2 **Partry Mountains**
Rep. of Ireland
119 C2 **Paru** *r.* Brazil
103 C4 **Pasadena** U.S.A.
30 A2 **Pasawng** Myanmar
110 C2 **Pascagoula** U.S.A.
78 C1 **Pașcani** Romania
102 C1 **Pasco** U.S.A.
70 C1 **Pasewalk** Ger.
97 D2 **Pasfield Lake** Can.
28 B1 **Pasir Putih** Malaysia
42 A2 **Pasni** Pak.
121 A5 **Paso Río Mayo** Arg.
103 B3 **Paso Robles** U.S.A.
123 D2 **Passa Tempo** Brazil
70 C2 **Passau** Ger.
120 C3 **Passo Fundo** Brazil
123 C2 **Passos** Brazil
56 C2 **Pastavy** Belarus
118 A2 **Pastaza** *r.* Peru
118 A1 **Pasto** Col.
29 C2 **Pasuruan** Indon.
56 B2 **Pasvalys** Lith.
121 A6 **Patagonia** *reg.* Arg.
43 C2 **Patan** Nepal
22 B1 **Patea** N.Z.
109 E2 **Paterson** U.S.A.

Pathein Myanmar *see*
Bassein
104 B2 **Pathfinder Reservoir** U.S.A.
29 C2 **Pati** Indon.
30 A1 **Pätkai Bum** *mts*
India/Myanmar
79 C3 **Patmos** *i.* Greece
43 E2 **Patna** India
49 C2 **Patnos** Turkey
122 B3 **Pato Branco** Brazil
120 C4 **Patos, Lagoa dos** *l.* Brazil
123 C1 **Patos de Minas** Brazil
120 B4 **Patquía** Arg.
79 B3 **Patra** Greece
43 C2 **Patratu** India
122 C1 **Patrocinio** Brazil
31 B3 **Pattani** Thai.
31 B2 **Pattaya** Thai.
96 B2 **Pattullo, Mount** Can.
97 D2 **Patuanak** Can.
112 B3 **Pátzcuaro** Mex.
72 B3 **Pau** France
72 B2 **Pauillac** France
30 A1 **Pauk** Myanmar
119 D2 **Paulistana** Brazil
119 E2 **Paulo Afonso** Brazil
91 D2 **Paulpietersburg** S. Africa
107 D2 **Pauls Valley** U.S.A.
30 A2 **Paungde** Myanmar
123 D1 **Pavão** Brazil
76 A1 **Pavia** Italy
56 B2 **Pāvilosta** Latvia
78 C2 **Pavlikeni** Bulg.
45 D1 **Pavlodar** Kazakh.
59 D2 **Pavlohrad** Ukr.
59 E1 **Pavlovsk** Rus. Fed.
59 D2 **Pavlovskaya** Rus. Fed.
28 B2 **Payakumbuh** Indon.
102 C2 **Payette** U.S.A.
102 C2 **Payette** *r.* U.S.A.
54 F2 **Pay-Khoy, Khrebet** *hills*
Rus. Fed.
120 C4 **Paysandú** Uru.
49 C1 **Pazar** Turkey
78 B2 **Pazardzhik** Bulg.
79 C3 **Pazarköy** Turkey
76 B1 **Pazin** Croatia
31 A2 **Pe** Myanmar
96 C2 **Peace** *r.* Can.
96 C2 **Peace River** Can.
103 E3 **Peale, Mount** U.S.A.
110 D2 **Pearl** *r.* U.S.A.
107 D3 **Pearsall** U.S.A.
89 C2 **Pebane** Moz.
77 D2 **Peć** Yugo.
123 D1 **Peçanha** Brazil
54 E2 **Pechora** Rus. Fed.
54 E2 **Pechora** *r.* Rus. Fed.
56 C2 **Pechory** Rus. Fed.
107 C2 **Pecos** U.S.A.
107 C3 **Pecos** *r.* U.S.A.
71 D2 **Pécs** Hungary
123 D1 **Pedra Azul** Brazil
122 C2 **Pedregulho** Brazil
119 D2 **Pedreiras** Brazil
41 C4 **Pedro, Point** Sri Lanka
119 D2 **Pedro Afonso** Brazil
122 B1 **Pedro Gomes** Brazil
120 C3 **Pedro Juan Caballero** Para.
64 C3 **Peebles** U.K.
111 E2 **Pee Dee** *r.* U.S.A.
94 C2 **Peel** *r.* Can.
66 A1 **Peel** Isle of Man
96 C2 **Peerless Lake** Can.
22 B2 **Pegasus Bay** N.Z.
69 E3 **Pegnitz** Ger.
30 A2 **Pegu** Myanmar
30 A2 **Pegu Yoma** *mts* Myanmar
121 B4 **Pehuajó** Arg.
69 E1 **Peine** Ger.

56 C2 **Peipus, Lake**
Estonia/Rus. Fed.
79 B3 **Peiraias** Greece
122 B2 **Peixe** *r.* Brazil
29 B2 **Pekalongan** Indon.
28 B1 **Pekan** Malaysia
28 B1 **Pekanbaru** Indon.
Peking China *see* Beijing
98 B2 **Pelee Island** Can.
27 C3 **Peleng** *i.* Indon.
60 I2 **Pelkosenniemi** Fin.
90 A2 **Pella** S. Africa
27 D3 **Pelleluhu Islands** P.N.G.
60 H2 **Pello** Fin.
96 A1 **Pelly** *r.* Can.
95 F2 **Pelly Bay** Can.
96 A1 **Pelly Mountains** Can.
120 C4 **Pelotas** Brazil
120 C3 **Pelotas, Rio das** *r.* Brazil
109 F1 **Pemadumcook Lake** U.S.A.
29 B1 **Pemangkat** Indon.
28 A1 **Pematangsiantar** Indon.
89 D2 **Pemba** Moz.
88 B2 **Pemba** Zambia
87 D3 **Pemba Island** Tanz.
96 B2 **Pemberton** Can.
105 D1 **Pembina** *r.* U.S.A.
98 C2 **Pembroke** Can.
67 A3 **Pembroke** U.K.
74 C1 **Peña Cerredo** *mt.* Spain
113 C2 **Peña Nevada, Cerro**
mt. Mex.
122 B2 **Penápolis** Brazil
74 B1 **Peñaranda de Bracamonte**
Spain
75 C1 **Peñarroya** *mt.* Spain
74 B2 **Peñarroya-Pueblonuevo**
Spain
74 B1 **Peñas, Cabo de** *c.* Spain
121 A5 **Penas, Golfo de** *g.* Chile
74 B1 **Peña Ubiña** *mt.* Spain
102 C1 **Pendleton** U.S.A.
96 B2 **Pendleton Bay** Can.
102 C1 **Pend Oreille Lake** U.S.A.
42 B3 **Penganga** *r.* India
91 D1 **Penge** S. Africa
38 C2 **Penglai** China
39 A3 **Pengshui** China
74 B2 **Peniche** Port.
66 B1 **Penicuik** U.K.
76 B2 **Penne** Italy
66 B1 **Pennines** *hills* U.K.
109 D2 **Pennsylvania** *state* U.S.A.
95 G2 **Penny Icecap** Can.
109 F2 **Penobscot** *r.* U.S.A.
20 B3 **Penola** Austr.
18 C3 **Penong** Austr.
66 B1 **Penrith** U.K.
110 C2 **Pensacola** U.S.A.
23 Q1 **Pensacola Mountains**
Antarctica
29 C1 **Pensiangan** *Sabah* Malaysia
96 C3 **Penticton** Can.
64 C1 **Pentland Firth** *sea chan.*
U.K.
67 B2 **Penygadair** *hill* U.K.
55 D3 **Penza** Rus. Fed.
67 A3 **Penzance** U.K.
108 B2 **Peoria** U.S.A.
75 C1 **Perales del Alfambra** Spain
19 E2 **Percy Isles** Austr.
54 F2 **Peregrebnoye** Rus. Fed.
118 A1 **Pereira** Col.
122 B2 **Pereira Barreto** Brazil
58 A2 **Peremyshlyany** Ukr.
57 E2 **Pereslavl'-Zalesskiy**
Rus. Fed.
59 C1 **Pereyaslav-Khmel'nyts'kyy**
Ukr.
121 B4 **Pergamino** Arg.

60 H3 **Perhonjoki** *r.* Fin.
99 C1 **Péribonca, Lac** *l.* Can.
120 B3 **Perico** Arg.
112 B2 **Pericos** Mex.
72 C2 **Périgueux** France
115 C4 **Perijá, Sierra de** *mts* Vene.
121 A5 **Perito Moreno** Arg.
69 E1 **Perleberg** Ger.
54 E3 **Perm'** Rus. Fed.
20 A2 **Pernatty Lagoon** *salt flat*
Austr.
73 C2 **Péronne** France
113 C3 **Perote** Mex.
72 C2 **Perpignan** France
67 A3 **Perranporth** U.K.
111 D2 **Perry** *FL* U.S.A.
111 D2 **Perry** *GA* U.S.A.
105 E2 **Perry** *IA* U.S.A.
107 C1 **Perryton** U.S.A.
105 F3 **Perryville** U.S.A.
67 B2 **Pershore** U.K.
59 D2 **Pershotravens'k** Ukr.
18 A3 **Perth** Austr.
64 C2 **Perth** U.K.
73 D3 **Pertuis** France
76 A2 **Pertusato, Capo** *c.* Corsica
France
118 A2 **Peru** *country* S. America
125 H4 **Peru-Chile Trench**
sea feature S. Pacific Ocean
76 B2 **Perugia** Italy
122 C2 **Peruíbe** Brazil
68 A2 **Péruwelz** Belgium
58 C2 **Pervomays'k** Ukr.
59 C2 **Pervomays'ke** Ukr.
57 F3 **Pervomayskiy** Rus. Fed.
59 D2 **Pervomays'kyy** Ukr.
76 B2 **Pesaro** Italy
76 B2 **Pescara** Italy
76 B2 **Pescara** *r.* Italy
42 B1 **Peshawar** Pak.
77 D2 **Peshkopi** Albania
77 C1 **Pesnica** Slovenia
57 E2 **Pestovo** Rus. Fed.
112 B3 **Petatlán** Mex.
108 B2 **Petenwell Lake** U.S.A.
20 A2 **Peterborough** Austr.
98 C2 **Peterborough** Can.
67 C2 **Peterborough** U.K.
64 D2 **Peterhead** U.K.
18 B2 **Petermann Ranges**
mts Austr.
97 D2 **Peter Pond Lake** Can.
96 A2 **Petersburg** *AK* U.S.A.
109 D3 **Petersburg** *VA* U.S.A.
69 D1 **Petershagen** Ger.
99 D1 **Petit Lac Manicouagan**
l. Can.
99 E1 **Petit Mécatina** *r.* Can.
113 C2 **Peto** Mex.
108 C1 **Petoskey** U.S.A.
48 B2 **Petra** Jordan
34 B2 **Petra Velikogo, Zaliv** *b.*
Rus. Fed.
79 B3 **Petrich** Bulg.
119 D2 **Petrolina** Brazil
45 C1 **Petropavlovsk** Kazakh.
51 L3 **Petropavlovsk-Kamchatsk..**
Rus. Fed.
78 B1 **Petroșani** Romania
57 F3 **Petrovskoye** Rus. Fed.
54 C2 **Petrozavodsk** Rus. Fed.
91 C2 **Petrusburg** S. Africa
91 C2 **Petrus Steyn** S. Africa
90 B3 **Petrusville** S. Africa
57 E2 **Petushki** Rus. Fed.
28 A1 **Peureula** Indon.
51 M2 **Pevek** Rus. Fed.
70 B2 **Pforzheim** Ger.
70 C2 **Pfunds** Austria

69 D3 **Pfungstadt** Ger.
91 C2 **Phahameng** S. Africa
91 D1 **Phalaborwa** S. Africa
42 B2 **Phalodi** India
31 A3 **Phangnga** Thai.
31 B2 **Phan Rang** Vietnam
31 B2 **Phan Thiêt** Vietnam
31 B3 **Phatthalung** Thai.
30 A2 **Phayao** Thai.
97 D2 **Phelps Lake** Can.
111 C2 **Phenix City** U.S.A.
31 A2 **Phet Buri** Thai.
31 B2 **Phichit** Thai.
109 D3 **Philadelphia** U.S.A.
104 C2 **Philip** U.S.A.
68 B2 **Philippeville** Belgium
68 A2 **Philippine** Neth.
32 B1 **Philippines** *country* Asia
32 B1 **Philippine Sea**
      N. Pacific Ocean
94 B2 **Philip Smith Mountains**
      U.S.A.
90 B3 **Philipstown** S. Africa
21 C3 **Phillip Island** Austr.
105 D3 **Phillipsburg** U.S.A.
91 C2 **Phiritona** S. Africa
31 B2 **Phitsanulok** Thai.
      Phnom Penh Cambodia *see*
      Phnum Pénh
106 A2 **Phnum Pénh** Cambodia
31 B2 **Phoenix** U.S.A.
31 B2 **Phon** Thai.
30 B1 **Phôngsali** Laos
30 B2 **Phrae** Thai.
31 A3 **Phuket** Thai.
31 B2 **Phumî Sâmraông** Cambodia
91 C2 **Phuthaditjhaba** S. Africa
76 A1 **Piacenza** Italy
76 B2 **Pianosa, Isola** *i.* Italy
78 C1 **Piatra Neamţ** Romania
119 D2 **Piauí** *r.* Brazil
76 B1 **Piave** *r.* Italy
85 B4 **Pibor** *r.* Sudan
85 B4 **Pibor Post** Sudan
110 C2 **Picayune** U.S.A.
120 B3 **Pichanal** Arg.
112 A2 **Pichilingue** Mex.
66 C1 **Pickering** U.K.
98 A1 **Pickle Lake** Can.
121 B5 **Pico Truncado** Arg.
21 D2 **Picton** Austr.
113 C3 **Piedras Negras** Guat.
112 B2 **Piedras Negras** Mex.
61 I3 **Pieksämäki** Fin.
60 I3 **Pielinen** *l.* Fin.
104 C2 **Pierre** U.S.A.
73 C3 **Pierrelatte** France
91 C2 **Pietermaritzburg** S. Africa
91 C1 **Pietersburg** S. Africa
76 C1 **Pietrosa** *mt.* Romania
96 C2 **Pigeon Lake** Can.
121 B4 **Pigüé** Arg.
60 I3 **Pihtipudas** Fin.
113 C3 **Pijijiapan** Mex.
104 C3 **Pikes Peak** U.S.A.
90 A3 **Piketberg** S. Africa
108 C3 **Pikeville** U.S.A.
71 D1 **Piła** Pol.
121 C4 **Pilar** Arg.
120 C3 **Pilar** Para.
21 C1 **Pilliga** Austr.
122 C1 **Pilões, Serra dos** *mts* Brazil
118 B3 **Pimenta Bueno** Brazil
121 C4 **Pinamar** Arg.
114 B2 **Pinar del Río** Cuba
71 E1 **Pińczów** Pol.
119 D2 **Pindaré** *r.* Brazil
79 B2 **Pindos** *mts* Greece

110 B2 **Pine Bluff** U.S.A.
18 C1 **Pine Creek** Austr.
104 B2 **Pinedale** U.S.A.
54 D2 **Pinega** Rus. Fed.
97 D2 **Pinehouse Lake** Can.
79 B3 **Pineios** *r.* Greece
96 C1 **Pine Point** Can.
104 C2 **Pine Ridge** U.S.A.
91 D2 **Pinetown** S. Africa
38 B2 **Pingdingshan** China
39 A3 **Pingguo** China
39 B3 **Pingjiang** China
38 A2 **Pingliang** China
39 C3 **P'ingtung** Taiwan
39 A3 **Pingxiang** *Guangxi* China
39 B3 **Pingxiang** *Jiangxi* China
38 B2 **Pingyin** China
119 D2 **Pinheiro** Brazil
69 D1 **Pinneberg** Ger.
113 C3 **Pinotepa Nacional** Mex.
56 C3 **Pinsk** Belarus
103 D3 **Pioche** U.S.A.
87 C3 **Piodi** Dem. Rep. Congo
71 E1 **Pionki** Pol.
71 D1 **Piotrków Trybunalski** Pol.
105 D2 **Pipestone** U.S.A.
99 C2 **Pipmuacan, Réservoir**
      resr Can.
122 B2 **Piquiri** *r.* Brazil
122 C1 **Piracanjuba** Brazil
122 C2 **Piracicaba** Brazil
123 D1 **Piracicaba** *r.* Brazil
122 C2 **Piraçununga** Brazil
122 C2 **Piraí do Sul** Brazil
122 C2 **Pirajuí** Brazil
122 B1 **Piranhas** Brazil
119 E2 **Piranhas** *r.* Brazil
123 D1 **Pirapora** Brazil
122 C1 **Pires do Rio** Brazil
119 D2 **Piripiri** Brazil
27 C3 **Piru** Indon.
76 B2 **Pisa** Italy
120 A2 **Pisagua** Chile
118 A3 **Pisco** Peru
70 C2 **Písek** Czech Rep.
47 D2 **Pishin** Iran
113 D2 **Pisté** Mex.
77 C2 **Pisticci** Italy
76 B2 **Pistoia** Italy
74 C1 **Pisuerga** *r.* Spain
102 B2 **Pit** *r.* U.S.A.
122 B2 **Pitanga** Brazil
123 D1 **Pitangui** Brazil
17 H6 **Pitcairn Islands** *terr.*
      S. Pacific Ocean
61 H2 **Piteå** Sweden
60 H2 **Piteälven** *r.* Sweden
78 B2 **Piteşti** Romania
43 C2 **Pithoragarh** India
64 C2 **Pitlochry** U.K.
96 B2 **Pitt Island** Can.
105 E3 **Pittsburg** U.S.A.
109 D2 **Pittsburgh** U.S.A.
109 E2 **Pittsfield** U.S.A.
21 D1 **Pittsworth** Austr.
123 C2 **Piumhi** Brazil
118 A2 **Piura** Peru
58 C2 **Pivdennyy Buh** *r.* Ukr.
99 E2 **Placentia** Can.
103 B3 **Placerville** U.S.A.
114 C2 **Placetas** Cuba
107 C2 **Plainview** U.S.A.
122 C1 **Planaltina** Brazil
110 B2 **Plaquemine** U.S.A.
74 B1 **Plasencia** Spain
115 C4 **Plato** Col.
105 D2 **Platte** *r.* U.S.A.
109 E2 **Plattsburgh** U.S.A.
69 F1 **Plau** Ger.
69 F2 **Plauen** Ger.

69 F1 **Plauer See** *l.* Ger.
57 E2 **Plavsk** Rus. Fed.
31 B2 **Plây Cu** Vietnam
97 E2 **Playgreen Lake** Can.
121 B4 **Plaza Huincul** Arg.
107 D3 **Pleasanton** U.S.A.
22 B2 **Pleasant Point** N.Z.
72 C2 **Pleaux** France
98 B1 **Pledger Lake** Can.
22 C1 **Plenty, Bay of** *g.* N.Z.
104 C1 **Plentywood** U.S.A.
54 D2 **Plesetsk** Rus. Fed.
99 C1 **Plétipi, Lac** *l.* Can.
68 C2 **Plettenberg** Ger.
90 B3 **Plettenberg Bay** S. Africa
78 B2 **Pleven** Bulg.
77 C2 **Pljevlja** Yugo.
77 C2 **Ploče** Croatia
71 D1 **Płock** Pol.
77 C2 **Pločno** *mt.* Bos.-Herz.
72 B2 **Ploemeur** France
78 C2 **Ploieşti** Romania
57 F2 **Ploskoye** Rus. Fed.
72 B2 **Plouzané** France
78 B2 **Plovdiv** Bulg.
56 B2 **Plungė** Lith.
56 C3 **Plyeshchanitsy** Belarus
115 D3 **Plymouth** Montserrat
67 A3 **Plymouth** U.K.
108 B2 **Plymouth** U.S.A.
56 C2 **Plyussa** Rus. Fed.
70 C2 **Plzeň** Czech Rep.
82 B3 **Pô** Burkina
76 B1 **Po** *r.* Italy
45 E2 **Pobedy, Pik** *mt.* China/Kyrg.
110 B1 **Pocahontas** U.S.A.
102 D2 **Pocatello** U.S.A.
58 B1 **Pochayiv** Ukr.
57 D3 **Pochep** Rus. Fed.
57 D3 **Pochinok** Rus. Fed.
113 C3 **Pochutla** Mex.
109 D3 **Pocomoke City** U.S.A.
123 C2 **Poços de Caldas** Brazil
57 D2 **Poddor'ye** Rus. Fed.
59 D1 **Podgorenskiy** Rus. Fed.
77 C2 **Podgorica** Yugo.
50 C3 **Podgornoye** Rus. Fed.
51 H2 **Podkamennaya Tunguska** *r.*
      Rus. Fed.
57 E2 **Podol'sk** Rus. Fed.
77 D2 **Podujevo** Yugo.
90 A2 **Pofadder** S. Africa
57 D3 **Pogar** Rus. Fed.
77 D2 **Pogradec** Albania
33 B2 **P'ohang** S. Korea
78 B2 **Poiana Mare** Romania
86 C3 **Poie** Dem. Rep. Congo
86 B3 **Pointe-Noire** Congo
94 D2 **Point Lake** Can.
108 C3 **Point Pleasant** U.S.A.
72 C2 **Poitiers** France
42 B2 **Pokaran** India
43 C2 **Pokhara** Nepal
51 J2 **Pokrovsk** Rus. Fed.
59 D2 **Pokrovskoye** Rus. Fed.
106 A1 **Polacca** U.S.A.
74 B1 **Pola de Lena** Spain
71 D1 **Poland** *country* Europe
56 C2 **Polatsk** Belarus
45 C3 **Pol-e Khomrī** Afgh.
29 C2 **Polewali** Indon.
86 B2 **Poli** Cameroon
70 C1 **Police** Pol.
77 C2 **Policoro** Italy
73 D2 **Poligny** France
32 B1 **Polillo Islands** Phil.
58 B1 **Polis'ke** Ukr.
71 D1 **Polkowice** Pol.
77 C3 **Pollino, Monte** *mt.* Italy
59 D2 **Polohy** Ukr.

58 B1 **Polonne** Ukr.
102 D1 **Polson** U.S.A.
59 C2 **Poltava** Ukr.
34 B2 **Poltavka** Rus. Fed.
59 D2 **Poltavskaya** Rus. Fed.
56 C2 **Põlva** Estonia
79 B2 **Polygyros** Greece
74 B2 **Pombal** Port.
76 B2 **Pomezia** Italy
60 I2 **Pomokaira** reg. Fin.
78 C2 **Pomorie** Bulg.
70 C1 **Pomorska, Zatoka** b. Pol.
123 D1 **Pompéu** Brazil
107 D1 **Ponca City** U.S.A.
115 D3 **Ponce** Puerto Rico
41 B3 **Pondicherry** India
95 F2 **Pond Inlet** Can.
74 B1 **Ponferrada** Spain
85 A4 **Pongo** watercourse Sudan
91 D2 **Pongola** r. S. Africa
96 C2 **Ponoka** Can.
122 B3 **Ponta Grossa** Brazil
122 C1 **Pontalina** Brazil
73 D2 **Pont-à-Mousson** France
73 D2 **Pontarlier** France
70 B2 **Pontcharra** France
110 B2 **Pontchartrain, Lake** U.S.A.
74 B2 **Ponte de Sor** Port.
97 D3 **Ponteix** Can.
118 C3 **Pontes-e-Lacerda** Brazil
74 B1 **Pontevedra** Spain
108 B2 **Pontiac** IL U.S.A.
108 C2 **Pontiac** MI U.S.A.
29 B2 **Pontianak** Indon.
72 B2 **Pontivy** France
119 C1 **Pontoetoe** Suriname
97 E2 **Ponton** Can.
67 B3 **Pontypool** U.K.
76 B2 **Ponziane, Isole** is Italy
67 C3 **Poole** U.K.
Poona India see Pune
20 B2 **Pooncarie** Austr.
120 B2 **Poopó, Lago de** l. Bol.
118 A1 **Popayán** Col.
51 I2 **Popigay** r. Rus. Fed.
20 B2 **Popiltah** Austr.
97 E2 **Poplar** r. Can.
105 E3 **Poplar Bluff** U.S.A.
86 B3 **Popokabaka**
 Dem. Rep. Congo
78 C2 **Popovo** Bulg.
71 E2 **Poprad** Slovakia
119 D3 **Porangatu** Brazil
42 A2 **Porbandar** India
94 B2 **Porcupine** r. Can./U.S.A.
76 B1 **Poreč** Croatia
61 H3 **Pori** Fin.
22 B2 **Porirua** N.Z.
56 C2 **Porkhov** Rus. Fed.
72 B2 **Pornic** France
51 K3 **Poronaysk** Rus. Fed.
79 B3 **Poros** Greece
61 E4 **Porsgrunn** Norway
65 C1 **Portadown** U.K.
65 D1 **Portaferry** U.K.
108 B2 **Portage** U.S.A.
97 E3 **Portage la Prairie** Can.
96 B3 **Port Alberni** Can.
74 B2 **Portalegre** Port.
107 C2 **Portales** U.S.A.
96 A2 **Port Alexander** U.S.A.
96 B2 **Port Alice** Can.
102 B1 **Port Angeles** U.S.A.
19 D4 **Port Arthur** Austr.
107 E3 **Port Arthur** U.S.A.
64 A3 **Port Askaig** U.K.
20 A2 **Port Augusta** Austr.
115 C3 **Port-au-Prince** Haiti
99 E1 **Port aux Choix** Can.
41 D3 **Port Blair** India

20 B3 **Port Campbell** Austr.
22 B3 **Port Chalmers** N.Z.
111 D3 **Port Charlotte** U.S.A.
115 C3 **Port-de-Paix** Haiti
96 A2 **Port Edward** Can.
123 D1 **Porteirinha** Brazil
119 C2 **Portel** Brazil
98 B2 **Port Elgin** Can.
91 C3 **Port Elizabeth** S. Africa
64 A3 **Port Ellen** U.K.
66 A1 **Port Erin** Isle of Man
90 A3 **Porterville** S. Africa
103 C3 **Porterville** U.S.A.
20 B3 **Port Fairy** Austr.
22 C1 **Port Fitzroy** N.Z.
86 A3 **Port-Gentil** Gabon
83 C4 **Port Harcourt** Nigeria
96 B2 **Port Hardy** Can.
 Port Harrison Can. see
 Inukjuak
99 D2 **Port Hawkesbury** Can.
18 A2 **Port Hedland** Austr.
67 A2 **Porthmadog** U.K.
99 E1 **Port Hope Simpson** Can.
108 C2 **Port Huron** U.S.A.
74 B2 **Portimão** Port.
21 C2 **Portland** N.S.W. Austr.
20 B3 **Portland** Vic. Austr.
109 E2 **Portland** ME U.S.A.
102 B1 **Portland** OR U.S.A.
96 A2 **Portland Canal** inlet Can.
65 C2 **Portlaoise** Rep. of Ireland
107 D3 **Port Lavaca** U.S.A.
20 A2 **Port Lincoln** Austr.
82 A4 **Port Loko** Sierra Leone
21 D2 **Port Macquarie** Austr.
96 B2 **Port McNeill** Can.
99 D2 **Port-Menier** Can.
27 D3 **Port Moresby** P.N.G.
64 A1 **Port Nis** U.K.
90 A2 **Port Nolloth** S. Africa
 Port-Nouveau-Québec Can.
 see Kangiqsualujjuaq
118 B2 **Porto Acre** Brazil
120 C4 **Porto Alegre** Brazil
119 C3 **Porto Artur** Brazil
119 C3 **Porto dos Gaúchos Óbidos**
 Brazil
118 C3 **Porto Esperidião** Brazil
76 B2 **Portoferraio** Italy
119 D2 **Porto Franco** Brazil
115 C4 **Port of Spain** Trin. and Tob.
76 B1 **Portogruaro** Italy
76 B2 **Portomaggiore** Italy
122 B2 **Porto Mendes** Brazil
120 C3 **Porto Murtinho** Brazil
119 D3 **Porto Nacional** Brazil
82 C4 **Porto-Novo** Benin
122 B2 **Porto Primavera, Represa**
 resr Brazil
119 C2 **Porto Santana** Brazil
123 E1 **Porto Seguro** Brazil
76 B2 **Porto Tolle** Italy
76 A2 **Porto Torres** Sardinia Italy
73 D3 **Porto-Vecchio** Corsica France
118 B2 **Porto Velho** Brazil
118 A2 **Portoviejo** Ecuador
20 B3 **Port Phillip Bay** Austr.
20 A2 **Port Pirie** Austr.
64 A2 **Portree** U.K.
96 B3 **Port Renfrew** Can.
65 C1 **Portrush** U.K.
84 B1 **Port Said** Egypt
111 C3 **Port St Joe** U.S.A.
91 C3 **Port St Johns** S. Africa
91 D3 **Port Shepstone** S. Africa
67 C3 **Portsmouth** U.K.
109 E2 **Portsmouth** NH U.S.A.
108 C3 **Portsmouth** OH U.S.A.

109 D3 **Portsmouth** VA U.S.A.
65 C1 **Portstewart** U.K.
84 B3 **Port Sudan** Sudan
110 C3 **Port Sulphur** U.S.A.
67 B3 **Port Talbot** U.K.
74 B2 **Portugal** country Europe
65 B2 **Portumna** Rep. of Ireland
73 C3 **Port-Vendres** France
61 I3 **Porvoo** Fin.
33 B2 **P'yongyang** S. Korea
120 C3 **Posadas** Arg.
57 E2 **Poshekhon'ye** Rus. Fed.
60 I2 **Posio** Fin.
26 C3 **Poso** Indon.
119 D3 **Posse** Brazil
69 E2 **Pößneck** Ger.
107 C2 **Post** U.S.A.
98 C1 **Poste-de-la-Baleine** Can.
90 B2 **Postmasburg** S. Africa
77 C2 **Posušje** Bos.-Herz.
107 E1 **Poteau** U.S.A.
77 C2 **Potenza** Italy
91 C1 **Potgietersrus** S. Africa
119 D2 **Poti** r. Brazil
49 C1 **P'ot'i** Georgia
83 D3 **Potiskum** Nigeria
109 D3 **Potomac, South Branch** r.
 U.S.A.
120 B2 **Potosí** Bol.
32 B1 **Pototan** Phil.
106 C3 **Potrero del Llano** Mex.
69 F1 **Potsdam** Ger.
109 E2 **Potsdam** U.S.A.
109 D2 **Pottstown** U.S.A.
109 D2 **Pottsville** U.S.A.
99 E2 **Pouch Cove** Can.
109 E2 **Poughkeepsie** U.S.A.
66 B2 **Poulton-le-Fylde** U.K.
123 C2 **Pouso Alegre** Brazil
31 B2 **Poŭthĭsăt** Cambodia
71 D2 **Považská Bystrica** Slovakia
77 C2 **Povlen** mt. Yugo.
74 B1 **Póvoa de Varzim** Port.
104 B2 **Powell** U.S.A.
103 D3 **Powell, Lake** resr U.S.A.
96 B3 **Powell River** Can.
122 B1 **Poxoréu** Brazil
 Poyang China see Boyang
39 B3 **Poyang Hu** l. China
77 D2 **Požarevac** Yugo.
113 C2 **Poza Rica** Mex.
77 C1 **Požega** Croatia
77 D2 **Požega** Yugo.
47 D2 **Pozm Tīāb** Iran
71 D1 **Poznań** Pol.
74 C2 **Pozoblanco** Spain
76 B2 **Pozzuoli** Italy
28 B2 **Prabumulih** Indon.
70 C2 **Prachatice** Czech Rep.
31 A2 **Prachuap Khiri Khan** Thai.
123 E1 **Prado** Brazil
70 C1 **Prague** Czech Rep.
 Praha Czech Rep. see
 Prague
107 C2 **Prairie Dog Town Fork** r.
 U.S.A.
108 A2 **Prairie du Chien** U.S.A.
28 A1 **Prapat** Indon.
122 C1 **Prata** Brazil
73 E3 **Prato** Italy
105 D3 **Pratt** U.S.A.
29 C2 **Praya** Indon.
31 B2 **Preăh Vihéar** Cambodia
57 F2 **Prechistoye** Rus. Fed.
97 D2 **Preeceville** Can.
56 C2 **Preili** Latvia
21 C2 **Premer** Austr.
73 C2 **Prémery** France
69 F1 **Premnitz** Ger.
70 C1 **Prenzlau** Ger.

31 A2 **Preparis Island** Cocos Is
31 A2 **Preparis North Channel**
  Cocos Is
31 A2 **Preparis South Channel**
  Cocos Is
71 D2 **Přerov** Czech Rep.
106 A2 **Prescott** U.S.A.
77 D2 **Preševo** Yugo.
120 B3 **Presidencia Roque Sáenz**
  Peña Arg.
119 D2 **Presidente Dutra** Brazil
122 B2 **Presidente Epitácio** Brazil
122 B2 **Presidente Prudente** Brazil
106 C3 **Presidio** U.S.A.
71 E2 **Prešov** Slovakia
109 F1 **Presque Isle** U.S.A.
69 F2 **Pressel** Ger.
66 B2 **Preston** U.K.
102 D2 **Preston** U.S.A.
64 R3 **Prestwick** U.K.
123 C1 **Preto** r. Brazil
91 C2 **Pretoria** S. Africa
79 B3 **Preveza** Greece
31 B2 **Prey Vêng** Cambodia
77 C2 **Priboj** Yugo.
103 D3 **Price** U.S.A.
56 B3 **Prienai** Lith.
90 B2 **Prieska** S. Africa
71 D2 **Prievidza** Slovakia
77 C2 **Prijedor** Bos.-Herz.
44 A2 **Prikaspiyskaya**
  Nizmennost' lowland
  Kazakh./Rus. Fed.
77 D2 **Prilep** Macedonia
59 D2 **Primorsko-Akhtarsk** Rus. Fed.
97 D2 **Primrose Lake** Can.
97 D2 **Prince Albert** Can.
90 B3 **Prince Albert** S. Africa
94 D2 **Prince Albert Peninsula**
  Can.
90 B3 **Prince Albert Road** S. Africa
94 C2 **Prince Alfred, Cape** Can.
90 A3 **Prince Alfred Hamlet**
  S. Africa
95 F2 **Prince Charles Island** Can.
23 E2 **Prince Charles Mountains**
  Antarctica
99 D2 **Prince Edward Island** prov.
  Can.
96 B3 **Prince George** Can.
94 E2 **Prince of Wales Island** Can.
96 A2 **Prince of Wales Island**
  U.S.A.
94 D1 **Prince of Wales Strait** Can.
94 D1 **Prince Patrick Island** Can.
04 E2 **Prince Regent Inlet**
  sea chan. Can.
96 A2 **Prince Rupert** Can.
19 D1 **Princess Charlotte Bay**
  Austr.
96 B2 **Princess Royal Island** Can.
96 B3 **Princeton** U.S.A.
102 B2 **Prineville** U.S.A.
58 B1 **Pripet** r. Belarus/Ukr.
58 A1 **Pripet Marshes** Belarus/Ukr.
77 D2 **Priština** Yugo.
69 F1 **Pritzwalk** Ger.
77 C2 **Privlaka** Croatia
57 F2 **Privolzhsk** Rus. Fed.
77 D2 **Prizren** Yugo.
119 C1 **Professor van Blommestein**
  Meer resr Suriname
113 D2 **Progreso** Mex.
49 C1 **Prokhladnyy** Rus. Fed.
77 D2 **Prokuplje** Yugo.
94 C3 **Prophet** r. Can.
96 B2 **Prophet River** Can.
19 D2 **Proserpine** Austr.
57 E3 **Protvino** Rus. Fed.
78 C2 **Provadiya** Bulg.

109 E2 **Providence** U.S.A.
114 B3 **Providencia, Isla de** i.
  Caribbean Sea
51 N2 **Providenya** Rus. Fed.
103 D2 **Provo** U.S.A.
97 C2 **Provost** Can.
122 B3 **Prudentópolis** Brazil
94 B2 **Prudhoe Bay** U.S.A.
68 C2 **Prüm** Ger.
73 D3 **Prunelli-di-Fiumorbo**
  Corsica France
71 E1 **Pruszków** Pol.
78 C1 **Prut** r. Europe
59 C1 **Pryluky** Ukr.
59 D2 **Prymors'k** Ukr.
107 D1 **Pryor** U.S.A.
  Prypyats' r. Belarus see Pripet
71 E2 **Przemyśl** Pol.
79 C3 **Psara** i. Greece
40 C1 **Psebay** Rus. Fed.
59 D3 **Pshekha** r. Rus. Fed.
56 C2 **Pskov** Rus. Fed.
56 C2 **Pskov, Lake**
  Estonia/Rus. Fed.
79 B2 **Ptolemaïda** Greece
77 C1 **Ptuj** Slovenia
118 A2 **Pucallpa** Peru
39 B3 **Pucheng** China
33 B2 **Puch'ŏn** S. Korea
71 D1 **Puck** Pol.
60 I2 **Pudasjärvi** Fin.
54 C2 **Pudozh** Rus. Fed.
  Puduchcheri India see
  Pondicherry
113 C3 **Puebla** Mex.
104 C3 **Puebla** U.S.A.
121 B4 **Puelén** Arg.
74 C2 **Puente-Genil** Spain
121 A5 **Puerto Aisén** Chile
120 B2 **Puerto Alegre** Bol.
113 C3 **Puerto Ángel** Mex.
114 B4 **Puerto Armuelles** Panama
118 B1 **Puerto Carreño** Col.
121 A5 **Puerto Cisnes** Chile
112 A2 **Puerto Cortés** Mex.
113 C3 **Puerto Escondido** Mex.
120 B2 **Puerto Frey** Bol.
118 B1 **Puerto Inírida** Col.
120 C2 **Puerto Isabel** Bol.
118 A2 **Puerto Leguizamo** Col.
112 A2 **Puerto Libertad** Mex.
74 C2 **Puertollano** Spain
121 B5 **Puerto Madryn** Arg.
118 B3 **Puerto Maldonado** Peru
121 A5 **Puerto Montt** Chile
121 A6 **Puerto Natales** Chile
118 B1 **Puerto Nuevo** Col.
112 A1 **Puerto Peñasco** Mex.
120 C3 **Puerto Pinasco** Para.
115 C3 **Puerto Plata** Dom. Rep.
118 A2 **Puerto Portillo** Peru
32 A2 **Puerto Princesa** Phil.
115 D3 **Puerto Rico** terr. West Indies
126 B3 **Puerto Rico Trench**
  sea feature Caribbean Sea
121 B6 **Puerto Santa Cruz** Arg.
112 B2 **Puerto Vallarta** Mex.
55 D3 **Pugachev** Rus. Fed.
42 B2 **Pugal** India
22 B2 **Pukaki, Lake** N.Z.
97 D2 **Pukatawagan** Can.
33 B1 **Pukchin** N. Korea
33 B1 **Pukch'ŏng** N. Korea
22 B1 **Pukekohe** N.Z.
33 B1 **Puksubaek-san** mt. N. Korea
76 B2 **Pula** Croatia
76 A3 **Pula** Sardinia Italy
120 B3 **Pulacayo** Bol.

60 I3 **Pulkkila** Fin.
102 C1 **Pullman** U.S.A.
32 B1 **Pulog, Mount** Phil.
118 A2 **Puná, Isla** i. Ecuador
22 B2 **Punakaiki** N.Z.
91 D1 **Punda Maria** S. Africa
41 B3 **Pune** India
33 B1 **P'ungsan** N. Korea
89 C2 **Púnguè** r. Moz.
121 B4 **Punta Alta** Arg.
121 A6 **Punta Arenas** Chile
76 A2 **Punta Balestrieri** mt.
  Sardinia Italy
114 B3 **Puntarenas** Costa Rica
118 A1 **Punto Fijo** Venez.
60 I3 **Puolanka** Fin.
38 B3 **Puqi** China
50 G2 **Pur** r. Rus. Fed.
43 C3 **Puri** India
68 B1 **Purmerend** Neth.
43 C2 **Pūrnia** India
43 C2 **Puruliya** India
118 B2 **Purus** r. Peru
29 B2 **Purwakarta** Indon.
33 B1 **Puryŏng** N. Korea
33 B2 **Pusan** S. Korea
56 C2 **Pushkinskiye Gory** Rus. Fed.
56 C2 **Pustoshka** Rus. Fed.
30 A1 **Putao** Myanmar
39 B3 **Putian** China
  Puting China see De'an
29 C2 **Puting, Tanjung** pt Indon.
69 F1 **Putlitz** Ger.
26 A2 **Putrajaya** Malaysia
70 C1 **Puttgarden** Ger.
118 A2 **Putumayo** r. Col.
29 C1 **Putusibau** Indon.
59 C1 **Putyvl'** Ukr.
95 F2 **Puvurnituq** Can.
38 B2 **Puyang** China
72 C3 **Puylaurens** France
67 A2 **Pwllheli** U.K.
31 A2 **Pyapon** Myanmar
50 G2 **Pyasina** r. Rus. Fed.
55 D3 **Pyatigorsk** Rus. Fed.
59 C2 **P'yatykhatky** Ukr.
30 A2 **Pyè** Myanmar
56 C3 **Pyetrykaw** Belarus
61 H3 **Pyhäjärvi** i. Fin.
60 H3 **Pyhäjoki** r. Fin.
60 I3 **Pyhäsalmi** Fin.
30 A2 **Pyinmana** Myanmar
33 B2 **Pyŏksŏng** N. Korea
33 B2 **P'yŏnggang** N. Korea
33 B2 **P'yŏngyang** N. Korea
103 C2 **Pyramid Lake** U.S.A.
75 H3 **Pyrenees** mts Europe
79 B3 **Pyrgos** Greece
59 C1 **Pyryatyn** Ukr.
71 C1 **Pyrzyce** Pol.
56 C2 **Pytalovo** Rus. Fed.
30 A2 **Pyu** Myanmar
79 B3 **Pyxaria** mt. Greece

Q

95 G1 **Qaanaaq** Greenland
91 C3 **Qacha's Nek** Lesotho
37 D2 **Qagan Nur** China
36 C2 **Qaidam Pendi** basin China
42 A1 **Qalāt** Afgh.
46 B2 **Qal'at Bīshah** Saudi Arabia
97 E1 **Qamanirjuaq Lake** l. Can.
  Qamanittuaq Can. see
  Baker Lake
46 B3 **Qam Hadil** Saudi Arabia
46 B2 **Qaryat al Ulyā** Saudi Arabia

95 H2 **Qasigiannguit** Greenland
47 D2 **Qaşr-e-Qand** Iran
49 C2 **Qaşr-e Shīrīn** Iran
95 H2 **Qassimiut** Greenland
46 B3 **Qa'tabah** Yemen
47 C2 **Qatar** *country* Asia
84 A2 **Qattâra Depression** Egypt
49 C1 **Qazax** Azer.
49 C1 **Qazimämmäd** Azer.
49 C2 **Qazvīn** Iran
84 B2 **Qena** Egypt
95 H2 **Qeqertarsuaq** *i.* Greenland
95 H2 **Qeqertarsuatsiaat** Greenland
95 H2 **Qeqertarsuup Tunua** *b.* Greenland
47 C2 **Qeshm** Iran
38 A3 **Qianjiang** *Chongqing* China
38 B2 **Qianjiang** *Hubei* China
33 A1 **Qian Shan** *mts* China
38 C2 **Qidong** China
39 A3 **Qijiang** China
38 C2 **Qijiaojing** China
95 G2 **Qikiqtarjuaq** Can.
42 A2 **Qila Ladgasht** Pak.
36 C2 **Qilian Shan** *mts* China
95 I2 **Qillak** *i.* Greenland
38 B3 **Qimen** China
95 G1 **Qimusseriarsuaq** *b.* Greenland
38 C2 **Qingdao** China
36 C2 **Qinghai Hu** *salt l.* China
36 C2 **Qinghai Nanshan** *mts* China
39 B3 **Qingyuan** *Guangdong* China
33 A1 **Qingyuan** *Liaoning* China
36 B2 **Qing Zang Gaoyuan** *plat.* China
38 B2 **Qingzhou** China
38 B2 **Qinhuangdao** China
38 A2 **Qin Ling** *mts* China
38 B2 **Qinyang** China
39 A3 **Qinzhou** China
39 B4 **Qionghai** China
36 C2 **Qionglai Shan** *mts* China
39 B4 **Qiongshan** China
37 E1 **Qiqihar** China
47 C2 **Qīr** Iran
34 B1 **Qitaihe** China
38 B2 **Qixian** China
Qogir Feng *mt.* China/Jammu and Kashmir *see* K2
49 D2 **Qom** Iran
49 D2 **Qomisheh** Iran
Qomolangma Feng *mt.* China/Nepal *see* Everest, Mount
Qoqek China *see* Tacheng
68 C1 **Quakenbrück** Ger.
31 B2 **Quang Ngai** Vietnam
31 B2 **Quang Tri** Vietnam
39 B3 **Quanzhou** *Fujian* China
39 B3 **Quanzhou** *Guangxi* China
76 A3 **Quartu Sant'Elena** *Sardinia* Italy
106 A2 **Quartzsite** U.S.A.
49 C1 **Quba** Azer.
21 C3 **Queanbeyan** Austr.
99 C2 **Québec** Can.
98 C1 **Québec** *prov.* Can.
69 E2 **Quedlinburg** Ger.
96 A2 **Queen Charlotte** Can.
96 A2 **Queen Charlotte Islands** Can.
96 B2 **Queen Charlotte Sound** *sea chan.* Can.
96 B2 **Queen Charlotte Strait** Can.
94 D1 **Queen Elizabeth Islands** Can.

94 E2 **Queen Maud Gulf** Can.
23 B2 **Queen Maud Land** *reg.* Antarctica
23 N1 **Queen Maud Mountains** Antarctica
20 B1 **Queensland** *state* Austr.
19 D4 **Queenstown** Austr.
22 A3 **Queenstown** N.Z.
91 C3 **Queenstown** S. Africa
89 C2 **Quelimane** Moz.
106 B2 **Quemado** U.S.A.
122 B2 **Queréncia do Norte** Brazil
113 B2 **Querétaro** Mex.
69 E2 **Querfurt** Ger.
96 B2 **Quesnel** Can.
96 B2 **Quesnel Lake** Can.
42 A1 **Quetta** Pak.
32 A2 **Quezon** Phil.
32 B1 **Quezon City** Phil.
88 A2 **Quibala** Angola
118 A1 **Quibdó** Col.
72 B2 **Quiberon** France
72 C3 **Quillan** France
121 C4 **Quilmes** Arg.
41 B4 **Quilon** India
19 D2 **Quilpie** Austr.
121 A4 **Quilpué** Chile
88 A1 **Quimbele** Angola
120 B3 **Quimilí** Arg.
72 B2 **Quimper** France
72 B2 **Quimperlé** France
105 E3 **Quincy** *IL* U.S.A.
109 E2 **Quincy** *MA* U.S.A.
31 B2 **Qui Nhon** Vietnam
75 C1 **Quinto** Spain
89 D2 **Quionga** Moz.
21 D2 **Quirindi** Austr.
89 C3 **Quissico** Moz.
88 A2 **Quitapa** Angola
118 A2 **Quito** Ecuador
119 E2 **Quixadá** Brazil
39 A3 **Qujing** China
20 A2 **Quorn** Austr.
47 C2 **Qurayat** Oman
45 C3 **Qürghonteppa** Tajik.
84 B2 **Quseir** Egypt
39 B3 **Quzhou** China

R

71 D2 **Raab** *r.* Austria
60 H3 **Raahe** Fin.
60 B1 **Raalte** Neth.
29 C2 **Raas** *i.* Indon.
29 C2 **Raba** Indon.
82 B1 **Rabat** Morocco
46 A2 **Rābigh** Saudi Arabia
58 B2 **Rābnița** Moldova
99 E2 **Race, Cape** Can.
110 B3 **Raceland** U.S.A.
31 B3 **Rach Gia** Vietnam
108 B2 **Racine** U.S.A.
46 B3 **Radā'** Yemen
78 C1 **Rădăuți** Romania
108 B3 **Radcliff** U.S.A.
42 B2 **Radhanpur** India
71 E1 **Radom** Pol.
71 D1 **Radomsko** Pol.
58 B1 **Radomyshl'** Ukr.
77 D2 **Radoviš** Macedonia
56 B2 **Radviliškis** Lith.
46 A2 **Radwá, Jabal** *mt.* Saudi Arabia
58 B1 **Radyvyliv** Ukr.
43 C2 **Rae Bareli** India
96 C1 **Rae-Edzo** Can.

96 C1 **Rae Lakes** Can.
68 C2 **Raeren** Belgium
22 C1 **Raetihi** N.Z.
120 B4 **Rafaela** Arg.
86 C2 **Rafaï** C.A.R.
46 B2 **Rafḥā'** Saudi Arabia
47 C1 **Rafsanjān** Iran
32 B2 **Ragang, Mount** *vol.* Phil.
77 B3 **Ragusa** *Sicily* Italy
27 C3 **Raha** Indon.
56 D3 **Rahachow** Belarus
42 B2 **Rahimyar Khan** Pak.
41 B3 **Raichur** India
43 C2 **Raigarh** India
96 C2 **Rainbow Lake** Can.
102 B1 **Rainier, Mount** *vol.* U.S.A.
98 A2 **Rainy Lake** Can.
97 E3 **Rainy River** Can.
43 C2 **Raipur** India
61 H3 **Raisio** Fin.
41 C3 **Rajahmundry** India
29 C1 **Rajang** *r.* Sarawak Malaysia
42 B2 **Rajanpur** Pak.
41 B4 **Rajapalaiyam** India
42 B2 **Rajasthan Canal** India
42 B2 **Rajgarh** India
42 B2 **Rajkot** India
42 B2 **Rajpur** India
43 C2 **Rajshahi** Bangl.
22 B2 **Rakaia** *r.* N.Z.
58 A2 **Rakhiv** Ukr.
59 D1 **Rakitnoye** Rus. Fed.
56 C2 **Rakke** Estonia
56 C2 **Rakvere** Estonia
111 E1 **Raleigh** U.S.A.
42 B2 **Ramgarh** India
49 C2 **Rāmhormoz** Iran
46 B3 **Ramlat Dahm** *des.* Saudi Arabia/Yemen
Ramlat Rabyānah *des.* Libya *see* Rebiana Sand Sea
78 C1 **Râmnicu Sărat** Romania
78 B1 **Râmnicu Vâlcea** Romania
57 E3 **Ramon'** Rus. Fed.
91 C1 **Ramotswa** Botswana
42 B2 **Rampur** India
30 A2 **Ramree Island** Myanmar
66 A1 **Ramsey** Isle of Man
67 D3 **Ramsgate** U.K.
43 C2 **Ranaghat** India
29 C1 **Ranau** *Sabah* Malaysia
121 A4 **Rancagua** Chile
43 C2 **Ranchi** India
61 F4 **Randers** Denmark
22 C2 **Rangiora** N.Z.
22 C1 **Rangitaiki** *r.* N.Z.
Rangoon Myanmar *see* Yangôn
43 C2 **Rangpur** Bangl.
97 E1 **Rankin Inlet** Can.
21 C2 **Rankin's Springs** Austr.
64 B2 **Rannoch Moor** *moorland* U.K.
42 B2 **Rann of Kachchh** *marsh* India
31 A3 **Ranong** Thai.
27 C3 **Ransiki** Indon.
29 C1 **Rantaupanjang** Indon.
28 A1 **Rantauprapat** Indon.
60 I2 **Ranua** Fin.
46 B2 **Ranyah, Wādī** *watercourse* Saudi Arabia
104 C2 **Rapid City** U.S.A.
56 B2 **Rapla** Estonia
42 A2 **Rapur** India
121 B5 **Rasa, Punta** *pt* Arg.
47 C2 **Ra's al Khaymah** U.A.E.
85 B3 **Ras Dashen** *mt.* Eth.
56 B2 **Raseiniai** Lith.
49 C2 **Rasht** Iran

42 A2 **Ras Koh** *mt.* Pak.
56 C2 **Rasony** Belarus
55 D3 **Rasskazovo** Rus. Fed.
47 C2 **Ras Tannūrah** Saudi Arabia
69 D1 **Rastede** Ger.
61 F3 **Rätan** Sweden
42 B2 **Ratangarh** India
31 A2 **Rat Buri** Thai.
30 A1 **Rathedaung** Myanmar
69 F1 **Rathenow** Ger.
65 C1 **Rathlin Island** U.K.
42 B2 **Ratlam** India
41 B3 **Ratnagiri** India
41 C4 **Ratnapura** Sri Lanka
58 A1 **Ratne** Ukr.
106 C1 **Raton** U.S.A.
64 D2 **Rattray Head** *hd* U.K.
69 E1 **Ratzeburg** Ger.
60 □B2 **Raufarhöfn** Iceland
22 C1 **Raukumara Range** *mts* N.Z.
61 H3 **Rauma** Fin.
29 C2 **Raung, Gunung** *vol.* Indon.
43 C2 **Raurkela** India
102 D1 **Ravalli** U.S.A.
49 C2 **Ravānsar** Iran
76 B2 **Ravenna** Italy
70 B2 **Ravensburg** Ger.
42 B1 **Ravi** *r.* Pak.
42 B1 **Rawalpindi** Pak.
71 D1 **Rawicz** Pol.
18 B3 **Rawlinna** Austr.
104 B2 **Rawlins** U.S.A.
121 B5 **Rawson** Arg.
41 C2 **Rāyagarha** India
37 E1 **Raychikhinsk** Rus. Fed.
46 B3 **Raydah** Yemen
55 E3 **Rayevskiy** Rus. Fed.
102 B1 **Raymond** U.S.A.
21 D2 **Raymond Terrace** Austr.
107 D3 **Raymondville** U.S.A.
113 C2 **Rayón** Mex.
31 B2 **Rayong** Thai.
46 A2 **Rayyis** Saudi Arabia
72 B2 **Raz, Pointe du** *pt* France
49 C2 **Razāzah, Buḩayrat ar** *l.* Iraq
78 C2 **Razgrad** Bulg.
78 B2 **Razim, Lacul** *lag.* Romania
78 B2 **Razlog** Bulg.
72 B2 **Ré, Île de** *i.* France
67 C3 **Reading** U.K.
109 D2 **Reading** U.S.A.
83 E2 **Rebiana Sand Sea** *des.* Libya
34 D1 **Rebun-tō** *i.* Japan
18 B3 **Recherche, Archipelago of the** *is* Austr.
57 D3 **Rechytsa** Belarus
119 E2 **Recife** Brazil
91 C3 **Recife, Cape** S. Africa
120 C3 **Reconquista** Arg.
110 B2 **Recklinghausen** Ger.
99 E1 **Red Bay** Can.
103 B2 **Red Bluff** U.S.A.
66 C1 **Redcar** U.K.
97 C2 **Redcliff** Can.
20 B2 **Red Cliffs** Austr.
96 C2 **Red Deer** Can.
94 D2 **Red Deer** *r.* Can.
97 C2 **Red Deer Lake** Can.
102 B2 **Redding** U.S.A.
67 C2 **Redditch** U.K.
105 D2 **Redfield** U.S.A.
98 A1 **Red Lake** Can.
105 E1 **Red Lakes** U.S.A.
102 E1 **Red Lodge** U.S.A.
102 B2 **Redmond** U.S.A.
105 D2 **Red Oak** U.S.A.
74 B2 **Redondo** Port.
127 B2 **Red Sea** Africa/Asia

96 B1 **Redstone** *r.* Can.
105 E2 **Red Wing** U.S.A.
105 D2 **Redwood Falls** U.S.A.
65 C2 **Ree, Lough** *l.* Rep. of Ireland
102 B2 **Reedsport** U.S.A.
22 B2 **Reefton** N.Z.
70 C2 **Regen** Ger.
123 E1 **Regência** Brazil
70 C2 **Regensburg** Ger.
82 C2 **Reggane** Alg.
77 C3 **Reggio di Calabria** Italy
76 B2 **Reggio nell'Emilia** Italy
78 B1 **Reghin** Romania
97 D2 **Regina** Can.
90 A1 **Rehoboth** Namibia
69 F2 **Reichenbach** Ger.
111 E1 **Reidsville** U.S.A.
67 C3 **Reigate** U.K.
73 C2 **Reims** France
69 E1 **Reinbek** Ger.
97 D2 **Reindeer** *r.* Can.
97 E2 **Reindeer Island** Can.
97 D2 **Reindeer Lake** Can.
60 F2 **Reine** Norway
68 C3 **Reinsfeld** Ger.
91 C2 **Reitz** S. Africa
90 B2 **Reivilo** S. Africa
97 D1 **Reliance** Can.
75 D2 **Relizane** Alg.
47 C2 **Remeshk** Iran
73 D2 **Remiremont** France
68 C2 **Remscheid** Ger.
70 B1 **Rendsburg** Ger.
109 D1 **Renfrew** Can.
28 B2 **Rengat** Indon.
58 B2 **Reni** Ukr.
60 D1 **Renmark** Austr.
68 D2 **Rennerod** Ger.
72 B2 **Rennes** France
97 D1 **Rennie Lake** Can.
76 B2 **Reno** *r.* Italy
103 C3 **Reno** U.S.A.
38 A3 **Renshou** China
108 B2 **Rensselaer** U.S.A.
43 C2 **Renukut** India
22 B2 **Renwick** N.Z.
23 B2 **Reo** Indon.
104 D3 **Republican** *r.* U.S.A.
95 F2 **Repulse Bay** Can.
118 A2 **Requena** Peru
75 C2 **Requena** Spain
122 B2 **Reserva** Brazil
120 C3 **Resistencia** Arg.
78 B1 **Reșița** Romania
94 E2 **Resolute Bay** Can.
95 G2 **Resolution Island** Can.
73 C2 **Rethel** France
79 B3 **Rethymno** Greece
81 H6 **Réunion** *terr.* Indian Ocean
75 D1 **Reus** Spain
70 B2 **Reutlingen** Ger.
96 C2 **Revelstoke** Can.
112 A3 **Revillagigedo, Islas** *is* Mex.
96 A2 **Revillagigedo Island** U.S.A.
43 C2 **Rewa** India
102 D2 **Rexburg** U.S.A.
60 □A3 **Reykjanestá** *pt* Iceland
60 □A3 **Reykjavík** Iceland
113 C2 **Reynosa** Mex.
56 C2 **Rēzekne** Latvia
68 C1 **Rhein** *r.* Ger. *see* Rhine
69 F1 **Rheine** Ger.
69 F1 **Rheinsberg** Ger.
68 C2 **Rhin** *r.* France *see* Rhine
69 F1 **Rhine** *r.* Europe
108 B1 **Rhinelander** U.S.A.
69 F1 **Rhinluch** *marsh* Ger.
69 F1 **Rhinow** Ger.
109 E2 **Rhode Island** *state* U.S.A.
79 C3 **Rhodes** Greece

79 C3 **Rhodes** *i.* Greece
78 B2 **Rhodope Mountains** Bulg./Greece
73 C3 **Rhône** *r.* France/Switz.
 Rhuthun U.K. *see* Ruthin
66 B2 **Rhyl** U.K.
122 C1 **Rianápolis** Brazil
28 B1 **Riau, Kepulauan** *is* Indon.
74 B1 **Ribadeo** Spain
74 B1 **Ribadesella** Spain
122 B2 **Ribas do Rio Pardo** Brazil
89 C2 **Ribáuè** Moz.
66 B2 **Ribble** *r.* U.K.
122 C1 **Ribeira** *r.* Brazil
122 C2 **Ribeirão Preto** Brazil
72 C2 **Ribérac** France
120 B2 **Riberalta** Bol.
70 C1 **Ribnitz-Damgarten** Ger.
108 A1 **Rice Lake** U.S.A.
91 D3 **Richards Bay** S. Africa
94 B2 **Richardson Mountains** Can.
103 D3 **Richfield** U.S.A.
102 C1 **Richland** U.S.A.
108 A2 **Richland Center** U.S.A.
21 D2 **Richmond** *N.S.W.* Austr.
19 D2 **Richmond** *Qld* Austr.
22 B2 **Richmond** N.Z.
90 B3 **Richmond** S. Africa
66 C1 **Richmond** U.K.
108 C3 **Richmond** *IN* U.S.A.
108 C3 **Richmond** *KY* U.S.A.
109 D3 **Richmond** *VA* U.S.A.
98 C2 **Rideau Lakes** Can.
103 C3 **Ridgecrest** U.S.A.
70 C1 **Riesa** Ger.
68 C1 **Rieste** Ger.
81 D2 **Riet** *r.* S. Africa
69 D2 **Rietberg** Ger.
76 B2 **Rieti** Italy
104 B3 **Rifle** U.S.A.
56 B2 **Rīga** Latvia
56 B2 **Riga, Gulf of** Estonia/Latvia
47 C2 **Rīgān** Iran
102 D2 **Rigby** U.S.A.
99 E1 **Rigolet** Can.
61 H3 **Riihimäki** Fin.
76 B1 **Rijeka** Croatia
102 C2 **Riley** U.S.A.
46 B2 **Rimah, Wādī al** *watercourse* Saudi Arabia
71 E2 **Rimavská Sobota** Slovakia
96 C2 **Rimbey** Can.
76 B2 **Rimini** Italy
99 D2 **Rimouski** Can.
61 F3 **Ringebu** Norway
61 E4 **Ringkøbing** Denmark
60 G2 **Ringvassøy** *i.* Norway
69 D1 **Rinteln** Ger.
118 A2 **Riobamba** Ecuador
118 B3 **Rio Branco** Brazil
122 C3 **Rio Branco do Sul** Brazil
122 B2 **Rio Brilhante** Brazil
122 C2 **Rio Claro** Brazil
121 B4 **Río Colorado** Arg.
121 B4 **Río Cuarto** Arg.
123 D2 **Rio de Janeiro** Brazil
121 B6 **Río Gallegos** Arg.
121 B6 **Río Grande** Arg.
120 C4 **Rio Grande** Brazil
112 B2 **Río Grande** Mex.
107 D3 **Rio Grande** *r.* Mex./U.S.A.
107 D3 **Rio Grande City** U.S.A.
118 A1 **Riohacha** Col.
118 A2 **Rioja** Peru
113 D2 **Río Lagartos** Mex.
73 C2 **Riom** France
120 B2 **Río Mulatos** Bol.
122 C3 **Rio Negro** Brazil
123 D1 **Rio Pardo de Minas** Brazil
106 B1 **Rio Rancho** U.S.A.

118 A2 **Río Tigre** Ecuador
122 B1 **Río Verde** Brazil
113 C2 **Río Verde** Mex.
122 B1 **Rio Verde de Mato Grosso** Brazil
58 C1 **Ripky** Ukr.
66 C2 **Ripley** U.K.
75 D1 **Ripoll** Spain
66 C1 **Ripon** U.K.
34 D1 **Rishiri-tō** i. Japan
61 E4 **Riser** Norway
90 B2 **Ritchie** S. Africa
31 A2 **Ritchie's Archipelago** is India
102 C1 **Ritzville** U.S.A.
120 B3 **Rivadavia** Arg.
76 B1 **Riva del Garda** Italy
114 B3 **Rivas** Nic.
120 C4 **Rivera** Uru.
97 D2 **Riverhurst** Can.
20 B2 **Riverina** reg. Austr.
90 B3 **Riversdale** S. Africa
103 C4 **Riverside** U.S.A.
104 B2 **Riverton** U.S.A.
99 D2 **Riverview** Can.
72 C3 **Rivesaltes** France
99 D2 **Rivière-du-Loup** Can.
58 B1 **Rivne** Ukr.
22 B2 **Riwaka** N.Z.
46 B2 **Riyadh** Saudi Arabia
49 C1 **Rize** Turkey
38 B2 **Rizhao** China
73 C2 **Roanne** France
109 D3 **Roanoke** U.S.A.
111 E1 **Roanoke** r. U.S.A.
111 E1 **Roanoke Rapids** U.S.A.
20 A3 **Robe** Austr.
69 F1 **Röbel** Ger.
60 H3 **Robertsfors** Sweden
90 A3 **Robertson** S. Africa
82 A4 **Robertsport** Liberia
99 C2 **Roberval** Can.
18 A2 **Robinson Range** hills Austr.
20 B2 **Robinvale** Austr.
97 D2 **Roblin** Can.
96 C2 **Robson, Mount** Can.
76 B3 **Rocca Busambra** mt. Sicily Italy
121 C4 **Rocha** Uru.
66 B2 **Rochdale** U.K.
122 B1 **Rochedo** Brazil
68 B2 **Rochefort** Belgium
72 B2 **Rochefort** France
105 E2 **Rochester** MN U.S.A.
109 E2 **Rochester** NH U.S.A.
109 D2 **Rochester** NY U.S.A.
108 B2 **Rockford** U.S.A.
19 E2 **Rockhampton** Austr.
111 D2 **Rock Hill** U.S.A.
18 A3 **Rockingham** Austr.
108 A2 **Rock Island** U.S.A.
104 B1 **Rock Springs** MT U.S.A.
107 C3 **Rocksprings** U.S.A.
104 B2 **Rock Springs** WY U.S.A.
104 C3 **Rocky Ford** U.S.A.
111 E1 **Rocky Mount** U.S.A.
96 C2 **Rocky Mountain House** Can.
92 D3 **Rocky Mountains** U.S.A.
68 B3 **Rocroi** France
70 C1 **Rødbyhavn** Denmark
99 E1 **Roddickton** Can.
72 C3 **Rodez** France
57 F2 **Rodniki** Rus. Fed.
        Rodos Greece see **Rhodes**
        Rodos i. Greece see **Rhodes**
18 A2 **Roebourne** Austr.
18 B1 **Roebuck Bay** Austr.
91 C1 **Roedtan** S. Africa
68 B2 **Roermond** Neth.

68 A2 **Roeselare** Belgium
95 F2 **Roes Welcome Sound** sea chan. Can.
110 B1 **Rogers** U.S.A.
90 B3 **Roggeveldberge** esc. S. Africa
60 G2 **Rognan** Norway
102 B2 **Rogue** r. U.S.A.
56 B2 **Roja** Latvia
28 B1 **Rokan** r. Indon.
56 C2 **Rokiškis** Lith.
58 B1 **Rokytne** Ukr.
122 B2 **Rolândia** Brazil
105 E3 **Rolla** U.S.A.
19 D2 **Roma** Austr.
27 C3 **Roma** i. Indon.
        Roma see **Rome**
91 C2 **Roma** Lesotho
107 D3 **Roma** U.S.A.
111 E2 **Romain, Cape** U.S.A.
78 C1 **Roman** Romania
78 B1 **Romania** country Europe
59 C3 **Roman-Kosh** mt. Ukr.
37 D1 **Romanovka** Rus. Fed.
73 D2 **Rombas** France
32 B1 **Romblon** Phil.
76 B2 **Rome** Italy
111 C2 **Rome** GA U.S.A.
109 E2 **Rome** NY U.S.A.
67 D3 **Romford** U.K.
73 C2 **Romilly-sur-Seine** France
59 C1 **Romny** Ukr.
72 C2 **Romorantin-Lanthenay** France
67 C3 **Romsey** U.K.
64 □ **Ronas Hill** hill U.K.
119 C3 **Roncador, Serra do** hills Brazil
74 B2 **Ronda** Spain
122 B2 **Rondon** Brazil
122 B1 **Rondonópolis** Brazil
42 B1 **Rondu** Jammu and Kashmir
39 A3 **Rong'an** China
39 A3 **Rongjiang** China
30 A1 **Rongklang Range** mts Myanmar
        Rongmei China see **Hefeng**
61 F4 **Rønne** Denmark
55 F4 **Ronne Ice Shelf** Antarctica
69 D1 **Ronnenberg** Ger.
68 A2 **Ronse** Belgium
68 B1 **Roordahuizum** Neth.
43 B2 **Roorkee** India
68 B2 **Roosendaal** Neth.
103 E2 **Roosevelt** U.S.A.
96 B2 **Roosevelt, Mount** Can.
23 K2 **Roosevelt Island** Antarctica
72 B3 **Roquefort** France
118 B1 **Roraima, Mount** Guyana
61 F3 **Røros** Norway
121 B4 **Rosario** Arg.
112 A1 **Rosario** Baja California Norte Mex.
112 B2 **Rosario** Sinaloa Mex.
112 B2 **Rosario** Sonora Mex.
119 C3 **Rosário Oeste** Brazil
112 A2 **Rosarito** Mex.
77 C3 **Rosarno** Italy
72 B2 **Roscoff** France
65 B2 **Roscommon** Rep. of Ireland
65 C2 **Roscrea** Rep. of Ireland
115 D3 **Roseau** Dominica
105 D1 **Roseau** U.S.A.
102 B2 **Roseburg** U.S.A.
107 D3 **Rosenberg** U.S.A.
69 D1 **Rosengarten** Ger.
70 C2 **Rosenheim** Ger.
97 C2 **Rosetown** Can.
90 A2 **Rosh Pinah** Namibia
78 C2 **Roşiori de Vede** Romania

61 F4 **Roskilde** Denmark
57 D3 **Roslavl'** Rus. Fed.
77 C2 **Rossano** Italy
65 B1 **Rossan Point** Rep. of Irelan[d]
23 K1 **Ross Ice Shelf** Antarctica
99 D2 **Rossignol, Lake** Can.
96 C3 **Rossland** Can.
65 C2 **Rosslare** Rep. of Ireland
82 A3 **Rosso** Maur.
73 D3 **Rosso, Capo** c. Corsica France
67 B3 **Ross-on-Wye** U.K.
59 D1 **Rossosh'** Rus. Fed.
96 A1 **Ross River** Can.
23 K2 **Ross Sea** Antarctica
60 F2 **Røssvatnet** l. Norway
47 C2 **Roştāq** Iran
97 D2 **Rosthern** Can.
70 C1 **Rostock** Ger.
57 E2 **Rostov** Rus. Fed.
59 D2 **Rostov-na-Donu** Rus. Fed.
60 H2 **Rosvik** Sweden
109 C2 **Roswell** U.S.A.
27 D2 **Rota** i. N. Mariana Is
27 C3 **Rote** i. Indon.
69 D1 **Rotenburg (Wümme)** Ger.
70 C2 **Roth** Ger.
66 C1 **Rothbury** U.K.
66 C2 **Rotherham** U.K.
64 B3 **Rothesay** U.K.
21 C2 **Roto** Austr.
73 D3 **Rotondo, Monte** mt. Corsica France
22 C1 **Rotorua** N.Z.
22 C1 **Rotorua, Lake** N.Z.
69 E2 **Rottenbach** Ger.
70 C2 **Rottenmann** Austria
68 B2 **Rotterdam** Neth.
70 B2 **Rottweil** Ger.
73 C1 **Roubaix** France
72 C2 **Rouen** France
        Roulers Belgium see **Roeselare**
21 D2 **Round Mountain** mt. Austr.
99 E2 **Round Pond** l. Can.
107 D2 **Round Rock** U.S.A.
102 E1 **Roundup** U.S.A.
64 C1 **Rousay** i. U.K.
98 C2 **Rouyn** Can.
60 I2 **Rovaniemi** Fin.
59 D2 **Roven'ki** Rus. Fed.
59 D2 **Roven'ky** Ukr.
76 B1 **Rovereto** Italy
31 B2 **Rôviĕng Tbong** Cambodia
76 B1 **Rovigo** Italy
76 B1 **Rovinj** Croatia
21 C1 **Rowena** Austr.
32 B2 **Roxas** Mindanao Phil.
32 B1 **Roxas** Mindoro Phil.
32 A1 **Roxas** Palawan Phil.
32 B1 **Roxas** Panay Phil.
20 A2 **Roxby Downs** Austr.
106 C1 **Roy** U.S.A.
108 B1 **Royale, Isle** i. U.S.A.
72 B2 **Royan** France
67 C2 **Royston** U.K.
58 C2 **Rozdil'na** Ukr.
59 C2 **Rozdol'ne** Ukr.
68 B3 **Rozoy-sur-Serre** France
55 D3 **Rtishchevo** Rus. Fed.
22 C1 **Ruapehu, Mount** vol. N.Z.
22 A3 **Ruapuke Island** N.Z.
46 B3 **Rub' al Khālī** des. Saudi Arabia
59 D2 **Rubizhne** Ukr.
45 E1 **Rubtsovsk** Rus. Fed.
103 C2 **Ruby Mountains** U.S.A.
34 C2 **Rudnaya Pristan'** Rus. Fed.
57 D3 **Rudnya** Rus. Fed.
44 C1 **Rudnyy** Kazakh.

50 E1 **Rudol'fa, Ostrov** *i.* Rus. Fed.
69 E2 **Rudolstadt** Ger.
87 D3 **Rufiji** *r.* Tanz.
121 B4 **Rufino** Arg.
89 B2 **Rufunsa** Zambia
38 C2 **Rugao** China
67 C2 **Rugby** U.K.
104 C1 **Rugby** U.S.A.
70 C1 **Rügen** *i.* Ger.
69 E2 **Ruhla** Ger.
56 B2 **Ruhnu** *i.* Estonia
68 C2 **Ruhr** *r.* Ger.
39 C3 **Rui'an** China
106 B2 **Ruidoso** U.S.A.
112 B2 **Ruiz** Mex.
87 D3 **Rukwa, Lake** Tanz.
64 A2 **Rum** *i.* U.K.
77 C1 **Ruma** Yugo.
46 B2 **Rumāh** Saudi Arabia
85 A4 **Rumbek** Sudan
73 D2 **Rumilly** France
18 C1 **Rum Jungle** Austr.
22 B2 **Runanga** N.Z.
66 B2 **Runcorn** U.K.
88 A2 **Rundu** Namibia
36 B2 **Ruoqiang** China
98 C1 **Rupert** *r.* Can.
98 C1 **Rupert Bay** Can.
89 C2 **Rusape** Zimbabwe
78 C2 **Ruse** Bulg.
45 D3 **Rushon** Tajik.
104 C2 **Rushville** U.S.A.
21 C3 **Rushworth** Austr.
97 D2 **Russell** Can.
22 B1 **Russell** N.Z.
110 C2 **Russellville** *AL* U.S.A.
110 B1 **Russellville** *AR* U.S.A.
108 B3 **Russellville** *KY* U.S.A.
69 D2 **Rüsselsheim** Ger.
50 D3 **Russian Federation** *country*
Asia/Europe
91 C2 **Rustenburg** S. Africa
110 B2 **Ruston** U.S.A.
66 B2 **Ruthin** U.K.
109 E2 **Rutland** U.S.A.
43 B1 **Rutog** China
87 E4 **Ruvuma** *r.* Moz./Tanz.
47 C2 **Ruweis** U.A.E.
45 C1 **Ruzayevka** Kazakh.
55 D3 **Ruzayevka** Rus. Fed.
87 C3 **Rwanda** *country* Africa
57 E3 **Ryazan'** Rus. Fed.
57 F3 **Ryazhsk** Rus. Fed.
54 C2 **Rybachiy, Poluostrov** *pen.*
Rus. Fed.
57 E2 **Rybinsk** Rus. Fed.
57 E2 **Rybinskoye**
Vodokhranilishche *resr*
Rus. Fed.
71 D1 **Rybnik** Pol.
57 E3 **Rybnoye** Rus. Fed.
67 D3 **Rye** U.K.
57 D3 **Ryl'sk** Rus. Fed.
35 C3 **Ryōtsu** Japan
Ryukyu Islands Japan *see*
Nansei-shotō
71 E1 **Rzeszów** Pol.
57 D2 **Rzhev** Rus. Fed.

S

47 C2 **Sa'ādatābād** Iran
69 E2 **Saale** *r.* Ger.
69 E2 **Saalfeld** Ger.
70 B2 **Saarbrücken** Ger.
56 B2 **Saaremaa** *i.* Estonia
60 I2 **Saarenkylä** Fin.

61 I3 **Saarijärvi** Fin.
70 B2 **Saarlouis** Ger.
48 B2 **Sab' Ābār** Syria
75 D1 **Sabadell** Spain
29 C1 **Sabah** *state* Malaysia
29 C2 **Sabalana** *i.* Indon.
123 D1 **Sabará** Brazil
76 B2 **Sabaudia** Italy
83 D2 **Sabhā** Libya
91 D2 **Sabie** *r.* Moz./S. Africa
113 B2 **Sabinas** Mex.
113 B2 **Sabinas Hidalgo** Mex.
99 D2 **Sable, Cape** Can.
111 D3 **Sable, Cape** U.S.A.
99 E2 **Sable Island** Can.
74 B1 **Sabugal** Port.
46 B3 **Şabyā** Saudi Arabia
44 B3 **Sabzevār** Iran
88 A2 **Sachanga** Angola
98 A1 **Sachigo Lake** *l.* Can.
33 B3 **Sach'on** S. Korea
94 C2 **Sachs Harbour** Can.
103 B3 **Sacramento** U.S.A.
106 B2 **Sacramento Mountains**
U.S.A.
103 B2 **Sacramento Valley** U.S.A.
91 C3 **Sada** S. Africa
75 C1 **Sádaba** Spain
46 B3 **Şa'dah** Yemen
30 A1 **Sadiya** India
35 C3 **Sadoga-shima** *i.* Japan
75 D2 **Sa Dragonera** *i.* Spain
61 F4 **Säffle** Sweden
106 B2 **Safford** U.S.A.
67 D2 **Saffron Walden** U.K.
82 B1 **Safi** Morocco
54 D2 **Safonovo** *Arkhangel'skaya*
Oblast' Rus. Fed.
57 D2 **Safonovo** *Smolenskaya*
Oblast' Rus. Fed.
46 B2 **Safrā' as Sark** *esc.*
Saudi Arabia
43 C2 **Saga** China
35 B4 **Saga** Japan
30 A1 **Sagaing** Myanmar
35 C3 **Sagamihara** Japan
43 B2 **Sagar** India
108 C2 **Saginaw** U.S.A.
108 C2 **Saginaw Bay** U.S.A.
74 B2 **Sagres** Port.
114 B2 **Sagua la Grande** Cuba
109 F1 **Saguenay** *r.* Can.
75 C2 **Sagunto** Spain
44 B2 **Sagyndyk, Mys** *pt* Kazakh.
74 B1 **Sahagún** Spain
82 C3 **Sahara** *des.* Africa
Şaḥārā el Gharbīya *des.*
Egypt *see* Western Desert
Şaḥārā el Sharqīya *des.*
Egypt *see* Eastern Desert
Saharan Atlas *mts* Alg. *see*
Atlas Saharien
43 B2 **Saharanpur** India
43 C2 **Saharsa** India
112 B2 **Sahuayo** Mex.
46 B2 **Şāḥūq** *reg.* Saudi Arabia
48 B2 **Saïda** Lebanon
43 C2 **Saidpur** Bangl.
Saigon Vietnam *see*
Hồ Chi Minh
30 A1 **Saiha** India
37 D2 **Saihan Tal** China
35 B4 **Saiki** Japan
61 I3 **Saimaa** *l.* Fin.
112 B1 **Sain Alto** Mex.
64 C3 **St Abb's Head** *hd* U.K.
67 C3 **St Albans** U.K.
67 B3 **St Alban's Head** *hd* U.K.
64 C2 **St Andrews** U.K.
68 B2 **St Anthonis** Neth.

99 E1 **St Anthony** Can.
102 D2 **St Anthony** U.S.A.
20 B3 **St Arnaud** Austr.
99 E1 **St-Augustin** Can.
99 E1 **St-Augustin** *r.* Can.
111 D3 **St Augustine** U.S.A.
67 A3 **St Austell** U.K.
72 C2 **St-Avertin** France
66 B1 **St Bees Head** *hd* U.K.
73 D3 **St-Bonnet-en-Champsaur**
France
67 A3 **St Bride's Bay** U.K.
72 B2 **St-Brieuc** France
98 C2 **St Catharines** Can.
67 C3 **St Catherine's Point** U.K.
105 E3 **St Charles** U.S.A.
108 C2 **St Clair, Lake** Can./U.S.A.
73 D2 **St-Claude** France
105 E1 **St Cloud** U.S.A.
108 A1 **St Croix** *r.* U.S.A.
115 D3 **St Croix Island** *i.*
Virgin Is (U.S.A.)
73 C2 **St-Dizier** France
99 C2 **Ste-Anne-des-Monts** Can.
73 D2 **St-Égrève** France
94 B2 **St Elias Mountains** Can.
99 D1 **Ste Marguerite** *r.* Can.
97 E2 **Ste Rose du Lac** Can.
72 B2 **Saintes** France
73 C2 **St-Étienne** France
76 A2 **St-Florent** Corsica France
73 C2 **St-Flour** France
104 C3 **St Francis** U.S.A.
73 D2 **St Gallen** Switz.
72 C3 **St-Gaudens** France
21 C1 **St George** Austr.
100 D3 **St George** U.S.A.
111 D3 **St George Island** U.S.A.
99 C2 **St-Georges** Can.
115 D3 **St George's** Grenada
65 C3 **St George's Channel**
Rep. of Ireland/U.K.
80 C5 **St Helena** *terr.*
S. Atlantic Ocean
90 A3 **St Helena Bay** S. Africa
90 A3 **St Helena Bay** *b.* S. Africa
66 B2 **St Helens** U.K.
102 B1 **St Helens, Mount** *vol.* U.S.A.
63 C4 **St Helier** Channel Is
68 B2 **St-Hubert** Belgium
109 E1 **St-Hyacinthe** Can.
108 C1 **St Ignace** U.S.A.
98 B2 **St Ignace Island** Can.
67 A3 **St Ives** U.K.
96 A2 **St James, Cape** Can.
99 C2 **St-Jean, Lac** *l.* Can.
72 B2 **St-Jean-d'Angély** France
72 B2 **St-Jean-de-Monts** France
98 C2 **St-Jean-sur-Richelieu** Can.
109 E1 **St-Jérôme** Can.
102 C1 **St Joe** *r.* U.S.A.
99 D2 **St John** Can.
109 F1 **St John** *r.* U.S.A.
115 D3 **St John's** Antigua
99 E2 **St John's** Can.
106 B2 **St Johns** U.S.A.
109 E2 **St Johnsbury** U.S.A.
105 E3 **St Joseph** U.S.A.
98 A1 **St Joseph, Lake** Can.
72 C2 **St-Julien** France
62 B2 **St Kilda** *i.* U.K.
115 D3 **St Kitts and Nevis** *country*
West Indies
68 A2 **St-Laureins** Belgium
St-Laurent, Golfe du Can.
see St Lawrence, Gulf of
119 C1 **St-Laurent-du-Maroni**
Fr. Guiana
99 D2 **St Lawrence** *inlet* Can.

99 D2 **St Lawrence, Gulf of** Can.
51 N2 **St Lawrence Island** U.S.A.
72 B2 **St-Lô** France
82 A3 **St Louis** Senegal
105 E3 **St Louis** U.S.A.
105 E1 **St Louis** *r.* U.S.A.
115 D3 **St Lucia** *country* West Indies
91 D2 **St Lucia Estuary** S. Africa
115 D3 **St Maarten** *i.* West Indies
72 B2 **St-Malo** France
72 B2 **St-Malo, Golfe de** *g.* France
90 A3 **St Martin, Cape** S. Africa
109 D2 **St Marys** Can.
98 C2 **St Maurice** *r.* Can.
73 D2 **St Moritz** Switz.
72 B2 **St-Nazaire** France
68 B2 **St-Niklaas** Belgium
72 C1 **St-Omer** France
97 C2 **St Paul** Can.
105 E2 **St Paul** U.S.A.
105 E2 **St Peter** U.S.A.
63 C4 **St Peter Port** Channel Is
57 D2 **St Petersburg** Rus. Fed.
111 D3 **St Petersburg** U.S.A.
99 E2 **St-Pierre**
        St Pierre and Miquelon
99 E2 **St Pierre and Miquelon** *terr.*
        N. America
72 B2 **St-Pierre-d'Oléron** France
73 C2 **St-Pourçain-sur-Sioule**
        France
99 D2 **St Quentin** Can.
73 C2 **St-Quentin** France
99 D2 **St Siméon** Can.
97 E2 **St Theresa Point** Can.
98 B2 **St Thomas** Can.
73 D3 **St-Tropez** France
73 D3 **St-Tropez, Cap de** *c.* France
70 C2 **St Veit an der Glan** Austria
20 A3 **St Vincent, Gulf** Austr.
115 D3 **St Vincent and the**
        Grenadines *i.* West Indies
68 C2 **St-Vith** Belgium
97 D2 **St Walburg** Can.
68 C3 **St Wendel** Ger.
72 C2 **St-Yrieix-la-Perche** France
27 D1 **Saipan** *i.* N. Mariana Is
120 B2 **Sajama, Nevado** *mt.* Bol.
90 B2 **Sak** *watercourse* S. Africa
35 C4 **Sakai** Japan
35 B4 **Sakaide** Japan
46 B2 **Sakākah** Saudi Arabia
104 C1 **Sakakawea, Lake** U.S.A.
79 D2 **Sakarya** Turkey
79 D2 **Sakarya** *r.* Turkey
34 C3 **Sakata** Japan
33 B1 **Sakchu** N. Korea
51 K3 **Sakhalin** *i.* Rus. Fed.
91 C2 **Sakhile** S. Africa
49 C1 **Şäki** Azer.
56 B3 **Šakiai** Lith.
37 E3 **Sakishima-shotō** *is* Japan
30 B2 **Sakon Nakhon** Thai.
90 B3 **Sakrivier** S. Africa
35 D3 **Sakura** Japan
59 C2 **Saky** Ukr.
61 G4 **Sala** Sweden
98 C2 **Salaberry-de-Valleyfield** Can.
56 B2 **Salacgrīva** Latvia
77 C2 **Sala Consilina** Italy
103 C4 **Salada, Laguna** *salt l.* Mex.
120 B4 **Salado** *r.* Arg.
113 C2 **Salado** *r.* Mex.
82 B4 **Salaga** Ghana
90 B1 **Salajwe** Botswana
83 D3 **Salal** Chad
46 A2 **Salālā** Sudan
47 C3 **Salālah** Oman
113 B2 **Salamanca** Mex.
74 B1 **Salamanca** Spain

74 B1 **Salas** Spain
27 C3 **Salawati** *i.* Indon.
26 C3 **Salayar** *i.* Indon.
116 B4 **Sala y Gómez, Isla** *i.*
        S. Pacific Ocean
72 C2 **Salbris** France
56 C3 **Šalčininkai** Lith.
74 C1 **Saldaña** Spain
90 A3 **Saldanha** S. Africa
56 B2 **Saldus** Latvia
21 C3 **Sale** Austr.
54 F2 **Salekhard** Rus. Fed.
41 B3 **Salem** India
105 E3 **Salem** *MO* U.S.A.
102 B2 **Salem** *OR* U.S.A.
64 B2 **Salen** U.K.
77 B2 **Salerno** Italy
66 B2 **Salford** U.K.
119 E2 **Salgado** *r.* Brazil
71 D2 **Salgótarján** Hungary
119 E2 **Salgueiro** Brazil
104 B3 **Salida** U.S.A.
79 C3 **Salihli** Turkey
56 C3 **Salihorsk** Belarus
89 C2 **Salima** Malawi
89 C2 **Salimo** Moz.
105 D3 **Salina** U.S.A.
76 B3 **Salina, Isola** *i.* Italy
113 C3 **Salina Cruz** Mex.
123 D1 **Salinas** Brazil
112 B2 **Salinas** Mex.
103 B3 **Salinas** U.S.A.
119 D2 **Salinópolis** Brazil
67 C3 **Salisbury** U.K.
109 D3 **Salisbury** *MD* U.S.A.
111 D1 **Salisbury** *NC* U.S.A.
67 B3 **Salisbury Plain** U.K.
119 D2 **Salitre** *r.* Brazil
60 I2 **Salla** Fin.
95 F2 **Salluit** Can.
43 C2 **Sallyana** Nepal
49 C2 **Salmās** Iran
102 D1 **Salmon** U.S.A.
102 C1 **Salmon** *r.* U.S.A.
96 C2 **Salmon Arm** Can.
102 C2 **Salmon River Mountains**
        U.S.A.
68 C3 **Salmtal** Ger.
61 H3 **Salo** Fin.
55 D4 **Sal'sk** Rus. Fed.
90 B3 **Salt** *watercourse* S. Africa
106 A2 **Salt** *r.* U.S.A.
120 B3 **Salta** Arg.
113 B2 **Saltillo** Mex.
102 D2 **Salt Lake City** U.S.A.
122 C2 **Salto** Brazil
120 C4 **Salto** Uru.
123 D1 **Salto da Divisa** Brazil
122 B2 **Salto del Guairá** Para.
103 C4 **Salton Sea** *salt l.* U.S.A.
111 D2 **Saluda** U.S.A.
76 A2 **Saluzzo** Italy
119 E3 **Salvador** Brazil
47 C2 **Salwah** Saudi Arabia
30 A2 **Salween** *r.* Myanmar
49 C2 **Şalyan** Azer.
70 C2 **Salzburg** Austria
69 E1 **Salzgitter** Ger.
69 D2 **Salzkotten** Ger.
69 E1 **Salzwedel** Ger.
112 B1 **Samalayuca** Mex.
34 D2 **Samani** Japan
32 B1 **Samar** *i.* Phil.
55 E3 **Samara** Rus. Fed.
29 C3 **Samarinda** Indon.
45 C3 **Samarkand** Uzbek.
49 C2 **Sāmarrā'** Iraq
49 C1 **Şamaxı** Azer.
87 C3 **Samba** Dem. Rep. Congo
29 C1 **Sambaliung** *mts* Indon.

43 C2 **Sambalpur** India
29 C2 **Sambar, Tanjung** *pt* Indon.
29 B1 **Sambas** Indon.
89 □E2 **Sambava** Madag.
58 A2 **Sambir** Ukr.
121 C4 **Samborombón, Bahía** *b.* Arg.
33 C4 **Samch'ŏk** S. Korea
49 C2 **Samdi Dag** *mt.* Turkey
87 D3 **Same** Tanz.
46 B2 **Samirah** Saudi Arabia
33 B1 **Samjiyŏn** N. Korea
17 G4 **Samoa** *country*
        S. Pacific Ocean
77 C1 **Samobor** Croatia
79 C3 **Samos** *i.* Greece
79 C3 **Samothraki** Greece
79 C2 **Samothraki** *i.* Greece
29 C2 **Sampit** Indon.
87 C3 **Sampwe** Dem. Rep. Congo
107 E2 **Sam Rayburn Reservoir**
        U.S.A.
48 B1 **Samsun** Turkey
49 C1 **Samtredia** Georgia
31 B3 **Samui, Ko** *i.* Thai.
31 B2 **Samut Songkhram** Thai.
82 B3 **San** Mali
46 B3 **Şan'ā'** Yemen
86 A2 **Sanaga** *r.* Cameroon
49 C2 **Sanandaj** Iran
114 B3 **San Andrés, Isla de** *i.*
        Caribbean Sea
106 B2 **San Andres Mountains**
        U.S.A.
113 C3 **San Andrés Tuxtla** Mex.
107 C2 **San Angelo** U.S.A.
107 D3 **San Antonio** U.S.A.
103 C4 **San Antonio, Mount** U.S.A.
75 D2 **San Antonio Abad** Spain
120 B3 **San Antonio de los Cobres**
        Arg.
121 B5 **San Antonio Oeste** Arg.
76 B2 **San Benedetto del Tronto**
        Italy
112 A3 **San Benedicto, Isla** *i.* Mex.
103 C4 **San Bernardino** U.S.A.
103 C4 **San Bernardino Mountains**
        U.S.A.
111 C3 **San Blas, Cape** U.S.A.
120 B2 **San Borja** Bol.
112 B2 **San Buenaventura** Mex.
32 B1 **San Carlos** Phil.
115 D4 **San Carlos** Venez.
121 A5 **San Carlos de Bariloche**
        Arg.
115 C4 **San Carlos del Zulia** Venez.
103 C4 **San Clemente Island** U.S.A.
72 C2 **Sancoins** France
118 A1 **San Cristóbal** Venez.
113 C3 **San Cristóbal de las Casas**
        Mex.
114 C2 **Sancti Spíritus** Cuba
91 D1 **Sand** *r.* S. Africa
29 C1 **Sandakan** *Sabah* Malaysia
61 E3 **Sandane** Norway
79 B2 **Sandanski** Bulg.
64 C1 **Sanday** *i.* U.K.
107 C2 **Sanderson** U.S.A.
118 B3 **Sandia** Peru
103 C4 **San Diego** U.S.A.
48 B2 **Sandıklı** Turkey
61 E4 **Sandnes** Norway
60 F2 **Sandnessjøen** Norway
86 C3 **Sandoa** Dem. Rep. Congo
71 E1 **Sandomierz** Pol.
57 E2 **Sandovo** Rus. Fed.
30 A2 **Sandoway** Myanmar
62 A2 **Sandoy** *i.* Faroe Is
102 C1 **Sandpoint** U.S.A.
39 B3 **Sandu** China
62 B1 **Sandur** Faroe Is

108 C2 **Sandusky** U.S.A.
90 A3 **Sandveld** *mts* S. Africa
61 F4 **Sandvika** Norway
61 G3 **Sandviken** Sweden
99 E1 **Sandwich Bay** Can.
97 D2 **Sandy Bay** Can.
19 E2 **Sandy Cape** Austr.
98 A1 **Sandy Lake** Can.
98 A1 **Sandy Lake** *l.* Can.
112 A1 **San Felipe**
       Baja California Norte Mex.
113 B2 **San Felipe** *Guanajuato* Mex.
118 B1 **San Felipe** Venez.
112 A2 **San Fernando**
       Baja California Norte Mex.
113 C2 **San Fernando** *Tamaulipas*
       Mex.
32 B1 **San Fernando** *Luzon* Phil.
32 B1 **San Fernando** *Luzon* Phil.
74 B2 **San Fernando** Spain
115 D3 **San Fernando** Trin. and Tob.
118 B1 **San Fernando de Apure**
       Venez.
111 D3 **Sanford** *FL* U.S.A.
109 E2 **Sanford** *ME* U.S.A.
120 B4 **San Francisco** Arg.
103 B3 **San Francisco** U.S.A.
75 D2 **San Francisco Javier** Spain
42 B3 **Sangamner** India
51 J2 **Sangar** Rus. Fed.
76 A3 **San Gavino Monreale**
       Sardinia Italy
69 E2 **Sangerhausen** Ger.
29 C1 **Sanggau** Indon.
86 B3 **Sangha** *r.* Congo
77 C3 **San Giovanni in Fiore** Italy
32 B2 **Sangir** *i.* Indon.
27 C2 **Sangir, Kepulauan** *is* Indon.
33 B2 **Sangju** S. Korea
29 C1 **Sangkulirang** Indon.
41 B3 **Sangli** India
86 D2 **Sangmélima** Cameroon
89 C3 **Sango** Zimbabwe
73 D2 **San Gottardo, Passo del**
       pass Switz.
104 B3 **Sangre de Cristo Range**
       mts U.S.A.
43 C2 **Sangsang** China
112 A2 **San Hipólito, Punta** *pt* Mex.
112 A2 **San Ignacio** Mex.
98 C1 **Sanikiluaq** Can.
29 A3 **Sanjiang** China
103 B3 **San Joaquin** *r.* U.S.A.
121 B5 **San Jorge, Golfo de** *g.* Arg.
114 B3 **San José** Costa Rica
32 B1 **San Jose** *Luzon* Phil.
32 B1 **San Jose** *Mindoro* Phil.
103 B3 **San Jose** U.S.A.
112 A2 **San José, Isla** *i.* Mex.
112 B2 **San José de Bavicora** Mex.
32 B1 **San José de Buenavista**
       Phil.
112 A2 **San José de Comondú** Mex.
112 B2 **San José del Cabo** Mex.
118 A1 **San José del Guaviare** Col.
120 B4 **San Juan** Arg.
114 B3 **San Juan** *r.* Costa Rica/Nic.
115 D3 **San Juan** Puerto Rico
103 D3 **San Juan** *r.* U.S.A.
75 D2 **San Juan Bautista** Spain
113 C3 **San Juan Bautista**
       Tuxtepec Mex.
102 B1 **San Juan Islands** U.S.A.
112 B2 **San Juanito** Mex.
104 B3 **San Juan Mountains** U.S.A.
121 B5 **San Julián** Arg.
43 C2 **Sankh** *r.* India
       Sankt-Peterburg Rus. Fed.
       see St Petersburg
48 B2 **Şanlıurfa** Turkey

106 B3 **San Lorenzo** Mex.
74 B2 **Sanlúcar de Barrameda**
       Spain
112 B2 **San Lucas** Mex.
121 B4 **San Luis** Arg.
113 B2 **San Luis de la Paz** Mex.
106 A2 **San Luisito** Mex.
103 B3 **San Luis Obispo** U.S.A.
113 B2 **San Luis Potosí** Mex.
112 A1 **San Luis Río Colorado** Mex.
107 D3 **San Marcos** U.S.A.
76 B2 **San Marino** *country* Europe
76 B2 **San Marino** San Marino
112 B2 **San Martín de Bolaños**
       Mex.
121 A5 **San Martín de los Andes**
       Arg.
121 B5 **San Matías, Golfo** *g.* Arg.
38 B2 **Sanmenxia** China
114 B3 **San Miguel** El Salvador
120 B3 **San Miguel de Tucumán**
       Arg.
113 C3 **San Miguel Sola de Vega**
       Mex.
39 B3 **Sanming** China
121 B4 **San Nicolás de los Arroyos**
       Arg.
103 C4 **San Nicolas Island** U.S.A.
91 C4 **Sannieshof** S. Africa
71 E2 **Sanok** Pol.
32 B1 **San Pablo** Phil.
112 B2 **San Pablo Balleza** Mex.
120 B3 **San Pedro** Arg.
120 B2 **San Pedro** Bol.
82 B4 **San-Pédro** Côte d'Ivoire
112 A2 **San Pedro** Mex.
106 A2 **San Pedro** *watercourse*
       U.S.A.
74 B2 **San Pedro, Sierra de** *mts*
       Spain
112 B2 **San Pedro de las Colonias**
       Mex.
114 B3 **San Pedro Sula** Hond.
76 A3 **San Pietro, Isola di** *i.*
       Sardinia Italy
112 A1 **San Quintín, Cabo** *c.* Mex.
121 B4 **San Rafael** Arg.
76 A2 **San Remo** Italy
114 B3 **San Salvador** El Salvador
120 B3 **San Salvador de Jujuy** Arg.
77 C2 **San Severo** Italy
77 C2 **Sanski Most** Bos.-Herz.
120 B2 **Santa Ana** Bol.
114 B3 **Santa Ana** El Salvador
112 A1 **Santa Ana** Mex.
103 C4 **Santa Ana** U.S.A.
112 B2 **Santa Bárbara** Mex.
103 C4 **Santa Barbara** U.S.A.
122 B2 **Santa Bárbara, Serra de**
       hills Brazil
120 B3 **Santa Catalina** Chile
118 B2 **Santa Clara** Col.
114 C2 **Santa Clara** Cuba
103 C4 **Santa Clarita** U.S.A.
77 C3 **Santa Croce, Capo** *c.* *Sicily*
       Italy
121 B6 **Santa Cruz** *r.* Arg.
120 B2 **Santa Cruz** Bol.
32 B1 **Santa Cruz** Phil.
103 B3 **Santa Cruz** U.S.A.
113 C3 **Santa Cruz Barillas** Guat.
123 E1 **Santa Cruz Cabrália** Brazil
75 D2 **Santa Cruz de Moya** Spain
82 A2 **Santa Cruz de Tenerife**
       Canary Is
103 C4 **Santa Cruz Island** U.S.A.
120 B4 **Santa Fé** Arg.
106 B1 **Santa Fe** U.S.A.
122 B1 **Santa Helena de Goiás**
       Brazil

121 B4 **Santa Isabel** Arg.
122 B1 **Santa Luisa, Serra de** *hills*
       Brazil
120 C3 **Santa Maria** Brazil
112 B1 **Santa María** *r.* Mex.
103 B4 **Santa Maria** U.S.A.
91 D2 **Santa Maria, Cabo de**
       c. Moz.
74 B2 **Santa Maria, Cabo de**
       c. Port.
119 D2 **Santa Maria das Barreiras**
       Brazil
77 C3 **Santa Maria di Leuca, Capo**
       c. Italy
118 A1 **Santa Marta** Col.
103 C4 **Santa Monica** U.S.A.
119 D3 **Santana** Brazil
74 C1 **Santander** Spain
76 A3 **Sant'Antioco** *Sardinia* Italy
76 A3 **Sant'Antioco, Isola di** *i.*
       Sardinia Italy
119 C2 **Santarém** Brazil
74 B2 **Santarém** Port.
122 B1 **Santa Rita do Araguaia**
       Brazil
121 B4 **Santa Rosa** Arg.
120 C3 **Santa Rosa** Brazil
103 B3 **Santa Rosa** *CA* U.S.A.
106 C2 **Santa Rosa** *NM* U.S.A.
114 B3 **Santa Rosa de Copán** Hond.
103 B4 **Santa Rosa Island** U.S.A.
112 A2 **Santa Rosalía** Mex.
120 C3 **Santiago** Brazil
121 A4 **Santiago** Chile
115 C3 **Santiago** Dom. Rep.
112 B2 **Santiago** Mex.
114 B4 **Santiago** Panama
32 B1 **Santiago** Phil.
74 B1 **Santiago de Compostela**
       Spain
112 B2 **Santiago Ixcuintla** Mex.
112 B2 **Santiago Papasquiaro** Mex.
75 D1 **Sant Jordi, Golf de** *g.* Spain
123 D2 **Santo Amaro de Campos**
       Brazil
123 C2 **Santo André** Brazil
120 C3 **Santo Ângelo** Brazil
122 B2 **Santo Antônio da Platina**
       Brazil
119 E3 **Santo Antônio de Jesus**
       Brazil
119 C2 **Santo Antônio do Içá** Brazil
123 C2 **Santo Antônio do Monte**
       Brazil
115 D3 **Santo Domingo** Dom. Rep.
106 D1 **Santo Domingo Pueblo**
       U.S.A.
79 C3 **Santorini** *i.* Greece
123 C2 **Santos** Brazil
120 C3 **Santo Tomé** Arg.
121 A5 **San Valentín, Cerro** *mt.*
       Chile
114 B3 **San Vicente** El Salvador
112 A1 **San Vicente** Mex.
118 A3 **San Vicente de Cañete**
       Peru
76 B2 **San Vincenzo** Italy
76 B3 **San Vito, Capo** *c.* *Sicily* Italy
39 A4 **Sanya** China
123 C2 **São Bernardo do Campo**
       Brazil
120 C3 **São Borja** Brazil
122 C2 **São Carlos** Brazil
119 C3 **São Félix** *Mato Grosso* Brazil
119 C2 **São Félix** *Pará* Brazil
123 C2 **São Fidélis** Brazil
123 D1 **São Francisco** Brazil
119 E3 **São Francisco** *r.* Brazil
122 C3 **São Francisco, Ilha de** *i.*
       Brazil

122 C3 São Francisco do Sul Brazil
120 C4 São Gabriel Brazil
123 D2 São Gonçalo Brazil
123 C1 São Gotardo Brazil
123 D2 São João da Barra Brazil
123 C2 São João da Boa Vista
        Brazil
 74 B1 São João da Madeira Port.
123 D1 São João do Paraíso Brazil
123 D2 São João Nepomuceno
        Brazil
122 C2 São Joaquim da Barra
        Brazil
122 C2 São José do Rio Preto
        Brazil
123 C2 São José dos Campos
        Brazil
122 C3 São José dos Pinhais Brazil
123 C2 São Lourenço Brazil
119 D2 São Luís Brazil
122 C2 São Manuel Brazil
122 C1 São Marcos r. Brazil
119 D2 São Marcos, Baía de b.
        Brazil
123 E1 São Mateus Brazil
123 C2 São Paulo Brazil
119 D2 São Raimundo Nonato Brazil
123 C1 São Romão Brazil
123 C2 São Sebastião, Ilha do i.
        Brazil
122 C2 São Sebastião do Paraíso
        Brazil
122 B1 São Simão Brazil
122 B1 São Simão, Barragem de
        resr Brazil
 27 C2 Sao-Siu Indon.
123 D2 São Tomé, Cabo de c. Brazil
 80 D3 São Tomé and Príncipe
        country Africa
123 C2 São Vicente Brazil
 74 B2 São Vicente, Cabo de c.
        Port.
 27 C3 Saparua Indon.
 57 F3 Sapozhok Rus. Fed.
 34 C2 Sapporo Japan
 77 C2 Sapri Italy
 49 C2 Saqqez Iran
 49 C2 Sarāb Iran
 31 B2 Sara Buri Thai.
 77 C2 Sarajevo Bos.-Herz.
 44 B1 Saraktash Rus. Fed.
109 E2 Saranac Lake U.S.A.
 77 D3 Sarandë Albania
 32 B2 Sarangani Islands Phil.
 55 D3 Saransk Rus. Fed.
 55 E3 Sarapul Rus. Fed.
111 D3 Sarasota U.S.A.
 58 B2 Sarata Ukr.
104 B2 Saratoga U.S.A.
109 E2 Saratoga Springs U.S.A.
 29 C1 Saratok Sarawak Malaysia
 55 D3 Saratov Rus. Fed.
 47 D2 Saravan Iran
 31 B2 Saravan Laos
 29 C1 Sarawak state Malaysia
 78 C2 Saray Turkey
 79 C3 Sarayköy Turkey
 47 D2 Sarbāz Iran
 42 B2 Sardarshahr India
        Sardegna i. Italy see Sardinia
 76 A2 Sardinia i. Italy
 60 G2 Sarektjåkkå mt. Sweden
 45 C3 Sar-e Pol Afgh.
126 B3 Sargasso Sea Atlantic Ocean
 42 B1 Sargodha Pak.
 83 D4 Sarh Chad
 47 D2 Sārī Iran
 79 C3 Sarıgöl Turkey
 49 C1 Sarıkamış Turkey

 29 C1 Sarikei Sarawak Malaysia
 19 D2 Sarina Austr.
 83 D2 Sarīr Tibesti des. Libya
 33 B2 Sariwŏn N. Korea
 79 C2 Sarıyer Turkey
 45 D2 Sarkand Kazakh.
 79 C2 Şarköy Turkey
 27 D3 Şarmi Indon.
108 C2 Sarnia Can.
 58 B1 Sarny Ukr.
 28 B2 Sarolangun Indon.
 79 B3 Saronikos Kolpos g. Greece
 79 C2 Saros Körfezi b. Turkey
 55 D3 Sarova Rus. Fed.
 73 D2 Sarrebourg France
 74 B1 Sarria Spain
 75 C1 Sarrión Spain
 73 D3 Sartène Corsica France
 71 D2 Sárvár Hungary
 44 B2 Sarykamyshkoye Ozero
        salt l. Turkm./Uzbek.
 45 D2 Saryozek Kazakh.
 45 D2 Saryshagan Kazakh.
 50 F3 Sarysu watercourse Kazakh.
 45 D3 Sary-Tash Kyrg.
 43 C2 Sasaram India
 35 A4 Sasebo Japan
 97 D2 Saskatchewan prov. Can.
 97 D2 Saskatchewan r. Can.
 97 D2 Saskatoon Can.
 51 I2 Saskylakh Rus. Fed.
 91 C2 Sasolburg S. Africa
 55 D3 Sasovo Rus. Fed.
 82 B4 Sassandra Côte d'Ivoire
 76 A2 Sassari Sardinia Italy
 70 C1 Sassnitz Ger.
 82 A3 Satadougou Mali
 91 C1 Satara S. Africa
 43 C2 Satna India
 42 B2 Satpura Range mts India
 31 B2 Sattahip Thai.
 78 B1 Satu Mare Romania
 31 B3 Satun Thai.
112 B2 Saucillo Mex.
 61 E4 Sauda Norway
 60 ☐B2 Sauðárkrókur Iceland
 46 B2 Saudi Arabia country Asia
 73 C3 Saugues France
 73 C2 Saulieu France
 98 B2 Sault Sainte Marie Can.
108 C1 Sault Ste Marie Can.
108 C1 Sault Ste Marie U.S.A.
 45 C1 Saumalkol' Kazakh.
 27 C3 Saumlakki Indon.
 72 B2 Saumur France
 88 B1 Saurimo Angola
 77 D2 Sava r. Europe
 59 E1 Savala r. Rus. Fed.
111 D2 Savannah GA U.S.A.
110 C1 Savannah TN U.S.A.
111 D2 Savannah r. U.S.A.
 31 B2 Savannakhét Laos
 98 A1 Savant Lake l. Can.
 79 C3 Savaştepe Turkey
 57 F2 Savino Rus. Fed.
 54 D2 Savinskiy Rus. Fed.
 76 A2 Savona Italy
 61 I3 Savonlinna Fin.
 60 I2 Savukoski Fin.
 42 B2 Sawai Madhopur India
 30 A2 Sawankhalok Thai.
104 B3 Sawatch Range mts U.S.A.
 21 D2 Sawtell Austr.
 27 C3 Sawu Sea Indon.
 47 C3 Sayḥūt Yemen
 37 D2 Saynshand Mongolia
109 D2 Sayre U.S.A.
112 B3 Sayula Jalisco Mex.
113 C3 Sayula Veracruz Mex.
 96 B2 Sayward Can.
 57 E2 Sazonovo Rus. Fed.

 82 B2 Sbaa Alg.
 66 B1 Scafell Pike hill U.K.
 77 C3 Scalea Italy
 64 C1 Scapa Flow inlet U.K.
 98 C2 Scarborough Can.
115 D3 Scarborough Trin. and Tob.
 66 C1 Scarborough U.K.
 32 A1 Scarborough Shoal
        sea feature Phil.
 64 A2 Scarinish U.K.
        Scarpanto i. Greece see
        Karpathos
 73 D2 Schaffhausen Switz.
 68 B1 Schagen Neth.
 70 C2 Schärding Austria
 68 A2 Scharendijke Neth.
 69 D1 Scharhörn sea feature Ger.
 69 D1 Scheeßel Ger.
 99 D1 Schefferville Can.
103 D3 Schell Creek Range mts
        U.S.A.
109 E2 Schenectady U.S.A.
 69 E3 Scheßlitz Ger.
 68 C1 Schiermonnikoog i. Neth.
 76 B1 Schio Italy
 69 F2 Schkeuditz Ger.
 69 E1 Schladen Ger.
 69 E2 Schleiz Ger.
 70 B1 Schleswig Ger.
 69 D2 Schloß Holte-Stukenbrock
        Ger.
 69 D2 Schlüchtern Ger.
 69 E3 Schlüsselfeld Ger.
 69 D2 Schmallenberg Ger.
 69 D1 Schneverdingen Ger.
 69 E1 Schönebeck (Elbe) Ger.
 69 E1 Schöningen Ger.
 68 B2 Schoonhoven Neth.
 27 D3 Schouten Islands P.N.G.
 70 C2 Schwandorf Ger.
 29 C2 Schwaner, Pegunungan
        mts Indon.
 69 E1 Schwarzenbek Ger.
 69 F2 Schwarzenberg Ger.
 90 A2 Schwarzrand mts Namibia
 70 C2 Schwaz Austria
 70 C1 Schwedt an der Oder Ger.
 69 E2 Schweinfurt Ger.
 69 E1 Schwerin Ger.
 69 E1 Schweriner See l. Ger.
 73 D2 Schwyz Switz.
 76 B3 Sciacca Sicily Italy
 63 B4 Scilly, Isles of U.K.
108 C3 Scioto r. U.S.A.
104 B1 Scobey U.S.A.
 21 D2 Scone Austr.
 23 R3 Scotia Ridge sea feature
        S. Atlantic Ocean
126 C8 Scotia Sea S. Atlantic Ocean
 64 C2 Scotland admin. div. U.K.
 96 B2 Scott, Cape Can.
 91 D3 Scottburgh S. Africa
104 C3 Scott City U.S.A.
104 C2 Scottsbluff U.S.A.
110 C2 Scottsboro U.S.A.
 64 B1 Scourie U.K.
109 D2 Scranton U.S.A.
 66 C2 Scunthorpe U.K.
 73 E2 Scuol Switz.
 97 E2 Seal r. Can.
 90 B3 Seal, Cape S. Africa
 20 B3 Sea Lake Austr.
107 D3 Sealy U.S.A.
110 B1 Searcy U.S.A.
 66 B1 Seascale U.K.
102 B1 Seattle U.S.A.
109 E2 Sebago Lake U.S.A.
112 A2 Sebastián Vizcaíno, Bahía
        b. Mex.
 78 B1 Sebeş Romania

28 B2 **Sebesi** i. Indon.
56 C2 **Sebezh** Rus. Fed.
48 B1 **Şebinkarahisar** Turkey
111 D3 **Sebring** U.S.A.
96 B3 **Sechelt** Can.
118 A2 **Sechura** Peru
41 B3 **Secunderabad** India
105 E3 **Sedalia** U.S.A.
73 C2 **Sedan** France
22 B2 **Seddon** N.Z.
106 A2 **Sedona** U.S.A.
69 E2 **Seeburg** Ger.
69 E1 **Seehausen (Altmark)** Ger.
90 A2 **Seeheim** Namibia
72 C2 **Sées** France
69 E2 **Seesen** Ger.
69 E1 **Seevetal** Ger.
88 A4 **Sefadu** Sierra Leone
91 C1 **Sefare** Botswana
28 B1 **Segamat** Malaysia
54 C2 **Segezha** Rus. Fed.
82 B3 **Ségou** Mali
74 C1 **Segovia** Spain
83 D2 **Séguédine** Niger
82 B4 **Séguéla** Côte d'Ivoire
107 D3 **Seguin** U.S.A.
75 C2 **Segura** r. Spain
74 C2 **Segura, Sierra de** mts Spain
88 B3 **Sehithwa** Botswana
61 H3 **Seinäjoki** Fin.
72 C2 **Seine** r. France
72 B2 **Seine, Baie de** b. France
71 E1 **Sejny** Pol.
28 B2 **Sekayu** Indon.
82 B4 **Sekondi** Ghana
27 C3 **Selaru** i. Indon.
29 C2 **Selatan, Tanjung** pt Indon.
94 A2 **Selawik** U.S.A.
66 C2 **Selby** U.K.
88 B3 **Selebi-Phikwe** Botswana
73 D2 **Sélestat** France
60 ⊓A3 **Selfoss** Iceland
82 A3 **Sélibabi** Maur.
106 A1 **Seligman** U.S.A.
84 A2 **Selîma Oasis** Sudan
79 C3 **Selimiye** Turkey
82 B3 **Sélingué, Lac de** l. Mali
57 D2 **Selizharovo** Rus. Fed.
61 E4 **Seljord** Norway
97 E2 **Selkirk** Can.
64 C3 **Selkirk** U.K.
96 C2 **Selkirk Mountains** Can.
110 C2 **Selma** AL U.S.A.
103 C3 **Selma** CA U.S.A.
57 D3 **Sel'tso** Rus. Fed.
118 A2 **Selvas** reg. Brazil
102 C1 **Selway** r. U.S.A.
97 D1 **Selwyn Lake** Can.
96 A1 **Selwyn Mountains** Can.
19 C2 **Selwyn Range** hills Austr.
28 B2 **Semangka, Teluk** b. Indon.
29 C2 **Semarang** Indon.
29 B1 **Sematan** Sarawak Malaysia
86 B2 **Sembé** Congo
49 C2 **Şemdinli** Turkey
59 C1 **Semenivka** Ukr.
54 D3 **Semenov** Rus. Fed.
29 C2 **Semeru, Gunung** vol. Indon.
57 E3 **Semiluki** Rus. Fed.
104 B2 **Seminoe Reservoir** U.S.A.
107 C2 **Seminole** U.S.A.
111 D2 **Seminole, Lake** U.S.A.
45 E1 **Semipalatinsk** Kazakh.
29 C1 **Semitau** Indon.
49 D2 **Semnān** Iran
29 C1 **Semporna** Sabah Malaysia
72 C2 **Semur-en-Auxois** France
118 B2 **Sena Madureira** Brazil
88 B2 **Senanga** Zambia
35 B4 **Sendai** Kagoshima Japan

35 D3 **Sendai** Miyagi Japan
82 A3 **Senegal** country Africa
82 A3 **Sénégal** r. Maur./Senegal
70 C1 **Senftenberg** Ger.
87 D3 **Sengerema** Tanz.
119 D3 **Senhor do Bonfim** Brazil
76 B2 **Senigallia** Italy
77 B2 **Senj** Croatia
60 G2 **Senja** i. Norway
90 B2 **Senlac** S. Africa
72 C2 **Senlis** France
31 B2 **Senmonorom** Cambodia
85 B3 **Sennar** Sudan
98 C2 **Senneterre** Can.
91 C3 **Senqu** r. Lesotho
73 C2 **Sens** France
77 D1 **Senta** Yugo.
96 B2 **Sentinel Peak** Can.
43 B2 **Seoni** India
33 B2 **Seoul** S. Korea
123 D2 **Sepetiba, Baía de** b. Brazil
27 D3 **Sepik** r. P.N.G.
29 C1 **Sepinang** Indon.
99 D1 **Sept-Îles** Can.
27 C3 **Seram** i. Indon.
27 C3 **Seram Sea** Indon.
28 B2 **Serang** Indon.
77 D2 **Serbia** aut. rep. Yugo.
57 E3 **Serebryanyye Prudy** Rus. Fed.
28 B1 **Seremban** Malaysia
87 D3 **Serengeti Plain** Tanz.
55 D3 **Sergach** Rus. Fed.
57 E2 **Sergiyev Posad** Rus. Fed.
29 C1 **Seria** Brunei
29 C1 **Serian** Sarawak Malaysia
79 B3 **Serifos** i. Greece
48 B2 **Şerik** Turkey
27 C3 **Sermata, Kepulauan** is Indon.
54 F3 **Serov** Rus. Fed.
88 B3 **Serowe** Botswana
74 B2 **Serpa** Port.
57 E3 **Serpukhov** Rus. Fed.
122 B1 **Serranópolis** Brazil
68 A3 **Serre** r. France
79 B2 **Serres** Greece
119 E3 **Serrinha** Brazil
123 D1 **Sêrro** Brazil
122 C2 **Sertãozinho** Brazil
29 C2 **Seruyan** r. Indon.
36 C2 **Sêrxu** China
88 A2 **Sesfontein** Namibia
76 B2 **Sessa Aurunca** Italy
75 D2 **See Salines, Cap de** c.
Spain
76 A2 **Sestri Levante** Italy
73 C3 **Sète** France
123 D1 **Sete Lagoas** Brazil
60 G2 **Setermoen** Norway
61 E4 **Setesdal** val. Norway
83 C1 **Sétif** Alg.
35 B4 **Seto-naikai** sea Japan
82 B1 **Settat** Morocco
66 B1 **Settle** U.K.
74 B2 **Setúbal** Port.
74 B2 **Setúbal, Baía de** b. Port.
98 A1 **Seul, Lac** l. Can.
44 A2 **Sevan, Lake** Armenia
Sevana Lich l. Armenia see
Sevan, Lake
59 C3 **Sevastopol'** Ukr.
73 C3 **Sévérac-le-Château** France
98 B1 **Severn** r. Can.
90 B2 **Severn** S. Africa
67 B3 **Severn** r. U.K.
54 D2 **Severnaya Dvina** r. Rus. Fed.
51 H1 **Severnaya Zemlya** is
Rus. Fed.
54 D2 **Severnyy** Nenetskiy
Avtonomnyy Okrug Rus. Fed.

54 F2 **Severnyy** Respublika Komi
Rus. Fed.
54 C2 **Severodvinsk** Rus. Fed.
54 C2 **Severomorsk** Rus. Fed.
59 D3 **Severskaya** Rus. Fed.
103 D3 **Sevier** r. U.S.A.
103 D3 **Sevier Lake** U.S.A.
Sevilla Spain see Seville
74 B2 **Seville** Spain
96 A2 **Sewell Inlet** Can.
96 C2 **Sexsmith** Can.
112 B2 **Sextín** r. Mex.
54 G1 **Seyakha** Rus. Fed.
81 H4 **Seychelles** country
Indian Ocean
60 ⊓C2 **Seyðisfjörður** Iceland
59 C1 **Seym** r. Rus. Fed./Ukr.
51 L2 **Seymchan** Rus. Fed.
21 C3 **Seymour** Austr.
113 D3 **Seymour** IN U.S.A.
107 D2 **Seymour** TX U.S.A.
73 C2 **Sézanne** France
79 B3 **Sfakia** Greece
78 C1 **Sfântu Gheorghe** Romania
83 D1 **Sfax** Tunisia
's-Gravenhage Neth. see
The Hague
64 A2 **Sgurr Alasdair** hill U.K.
38 A2 **Shaanxi** prov. China
59 D2 **Shabel'sk** Rus. Fed.
45 D3 **Shache** China
23 R1 **Shackleton Range** mts
Antarctica
67 D3 **Shaftesbury** U.K.
43 C2 **Shahdol** India
45 C3 **Shah Fuladi** mt. Afgh.
43 B2 **Shahjahanpur** India
49 D2 **Shahr-e Kord** Iran
57 E2 **Shakhovskaya** Rus. Fed.
45 C3 **Shakhrisabz** Uzbek.
59 E2 **Shakhty** Rus. Fed.
54 D3 **Shakhun'ya** Rus. Fed.
34 D2 **Shakotan-misaki** c. Japan
36 C2 **Shaluli Shan** mts China
97 F2 **Shamattawa** Can.
107 C1 **Shamrock** U.S.A.
36 C2 **Shandan** China
38 B2 **Shandong** prov. China
38 C2 **Shandong Bandao** pen.
China
89 B2 **Shangani** r. Zimbabwe
38 C2 **Shanghai** China
38 C2 **Shanghai** mun. China
39 B3 **Shanghang** China
38 B2 **Shangqiu** China
39 B3 **Shangrao** China
38 B2 **Shangshui** China
38 C2 **Shangyu** China
37 E1 **Shangzhi** China
38 A2 **Shangzhou** China
65 B2 **Shannon** r. Rep. of Ireland
65 B2 **Shannon, Mouth of the**
Rep. of Ireland
39 B3 **Shantou** China
38 B2 **Shanxi** prov. China
39 B3 **Shaoguan** China
39 B3 **Shaowu** China
38 B2 **Shaoxing** China
39 B3 **Shaoyang** China
84 C2 **Shaqrā'** Saudi Arabia
58 B2 **Sharhorod** Ukr.
47 C2 **Sharjah** U.A.E.
56 C2 **Sharkawshchyna** Belarus
18 A2 **Shark Bay** Austr.
46 A2 **Sharm el Sheikh** Egypt
108 C2 **Sharon** U.S.A.
54 D3 **Shar'ya** Rus. Fed.
89 B3 **Shashe** r. Botswana/
Zimbabwe
85 B4 **Shashemenē** Eth.

102 B2 **Shasta, Mount** vol. U.S.A.
102 B2 **Shasta Lake** U.S.A.
57 E2 **Shatura** Rus. Fed.
97 D3 **Shaunavon** Can.
108 B2 **Shawano** U.S.A.
99 C2 **Shawinigan** Can.
107 D1 **Shawnee** U.S.A.
18 B2 **Shay Gap** Austr.
57 E3 **Shchekino** Rus. Fed.
57 E2 **Shchelkovo** Rus. Fed.
57 E3 **Shchigry** Rus. Fed.
59 C1 **Shchors** Ukr.
56 B3 **Shchuchyn** Belarus
59 D1 **Shebekino** Rus. Fed.
45 C3 **Sheberghān** Afgh.
108 B2 **Sheboygan** U.S.A.
59 D3 **Shebsh** r. Rus. Fed.
65 C2 **Sheelin, Lough** l.
         Rep. of Ireland
66 C2 **Sheffield** U.K.
57 E2 **Sheksna** Rus. Fed.
57 E2 **Sheksninskoye**
         Vodokhranilishche resr
         Rus. Fed.
51 M2 **Shelagskiy, Mys** pt Rus. Fed.
99 D2 **Shelburne** Can.
102 D1 **Shelby** U.S.A.
108 B3 **Shelbyville** IN U.S.A.
110 C1 **Shelbyville** TN U.S.A.
51 L2 **Shelikhova, Zaliv** g.
         Rus. Fed.
97 D2 **Shellbrook** Can.
102 B1 **Shelton** U.S.A.
105 D2 **Shenandoah** U.S.A.
109 D3 **Shenandoah** r. U.S.A.
109 D3 **Shenandoah Mountains**
         U.S.A.
86 A2 **Shendam** Nigeria
54 D2 **Shenkursk** Rus. Fed.
33 A1 **Shenyang** China
39 B3 **Shenzhen** China
58 B1 **Shepetivka** Ukr.
21 C3 **Shepparton** Austr.
67 D3 **Sheppey, Isle of** i. U.K.
99 D2 **Sherbrooke** N.S. Can.
99 C2 **Sherbrooke** Que. Can.
84 B3 **Shereiq** Sudan
104 B2 **Sheridan** U.S.A.
107 D2 **Sherman** U.S.A.
68 B2 **'s-Hertogenbosch** Neth.
64 □ **Shetland Islands** is U.K.
44 B2 **Shetpe** Kazakh.
         Shevchenko Kazakh. see
         Aktau
105 D1 **Sheyenne** r. U.S.A.
47 B3 **Shibām** Yemen
34 D2 **Shibetsu** Japan
39 B3 **Shicheng** China
64 B2 **Shiel, Loch** l. U.K.
45 E2 **Shihezi** China
         Shijiao China see Fogang
38 B2 **Shijiazhuang** China
42 A2 **Shikarpur** Pak.
35 B4 **Shikoku** i. Japan
34 D2 **Shikotsu-ko** l. Japan
54 D2 **Shilega** Rus. Fed.
43 C2 **Shiliguri** India
43 D2 **Shillong** India
57 F3 **Shilovo** Rus. Fed.
85 C3 **Shimbiris** mt. Somalia
35 C3 **Shimizu** Japan
43 B3 **Shimoga** India
35 B4 **Shimonoseki** Japan
64 B1 **Shin, Loch** l. U.K.
35 C4 **Shingū** Japan
91 D1 **Shingwedzi** S. Africa
91 D1 **Shingwedzi** r. S. Africa
87 D3 **Shinyanga** Tanz.
35 C4 **Shiono-misaki** c. Japan
106 B1 **Shiprock** U.S.A.

39 A3 **Shiqian** China
38 A2 **Shiquan** China
         Shiquanhe China see Gar
         Shiquan He r. China/Pak. see
         Indus
35 C3 **Shirane-san** mt. Japan
49 D3 **Shīrāz** Iran
34 D2 **Shiretoko-misaki** c. Japan
34 D2 **Shiriya-zaki** c. Japan
42 B2 **Shiv** India
43 B2 **Shivpuri** India
38 B2 **Shiyan** China
38 A2 **Shizuishan** China
35 C4 **Shizuoka** Japan
57 D3 **Shklow** Belarus
77 C2 **Shkodër** Albania
51 H1 **Shmidta, Ostrov** i. Rus. Fed.
103 D3 **Shoshone** U.S.A.
103 C3 **Shoshone Mountains** mts
         U.S.A.
91 C1 **Shoshong** Botswana
59 C1 **Shostka** Ukr.
38 B2 **Shouxian** China
106 A2 **Show Low** U.S.A.
59 C2 **Shpola** Ukr.
110 B2 **Shreveport** U.S.A.
67 B2 **Shrewsbury** U.K.
30 A1 **Shuangjiang** China
55 E4 **Shubarkuduk** Kazakh.
84 B1 **Shubrā el Kheima** Egypt
57 D2 **Shugozero** Rus. Fed.
88 B2 **Shumba** Zimbabwe
78 C2 **Shumen** Bulg.
56 C2 **Shumilina** Belarus
57 D3 **Shumyachi** Rus. Fed.
94 A2 **Shungnak** U.S.A.
46 B3 **Shuqrah** Yemen
57 F2 **Shushkodom** Rus. Fed.
49 C2 **Shushtar** Iran
96 C2 **Shuswap Lake** Can.
57 F2 **Shuya** Rus. Fed.
57 F2 **Shuyskoye** Rus. Fed.
30 A1 **Shwebo** Myanmar
30 A1 **Shwedwin** Myanmar
30 A2 **Shwegyin** Myanmar
45 C2 **Shymkent** Kazakh.
59 C2 **Shyroke** Ukr.
27 C3 **Sia** Indon.
42 A2 **Siahan Range** mts Pak.
42 B1 **Sialkot** Pak.
32 B2 **Siargao** i. Phil.
28 A2 **Siberut** i. Indon.
42 A2 **Sibi** Pak.
78 B1 **Sibiu** Romania
28 A1 **Sibolga** Indon.
30 A1 **Sibsagar** India
29 C1 **Sibu** Sarawak Malaysia
86 B3 **Sibut** C.A.R.
32 B1 **Sibuyan** i. Phil.
32 B1 **Sibuyan Sea** Phil.
96 C2 **Sicamous** Can.
31 A3 **Sichon** Thai.
38 A2 **Sichuan** prov. China
38 A3 **Sichuan Pendi** basin China
73 D3 **Sicié, Cap** c. France
         Sicilia i. Italy see Sicily
76 B3 **Sicilian Channel** Italy/Tunisia
76 B3 **Sicily** i. Italy
118 A3 **Sicuani** Peru
42 B2 **Siddhapur** India
79 C3 **Sideros, Akra** pt Greece
75 D2 **Sidi Aïssa** Alg.
75 D2 **Sidi Ali** Alg.
82 B1 **Sidi Bel Abbès** Alg.
82 A2 **Sidi Ifni** Morocco
28 A1 **Sidikalang** Indon.
64 C2 **Sidlaw Hills** U.K.
67 B3 **Sidmouth** U.K.

102 B1 **Sidney** Can.
104 C1 **Sidney** MT U.S.A.
104 C2 **Sidney** NE U.S.A.
108 C2 **Sidney** OH U.S.A.
111 D2 **Sidney Lanier, Lake** U.S.A.
122 B2 **Sidrolândia** Brazil
71 E1 **Siedlce** Pol.
68 C2 **Sieg** r. Ger.
68 D2 **Siegen** Ger.
31 B2 **Siĕmréab** Cambodia
76 B2 **Siena** Italy
71 D1 **Sieradz** Pol.
121 B5 **Sierra Grande** Arg.
82 A4 **Sierra Leone** country Africa
112 B2 **Sierra Mojada** Mex.
106 A2 **Sierra Vista** U.S.A.
73 D2 **Sierre** Switz.
79 B3 **Sifnos** i. Greece
75 C2 **Sig** Alg.
95 H2 **Sigguup Nunaa** pen.
         Greenland
71 E2 **Sighetu Marmaţiei** Romania
78 B1 **Sighişoara** Romania
28 A1 **Sigli** Indon.
60 □B2 **Siglufjörður** Iceland
70 B2 **Sigmaringen** Ger.
68 B3 **Signy-l'Abbaye** France
74 C1 **Sigüenza** Spain
82 B3 **Siguiri** Guinea
55 B2 **Sigulda** Latvia
31 B2 **Sihanoukville** Cambodia
60 I3 **Siilinjärvi** Fin.
49 C2 **Siirt** Turkey
28 B2 **Sijunjung** Indon.
42 B2 **Sikar** India
82 B3 **Sikasso** Mali
105 F3 **Sikeston** U.S.A.
34 B2 **Sikhote-Alin'** mts Rus. Fed.
79 C3 **Sikinos** i. Greece
112 B2 **Silao** Mex.
43 D2 **Silchar** India
45 D1 **Siletiteniz, Ozero**
         salt l. Kazakh.
43 C2 **Silgarhi** Nepal
48 B2 **Silifke** Turkey
43 C1 **Siling Co** salt l. China
78 C2 **Silistra** Bulg.
48 A1 **Silivri** Turkey
61 F3 **Siljan** l. Sweden
61 E4 **Silkeborg** Denmark
56 C2 **Sillamäe** Estonia
110 B1 **Siloam Springs** U.S.A.
91 D2 **Silobela** S. Africa
86 C1 **Šilutė** Lith.
49 C2 **Silvan** Turkey
106 B2 **Silver City** U.S.A.
104 B3 **Silverton** U.S.A.
30 B1 **Simao** China
98 C2 **Simard, Lac** l. Can.
79 C3 **Simav** Turkey
79 C3 **Simav Dağları** mts Turkey
86 C2 **Simba** Dem. Rep. Congo
109 D2 **Simcoe, Lake** Can.
28 A1 **Simeuluë** i. Indon.
59 C3 **Simferopol'** Ukr.
78 B1 **Şimleu Silvaniei** Romania
68 C3 **Simmern (Hunsrück)** Ger.
97 D2 **Simonhouse** Can.
19 C2 **Simpson Desert** Austr.
61 F4 **Simrishamn** Sweden
28 A1 **Sinabang** Indon.
84 B2 **Sinai** pen. Egypt
39 A3 **Sinan** China
33 B2 **Sinanju** N. Korea
30 A1 **Sinbo** Myanmar
118 A1 **Sincelejo** Col.
79 C3 **Sındırgı** Turkey
54 E2 **Sindor** Rus. Fed.
79 C2 **Sinekçi** Turkey
74 B2 **Sines** Port.

74 B2 **Sines, Cabo de** c. Port.
43 C2 **Singahi** India
28 B1 **Singapore** country Asia
29 C2 **Singaraja** Indon.
87 D3 **Singida** Tanz.
30 A1 **Singkaling Hkamti** Myanmar
29 A1 **Singkawang** Indon.
28 A1 **Singkil** Indon.
21 D2 **Singleton** Austr.
30 A1 **Singu** Myanmar
76 A2 **Siniscola** Sardinia Italy
77 C2 **Sinj** Croatia
84 B3 **Sinkat** Sudan
Sinkiang aut. reg. China see
Xinjiang Uygur Zizhiqu
48 B1 **Sinop** Turkey
33 B1 **Sinp'o** N. Korea
29 C1 **Sintang** Indon.
107 D3 **Sinton** U.S.A.
33 A1 **Sinŭiju** N. Korea
71 D2 **Siófok** Hungary
73 D2 **Sion** Switz.
105 D2 **Sioux Center** U.S.A.
105 D2 **Sioux City** U.S.A.
105 D2 **Sioux Falls** U.S.A.
98 A1 **Sioux Lookout** Can.
33 A1 **Siping** China
97 E2 **Sipiwesk Lake** Can.
28 A2 **Sipura** i. Indon.
61 E4 **Sira** r. Norway
Siracusa Italy see Syracuse
19 C1 **Sir Edward Pellew Group**
is Austr.
84 B1 **Sirhān, Wādī an**
watercourse Saudi Arabia
47 C2 **Sīrīk** Iran
30 B2 **Siri Kit Dam** Thai.
96 B1 **Sir James MacBrien,**
Mount Can.
47 C2 **Sīrjān** Iran
42 B2 **Şırnak** Turkey
42 B2 **Sirohi** India
42 B2 **Sirsa** India
78 B2 **Sirte** Libya
83 D1 **Sirte, Gulf of** Libya
56 B2 **Širvintos** Lith.
110 C2 **Sisal** Mex.
90 B1 **Sishen** S. Africa
49 C2 **Sisian** Armenia
97 D2 **Sisipuk Lake** Can.
31 B2 **Sisŏphŏn** Cambodia
73 D3 **Sisteron** France
43 C2 **Sitapur** India
91 G4 **Siteki** Swaziland
96 A2 **Sitka** U.S.A.
30 A2 **Sittang** r. Myanmar
68 B2 **Sittard** Neth.
30 A1 **Sittwe** Myanmar
29 C2 **Situbondo** Indon.
48 B2 **Sivas** Turkey
79 C3 **Sivaslı** Turkey
79 C3 **Siverek** Turkey
51 C3 **Sivrihisar** Turkey
84 A2 **Siwa** Egypt
42 B1 **Siwalik Range** mts
India/Nepal
73 D3 **Six-Fours-les-Plages** France
38 B2 **Sixian** China
91 C2 **Siyabuswa** S. Africa
61 F4 **Sjælland** i. Denmark
77 D2 **Sjenica** Yugo.
60 G2 **Sjøvegan** Norway
59 C2 **Skadovs'k** Ukr.
61 F4 **Skagen** Denmark
61 E4 **Skagerrak** str.
Denmark/Norway
102 B1 **Skagit** r. U.S.A.
96 A2 **Skagway** U.S.A.
42 B1 **Skardu** Jammu and Kashmir
71 E1 **Skarżysko-Kamienna** Pol.

71 D2 **Skawina** Pol.
96 B2 **Skeena** r. Can.
96 B2 **Skeena Mountains** Can.
60 D2 **Skegness** U.K.
60 H3 **Skellefteå** Sweden
60 H3 **Skellefteälven** r. Sweden
65 C2 **Skerries** Rep. of Ireland
79 B3 **Skiathos** i. Greece
65 B3 **Skibbereen** Rep. of Ireland
60 □B2 **Skíðadals-jökull** glacier
Iceland
66 B1 **Skiddaw** hill U.K.
61 E4 **Skien** Norway
71 E1 **Skierniewice** Pol.
83 C1 **Skikda** Alg.
20 B3 **Skipton** Austr.
66 B2 **Skipton** U.K.
61 E4 **Skive** Denmark
60 H1 **Skjervøy** Norway
79 B3 **Skopelos** i. Greece
57 E3 **Skopin** Rus. Fed.
77 D2 **Skopje** Macedonia
61 F4 **Skövde** Sweden
109 F2 **Skowhegan** U.S.A.
56 B2 **Skrunda** Latvia
96 A1 **Skukum, Mount** Can.
91 D1 **Skukuza** S. Africa
56 B2 **Skuodas** Lith.
64 A2 **Skye** i. U.K.
79 B3 **Skyros** Greece
79 B3 **Skyros** i. Greece
61 F4 **Slagelse** Denmark
65 C2 **Slaney** r. Rep. of Ireland
56 C2 **Slantsy** Rus. Fed.
77 C1 **Slatina** Croatia
78 B2 **Slatina** Romania
97 C1 **Slave** r. Can.
82 C4 **Slave Coast** Africa
96 C2 **Slave Lake** Can.
50 G3 **Slavgorod** Rus. Fed.
77 C1 **Slavonski Brod** Croatia
58 B1 **Slavuta** Ukr.
58 C1 **Slavutych** Ukr.
59 D2 **Slavyansk-na-Kubani**
Rus. Fed.
57 D3 **Slawharad** Belarus
71 D1 **Slawno** Pol.
65 A2 **Slea Head** hd Rep. of Ireland
98 C1 **Sleeper Islands** Can.
65 C1 **Slieve Donard** hill U.K.
65 B1 **Slieve Gamph** hills
Rep. of Ireland
65 B1 **Sligo** Rep. of Ireland
65 B1 **Sligo Bay** Rep. of Ireland
61 G4 **Slite** Sweden
78 C2 **Sliven** Bulg.
78 C2 **Slobozia** Romania
96 C3 **Slocan** Can.
56 C3 **Slonim** Belarus
68 B1 **Sloten** Neth.
67 C3 **Slough** U.K.
71 D2 **Slovakia** country Europe
76 B1 **Slovenia** country Europe
59 D2 **Slov"yans'k** Ukr.
58 B1 **Sluch** r. Ukr.
71 D1 **Słupsk** Pol.
56 C3 **Slutsk** Belarus
65 A2 **Slyne Head** hd
Rep. of Ireland
99 D1 **Smallwood Reservoir** Can.
56 C3 **Smalyavichy** Belarus
56 C3 **Smarhon'** Belarus
97 D2 **Smeaton** Can.
77 D2 **Smederevo** Yugo.
77 D2 **Smederevska Palanka**
Yugo.
59 C2 **Smila** Ukr.
56 C2 **Smiltene** Latvia
96 B2 **Smithers** Can.
111 E1 **Smithfield** U.S.A.

109 D3 **Smith Mountain Lake** U.S.A.
98 C2 **Smiths Falls** Can.
105 D3 **Smoky Hills** U.S.A.
60 E3 **Smøla** i. Norway
57 D3 **Smolensk** Rus. Fed.
78 B2 **Smolyan** Bulg.
98 B2 **Smooth Rock Falls** Can.
Smyrna Turkey see İzmir
60 □B3 **Snæfell** mt. Iceland
66 A1 **Snaefell** hill Isle of Man
100 B2 **Snake** r. U.S.A.
102 D2 **Snake River Plain** U.S.A.
96 C1 **Snare Lake** Can.
68 B1 **Sneek** Neth.
65 B3 **Sneem** Rep. of Ireland
90 B3 **Sneeuberge** mts S. Africa
76 B1 **Snežnik** mt. Slovenia
59 C2 **Snihurivka** Ukr.
61 E3 **Snøhetta** mt Norway
97 D1 **Snowbird Lake** l. Can.
66 A2 **Snowdon** mt. U.K.
Snowdrift Can. see Łutselk'e
97 C1 **Snowdrift** r. Can.
106 A2 **Snowflake** U.S.A.
97 D2 **Snow Lake** Can.
20 A2 **Snowtown** Austr.
21 C3 **Snowy** r. Austr.
21 C3 **Snowy Mountains** Austr.
107 C2 **Snyder** U.S.A.
89 □D2 **Soalala** Madag.
85 B4 **Sobat** r. Sudan
68 C3 **Sobernheim** Ger.
57 F2 **Sobinka** Rus. Fed.
110 D3 **Sobradinho, Barragem de**
resr Brazil
119 D2 **Sobral** Brazil
55 C4 **Sochi** Rus. Fed.
33 B2 **Sŏch'ŏn** S. Korea
118 A1 **Socorro** Col.
106 B2 **Socorro** U.S.A.
112 A3 **Socorro, Isla** i. Mex.
24 B4 **Socotra** i. Yemen
31 B3 **Soc Trăng** Vietnam
74 C2 **Socuéllamos** Spain
60 I? **Sodankylä** Fin.
102 D2 **Soda Springs** U.S.A.
61 G3 **Söderhamn** Sweden
61 G4 **Södertälje** Sweden
84 A3 **Sodiri** Sudan
85 B4 **Sodo** Eth.
61 G3 **Södra Kvarken** str.
Fin./Sweden
68 D2 **Soest** Ger.
78 B2 **Sofia** Bulg.
Sofiya Bulg. see Sofia
36 C2 **Sog** China
61 E3 **Sognefjorden** inlet Norway
79 D2 **Söğüt** Turkey
84 B2 **Sohâg** Egypt
68 B2 **Soignies** Belgium
72 C2 **Soissons** France
58 A1 **Sokal'** Ukr.
79 C3 **Söke** Turkey
49 C1 **Sokhumi** Georgia
82 C4 **Sokodé** Togo
57 F2 **Sokol** Rus. Fed.
69 F2 **Sokolov** Czech Rep.
83 C3 **Sokoto** Nigeria
83 C3 **Sokoto** r. Nigeria
58 B2 **Sokyryany** Ukr.
41 B3 **Solāpur** India
103 B3 **Soledad** U.S.A.
57 F2 **Soligalich** Rus. Fed.
67 C2 **Solihull** U.K.
54 E3 **Solikamsk** Rus. Fed.
55 E3 **Sol'-Iletsk** Rus. Fed.
68 C2 **Solingen** Ger.
60 G3 **Sollefteå** Sweden
61 G4 **Sollentuna** Sweden
69 D2 **Solling** hills Ger.

57 E2 **Solnechnogorsk** Rus. Fed.
28 B2 **Solok** Indon.
17 E3 **Solomon Islands** country
S. Pacific Ocean
73 D2 **Solothurn** Switz.
69 D1 **Soltau** Ger.
57 D2 **Sol'tsy** Rus. Fed.
64 C3 **Solway Firth** est. U.K.
88 B2 **Solwezi** Zambia
79 C3 **Soma** Turkey
85 C4 **Somalia** country Africa
88 B1 **Sombo** Angola
77 C1 **Sombor** Yugo.
112 B2 **Sombrerete** Mex.
108 C3 **Somerset** U.S.A.
91 C3 **Somerset East** S. Africa
94 E2 **Somerset Island** Can.
90 A3 **Somerset West** S. Africa
69 E2 **Sömmerda** Ger.
43 C2 **Son** r. India
61 E4 **Sønderborg** Denmark
69 E2 **Sondershausen** Ger.
Søndre Strømfjord inlet
Greenland see
Kangerlussuaq
30 B1 **Sông Da, Hô** resr Vietnam
87 D4 **Songea** Tanz.
33 B1 **Sŏnggan** N. Korea
33 B1 **Songhua Hu** resr China
Sŏngjin N. Korea see
Kimch'aek
31 B3 **Songkhla** Thai.
37 E1 **Songling** China
33 B2 **Sŏngnam** S. Korea
33 B2 **Songnim** N. Korea
88 A1 **Songo** Angola
89 C2 **Songo** Moz.
37 E1 **Songyuan** China
Sonid Youqi China see
Saihan Tal
57 E2 **Sonkovo** Rus. Fed.
30 B1 **Son La** Vietnam
42 A2 **Sonmiani** Pak.
69 E2 **Sonneberg** Ger.
112 A2 **Sonora** r. Mex.
103 B3 **Sonora** CA U.S.A.
107 C2 **Sonora** TX U.S.A.
106 A2 **Sonoyta** Mex.
85 A4 **Sopo** watercourse Sudan
71 D2 **Sopron** Hungary
76 B2 **Sora** Italy
98 C2 **Sorel** Can.
19 D4 **Sorell** Austr.
74 C1 **Soria** Spain
44 B2 **Sor Mertvyy Kultuk** dry lake
Kazakh.
58 B2 **Soroca** Moldova
122 C2 **Sorocaba** Brazil
55 E3 **Sorochinsk** Rus. Fed.
27 D2 **Sorol** atoll Micronesia
27 C3 **Sorong** Indon.
87 D2 **Soroti** Uganda
60 H1 **Sørøya** i. Norway
60 G2 **Sorsele** Sweden
32 B1 **Sorsogon** Phil.
54 C2 **Sortavala** Rus. Fed.
60 G2 **Sortland** Norway
33 B2 **Sŏsan** S. Korea
91 C2 **Soshanguve** S. Africa
57 E3 **Sosna** r. Rus. Fed.
121 B4 **Sosneado** mt. Arg.
54 E2 **Sosnogorsk** Rus. Fed.
54 D2 **Sosnovka** Rus. Fed.
56 C2 **Sosnovyy Bor** Rus. Fed.
71 D1 **Sosnowiec** Pol.
59 D2 **Sosyka** r. Rus. Fed.
113 C2 **Soto la Marina** Mex.
86 B2 **Souanké** Congo
72 C3 **Souillac** France
Sŏul S. Korea see Seoul

72 B2 **Soulac-sur-Mer** France
72 B3 **Soulom** France
48 C2 **Soûr** Lebanon
75 D2 **Sour el Ghozlane** Alg.
97 D3 **Souris** Man. Can.
99 D2 **Souris** P.E.I. Can.
97 E3 **Souris** r. Can.
119 E2 **Sousa** Brazil
83 D1 **Sousse** Tunisia
72 B3 **Soustons** France
90 B3 **South Africa, Republic of**
country Africa
67 C3 **Southampton** U.K.
95 F2 **Southampton Island** Can.
41 D3 **South Andaman** i. India
20 A1 **South Australia** state Austr.
98 B2 **South Baymouth** Can.
108 B2 **South Bend** U.S.A.
111 D2 **South Carolina** state U.S.A.
124 B4 **South China Sea**
N. Pacific Ocean
104 C2 **South Dakota** state U.S.A.
67 C3 **South Downs** hills U.K.
97 D2 **Southend** Can.
67 D3 **Southend-on-Sea** U.K.
22 B2 **Southern Alps** mts N.Z.
18 A3 **Southern Cross** Austr.
97 E2 **Southern Indian Lake** Can.
127 **Southern Ocean**
111 E1 **Southern Pines** U.S.A.
64 B3 **Southern Uplands** hills U.K.
117 F6 **South Georgia and South**
Sandwich Islands terr.
S. Atlantic Ocean
64 A2 **South Harris** pen. U.K.
97 E1 **South Henik Lake** l. Can.
22 B2 **South Island** N.Z.
103 B3 **South Lake Tahoe** U.S.A.
96 B1 **South Nahanni** r. Can.
23 Q4 **South Orkney Islands**
S. Atlantic Ocean
104 C2 **South Platte** r. U.S.A.
66 B2 **Southport** U.K.
111 E2 **Southport** U.S.A.
64 C1 **South Ronaldsay** i. U.K.
91 D3 **South Sand Bluff** pt
S. Africa
97 D2 **South Saskatchewan** r. Can.
97 E2 **South Seal** r. Can.
23 P3 **South Shetland Islands**
Antarctica
66 C1 **South Shields** U.K.
22 B1 **South Taranaki Bight** b. N.Z.
98 C1 **South Twin Island** Can.
64 A2 **South Uist** i. U.K.
21 D2 **South West Rocks** Austr.
67 D2 **Southwold** U.K.
77 C3 **Soverato** Italy
56 B2 **Sovetsk** Rus. Fed.
54 F2 **Sovetskiy** Rus. Fed.
59 C2 **Sovyets'kyy** Ukr.
91 C2 **Soweto** S. Africa
34 D1 **Sōya-misaki** c. Japan
58 C1 **Sozh** r. Europe
78 C2 **Sozopol** Bulg.
74 C1 **Spain** country Europe
67 C2 **Spalding** U.K.
103 D2 **Spanish Fork** U.S.A.
65 D2 **Spanish Point**
Rep. of Ireland
76 B3 **Sparagio, Monte** mt. Sicily
Italy
103 C3 **Sparks** U.S.A.
108 A2 **Sparta** U.S.A.
111 D2 **Spartanburg** U.S.A.
79 B3 **Sparti** Greece
77 C3 **Spartivento, Capo** c. Italy
57 D3 **Spas-Demensk** Rus. Fed.
57 F2 **Spas-Klepiki** Rus. Fed.
34 B2 **Spassk-Dal'niy** Rus. Fed.

57 F3 **Spassk-Ryazanskiy**
Rus. Fed.
79 B3 **Spatha, Akra** pt Greece
104 C2 **Spearfish** U.S.A.
107 C1 **Spearman** U.S.A.
105 D2 **Spencer** U.S.A.
20 A2 **Spencer Gulf** est. Austr.
66 C1 **Spennymoor** U.K.
22 B2 **Spenser Mountains** N.Z.
69 D3 **Spessart** reg. Ger.
64 C2 **Spey** r. U.K.
70 B2 **Speyer** Ger.
68 C1 **Spiekeroog** i. Ger.
68 B2 **Spijkenisse** Neth.
96 C2 **Spirit River** Can.
71 E2 **Spišská Nová Ves** Slovakia
50 C1 **Spitsbergen** i. Svalbard
70 C2 **Spittal an der Drau** Austria
77 C2 **Split** Croatia
97 E2 **Split Lake** Can.
97 E2 **Split Lake** l. Can.
102 C1 **Spokane** U.S.A.
108 A1 **Spooner** U.S.A.
70 C1 **Spree** r. Ger.
90 A2 **Springbok** S. Africa
99 E2 **Springdale** Can.
110 B1 **Springdale** U.S.A.
69 D1 **Springe** Ger.
106 C1 **Springer** U.S.A.
106 B2 **Springerville** U.S.A.
104 C3 **Springfield** CO U.S.A.
108 B3 **Springfield** IL U.S.A.
109 E2 **Springfield** MA U.S.A.
105 E3 **Springfield** MO U.S.A.
108 C3 **Springfield** OH U.S.A.
102 B2 **Springfield** OR U.S.A.
91 C3 **Springfontein** S. Africa
99 D2 **Springhill** Can.
111 D3 **Spring Hill** U.S.A.
22 B2 **Springs Junction** N.Z.
66 D2 **Spurn Head** hd U.K.
96 B3 **Squamish** Can.
77 C3 **Squillace, Golfo di** g. Italy
Srbija aut. rep. Yugo. see
Serbia
78 C2 **Sredets** Bulg.
51 L3 **Sredinnyy Khrebet** mts
Rus. Fed.
51 L2 **Srednekolymsk** Rus. Fed.
57 E3 **Sredne-Russkaya**
Vozvyshennost' hills
Rus. Fed.
51 I2 **Sredne-Sibirskoye**
Ploskogor'ye plat. Rus. Fed.
78 B2 **Srednogorie** Bulg.
37 D1 **Sretensk** Rus. Fed.
29 C1 **Sri Aman** Sarawak Malaysia
41 B4 **Sri Jayewardenepura Kott**
Sri Lanka
41 C3 **Srikakulam** India
41 C4 **Sri Lanka** country Asia
42 B1 **Srinagar**
Jammu and Kashmir
41 B3 **Srivardhan** India
69 D1 **Stade** Ger.
69 E1 **Stadensen** Ger.
68 C1 **Stadskanaal** Neth.
69 D2 **Stadtallendorf** Ger.
69 D1 **Stadthagen** Ger.
69 E2 **Staffelstein** Ger.
67 B2 **Stafford** U.K.
67 C3 **Staines** U.K.
59 D2 **Stakhanov** Ukr.
Stalingrad Rus. Fed. see
Volgograd
71 E1 **Stalowa Wola** Pol.
67 C2 **Stamford** U.K.
109 E2 **Stamford** CT U.S.A.
107 D2 **Stamford** TX U.S.A.
90 A1 **Stampriet** Namibia

60 F2	**Stamsund** Norway	
91 C2	**Standerton** S. Africa	
108 C2	**Standish** U.S.A.	
91 D2	**Stanger** S. Africa	
121 C6	**Stanley** Falkland Is	
104 C1	**Stanley** U.S.A.	
51 I3	**Stanovoye Nagor'ye** *mts* Rus. Fed.	
51 J3	**Stanovoy Khrebet** *mts* Rus. Fed.	
21 D1	**Stanthorpe** Austr.	
71 E1	**Starachowice** Pol.	
	Stara Planina *mts* Bulg./Yugo. *see* **Balkan Mountains**	
57 D2	**Staraya Russa** Rus. Fed.	
57 D2	**Staraya Toropa** Rus. Fed.	
78 C2	**Stara Zagora** Bulg.	
71 D1	**Stargard Szczeciński** Pol.	
110 C2	**Starkville** U.S.A.	
59 D2	**Starobil's'k** Ukr.	
57 D3	**Starodub** Rus. Fed.	
71 D1	**Starogard Gdański** Pol.	
58 B2	**Starokostyantyniv** Ukr.	
59 D2	**Starominskaya** Rus. Fed.	
59 D2	**Staroshcherbinovskaya** Rus. Fed.	
59 D2	**Starotitarovskaya** Rus. Fed.	
57 F3	**Staroyur'yevo** Rus. Fed.	
67 B3	**Start Point** U.K.	
56 C3	**Starya Darohi** Belarus	
57 E3	**Staryy Oskol** Rus. Fed.	
69 E2	**Staßfurt** Ger.	
109 D2	**State College** U.S.A.	
111 D2	**Statesboro** U.S.A.	
111 D1	**Statesville** U.S.A.	
61 E4	**Stavanger** Norway	
55 D4	**Stavropol'** Rus. Fed.	
55 D4	**Stavropol'skaya Vozvyshennost'** *hills* Rus. Fed.	
20 B3	**Stawell** Austr.	
91 C2	**Steadville** S. Africa	
104 B2	**Steamboat Springs** U.S.A.	
69 E2	**Stedten** Ger.	
96 C2	**Steen River** Can.	
102 C2	**Steens Mountain** U.S.A.	
68 C1	**Steenwijk** Neth.	
94 D2	**Stefansson Island** Can.	
69 E3	**Steigerwald** *mts* Ger.	
97 E3	**Steinbach** Can.	
68 C1	**Steinfurt** Ger.	
88 A3	**Steinhausen** Namibia	
60 F3	**Steinkjer** Norway	
90 A2	**Steinkopf** S. Africa	
90 B2	**Stella** S. Africa	
73 D2	**Stenay** France	
69 E1	**Stendal** Ger.	
	Stepanakert Azer. *see* **Xankändi**	
99 E2	**Stephenville** Can.	
107 D2	**Stephenville** U.S.A.	
90 B3	**Sterling** S. Africa	
104 C2	**Sterling** CO U.S.A.	
108 B2	**Sterling** IL U.S.A.	
55 E3	**Sterlitamak** Rus. Fed.	
69 E1	**Sternberg** Ger.	
96 C2	**Stettler** Can.	
108 C2	**Steubenville** U.S.A.	
67 C3	**Stevenage** U.K.	
97 E2	**Stevenson Lake** Can.	
94 B2	**Stevens Village** U.S.A.	
96 B2	**Stewart** Can.	
94 B2	**Stewart** r. Can.	
22 A3	**Stewart Island** N.Z.	
95 F2	**Stewart Lake** Can.	
70 C2	**Steyr** Austria	
90 B3	**Steytlerville** S. Africa	
96 A2	**Stikine** r. Can.	
96 A2	**Stikine Plateau** Can.	
90 B3	**Stilbaai** S. Africa	
107 D1	**Stillwater** U.S.A.	
77 D2	**Štip** Macedonia	
64 C2	**Stirling** U.K.	
60 F3	**Stjørdalshalsen** Norway	
71 D2	**Stockerau** Austria	
61 G4	**Stockholm** Sweden	
66 B2	**Stockport** U.K.	
103 B3	**Stockton** U.S.A.	
66 C1	**Stockton-on-Tees** U.K.	
31 B2	**Stœng Trêng** Cambodia	
64 B1	**Stoer, Point of** U.K.	
66 B2	**Stoke-on-Trent** U.K.	
77 C2	**Stolac** Bos.-Herz.	
68 C2	**Stolberg (Rheinland)** Ger.	
56 C3	**Stolin** Belarus	
69 F2	**Stollberg** Ger.	
69 D1	**Stolzenau** Ger.	
64 C2	**Stonehaven** U.K.	
97 E2	**Stonewall** Can.	
97 D2	**Stony Rapids** Can.	
60 G2	**Storavan** l. Sweden	
61 F4	**Store Bælt** *sea chan.* Denmark	
60 F3	**Støren** Norway	
60 F2	**Storforshei** Norway	
94 D2	**Storkerson Peninsula** Can.	
105 D2	**Storm Lake** U.S.A.	
61 E3	**Stornosa** *mt.* Norway	
64 A1	**Stornoway** U.K.	
54 E2	**Storozhevsk** Rus. Fed.	
58 B2	**Storozhynets'** Ukr.	
60 F3	**Storsjön** l. Sweden	
60 H2	**Storsteinnes** Norway	
60 G2	**Storuman** Sweden	
67 C2	**Stour** r. *England* U.K.	
67 C2	**Stour** r. *England* U.K.	
98 A1	**Stout Lake** Can.	
56 C3	**Stowbtsy** Belarus	
65 C1	**Strabane** U.K.	
70 C2	**Strakonice** Czech Rep.	
70 C1	**Stralsund** Ger.	
90 A3	**Strand** S. Africa	
61 E3	**Stranda** Norway	
65 D1	**Strangford Lough** *inlet* U.K.	
64 B3	**Stranraer** U.K.	
73 D2	**Strasbourg** France	
108 C2	**Stratford** Can.	
22 B1	**Stratford** N.Z.	
107 C1	**Stratford** U.S.A.	
67 C2	**Stratford-upon-Avon** U.K.	
96 C2	**Strathmore** Can.	
64 C2	**Strathspey** *val.* U.K.	
70 C2	**Straubing** Ger.	
19 C3	**Streaky Bay** Austr.	
100 D2	**Streator** U.S.A.	
78 B2	**Strehaia** Romania	
79 B2	**Strimonas** r. Greece	
121 B5	**Stroeder** Arg.	
69 D1	**Ströhen** Ger.	
77 C3	**Stromboli, Isola** i. Italy	
64 C1	**Stromness** U.K.	
60 G3	**Strömsund** Sweden	
64 C1	**Stronsay** i. U.K.	
21 D2	**Stroud** Austr.	
67 B3	**Stroud** U.K.	
68 C1	**Strücklingen (Saterland)** Ger.	
77 D2	**Struga** Macedonia	
56 C2	**Strugi-Krasnyye** Rus. Fed.	
90 B3	**Struis Bay** S. Africa	
77 D2	**Strumica** Macedonia	
90 B2	**Strydenburg** S. Africa	
58 A2	**Stryy** Ukr.	
96 B2	**Stuart Lake** Can.	
98 A1	**Stull Lake** Can.	
57 E3	**Stupino** Rus. Fed.	
108 B2	**Sturgeon Bay** U.S.A.	
98 C2	**Sturgeon Falls** Can.	
98 A2	**Sturgeon Lake** Can.	
108 B2	**Sturgis** MI U.S.A.	
104 C2	**Sturgis** SD U.S.A.	
18 B1	**Sturt Creek** *watercourse* Austr.	
20 B1	**Sturt Stony Desert** Austr.	
91 C3	**Stutterheim** S. Africa	
70 B2	**Stuttgart** Ger.	
110 B2	**Stuttgart** U.S.A.	
60 □A2	**Stykkishólmur** Iceland	
58 B1	**Styr** r. Belarus/Ukr.	
123 D1	**Suaçuí Grande** r. Brazil	
84 B3	**Suakin** Sudan	
46 A3	**Suara, Mount** Eritrea	
77 C1	**Subotica** Yugo.	
78 C1	**Suceava** Romania	
65 B2	**Suck** r. Rep. of Ireland	
120 B2	**Sucre** Bol.	
122 B2	**Sucuriú** r. Brazil	
57 E2	**Suda** Rus. Fed.	
59 C3	**Sudak** Ukr.	
85 B3	**Sudan** *country* Africa	
98 B2	**Sudbury** Can.	
85 A4	**Sudd** *swamp* Sudan	
57 F2	**Sudislavl'** Rus. Fed.	
57 F2	**Sudogda** Rus. Fed.	
62 B1	**Suðuroy** i. Faroe Is	
75 C2	**Sueca** Spain	
84 B2	**Suez** Egypt	
84 B2	**Suez, Gulf of** Egypt	
48 B2	**Suez Canal** Egypt	
109 D3	**Suffolk** U.S.A.	
47 C2	**Suhār** Oman	
37 D1	**Sühbaatar** Mongolia	
69 E2	**Suhl** Ger.	
77 C1	**Suhopolje** Croatia	
38 C2	**Suide** China	
04 D□	**Suifenhe** China	
37 E1	**Suihua** China	
38 A2	**Suining** China	
38 B2	**Suiping** China	
38 B2	**Suizhou** China	
42 B2	**Sujangarh** India	
42 B1	**Sujanpur** India	
42 A2	**Sujawal** Pak.	
28 B2	**Sukabumi** Indon.	
29 D2	**Sukadana** Indon.	
57 E3	**Sukhinichi** Rus. Fed.	
57 F2	**Sukhona** r. Rus. Fed.	
30 A2	**Sukhothai** Thai.	
42 A2	**Sukkur** Pak.	
57 E2	**Sukromny** Rus. Fed.	
27 C3	**Sula, Kepulauan** is Indon.	
42 A1	**Sulaiman Ranges** *mts* Pak.	
26 C3	**Sulawesi** i. Indon.	
118 A2	**Sullana** Peru	
105 E3	**Sullivan** U.S.A.	
107 D2	**Sulphur Springs** U.S.A.	
32 B2	**Sulu Archipelago** is Phil.	
32 A2	**Sulu Sea** N. Pacific Ocean	
69 E3	**Sulzbach-Rosenberg** Ger.	
47 C2	**Sumāil** Oman	
28 A1	**Sumatera** i. Indon.	
	Sumatra i. Indon. *see* **Sumatera**	
26 C3	**Sumba** i. Indon.	
29 C2	**Sumbawa** i. Indon.	
29 C2	**Sumbawabesar** Indon.	
87 D3	**Sumbawanga** Tanz.	
88 A2	**Sumbe** Angola	
64 □	**Sumburgh** U.K.	
64 □	**Sumburgh Head** hd U.K.	
29 C2	**Sumenep** Indon.	
35 D4	**Sumisu-jima** i. Japan	
99 D2	**Summerside** Can.	
108 C2	**Summersville** U.S.A.	
96 B2	**Summit Lake** Can.	
71 D2	**Šumperk** Czech Rep.	
49 C1	**Sumqayıt** Azer.	
111 D2	**Sumter** U.S.A.	
59 C1	**Sumy** Ukr.	

43 D2 **Sunamganj** Bangl.
33 B2 **Sunan** N. Korea
47 C2 **Şunaynah** Oman
20 B3 **Sunbury** Austr.
109 D2 **Sunbury** U.S.A.
33 B2 **Sunch'ŏn** N. Korea
33 B3 **Sunch'ŏn** S. Korea
91 C2 **Sun City** S. Africa
28 B2 **Sunda, Selat** str. Indon.
104 C2 **Sundance** U.S.A.
43 C2 **Sundarbans** reg. Bangl./India
66 C1 **Sunderland** U.K.
96 C2 **Sundre** Can.
61 G3 **Sundsvall** Sweden
91 D2 **Sundumbili** S. Africa
28 B2 **Sungailiat** Indon.
28 B2 **Sungaipenuh** Indon.
28 B1 **Sungei Petani** Malaysia
48 B1 **Sungurlu** Turkey
61 E3 **Sunndalsøra** Norway
102 C1 **Sunnyside** U.S.A.
103 B3 **Sunnyvale** U.S.A.
51 I2 **Suntar** Rus. Fed.
42 A2 **Suntsar** Pak.
82 B4 **Sunyani** Ghana
50 D2 **Suoyarvi** Rus. Fed.
106 A2 **Superior** AZ U.S.A.
105 D2 **Superior** NE U.S.A.
108 A1 **Superior** WI U.S.A.
108 B1 **Superior, Lake** Can./U.S.A.
57 D3 **Suponevo** Rus. Fed.
49 C2 **Sūq ash Shuyūkh** Iraq
38 B2 **Suqian** China
46 A2 **Sūq Suwayq** Saudi Arabia
47 C2 **Şūr** Oman
42 A2 **Surab** Pak.
29 C2 **Surabaya** Indon.
29 C2 **Surakarta** Indon.
42 B2 **Surat** India
42 B2 **Suratgarh** India
31 A3 **Surat Thani** Thai.
57 D3 **Surazh** Rus. Fed.
77 D2 **Surdulica** Yugo.
42 B2 **Surendranagar** India
50 F2 **Surgut** Rus. Fed.
32 B2 **Surigao** Phil.
31 B2 **Surin** Thai.
119 C1 **Suriname** country S. America
Surt Libya see Sirte
Surt, Khalīj g. Libya see
Sirte, Gulf of
28 B2 **Surulangun** Indon.
57 F2 **Susanino** Rus. Fed.
103 B2 **Susanville** U.S.A.
48 B1 **Suşehri** Turkey
99 C2 **Sussex** Can.
69 D1 **Süstedt** Ger.
68 C1 **Sustrum** Ger.
51 K2 **Susuman** Rus. Fed.
79 C3 **Susurluk** Turkey
43 B1 **Sutak** Jammu and Kashmir
90 B3 **Sutherland** S. Africa
67 C2 **Sutton Coldfield** U.K.
34 D2 **Suttsu** Japan
57 E3 **Suvorov** Rus. Fed.
71 E1 **Suwałki** Pol.
31 B2 **Suwannaphum** Thai.
111 D3 **Suwannee** r. U.S.A.
Suweis, Qanâ el canal Egypt
see Suez Canal
33 B2 **Suwŏn** S. Korea
47 C2 **Sūzā** Iran
57 F2 **Suzdal'** Rus. Fed.
38 B2 **Suzhou** Anhui China
38 C2 **Suzhou** Jiangsu China
35 C3 **Suzu** Japan
35 C3 **Suzu-misaki** pt Japan
50 B1 **Svalbard** terr. Arctic Ocean
59 D2 **Svatove** Ukr.
31 B2 **Svay Riĕng** Cambodia

61 F3 **Sveg** Sweden
56 C2 **Švenčionys** Lith.
61 F4 **Svendborg** Denmark
Sverdlovsk Rus. Fed. see
Yekaterinburg
77 D2 **Sveti Nikole** Macedonia
56 B3 **Svetlogorsk** Rus. Fed.
56 B3 **Svetly** Rus. Fed.
61 I3 **Svetogorsk** Rus. Fed.
78 C2 **Svilengrad** Bulg.
78 B2 **Svinecea Mare, Vârful** mt.
Romania
78 C2 **Svishtov** Bulg.
71 D2 **Svitavy** Czech Rep.
59 C2 **Svitlovods'k** Ukr.
37 E1 **Svobodnyy** Rus. Fed.
60 F2 **Svolvær** Norway
56 C3 **Svyetlahorsk** Belarus
111 D2 **Swainsboro** U.S.A.
88 A3 **Swakopmund** Namibia
20 B3 **Swan Hill** Austr.
96 C2 **Swan Hills** Can.
97 D2 **Swan Lake** l. Can.
97 D2 **Swan River** Can.
21 D2 **Swansea** Austr.
67 B3 **Swansea** U.K.
91 C2 **Swartruggens** S. Africa
Swatow China see
Shantou
91 D2 **Swaziland** country
Africa
61 G3 **Sweden** country Europe
107 C2 **Sweetwater** U.S.A.
104 B2 **Sweetwater** r. U.S.A.
90 B3 **Swellendam** S. Africa
71 D1 **Świdnica** Pol.
71 D1 **Świdwin** Pol.
71 D1 **Świebodzin** Pol.
71 D1 **Świecie** Pol.
97 D2 **Swift Current** Can.
65 C1 **Swilly, Lough** inlet
Rep. of Ireland
67 C2 **Swindon** U.K.
70 C1 **Świnoujście** Pol.
73 D2 **Switzerland** country
Europe
65 C2 **Swords** Rep. of Ireland
56 C3 **Syanno** Belarus
57 D2 **Sychevka** Rus. Fed.
21 D2 **Sydney** Austr.
99 D2 **Sydney** Can.
99 D2 **Sydney Mines** Can.
59 D2 **Syeverodonets'k** Ukr.
54 E2 **Syktyvkar** Rus. Fed.
110 C2 **Sylacauga** U.S.A.
43 D2 **Sylhet** Bangl.
70 B1 **Sylt** i. Ger.
79 C3 **Symi** i. Greece
59 D2 **Synel'nykove** Ukr.
104 C3 **Syracuse** KS U.S.A.
109 D2 **Syracuse** NY U.S.A.
48 C2 **Syrdar'ya** r. Asia
46 B2 **Syria** country Asia
31 A2 **Syriam** Myanmar
Syrian Desert Asia see
Bādiyat ash Shām
79 B3 **Syros** i. Greece
55 D3 **Syzran'** Rus. Fed.
70 C1 **Szczecin** Pol.
71 D1 **Szczecinek** Pol.
71 E1 **Szczytno** Pol.
71 E2 **Szeged** Hungary
71 D2 **Székesfehérvár** Hungary
71 D2 **Szekszárd** Hungary
71 E2 **Szentes** Hungary
71 D2 **Szentgotthárd** Hungary
71 D2 **Szigetvár** Hungary
71 E2 **Szolnok** Hungary
71 D2 **Szombathely** Hungary

T

46 B2 **Tābah** Saudi Arabia
44 B3 **Tabas** Iran
49 D3 **Tābask, Kūh-e** mt. Iran
118 B2 **Tabatinga** Brazil
82 B2 **Tabelbala** Alg.
97 C3 **Taber** Can.
70 C2 **Tábor** Czech Rep.
87 D3 **Tabora** Tanz.
82 B4 **Tabou** Côte d'Ivoire
49 C2 **Tabrīz** Iran
46 A2 **Tabūk** Saudi Arabia
45 E2 **Tacheng** China
70 C2 **Tachov** Czech Rep.
32 B1 **Tacloban** Phil.
118 A3 **Tacna** Peru
102 B1 **Tacoma** U.S.A.
120 C4 **Tacuarembó** Uru.
106 B3 **Tacupeto** Mex.
85 C3 **Tadjoura** Djibouti
48 B2 **Tadmur** Syria
97 E2 **Tadoule Lake** Can.
33 B2 **Taegu** S. Korea
33 B2 **Taejŏn** S. Korea
33 B3 **Taejŏng** S. Korea
33 B2 **T'aepaek** S. Korea
75 C1 **Tafalla** Spain
120 B3 **Tafí Viejo** Arg.
47 D2 **Taftān, Kūh-e** mt. Iran
59 D2 **Taganrog** Rus. Fed.
59 D2 **Taganrog, Gulf of**
Rus. Fed./Ukr.
30 A1 **Tagaung** Myanmar
32 B1 **Tagaytay City** Phil.
32 B2 **Tagbilaran** Phil.
32 B1 **Tagudin** Phil.
32 B2 **Tagum** Phil.
74 B2 **Tagus** r. Port./Spain
83 C2 **Tahan, Gunung** mt. Malaysia
83 C2 **Tahat, Mont** mt. Alg.
37 E1 **Tahe** China
107 E1 **Tahlequah** U.S.A.
103 B3 **Tahoe, Lake** U.S.A.
103 B3 **Tahoe City** U.S.A.
94 D2 **Tahoe Lake** Can.
83 C3 **Tahoua** Niger
47 C2 **Tahrūd** Iran
96 B3 **Tahsis** Can.
38 B2 **Tai'an** China
Taibus Qi China see
Baochang
39 C3 **T'aichung** Taiwan
22 C1 **Taihape** N.Z.
38 C2 **Tai Hu** l. China
20 A3 **Tailem Bend** Austr.
39 C3 **T'ainan** Taiwan
123 D1 **Taiobeiras** Brazil
39 C3 **T'aipei** Taiwan
28 B1 **Taiping** Malaysia
39 B3 **Taishan** China
121 A5 **Taitao, Península de** pen.
Chile
39 C3 **T'aitung** Taiwan
60 I2 **Taivalkoski** Fin.
60 H2 **Taivaskero** hill Fin.
39 C3 **Taiwan** country Asia
39 B3 **Taiwan Strait** China/Taiwan
38 B2 **Taiyuan** China
38 B2 **Taizhou** Jiangsu China
39 C3 **Taizhou** Zhejiang China
46 B3 **Ta'izz** Yemen
45 D3 **Tajikistan** country Asia
43 B2 **Taj Mahal** India
Tajo r. Port. see Tagus
26 A1 **Tak** Thai.
22 B2 **Takaka** N.Z.
35 B4 **Takamatsu** Japan

35 C3 Takaoka Japan
22 B1 Takapuna N.Z.
35 C3 Takasaki Japan
90 B1 Takatokwane Botswana
35 C3 Takayama Japan
35 C3 Takefu Japan
28 A1 Takengon Indon.
31 B2 Takêv Cambodia
31 B2 Ta Khmau Cambodia
34 D2 Takikawa Japan
96 B2 Takla Lake Can.
96 B2 Takla Landing Can.
45 E3 Taklimakan Shamo des.
        China
96 A2 Taku r. Can./U.S.A.
31 A3 Takua Pa Thai.
83 C4 Takum Nigeria
56 C3 Talachyn Belarus
42 B1 Talagang Pak.
118 A2 Talara Peru
42 A2 Talar-i-Band mts Pak.
27 C2 Talaud, Kepulauan is Indon.
74 C2 Talavera de la Reina Spain
121 A4 Talca Chile
121 A4 Talcahuano Chile
57 E2 Taldom Rus. Fed.
45 D2 Taldykorgan Kazakh.
27 C3 Taliabu i. Indon.
32 B1 Talisay Phil.
29 C2 Taliwang Indon.
49 C2 Tall 'Afar Iraq
111 D2 Tallahassee U.S.A.
56 B2 Tallinn Estonia
110 B2 Tallulah U.S.A.
72 B2 Talmont-St-Hilaire France
58 C2 Tal'ne Ukr.
85 B3 Talodi Sudan
59 E1 Talovaya Rus. Fed.
94 E2 Taloyoak Can.
56 B2 Talsi Latvia
120 A3 Taltal Chile
97 C1 Taltson r. Can.
28 A1 Talu Indon.
21 C1 Talwood Austr.
82 B4 Tamale Ghana
83 C2 Tamanrasset Alg.
67 A3 Tamar r. U.K.
113 C2 Tamazunchale Mex.
82 A3 Tambacounda Senegal
29 B1 Tambelan, Kepulauan
        is Indon.
59 E1 Tambov Rus. Fed.
113 C2 Tamiahua, Laguna de
        lag. Mex.
111 D3 Tampa U.S.A.
111 D3 Tampa Bay U.S.A.
61 H3 Tampere Fin.
113 C2 Tampico Mex.
37 D1 Tamsagbulag Mongolia
70 C2 Tamsweg Austria
21 D2 Tamworth Austr.
67 C2 Tamworth U.K.
87 E3 Tana r. Kenya
35 C4 Tanabe Japan
60 I1 Tana Bru Norway
85 B3 T'ana Häyk' I. Eth.
29 C2 Tanahgrogot Indon.
26 C3 Tanahjampea i. Indon.
18 C1 Tanami Desert Austr.
94 A2 Tanana U.S.A.
76 A1 Tanaro r. Italy
33 B1 Tanch'ŏn N. Korea
32 B2 Tandag Phil.
78 C2 Ţăndărei Romania
121 C4 Tandil Arg.
42 A2 Tando Adam Pak.
42 A2 Tando Muhammad Khan
        Pak.
82 B2 Tanezrouft reg. Alg./Mali
87 D3 Tanga Tanz.

87 C3 Tanganyika, Lake Africa
        Tanger Morocco see Tangier
69 E1 Tangermünde Ger.
43 C1 Tanggula Shan mts China
82 B1 Tangier Morocco
43 C1 Tangra Yumco salt l. China
38 B2 Tangshan China
36 C2 Taniantaweng Shan mts
        China
27 C3 Tanimbar, Kepulauan
        is Indon.
32 B2 Tanjay Phil.
28 A1 Tanjungbalai Indon.
28 B2 Tanjungkarang-Telukbetung
        Indon.
29 B2 Tanjungpandan Indon.
28 B1 Tanjungpinang Indon.
29 C1 Tanjungredeb Indon.
29 C1 Tanjungselor Indon.
42 B1 Tank Pak.
83 C3 Tanout Niger
43 C2 Tansen Nepal
84 B1 Tanta Egypt
87 D3 Tanzania country Africa
37 E1 Taonan China
106 B1 Taos U.S.A.
82 B2 Taoudenni Mali
56 C2 Tapa Estonia
113 C3 Tapachula Mex.
119 C2 Tapajós r. Brazil
28 A1 Tapaktuan Indon.
113 C3 Tapanatepec Mex.
118 B2 Tapauá Brazil
82 B4 Tapeta Liberia
42 B2 Tāpi r. India
109 D3 Tappahannock U.S.A.
118 B2 Tapurucuara Brazil
122 B1 Taquari Brazil
122 A1 Taquari r. Brazil
122 B1 Taquari, Serra do hills Brazil
122 C2 Taquaritinga Brazil
83 D4 Taraba r. Nigeria
        Tarabulus Libya see Tripoli
56 A3 Tarakan Indon.
        Taranaki, Mount vol. N.Z.
        see Egmont, Mt
74 C1 Tarancón Spain
77 C2 Taranto Italy
77 C2 Taranto, Golfo di g. Italy
118 A2 Tarapoto Peru
59 E2 Tarasovskiy Rus. Fed.
118 A2 Tarauacá Brazil
118 B2 Tarauacá r. Brazil
45 D2 Taraz Kazakh.
75 C1 Tarazona Spain
45 E2 Tarbagatay, Khrebet
        mts Kazakh.
64 A2 Tarbert Scotland U.K.
64 B3 Tarbert Scotland U.K.
72 C3 Tarbes France
64 B2 Tarbet U.K.
19 C3 Tarcoola Austr.
21 D2 Taree Austr.
78 C2 Târgoviște Romania
78 B1 Târgu Jiu Romania
78 B1 Târgu Mureș Romania
78 C1 Târgu Neamţ Romania
47 C2 Tarif U.A.E.
120 B3 Tarija Bol.
47 B3 Tarīm Yemen
45 E2 Tarim He r. China
45 E3 Tarim Pendi basin China
27 D3 Taritatu r. Indon.
50 G2 Tarko-Sale Rus. Fed.
82 B4 Tarkwa Ghana
32 B1 Tarlac Phil.
60 G2 Tärnaby Sweden
45 C3 Tarnak r. Afgh.
78 B1 Târnăveni Romania

71 E1 Tarnobrzeg Pol.
71 E1 Tarnów Pol.
82 B1 Taroudannt Morocco
76 B2 Tarquinia Italy
75 D1 Tarragona Spain
75 D1 Tàrrega Spain
48 B2 Tarsus Turkey
120 B3 Tartagal Arg.
72 B3 Tartas France
56 C2 Tartu Estonia
48 B2 Ţarţūs Syria
123 D1 Tarumirim Brazil
57 E3 Tarusa Rus. Fed.
76 B1 Tarvisio Italy
        Tashi Chho Bhutan see
        Thimphu
49 D3 Tashk, Daryācheh-ye I. Iran
45 C2 Tashkent Uzbek.
99 D1 Tasiujaq Can.
45 E2 Taskesken Kazakh.
22 B2 Tasman Bay N.Z.
19 D4 Tasmania state Austr.
22 B2 Tasman Mountains N.Z.
124 D8 Tasman Sea
        S. Pacific Ocean
83 C2 Tassili du Hoggar plat. Alg.
83 C2 Tassili n'Ajjer plat. Alg.
71 D2 Tatabánya Hungary
58 B2 Tatarbunary Ukr.
51 K3 Tatarskiy Proliv str.
        Rus. Fed.
35 C4 Tateyama Japan
96 C1 Tathlina Lake Can.
46 B3 Tathlīth Saudi Arabia
46 B2 Tathlīth, Wādī watercourse
        Saudi Arabia
21 C3 Tathra Austr.
30 A1 Tatkon Myanmar
96 B2 Tatla Lake Can.
42 A2 Tatta Pak.
122 C1 Tatul Brazil
107 C2 Tatum U.S.A.
49 C2 Tatvan Turkey
119 D2 Taua Brazil
123 C2 Taubaté Brazil
69 D3 Tauberbischofsheim Ger.
22 C1 Taumarunui N.Z.
30 A1 Taunggyi Myanmar
30 A2 Taunqup Myanmar
87 B3 Taunton U.K.
68 C2 Taunus hills Ger.
22 C1 Taupo N.Z.
22 C1 Taupo, Lake N.Z.
56 B2 Tauragé Lith.
22 C1 Tauranga N.Z.
79 C3 Tavas Turkey
54 F3 Tavda Rus. Fed.
74 B2 Tavira Port.
67 A3 Tavistock U.K.
31 A2 Tavoy Myanmar
79 C3 Tavşanlı Turkey
67 A3 Taw r. U.K.
108 C2 Tawas City U.S.A.
29 C1 Tawau Sabah Malaysia
32 A2 Tawitawi i. Phil.
113 C3 Taxco Mex.
45 D3 Taxkorgan China
64 C2 Tay r. U.K.
64 C2 Tay, Firth of est. U.K.
64 B2 Tay, Loch I. U.K.
96 B2 Taylor Can.
107 D2 Taylor U.S.A.
108 B3 Taylorville U.S.A.
46 A2 Taymā' Saudi Arabia
51 H2 Taymura r. Rus. Fed.
51 H2 Taymyr, Ozero I. Rus. Fed.
51 G2 Taymyr, Poluostrov pen.
        Rus. Fed.
31 B2 Tây Ninh Vietnam
32 A1 Taytay Phil.

50 G2 Taz r. Rus. Fed.
82 B1 Taza Morocco
97 D2 Tazin Lake Can.
54 G2 Tazovskaya Guba sea chan. Rus. Fed.
49 C1 T'bilisi Georgia
59 E2 Tbilisskaya Rus. Fed.
86 B3 Tchibanga Gabon
86 B2 Tcholliré Cameroon
71 D1 Tczew Pol.
112 B2 Teacapán Mex.
22 A3 Te Anau N.Z.
22 A3 Te Anau, Lake N.Z.
113 C3 Teapa Mex.
22 C1 Te Awamutu N.Z.
83 C1 Tébessa Alg.
28 B2 Tebingtinggi Sumatera Indon.
28 A1 Tebingtinggi Sumatera Indon.
82 B4 Techiman Ghana
112 B3 Tecomán Mex.
112 B2 Tecoripa Mex.
113 B3 Técpan Mex.
112 B2 Tecuala Mex.
78 C1 Tecuci Romania
44 C3 Tedzhen Turkm.
44 C3 Tedzhen r. Turkm.
36 C1 Teeli Rus. Fed.
66 C1 Tees r. U.K.
79 C3 Tefenni Turkey
29 B2 Tegal Indon.
114 B3 Tegucigalpa Hond.
83 C3 Teguidda-n-Tessoumt Niger
82 B4 Téhini Côte d'Ivoire
49 D2 Tehrān Iran
113 C3 Tehuacán Mex.
113 C3 Tehuantepec, Golfo de g. Mex.
113 C3 Tehuantepec, Istmo de isth. Mex.
67 A2 Teifi r. U.K.
113 B3 Tejupilco Mex.
22 B2 Tekapo, Lake N.Z.
113 D2 Tekax Mex.
84 B3 Tekezē Wenz r. Eritrea/Eth.
79 C2 Tekirdağ Turkey
22 C1 Te Kuiti N.Z.
43 C2 Tel r. India
49 C1 T'elavi Georgia
48 B2 Tel Aviv-Yafo Israel
113 D2 Telchac Puerto Mex.
96 A2 Telegraph Creek Can.
122 B2 Telêmaco Borba Brazil
67 B2 Telford U.K.
28 A2 Telo Indon.
54 E2 Tel'pos-Iz, Gora mt. Rus. Fed.
56 B2 Telšiai Lith.
28 B1 Teluk Anson Malaysia
29 B1 Telukbatang Indon.
28 A1 Telukdalam Indon.
98 C2 Temagami Lake Can.
29 C2 Temanggung Indon.
91 C2 Temba S. Africa
28 B2 Tembilahan Indon.
88 A1 Tembo Aluma Angola
67 B2 Teme r. U.K.
28 B1 Temerloh Malaysia
45 D1 Temirtau Kazakh.
21 C2 Temora Austr.
107 D2 Temple U.S.A.
65 C2 Templemore Rep. of Ireland
113 C2 Tempoal Mex.
59 D2 Temryuk Rus. Fed.
121 A4 Temuco Chile
22 B2 Temuka N.Z.
113 C2 Tenabo Mex.
41 C3 Tenali India
31 A2 Tenasserim Myanmar
67 A3 Tenby U.K.

85 C3 Tendaho Eth.
73 D3 Tende France
76 A2 Tende, Col de pass France/Italy
41 D4 Ten Degree Channel India
35 D3 Tendō Japan
82 B3 Ténenkou Mali
83 D2 Ténéré du Tafassâsset des. Niger
82 A2 Tenerife i. Canary Is
75 D2 Ténès Alg.
29 C2 Tengah, Kepulauan is Indon.
30 A1 Tengchong China
29 C2 Tenggarong Indon.
38 A2 Tengger Shamo des. China
39 B3 Tengxian China
87 C4 Tenke Dem. Rep. Congo
82 B3 Tenkodogo Burkina
19 C1 Tennant Creek Austr.
110 C1 Tennessee r. U.S.A.
110 C1 Tennessee state U.S.A.
113 C3 Tenosique Mex.
21 D1 Tenterfield Austr.
122 B2 Teodoro Sampaio Brazil
123 D1 Teófilo Otôni Brazil
113 C3 Teopisca Mex.
112 B2 Tepache Mex.
22 B1 Te Paki N.Z.
112 B2 Tepalcatepec Mex.
112 B2 Tepatitlán Mex.
112 B2 Tepehuanes Mex.
77 D2 Tepelenë Albania
112 B2 Tepic Mex.
70 C1 Teplice Czech Rep.
57 E3 Teploye Rus. Fed.
112 B2 Tequila Mex.
76 B2 Teramo Italy
57 E3 Terbuny Rus. Fed.
58 B2 Terebovlya Ukr.
55 D4 Terek r. Rus. Fed.
119 D2 Teresina Brazil
123 D2 Teresópolis Brazil
31 A3 Teressa Island India
48 B1 Terme Turkey
45 C3 Termez Uzbek.
76 B3 Termini Imerese Sicily Italy
113 C3 Términos, Laguna de lag. Mex.
77 B2 Termoli Italy
27 C2 Ternate Indon.
68 A2 Terneuzen Neth.
76 B2 Terni Italy
58 B2 Ternopil' Ukr.
96 B2 Terrace Can.
98 B2 Terrace Bay Can.
90 B2 Terra Firma S. Africa
108 B3 Terre Haute U.S.A.
99 E2 Terrenceville Can.
68 B1 Terschelling i. Neth.
76 A3 Tertenia Sardinia Italy
75 C1 Teruel Spain
60 H2 Tervola Fin.
77 C2 Tešanj Bos.-Herz.
84 B3 Teseney Eritrea
34 D2 Teshio-gawa r. Japan
96 A1 Teslin Can.
96 A1 Teslin Lake Can.
122 B1 Tesouro Brazil
83 C3 Tessaoua Niger
89 C2 Tete Moz.
58 C1 Teteriv r. Ukr.
69 F1 Teterow Ger.
58 B2 Tetiyiv Ukr.
82 B1 Tétouan Morocco
77 D2 Tetovo Macedonia
76 B2 Teuco r. Arg.
112 B2 Teul de González Ortega Mex.
69 D1 Teutoburger Wald hills Ger.
76 B2 Tevere r. Italy

22 A3 Teviot N.Z.
19 E2 Tewantin Austr.
22 C2 Te Wharau N.Z.
107 E2 Texarkana U.S.A.
21 D1 Texas Austr.
107 D2 Texas state U.S.A.
107 E3 Texas City U.S.A.
68 B1 Texel i. Neth.
107 D2 Texoma, Lake U.S.A.
91 C2 Teyateyaneng Lesotho
57 F2 Teykovo Rus. Fed.
57 F2 Teza r. Rus. Fed.
43 D2 Tezpur India
30 A1 Tezu India
97 E1 Tha-anne r. Can.
91 C2 Thabana-Ntlenyana mt. Lesotho
91 C2 Thaba Putsoa mt. Lesotho
91 C1 Thabazimbi S. Africa
91 C2 Thabong S. Africa
31 A2 Thagyettaw Myanmar
30 B1 Thai Binh Vietnam
31 B2 Thailand country Asia
31 B2 Thailand, Gulf of Asia
30 B1 Thai Nguyên Vietnam
31 A3 Thalang Thai.
42 B1 Thal Desert Pak.
69 E2 Thale (Harz) Ger.
30 B2 Tha Li Thai.
91 C1 Thamaga Botswana
84 C3 Thamar, Jabal mt. Yemen
47 C3 Thamarīt Oman
98 B2 Thames r. Can.
22 C1 Thames N.Z.
67 D3 Thames est. U.K.
67 D3 Thames r. U.K.
31 A2 Thanbyuzayat Myanmar
30 B2 Thanh Hoa Vietnam
41 B3 Thanjavur India
42 A2 Thano Bula Khan Pak.
30 B1 Than Uyen Vietnam
42 A2 Thar Desert India/Pak.
20 B1 Thargomindah Austr.
30 A2 Tharrawaddy Myanmar
49 C2 Tharthār, Buḩayrat ath l. Iraq
79 B2 Thasos i. Greece
30 B1 Thât Khê Vietnam
30 A2 Thaton Myanmar
30 A1 Thaungdut Myanmar
30 A2 Thayetmyo Myanmar
30 A1 Thazi Myanmar
114 C2 The Bahamas country West Indies
66 B1 The Cheviot hill U.K.
102 B1 The Dalles U.S.A.
67 C2 The Fens reg. U.K.
82 A3 The Gambia country Africa
84 B2 The Great Oasis Egypt
47 C2 The Gulf Asia
68 B1 The Hague Neth.
97 E1 Thelon r. Can.
69 E2 Themar Ger.
64 A1 The Minch sea chan. U.K.
118 B2 Theodore Roosevelt r. Braz.
97 D2 The Pas Can.
79 B2 Thermaikos Kolpos g. Greece
104 B2 Thermopolis U.S.A.
21 C3 The Rock Austr.
98 B2 Thessalon Can.
79 B2 Thessaloniki Greece
67 D2 Thetford U.K.
99 C2 Thetford Mines Can.
30 A1 The Triangle mts Myanmar
99 D1 Thévenet, Lac l. Can.
67 D2 The Wash b. U.K.
107 D2 The Woodlands U.S.A.
110 B3 Thibodaux U.S.A.
97 E2 Thicket Portage Can.

105 D1 **Thief River Falls** U.S.A.
73 C2 **Thiers** France
87 D3 **Thika** Kenya
41 B4 **Thiladhunmathee Atoll** Maldives
43 C2 **Thimphu** Bhutan
73 D2 **Thionville** France
Thira i. Greece see Santorini
66 C1 **Thirsk** U.K.
Thiruvananthapuram India see Trivandrum
61 E4 **Thisted** Denmark
97 E1 **Thlewiaza** r. Can.
30 A2 **Thoen** Thai.
91 D1 **Thohoyandou** S. Africa
69 E1 **Thomasburg** Ger.
65 C2 **Thomastown** Rep. of Ireland
111 D2 **Thomasville** U.S.A.
68 C2 **Thommen** Belgium
97 E2 **Thompson** Can.
96 E3 **Thompson** r. U.S.A.
102 C1 **Thompson Falls** U.S.A.
96 B2 **Thompson Sound** Can.
64 C3 **Thornhill** U.K.
23 C2 **Thorshavnheiane** reg. Antarctica
72 B2 **Thouars** France
96 C2 **Three Hills** Can.
31 A2 **Three Pagodas Pass** Myanmar/Thai.
82 B4 **Three Points, Cape** Ghana
31 B2 **Thu Dau Mot** Vietnam
68 B2 **Thuin** Belgium
89 B3 **Thuli** Zimbabwe
98 B2 **Thunder Bay** Can.
31 A3 **Thung Song** Thai.
69 E2 **Thüringer Becken** reg. Ger.
69 E2 **Thüringer Wald** mts Ger.
65 C2 **Thurles** Rep. of Ireland
64 C1 **Thurso** U.K.
64 C1 **Thurso** r. U.K.
119 D2 **Tianguá** Brazil
38 B2 **Tianjin** China
38 B2 **Tianjin** mun. China
39 A3 **Tianlin** China
38 B2 **Tianmen** China
38 A2 **Tianshui** China
122 B2 **Tibagi** r. Brazil
86 B2 **Tibati** Cameroon
Tiberias, Lake l. Israel see Galilee, Sea of
83 D2 **Tibesti** mts Chad
Tibet aut. reg. China see Xizang Zizhiqu
Tibet, Plateau of China see Qing Zang Gaoyuan
20 B1 **Tibooburra** Austr.
112 A2 **Tiburón, Isla** i. Mex.
82 B3 **Tichît** Maur.
82 A2 **Tichla** Western Sahara
113 D2 **Ticul** Mex.
82 A3 **Tidjikja** Maur.
68 B2 **Tiel** Neth.
33 A1 **Tieling** China
68 A2 **Tielt** Belgium
68 B2 **Tienen** Belgium
36 B2 **Tien Shan** mts China/Kyrg.
Tientsin China see Tianjin
61 G3 **Tierp** Sweden
113 C3 **Tierra Blanca** Mex.
113 C3 **Tierra Colorada** Mex.
121 B6 **Tierra del Fuego, Isla Grande de** i. Arg./Chile
122 C2 **Tietê** Brazil
Tiflis Georgia see T'bilisi
111 D2 **Tifton** U.S.A.
58 B2 **Tighina** Moldova
99 D2 **Tignish** Can.
118 A2 **Tigre** r. Ecuador/Peru
49 C2 **Tigris** r. Asia

113 C2 **Tihuatlán** Mex.
112 A1 **Tijuana** Mex.
59 E2 **Tikhoretsk** Rus. Fed.
57 D2 **Tikhvin** Rus. Fed.
57 D2 **Tikhvinskaya Gryada** ridge Rus. Fed.
22 C1 **Tikokino** N.Z.
49 C2 **Tikrit** Iraq
51 J2 **Tiksi** Rus. Fed.
68 B2 **Tilburg** Neth.
120 B3 **Tilcara** Arg.
20 B1 **Tilcha** Austr.
82 C3 **Tillabéri** Niger
102 B1 **Tillamook** U.S.A.
31 A3 **Tillanchong Island** India
79 C3 **Tilos** i. Greece
20 B2 **Tilpa** Austr.
54 F2 **Til'tim** Rus. Fed.
57 E3 **Tim** Rus. Fed.
54 D2 **Timanskiy Kryazh** ridge Rus. Fed.
22 B2 **Timaru** N.Z.
59 D2 **Timashevsk** Rus. Fed.
82 B3 **Timbedgha** Maur.
18 C1 **Timber Creek** Austr.
Timbuktu Mali see Tombouctou
82 C2 **Timimoun** Alg.
78 B1 **Timiş** r. Romania
78 B1 **Timişoara** Romania
98 B2 **Timmins** Can.
57 E2 **Timokhino** Rus. Fed.
119 D2 **Timon** Brazil
27 C3 **Timor** i. Indon.
26 C3 **Timor Sea** Austr./Indon.
61 G3 **Timrå** Sweden
82 B2 **Tindouf** Alg.
43 C2 **Tingri** China
61 F4 **Tingsryd** Sweden
27 D2 **Tinian** i. N. Mariana Is
120 B3 **Tinogasta** Arg.
79 C3 **Tinos** Greece
79 C3 **Tinos** i. Greece
83 C2 **Tinrhert, Plateau du** Alg.
30 A1 **Tinsukia** India
76 B1 **Tipasa** Alg.
65 B2 **Tipperary** Rep. of Ireland
77 C2 **Tirana** Albania
Tiranë Albania see Tirana
76 B1 **Tirano** Italy
58 B2 **Tiraspol** Moldova
79 C3 **Tire** Turkey
64 A2 **Tiree** i. U.K.
42 B1 **Tirich Mir** mt. Pak.
41 B3 **Tiruchchirāppalli** India
41 D4 **Tirunelveli** India
41 B3 **Tirupati** India
41 B3 **Tiruppattur** India
77 D1 **Tisa** r. Europe
97 D2 **Tisdale** Can.
75 D2 **Tissemsilt** Alg.
120 B2 **Titicaca, Lago** l. Bol./Peru
43 C2 **Titlagarh** India
78 C2 **Titu** Romania
111 D3 **Titusville** U.S.A.
67 B3 **Tiverton** U.K.
76 B2 **Tivoli** Italy
47 C2 **Tīwī** Oman
113 C3 **Tizimín** Mex.
75 D2 **Tizi Ouzou** Alg.
113 C3 **Tiznit** Morocco
113 C3 **Tlacotalpán** Mex.
113 C3 **Tlahualilo** Mex.
113 C3 **Tlapa** Mex.
113 C3 **Tlaxcala** Mex.
113 C3 **Tlaxiaco** Mex.
82 B1 **Tlemcen** Alg.
91 C1 **Tlokweng** Botswana
96 B2 **Toad River** Can.

89 □D2 **Toamasina** Madag.
28 A1 **Toba, Danau** l. Indon.
42 A1 **Toba and Kakar Ranges** mts Pak.
115 D3 **Tobago** i. Trin. and Tob.
27 C2 **Tobelo** Indon.
98 B2 **Tobermory** Can.
64 A2 **Tobermory** U.K.
97 D2 **Tobin Lake** l. Can.
28 B2 **Toboali** Indon.
44 C1 **Tobol** r. Kazakh./Rus. Fed.
54 F3 **Tobol'sk** Rus. Fed.
119 D2 **Tocantinópolis** Brazil
119 D2 **Tocantins** r. Brazil
111 D2 **Toccoa** U.S.A.
76 A1 **Toce** r. Italy
120 A3 **Tocopilla** Chile
21 C3 **Tocumwal** Austr.
112 A2 **Todos Santos** Mex.
96 B3 **Tofino** Can.
64 □ **Toft** U.K.
27 C3 **Togian, Kepulauan** is Indon.
82 C4 **Togo** country Africa
42 B2 **Tohana** India
94 B2 **Tok** U.S.A.
84 B3 **Tokar** Sudan
37 E3 **Tokara-rettō** is Japan
59 E1 **Tokarevka** Rus. Fed.
17 G3 **Tokelau** terr. S. Pacific Ocean
45 D2 **Tokmak** Kyrg.
59 D2 **Tokmak** Ukr.
22 C1 **Tokoroa** N.Z.
36 B2 **Toksun** China
35 B4 **Tokushima** Japan
35 C3 **Tōkyō** Japan
89 □D3 **Tôlañaro** Madag.
122 B2 **Toledo** Brazil
74 C2 **Toledo** Spain
108 C2 **Toledo** U.S.A.
74 C2 **Toledo, Montes de** mts Spain
110 B2 **Toledo Bend Reservoir** U.S.A.
89 □D3 **Toliara** Madag.
26 C2 **Tolitoli** Indon.
76 B1 **Tolmezzo** Italy
72 B3 **Tolosa** Spain
113 C3 **Toluca** Mex.
55 D3 **Tol'yatti** Rus. Fed.
108 A2 **Tomah** U.S.A.
34 D2 **Tomakomai** Japan
74 B2 **Tomar** Port.
71 E1 **Tomaszów Lubelski** Pol.
71 E1 **Tomaszów Mazowiecki** Pol.
112 B3 **Tomatlán** Mex.
110 C2 **Tombigbee** r. U.S.A.
123 D2 **Tombos** Brazil
82 B3 **Tombouctou** Mali
88 A2 **Tombua** Angola
91 C1 **Tom Burke** S. Africa
21 C2 **Tomingley** Austr.
26 C3 **Tomini, Teluk** g. Indon.
77 C2 **Tomislavgrad** Bos.-Herz.
18 A2 **Tom Price** Austr.
50 C3 **Tomsk** Rus. Fed.
61 F4 **Tomtabacken** hill Sweden
113 C3 **Tonalá** Mex.
118 B2 **Tonantins** Brazil
27 C2 **Tondano** Indon.
17 G4 **Tonga** country S. Pacific Ocean
39 B3 **Tongcheng** China
38 A2 **Tongchuan** China
39 A3 **Tongdao** China
33 B2 **Tongduch'ŏn** S. Korea
68 B2 **Tongeren** Belgium
33 B2 **Tonghae** S. Korea
30 B1 **Tonghai** China
33 B1 **Tonghua** China
33 B2 **Tongjosŏn-man** b. N. Korea

30 B1 **Tongking, Gulf of** China/Vietnam
37 E2 **Tongliao** China
38 B2 **Tongling** China
20 B2 **Tongo** Austr.
39 A3 **Tongren** China
Tongshan China see **Xuzhou**
37 E2 **Tongshi** China
Tongtian He r. China see **Yangtze**
64 B1 **Tongue** U.K.
33 B3 **T'ongyŏng** S. Korea
37 E2 **Tongyu** China
33 A1 **Tongyuanpu** China
42 B2 **Tonk** India
31 B2 **Tônlé Sab** l. Cambodia
103 C3 **Tonopah** U.S.A.
61 F4 **Tønsberg** Norway
103 D2 **Tooele** U.S.A.
20 B2 **Tooleybuc** Austr.
21 D1 **Toowoomba** Austr.
105 D3 **Topeka** U.S.A.
112 B2 **Topia** Mex.
112 B2 **Topolobampo** Mex.
54 C2 **Topozero, Ozero** l. Rus. Fed.
102 B1 **Toppenish** U.S.A.
79 C3 **Torbalı** Turkey
44 B3 **Torbat-e Heydarīyeh** Iran
44 C3 **Torbat-e Jām** Iran
74 C1 **Tordesillas** Spain
75 D1 **Tordesilos** Spain
69 F2 **Torgau** Ger.
68 A2 **Torhout** Belgium
Torino Italy see **Turin**
122 B1 **Torixoreu** Brazil
74 B1 **Tormes** r. Spain
60 H2 **Torneälven** r. Sweden
95 G3 **Torngat Mountains** Can.
60 H2 **Tornio** Fin.
74 B1 **Toro** Spain
98 C2 **Toronto** Can.
87 D2 **Tororo** Uganda
48 B2 **Toros Dağları** mts Turkey
67 B3 **Torquay** U.K.
74 B2 **Torrão** Port.
74 B1 **Torre** mt. Port.
75 D1 **Torreblanca** Spain
74 B1 **Torre de Moncorvo** Port.
74 C1 **Torrelavega** Spain
74 C2 **Torremolinos** Spain
20 A2 **Torrens, Lake** salt flat Austr.
75 C2 **Torrent** Spain
112 B2 **Torreón** Mex.
74 B2 **Torres Novas** Port.
74 B2 **Torres Vedras** Port.
75 C2 **Torrevieja** Spain
64 B2 **Torridon** U.K.
74 C2 **Torrijos** Spain
109 E2 **Torrington** CT U.S.A.
104 C2 **Torrington** WY U.S.A.
75 D1 **Torroella de Montgri** Spain
62 B1 **Tórshavn** Faroe Is
76 A3 **Tortolì** Sardinia Italy
75 D1 **Tortosa** Spain
71 D1 **Toruń** Pol.
65 B1 **Tory Island** Rep. of Ireland
57 D2 **Torzhok** Rus. Fed.
90 B2 **Tosca** S. Africa
57 D2 **Tosno** Rus. Fed.
120 B3 **Tostado** Arg.
69 D1 **Tostedt** Ger.
48 B1 **Tosya** Turkey
54 D3 **Tot'ma** Rus. Fed.
35 B3 **Tottori** Japan
82 B4 **Touba** Côte d'Ivoire
88 B1 **Toubkal, Jbel** mt. Morocco
82 B3 **Tougan** Burkina
83 C1 **Touggourt** Alg.
73 D2 **Toul** France

39 C3 **Touliu** Taiwan
73 D3 **Toulon** France
72 C3 **Toulouse** France
30 A2 **Toungoo** Myanmar
68 A2 **Tournai** Belgium
72 C2 **Tournus** France
119 E2 **Touros** Brazil
72 C2 **Tours** France
83 D2 **Tousside, Pic** mt. Chad
90 B3 **Touwsrivier** S. Africa
34 D2 **Towada** Japan
102 D1 **Townsend** U.S.A.
19 D1 **Townsville** Austr.
45 E2 **Toxkan He** r. China
34 D2 **Tōya-ko** l. Japan
35 C3 **Toyama** Japan
35 C3 **Toyota** Japan
83 C1 **Tozeur** Tunisia
49 C1 **Tqvarch'eli** Georgia
48 B2 **Trâblous** Lebanon
48 B1 **Trabzon** Turkey
74 B2 **Trafalgar, Cabo** c. Spain
96 C3 **Trail** Can.
56 B3 **Trakai** Lith.
65 B2 **Tralee** Rep. of Ireland
65 C2 **Tramore** Rep. of Ireland
31 A3 **Trang** Thai.
23 I2 **Transantarctic Mountains** Antarctica
Transylvanian Alps mts Romania see **Carpaţii Meridionali**
76 B3 **Trapani** Sicily Italy
21 C3 **Traralgon** Austr.
31 B2 **Trat** Thai.
70 C2 **Traunstein** Ger.
108 B2 **Traverse City** U.S.A.
71 D2 **Třebíč** Czech Rep.
77 C2 **Trebinje** Bos.-Herz.
71 E2 **Trebišov** Slovakia
77 C1 **Trebnje** Slovenia
121 C4 **Treinta-y-Tres** Uru.
121 B5 **Trelew** Arg.
61 F4 **Trelleborg** Sweden
98 C2 **Tremblant, Mont** hill Can.
77 C2 **Tremiti, Isole** is Italy
102 D2 **Tremonton** U.S.A.
75 D1 **Tremp** Spain
71 D2 **Trenčín** Slovakia
121 B4 **Trenque Lauquén** Arg.
66 C2 **Trent** r. U.K.
76 B1 **Trento** Italy
109 D2 **Trenton** Can.
108 B2 **Trenton** MO U.S.A.
109 E2 **Trenton** NJ U.S.A.
99 E2 **Trepassey** Can.
121 B4 **Tres Arroyos** Arg.
123 C2 **Três Corações** Brazil
122 B2 **Três Lagoas** Brazil
121 A5 **Tres Lagos** Arg.
123 C1 **Três Marias, Represa** resr Brazil
123 C2 **Três Pontas** Brazil
121 B5 **Tres Puntas, Cabo** c. Arg.
123 D2 **Três Rios** Brazil
69 F1 **Treuenbrietzen** Ger.
76 A1 **Treviglio** Italy
76 B1 **Treviso** Italy
67 A3 **Trevose Head** hd U.K.
77 C3 **Tricase** Italy
41 B3 **Trichur** India
21 C3 **Trida** Austr.
68 C3 **Trier** Ger.
76 B1 **Trieste** Italy
77 C1 **Triglav** mt. Slovenia
27 D3 **Trikora, Puncak** mt. Indon.
65 C2 **Trim** Rep. of Ireland
41 C4 **Trincomalee** Sri Lanka
122 C1 **Trindade** Brazil

120 B2 **Trinidad** Bol.
115 D3 **Trinidad** i. Trin. and Tob.
104 C3 **Trinidad** U.S.A.
115 D3 **Trinidad and Tobago** country West Indies
99 E2 **Trinity Bay** Can.
79 B3 **Tripoli** Greece
Tripoli Lebanon see **Trâblous**
83 D1 **Tripoli** Libya
117 G5 **Tristan da Cunha** i. S. Atlantic Ocean
41 B4 **Trivandrum** India
76 B2 **Trivento** Italy
71 D2 **Trnava** Slovakia
77 C2 **Trogir** Croatia
77 C2 **Troia** Italy
68 C2 **Troisdorf** Ger.
99 C2 **Trois-Rivières** Can.
54 E2 **Troitsko-Pechorsk** Rus. Fed.
119 C2 **Trombetas** r. Brazil
91 C3 **Trompsburg** S. Africa
60 G2 **Tromsø** Norway
60 F3 **Trondheim** Norway
96 C2 **Trout Lake** Can.
96 B1 **Trout Lake** l. N.W.T. Can.
98 A1 **Trout Lake** l. Ont. Can.
67 B3 **Trowbridge** U.K.
110 C2 **Troy** AL U.S.A.
109 E2 **Troy** NY U.S.A.
73 C2 **Troyes** France
77 D2 **Trstenik** Yugo.
57 D3 **Trubchevsk** Rus. Fed.
74 B1 **Truchas** Spain
47 C2 **Trucial Coast** U.A.E.
114 B3 **Trujillo** Hond.
118 A2 **Trujillo** Peru
74 B2 **Trujillo** Spain
115 C4 **Trujillo** Venez.
110 B1 **Trumann** U.S.A.
99 D2 **Truro** Can.
67 A3 **Truro** U.K.
106 B2 **Truth or Consequences** U.S.A.
71 D1 **Trutnov** Czech Rep.
61 F3 **Trysil** Norway
71 D1 **Trzebiatów** Pol.
36 B1 **Tsagaannuur** Mongolia
89 □D2 **Tsaratanana, Massif du** mts Madag.
78 C2 **Tsarevo** Bulg.
90 A2 **Tses** Namibia
90 B1 **Tsetseng** Botswana
36 C1 **Tsetserleg** Mongolia
90 B2 **Tshabong** Botswana
90 B1 **Tshane** Botswana
59 D2 **Tshchikskoye Vodokhranilishche** resr Rus. Fed.
86 B3 **Tshela** Dem. Rep. Congo
86 C3 **Tshikapa** Dem. Rep. Congo
86 C3 **Tshikapa** r. Dem. Rep. Congo
91 D1 **Tshipise** S. Africa
86 C3 **Tshitanzu** Dem. Rep. Congo
86 C3 **Tshuapa** r. Dem. Rep. Congo
55 D4 **Tsimlyanskoye Vodokhranilishche** resr Rus. Fed.
Tsingtao China see **Qingdao**
Tsining China see **Jining**
89 □D2 **Tsiroanomandidy** Madag.
91 C3 **Tsomo** S. Africa
35 C4 **Tsu** Japan
35 D3 **Tsuchiura** Japan
34 D2 **Tsugarū-kaikyō** str. Japan
88 A2 **Tsumeb** Namibia
90 A1 **Tsumis Park** Namibia
88 B2 **Tsumkwe** Namibia
35 C3 **Tsuruga** Japan
34 C3 **Tsuruoka** Japan

35 A4 **Tsushima** *is* Japan
Tsushima-kaikyō *str.* Japan/S. Korea *see* Korea Strait
35 B3 **Tsuyama** Japan
91 C2 **Tswelelang** S. Africa
59 C2 **Tsyurupyns'k** Ukr.
Tthenaagoo Can. *see* Nahanni Butte
27 C3 **Tual** Indon.
65 B2 **Tuam** Rep. of Ireland
59 D3 **Tuapse** Rus. Fed.
22 A3 **Tuatapere** N.Z.
106 A1 **Tuba City** U.S.A.
29 C2 **Tuban** Indon.
120 D3 **Tubarão** Brazil
70 B2 **Tübingen** Ger.
83 E1 **Tubruq** Libya
120 C2 **Tucavaca** Bol.
96 B1 **Tuchitua** Can.
106 A2 **Tucson** U.S.A.
107 C1 **Tucumcari** U.S.A.
118 B1 **Tucupita** Venez.
119 D2 **Tucuruí** Brazil
119 D2 **Tucuruí, Represa** *resr* Brazil
75 C1 **Tudela** Spain
74 B1 **Tuela** *r.* Port.
30 A1 **Tuensang** India
91 D2 **Tugela** *r.* S. Africa
32 B1 **Tuguegarao** Phil.
27 C3 **Tukangbesi, Kepulauan** *is* Indon.
94 C2 **Tuktoyaktuk** Can.
56 B2 **Tukums** Latvia
57 E3 **Tula** Rus. Fed.
113 C2 **Tulancingo** Mex.
103 C3 **Tulare** U.S.A.
106 B2 **Tularosa** U.S.A.
78 C1 **Tulcea** Romania
58 B2 **Tul'chyn** Ukr.
97 E1 **Tulemalu Lake** Can.
107 C2 **Tulia** U.S.A.
110 C1 **Tullahoma** U.S.A.
65 C2 **Tullamore** Rep. of Ireland
72 C2 **Tulle** France
19 D1 **Tully** Austr.
107 E1 **Tuloa** U.S.A.
118 A1 **Tumaco** Col.
61 G4 **Tumahole** S. Africa
61 G4 **Tumba** Sweden
86 B3 **Tumba, Lac** *l.* Dem. Rep. Congo
21 C3 **Tumbarumba** Austr.
118 A2 **Tumbes** Peru
96 B2 **Tumbler Ridge** Can.
20 A2 **Tumby Bay** Austr.
33 B1 **Tumen** China
119 G2 **Tumereng** Guyana
32 A2 **Tumindao** *i.* Phil.
42 A2 **Tump** Pak.
119 C1 **Tumucumaque, Serra** *hills* Brazil
21 C3 **Tumut** Austr.
17 D3 **Tunbridge Wells, Royal** U.K.
48 B2 **Tunceli** Turkey
21 D2 **Tuncurry** Austr.
87 D4 **Tunduru** Tanz.
78 C2 **Tundzha** *r.* Bulg.
96 B1 **Tungsten** Can.
83 D1 **Tunis** Tunisia
83 C1 **Tunisia** *country* Africa
118 A1 **Tunja** Col.
60 F3 **Tunnsjøen** *l.* Norway
Tunxi China *see* Huangshan
122 B2 **Tupã** Brazil
122 C1 **Tupaciguara** Brazil

110 C2 **Tupelo** U.S.A.
120 B3 **Tupiza** Bol.
51 H2 **Tura** Rus. Fed.
54 F3 **Tura** *r.* Rus. Fed.
46 B2 **Turabah** Saudi Arabia
51 J3 **Turana, Khrebet** *mts* Rus. Fed.
22 C1 **Turangi** N.Z.
44 B2 **Turan Lowland** Asia
46 A1 **Turayf** Saudi Arabia
56 B2 **Turba** Estonia
42 A2 **Turbat** Pak.
118 A1 **Turbo** Col.
78 B1 **Turda** Romania
Turfan China *see* Turpan
44 C2 **Turgay** Kazakh.
79 C3 **Turgutlu** Turkey
48 B1 **Turhal** Turkey
75 C2 **Turia** *r.* Spain
76 A1 **Turin** Italy
54 F3 **Turinsk** Rus. Fed.
58 A1 **Turiys'k** Ukr.
87 D2 **Turkana, Lake** *salt l.* Eth./Kenya
45 C2 **Turkestan** Kazakh.
48 B2 **Turkey** *country* Asia
44 B2 **Turkmenbashi** Turkm.
44 B2 **Turkmenistan** *country* Asia
115 C2 **Turks and Caicos Islands** *terr.* West Indies
61 H3 **Turku** Fin.
103 B3 **Turlock** U.S.A.
22 C2 **Turnagain, Cape** N.Z.
68 B2 **Turnhout** Belgium
97 D2 **Turnor Lake** Can.
78 B2 **Turnu Măgurele** Romania
36 B2 **Turpan** China
45 D2 **Turugart Pass** China/Kyrg.
110 C2 **Tuscaloosa** U.S.A.
110 C2 **Tuskegee** U.S.A.
41 B4 **Tuticorin** India
88 B3 **Tutume** Botswana
17 F3 **Tuvalu** *country* S. Pacific Ocean
46 B2 **Tuwayq, Jabal** *hills* Saudi Arabia
46 B2 **Tuwayq, Jabal** *mts* Saudi Arabia
46 A2 **Tuwwal** Saudi Arabia
112 B2 **Tuxpan** *Nayarit* Mex.
113 C2 **Tuxpan** *Veracruz* Mex.
113 C3 **Tuxtla Gutiérrez** Mex.
30 B1 **Tuyên Quang** Vietnam
31 B2 **Tuy Hoa** Vietnam
48 B2 **Tuz Gölü** *salt l.* Turkey
49 C2 **Tuz Khurmātū** Iraq
77 C2 **Tuzla** Bos.-Herz.
59 E2 **Tuzlov** *r.* Rus. Fed.
57 E2 **Tver'** Rus. Fed.
66 B1 **Tweed** *r.* U.K.
90 A2 **Twee Rivier** Namibia
103 C4 **Twentynine Palms** U.S.A.
99 E2 **Twillingate** Can.
102 D2 **Twin Falls** U.S.A.
105 E1 **Two Harbors** U.S.A.
97 C2 **Two Hills** Can.
107 D2 **Tyler** U.S.A.
51 J3 **Tynda** Rus. Fed.
61 F3 **Tynset** Norway
79 B3 **Tyrnavos** Greece
20 B3 **Tyrrell, Lake** *dry lake* Austr.
76 B2 **Tyrrhenian Sea** France/Italy
44 B2 **Tyub-Karagan, Mys** *pt* Kazakh.
55 E3 **Tyul'gan** Rus. Fed.
54 F3 **Tyumen'** Rus. Fed.
51 J2 **Tyung** *r.* Rus. Fed.
67 A3 **Tywi** *r.* U.K.
91 D1 **Tzaneen** S. Africa

U

88 B2 **Uamanda** Angola
118 B2 **Uaupés** Brazil
123 D2 **Ubá** Brazil
123 D1 **Ubaí** Brazil
119 E3 **Ubaitaba** Brazil
86 B3 **Ubangi** *r.* C.A.R./Dem. Rep. Congo
35 B4 **Ube** Japan
74 C2 **Úbeda** Spain
122 C1 **Uberaba** Brazil
122 C1 **Uberlândia** Brazil
91 D2 **Ubombo** S. Africa
31 B2 **Ubon Ratchathani** Thai.
87 C3 **Ubundu** Dem. Rep. Congo
118 A2 **Ucayali** *r.* Peru
42 B2 **Uch** Pak.
45 E2 **Ucharal** Kazakh.
34 D2 **Uchiura-wan** *b.* Japan
51 J3 **Uchur** *r.* Rus. Fed.
96 B3 **Ucluelet** Can.
42 B2 **Udaipur** India
59 C1 **Uday** *r.* Ukr.
61 F4 **Uddevalla** Sweden
60 G2 **Uddjaure** *l.* Sweden
68 B2 **Uden** Neth.
42 B1 **Udhampur** Jammu and Kashmir
76 B1 **Udine** Italy
57 E2 **Udomlya** Rus. Fed.
30 D2 **Udon Thani** Thai.
41 B3 **Udupi** India
51 K3 **Udyl', Ozero** *l.* Rus. Fed.
35 C3 **Ueda** Japan
26 C3 **Uekuli** Indon.
86 C2 **Uele** *r.* Dem. Rep. Congo
69 E1 **Uelzen** Ger.
87 C2 **Uere** *r.* Dem. Rep. Congo
55 E3 **Ufa** Rus. Fed.
87 D3 **Ugalla** *r.* Tanz.
87 D2 **Uganda** *country* Africa
57 F2 **Uglich** Rus. Fed.
57 D2 **Uglovka** Rus. Fed.
57 D3 **Ugra** Rus. Fed.
71 D2 **Uherské Hradiště** Czech Rep.
69 E2 **Uichteritz** Ger.
64 A2 **Uig** U.K.
88 A1 **Uíge** Angola
33 B2 **Uijŏngbu** S. Korea
103 D2 **Uinta Mountains** U.S.A.
88 A3 **Uis Mine** Namibia
33 B2 **Úisŏng** S. Korea
91 C3 **Uitenhage** S. Africa
68 C1 **Uithuizen** Neth.
42 B2 **Ujjain** India
26 B3 **Ujung Pandang** Indon.
57 F3 **Ukholovo** Rus. Fed.
30 A1 **Ukhrul** India
54 E2 **Ukhta** Rus. Fed.
103 B3 **Ukiah** U.S.A.
95 H2 **Ukkusissat** Greenland
56 B2 **Ukmergė** Lith.
58 C2 **Ukraine** *country* Europe
37 D1 **Ulaanbaatar** Mongolia
36 C1 **Ulaangom** Mongolia
Ulan Bator Mongolia *see* Ulaanbaatar
Ulanhad China *see* Chifeng
37 E1 **Ulanhot** China
55 D4 **Ulan-Khol** Rus. Fed.
37 D1 **Ulan-Ude** Rus. Fed.
43 D1 **Ulan Ul Hu** *l.* China
33 B2 **Ulchin** S. Korea
Uleåborg Fin. *see* Oulu
56 C2 **Ülenurme** Estonia
41 B3 **Ulhasnagar** India

37 D1 **Uliastai** China
36 C1 **Uliastay** Mongolia
27 D2 **Ulithi** *atoll* Micronesia
21 D3 **Ulladulla** Austr.
64 B2 **Ullapool** U.K.
66 B1 **Ullswater** *l.* U.K.
33 C2 **Ullŭng-do** *i.* S. Korea
70 B2 **Ulm** Ger.
33 B2 **Ulsan** S. Korea
64 □ **Ulsta** U.K.
65 C1 **Ulster** *reg.*
        Rep. of Ireland/U.K.
20 B3 **Ultima** Austr.
79 C3 **Ulubey** Turkey
79 C2 **Uludağ** *mt.* Turkey
91 D2 **Ulundi** S. Africa
45 E2 **Ulungur Hu** *l.* China
        Uluru *hill* Austr. *see*
        Ayers Rock
66 B1 **Ulverston** U.K.
55 D3 **Ul'yanovsk** Rus. Fed.
104 C3 **Ulysses** U.S.A.
58 C2 **Uman'** Ukr.
54 C2 **Umba** Rus. Fed.
27 D3 **Umboi** *i.* P.N.G.
60 H3 **Umeå** Sweden
60 H3 **Umeälven** *r.* Sweden
95 I2 **Umiivip Kangertiva** *inlet*
        Greenland
94 D2 **Umingmaktok** Can.
91 D2 **Umlazi** S. Africa
85 A3 **Umm Keddada** Sudan
46 A2 **Umm Lajj** Saudi Arabia
85 B3 **Umm Ruwaba** Sudan
83 E1 **Umm Sa'ad** Libya
102 B2 **Umpqua** *r.* U.S.A.
88 A2 **Umpulo** Angola
91 C3 **Umtata** S. Africa
122 B2 **Umuarama** Brazil
77 C1 **Una** *r.* Bos.-Herz./Croatia
123 E1 **Una** Brazil
122 C1 **Unaí** Brazil
46 B2 **'Unayzah** Saudi Arabia
104 C1 **Underwood** U.S.A.
57 D3 **Unecha** Rus. Fed.
21 C2 **Ungarie** Austr.
20 A2 **Ungarra** Austr.
95 G2 **Ungava, Péninsule d'**
        pen. Can.
95 G3 **Ungava Bay** Can.
33 C1 **Unggi** N. Korea
58 B2 **Ungheni** Moldova
        Unguja *i.* Tanz. *see*
        Zanzibar Island
122 B3 **União da Vitória** Brazil
118 B2 **Unini** *r.* Brazil
110 C1 **Union City** U.S.A.
90 B3 **Uniondale** S. Africa
109 D3 **Uniontown** U.S.A.
47 C2 **United Arab Emirates**
        country Asia
63 C3 **United Kingdom** *country*
        Europe
100 D3 **United States of America**
        country N. America
97 D2 **Unity** Can.
64 □ **Unst** *i.* U.K.
69 E2 **Unstrut** *r.* Ger.
57 E3 **Upa** *r.* Rus. Fed.
87 C3 **Upemba, Lac** *l.*
        Dem. Rep. Congo
90 B2 **Upington** S. Africa
102 B2 **Upper Alkali Lake** U.S.A.
96 C2 **Upper Arrow Lake** Can.
102 B2 **Upper Klamath Lake** U.S.A.
96 B1 **Upper Liard** Can.
65 C1 **Upper Lough Erne** *l.* U.K.
61 G4 **Uppsala** Sweden
46 B2 **'Uqlat aş Şuqūr**
        Saudi Arabia

        Urad Qianqi China *see*
        Xishanzui
44 B2 **Ural** *r.* Kazakh./Rus. Fed.
21 D2 **Uralla** Austr.
        Ural Mountains Rus. Fed.
        see Ural'skiy Khrebet
44 B1 **Ural'sk** Kazakh.
55 E3 **Ural'skiy Khrebet** *mts*
        Rus. Fed.
87 D3 **Urambo** Tanz.
21 C3 **Urana** Austr.
97 C2 **Uranium City** Can.
54 F2 **Uray** Rus. Fed.
66 C1 **Ure** *r.* U.K.
54 D3 **Uren'** Rus. Fed.
112 A2 **Ures** Mex.
44 C2 **Urgench** Uzbek.
68 B1 **Urk** Neth.
79 C3 **Urla** Turkey
77 D2 **Uroševac** Yugo.
112 B2 **Uruáchic** Mex.
119 D3 **Uruaçu** Brazil
112 B3 **Uruapan** Mex.
118 A3 **Urubamba** *r.* Peru
119 C2 **Urucara** Brazil
119 D2 **Uruçuí** Brazil
119 C2 **Urucurituba** Brazil
120 C3 **Uruguaiana** Brazil
121 C4 **Uruguay** *country* S. America
        Urumchi China *see* Ürümqi
36 B2 **Ürümqi** China
21 D2 **Urunga** Austr.
78 C2 **Urziceni** Romania
35 B4 **Usa** Japan
50 E2 **Usa** *r.* Rus. Fed.
79 C3 **Uşak** Turkey
50 G1 **Ushakova, Ostrov** *i.*
        Rus. Fed.
45 D2 **Ushtobe** Kazakh.
121 B6 **Ushuaia** Arg.
54 E2 **Usinsk** Rus. Fed.
56 C3 **Ushodni** Belarus
57 E3 **Usman'** Rus. Fed.
54 D2 **Usogorsk** Rus. Fed.
72 C2 **Ussel** France
34 B2 **Ussuriysk** Rus. Fed.
76 B3 **Ustica, Isola di** *i.* Sicily Italy
51 I3 **Ust'-Ilimsk** Rus. Fed.
54 E2 **Ust'-Ilych** Rus. Fed.
71 D1 **Ustka** Pol.
51 L3 **Ust'-Kamchatsk** Rus. Fed.
45 E2 **Ust'-Kamenogorsk** Kazakh.
54 F2 **Ust'-Kara** Rus. Fed.
54 E2 **Ust'-Kulom** Rus. Fed.
51 I3 **Ust'-Kut** Rus. Fed.
59 D2 **Ust'-Labinsk** Rus. Fed.
56 C2 **Ust'-Luga** Rus. Fed.
54 E2 **Ust'-Nem** Rus. Fed.
51 K2 **Ust'-Nera** Rus. Fed.
51 K2 **Ust'-Omchug** Rus. Fed.
51 H3 **Ust'-Ordynskiy** Rus. Fed.
54 E2 **Ust'-Tsil'ma** Rus. Fed.
54 D2 **Ust'-Ura** Rus. Fed.
44 B2 **Ustyurt Plateau**
        Kazakh./Uzbek.
57 E2 **Ustyuzhna** Rus. Fed.
57 D2 **Usvyaty** Rus. Fed.
103 D3 **Utah** *state* U.S.A.
103 D3 **Utah Lake** U.S.A.
61 I4 **Utena** Lith.
109 D2 **Utica** U.S.A.
75 C2 **Utiel** Spain
96 C2 **Utikuma Lake** Can.
68 B1 **Utrecht** Neth.
74 B2 **Utrera** Spain
60 I2 **Utsjoki** Fin.
35 C3 **Utsunomiya** Japan
55 D4 **Utta** Rus. Fed.
30 B2 **Uttaradit** Thai.
95 G1 **Uummannaq** Greenland

95 H2 **Uummannaq Fjord** *inlet*
        Greenland
61 H3 **Uusikaupunki** Fin.
107 D3 **Uvalde** U.S.A.
87 D3 **Uvinza** Tanz.
36 C1 **Uvs Nuur** *salt l.* Mongolia
35 B4 **Uwajima** Japan
46 A2 **'Uwayrid, Ḩarrat al** *lava field*
        Saudi Arabia
84 A2 **Uweinat, Jebel** *mt.* Sudan
51 H3 **Uyar** Rus. Fed.
83 C4 **Uyo** Nigeria
120 B3 **Uyuni, Salar de** *salt flat* Bol.
44 C2 **Uzbekistan** *country* Asia
72 C2 **Uzerche** France
73 C3 **Uzès** France
58 C1 **Uzh** *r.* Ukr.
58 A2 **Uzhhorod** Ukr.
77 C2 **Užice** Yugo.
57 E3 **Uzlovaya** Rus. Fed.
79 C3 **Üzümlü** Turkey
79 C2 **Uzunköprü** Turkey

V

91 B2 **Vaal** *r.* S. Africa
91 C2 **Vaal Dam** S. Africa
91 C1 **Vaalwater** S. Africa
60 H3 **Vaasa** Fin.
71 D2 **Vác** Hungary
120 C3 **Vacaria** Brazil
122 B2 **Vacaria, Serra** *hills* Brazil
103 B3 **Vacaville** U.S.A.
42 B2 **Vadodara** India
60 I1 **Vadsø** Norway
73 D2 **Vaduz** Liechtenstein
62 B1 **Vágar** *i.* Faroe Is
62 B1 **Vágur** Faroe Is
71 D2 **Váh** *r.* Slovakia
56 B2 **Vaida** Estonia
104 B3 **Vail** U.S.A.
47 C2 **Vakīlābād** Iran
76 B1 **Valdagno** Italy
57 D2 **Valday** Rus. Fed.
57 D2 **Valdayskaya**
        Vozvyshennost' *hills*
        Rus. Fed.
74 B2 **Valdecañas, Embalse de**
        resr Spain
61 G4 **Valdemarsvik** Sweden
73 D2 **Val-de-Meuse** France
74 C2 **Valdepeñas** Spain
121 B5 **Valdés, Península** *pen.* Arg.
121 A4 **Valdivia** Chile
98 C2 **Val-d'Or** Can.
111 D2 **Valdosta** U.S.A.
96 C2 **Valemount** Can.
73 C3 **Valence** France
75 C2 **Valencia** Spain
118 B1 **Valencia** Venez.
75 D2 **Valencia, Golfo de** *g.* Spain
68 A2 **Valenciennes** France
104 C2 **Valentine** U.S.A.
32 B1 **Valenzuela** Phil.
118 A1 **Valera** Venez.
77 C2 **Valjevo** Yugo.
56 C2 **Valka** Latvia
61 H3 **Valkeakoski** Fin.
68 B2 **Valkenswaard** Neth.
59 D2 **Valky** Ukr.
23 D2 **Valkyrie Dome** *ice feature*
        Antarctica
113 D2 **Valladolid** Mex.
74 C1 **Valladolid** Spain
75 C2 **Vall de Uxó** Spain
61 E4 **Valle** Norway
113 C2 **Vallecillos** Mex.

118 B1 **Valle de la Pascua** Venez.
118 A1 **Valledupar** Col.
113 C2 **Valle Hermoso** Mex.
103 B3 **Vallejo** U.S.A.
120 A3 **Vallenar** Chile
105 D1 **Valley City** U.S.A.
102 B2 **Valley Falls** U.S.A.
96 C2 **Valleyview** Can.
75 D1 **Valls** Spain
97 D3 **Val Marie** Can.
56 C2 **Valmiera** Latvia
56 C3 **Valozhyn** Belarus
122 B2 **Valparaíso** Brazil
121 A4 **Valparaíso** Chile
73 C3 **Valréas** France
27 D3 **Vals, Tanjung** c. Indon.
42 B2 **Valsåd** India
90 B2 **Valspan** S. Africa
59 D1 **Valuyki** Rus. Fed.
74 B2 **Valverde del Camino** Spain
49 C2 **Van** Turkey
109 F1 **Van Buren** U.S.A.
96 B3 **Vancouver** Can.
102 B1 **Vancouver** U.S.A.
96 B3 **Vancouver Island** Can.
108 B3 **Vandalia** U.S.A.
91 C2 **Vanderbijlpark** S. Africa
96 B2 **Vanderhoof** Can.
56 C2 **Vändra** Estonia
61 F4 **Vänern** l. Sweden
61 F4 **Vänersborg** Sweden
89 ☐D3 **Vangaindrano** Madag.
49 C2 **Van Gölü** salt l. Turkey
106 C2 **Van Horn** U.S.A.
27 D3 **Vanimo** P.N.G.
51 K3 **Vanino** Rus. Fed.
72 B2 **Vannes** France
27 D3 **Van Rees, Pegunungan** mts Indon.
90 A3 **Vanrhynsdorp** S. Africa
61 H3 **Vantaa** Fin.
17 E4 **Vanuatu** country S. Pacific Ocean
108 C2 **Van Wert** U.S.A.
90 B3 **Vanwyksvlei** S. Africa
90 B2 **Van Zylsrus** S. Africa
43 C2 **Varanasi** India
60 I1 **Varangerfjorden** sea chan. Norway
60 I1 **Varanger Halvøya** pen. Norway
77 C1 **Varaždin** Croatia
61 F4 **Varberg** Sweden
77 D2 **Vardar** r. Macedonia
61 E4 **Varde** Denmark
60 J1 **Varde** Norway
68 D1 **Varel** Ger.
56 B3 **Varèna** Lith.
76 A1 **Varese** Italy
123 C2 **Varginha** Brazil
61 I3 **Varkaus** Fin.
78 C2 **Varna** Bulg.
61 F4 **Värnamo** Sweden
123 D1 **Várzea da Palma** Brazil
54 C2 **Varzino** Rus. Fed.
    Vasa Fin. see **Vaasa**
56 C2 **Vasknarva** Estonia
78 C1 **Vaslui** Romania
61 G4 **Västerås** Sweden
61 G3 **Västerdalälven** r. Sweden
56 A2 **Västerhaninge** Sweden
61 G4 **Västervik** Sweden
76 B2 **Vasto** Italy
58 C1 **Vasyl'kiv** Ukr.
72 C2 **Vatan** France
76 B2 **Vatican City** Europe
60 ☐B3 **Vatnajökull** ice cap Iceland
78 C1 **Vatra Dornei** Romania
61 F4 **Vättern** l. Sweden
106 B2 **Vaughn** U.S.A.

73 C3 **Vauvert** France
56 B3 **Vawkavysk** Belarus
61 F4 **Växjö** Sweden
54 E1 **Vaygach, Ostrov** i. Rus. Fed.
69 D1 **Vechta** Ger.
78 C2 **Vedea** r. Romania
68 C1 **Veendam** Neth.
68 B1 **Veenendaal** Neth.
97 C2 **Vegreville** Can.
74 B2 **Vejer de la Frontera** Spain
61 E4 **Vejle** Denmark
77 D2 **Velbůzhdki Prokhod** pass Macedonia
68 B2 **Veldhoven** Neth.
77 B2 **Velebit** mts Croatia
68 C2 **Velen** Ger.
77 C1 **Velenje** Slovenia
77 D2 **Veles** Macedonia
74 C2 **Vélez-Málaga** Spain
123 D1 **Velhas** r. Brazil
77 D2 **Velika Plana** Yugo.
56 C2 **Velikaya** r. Rus. Fed.
57 D2 **Velikiye Luki** Rus. Fed.
57 D2 **Velikiy Novgorod** Rus. Fed.
54 D2 **Velikiy Ustyug** Rus. Fed.
78 C2 **Veliko Tŭrnovo** Bulg.
76 B2 **Veli Lošinj** Croatia
57 D2 **Velizh** Rus. Fed.
54 D2 **Vel'sk** Rus. Fed.
69 F1 **Velten** Ger.
59 D1 **Velykyy Burluk** Ukr.
76 B2 **Venafro** Italy
122 C2 **Venceslau Bráz** Brazil
72 C2 **Vendôme** France
57 E3 **Venev** Rus. Fed.
    Venezia Italy see **Venice**
118 B1 **Venezuela** country S. America
118 A1 **Venezuela, Golfo de** g. Venez.
76 B1 **Venice** Italy
111 D3 **Venice** U.S.A.
76 D1 **Venice, Gulf of** Europe
68 C2 **Venlo** Neth.
68 B2 **Venray** Neth.
56 B2 **Venta** r. Latvia/Lith.
56 B2 **Venta** Lith.
91 C3 **Venterstad** S. Africa
67 C3 **Ventnor** U.K.
56 B2 **Ventpils** Latvia
103 C4 **Ventura** U.S.A.
107 C3 **Venustiano Carranza, Presa** resr Mex.
75 C2 **Vera** Spain
113 C3 **Veracruz** Mex.
42 B2 **Veraval** India
76 A1 **Verbania** Italy
76 A1 **Vercelli** Italy
73 D3 **Vercors** reg. France
60 F3 **Verdalsøra** Norway
122 B1 **Verde** r. Goiás Brazil
122 B2 **Verde** r. Mato Grosso do Sul Brazil
112 B2 **Verde** r. Mex.
106 A2 **Verde** r. U.S.A.
123 D1 **Verde Grande** r. Brazil
69 D1 **Verden (Aller)** Ger.
122 B1 **Verdinho, Serra do** mts Brazil
76 A2 **Verdon** r. France
72 D2 **Verdun** France
91 C2 **Vereeniging** S. Africa
74 B1 **Verín** Spain
59 D3 **Verkhnebakanskiy** Rus. Fed.
60 J2 **Verkhnetulomskiy** Rus. Fed.
59 E1 **Verkhniy Mamon** Rus. Fed.
57 E3 **Verkhov'ye** Rus. Fed.
58 A2 **Verkhovyna** Ukr.
51 J2 **Verkhoyanskiy Khrebet** mts Rus. Fed.

97 C2 **Vermilion** Can.
105 D2 **Vermillion** U.S.A.
98 A2 **Vermilion Bay** Can.
109 E2 **Vermont** state U.S.A.
103 E2 **Vernal** U.S.A.
96 C2 **Vernon** Can.
107 D2 **Vernon** U.S.A.
111 D3 **Vero Beach** U.S.A.
79 B2 **Veroia** Greece
76 B1 **Verona** Italy
72 C2 **Versailles** France
72 B2 **Vertou** France
91 D2 **Verulam** S. Africa
68 B2 **Verviers** Belgium
73 C2 **Vervins** France
73 D3 **Vescovato** Corsica France
55 E3 **Veselaya, Gora** mt. Rus. Fed.
59 C2 **Vesele** Ukr.
73 D2 **Vesoul** France
60 F2 **Vesterålen** is Norway
60 F2 **Vestfjorden** sea chan. Norway
62 B1 **Vestmanna** Faroe Is
61 E3 **Vestnes** Norway
76 B2 **Vesuvio** vol. Italy
57 E2 **Ves'yegonsk** Rus. Fed.
61 G4 **Vetlanda** Sweden
54 D3 **Vetluga** Rus. Fed.
68 A2 **Veurne** Belgium
73 D2 **Vevey** France
59 D1 **Veydelevka** Rus. Fed.
48 B1 **Vezirköprü** Turkey
119 D2 **Viana** Brazil
74 B1 **Viana do Castelo** Port.
    Vlangchan Laos see **Vientiane**
30 B1 **Viangphoukha** Laos
122 C1 **Vianópolis** Brazil
76 B2 **Viareggio** Italy
61 E4 **Viborg** Denmark
77 C3 **Vibo Valentia** Italy
30 B2 **Vic** Spain
112 A1 **Vicente Guerrero** Mex.
76 B1 **Vicenza** Italy
73 C2 **Viohy** France
110 B2 **Vicksburg** U.S.A.
123 D2 **Viçosa** Brazil
20 A3 **Victor Harbor** Austr.
18 C1 **Victoria** r. Austr.
20 B3 **Victoria** state Austr.
96 B3 **Victoria** Can.
121 A4 **Victoria** Chile
107 D3 **Victoria** U.S.A.
87 D3 **Victoria, Lake** Africa
20 B2 **Victoria, Lake** Austr.
30 A1 **Victoria, Mount** Myanmar
27 D3 **Victoria, Mount** P.N.G.
88 B2 **Victoria Falls** waterfall Zambia/Zimbabwe
94 D2 **Victoria Island** Can.
18 C1 **Victoria River Downs** Austr.
90 B3 **Victoria West** S. Africa
103 C4 **Victorville** U.S.A.
78 C2 **Videle** Romania
60 ☐A2 **Víðidalsá** Iceland
121 B5 **Viedma** Arg.
121 A5 **Viedma, Lago** l. Arg.
68 B2 **Vielsalm** Belgium
69 E2 **Vienenburg** Ger.
71 D3 **Vienna** Austria
73 C2 **Vienne** France
72 C2 **Vienne** r. France
30 B2 **Vientiane** Laos
68 C2 **Viersen** Ger.
72 C2 **Vierzon** France
112 B2 **Viesca** Mex.
77 C2 **Vieste** Italy
30 B2 **Vietnam** country Asia
30 B1 **Viêt Tri** Vietnam

32 B1 Vigan Phil.
76 A1 Vigevano Italy
74 B1 Vigo Spain
41 C3 Vijayawada India
60 ☐B3 Vík Iceland
97 C2 Viking Can.
74 B2 Vila Franca de Xira Port.
74 B2 Vilagarcía de Arousa Spain
74 B1 Vilalba Spain
74 B1 Vila Nova de Gaia Port.
75 D1 Vilanova i la Geltrú Spain
74 B1 Vila Real Port.
74 B1 Vilar Formoso Port.
123 D2 Vila Velha Brazil
118 A3 Vilcabamba, Cordillera mts Peru
60 G3 Vilhelmina Sweden
118 B3 Vilhena Brazil
56 C2 Viljandi Estonia
56 B3 Vilkaviškis Lith.
51 H1 Vil'kitskogo, Proliv str. Rus. Fed.
112 B1 Villa Ahumada Mex.
74 B1 Villablino Spain
70 C2 Villach Austria
112 A2 Villa Constitución Mex.
112 B2 Villa de Cos Mex.
120 B4 Villa Dolores Arg.
113 C3 Villa Flores Mex.
113 C3 Villagrán Mex.
113 C3 Villahermosa Mex.
112 A2 Villa Insurgentes Mex.
120 B4 Villa María Arg.
120 B3 Villa Montes Bol.
112 B2 Villanueva Mex.
74 B2 Villanueva de la Serena Spain
74 C2 Villanueva de los Infantes Spain
120 C3 Villa Ocampo Arg.
76 A3 Villaputzu Sardinia Italy
120 C3 Villarrica Para.
74 C2 Villarrobledo Spain
120 B3 Villa Unión Arg.
112 A2 Villa Unión Durango Mex.
112 B2 Villa Unión Sinaloa Mex.
118 A1 Villavicencio Col.
120 B3 Villazon Bol.
75 C2 Villena Spain
72 C3 Villeneuve-sur-Lot France
110 B2 Ville Platte U.S.A.
73 C2 Villeurbanne France
70 B2 Villingen Ger.
56 C3 Vilnius Lith.
59 C2 Vil'nohirs'k Ukr.
59 D2 Vil'nyans'k Ukr.
68 B2 Vilvoorde Belgium
56 C3 Vilyeyka Belarus
51 J2 Vilyuy r. Rus. Fed.
61 G4 Vimmerby Sweden
121 A4 Viña del Mar Chile
75 D1 Vinaròs Spain
108 B3 Vincennes U.S.A.
23 G3 Vincennes Bay Antarctica
109 D3 Vineland U.S.A.
30 B2 Vinh Vietnam
31 B2 Vinh Long Vietnam
107 D1 Vinita U.S.A.
58 B2 Vinnytsya Ukr.
23 O2 Vinson Massif mt. Antarctica
61 E3 Vinstra Norway
76 B1 Vipiteno Italy
32 B1 Virac Phil.
97 D3 Virden Can.
72 B2 Vire France
88 A2 Virei Angola
123 D1 Virgem da Lapa Brazil
106 A1 Virgin r. U.S.A.
91 C2 Virginia S. Africa
105 E1 Virginia U.S.A.

109 D3 Virginia state U.S.A.
109 D3 Virginia Beach U.S.A.
103 C3 Virginia City U.S.A.
115 D3 Virgin Islands (U.K.) terr. West Indies
115 D3 Virgin Islands (U.S.A.) terr. West Indies
31 B2 Virôchey Cambodia
77 C1 Virovitica Croatia
68 B3 Virton Belgium
56 B2 Virtsu Estonia
77 C2 Vis i. Croatia
56 C2 Visaginas Lith.
103 C3 Visalia U.S.A.
42 B2 Visavadar India
32 B1 Visayan Sea Phil.
61 G4 Visby Sweden
94 D2 Viscount Melville Sound sea chan. Can.
119 D2 Viseu Brazil
74 B1 Viseu Port.
41 C3 Vishakhapatnam India
56 C2 Viški Latvia
77 C2 Visoko Bos.-Herz.
76 B2 Viterbo Italy
51 I3 Vitim r. Rus. Fed.
123 D2 Vitória Brazil
119 D3 Vitória da Conquista Brazil
74 C1 Vitoria-Gasteiz Spain
72 B2 Vitré France
73 C2 Vitry-le-François France
57 D2 Vitsyebsk Belarus
73 D2 Vittel France
76 B3 Vittoria Sicily Italy
76 B1 Vittorio Veneto Italy
74 B1 Viveiro Spain
112 A2 Vizcaíno, Sierra mts Mex.
78 C2 Vize Turkey
41 C3 Vizianagaram India
68 B2 Vlaardingen Neth.
55 D4 Vladikavkaz Rus. Fed.
57 F2 Vladimir Rus. Fed.
34 B2 Vladivostok Rus. Fed.
77 D2 Vlasotince Yugo.
54 E1 Vlieland i. Neth.
68 A2 Vlissingen Neth.
77 C2 Vlorë Albania
70 C2 Vöcklabruck Austria
69 D2 Vogelsberg hills Ger.
87 D3 Voi Kenya
73 D2 Voiron France
99 D1 Voisey Bay Can.
77 C1 Vojvodina prov. Yugo.
60 J3 Voknavolok Rus. Fed.
Volcano Bay b. Japan see Uchiura-wan
57 E2 Volga Rus. Fed.
57 E2 Volga r. Rus. Fed.
57 E2 Volgodonsk Rus. Fed.
55 D4 Volgograd Rus. Fed.
57 D2 Volkhov Rus. Fed.
57 D1 Volkhov r. Rus. Fed.
69 E2 Volkstedt Ger.
59 D2 Volnovakha Ukr.
58 B2 Volochys'k Ukr.
59 D2 Volodars'ke Ukr.
58 B1 Volodars'k-Volyns'kyy Ukr.
58 B1 Volodymyrets' Ukr.
58 A1 Volodymyr-Volyns'kyy Ukr.
57 E2 Vologda Rus. Fed.
57 E2 Volokolamsk Rus. Fed.
59 D1 Volokonovka Rus. Fed.
79 B3 Volos Greece
56 C2 Volosovo Rus. Fed.
57 D2 Volot Rus. Fed.
57 E3 Volovo Rus. Fed.
55 D3 Vol'sk Rus. Fed.
82 C4 Volta, Lake resr Ghana
123 D2 Volta Redonda Brazil

55 D4 Volzhskiy Rus. Fed.
60 ☐C2 Vopnafjörður Iceland
56 C3 Voranava Belarus
54 F2 Vorkuta Rus. Fed.
56 B2 Vormsi i. Estonia
57 E3 Voronezh Rus. Fed.
57 E3 Voronezh r. Rus. Fed.
59 E1 Vorontsovka Rus. Fed.
59 C2 Vorskla r. Rus. Fed.
56 C2 Võrtsjärv l. Estonia
56 C2 Võru Estonia
90 B3 Vosburg S. Africa
73 D2 Vosges mts France
57 E2 Voskresensk Rus. Fed.
61 E3 Voss Norway
51 K2 Vostochno-Sibirskoye More sea Rus. Fed.
51 H3 Vostochnyy Sayan mts Rus. Fed.
54 E3 Votkinsk Rus. Fed.
122 C2 Votuporanga Brazil
68 B3 Vouziers France
60 J2 Voynitsa Rus. Fed.
59 C2 Voznesens'k Ukr.
61 E4 Vrådal Norway
34 B2 Vrangel' Rus. Fed.
51 N2 Vrangelya, Ostrov i. Rus. Fed.
77 D2 Vranje Yugo.
78 C2 Vratnik pass Bulg.
78 B2 Vratsa Bulg.
77 C1 Vrbas r. Bos.-Herz.
77 C1 Vrbas Yugo.
90 A3 Vredenburg S. Africa
90 A3 Vredendal S. Africa
68 B3 Vresse Belgium
77 D1 Vršac Yugo.
90 B2 Vryburg S. Africa
91 D2 Vryheid S. Africa
57 D1 Vsevolozhsk Rus. Fed.
77 D2 Vučitrn Yugo.
77 C1 Vukovar Croatia
54 E2 Vuktyl' Rus. Fed.
91 C2 Vukuzakhe S. Africa
77 B3 Vulcano, Isola i. Italy
31 B2 Vung Tau Vietnam
42 B2 Vyara India
Vyatka Rus. Fed. see Kirov
57 D2 Vyaz'ma Rus. Fed.
61 I3 Vyborg Rus. Fed.
56 C2 Vyerkhnyadzvinsk Belarus
55 D3 Vyksa Rus. Fed.
58 A2 Vylkove Ukr.
58 B2 Vynohradiv Ukr.
57 D2 Vypolzovo Rus. Fed.
57 D2 Vyritsa Rus. Fed.
59 D2 Vyselki Rus. Fed.
58 C1 Vyshhorod Ukr.
57 D2 Vyshniy-Volochek Rus. Fed.
71 D2 Vyškov Czech Rep.
54 C2 Vytegra Rus. Fed.

W

82 B3 Wa Ghana
68 B2 Waal r. Neth.
68 B2 Waalwijk Neth.
96 C2 Wabasca r. Can.
96 C2 Wabasca-Desmarais Can.
108 B3 Wabash r. U.S.A.
85 C4 Wabē Gestro r. Eth.
85 C4 Wabē Shebelē Wenz r. Eth.
97 E2 Wabowden Can.
111 D3 Waccasassa Bay U.S.A.
69 D2 Wächtersbach Ger.
107 D2 Waco U.S.A.

42 A2 Wad Pak.
83 D2 Waddān Libya
68 B1 Waddeneilanden *is* Neth.
68 B1 Waddenzee *sea chan.* Neth.
96 B2 Waddington, Mount Can.
68 B1 Waddinxveen Neth.
97 D2 Wadena Can.
105 D1 Wadena U.S.A.
84 B2 Wadi Halfa Sudan
84 B3 Wad Medani Sudan
38 C2 Wafangdian China
68 B2 Wageningen Neth.
95 F2 Wager Bay Can.
21 C3 Wagga Wagga Austr.
105 D2 Wahoo U.S.A.
105 D1 Wahpeton U.S.A.
22 B2 Waiau r. N.Z.
27 C3 Waigeo *i.* Indon.
22 B2 Waikabubak Indon.
20 A2 Waikerie Austr.
22 B2 Waimate N.Z.
43 B3 Wainganga *r.* India
26 C3 Waingapu Indon.
97 C2 Wainwright Can.
22 C1 Waiouru N.Z.
22 B1 Waipara N.Z.
22 C2 Waipawa N.Z.
22 B1 Wairau *r.* N.Z.
22 C1 Wairoa N.Z.
22 B2 Waitaki *r.* N.Z.
22 B1 Waitara N.Z.
22 B1 Waiuku N.Z.
87 E2 Wajir Kenya
35 C3 Wakasa-wan *b.* Japan
22 A3 Wakatipu, Lake N.Z.
97 D2 Wakaw Can.
35 C4 Wakayama Japan
104 D3 WaKeeney U.S.A.
22 B2 Wakefield N.Z.
66 C2 Wakefield U.K.
34 D1 Wakkanai Japan
91 D2 Wakkerstroom S. Africa
71 D1 Wałbrzych Pol.
21 D2 Walcha Austr.
68 C1 Walchum Ger.
71 D1 Wałcz Pol.
67 B2 Wales *admin. div.* U.K.
21 C2 Walgett Austr.
87 C3 Walikale Dem. Rep. Congo
103 C3 Walker Lake *l.* U.S.A.
20 A2 Wallaroo Austr.
66 B2 Wallasey U.K.
102 C1 Walla Walla U.S.A.
69 D3 Walldürn Ger.
21 C2 Wallendbeen Austr.
17 F4 Wallis and Futuna Islands
        terr. S. Pacific Ocean
64 □ Walls U.K.
66 B1 Walney, Isle of *i.* U.K.
67 C2 Walsall U.K.
104 C3 Walsenburg U.S.A.
69 D1 Walsrode Ger.
111 D2 Walterboro U.S.A.
88 A3 Walvis Bay Namibia
86 C3 Wamba Dem. Rep. Congo
20 B1 Wanaaring Austr.
22 A2 Wanaka N.Z.
22 A2 Wanaka, Lake N.Z.
98 B2 Wanapitei Lake Can.
122 B3 Wanda Arg.
34 B1 Wanda Shan *mts* China
30 A1 Wanding China
22 C1 Wanganui N.Z.
21 C3 Wangaratta Austr.
68 C1 Wangerooge *i.* Ger.
33 B1 Wangqing China
30 A1 Wan Hsa-la Myanmar
39 B4 Wanning China
68 B2 Wanroij Neth.
67 C3 Wantage U.K.

38 A2 Wanxian China
38 A2 Wanyuan China
41 B3 Warangal India
69 D2 Warburg Ger.
18 B2 Warburton Austr.
20 A1 Warburton *watercourse*
        Austr.
43 B2 Wardha India
64 C1 Ward Hill U.K.
96 B2 Ware Can.
69 F1 Waren Ger.
68 C2 Warendorf Ger.
21 D1 Warialda Austr.
90 A2 Warmbad Namibia
103 C3 Warm Springs U.S.A.
102 C2 Warner Lakes U.S.A.
111 D2 Warner Robins U.S.A.
120 B2 Warnes Bol.
20 B3 Warracknabeal Austr.
21 C2 Warrego *r.* Austr.
21 C2 Warren Austr.
110 B2 Warren *AR* U.S.A.
108 C2 Warren *OH* U.S.A.
109 D2 Warren *PA* U.S.A.
65 C1 Warrenpoint U.K.
105 E3 Warrensburg U.S.A.
90 B2 Warrenton S. Africa
83 C4 Warri Nigeria
66 B2 Warrington U.K.
20 B3 Warrnambool Austr.
71 E1 Warsaw Pol.
        Warszawa Pol. *see* Warsaw
71 C1 Warta *r.* Pol.
21 D1 Warwick Austr.
67 C2 Warwick U.K.
103 C3 Wasco U.S.A.
104 C1 Washburn U.S.A.
109 D3 Washington *DC* U.S.A.
105 E2 Washington *IA* U.S.A.
108 B3 Washington *IN* U.S.A.
105 E3 Washington *MO* U.S.A.
111 E1 Washington *NC* U.S.A.
108 C2 Washington *PA* U.S.A.
102 B1 Washington *state* U.S.A.
109 E2 Washington, Mount U.S.A.
108 C3 Washington Court House
        U.S.A.
42 A2 Washuk Pak.
98 C1 Waskaganish Can.
97 E2 Waskaiowaka Lake Can.
90 A2 Wasser Namibia
98 C2 Waswanipi, Lac *l.* Can.
26 C3 Watampone Indon.
109 E2 Waterbury U.S.A.
97 D2 Waterbury Lake Can.
65 C2 Waterford Rep. of Ireland
65 C2 Waterford Harbour
        Rep. of Ireland
105 E2 Waterloo U.S.A.
91 C1 Waterpoort S. Africa
109 D2 Watertown *NY* U.S.A.
105 D2 Watertown *SD* U.S.A.
108 B2 Watertown *WI* U.S.A.
109 F2 Waterville U.S.A.
67 C3 Watford U.K.
104 C1 Watford City U.S.A.
97 D2 Wathaman *r.* Can.
107 D1 Watonga U.S.A.
97 D2 Watrous Can.
87 C2 Watsa Dem. Rep. Congo
108 B2 Watseka U.S.A.
86 C3 Watsi Kengo
        Dem. Rep. Congo
96 B1 Watson Lake Can.
103 B3 Watsonville U.S.A.
27 C3 Watubela, Kepulauan
        is Indon.
27 D3 Wau P.N.G.
85 A4 Wau Sudan
21 D2 Wauchope Austr.

108 B2 Waukegan U.S.A.
107 D2 Waurika U.S.A.
108 B2 Wausau U.S.A.
67 D2 Waveney *r.* U.K.
105 E2 Waverly U.S.A.
111 D2 Waycross U.S.A.
105 D2 Wayne U.S.A.
111 D2 Waynesboro *GA* U.S.A.
109 D3 Waynesboro *VA* U.S.A.
111 D1 Waynesville U.S.A.
42 B1 Wazirabad Pak.
66 C1 Wear *r.* U.K.
107 D2 Weatherford U.S.A.
102 B2 Weaverville U.S.A.
98 B1 Webequie Can.
85 C4 Webi Shabeelle *r.* Somalia
105 D1 Webster U.S.A.
105 E2 Webster City U.S.A.
23 Q2 Weddell Sea Antarctica
68 B2 Weert Neth.
21 C2 Wee Waa Austr.
68 C2 Wegberg Ger.
71 E1 Węgorzewo Pol.
69 F3 Weiden in der Oberpfalz
        Ger.
38 B2 Weifang China
38 C2 Weihai China
21 C1 Weilmoringle Austr.
69 E2 Weimar Ger.
38 A2 Weinan China
21 C1 Weipa Austr.
21 C1 Weir *r.* Austr.
108 C2 Weirton U.S.A.
30 B1 Weishan China
69 E2 Weißenfels Ger.
70 C2 Weißkugel *mt.* Austria/Italy
71 D1 Wejherowo Pol.
108 C3 Welch U.S.A.
85 B3 Weldiya Eth.
91 C2 Welkom S. Africa
67 C2 Welland *r.* U.K.
19 C1 Wellesley Islands Austr.
21 C2 Wellington Austr.
22 B3 Wellington N.Z.
90 A3 Wellington S. Africa
105 D3 Wellington U.S.A.
121 A5 Wellington, Isla *i.* Chile
21 C3 Wellington, Lake Austr.
96 B2 Wells Can.
67 B3 Wells U.K.
102 D2 Wells U.S.A.
18 B2 Wells, Lake *salt flat* Austr.
22 B1 Wellsford N.Z.
66 D2 Wells-next-the-Sea U.K.
70 C2 Wels Austria
67 B2 Welshpool U.K.
91 C2 Wembesi S. Africa
98 C1 Wemindji Can.
102 B1 Wenatchee U.S.A.
39 B4 Wenchang China
82 B4 Wenchi Ghana
38 C2 Wendeng China
69 E1 Wendisch Evern Ger.
85 B4 Wendo Eth.
102 D2 Wendover U.S.A.
39 B3 Wengyuan China
39 C3 Wenling China
39 A3 Wenshan China
20 B2 Wentworth Austr.
39 C3 Wenzhou China
91 C2 Wepener S. Africa
90 B2 Werda Botswana
69 F2 Werdau Ger.
69 F1 Werder Ger.
69 F3 Wernberg-Köblitz Ger.
69 E2 Wernigerode Ger.
69 D2 Werra *r.* Ger.
21 D2 Werris Creek Austr.
69 D3 Wertheim Ger.
68 C2 Wesel Ger.

69 E1 **Wesendorf** Ger.
69 D1 **Weser** r. Ger.
69 D1 **Weser** sea chan. Ger.
19 C1 **Wessel, Cape** Austr.
19 C1 **Wessel Islands** Austr.
91 C2 **Wesselton** S. Africa
48 B2 **West Bank** terr. Asia
108 B2 **West Bend** U.S.A.
67 C2 **West Bromwich** U.K.
68 C2 **Westerburg** Ger.
68 C1 **Westerholt** Ger.
18 B2 **Western Australia** state Austr.
90 B3 **Western Cape** prov. S. Africa
84 A2 **Western Desert** des. Egypt
41 B3 **Western Ghats** mts India
82 A2 **Western Sahara** terr. Africa
Western Samoa country S. Pacific Ocean see **Samoa**
68 A2 **Westerschelde** est. Neth.
68 C1 **Westerstede** Ger.
68 C2 **Westerwald** hills Ger.
121 B6 **West Falkland** i. Falkland Is
108 B3 **West Frankfort** U.S.A.
115 D2 **West Indies** N. America
64 A1 **West Loch Roag** b. U.K.
96 C2 **Westlock** Can.
68 B2 **Westmalle** Belgium
110 B1 **West Memphis** U.S.A.
108 C3 **Weston** U.S.A.
67 B3 **Weston-super-Mare** U.K.
111 D3 **West Palm Beach** U.S.A.
105 E3 **West Plains** U.S.A.
105 D2 **West Point** U.S.A.
22 B2 **Westport** N.Z.
65 B2 **Westport** Rep. of Ireland
97 D2 **Westray** Can.
64 C1 **Westray** i. U.K.
68 B1 **West-Terschelling** Neth.
65 B1 **West Town** Rep. of Ireland
108 C3 **West Virginia** state U.S.A.
21 C2 **West Wyalong** Austr.
102 D2 **West Yellowstone** U.S.A.
27 C3 **Wetar** i. Indon.
96 C2 **Wetaskiwin** Can.
69 D2 **Wetzlar** Ger.
27 D3 **Wewak** P.N.G.
65 C2 **Wexford** Rep. of Ireland
97 D2 **Weyakwin** Can.
97 D3 **Weyburn** Can.
69 D1 **Weyhe** Ger.
67 B3 **Weymouth** U.K.
22 C1 **Whakatane** N.Z.
97 E1 **Whale Cove** Can.
64 □ **Whalsay** i. U.K.
22 B1 **Whangarei** N.Z.
66 C2 **Wharfe** r. U.K.
96 C1 **Wha Ti** Can.
104 C2 **Wheatland** U.S.A.
99 E2 **White Bay** Can.
104 C1 **White Butte** mt. U.S.A.
20 B2 **White Cliffs** Austr.
96 C2 **Whitecourt** Can.
102 D1 **Whitefish** U.S.A.
66 B1 **Whitehaven** U.K.
65 D1 **Whitehead** U.K.
96 A1 **Whitehorse** Can.
110 B3 **White Lake** l. U.S.A.
103 C3 **White Mountain Peak** U.S.A.
84 B3 **White Nile** r. Sudan/Uganda
54 C2 **White Sea** Rus. Fed.

102 D1 **White Sulphur Springs** U.S.A.
111 E2 **Whiteville** U.S.A.
82 B3 **White Volta** watercourse Burkina/Ghana
106 B2 **Whitewater Baldy** mt. U.S.A.
98 A1 **Whitewater Lake** Can.
97 D2 **Whitewood** Can.
64 B3 **Whithorn** U.K.
22 C1 **Whitianga** N.Z.
103 C3 **Whitney, Mount** U.S.A.
19 D2 **Whitsunday Island** Austr.
20 A2 **Whyalla** Austr.
30 A1 **Wiang Phran** Thai.
68 A2 **Wichelen** Belgium
105 D3 **Wichita** U.S.A.
107 D2 **Wichita Falls** U.S.A.
64 C1 **Wick** U.K.
106 A2 **Wickenburg** U.S.A.
65 C2 **Wicklow** Rep. of Ireland
65 D2 **Wicklow Head** hd Rep. of Ireland
65 C2 **Wicklow Mountains** Rep. of Ireland
66 B2 **Widnes** U.K.
69 D1 **Wiehengebirge** hills Ger.
68 C2 **Wiehl** Ger.
71 D1 **Wieluń** Pol.
Wien Austria see **Vienna**
71 D2 **Wiener Neustadt** Austria
68 B1 **Wieringerwerf** Neth.
68 D2 **Wiesbaden** Ger.
68 C1 **Wiesmoor** Ger.
71 D1 **Wieżyca** hill Pol.
67 C3 **Wight, Isle of** i. U.K.
64 B3 **Wigtown** U.K.
68 B2 **Wijchen** Neth.
20 B2 **Wilcannia** Austr.
91 C3 **Wild Coast** S. Africa
91 C2 **Wilge** r. S. Africa
68 D1 **Wilhelmshaven** Ger.
109 D2 **Wilkes-Barre** U.S.A.
23 H3 **Wilkes Land** reg. Antarctica
97 D2 **Wilkie** Can.
106 B2 **Willcox** U.S.A.
68 B2 **Willebroek** Belgium
115 D3 **Willemstad** Neth. Antilles
20 B3 **William, Mount** Austr.
20 A1 **William Creek** Austr.
106 A1 **Williams** U.S.A.
109 D2 **Williamsburg** U.S.A.
96 B2 **Williams Lake** Can.
108 C3 **Williamson** U.S.A.
109 D2 **Williamsport** U.S.A.
111 E1 **Williamston** U.S.A.
90 B3 **Williston** S. Africa
104 C1 **Williston** U.S.A.
96 B2 **Williston Lake** Can.
103 B3 **Willits** U.S.A.
105 D1 **Willmar** U.S.A.
90 B3 **Willowmore** S. Africa
91 C3 **Willowvale** S. Africa
18 B2 **Wills, Lake** salt flat Austr.
20 A3 **Willunga** Austr.
20 A2 **Wilmington** Austr.
109 D3 **Wilmington** DE U.S.A.
111 E2 **Wilmington** NC U.S.A.
68 D2 **Wilnsdorf** Ger.
111 E1 **Wilson** U.S.A.
21 C3 **Wilson's Promontory** pen. Austr.
68 B3 **Wiltz** Lux.
18 B2 **Wiluna** Austr.
67 C3 **Winchester** U.K.
108 C3 **Winchester** KY U.S.A.
109 D3 **Winchester** VA U.S.A.
66 B1 **Windermere** l. U.K.
88 A3 **Windhoek** Namibia
105 D2 **Windom** U.S.A.
19 D2 **Windorah** Austr.

104 B2 **Wind River Range** mts U.S.A.
21 D2 **Windsor** Austr.
98 B2 **Windsor** Can.
115 D3 **Windward Islands** Caribbean Sea
115 C3 **Windward Passage** Cuba/Haiti
105 D3 **Winfield** U.S.A.
68 A2 **Wingene** Belgium
21 D2 **Wingham** Austr.
98 B1 **Winisk** Can.
98 B1 **Winisk** r. Can.
98 B1 **Winisk Lake** Can.
31 A2 **Winkana** Myanmar
97 E3 **Winkler** Can.
82 B4 **Winneba** Ghana
108 B2 **Winnebago, Lake** U.S.A.
102 C2 **Winnemucca** U.S.A.
104 C2 **Winner** U.S.A.
110 B2 **Winnfield** U.S.A.
105 E1 **Winnibigoshish, Lake** U.S.
97 E3 **Winnipeg** Can.
97 E2 **Winnipeg** r. Can.
97 E2 **Winnipeg, Lake** Can.
97 D2 **Winnipegosis, Lake** Can.
109 E2 **Winnipesaukee, Lake** U.S.A.
110 B2 **Winnsboro** U.S.A.
105 E2 **Winona** MN U.S.A.
110 C2 **Winona** MS U.S.A.
68 C1 **Winschoten** Neth.
69 D1 **Winsen (Aller)** Ger.
69 E1 **Winsen (Luhe)** Ger.
106 A1 **Winslow** U.S.A.
111 D1 **Winston-Salem** U.S.A.
69 D2 **Winterberg** Ger.
111 D3 **Winter Haven** U.S.A.
68 C2 **Winterswijk** Neth.
73 D2 **Winterthur** Switz.
19 D2 **Winton** Austr.
22 A3 **Winton** N.Z.
20 A2 **Wirrabara** Austr.
67 D2 **Wisbech** U.K.
108 A2 **Wisconsin** r. U.S.A.
108 B2 **Wisconsin** state U.S.A.
108 B2 **Wisconsin Rapids** U.S.A.
71 D1 **Wisła** r. Pol.
69 E1 **Wismar** Ger.
91 C2 **Witbank** S. Africa
66 D2 **Withernsea** U.K.
68 B1 **Witmarsum** Neth.
67 C3 **Witney** U.K.
91 D2 **Witrivier** S. Africa
69 E1 **Wittenberge** Ger.
69 E1 **Wittenburg** Ger.
69 E1 **Wittingen** Ger.
68 C1 **Wittlich** Ger.
68 C1 **Wittmund** Ger.
69 F1 **Wittstock** Ger.
88 A3 **Witvlei** Namibia
69 D2 **Witzenhausen** Ger.
71 D1 **Władysławowo** Pol.
71 D1 **Włocławek** Pol.
21 C3 **Wodonga** Austr.
27 C3 **Wokam** i. Indon.
67 C3 **Woking** U.K.
69 F2 **Wolfen** Ger.
69 E1 **Wolfenbüttel** Ger.
69 D2 **Wolfhagen** Ger.
104 B1 **Wolf Point** U.S.A.
69 E1 **Wolfsburg** Ger.
68 C3 **Wolfstein** Ger.
99 D2 **Wolfville** Can.
70 C1 **Wolgast** Ger.
70 C1 **Wolin** Pol.
97 D2 **Wollaston Lake** Can.
97 D2 **Wollaston Lake** l. Can.
94 D2 **Wollaston Peninsula** Can.
21 D2 **Wollongong** Austr.
69 E2 **Wolmirsleben** Ger.

69 E1 **Wolmirstedt** Ger.
68 C1 **Wolvega** Neth.
67 B2 **Wolverhampton** U.K.
33 B2 **Wŏnju** S. Korea
96 B2 **Wonowon** Can.
33 B2 **Wŏnsan** N. Korea
21 C3 **Wonthaggi** Austr.
20 A2 **Woocalla** Austr.
19 C1 **Woodah, Isle** i. Austr.
67 D2 **Woodbridge** U.K.
104 B3 **Woodland Park** U.S.A.
18 C2 **Woodroffe, Mount** Austr.
19 C1 **Woods, Lake** salt flat Austr.
97 E3 **Woods, Lake of the**
       Can./U.S.A.
21 C3 **Woods Point** Austr.
99 D2 **Woodstock** N.B. Can.
108 C2 **Woodstock** Ont. Can.
22 C2 **Woodville** N.Z.
107 D1 **Woodward** U.S.A.
21 D2 **Woolgoolga** Austr.
20 A2 **Woomera** Austr.
108 C2 **Wooster** U.S.A.
90 A3 **Worcester** S. Africa
67 B2 **Worcester** U.K.
109 E2 **Worcester** U.S.A.
70 C2 **Wörgl** Austria
66 B1 **Workington** U.K.
66 C2 **Worksop** U.K.
104 B2 **Worland** U.S.A.
69 D3 **Worms** Ger.
67 C3 **Worthing** U.K.
105 D2 **Worthington** U.S.A.
26 C1 **Wotu** Indon.
27 C3 **Wowoni** i. Indon.
       Wrangel Island Rus. Fed.
       see **Vrangelya, Ostrov**
96 A2 **Wrangell** U.S.A.
64 B1 **Wrath, Cape** U.K.
104 C2 **Wray** U.S.A.
90 A2 **Wreck Point** S. Africa
66 B2 **Wrexham** U.K.
104 B2 **Wright** U.S.A.
31 A2 **Wrightmyo** India
96 B1 **Wrigley** Can.
71 D1 **Wrocław** Pol.
71 D1 **Września** Pol.
38 B2 **Wu'an** China
38 A2 **Wudu** China
38 A2 **Wuhai** China
38 B2 **Wuhan** China
38 B2 **Wuhu** China
       Wujin China see **Changzhou**
83 C4 **Wukari** Nigeria
30 B1 **Wuliang Shan** mts China
27 C3 **Wuliaru** i. Indon.
39 A3 **Wumeng Shan** mts China
98 B1 **Wunnummin Lake** Can.
69 F2 **Wunsiedel** Ger.
69 D1 **Wunstorf** Ger.
30 A1 **Wuntho** Myanmar
68 C2 **Wuppertal** Ger.
90 A3 **Wuppertal** S. Africa
69 E2 **Wurzbach** Ger.
69 D3 **Würzburg** Ger.
69 F2 **Wurzen** Ger.
36 C2 **Wuwei** China
38 A2 **Wuxi** Chongqing China
38 C2 **Wuxi** Jiangsu China
       Wuxing China see **Huzhou**
39 A3 **Wuxuan** China
       Wuyang China see **Zhenyuan**
37 E1 **Wuyiling** China
39 B3 **Wuyishan** China
39 B3 **Wuyi Shan** mts China
38 A1 **Wuyuan** China
38 A2 **Wuzhong** China
39 B3 **Wuzhou** China
21 C2 **Wyangala Reservoir** Austr.
20 B3 **Wycheproof** Austr.
67 B3 **Wye** r. U.K.
18 B1 **Wyndham** Austr.
110 B1 **Wynne** U.S.A.
97 D2 **Wynyard** Can.
104 B2 **Wyoming** state U.S.A.
71 E1 **Wyszków** Pol.
108 C3 **Wytheville** U.S.A.

X

85 D3 **Xaafuun** Somalia
89 C3 **Xai-Xai** Moz.
38 A1 **Xamba** China
30 B1 **Xam Hua** Laos
88 A2 **Xangongo** Angola
49 C2 **Xankändi** Azer.
79 B2 **Xanthi** Greece
118 B3 **Xapuri** Brazil
75 C2 **Xàtiva** Spain
       Xiaguan China see **Dali**
39 B3 **Xiamen** China
38 A2 **Xi'an** China
38 A3 **Xianfeng** China
38 B2 **Xiangfan** China
       Xiangjiang China see
       Huichang
30 B2 **Xiangkhoang** Laos
39 B3 **Xiangtan** China
       Xiangyang China see
       Xiangfan
38 B2 **Xiantao** China
38 A2 **Xianyang** China
38 B2 **Xiaogan** China
37 E1 **Xiao Hinggan Ling** mts
       China
38 C2 **Xiaoshan** China
30 B1 **Xichang** China
113 C2 **Xicohténcatl** Mex.
38 A2 **Xifeng** Gansu China
39 A3 **Xifeng** Guizhou China
43 C2 **Xigazê** China
51 I4 **Xilinhot** China
38 B2 **Xincai** China
36 C2 **Xinghai** China
38 B2 **Xinghua** China
39 B3 **Xingning** China
38 A2 **Xingping** China
38 B2 **Xingtai** China
119 C2 **Xingu** r. Brazil
39 A3 **Xingyi** China
39 B3 **Xinhua** China
36 C2 **Xining** China
43 C1 **Xinjiang Uygur Zizhiqu**
       aut. reg. China
       Xinjing China see **Jingxi**
33 A1 **Xinmin** China
39 B3 **Xinning** China
38 B2 **Xintai** China
38 B2 **Xinxiang** China
38 B2 **Xinyang** China
39 B3 **Xinyu** China
37 D2 **Xinzhou** Shanxi China
38 B2 **Xinzhou** Shanxi China
74 B1 **Xinzo de Limia** Spain
       Xiongshan China see
       Zhenghe
36 C2 **Xiqing Shan** mts China
119 D3 **Xique Xique** Brazil
38 A1 **Xishanzui** China
39 A3 **Xiushan** China
39 B3 **Xiuying** China
38 B2 **Xixia** China
43 C1 **Xizang Zizhiqu** aut. reg.
       China
39 A3 **Xuanwei** China
38 B2 **Xuanzhou** China
38 B2 **Xuchang** China

       Xucheng China see **Xuwen**
85 C4 **Xuddur** Somalia
       Xujiang China see
       Guangchang
39 B3 **Xun Jiang** r. China
39 B3 **Xunwu** China
39 B3 **Xuwen** China
39 A3 **Xuyong** China
38 B2 **Xuzhou** China

Y

85 B4 **Yabēlo** Eth.
37 D1 **Yablonovyy Khrebet** mts
       Rus. Fed.
111 D1 **Yadkin** r. U.S.A.
43 C2 **Yadong** China
57 E2 **Yagnitsa** Rus. Fed.
86 B1 **Yagoua** Cameroon
96 C3 **Yahk** Can.
112 B2 **Yahualica** Mex.
48 B2 **Yahyalı** Turkey
35 C4 **Yaizu** Japan
102 B1 **Yakima** U.S.A.
82 B3 **Yako** Burkina
34 D2 **Yakumo** Japan
94 B3 **Yakutat** U.S.A.
51 J2 **Yakutsk** Rus. Fed.
59 D2 **Yakymivka** Ukr.
31 B3 **Yala** Thai.
21 C3 **Yallourn** Austr.
79 C2 **Yalova** Turkey
59 C3 **Yalta** Ukr.
33 A1 **Yalu Jiang** r. China/N. Korea
35 D3 **Yamagata** Japan
35 B4 **Yamaguchi** Japan
54 F1 **Yamal, Poluostrov** pen.
       Rus. Fed.
21 D1 **Yamba** Austr.
85 A4 **Yambio** Sudan
78 C2 **Yambol** Bulg.
59 G2 **Yamburg** Rus. Fed.
30 A1 **Yamethin** Myanmar
82 B4 **Yamoussoukro** Côte d'Ivoire
58 B2 **Yampil'** Ukr.
43 C2 **Yamuna** r. India
43 D2 **Yamzho Yumco** l. China
51 K2 **Yana** r. Rus. Fed.
38 A2 **Yan'an** China
118 A3 **Yanaoca** Peru
46 A2 **Yanbu' al Baḥr** Saudi Arabia
38 C2 **Yancheng** China
18 A3 **Yanchep** Austr.
39 B3 **Yangcheng** China
39 B3 **Yangchun** China
33 B2 **Yangdok** N. Korea
39 B3 **Yangjiang** China
30 A2 **Yangôn** Myanmar
38 B2 **Yangquan** China
39 B3 **Yangshuo** China
38 C3 **Yangtze** r. China
37 E2 **Yangtze, Mouths of the**
       China
38 B2 **Yangzhou** China
33 B2 **Yanji** China
105 D2 **Yankton** U.S.A.
51 K2 **Yano-Indigirskaya**
       Nizmennost' lowland
       Rus. Fed.
51 K2 **Yanskiy Zaliv** g. Rus. Fed.
21 C1 **Yantabulla** Austr.
38 C2 **Yantai** China
86 B2 **Yaoundé** Cameroon
27 D3 **Yap** i. Micronesia
27 D3 **Yapen** i. Indon.
27 D3 **Yapen, Selat** sea chan.
       Indon.

112 A2 **Yaqui** r. Mex.
19 D2 **Yaraka** Austr.
54 D3 **Yaransk** Rus. Fed.
46 B3 **Yarīm** Yemen
45 D3 **Yarkant He** r. China
43 D2 **Yarlung Zangbo** r. China
99 D2 **Yarmouth** Can.
54 F2 **Yarongo** Rus. Fed.
57 E2 **Yaroslavl'** Rus. Fed.
34 B2 **Yaroslavskiy** Rus. Fed.
21 C3 **Yarram** Austr.
57 D2 **Yartsevo** Rus. Fed.
57 E3 **Yasnogorsk** Rus. Fed.
31 B2 **Yasothon** Thai.
21 C2 **Yass** Austr.
79 C3 **Yatağan** Turkey
97 E1 **Yathkyed Lake** Can.
35 B4 **Yatsushiro** Japan
118 B2 **Yavari** r. Brazil/Peru
43 B2 **Yavatmāl** India
58 A2 **Yavoriv** Ukr.
35 B4 **Yawatahama** Japan
49 D2 **Yazd** Iran
110 B2 **Yazoo City** U.S.A.
79 B3 **Ydra** i. Greece
31 A2 **Ye** Myanmar
45 D3 **Yecheng** China
112 B2 **Yécora** Mex.
57 E3 **Yefremov** Rus. Fed.
57 E2 **Yegor'yevsk** Rus. Fed.
85 B4 **Yei** Sudan
54 F3 **Yekaterinburg** Rus. Fed.
57 E3 **Yelets** Rus. Fed.
82 A3 **Yélimané** Mali
64 □ **Yell** i. U.K.
96 C1 **Yellowknife** Can.
       Yellow River r. China see
       Huang He
37 E2 **Yellow Sea** N. Pacific Ocean
104 C1 **Yellowstone** r. U.S.A.
104 A2 **Yellowstone Lake** U.S.A.
56 C3 **Yel'sk** Belarus
46 B3 **Yemen** country Asia
54 E2 **Yemva** Rus. Fed.
59 D2 **Yenakiyeve** Ukr.
30 A1 **Yenangyaung** Myanmar
30 B1 **Yên Bai** Vietnam
82 B4 **Yendi** Ghana
79 C3 **Yenice** Turkey
79 C3 **Yenifoça** Turkey
36 C1 **Yenisey** r. Rus. Fed.
21 C2 **Yeoval** Austr.
67 B3 **Yeovil** U.K.
19 E2 **Yeppoon** Austr.
51 I2 **Yerbogachen** Rus. Fed.
49 C1 **Yerevan** Armenia
45 D1 **Yereymentau** Kazakh.
55 D3 **Yershov** Rus. Fed.
33 B2 **Yesan** S. Korea
45 C1 **Yesil'** Kazakh.
79 C3 **Yeşilova** Turkey
67 A3 **Yes Tor** hill U.K.
21 D1 **Yetman** Austr.
30 A1 **Yeu** Myanmar
72 B2 **Yeu, Île d'** i. France
59 C2 **Yevpatoriya** Ukr.
59 D2 **Yeysk** Rus. Fed.
56 C2 **Yezyaryshcha** Belarus
39 A3 **Yibin** China
38 B2 **Yichang** China
37 E1 **Yichun** Heilong. China
39 B3 **Yichun** Jiangxi China
78 C2 **Yıldız Dağları** mts Turkey
48 B2 **Yıldızeli** Turkey
38 A2 **Yinchuan** China
33 B1 **Yingchengzi** China
39 B3 **Yingde** China
38 C1 **Yingkou** China
38 B2 **Yingshan** Hubei China
38 A2 **Yingshan** Sichuan China

39 B3 **Yingtan** China
45 E2 **Yining** China
85 B4 **Yirga Alem** Eth.
38 B2 **Yishui** China
36 C2 **Yiwu** China
39 B3 **Yiyang** China
39 A3 **Yizhou** China
60 I2 **Yli-Kitka** l. Fin.
60 H2 **Ylitornio** Fin.
60 H3 **Ylivieska** Fin.
29 C2 **Yogyakarta** Indon.
86 B2 **Yoko** Cameroon
35 C3 **Yokohama** Japan
83 D4 **Yola** Nigeria
35 D3 **Yonezawa** Japan
39 B3 **Yong'an** China
39 B3 **Yongchun** China
38 A2 **Yongdeng** China
33 B2 **Yŏngdŏk** S. Korea
39 C3 **Yongkang** China
30 B1 **Yongsheng** China
39 B3 **Yongzhou** China
118 A1 **Yopal** Col.
18 A3 **York** Austr.
66 C2 **York** NE U.S.A.
105 D2 **York** NE U.S.A.
109 D3 **York** PA U.S.A.
19 D1 **York, Cape** Austr.
20 A3 **Yorke Peninsula** Austr.
20 A3 **Yorketown** Austr.
66 C2 **Yorkshire Wolds** hills U.K.
97 D2 **Yorkton** Can.
55 D3 **Yoshkar-Ola** Rus. Fed.
65 C3 **Youghal** Rep. of Ireland
21 C2 **Young** Austr.
20 A3 **Younghusband Peninsula**
       Austr.
108 C2 **Youngstown** U.S.A.
82 B3 **Youvarou** Mali
45 E2 **Youyi Feng** mt.
       China/Rus. Fed.
48 B2 **Yozgat** Turkey
102 B2 **Yreka** U.S.A.
       Yr Wyddfa mt. U.K. see
       Snowdon
73 C2 **Yssingeaux** France
61 F4 **Ystad** Sweden
       Ysyk-Köl Kyrg. see Balykchy
45 D2 **Ysyk-Köl** salt l. Kyrg.
60 □A3 **Ytri-Rangá** r. Iceland
30 B1 **Yuanjiang** China
30 B1 **Yuan Jiang** r. China
30 B1 **Yuanmou** China
103 B3 **Yuba City** U.S.A.
34 D2 **Yūbari** Japan
113 C3 **Yucatán** pen. Mex.
114 B2 **Yucatan Channel** Cuba/Mex.
38 B2 **Yuci** China
18 C2 **Yuendumu** Austr.
39 B3 **Yueyang** China
54 F2 **Yugorsk** Rus. Fed.
77 D2 **Yugoslavia** country Europe
51 L2 **Yukagirskoye Ploskogor'ye**
       plat. Rus. Fed.
94 A2 **Yukon** r. Can./U.S.A.
96 A1 **Yukon Territory** admin. div.
       Can.
39 B3 **Yulin** Guangxi China
38 A2 **Yulin** Shaanxi China
30 B1 **Yulongxue Shan** mt. China
104 C2 **Yuma** AZ U.S.A.
104 C2 **Yuma** CO U.S.A.
36 C2 **Yumen** China
48 B2 **Yunak** Turkey
38 B2 **Yuncheng** China
39 B3 **Yunfu** China
30 B1 **Yunnan** prov. China
20 A2 **Yunta** Austr.
38 B2 **Yunyang** China
118 A2 **Yurimaguas** Peru

45 E3 **Yurungkax He** r. China
39 C3 **Yü Shan** mt. Taiwan
36 C2 **Yushu** China
       Yushuwan China see
       Huaihua
49 C1 **Yusufeli** Turkey
45 E3 **Yutian** China
30 B1 **Yuxi** China
34 D2 **Yuzhno-Kuril'sk** Rus. Fed.
51 K3 **Yuzhno-Sakhalinsk**
       Rus. Fed.
59 C2 **Yuzhnoukrayinsk** Ukr.
72 C2 **Yvetot** France

Z

68 B1 **Zaandam** Neth.
37 D1 **Zabaykal'sk** Rus. Fed.
46 B3 **Zabīd** Yemen
44 C3 **Zābol** Iran
47 D2 **Zāboli** Iran
112 B3 **Zacapu** Mex.
112 B2 **Zacatecas** Mex.
113 C3 **Zacatepec** Mex.
113 C3 **Zacatlán** Mex.
79 B3 **Zacharo** Greece
112 B2 **Zacoalco** Mex.
113 C2 **Zacualtipán** Mex.
77 C2 **Zadar** Croatia
31 A3 **Zadetkyi Kyun** i. Myanmar
57 E3 **Zadonsk** Rus. Fed.
74 B2 **Zafra** Spain
84 B1 **Zagazig** Egypt
77 C1 **Zagreb** Croatia
49 C2 **Zagros, Kūhhā-ye** mts Iran
47 D2 **Zāhedān** Iran
48 B2 **Zahlé** Lebanon
46 B3 **Zahrān** Saudi Arabia
       Zaire country Africa see
       Congo, Democratic Republic of
77 D2 **Zaječar** Yugo.
57 E3 **Zakharovo** Rus. Fed.
49 C2 **Zākhō** Iraq
79 B3 **Zakynthos** Greece
       Zakynthos i. Greece see
       Zante
71 D2 **Zalaegerszeg** Hungary
78 B1 **Zalău** Romania
46 B2 **Zalim** Saudi Arabia
85 A3 **Zalingei** Sudan
46 A2 **Zalmā, Jabal az** mt.
       Saudi Arabia
96 C2 **Zama City** Can.
       Zambeze r. Moz. see
       Zambezi
88 B2 **Zambezi** Zambia
88 C2 **Zambezi** r. Zambia
88 B2 **Zambia** country Africa
32 B2 **Zamboanga** Phil.
32 B2 **Zamboanga Peninsula** Phil.
74 B1 **Zamora** Spain
112 B3 **Zamora de Hidalgo** Mex.
71 E1 **Zamość** Pol.
43 B2 **Zanda** China
68 B2 **Zandvliet** Belgium
108 C3 **Zanesville** U.S.A.
47 C2 **Zanjān** Iran
79 B3 **Zante** i. Greece
87 D3 **Zanzibar** Tanz.
87 D3 **Zanzibar Island** Tanz.
57 E3 **Zaokskiy** Rus. Fed.
83 C2 **Zaouatallaz** Alg.
38 B2 **Zaozhuang** China
57 D2 **Zapadnaya Dvina** r. Europe
57 D2 **Zapadnaya Dvina** Rus. Fed.
36 B1 **Zapadnyy Sayan** reg.
       Rus. Fed.

107 D3 **Zapata** U.S.A.
60 J2 **Zapolyarnyy** Rus. Fed.
59 D2 **Zaporizhzhya** Ukr.
69 E2 **Zappendorf** Ger.
48 B2 **Zara** Turkey
113 B3 **Zaragoza** Mex.
75 C1 **Zaragoza** Spain
44 B3 **Zarand** Iran
44 C3 **Zaranj** Afgh.
56 C2 **Zarasai** Lith.
57 E3 **Zaraysk** Rus. Fed.
118 B1 **Zaraza** Venez.
83 C3 **Zaria** Nigeria
58 B1 **Zarichne** Ukr.
49 D3 **Zarqān** Iran
34 B2 **Zarubino** Rus. Fed.
71 C1 **Żary** Pol.
83 D1 **Zarzis** Tunisia
91 C3 **Zaskar Mountains** India
91 C3 **Zastron** S. Africa
37 E1 **Zavitinsk** Rus. Fed.
71 D1 **Zawiercie** Pol.
45 E2 **Zaysan, Ozero** l. Kazakh.
36 C3 **Zayü** China
58 B1 **Zdolbuniv** Ukr.
   Zealand i. Denmark see
   Sjælland
68 A2 **Zeebrugge** Belgium
91 C2 **Zeerust** S. Africa
18 C2 **Zeil, Mount** Austr.
69 F2 **Zeitz** Ger.
56 B3 **Zelenogradsk** Rus. Fed.
50 E1 **Zemlya Aleksandry** i.
   Rus. Fed.
50 E1 **Zemlya Frantsa-Iosifa** is
   Rus. Fed.
50 F1 **Zemlya Vil'cheka** i.
   Rus. Fed.
75 D2 **Zemmora** Alg.
113 C3 **Zempoaltépetl, Nudo de** mt.
   Mex.
33 B1 **Zengfeng Shan** mt. China
73 D2 **Zermatt** Switz.
59 E2 **Zernograd** Rus. Fed.
69 E2 **Zeulenroda** Ger.
60 D2 **Zeven** Ger.
68 C2 **Zevenaar** Neth.
51 J3 **Zeya** Rus. Fed.
47 C2 **Zeydābād** Iran
51 J3 **Zeyskoye**
   Vodokhranilishche resr
   Rus. Fed.
71 D1 **Zgierz** Pol.
43 C2 **Zhabdün** China
56 B3 **Zhabinka** Belarus
44 A2 **Zhalpaktal** Kazakh.
45 C1 **Zhaltyr** Kazakh.
44 B2 **Zhanaozen** Kazakh.
   Zhangde China see Anyang
38 B1 **Zhangjiakou** China
39 B3 **Zhangping** China
39 B3 **Zhangshu** China
36 C2 **Zhangye** China
39 B3 **Zhangzhou** China
39 B3 **Zhanjiang** China
39 B3 **Zhao'an** China
39 B3 **Zhaoqing** China
39 A3 **Zhaotong** China
43 C1 **Zhari Namco** salt l. China
45 E2 **Zharkent** Kazakh.
57 D2 **Zharkovskiy** Rus. Fed.
45 E2 **Zharma** Kazakh.
58 C2 **Zhashkiv** Ukr.
39 C3 **Zhejiang** prov. China
50 F1 **Zhelaniya, Mys** c. Rus. Fed.
57 E2 **Zheleznogorsk** Rus. Fed.
38 A2 **Zhenba** China
39 A3 **Zheng'an** China
39 B3 **Zhenghe** China
38 B2 **Zhengzhou** China

38 B2 **Zhenjiang** China
39 A3 **Zhenyuan** China
59 E1 **Zherdevka** Rus. Fed.
54 D2 **Zheshart** Rus. Fed.
45 C2 **Zhezkazgan** Karagandinskaya
   Oblast' Kazakh.
45 C2 **Zhezkazgan** Karagandinskaya
   Oblast' Kazakh.
51 J2 **Zhigansk** Rus. Fed.
   Zhi Qu r. China see Yangtze
44 C1 **Zhitikara** Kazakh.
56 D3 **Zhlobin** Belarus
58 B2 **Zhmerynka** Ukr.
42 A1 **Zhob** Pak.
51 L1 **Zhokhova, Ostrov** i.
   Rus. Fed.
30 A1 **Zhongdian** China
   Zhonghe China see Xiushan
38 A2 **Zhongning** China
39 B3 **Zhongshan** China
   Zhongshan China see
   Lupanshui
38 A2 **Zhongwei** China
   Zhongxin China see
   Zhongdian
38 B2 **Zhoukou** China
38 C2 **Zhoushan** China
59 C2 **Zhovti Vody** Ukr.
33 A2 **Zhuanghe** China
38 B2 **Zhucheng** China
57 D3 **Zhukovka** Rus. Fed.
57 E2 **Zhukovskiy** Rus. Fed.
38 B2 **Zhumadian** China
   Zhuoyang China see Suiping
39 B3 **Zhuzhou** Hunan China
39 B3 **Zhuzhou** Hunan China
58 A2 **Zhydachiv** Ukr.
56 C3 **Zhytkavichy** Belarus
58 B1 **Zhytomyr** Ukr.
71 D2 **Žiar nad Hronom** Slovakia
38 B2 **Zibo** China
71 C1 **Zielona Góra** Pol.
30 A1 **Zigaing** Myanmar
39 A3 **Zigong** China
38 B2 **Zigui** China
82 A3 **Ziguinchor** Senegal
112 B3 **Zihuatanejo** Mex.
71 D2 **Žilina** Slovakia
51 H3 **Zima** Rus. Fed.
113 C2 **Zimapán** Mex.
89 C3 **Zimbabwe** country Africa
82 A4 **Zimmi** Sierra Leone
78 C2 **Zimnicea** Romania
83 C3 **Zinder** Niger
46 B3 **Zinjibār** Yemen
71 D2 **Zirc** Hungary
30 A1 **Ziro** India
47 C2 **Zīr Rūd** Iran
71 D2 **Zistersdorf** Austria
113 B3 **Zitácuaro** Mex.
71 C1 **Zittau** Ger.
55 E3 **Zlatoust** Rus. Fed.
71 D2 **Zlín** Czech Rep.
57 D3 **Zlynka** Rus. Fed.
57 E3 **Zmiyevka** Rus. Fed.
59 D2 **Zmiyiv** Ukr.
57 E3 **Znamenka** Orlovskaya Oblast'
   Rus. Fed.
59 E1 **Znamenka** Tambovskaya
   Oblast' Rus. Fed.
59 C2 **Znam"yanka** Ukr.
71 D2 **Znojmo** Czech Rep.
59 D1 **Zolochiv** Kharkivs'ka Oblast'
   Ukr.
58 A2 **Zolochiv** L'vivs'ka Oblast' Ukr.
59 C2 **Zolotonosha** Ukr.
57 E3 **Zolotukhino** Rus. Fed.
89 C2 **Zomba** Malawi
48 B1 **Zonguldak** Turkey
73 D3 **Zonza** Corsica France

82 B4 **Zorzor** Liberia
83 D2 **Zouar** Chad
82 A2 **Zouérat** Maur.
77 D1 **Zrenjanin** Yugo.
57 D2 **Zubtsov** Rus. Fed.
73 D2 **Zug** Switz.
49 C1 **Zugdidi** Georgia
74 B2 **Zújar** r. Spain
68 C2 **Zülpich** Ger.
89 C2 **Zumbo** Moz.
113 C3 **Zumpango** Mex.
106 B1 **Zuni Mountains** U.S.A.
39 A3 **Zunyi** China
77 C1 **Županja** Croatia
73 D2 **Zürich** Switz.
68 C1 **Zutphen** Neth.
83 D1 **Zuwārah** Libya
58 C2 **Zvenyhorodka** Ukr.
89 C3 **Zvishavane** Zimbabwe
71 D2 **Zvolen** Slovakia
77 C2 **Zvornik** Bos.-Herz.
82 B4 **Zwedru** Liberia
91 C3 **Zwelitsha** S. Africa
71 D2 **Zwettl** Austria
69 F2 **Zwickau** Ger.
68 C1 **Zwolle** Neth.
51 L2 **Zyryanka** Rus. Fed.